Al-Kafi
Volume 1 of 8

English Translation

Al-Kafi

Volume 1 of 8
('Usul al-Kafi)

English Translation

Second Edition

Compiled by
Thiqatu al-Islam, Abu Ja'far Muhammad
ibn Ya'qub al-Kulayni

Translated by
Muhammad Sarwar

Published by
The Islamic Seminary Inc.
www.theislamicseminary.org

The Islamic Seminary Inc., New York
© 2015 by The Islamic Seminary Inc.
All rights reserved
Second Edition 2015
Printed in the United States of America.

ISBN: 978-0-9914308-6-4

Al-Kafi, Volume 1 of 8. English Translation – 2nd ed.
Rabi' al-Awwal 1436
January 2015

Note to Readers

Dear respected readers, please note the following:

The English translation of this volume from Kitab al-Kafi is now, by the will of Allah, in your hands. It was only because of the beauty of the words of Ahl al-Bayt *'Alayhim al-Salam* that made it all possible. The magnitude of this project had become quite large and complex due to two language texts and it was sometimes difficult to handle.

All comments, suggestions and corrections will be very much appreciated. In fact it will be your participation in the good cause and rewarding in the sight of Allah, most Majestic, most Glorious. Please e-mail your comments, suggestions or corrections to: info@theislamicseminary.org.

With thanks,

The Islamic Seminary
www.theislamicseminary.org

Contents

Part One: The Book of Intelligence and Ignorance

Part Two: The Book on the Excellence of Knowledge

Part Three: The Book on the Oneness of Allah

Part Four: The Book about People with Divine Authority

Chapters on History

Introduction to the Arabic Version

In the Name of Allah, the Beneficent, the Merciful

Materials in the beginning of this introduction are the same as those quoted from the introduction of Wasa'il al-Shia.

1. Biography of al-Kulayni

Kulayn was born in a village 27 kilometers south west of the city of Ray, a well-known city in Iran. The ruins of the village still are near Tehran, Iran. Muhammad ibn Ya'qub al-Kulayni, the compiler of *al-Kafi* was born in this village.

Further evidence that he was born therein is the fact that in history he is called the religious scholar of Shi'a of Ray in his time.

Muhammad ibn Ya'qub ibn Ishaq al-Kulayni al-Razi al-Baghdadi was from a noble family of Kulayn. Outstanding scholars in jurisprudence and *Hadith* came from this family. Al-Kulayni himself was the most prominent religious figure of his time in Ray. He lived in Baghdad, Iraq also. He lived in the gate of Kufa, Baghdad, Iraq as the chief of the Shi'a scholars in jurisprudence during the rule of al-Muqtadir, the 'Abbassid Caliph. Al-Kulayni, of all other compilers of *Hadith*, alone was a contemporary of all the four successive special representatives and ambassadors of Imam al-Mahdi, the twelfth Imam *'Alayhi al-Salam*, He had the chance to collect *Hadith* from the proper sources. *Al-Kafi, the book* is a unique collection of *Hadith*. *Al-Kulayni* compiled this book on request from a prominent Shi'a scholar (as mentioned in his introduction to *al-Kafi*).

Prominent scholars of Islamic studies in search of knowledge would meet him at his place to discuss, exchange notes and to confer with him for better understanding of the issues.

xv

Al-Kulayni was a great scholar, a reliable narrator of *Hadith* and a man of great learning. He was of the outstanding scholars of law and an authority in the science of *Hadith*. He was a man of great chastity, piety, integrity and holiness.

His book *al-Kafi,* no doubt, is a treasure of Islamic literature, *Shari'ah* (law), Divine commandments and prohibitions, in the form of texts of the *Sunnah,* the statements, actions and the approvals of the Holy Prophet and the twelve A'immah, *'Alayhim al-Salam.* It is a text of the basis of the Islamic education and culture.

Al-Kulayni has himself prefaced his book, *al-Kafi* and has also provided certain explanatory notes in certain chapters, which shows his skill and proficiency in writing and in Arabic literature.

He was well versed in categorizing the narrators of *Hadith* and the texts of *Hadith.* He is the author of a book in the science of *Hadith* and an expert in scrutinizing the narrators. He was a great scholar of theology and he has written a book refuting *al-Qaramitah* (one of the several names applied to the sect of Isma'ilies who were once very active in politics).

His two books (1) Letters of *A'immah, 'Alayhim al-Salam,* (2) And poems in praises of the *A'immah, 'Alayhim al-Salam,* show his interest in linguistics.

His book on the interpretation of dreams is of the best books on the subject.

2. Words of Appreciation for His Efforts

Al-Najashi has said, "In our people al-Kulayni was the chief scholar in Ray, Iran. He was the most reliable in the matters of *Hadith.*" (ar-Rijal, an-Najashi, p.266)

Al-'Allama al-Hilli has confirmed this and ibn Dawud also has expressed similar words about him. (*Khulasat al-aqwal,* p.71. ar-Rijal, Ibn Dawud at the back of the leaf 48).

Al-Tusi, the great scholar has called him the most dependable expert in *Hadith,* the man of highest esteem and a scholar in *Hadith.* (*al-Fihrist,* ash-Shaykh at-Tusi, p.135, 34. ar-Rijal, ash-Shaykh at-Tusi, at the back of the leaf 119.)

Al-Sayyid Radi al-Din ibn Tawus has said, "Muhammad ibn Ya'qub al-Kulayni is universally accepted for his leadership and reliability." (*al-Fihrist,* ash-Shaykh at-Tusi, p.135.)

He has also said, "Muhammad ibn Ya'qub, al-Kulayni is the most eloquent and the most truthful in the knowledge of *Hadith.*" (*Faraj* al-Mahmum p.90.)

Ibn al-Athir has called him to be of the outstanding leaders of the Shi'a and their great scholar. (al-Kamil, Ibn al-Athir, vol.VlII, p.128.)

He has also described him as "A reformer of the Shi'a at the end of the third century, as their leader and as a renowned scholar among them." (*Munth'a* al-Maqal, p.298; *Rawdat al-jannat,* p.551; Lulu'at al-bahrayn, p. 237; al-Wajizah, al-Baha'i al-'Amili, p.184).

Al-Tayyibi has called him the reviver of the *'Ummah,* the whole Muslim community at the end of that century . . . He was among the most learned in Islamic jurisprudence. (*Rawdat al-jannat,* p.551)

Ibn Hajar has said, "He was one among the Shi'a scholars of law and an author of their school." (*Lisan* al-mizan, vol.V, p.433.)

He has also said, "Abu Ja'far Muhammad ibn Ya'qub al-Kulayni was among the chief scholars of the Shi 'a world in the days of al-Muqtadir." (*Rawdat al-jannat,* p.551, quoted from al-Tabsir)

Al-Shaykh Husayn ibn 'Abd al-Samad al-Harithi al-Hamdani has said, "Muhammad ibn Ya'qub al-Kulayni was the religious chief of his time and an outstanding, noble minded and highly learned scholar. He was the most reliable person in *Hadith,* the best critic and the most conversant in it." (*Wusul* al-akhyar, p.69.)

Al-Qadi Nur Allah al-Shushtari placed him at the top of the scholars of *Hadith* and the chief guardian thereof. (*Majalis* al-mu'minin, p.194)

Muhammad Taqi al-Majlisi, the great scholar has said:

"He is unparalleled among all the scholars we have seen. The study of his compiling *Hadith,* his manner of editing them, proves him to be a divinely gifted scholar. May Allah grant him the highest rewards reserved for the doers of the good for his services to Islam and the Muslim community." (*Sharh* Mashyakhat, Man *la yahduruhu al-faqih,* p.267.)

He also has called him, "The *shaykh* (the chief) *al-Sadiq* (the most truthful) and *Thiqatu al-Islam* (the most trustworthy in Islamic learning), as one acceptable to people of all classes. Both Shi'a and non-Shi'a have praised him." (*Mir'a t al-'uqul,* vol.11 p.3.)

Mirza 'Abd Allah al-Afandi has said, "The person generally referred to with the title *Thiqatu al-Islam* (the most trustworthy in Islamic issues) is Muhammad ibn Ya'qub ibn Ishaq al-Kulayni al-Razi, the compiler of the book *al-Kafi.* He is the earliest religious chief of the Muslim world in the sight of the masses and the elite alike and the Mufti, scholar of law for both the Shi'a and the Sunni Muslims." (*Riyaz* al-'ulama ', p.226)

3. His Compilations

1. Kitab Tafsir al-Ru'ya (*al-Fihrist,* at Tusi, p.135; ar-Rijal, an-Najashi, p.267; Ma'a-lim al-'ulama', p.88.)

2. Kitab al-Rijal (ar-Rijal, an-Najashi, p.267)

3. Kitab al-Radd 'Ala al-Qaramita. (ar-Rijal, an-Najashi, p.268; *al-Fihrist,* at-Tusi, p.125; Ma'alim al-'ulama' p.88; *Kashf al-hujub wa'l-astar,* p.442.)

4. Kitab al-Rasa'il (*al-Fihrist,* at-Tusi, p.135; *Ma'-alim al-'ulama',* p.88; *Kashf al-hujub,* p.291.), Rasa'il al-*A'immah 'Alayhim al-Salam,* ar-Rijal, an-Najashi, p.267.)

5. Kitab *al-Kafi* (*Kashf al-hujub* wa'l-astar, p.418-420)

6. Kitab ma qila fi al-*A'immah, 'Alayhi al-Salam* (ar-Rijal, an-Najashi, p.267)

4. Al-Kafi

This book was known as al-Kulayni (ibid p.266.) and also *al-Kafi* (ar-Rijal, an-Najashi, p.266; at-Fihrist, at-Tusi, p.135; Ma'a-lim al-ulama', p.88). In reply to one of his friends, al-Kulayni has explained why he compiled this book.

"Allah, the Most Majestic, the Most Gracious, has made the compilation of the book that you had wished for possible. I hope it will prove to be up to your expectations. It may have shortcomings but our intentions have not been insincere to provide good advice. Providing good advice to our people is obligatory. We also hoped to be considered as partners in all benefits of this book up to the end of time." (*Usul al-Kafi,* p.8)

It took twenty years to complete *al-Kafi.* (*ar-Rijid,* an-Najashi, p.266)

5. Distinctive Features

1. The compiler of *al-Kafi,* al-Kulayni was a contemporary of the four successive special representatives of Imam al-Mahdi *'Alayhi al-Salam,* as al-Sayyid ibn Tawus has pointed out, "All the works and the collections (of *Hadith*) of al-Shaykh Muhammad ibn Ya'qub al-Kulayni had been completed during the life time of the special representatives of Imam al-Mahdi *'Alayhi al-Salam.* It is a ground to believe the veracity of his collection of *Hadith.*" (*Kashf al-mahajjah, p.159; Mustadrak al-wasa'il,* vol.111, pp.532, 533, 546)

2. The compiler, except in the case of a few *Hadith,* has named the whole chain of narrators up to the infallible Imam, *'Alayhi al-Salam.* In certain cases he deletes the first narrator probably because he quotes from the original book that narrates directly from the Imam, *'Alayhi al-Salam.* (al-Wafi, vol.1, part 1, p.13)

3. Al-Kulayni's, according to great scholars, method of collecting and grading *Ahadith* in a chapter is by the order of the authenticity and the clarity of their meaning. It is, therefore, the last *Hadith* of every chapter that are always very general, unclear and problematic.

4. The compiler generally has avoided the *Ahadith* that are contradictory. Under the heading of a chapter he has recorded those *Ahadith* that relate best. (*Rawdat al-jannat,* pp.219, 222)

6. Commentaries of al-Kafi

The famous commentaries of *al-Kafi* are as follows.

1. The commentary of al-Mawla Sadr al-Din Shirazi (D. 1050/1640)
2. The commentary of al-Mawla Muhammad Salih Mazandarani (D.1081/1670); published in Tehran in twelve volumes in 1382/1962-1388/1968

Mir'at *al-'Uqul fi sharh akhbar al-Rasul* of al-Mawla Muhammad Baqir ibn Muhammad Taqi, al-'Allama al-Majlisi (1037/1628-111-1/1700) published in Tehran 1321/1903 in four volumes.

7. The Year of al-Kulayni's Death

According to al-Najashi, al-Kulayni (the compiler) died in Baghdad 329/941, (*ar-Rijal,* an-Najashi, p.267; Khulasat al-aqwal, p.71) and according to al-Tusi, he died in 328/940.(*al-Fihrist,* at-Tusi, p.126) However, al-Tusi afterwards agreed with al-Najashi as mentioned in his book *al-Rijal (ar-Rijal,* at-Tusi, p.495) compiled later on.

Al-Sayyid Radi al-Din ibn Tawus has said, "Shaykh Muhammad ibn Ya'qub, al-Kulayni was a contemporary of all the four special representatives of Imam al-Mahdi, *'Alayhi al-Salam,* namely:

1. 'Uthman ibn Sa'id al-'Amri

2. Abu Ja'far Muhammad, son of al-'Amri

3. Abu al-Qasim Husayn ibn Ruh

4. 'Ali ibn Muhammad al-Samuri

Al-Samuri died after the death of al-Kulayni. Al-Samuri died in the month of Sha'ban 329 AH. (941 AD.) and al-Kulayni died in 328/940. Both died in Baghdad. (*Kashf al-mahajjah,* p.159)

Ibn al-Athir and ibn Hajar both say that al-Kulayni died in 328/940. (al-Kamil, Ibn al-Athir, vol.Vlll, p.128; Lisan al-mizan, vol.V, p.433)

Al-Shaykh al-Baha'i al-'Amili has said in his book *al-Wajiza* that al-Kulayni died in 329/941 or 330/942. (*al-Wajizah,* p.184)

8. His Grave in Baghdad

Al-Kulayni was buried in Baghdad near Bab al-Kufa. (*ar-Rijal*, at-Tusi, p.496; *ar-Rijal*, an-Najashi, p.267; *Khulasat al-aqwal*, p.71, *Luluat al-bahrayn*, p.237; Nukhbat al-maqal, p.98) His shrine can be found in the eastern part of Baghdad on the bank of the River Tigris (Dajlah) near al-Jisr al-'Atiq, (the old bridge). (ar-Rijal, an-Najashi, p.267; *al-Fihrist*, at-Tusi, p.136; *Khulasat al-aqwal*)

9. A Note about Narrators

(a) Wherever al-Kulayni says, "A number of our people have narrated from Ahmad ibn Muhammad ibn 'Isa", people therein are:

1.   Abu Ja'far Muhammad ibn Yahya al-'Attar al-Qumi
2.   Ali ibn Musa ibn Ja'far al-Kamandani
3.   Abu Sulayman Dawud ibn Kawra al-Qumi
4.   Abu Ali Ahmad ibn Idris ibn Ahmad al-Ash'ari al-Qumi
5.   Abu al-Hassan Ali ibn Ibrahim ibn Hashim al-Qumi

(b) Wherever al-Kulayni says, "A number of our people have narrated from Ahmad ibn Muhammad ibn Khalid al-Barqi", the people therein are:

1.   Abu al-Hassan Ali ibn Ibrahim ibn Hashim al-Qumi
2.   Ali ibn Muhammad ibn 'Abd Allah ibn 'Udhayna
3.   Ahmad ibn Abd Allah ibn 'Umayya
4.   Ali ibn al-Husayn al-Sa'd Abadi

(c) Wherever al-Kulayni says, "A number of our people have narrated from Sahl ibn Ziyad", the people therein are:

1.   Abu al-Hassan Ali ibn Muhammad ibn Ibrahim ibn Aban al-Razi, known as 'Allan al-Kulayni
2.   Abu al-Husayn Muhammad ibn abu 'Abd Allah Ja'far ibn Muhammad ibn 'Awn al-Asadi al-Kufi, resident of Ray
3.   Muhammad ibn al-Husayn ibn Farrukh al-Saffar al-Qumi
4.   Muhammad ibn 'Aqil al-Kulayni

(d) Wherever al-Kulayni says, "A number of our people have narrated from Ja'far ibn Muhammad from al-Hassan ibn Ali ibn Faddal," of such people one is abu 'Abd Allah al-Husayn ibn Muhammad ibn 'Imran ibn abu Bakr al-Ash'ari al- Qumi.

(a) Wherever al-Kulayni says, "He, *'Alayhi al-Salam*, has said so and so," it is a reference to the Holy Prophet.

(b) Wherever al-Kulayni says, "abu Ja'far has said so and so," it is a reference to Imam Muhammad ibn Ali Zayn al-'Abidin.

(c) Wherever al-Kulayni says, "abu 'Abd Allah has said so and so," it is a reference to Imam Ja'far al-Sadiq.

(d) Wherever al-Kulayni says, "abu al-Hassan has said so and so, " it is a reference to Imam Musa al-Kazim.

(e) Wherever al-Kulayni says, "abu Ibrahim or the scholar or faqih or shaykh or the man has said so and so," it is a reference to Imam Musa al-Kazim.

(f) Wherever al-Kulayni says, "abu Ja'far al-Thani has said so and so," it is a reference to Imam Muhammad ibn Ali, al-Taqi.

(g) Wherever al-Kulayni says, "abu al-Hassan al-Thani has said so and so," it is a reference to Imam Ali al-Rida.

(h) Wherever al-Kulayni says, "abu al-Hassan al-Thalith has said so and so," it is a reference to Imam Ali ibn Muhammad al-Hadi.

(i) Wherever al-Kulayni says, "al-'Askari has said so and so," it is a reference to Imam al-Hassan ibn Ali ibn Muhammad or his father very rarely which is understandable from existing indications.

10. Introduction by al-Kulayni

In Praise of Allah, the Beneficent, the Merciful

All praise belongs to Allah Who is praised for His bounties, worshipped for His Might, obeyed in His Rule and feared for His Majesty. He possesses all that is attractive; His commands pervade in all of His creation. He is High, the Most High. He is near in His Highness and the Most High above being seen. His being the first has had no beginning and He is eternal. He existed before the existence of all things and He is the eternal Who guards all things. He is the overwhelming power and the preservation of the things does not burden Him. He is the only Almighty in His kingdom and only power to compel what is to compel. Through wisdom He has revealed His authority over His creation. He created all things in their origin new and at the very beginning through His might and wisdom and nothing existed to invalidate His being the originator of all things. No other cause existed to compete His invention. He alone created what He wished as He wished to reveal His wisdom and the reality of His Lordship. Reason is not able to grasp Him. Imagination is not able to reach Him. Eyes are not able to see Him. Measurement is not able to limit Him. Statements fail to describe Him. Eyes turn dull in trying to see Him. Describing Him by means of qualities loses the right path.

He is veiled without any barrier and is concealed without any covering. He is known but is not seen and is described without a form. He is characterized without a body. There is no Lord except Allah, the Most Great, the Most

High. Imagination loses the right path in trying to reach His reality. Intelligent becomes exhausted and is not able to reach Him. So also is the case with imaginations and eyesight. He is all hearing and all knowing. Allah has established His authority over His creatures through His messengers, *'Alayhi al-Salam*, and has explained things with evidence. He has sent His messengers with glad news and warnings. So that those who would find salvation would do so with proper evidence and those to be destroyed would become so for ignoring proper evidence. So that people may learn about their Lord what they are ignorant of and know Him through His Lordship after that they were ignorant of this fact, so that they believe in Him as the only One Lord after their considering other things to be like Him.

I thank Him in a way that to be a cure for the souls, a thankfulness of a degree to please Him, enough to fulfil the duty to express gratitude for His favors to us in the form of His pleasant blessings, graceful bounties and beautiful trials.

I testify that there is no Lord except Allah alone Who has no partners. He is the only Lord, the only self-sufficient Who has no companion or children.

I testify that Muhammad, *'Alayhi al-Salam*, is His servant. He is His chosen one, His messenger whom He sent at a time of lapse of messengers and at the time of the long sleep of the nations, wide spread of ignorance, mischief and shortages of authority, blindness to the truth, prevailing injustice and the disappearance of religion.

Allah sent His book to him (Muhammad) that contains the statements and explanations, a reading in straightforward Arabic language so that people may become pious.

Allah has explained and organized this book for the people and with knowledge He has given the details. He has explained a religion in it, certain obligations are made obligatory therein and certain matters are declared for His creature in it. It contains signs that lead to salvation and evidence that call to guidance.

He (Muhammad), preached His message and executed His commands. He fulfilled his responsibilities with patience for the sake of his Lord. He worked hard for His cause, gave good advice to his followers and invited them to salvation. He encouraged them to speak of (Allah), gave them guidance to the right path after his passing away through a system, reason, basis for the people and signs that he established for them so that they are not misled after him. It was all due to his kindness and sympathy for them.

When his life ended and his days were over, Allah took his soul to Himself. With Allah he is well pleased for his deeds. His reward is a good deal and his position very great. He left this world leaving behind among his followers the Book of Allah and the executor of his will, Amir al-Mu'minin, Ali, *'Alayhi al-Salam*, the master of the believers and the leader (Imam) for pious people.

The twine that he left behind was a united companion. They each acknowledge and speak in support of the other.

The Imam speaks of Allah from the Book. He speaks of what Allah has made obligatory on His servants, of obedience to Him, of obedience to the Imam, *'Alayhi al-Salam*, and of the acknowledgement of Leadership with Divine Authority. He speaks of His rights that are meant to be for the completion of religion, His commandments, establishment of His authority, seeking guidance in His light from its mines, His chosen and select people who have received goodness from Him.

Allah through the *A'immah* of guidance from the family of His Prophet, *'Alayhi al-Salam*, has explained His religion. Through them He has clarified the ways of His system. Through them He has opened the inside of His knowledge. He has made them to be the path to know Him, the sources of knowledge of His religion, the medium between Him and His creatures, the gate that lead to know His rights and has given them the knowledge of His hidden secret.

Whenever, an Imam from them left this world He established a clearly known successor for that Imam for His creatures as a bright guide, an Imam and guardian with the truth and justice. Allah and those who preach for Him and supervise over His creatures have established their authority. Through their guidance people follow the religion and through their light people of the lands find their way.

Allah has made them, (*A'immah*) the life for people, the light in darkness, the key to the words and the pillars of Islam. He has based the system of His obedience and the fulfillment of obligation submission to them (*A'immah*) in all that one needs to know and ask them what one is ignorant of. He has prohibited others from engaging in what they are ignorant of and from rejecting what they do not know. It is because Allah has willed to save, from His creatures whoever He wills, from injustice and darkness.

May Allah grant blessings upon Muhammad, *'Alayhi al-Salam*, and the select members of his family whom Allah has thoroughly cleansed.

After my words about Allah and His Messenger in the above, herein below is my response to your note.

I have understood your concerns about the conditions of the people of our times who seem to have agreed up on ignorance to be the standard and authority in their dealings. They cooperate and work together to establish the ways and the manners of ignorance and distance themselves from knowledge and the people of knowledge. Consequently, knowledge is almost banished and the sources of knowledge are about to depart the people. It is all because they rely so much on ignorance (ignorant people) and lose the (blessing of) people of knowledge.

You have asked, "Can the dealings of the people be considered proper in following a religion without knowing the rules and laws therein that show what is lawful or otherwise? Can they decide and settle all matters on the basis of what they feel is good and live a life in such a manner? Can they just do what their ancestors had been doing and rely on their own understanding of the issues great or small?"

To understand the answer to your question, note the following O brother in faith, may Allah grant you blessings:

Allah, the Most Holy, the Most High, has created human beings and has given them distinction over the animals. He has given them the ability to understand and distinguish good from bad. Human beings have been given the ability to understand Allah's commands and prohibitions.

There are two kinds of people. (a) There are those who are physically and mentally safe and sound and (b) those who lack such abilities. Safe and sound people are held responsible to follow the commands and prohibitions of Allah. Those who lack such abilities are exempt because of their inability to learn, discipline and fulfill responsibilities. Allah, the Most Majestic, the Most Gracious, has designed education, good manners and moral discipline to serve as means of survival for the people who are safe and sound. Had it been permissible for safe and sound people to follow ignorance it would have been permissible for them not to become obligated to fulfill responsibilities. Such a condition amounts to make the coming of the Divine messengers and education useless. Ignoring the book of guidance, the Divine messengers and education destroys the whole civilization. This is a return to atheism. The justice and wisdom of Allah, the Most Majestic, the Most Gracious, required the creation of creatures, who can understand the commands and prohibitions of Allah so that people do not live a useless life. Instead they realize the greatness of Allah They acknowledge His Oneness and that He is the Lord. They must know that He is their Creator Who gives them sustenance. The proof of His existence is so clear and obvious. The signs of His authority are shinning and manifest. His lighthouses are visible everywhere and call people to believe in Allah, the Most Majestic, and the Most Gracious. Each sign testifies to the existence of the Lord and the One Who deserves to be worshipped. Such proofs that exist in each sign are proofs of the effect of the creation in them. Each creature is a marvelous proof of His plan. He invites them to know Him so that they will not remain ignorant of His existence and ignorant of His religion and laws.

People of wisdom do not consider ignorance of his existence a permissible attitude, as is the case of denying His religion. Allah, the Most Majestic, the Most Gracious, said:

"Did they not make a covenant (with Allah) in the Book not to speak anything other than the Truth about Allah and to study its contents well? (7:169) They call a lie something that is beyond the limit of their knowledge . . ." (10:39)

People are bound to obey the commands of Allah and His prohibitions. It is not permissible for them to follow ignorance (ignorant people).

It is obligatory for them to ask if they do not already know and to acquire proper understanding of religion.

Allah, the Most Majestic, the Most Gracious, has said, "Not all believers have to become specialists in religious learning. Why do not certain people from each group of believers seek to become specialists in religious learning and, after completing their studies, guide their group so that they will have fear of Allah." (9:122)

If people who are physically and mentally safe and sound were permitted to stay ignorant Allah would not have asked them to ask and learn. He did not need to send any messengers, books and guidance. In such case, they would have lived like animals or like people physically and mentally defective and if so they did not remain in existence even for a blinking of an eye.

In fact, it is not permissible for them to live without discipline and education. Thus, it became necessary for those physically and mentally sound to find instructors to educate and discipline them and provide answer to their questions.

The best and most important education for people of reason, the education worthwhile for one to study assiduously is the religious education. The education that teaches one about the Creator, His Oneness and how to worship Him, is the most important one. It is important to be educated in the issues of *Shari'ah*, His laws of guidance, His commandments, prohibitions, warnings and discipline. This is necessary because there is solid evidence to support the need for such education, that responsibility is real, life is short, indifference and procrastination is not acceptable.

The condition for a worship to be proper and acceptable is to fulfil all the obligations on the basis of certainty, knowledge and proper understanding. Only then the worshiper is considered praiseworthy in the sight of Allah and deserving rewards and His great blessings.

On the other hand, one who acts without proper knowledge and understanding does not know what and for what reason one is acting. Ignorant people do not have trust in what they do. They do not acknowledge anything because acknowledgement does not come without doubt free knowledge of the subject to be acknowledged.

The person who has doubts is not like a person who has certainty of the matters of piety, humbleness before the Lord and the need to seek nearness to Him. Allah, the Most Majestic, the Most Gracious, has said, "Those who have witnessed the truth only they have proper knowledge." (43:87)

Only the testimony of those who possess proper knowledge is accepted and it is because of the knowledge of the subject of the testimony. Without the knowledge of the subject of the testimony it is not accepted. The acceptance of the deeds of the people who act with doubts is up to Allah to decide. He may accept such deeds because of His grace or He may refuse to accept because of the absence of the conditions such as knowledge and certainty. It is Knowledge, proper understanding and certainty that separate one from those mentioned in the following words of Allah, the Most Majestic, the Most Gracious, "Certain people worship Allah to achieve worldly gains. They are confident when they are prosperous, but when they face hardships they turn away from (worship). They are lost in this life and will be lost in the life to come. Such loss is indeed destructive." (22:11)

It is all because of acting without knowledge and certainty in the beginning and in the end.

The scholar has said, "One who accepts the faith with certainty remains in it steadfast and the faith benefits him. Those who accept the faith without certainty they leave it just as they came in."

He has also said, "Those who get their religion from the Book of Allah and the *Sunnah* of the Messenger of Allah, the strength of their faith is as such that mountains may be destroyed but not their faith. Those who get their religion from the words of the people they may reject it"

He has also said, "Those who do not know us through the Holy Quran they fail to protect themselves against mischief."

This is why so many religions have emerged in our times as well as disgraceful systems that almost have entered the level of disbelief. This is because of the opportunity that Allah has provided for everyone. One whose faith in the will of Allah is to remain solid He makes the means that to make it so happen, available. He then gets his religion from the Book of Allah and the *Sunnah* of His Messenger, *'Alayhi al-Salam*, with certainty and proper understanding. His religion is stronger than the heavy mountains. Those whose faith in the will of Allah is to be temporary and bound to failure, - may He grant us refuge- He gives them the opportunity to follow certain ideas that are devoid of Divine authority. They follow what seems good to one to follow and such other matters like following what others do, certain interpretations and so on without proper understand and certainty. In such case Allah may or may not accept their deeds. They may live as a believer in the morning and a unbeliever in the evening or vice versa. It is because such people may easily follow the influential elements in the society or act upon what they feel is good.

The scholar, *'Alayhi al-Salam*, has said, "Allah, the Most Majestic, the Most Gracious, has created the prophets with prophet-hood they can be nothing but prophets. He has created the executors of the will of the prophets as the executors thus they can be nothing but the executors of the wills of the prophets. He has given temporary faith to certain people. He may complete it for them or remove it from them as mentioned in this expression of Quran, "The established faith the temporary faith." (6:98)

You have mentioned that you are confused in the issues of the verification of *Hadith* due to the difference in variously narrated texts and that you know the reason for variation but you do not find reliable people to discuss with. You have said that you wish you had a book sufficient (*Kafi*) that contained all issues of the religion. A book that provides a student all the material that he needs is urgently needed. A book is needed that can help people to have proper guidance in the matters of religion to follow the correct instructions of the truthful people, *'Alayhi al-Salam*, and the prevailing *Sunnah*, the basis of practices. So that one can fulfil his responsibilities toward Allah, the Most Majestic, the Most Gracious, and follow the *Sunnah* of (the Holy Prophet).

You have said, that you hope such a book, Allah willing, will help our brothers in faith to find the right guidance.

My brother in faith, may Allah grant you proper guidance, please note that there is no other way to sort out the confusion that comes from the variation of the narration of the scholars except by the help of the principles that the scholar, *'Alayhi al-Salam*, has set. "Compare a narration with the text of the Holy Quran. Whatever agrees with the Holy Quran is acceptable and what does not agree is rejected."

Also he has said, "Leave alone what agrees with the views of the others because the right is in what is opposite to them."

Also there are his (Imam's), *'Alayhi al-Salam*,) words, "Follow what is unanimously agreed upon because there is no harm in what is unanimously agreed upon."

We are only able to apply such principles to a very few of such cases. We do not find anything better and more precautionary than to refer to the scholar (Imam), *'Alayhi al-Salam* and accept that which is within the limit of his (Imam's), *'Alayhi al-Salam*, words, "Whichever you follow in submission and obedience is excusable for you."

Allah, the Most Majestic, the Most Gracious, has made the compilation of the book that you had wished for possible. I hope it will prove to be up to your expectations. It may have shortcomings, but our intentions have not been insincere to provide good advice because to provide good advice to our people is obligatory. We also hoped to be considered as partners in all benefits of this book up to the end of time.

The Lord is one, the Messenger is one, the last prophet, *'Alayhi al-Salam*, is one and the *Shari'ah* is one. What Muhammad, *'Alayhi al-Salam*, has made lawful will remain lawful up to the Day of Judgment and what he has made unlawful will remain unlawful to the Day of Judgment.

We extended the Book on 'People with Divine Authority' to a certain degree although not as it should have been done because we did not like to be deprived of the benefits thereof.

I hope Allah, the Most Majestic, the Most Gracious, will approve what is based on our intentions. If life will give us a chance we intend to compile a book of a bigger volume to serve the causes as they should be served, by the will of Allah, the Most High. From Him comes the power and means. From Him one expects help and increase in rewards and opportunity.

May Allah grant blessings up on Muhammad and his purified family.

The first thing is the book of Intelligence and the excellence of knowledge, the excellence of the people of knowledge, the defects of the people of ignorance and its harms. Intelligence is the focal point and the axes of the matters. On the basis of Intelligence come the rewards and sufferings and Allah is the best One to provide good opportunities.

An Outline of the Number of Volumes, Sections and Sub-divisions of Kitab al-Kafi

Part 1 - Al-'Usul (Principles)

Volume 1

This part of the book consists of *Ahadith* on the principles of beliefs and it is called 'Usul (principles) in *al-Kafi*.

The sections or chapters in volume 1 are as follows:

1. The Book of Intelligence and Ignorance (*Kitab al-'Aql wa al-Jahl*)
2. The Book of the Excellence of Knowledge (*Kitabu Fad al-'Ilm*)
3. The Book on Oneness of Allah (*Kitab al-Tawhid*)
4. The Book about the people who possess Divine Authority (*Kitab al-Hujja*)

Volume 2

Sections or Chapters in Volume 2:

5. The Book on Belief and Disbelief (*Kitab al-'Iman wa al-Kufr*)
6. The Book on Prayers (*Kitab al-Du'a'*)
7. The Book on the Excellence of the Holy Quran (*Kitabu Fadl al-Quran*)
8. The Book of Social Discipline (*Kitab al-'Ishra*)

PART 2 - Al-*Furu'* (Branches)

Volumes 3-7

This part consists of *Ahadith* on Islamic practical laws such as:

> The acts of worship (*'Ibadat*)
>
> Business transactions (*mu'amalat*)
>
> Judicial laws (*al-Qada'*)

Furu' al-Kafi (volume 3 – 7): The rules of conduct, the practical laws of the Islamic system, consists of the following:

9. The Book of Laws of Cleanliness (*Kitab al-Tahara*)
10. The Book of Laws of Menstruation (*Kitab al-Hayd*)
11. The Book of Laws about the dying people and their burials (*Kitab al-Jana'iz*)
12. The Book of Laws of Prayer (*Kitab al-Salat*)
13. The Book of Laws of Charities, Taxes (*Kitab al-Zakat*)

PART 3 - Al- Rawdah (Garden of Flowers (Hadith))

Volume 8

This part consists of miscellaneous *Ahadith* of both the *'Usul* and *Furu'* of *al-Kafi*. The topics are not arranged and organized as in the other volumes. The chapters are not in alphabetical order of *Ahadith* or narrators.

This volume comprises about six hundred *Hadith* on various topics and is a treasure of knowledge of the matters of belief, spiritual discipline, interpretations of many verses of the Holy Quran, accounts of the noble manners of the Holy Prophet and infallible members of his family and information about the system of this and the next life.

In the Name of Allah, the Beneficient, the Merciful

Part One:
The Book of Intelligence and Ignorance

Chapter 1

Hadith 1, Chapter 1, hadith 1
(The Bearers of this Hadith in consecutive order):
Abu Ja'far Muhammad ibn Ya'qub has narrated from a number of our people of whom one is Muhammad ibn Yahya al-'Attar who narrated from Ahmad ibn Muhammad from Hassan ibn Mahbub from 'Ala' ibn Razin from Muhammad ibn Muslim from abu Ja'far, *'Alayhi al-Salam*, who has said the following: (The Text of this Hadith):
"When Allah created Intelligence He induced it to speak and said, 'Come forward.' Intelligence then did come forward. He then said, 'Go back.' Intelligence then did go back. Thereupon Allah said, 'I swear by My Honor and Glory that I have not created any creature more beloved to Me than you. I will not perfect you in anyone except those whom I love. I, however, will command only you to do (certain) things and prohibit only you from committing certain others. I will grant blessings (rewards) to you only and will hold only you responsible for the consequences (of your acts).'"

H 2, Ch. 1, h 2
'Ali ibn Muhammad has narrated from Sahl ibn Ziyad, from 'Amr ibn 'Uthman, from Mufaddal Ali ibn Salih from Sa'd ibn Tarif from Asbagh ibn Nubatah, from (Imam) Ali, *'Alayhi al-Salam*, who has said the following:
"Once Jibril (Gabriel) came to Adam, *'Alayhi al-Salam*, and said, 'I am ordered to offer you three choices. You may choose one and leave the other two.' Adam then asked, 'What are those three things?' Gabriel replied, 'They are Intelligence, Bashfulness and Religion.'

"Adam then said, 'I choose Intelligence.' Jibril (Gabriel) then asked Bashfulness and Religion to return and leave Intelligence with Adam. They said to Jibril, 'O Jibril, we are commanded to be with Intelligence wherever it may exist. Jibril then said, 'It then is up to you.' He then ascended to heaven."

H 3, Ch. 1, h 3
Ahmad ibn 'Idris has narrated from Muhammad ibn 'Abd al-Jabbar, from certain persons of our people in a *marfu'* manner, who have ascribed it to abu 'Abd Allah, *'Alayhi al-Salam*, who has said the following:
"When I asked abu 'Abd Allah, 'What is Intelligence,' He replied, 'It is a fact with whose help one worships Allah, the Merciful, and attains paradise.' I then asked, 'What was the thing with Mu'awiya?' 'It was shrewdness. It was mischief which is similar to Intelligence but is not Intelligence,' the Imam replied."

H 4, Ch. 1, h 4

Muhammad ibn Yahya has narrated from Ahmad ibn Muhammad ibn 'Isa from ibn Faddal from al-Hassan ibn al-Jahm, who has said the following:

"I heard (Imam) al-Rida, *'Alayhi al-Salam*, saying, 'The friend of a person is his/her intelligence and the enemy of a person is his/her Ignorance.'"

H 5, Ch. 1, h 5

It is narrated from him from Ahmad ibn Muhammad from ibn Faddal from al-Hassan ibn al-Jahm, who has said the following:

"Once, I said to abu al-Hassan, 'We know certain people who have a great deal of love for *Ahl al-Bayt* (family of the Holy Prophet), *'Alayhi al-Salam*, but they do not have much determination and understanding of the cause of *Imamat* (Leadership with Divine Authority).' The Imam replied, 'They are not of the ones that Allah has admonished. What Allah has said is, 'People of Intelligence and understanding take a lesson.'"

H 6, Ch. 1, h 6

Ahmad ibn Idris has narrated from Muhammad ibn Hassa'n from abu Muhammad al-Razi from Sayf ibn 'Umayra from Ishaq ibn 'Ammar from abu 'Abd Allah, *'Alayhi al-Salam*, who has said the following:

"One who has Intelligence has religion also and one who has religion enters paradise."

H 7, Ch. 1, h 7

A number of our people have narrated from Ahmad ibn Muhammad ibn Khalid from al-Hassan ibn Ali ibn Yaqtin from Muhammad ibn Sinan ibn abu al-Jarud from abu Ja'far, *'Alayhi al-Salam*, who has said the following:

"Allah, on the Day of Judgment, will hold everyone accountable, proportionate to the degree of the Intelligence that He had given them in their worldly life."

H 8, Ch. 1, h 8

Ali ibn Muhammad ibn 'Abd Allah has narrated from Ibrahim ibn Ishaq al-Ahmar from Muhammad ibn Sulayman al-Daylami his father who has said the following:

"Once I mentioned a certain person's Intelligence, worship, religion and merits before Imam abu 'Abd Allah, *'Alayhi al-Salam.* The Imam, *'Alayhi al-Salam*, asked, 'How is his Intelligence?' I replied, 'I do not know.' Then the Imam said, 'The degree of reward is based on the degree of intelligence. A man of Banu Israel worshipped Allah on an island in the ocean. The island was lush green, with many trees and abundant water. Once an angel passed by the worshipper and asked Allah to show how much reward and blessings the worshipper would receive for his good deeds. Allah showed the rewards due to the worshipper to the angel and the angel considered them to be very little. Allah then told the angel to stay with the worshipper as a companion. The angel then appeared to the worshipper in the form of a human being. The worshipper asked, "Who are you?" "I have heard about your great deeds of worship and your spiritual position at this place and I wish to join you to worship Allah along with you," the angel replied. He spent that day with the worshipper and the next day the angel said to the worshipper, "Your place is beautiful and it should be used only for worship." "Yes, it is but it has one defect," the worshipper responded. "What is that?" the angel inquired.

"Our Lord does not have an animal. I wish He had a donkey so we could make the donkey graze all the grass around. All this grass is a waste," the worshipper replied. "Is it true that your Lord does not have any donkeys?" asked the angel. "Had our Lord had a donkey all this grass would not have turned into waste," the worshipper answered with sadness. Allah then revealed to the angel, "We will reward him according to the degree of his Intelligence.'"

H 9, Ch. 1, h 9

Ali ibn Ibrahim has narrated from his father from al-Nawfali from al-Sakuni from abu 'Abd Allah, *'Alayhi al-Salam,* who has said the following:

"The Holy Prophet has said, 'If you hear good things about a man, you should examine how good his Intelligence is; he will be rewarded according to his Intelligence.'"

H 10, Ch. 1, h 10

Muhammad ibn Yahya has narrated from Ahmad ibn Muhammad from ibn Mahbub from 'Abd Allah ibn Sinan who has said the following:

"I mentioned a person, who would overdo acts of his Wudu and prayer, to Imam abu 'Abd Allah, *'Alayhi al-Salam,* and added that he is a man of good Intelligence. The Imam, *'Alayhi al-Salam,* then said, 'What kind of intelligence is it that allows him to obey Satan?' I then asked the Imam, 'How would he be considered as obeying Satan?' The Imam, *'Alayhi al-Salam,* said, 'Ask him wherefrom this thing (overdoing) comes to him. He will certainly say, "It comes from Satan."'"

H 11, Ch. 1, h 11

A number of our people have narrated Ahmad ibn Muhammad ibn Khalid from certain persons of his people in a *marfu'* manner from the Holy Prophet, *'Alayhi al-Salam,* who has said the following:

"Allah has not distributed anything among people more excellent than Intelligence. An Intelligent person's sleeping is better than an ignorant person's worshipping for the whole night. An Intelligent person's staying at home is better than an ignorant person's journey in search of success and good deeds. Allah did not send any prophet or messenger before the completion of his Intelligence and before allowing it to become greater than the Intelligence of all of his followers. A prophet's mere thinking is better than the achievement of all the people striving for virtue and good deeds. People do not fulfill their obligations to Allah without having an understanding of Him. All the worshippers will not be able to achieve with the virtue of their worship what a person of intelligence achieves. It is the people of intelligence who are considered people of proper understanding in chapter 2:269 of the Holy Quran, 'Only people of understanding realize this.'"

H 12, Ch. 1, h 12

Abu 'Abd Allah al-Ash'ari has narrated from certain persons of our people in a *marfu'* manner from Hisham ibn al-Hakam who has said the following:

"Abu al-Hassan Musa ibn Ja'far, *'Alayhi al-Salam,* said to me the following, 'O Hisham, Allah has given good news to the people of reason (intelligence) and understanding in His book in the following words, "Give the good news to those of My servants who hear certain words but follow only the good words. These are the ones whom Allah has given guidance and they are the people of understanding." (39:20, Holy Quran)

"O Hisham, it is certain that Allah, the Most Gracious, the Most High, has made Intelligence a criterion for people (to refer to) in discerning right from wrong. He supported the messengers with the (ability) to communicate and has guided them to His own Lordship with proofs, saying, 'Your Lord is the only Lord. No one deserves worship except Allah, the Beneficent, the Merciful.' (2:163)

"Of the signs of His existence are the creation of the heavens and earth, the alternation of nights and days, the ships that sail in the sea for the benefit of the people. (Also of such signs are) the water that Allah sends from the sky to revive the dead earth where He has scattered all kinds of animals, the winds of all directions and the clouds that are rendered for service between the sky and the earth. Such are evidence (of His existence) for those who use their Intelligence." (2:164)

"O Hisham, Allah has mentioned the above facts as proof of His existence and that those facts depend upon the Will of One Who has designed them, saying: 'Allah has made the day and the night, the sun and the moon, and all the stars subservient to you by His command. In this there is evidence of the truth for people of understanding.' (16:12)

"It is He Who created you from clay, turning it into a living germ, then into a clot of blood, and then brings you forth as a child. He then makes you grow into manhood and become old. He causes certain ones of you to live for the appointed time and others of you to die before, so that perhaps you may have understanding. (40:67)

"In the heavens and the earth there is evidence (of the Truth) for the believers (45:3). In your creation and in that of the beasts living on earth there is evidence of the Truth for the people who have strong faith (45:4). In the alternation of the night and the day, the sustenance, which Allah has sent down from the sky to revive the barren earth and in the changing of the direction of the winds there is evidence of the Truth for the people of understanding. (45:5)

"Know that Allah brings the dead earth back to life. We have explained Our revelations to you so that you may perhaps have understanding." (57:17)

"In the earth there are adjacent pieces of land, vineyards, farms, date palms of single and many roots which are all watered by the same water. We have made some yield a better food than others. All this is evidence (of the existence of Allah) for the people who understand." (13:4)

"Also, of the evidence of His existence are His showing you lightning, which gives you fear and hope, and His sending water down from the sky, which revives the earth after its death. In this there is evidence (of the truth) for the people of understanding." (30:24)

"(Muhammad), say, 'Allow me to tell you about what your Lord has commanded: Do not consider anything equal to Allah; be kind to your parents; do not murder

4

your children out of fear of poverty; We give sustenance to you and to them. Do not even approach indecency either in public or in private. Take not a life, which Allah has made sacred except by way of justice and law. Thus does He command you that you may learn wisdom.' (6:151)

"Allah has told you this parable about yourselves: Could your slaves share your wealth equally with you and could you fear them as you fear yourselves? Thus do We clarify the evidence (of the Truth) for the people of understanding." (30:28).

"O Hisham, Allah then has given good advice to the people of intelligence and has encouraged them to become interested in the life to come. He has said, "The worldly life is but useless amusement and childish plaything (compared to) the life hereafter which is far better and is only for the pious ones. Will you not then understand?" (6:32)

"O Hisham, Allah then has given warnings to those who do not think about the punishment that may come upon them from Allah, saying, 'Then We totally destroyed the others. (37:136) You do pass by (their ruined town) in the morning and at night (37:137) why do you then not understand?' (37:138)

"We will bring torment from the sky on this town because of the evil deeds of its inhabitants." (29:34) 'We left manifest evidence (of the truth) there for the people of understanding.' (29:35)

"O Hisham, intelligence comes with knowledge. Allah has said, 'These are parables which We tell to human beings, but only the learned ones understand them.' (29:43)

"O Hisham, Allah has then expressed dislike toward those who do not understand, saying, 'When certain people are asked to follow the revelations of Allah, they say, "We would rather follow what our fathers have followed," even though their fathers had no understanding and could not find the true guidance.' (2:170)

"Preaching to unbelievers is like talking to the ones who cannot hear anything except yells and shouts. They are deaf, dumb, and blind; they have no understanding." (2:171)

"Certain ones of them listen to you, but are you to make the deaf hear even if they have no understanding?" (10:43)

"Do you think that most of them listen and understand? They are like cattle, or even more straying and confused." (25:44)

"They will not fight you united except with the protection of fortified towns or from behind walls. Their fight among them is strong. You think they are united, but in fact, their hearts are divided. They are a people who have no understanding." (59:14)

5

"Would you order people to do good deeds and forget to do them yourselves even though you read the Book? Why do you not think?" (2:44)

"O Hisham, Allah then has expressed dislikes towards the multitudes, saying, 'Most of the people in the land will lead you away from Allah's guidance if you follow them; they only follow their own conjecture and preach falsehood.' (6:116)

"If you ask them, 'Who has created the heavens and the earth,' they will certainly say, 'Allah has created them.' Say, 'It is only Allah who deserves all praise, but most of them do not know.'" (31:25)

"(If you) ask them, 'Who has sent down water from the sky to revive the dead earth?' They will say, 'Allah has done it.' Say, 'It is only Allah Who deserves all praise,' but many of them do not understand." (29:63)

"O Hisham, Allah then has praised those fewer in number saying; 'Only few of My servants are grateful.' (34:13) He has said, 'How few are they!' (38:24)

"A believing person from the people of the Pharaoh who concealed his faith said, 'Would you kill a man just because he says Allah is my Lord?' (40:28)

"No one believed in him, except a few." (11:40)

"(Muhammad), tell them, 'Allah certainly has the Power to show such miracles but many of them are ignorant.' (6:37)

"Many of them have no understanding." (5:103)

"Many of them do not realize."

"O Hisham, Allah has then mentioned the people of Intelligence in the best manners with the best of characteristics saying, 'Allah gives wisdom to whoever He wants. Whoever is given wisdom, has, certainly, received much good. Only people of Intelligence can grasp this.' (2:269)

". . . Those who have a firm grounding in knowledge say, 'We believe in it. All its verses are from our Lord.' No one can grasp this fact except the people of Intelligence." (3:7)

"The creation of the heavens and the earth and the alternation of the day and the night are evidence (of the existence of Allah) for people of Intelligence." (3:190)

"Can a person who knows that what is revealed to you from your Lord is the Truth, be considered equal to a blind person? Only those who have understanding take heed." (13:19)

"Can this one be considered equal to one who worships Allah during the night, prostrating and standing, who has fear of the Day of Judgment and who has hope in the mercy of his Lord?" Say, 'Are those who know equal to those who do not know?' Only the people of Intelligence take heed." (39:9)

"It is a blessed Book which We have revealed for you so that they will reflect upon its verses and the people of understanding will take heed." (38:29)

"To Moses We had given guidance and to the children of Israel We had given the Book (40:53) as their inheritance and as a guide and a reminder to the people of understanding." (40:54)

"Keep on reminding them. This benefits the believers." (51:55).

"O Hisham, Allah says in His book, 'This is a reminder for the ones who understand, listen, and see.' (50:37) It means Intelligence.

"'We gave wisdom to Luqman (31:12),' means: Allah gave Luqman Intelligence and understanding.

"O Hisham, Luqman said to his son, 'Revere the Truth; you will be the most intelligent among men. Cleverness in the presence of Intelligence has a very small value. My son, the world is a very deep ocean in which many people have drowned. You must take piety before Allah as a ship, faith as supplies therein, trust in Allah as the sails, Intelligence as captain, knowledge as guide and patience as passengers.'

"O Hisham, for everything there is a guide. The guide for Intelligence is thinking. The guide for thinking is silence. For everything there is a means of mobility. The means of mobility for Intelligence is humble attitude. To disobey a prohibition (of Allah) is enough proof of one's ignorance."

"O Hisham, Allah sent His messengers to people for no reason other than their acquiring understanding about Him. Those who obey Him better have better understanding about Him. Those who are more knowledgeable in the commandment of Allah are the ones who have more powerful Intelligence, and those who have more powerful Intelligence are of a higher degree of excellence in this world and in the next life.

"O Hisham, Allah has established two complete kinds of authority and criteria for people (to refer to) to discern right from wrong: (a) the apparent, the manifest authority and criteria, and (b) the internal, the hidden authority and criteria.

"The prophets and messengers and *'A'immah* are the apparent, manifest authorities and criteria and Intelligence is the hidden, the internal authority and criterion.

"O Hisham, a man of Intelligence is the one whose thankfulness does not diminish because of large wealth and prohibited matters cannot overpower his patience.

"O Hisham, one who supports three things against another three kinds of things he is headed to the destruction of his own Intelligence: (1) darkening of one's ability to think with daydreaming, (2) the abolishment of the sparks of one's wisdom with excessive bluffs and (3) the extinguishing of the lights of good lessons from experience by the desires of one's soul. It is like supporting one's desire to destroy one's own Intelligence. One who destroys his own Intelligence has destroyed his own worldly life as well as the life to come.

"O Hisham, how can you expect to have pure deeds before Allah when you have such things that keep you away from the facts that matter to Allah, your Lord, and you have obeyed your desires against your own Intelligence?

"O Hisham, maintaining patience in loneliness is a sign of the strength of Intelligence. One who has understanding about Allah keeps himself aloof from the people of this world and those interested in it. He becomes interested in what is with Allah. Allah then gives him comfort in his fear and company when he is lonely. Allah gives him riches in his poverty and honor without the existence of his tribesmen.

"O Hisham, Truth is established to obey Allah. There is no salvation without obedience to Allah. Obedience comes only from knowledge, which comes from learning that receives strength from Intelligence. The only knowledge of value is that of one who knows about the Lord and Intelligence discerns the valuable knowledge.

"O Hisham, smaller degrees of deeds with knowledge are accepted with double value, and deeds, even in great deals, of those who ignorantly follow their desires are rejected.

"O Hisham, a person of Intelligence is pleased with little things of the world with wisdom, but he does not agree with a little wisdom with the entire world and, in this way, such people strike a gainful bargain.

"O Hisham, the people of Intelligence stay away from what is more than the basic lawful necessities of life. How then would they not stay away from the sins in this world? To stay away from what is more than the bare necessities of life is only extra virtue but staying away from sins is obligatory.

"O Hisham, a man of Intelligence observes the world and the people of the world and finds out that the worldly gains come only through hard work and labor. He finds out that gains of the life hereafter also come through hard work and labor. He then accepts the kind of gain that is more durable.

"O Hisham, people of Intelligence hold themselves back from the worldly things and strengthen their interest in the gains of the life hereafter. They have learned that the worldly gains are sought after and are wanted and so also are the gains of the life hereafter. One who seeks the gains of the life hereafter, the world will seek him out to deliver to him his livelihood, but one who seeks the worldly gains, the hereafter would also seek to find him. Death will then approach him and it will destroy his world and leave him with no opportunity in the life hereafter (because he did not seek such achievements).

"O Hisham, one who wants self-sufficiency without property, comfort for his heart from the evil of jealousy and the safety of his religion should pray to Allah, the Most Glorious, to perfect his Intelligence. The person of Intelligence is satisfied with the basic necessities and one who is content with basic necessities is self-sufficient and free of needs. One who is not satisfied with basic necessities is never free from want.

"O Hisham, Allah has stated the following on behalf of the people of virtue, who say, 'Lord, do not cause our hearts to deviate from Your guidance, and grant us mercy. You are the Most Awarding One.' (3:8) They know that hearts may deviate and turn toward blindness and destruction.

"It is certain that those who do not fear Allah have no understanding about Him. One who does not have proper understanding about Allah, his heart does not establish about Allah any stable knowledge of the degree of certainty whereby one having clear awareness can find and realize the fact of such quality in his heart. No one can be as such except those whose deeds confirm their words, and their private life agrees with their public activities. This is because Allah, Sacrosanct are Whose names, has not shown what is private and unknown of Intelligence except through what is public and speaks for it.

"O Hisham, the commander of the true believers, Imam Ali, 'Alayhi al-Salam, has said, 'Allah is worshipped better by no means other than Intelligence. No one's Intelligence reaches perfection until therewith are found various qualities. Disbelief and evil should not emerge there-from. Wisdom and goodness should be expected to exist therewith. The extra part of the property of a person of Intelligence is given in charity, the extra of his words are restrained and his share of the worldly things is only the basic necessities. He never considers himself to have learned enough. To be with Allah, although in a very humble state, is far better to him (a person of Intelligence) than to live very much honored with others. Humbleness is more beloved to him than being treated as a dignitary. He considers virtuous deeds of others a great deal and his own virtuous deeds as insignificant. He considers all the other people better than himself and his own self as the worst of all, and this is summing up (victory over) all things.'

"O Hisham, a man of Intelligence never speaks a lie even though it (the lie) may satisfy his desires.

"O Hisham, one who does not maintain honorable kindness has no religion and one cannot have such noble character without Intelligence. A person of the greatest value among people is one who does not consider the worldly gains his fortune. Nothing can become an adequate price for your body other than paradise. Do not sell (yourself) for anything other than paradise.

"O Hisham, the commander of the true believers, Imam Ali, *'Alayhi al-Salam*, has said, 'Three noble qualities in man are of the signs of the existence of Intelligence. He (a) replies when questioned, (b) speaks up only when everyone else fails to speak, and (c) offers his advice when it is beneficial to his people. One who has none of these qualities is a fool.' He also has said, 'No one other than a person who has all of the above or a few of such qualities should chair a gathering, and if one does so without having any of such qualities he is a fool.'

"Imam Hassan ibn Ali, *'Alayhi al-Salam*, has said, 'If you ask for help do so from a proper source.' He was asked, 'O grandson of the Holy Prophet, who are the proper sources?' He replied, 'They are those about whom Allah has spoken in His book saying, "Only those who have understanding will take heed and they are the people of Intelligence."'"

"Imam Ali ibn al-Hussein, *'Alayhi al-Salam*, has said, 'Sitting in the company of virtuous people leads one to virtue, and association with the scholars is a means of strengthening one's Intelligence. Obedience to the authorities that practice justice is an honor. The investment of wealth for profit is a dignifying practice. Guiding one who asks for guidance is an expression of gratitude. To restrain one's harmful behaviors and deeds is the perfection of one's Intelligence in which there is comfort for the body in the short and the long terms.'

"O Hisham, a man of Intelligence does not speak to one who is feared for his calling one a liar. He does not ask for help from those that he fears may deny him. He does not count on what is not within his abilities. He does not maintain any hope in that which may involve agony and harshness. He does not take any steps toward that which he fears may not be achieved due to his inability."

H 13, Ch. 1, h 13
Ali ibn Muhammad has narrated from Sahl ibn Ziyad in a marfu' manner Amir al-Mu'minin Ali, *'Alayhi al-Salam*, who has said the following:
"Intelligence for one is a complete cover (protection). Extra knowledge and skills are evident beauty. Veil your physical shortcomings with your extra knowledge and skills. Fight your desires with help from your Intelligence. In so doing friendship is secured and love becomes manifest for you."

H 14, Ch. 1, h 14
A number of our people have narrated from Ahmad ibn Muhammad from Ali ibn Hadid from Sama'a ibn Mihran who has said the following:
"Once with a gathering of his followers I was in the presence of Imam abu 'Abd Allah, *'Alayhi al-Salam*. A discussion on Intelligence and Ignorance began to emerge among them. Thereupon, Imam abu 'Abd Allah said, 'First, you must recognize Intelligence and its army as well as Ignorance and its army, only then do you find proper guidance.' I then said, 'May Allah keep my soul in service to your cause, we only learn what you teach us.' The Imam, *'Alayhi al-Salam*, said, 'Allah, the Glorious, the Majestic from His light created Intelligence and it was the first creature of the spiritual world on the right side of the Throne. He then told him to move backwards and Intelligence moved backwards. He then told him

to come forward. Intelligence came forward. Allah, the Most Holy, the Most High said, "I have created you a great creature and honored you above all others of My creatures."' The Imam, *'Alayhi al-Salam*, continued, 'Allah then created Ignorance from a salty, dark ocean and told it, "Move backwards," it moved backwards. He then called it to come forward but it did not come forward. He then said to it, "Did you shun coming forward?" He then pronounced it condemned. He then assigned seventy-five armies for Intelligence. When Ignorance saw all the honors Allah had granted to Intelligence it bore hidden animosity toward Intelligence and said, "Lord, this creature is just like me. You created and honored it and gave it power. However, I have no power against it. Give me also likewise armies." The Lord then said, "I will give you also an army but if you disobey Me I will then expel you and your army from My mercy." Ignorance then said, "I agree." Allah gave it seventy-five armies and it was out of the army of Intelligence."'

The Armies of Intelligence / The Armies of Ignorance

Goodness is the minister of Intelligence / Evil is the minister of Ignorance

Belief / Disbelief

Professing / Refusal

Hope / Despair

Justice / Injustice

Consent / Disapproval

Thankfulness / Ungratefulness

Expectation / Hopelessness

Reliance / Greed

Soft-heartedness / Hard-heartedness

Mercy / Anger

Knowledge / Ignorance

Understanding / Foolishness

Chastity / Recklessness

Restraint / Yearning

Relenting / Relentlessness

11

Cautiousness / Impudence

Humbleness / Arrogance

Relaxation / Haste

Forbearance / Silliness

Quietness / Bluffing

Peacefulness / Contempt

Acceptance / Doubt

Patience / Impatience

Forgiving / Revenge

Self-reliance / Poverty

Remembrance / Forgetfulness

Sympathy / Detachment

Self-contentedness / Covetousness

Munificence / Avariciousness

Affection / Animosity

Loyalty / Infidelity

Obedience / Disobedience

Subservience / Supremacy

Security / Affliction

Love / Hatred

Truthfulness / Duplicity

Truth / Falsehood

Trustworthiness / Treachery

Sincerity / Distortion

Sharp-wittedness / Feeble-mindedness

Comprehension / Simple-mindedness

Cognizance / Refusal

Safekeeping / Feeling evil satisfaction

Security unseen / Intemperance

Protectiveness / Unmasking

Prayer / Failing to Pray

Fasting / Consuming Food

Hard work / Passivity

Hajj / Disregard of covenant

Soundness of words / Scandal

Kindness to parents / Rudeness to parents

Factualness / Bragging

Legitimacy / Wickedness

Guardedness / Frivolity

Concealment / Flamboyance

Fairness / Taking sides

Peacefulness / Rebelliousness

Cleanliness / Filthiness

Bashfulness / Ill-manners

Impartiality / Aggression

Comfort / Exhaustion

Ease / Hardship

Blessedness / Lack of blessings

Tranquility / Suffering

Stability / Aggrandizement

Wisdom / Desires

Dignity / Meanness

Fortunateness / Misfortune

Repentance / Persistence

Seeking forgiveness / Keeping pride

Conservativeness / Heedlessness

Invocation / Withholding

Vitality / Lethargy

Happiness / Sorrow

Friendliness / Aversion

Generosity / Stinginess

"No one other than a prophet or his successor or a true believer, whose strength of faith Allah has already tested, can have the whole army of Intelligence with all such characteristics. However, certain persons of our followers and friends may acquire a few of such characteristics so that they may reach perfection, repulse the army of Ignorance and purify themselves from evil. In such a case they will also be found at the high position of the prophets and the successors of the prophets. This progress can be made only after knowing, with certainty, Intelligence and its armies and Ignorance and its armies. May Allah provide us and you the opportunity to obey Him and work to please Him."

H 15, Ch. 1, h 15
A group of our people has narrated from Ahmad ibn Muhammad ibn 'Isa from al-Hassan ibn Ali ibn Faddal from certain persons of our people from abu 'Abd Allah who has said the following:
"The Holy Prophet never spoke to people from the height and with the full power of his Intelligence. The Holy Prophet, *'Alayhi al-Salam*, has said, 'We, the community of the prophets, are commanded to speak to people up to the level of their Intelligence and understanding.'"

H 16, Ch. 1, h 16
Ali ibn Muhammad has narrated from Sahl ibn Ziyad from al-Nawfali from al-Sakuni from Ja'far from his father, *'Alayhi al-Salam*, from Amir al-Mu'minin Ali, *'Alayhi al-Salam*, who has said the following:
"Greed motivates the hearts of ignorant people; longings and yearnings keep them as hostages, and deceit clings to them."

H 17, Ch. 1, h 17

Ali ibn Ibrahim has narrated from his father from Ja'far ibn Muhammad al-Ash'ari from 'Ubayd Allah al-Dihqan from Durust from Ibrahim ibn 'Abd al-Hamid from abu 'Abd Allah, *'Alayhi al-Salam*, who has said the following:

"The most perfect in Intelligence are those who are the best in moral discipline."

H 18, Ch. 1, h 18

Ali has narrated from his father from abu Hashim al-Ja'fari who has said the following:

"Once, we were in the presence of Imam al-Rida, *'Alayhi al-Salam*, when a discussion about Intelligence and discipline took place and the Imam said, 'O abu Hashim, Intelligence is a present from Allah but discipline is a skill and burden. One who pretends to be a well-disciplined one demonstrates it (discipline) with commanding skill and full control. But to pretend to be a person of Intelligence increases for one nothing but Ignorance.'"

H 19, Ch. 1, h 19

Ali ibn Ibrahim has narrated from his father from Yahya ibn al-Mubarak from 'Abd Allah ibn Jabla from ibn Ishaq ibn 'Ammar from abu 'Abd Allah *'Alayhi al-Salam*, who has said the following:

"Once I asked Imam abu 'Abd Allah, *'Alayhi al-Salam*, 'May Allah keep my soul in service for your cause, I have a neighbor who prays a great deal, generously gives in charity and very often visits Makkah and he seems to be acceptable.' The Imam, *'Alayhi al-Salam*, asked, 'How is his Intelligence, O ibn Ishaq?' I then said, 'May Allah keep my soul in service to your cause, he does not have much Intelligence.' 'Nothing from what he does will be raised up (to heaven),' replied the Imam."

H 20, Ch. 1, h 20

Al-Husayn ibn Muhammad has narrated from Ahmad ibn Muhammad al-Sayyari from abu Ya'qub al-Baghdadi who has said the following:

"Once ibn Sikkiyt asked Imam abu al-Hassan, *'Alayhi al-Salam*, 'Why did Allah send Moses with miracles that appeared through his staff and his hand and means of magic? Why did He send Jesus with miraculous means of medical tasks and Prophet Muhammad, *'Alayhi al-Salam*, with miracles that appeared in his speech and sermons?'

"The Imam, *'Alayhi al-Salam*, replied, 'When Moses was sent, magic was very popular among the people. He showed a magic of such form that was not possible for others to perform. He was given such means that destroyed the magical effects of other people's magic and established the Truth of the message of Allah among them. Allah sent Jesus at a time when serious (chronic) illnesses existed among the people and they needed medical treatment. Jesus brought from Allah what the people did not have. He brought from Allah the means to bring the dead back to life, cure the sick and the lepers by the permission of Allah. Thus, he established the truth of the message of Allah among the people.

"Allah sent Prophet Muhammad, *'Alayhi al-Salam*, at a time when oratory and speech were very popular among the people - I think he said poetry (uncertainty is from narrator). He brought to the people from Allah the good advice and wisdom that showed the falsehood in their speeches. Thus, he established the truthfulness of the message of Allah among them.' Ibn al-Sikkiyt then said, 'I swear by Allah that I have never seen anyone like you. What is the proof to establish the Truth of the message of Allah among people today?' The Imam then said, 'It is Intelligence. Intelligence recognizes those who speak the Truth from Allah, thus, one acknowledges their truth. Intelligence recognizes the lies of those who lie in the name of Allah,' Ibn al-Sikkiyt then said, 'This, by Allah, is the answer.'"

H 21, Ch. 1, h 21

Al-Husayn ibn Muhammad has narrated from Mu'alla ibn Muhammad from al-Washsha' from al-Muthanna al-Hannat from al-Qutayba al-A'sha' from ibn abu Ya'fur from a slave of clan of Shayban from abu Ja'far, *'Alayhi al-Salam*, who has said the following:

"When al-Qa'im (the one who will rise with Divine Authority), the guardian, of our family will appear in public, Allah will place His hand over the heads of His servants. Thus, He will join their Intelligence together and complete their understanding."

H 22, Ch. 1, h 22

Ali ibn Muhammad has narrated from Sahl ibn Ziyad from Muhammad ibn Sulayman from Ali ibn Ibrahim from 'Abd Allah ibn Sinan from abu 'Abd Allah, *'Alayhi al-Salam*, who has said the following:

"The authority of Allah among the people (His criterion to discern right from wrong) is the Prophet, *'Alayhi al-Salam* and the authority to judge between Allah and the people is Intelligence."

H 23, Ch. 1, h 23

A number of our people have narrated from Ahmad ibn Muhammad in a *mursal* manner from abu 'Abd Allah, *'Alayhi al-Salam*, who has said the following:

"Intelligence is the support for man. From Intelligence come insightfulness, understanding, memory and knowledge; and with Intelligence he gains perfection. Intelligence is his guide, his instructor and the key to his affairs. When his Intelligence is supported with light, he becomes a scholar, a keeper (of knowledge), an intelligent recaller and a man of understanding. Through Intelligence he learns the answer to how, why, where or when. He learns who helps and who harms him. When he learns these (facts) he learns the channels, the connections and the differentiating factors. He then establishes pure belief in the Oneness of Allah and acknowledges the need to obey Him. When he does so he finds the proper remedy for what he has lost and the right approach to whatever may confront him. He knows well his present involvement, why he is here, where he has come from and to what end he is headed. He will have all these because of Intelligence."

H 24, Ch. 1, h 24

Ali ibn Muhammad has narrated from Sahl ibn Ziyad from 'Isma'il ibn Mihran from certain persons of his people from abu 'Abd Allah, *'Alayhi al-Salam*, who has said the following:

"Intelligence is the guide of a true believer."

H 25, Ch. 1, h 25

Al-Husayn ibn Muhammad has narrated from Mu'alla ibn Muhammad from al-Washsha' from Hammad ibn 'Uthman from al-Sariy ibn Khalid from abu 'Abd Allah, *'Alayhi al-Salam,* who has said the following: "The Messenger of Allah has said, 'O Ali, no poverty is more severe than Ignorance and no property is more valuable than Intelligence."

H 26, Ch. 1, h 26

Muhammad ibn al-Hassan has narrated from Sahl ibn Ziyad from ibn abu Najran from al-'Ala' ibn Razin from Muhammad ibn Muslim from abu Ja'far, *'Alayhi al-Salam,* who has said the following:

"When Allah created Intelligence He said, 'Come forward.' It came forward. He then said, 'Go back.' It went back. Then Allah said, 'I swear by My Honor and Glory that I have not created any creature more beautiful than you. I will command only you to do certain things and prohibit only you from doing certain things. I will grant blessings (rewards) to you only and will hold only you responsible for the consequences of your deeds.'"

H 27, Ch. 1, h 27

A number of our people have narrated from Ahmad ibn Muhammad from al-Haytham ibn abu Masruq al-Nahdi from al-Husayn ibn Khalid from Ishaq ibn 'Ammar who has said the following:

"Once I said to abu 'Abd Allah, *'Alayhi al-Salam,* 'A man comes to me and I speak to him. As soon as I speak only a part of what I want to say he understands all that I want to say. There are other people who come to me and I speak to them all that I want to speak and only then do they understand all of my statements and explain to me what I meant. There are still others to whom I speak at length but they ask me to repeat what I have already expressed to them.' The Imam, *'Alayhi al-Salam,* then said, 'O Ishaq, do you know why this is?' I replied, 'No, I do not know.' The Imam then said the following, 'Those to whom you speak only part of what you want to say and they understand the rest are those whose Intelligence is mixed to take shape with their nature (*Nutfah*). Those who understand you only when you complete your speech are those whose Intelligence is mixed with them in the womb of their mothers. Those who ask you to repeat what you already said are those whose Intelligence is combined with them when they grow up. It is such people who ask you to repeat your statement.'"

H 28, Ch. 1, h 28

A number of our people have narrated from Ahmad ibn Muhammad from certain persons of our people in a *marfu'* manner from abu 'Abd Allah, *'Alayhi al-Salam,* who has said the following:

"The Holy Prophet, *'Alayhi al-Salam,* has said, 'When you find a man who prays and fasts a great deal, do not become proud of him until you see how his Intelligence is.'"

H 29, Ch. 1, h 29

Certain persons of our people have narrated in a *marfu'* manner from Mufaddal ibn 'Umar from abu 'Abd Allah, *'Alayhi al-Salam,* who has said the following:

"O Mufaddal, one can never gain success until he understands and one can never understand until he acquires knowledge. One who understands can very soon excel. One who exercises patience can very soon triumph. Knowledge serves one as a shield, truth is honor, ignorance is humiliation, sharp-wittedness is glory, generosity is success and moral excellence attracts friendship. One who possesses the wisdom of his time does not become frustrated by confusion. Strong determination creates pessimism. In the task of connecting a man and wisdom the existence of the scholar is the blessing. The ignorant ones face misfortunes in between: without wisdom and the scholar. Allah is the guardian of those who know Him. He is the enemy of those who pretend to know Him. A person of Intelligence is forgiving and an ignorant person is treacherous. If you like to be honored you must become kindhearted. If you like to be insulted then show harshness in your manners. One whose origin is noble is kindhearted. One whose element is rough, his liver is thick. The extremist falls into crisis. One who is afraid of the consequences desists from involvement in what he has no knowledge of. One who engages in an affair without knowing anything about it is headed to land in his own loss. One who does not know does not understand; and one who does not understand, does not agree to become peaceful. One who does not agree and submit is not respected; and one who is not respected is broken. One who is so broke is blamable; and one who is in such a condition must become regretful for his own self."

H 30, Ch. 1, h 30

Muhammad ibn Yahya has narrated from in a *marfu'* manner from Amir al-Mu'minin Ali, *'Alayhi al-Salam*, who has said the following:

"If one guarantees for me to firmly establish in himself one good quality I will credit him for it and forgive his other shortcomings. But I will not forgive him for his losing Intelligence and religion; abandoning religion is departing peace and security. Thus, life with fear and insecurity is unpleasant. Loss of Intelligence is loss of life. A person without Intelligence can be compared with no other thing but the dead."

H 31, Ch. 1, h 31

Ali ibn Ibrahim ibn Hashim has narrated from Musa ibn Ibrahim from al-Muharibi from al-Hassan ibn Musa from Musa ibn 'Abd Allah from Maymun ibn Ali from abu 'Abd Allah, *'Alayhi al-Salam*, who has said the following:

"Amir al-Mu'minin Ali, *'Alayhi al-Salam*, has said, 'Self-glorification is an indication of the weakness of one's Intelligence.'"

H 32, Ch. 1, h 32

Abu 'Abd Allah al-'Asimiy has narrated from Ali ibn al-Hassan from Ali ibn Asbat from al-Hassan ibn al-Jahm from abu al-Hassan al-Rida, *'Alayhi al-Salam*, who has said the following:

"Our people mentioned Intelligence and spoke about it in the presence of Imam al-Rida, *'Alayhi al-Salam*, and he said, 'Of the religious people, those who have no Intelligence deserve no credit.' I then asked, 'May Allah keep my soul in your service, of the people who support this cause (*al-walayah*) we know a group who are considered acceptable in our opinion but they do not have such Intelligence.' The Imam then said, 'They are not of the people whom Allah has addressed when He created Intelligence and said to it, "Come forward." It came forward. He then said, 'Go back.' It went back. Then Allah said, 'I swear by My Honor and Glory that I have not created anything better and more beloved to Me than you. I will grant blessings (rewards) to you only and will hold only you responsible for the consequences (of your deeds).'"

H 33, Ch. 1, h 33
Ali ibn Muhammad has narrated from Ahmad ibn Muhammad ibn Khalid from his father from certain persons of our people from abu 'Abd Allah, *'Alayhi al-Salam*, who has said the following:
"The only thing (standing) between belief and disbelief is lack of Intelligence. People asked the Imam, 'How is that, O great-great-great-great grandson of the Holy Prophet?' The Imam replied, 'Human beings center their expectations on other creatures. If they become sincere to Allah He will grant their wish and fulfill their expectations more quickly.'"

H 34, Ch. 1, h 34
A number of our people have narrated from Sahl ibn Ziyad from 'Ubayd Allah al-Dihqan from Ahmad ibn 'Umar al-Halabi from Yahya ibn 'Imran from abu 'Abd Allah, *'Alayhi al-Salam*, who has said the following:
"Amir al-Mu'minin Ali, *'Alayhi al-Salam*, would often say, 'Through Intelligence the depths of wisdom are approached and with wisdom the depths of Intelligence are reached. Good policies are of the virtuous moral discipline.' He would also say, 'Thinking is life for the intelligent heart just as light helps one to walk in darkness with ease and without waiting for a long time.'"

(a) A number of our people have narrated from 'Abd Allah al-Bazzaz from Muhammad ibn 'Abd al-Rahman ibn Hammad from al-Hassan ibn 'Ammar from abu 'Abd Allah, *'Alayhi al-Salam*, in a long *Hadith* the following:
"The first, the beginning, the force and the structure of something is that without which it is of no benefit. The thing that Allah has made a beauty and a light for His creatures, the people, is Intelligence. With Intelligence, people come to know their Creator and that they are created. That He is the One Who has designed them and they are the ones who are being maintained. That it is the Creator Who is Eternal and it is the creatures who are mortals. It is Intelligence with which they reason from His creatures, like the heavens, the earth, the sun, the moon, the night and the day. In this way they learn that they and the creatures have a Creator and Maintainer Who is Eternal. With Intelligence they learn about good and bad. That darkness is in Ignorance and light is in knowledge. Such are facts that they learn with Intelligence.

People asked the Imam, *'Alayhi al-Salam*, 'Can Intelligence alone be enough for people?' The Imam, *'Alayhi al-Salam*, then replied, 'The man of Intelligence, with the guidance of Intelligence, a dependable authority for him from Allah, a beauty and guide for him, he (the Intelligent person) learns that Allah is the Truth and that He is his Lord. With Intelligence one learns that his Creator loves certain things and that He dislikes certain things. The Lord must be obeyed. Certain acts are disobedience to Him. Nothing but Intelligence shows him all these facts. One also (with Intelligence) learns that only with knowledge and searching may one reach the Creator. That one may not benefit from his Intelligence if he cannot learn the truth about Him through his knowledge. It then is necessary for a person of Intelligence to acquire knowledge and proper moral discipline without which nothing else is dependable.'"

(b) Ali ibn Muhammad has narrated from certain persons of his people from ibn abu 'Umayr from al-Nadr ibn Suwayd from Humran and Safwan ibn Mihran al-Jammal who have said we heard Imam abu 'Abd Allah, *'Alayhi al-Salam*, say the following:

"No wealth is more profitable than Intelligence, no poverty is more crushing than foolishness and no effort of seeking support is more supportive than seeking consultation."

This is the end of the Book of Intelligence and Ignorance. All praise belongs to Allah. O Allah, send peace and blessings upon Muhammad and his Holy family.

In the Name of Allah, the Beneficent, the Merciful

Part Two:
The Book on the Excellence of Knowledge

Chapter 1 - The Necessity to Seek Knowledge and the Exhortation to Learn

H 35, Ch. 1, h 1

Muhammad ibn Ya'qub has narrated from Ali ibn Ibrahim ibn Hashim from his father from al-Hassan ibn abu al-Husayn al-Farisi from 'Abd al-Rahman ibn Zayd from his father from abu 'Abd Allah, *'Alayhi al-Salam*, who has said the following:

"The Messenger of Allah has said, 'Seeking knowledge is obligatory for every Muslim. (People should) know that Allah loves those who seek knowledge.'"

H 36, Ch. 1, h 2

Muhammad ibn Yahya has narrated from Muhammad ibn al-Husayn from Muhammad ibn 'Abd Allah from 'Isa ibn 'Abd Allah al-'Amri from abu 'Abd Allah, *'Alayhi al-Salam*, who has said the following:

"Seeking knowledge is obligatory."

H 37, Ch. 1, h 3

Ali ibn Ibrahim has narrated from Muhammad ibn 'Isa from Yunus ibn 'Abd al-Rahman from certain persons of his people who have said the following:

"Once abu al-Hassan, *'Alayhi al-Salam*, was asked, 'Is it permissible for people not to seek what (religious knowledge) they need?' The Imam, *'Alayhi al-Salam*, said, 'No, (it is not permissible to disregard learning).'"

H 38, Ch. 1, h 4

Ali ibn Muhammad and others have narrated from Sahl ibn Ziyad and Muhammad ibn Yahya from Ahmad ibn Muhammad ibn 'Isa all from ibn Mahbub from Hisham ibn Salim from abu Hamza from abu Ishaq al-Subay'i from one who narrated to him who has said the following:

"I heard Amir al-Mu'minin Ali, *'Alayhi al-Salam*, saying, 'O people, you must know that religion becomes complete through seeking knowledge and acting accordingly. You must know that seeking knowledge is of a stronger imperative nature for you than seeking wealth. In wealth everyone's share is guaranteed. A just person has already divided wealth among you. He and my sword guarantee that you receive your share. Knowledge, however, is stored with those who possess it. You are commanded to seek knowledge from its sources (from those who possess it). You must seek knowledge.'"

H 39, Ch. 1, h 5

A number of our people have narrated from Ahmad ibn Muhammad al-Barqi from Ya'qub ibn Yazid from abu 'Abd Allah, a man of our people narrated in a marfu' manner from abu 'Abd Allah, *'Alayhi al-Salam*, from the Holy Prophet, *'Alayhi al-Salam*, who has said the following:

"Seeking knowledge is obligatory."

21

In another *Hadith* Imam abu 'Abd Allah, *'Alayhi al-Salam*, has narrated from the Holy Prophet who has said, "Seeking knowledge is obligatory for every Muslim. Allah, certainly, loves those who seek knowledge."

H 40, Ch. 1, h 6

Ali ibn Muhammad ibn 'Abd Allah has narrated from Ahmad ibn Muhammad ibn Khalid from 'Uthman ibn 'Isa from Ali ibn abu Hamza who has said the following:

"I heard Imam abu 'Abd Allah, *'Alayhi al-Salam*, saying, 'Acquire a good understanding of religion; those of you who do not have good understanding in religion are like the Bedouins. Allah has said in His book, "Why do not certain people from each group of believers seek to become specialists in religious learning and, after completing their studies, guide their group so that they will have fear of Allah?'" (9:122)

H 41, Ch. 1, h 7

Al-Husayn ibn Muhammad has narrated from Ja'far ibn Muhammad from al-Qasim ibn al-Rabi' from Mufaddl ibn 'Umar who has said the following:

"I heard abu 'Abd Allah, *'Alayhi al-Salam*, saying, 'It is necessary for you to have good understanding of religion of Allah. Do not be like Bedouins; on the Day of Judgment Allah will not look to those who do not gain a good understanding of religion, and none of their deeds will be cleansed.'"

H 42, Ch. 1, h 8

Muhammad ibn 'Isma'il has narrated from al-Fadl ibn Shadhan from ibn abu 'Umayr from Jamil ibn Durraj from Aban ibn Taghlib from abu 'Abd Allah, *'Alayhi al-Salam*, who has said the following:

"I like to teach my associates and followers to have good understanding of religion even if it may become necessary to use my whip on their heads."

H 43, Ch. 1, h 9

Ali ibn Muhammad has narrated from Sahl ibn Ziyad from Muhammad ibn 'Isa from one who narrated to him from abu 'Abd Allah, *'Alayhi al-Salam*, the following:

"The narrator has said that a man once said to the Imam, *'Alayhi al-Salam*, 'May Allah keep my soul in your service, what (do you say) about a man who believes in this fact (the Leadership of *Ahl al-Bayt* with Divine Authority) but remains at home and does not acquaint himself with his brethren?'

"Abu 'Abd Allah, *'Alayhi al-Salam*, said, 'How then does he achieve good understanding of his religion?'"

Chapter 2 - The Quality of Knowledge, Its Excellence and the Excellence of the Scholars

H 44, Ch. 2, h 1

Muhammad ibn al-Hassan has narrated from Ali ibn Muhammad from Sahl ibn Ziyad from Muhammad ibn 'Isa from 'Ubayd Allah al-Dihqan from Durust al-Wasiti from Ibrahim ibn 'Abd al-Hamid from abu al-Hassan Musa, *'Alayhi al-Salam*, who has said the following:

"Once the Holy Prophet, *'Alayhi al-Salam*, entered the Mosque and found a group of people gathered around a man. He asked, 'Who is he?' It was said that he was an 'Allama. Then he asked, 'What is that?' They replied that he is an expert in genealogy, chronology, and the history of the pre-Islamic days of darkness and poetry of Arabs. The Holy Prophet, *'Alayhi al-Salam*, then told them, 'There are only three kinds of Knowledge: A strong sign, a justly enjoined obligation or an established tradition. Other than these are only something extra.'"

H 45, Ch. 2, h 2

Muhammad ibn Yahya has narrated from Ahmad ibn Muhammad ibn 'Isa from Muhammad ibn Khalid from abu al-Bakhtari from abu 'Abd Allah, *'Alayhi al-Salam*, who has said the following:

"The scholars are the heirs of the prophets because the prophets did not leave any Dirham or Dinar (units of money) as their legacy. What they left was certain pieces of their statements. Those who acquired anything of these pieces of their statements have certainly gained a colossal share. You must be very careful, when acquiring such knowledge, to know from what kind of people you receive them. After (the death of) every one of us (the *Ahl al-Bayt*, family of the Holy Prophet, *'Alayhi al-Salam*), there comes a just person who removes (and exposes) from (the texts of *Shari'a*) the forgeries of the exaggerators, the materials of the fallacious ones that might have been made to infiltrate and the interpretations of the ignorant ones."

H 46, Ch. 2, h 3

Al-Hassan ibn Muhammad has narrated from Mu'alla ibn Muhammad from al-Hassan ibn Ali al-Washsha' from Hammad ibn 'Uthman from abu 'Abd Allah, *'Alayhi al-Salam*, who has said the following:

"When Allah wants goodness for a person He grants him *Fiqh* (good understanding of religion)."

H 47, Ch. 2, h 4

Muhammad ibn 'Isma'il has narrated from Fadl ibn Shadhan from Hammad ibn 'Isa from Rab'i ibn 'Abd Allah from a man from abu Ja'far, *'Alayhi al-Salam*, who has said the following:

"The entirety of excellence and perfection is in (a) good understanding of religion, (b) exercising patience in hardships and (c) proper planning for one's means of living."

H 48, Ch. 2, h 5

Muhammad ibn Yahya has narrated from Ahmad ibn Muhammad ibn 'Isa from Muhammad ibn Sinan from 'Isma'il ibn Jabir from abu 'Abd Allah, *'Alayhi al-Salam*, who has said the following:

"Scholars are trustworthy people; the pious ones are the strongholds (against the spread of evil) and the successors (of the Holy Prophet, *'Alayhi al-Salam*), are the leaders. In another *Hadith* it is said, 'The scholars are the lighthouses, the pious people are the strongholds (against evil) and the successors (of the Holy Prophet) are the leaders.'"

H 49, Ch. 2, h 6

Ahmad ibn Idris has narrated from Muhammad ibn Hassa'n from Idris ibn al-Hassan from abu Ishaq al-Kindi from Bashir al-Dahhan from abu 'Abd Allah, *'Alayhi al-Salam*, who has said the following:

"O Bashir, there is nothing good in those of our people (followers) who do not acquire good understanding of religion (*Fiqh*). If someone among them may not have good understanding of religion, he needs to ask those who oppose us. When he needs them they lead him astray without his even realizing."

H 50, Ch. 2, h 7
Ali ibn Muhammad has narrated from Sahl ibn Ziyad from al-Nawfali from al-Sakuni from abu 'Abd Allah, *'Alayhi al-Salam*, has narrated from his ancestors from the Holy Prophet, *'Alayhi al-Salam*, who has said the following:

"There is nothing good in life without two kinds of people: a scholar who is obeyed, and an audience who listens carefully."

H 51, Ch. 2, h 8
Ali ibn Ibrahim has narrated from his father from ibn abu 'Umayr and Muhammad ibn Yahya from Ahmad ibn Muhammad from ibn abu 'Umayr from Sayf ibn 'Amira from abu Hamza from abu Ja'far, *'Alayhi al-Salam*, who has said the following:

"A scholar who benefits from his knowledge is better than seventy thousand worshippers."

H 52, Ch. 2, h 9
Al-Hassan ibn Muhammad has narrated from Ahmad ibn Ishaq from Su'dan ibn Muslim from Mu'awiya ibn 'Ammar who has said the following:

"Once, I asked (Imam) abu 'Abd Allah, *'Alayhi al-Salam*, 'There is a man who recounts your *Hadith* and spreads them among people and ties them to their hearts and the hearts of your followers. Also there is a worshipper among your followers who does not narrate your *Hadith*. Which of these two people is better?' The Imam replied, 'The one who narrates our *Hadith* and ties them up to the hearts of our followers is better than one thousand worshippers.'"

Chapter 3 - Kinds of People

H 53, Ch. 3, h 1
Ali ibn Muhammad from Sahl ibn Ziyad and Muhammad ibn Yahya from Ahmad ibn Muhammad ibn 'Isa all from ibn Mahbub from abu 'Usama from Hisham ibn Salim from abu Hamza from abu Ishaq al-Sabiy'i from one who narrated it from a reliable source from Imam Ali, *'Alayhi al-Salam*, who has said the following:

"After the Holy Prophet, people become of three kinds. One group went to a divinely well-guided scholar. Allah had given him a high degree of knowledge that made him independent of the knowledge of the others. The second group was the ignorant group, which claimed to have knowledge but in fact had no knowledge. This was an egotist group. Worldly attractions had made them lose sight of the truth and they misled other people. The third group consisted of people who learned from a divinely guided scholar. He taught them for the sake of Allah and for their salvation. It then was clear that those who claimed (to be scholars when, in fact, they were not) and those who forged certain matters (in *Shari'a*) were destroyed."

H 54, Ch. 3, h 2
Al-Husayn ibn Muhammad al-Ash'ari has narrated from Mu'alla ibn Muhammad from al-Hassan ibn Ali al-Washsha' from Ahmad ibn 'A'idh from abu Khadija Salim ibn Mukram from abu 'Abd Allah, *'Alayhi al-Salam*, who has said the following:

"People are of three kinds: Scholars, the learning group (students) and the garbled ones (who do not have any opinion in life)."

H 55, Ch. 3, h 3

Muhammad ibn Yahya has narrated from 'Abd Allah ibn Muhammad from Ali ibn al-Hakam from al-'Ala' ibn Razin from Muhammad ibn Muslim from abu Hamza al-Thumali who has said the following:

"Once abu 'Abd Allah, *'Alayhi al-Salam*, said to me, 'Be a scholar or a student or love the scholars. Do not become of the fourth group lest you be destroyed due to hating them (the scholars).'"

H 56, Ch. 3, h 4

Ali ibn Ibrahim has narrated from Muhammad ibn 'Isa from Yunus from Jamil who has said the following:

"I heard Imam abu 'Abd Allah, *'Alayhi al-Salam*, saying, 'People become of three groups: Scholars, those who learn, and garbled ones. We are the scholars. Our followers are the ones who learn. The rest of the people are garbled ones (who do not have any meaningful opinion in life).'"

Chapter 4 - The Reward for the Scholars and Those Who Seek Knowledge

H 57, Ch. 4, h 1

Muhammad ibn al-Hassan and Ali ibn Muhammad has narrated from Sahl ibn Ziyad and Muhammad ibn Yahya from Ahmad ibn Muhammad, all from Ja'far ibn Muhammad al-Ash'ari from 'Abd Allah ibn Maymun al-Qaddah and Ali ibn Ibrahim from his father from Hammad ibn 'Isa from al-Qaddah from abu 'Abd Allah, *'Alayhi al-Salam*, who has said the following:

"The Holy Prophet has said, 'If one sets out on a journey to seek knowledge, Allah will lead him to the path that takes him to paradise. The angels will stretch their wings for the pleasure of the seeker of knowledge, and all that is in heaven and earth, even the whales in the oceans will ask (Allah) to forgive him. The excellence of the scholar over other people is like the brilliance of the moon over other stars during a full-moon night. Scholars are the heirs of the prophets. The prophets did not leave any Dirham or Dinar (wealth) as their legacy but left knowledge as their legacy. Whoever acquires a share from such legacy has gained an enormous share.'"

H 58, Ch. 4, h 2

Muhammad ibn Yahya has narrated from Ahmad ibn Muhammad from al-Hassan ibn Mahbub from Jamil ibn Salih from Muhammad ibn Muslim from abu Ja'far, *'Alayhi al-Salam*, who has said the following:

"Those of you who teach will have the same reward as those who learn as well as their higher position over the student. Learn knowledge from those who possess knowledge and teach it to your brethren just as the scholars have taught you."

H 59, Ch. 4, h 3

Ali ibn Ibrahim has narrated from Ahmad ibn Muhammad al-Barqi from Ali ibn al-Hakam from Ali ibn abu Hamza from abu Basir from abu 'Abd Allah, *'Alayhi al-Salam*, who has said the following:

"Whoever teaches something good will receive a reward each time his student practices such knowledge." Abu Basir has said, 'I asked the Imam, would this apply to the student if he teaches other people?' The Imam, *'Alayhi al-Salam*, said, 'Yes, it applies to him even if he teaches it to all people.' I then asked, 'Will it apply to him if he will already be dead?' The Imam, *'Alayhi al-Salam*, responded, 'Yes, even if he will die.'"

H 60, Ch. 4, h 4
Through the same chain of narrators it is narrated from Muhammad ibn 'Abd al-Hamid from al-'Ala' ibn Razin from abu 'Ubayda al-Hadhdha' from abu Ja'far, *'Alayhi al-Salam*, who has said the following:

"Whoever teaches a chapter of guidance will receive a reward equal to the rewards of all of those who practice such guidance without any reduction in the rewards of the later ones. Whoever introduces a chapter of misguidance will suffer for each time others practice it without any reduction in the suffering of whoever may practice such misguidance."

H 61, Ch. 4, h 5
Al-Husayn ibn Muhammad has narrated from Ali ibn Muhammad ibn Sa'd in a *marfu'* manner from abu Hamza from Ali ibn al-Husayn, *'Alayhi al-Salam*, who has said the following:

"If only people knew how much reward there is for seeking knowledge, they would seek it even if they had to shed their blood for it or dive in large waves. Allah, the Blessed and the Most High revealed to Daniel saying, 'The most hated among My creatures are the ignorant ones who disrespect the scholars and do not follow them. The most beloved to Me in My servants are the pious ones who work hard to become deserving of greater rewards, who always stay close to the scholars, follow the forbearing people and accept (the advice of) people of wisdom.'"

H 62, Ch. 4, h 6
Ali ibn Ibrahim has narrated from his father from al-Qasim ibn Muhammad from Sulayman ibn Dawud al-Minqari from Hafs ibn Ghiyath who has said that abu 'Abd Allah, *'Alayhi al-Salam*, said the following:

"Whoever acquires knowledge and practices what he has learned and teaches it to others for the sake of Allah, will be called a great person among the angels of heavens. It will be said: 'He learned for the sake of Allah, practiced for the sake of Allah and taught for the sake of Allah.'"

Chapter 5 - The Qualities of the Scholars

H 63, Ch. 5, h 1
Muhammad ibn Yahya al-'Attar has narrated from Ahmad ibn Muhammad ibn 'Isa from al-Hassan ibn Mahbub from Mu'awiya ibn Wahab who has said the following:

"I heard Imam abu 'Abd Allah, *'Alayhi al-Salam*, saying, 'Seek knowledge and beautify it with forbearance and dignity. Be humble to your students and to those from whom you learn. Do not be a tyrant scholar, otherwise your falsehood destroys the truth in you.'"

H 64, Ch. 5, h 2
Ali ibn Ibrahim has narrated from Muhammad ibn 'Isa from Yunus from Hammad ibn 'Uthman from al-Harith ibn Mughirah al-Nasri from abu 'Abd Allah, *'Alayhi al-Salam*, who about the words of Allah, the Most Majestic, the Most Gracious, has said the following:

"'Only Allah's knowledgeable servants fear Him . . .' (35:28) means that scholars are those whose deeds testify to the truthfulness of their words; otherwise, they are not scholars."

H 65, Ch. 5, h 3

A number of our people have narrated from Ahmad ibn Muhammad al-Barqi from 'Isma'il ibn Mihran from abu Sa'id al-Qammat from al-Halabi from abu 'Abd Allah, *'Alayhi al-Salam*, who has said the following:

"Once Imam Ali, *'Alayhi al-Salam*, said, 'Do you want me to describe to you the true *Faqih* (the person who truly has a good understanding of religion)? A true *Faqih* is one who does not cause people to despair from the mercy of Allah or to become indifferent toward and unconcerned about the punishment of Allah, who does not allow them to consider disobedience to Allah as permissible and who does not abandon the Holy Quran despite the existence of other matters' attractions. You must know that there is no goodness in knowledge without good understanding (*Fiqh*). You must know that there is nothing good in a recitation without thinking about it. You must know that there is nothing good in worship without thoughtfulness.' In another *Hadith* he has said, "You must know that there is nothing good in knowledge without good understanding. You must know that there is nothing good in a recitation without thinking about it. You must know that there is nothing good in worship without having a good understanding of religion. You must know that there is nothing good in performing the acts of Hajj and so forth without piety.'"

H 66, Ch. 5, h 4

Muhammad ibn Yahya has narrated from Ahmad ibn Muhammad ibn 'Isa and Muhammad ibn 'Isma'il from al-Fadl ibn Shadhan al-Niysaburi, all from Safwan ibn Yahya from abu al-Hassan al-Rida, *'Alayhi al-Salam*, who has said the following:

"Of the signs of *Fiqh* (good understanding of religion) are forbearance and silence."

H 67, Ch. 5, h 5

Ahmad ibn 'Abd Allah from Ahmad ibn Muhammad al-Barqi from certain persons of his people in a marfu' manner *(rafa'ahu)* from Amir al-Mu'minin Ali, *'Alayhi al-Salam*, *'Alayhi al-Salam*, who has said the following:

"Foolishness and arrogance are not found in the hearts of scholars."

H 68, Ch. 5, h 6

Through the same chain of narrators it is narrated from Muhammad ibn Khalid from Muhammad ibn Sinan in a *marfu'* manner *(rafa'ahu)* from Jesus son of Mary who has said the following to his disciples:

"'O disciples, I need your help; so help me.' They replied, 'Your request is granted, O Spirit of Allah.' Jesus then got up and washed their feet. To this the disciples said, 'We should have served you, O Spirit of Allah.' Jesus then said, 'The people who must serve others are the scholars. I acted in this humble way so that you will act among people in the humble way I acted before you.' Jesus then said, 'It is with humility that wisdom is established but not with arrogance, just as plants grow in plain, soft ground but not on hard ground and rocks.'"

H 69, Ch. 5, h 7

Ali ibn Ibrahim has narrated from his father from Ali ibn Ma'bad from the person whom he mentioned from Mu'awiya ibn Wahab from abu 'Abd Allah, *'Alayhi al-Salam*, who has said the following:

"Imam Ali, *'Alayhi al-Salam*, would often say, 'O seekers of knowledge (note that) a scholar has three signs: Knowledge, forbearance and calmness. A pretending scholar has three qualities: He quarrels with those higher than he through disobedience. He does injustice to those below him in position through domination and he becomes a supporter of the unjust.'"

Chapter 6 - The Rights of the Scholars

H 70, Ch. 6, h 1

Ali ibn Muhammad ibn 'Abd Allah has narrated from Ahmad ibn Muhammad from Muhammad ibn Khalid from Sulayman ibn Ja'far al-Ja'fari from the person who he mentioned from abu 'Abd Allah, *'Alayhi al-Salam*, who has said the following:

"Imam Ali, *'Alayhi al-Salam*, has said, 'One of the rights of a scholar is that one must not ask him a great many questions and must not latch on to his garment (excessive questioning). When one would enter in his presence while other people are there, one should offer greeting of peace to everyone and special greetings to the scholar alone. One must sit before him and not behind him. One must not blink his eyes before him or make hand gestures and must not speak much in his presence that such as so and so said so and so contrary to what he says. The length of his meeting must not disappoint one because the case of a scholar is like a fruit-bearing tree in which case one needs to wait until the tree lets fruits fall onto one. The reward for a scholar is greater than that for those who fast and perform prayers very often and for those who fight for the cause of Allah.'"

Chapter 7 - The Loss of a Scholar

H 71, Ch. 7, h 1

A number of our people have narrated from Ahmad ibn Muhammad ibn Khalid from 'Uthman ibn 'Isa from abu Ayyub al-Khazzaz from Sulayman ibn Khalid from abu 'Abd Allah, *'Alayhi al-Salam*, who has said the following:

"Of the deaths of the true believers the one that Satan loves most is the death of a *Faqih* (one who has very good understanding of religion and its laws)."

H 72, Ch. 7, h 2

Ali ibn Ibrahim has narrated from his father from ibn abu 'Umayr from certain persons of his people from abu 'Abd Allah, *'Alayhi al-Salam*, who has said the following:

"When a true believer who is a *Faqih* dies, it causes an irreparable damage in the Islamic system."

H 73, Ch. 7, h 3

Muhammad ibn Yahya has narrated from Ahmad ibn Muhammad from ibn Mahbub from Ali ibn abu Hamza who has said the following:

"I heard (Imam) abu al-Hassan Musa ibn Ja'far, *'Alayhi al-Salam*, saying, 'When a true believer dies the angels and places of earth, where he worshipped Allah, weep because of his death. Also the doors of the heavens through which his good deeds had been raised weep and it (his death) causes an irreparable damage in the

Islamic system, because the true believing *Fuqaha* (people of proper understanding in religion and its laws) are the strongholds of the Islamic system, just as the fortress around a city is a stronghold for it.'"

H 74, Ch. 7, h 4

From him (Muhammad ibn Yahya) from Ahmad from ibn Mahbub from abu Ayyub al-Khazzaz from Sulayman ibn Khalid from abu 'Abd Allah, *'Alayhi al-Salam*, who has said the following:

"Of the deaths of the true believers the one that Satan loves most is the death of a *Faqih,* (one who has good understanding of religion and its laws)."

H 75, Ch. 7, h 5

Ali ibn Muhammad has narrated from Sahl ibn Ziyad from Ali ibn Asbat from his uncle Ya'qub ibn Salim from Dawud ibn Farqad who has said the following:

"Imam abu 'Abd Allah, *'Alayhi al-Salam*, has said, 'My father would often say, "Allah does not take back the knowledge that He has sent down. But when the scholar dies it (his death) takes away his knowledge and after this the unjust ones (disobedient to laws) come. They go astray and mislead people. There is no good in things that have no basis and foundation."'"

H 76, Ch. 7, h 6

A number of our people have narrated from Ahmad ibn Muhammad from Muhammad ibn Ali from the person who he mentioned from Jabir from abu Ja'far, *'Alayhi al-Salam*, who has said the following:

"Imam Ali ibn al-Husayn, *'Alayhi al-Salam*, would say, 'My soul shows generosity in accepting the quickening of our death or being murdered. It is due to the words of Allah that say, 'Have they not considered that We have taken over the land and reduced its borders?' (13:41) The reference here is to the death of the scholars."

Chapter 8 - Meeting the Scholars and Associating with Them

H 77, Ch. 8, h 1

Ali ibn Ibrahim has narrated from Muhammad ibn 'Isa from Yunus in a *marfu'* manner *(rafa'ahu)* from Luqman the wise, who has said the following to his son:

"My son, choose your own meeting place. If you find a people who speak of Allah, the Glorious, the Majestic, sit with them. If you know already, you benefit from your knowledge and if you are ignorant they teach you. Perhaps Allah may cover them with the shadow of His mercy and you may be covered along with them. If you see a people who do not speak of Allah, do not sit with them; even if you had knowledge it would not benefit you, and if you were ignorant they increase your ignorance. Perhaps Allah may cover them with the shadow of His punishment which may catch you also along with them."

H 78, Ch. 8, h 2

Ali ibn Ibrahim has narrated from his father and Muhammad ibn Yahya from Ahmad ibn Muhammad ibn 'Isa, all from ibn Mahbub from Durust ibn abu Mansur from Ibrahim ibn 'Abd al-Hamid from abu al-Hassan Musa ibn Ja'far, *'Alayhi al-Salam*, who has said the following:

"Speaking to a scholar, even at a trash collection, is better than speaking to an ignorant person at the best furnished palace."

H 79, Ch. 8, h 3

A number of our people have narrated from Ahmad ibn Muhammad al-Barqi from Sharif ibn Sabiq from al-Fadl ibn abu Qurrah from abu 'Abd Allah, *'Alayhi al-Salam*, who has said the following:

"The Holy Prophet has said, 'Once the disciples asked Jesus, "O the Spirit of Allah, who should we associate with?" Jesus replied, "Associate with those whose visit reminds you of Allah, whose speech and logic increase your knowledge and whose deeds attract you to the next life.'"'

H 80, Ch. 8, h 4

Muhammad ibn 'Isma'il has narrated from al-Fadl ibn Shadhan from ibn abu 'Umayr from Mansur ibn Hazim from abu 'Abd Allah, *'Alayhi al-Salam*, who has said the following:

"The Holy Prophet has said, 'Association with religious people is an honor in this life as well as in the next life.'"

H 81, Ch. 8, h 5

Ali ibn Ibrahim has narrated from his father from al-Qasim ibn Muhammad al-Asbahani from Sulayman ibn Dawud al-Minqari from Sufyan ibn 'Uyayna from Mis'ar ibn Kidam who has said the following:

"I heard (Imam) abu Ja'far, *'Alayhi al-Salam*, saying, 'A meeting with one whom I trust gives more strength to my soul than working for one whole year.'"

Chapter 9 - Asking the Scholar and Discussing with Him

H 82, Ch. 9, h 1

Ali ibn Ibrahim has narrated from his father from ibn abu 'Umayr from certain persons of our people from abu 'Abd Allah, *'Alayhi al-Salam*, who has said the following:

"About a person who had smallpox and needed a formal bath due to sexual activities, and to whom certain people had given a bath and then he died, the Imam said, 'They have killed him. Why did they not ask about it? The medicine for the illness due to ignorance is, certainly, to ask.'"

H 83, Ch. 9, h 2

Muhammad ibn Yahya has narrated from Ahmad ibn Muhammad ibn 'Isa from Hammed ibn 'Isa from Hariz from Zurara, Muhammad ibn Muslim and Burayd al-'Ijli who has said the following:

"(Imam) abu 'Abd Allah, *'Alayhi al-Salam*, has said, 'People are destroyed only because they do not ask (about what they do not know).'"

H 84, Ch. 9, h 3

Ali ibn Muhammad has narrated from Sahl ibn Ziyad from Ja'far ibn Muhammad al-Ash'ari from 'Abd Allah ibn Maymun al-Qaddah from abu 'Abd Allah, *'Alayhi al-Salam*, who has said the following:

"This knowledge (the knowledge of the Holy Prophet and *Ahl al-Bayt*, *'Alayhim al-Salam*) is under lock and the key to its asking."

Ali ibn Ibrahim has narrated from his father from al-Nawfali, from al-Sakuni from Imam abu 'Abd Allah, *'Alayhi al-Salam*, a similar *Hadith*.

H 85, Ch. 9, h 4

Ali ibn Ibrahim has narrated from Muhammad ibn 'Isa ibn 'Ubayd from Yunus ibn 'Abd al-Rahman from abu Ja'far al-Awwal from abu 'Abd Allah, *'Alayhi al-Salam*, who has said the following:

"People can do nothing until they ask, acquire proper understanding of religion and know their Imam; and then they can follow what the Imam says even if he, *'Alayhi al-Salam*, would say something differently under (*taqiyah*) pressure."

H 86, Ch. 9, h 5
Ali has narrated from Muhammad ibn 'Isa from Yunus from the person who he mentioned from abu 'Abd Allah, *'Alayhi al-Salam*, who has said the following:
"The Holy Prophet has said, 'Woe is to a man who does not reserve time every Friday for learning about his religion and make it a habit to ask about his religion.'" In another *Hadith* it says, "Woe is to every such Muslim."

H 87, Ch. 9, h 6
Ali ibn Ibrahim has narrated from his father from ibn abu 'Umayr from 'Abd Allah ibn Sinan from abu 'Abd Allah, *'Alayhi al-Salam*, who has said the following:
"The Holy Prophet has said, 'Allah, the Majestic, the Glorious, says, "Discussions in knowledge among My servants are of the matters that bring the dead hearts to life only, if such discussions lead them to My commandments."'"

H 88, Ch. 9, h 7
Muhammad ibn Yahya has narrated from Ahmad ibn Muhammad ibn 'Isa from Muhammad ibn Sinan from abu al-Jarud from abu Ja'far, *'Alayhi al-Salam*, who has said the following:
"I heard abu Ja'far, *'Alayhi al-Salam*, saying, 'May Allah grant forgiveness to a man who revives knowledge.' Abu al-Jarud has said, 'I asked the Imam, "What is reviving knowledge?" The Imam, *'Alayhi al-Salam*, replied, saying, 'It is knowledge discussed among religious people and people of piety.'"

H 89, Ch. 9, h 8
Muhammad ibn Yahya has narrated from Ahmad ibn Muhammad from 'Abd Allah ibn Muhammad al-Hajjal from certain persons of our people in a *marfu'* manner from the Messenger of Allah who has said the following:
"Discuss facts, meet each other and speak to each other; speaking is brightness for hearts. Hearts stain just as swords do. Speaking cleanses them up."

Note: In certain manuscripts it is 'Hadid' (Iron) instead of '*Hadith*,' (speaking) at the end of the sentence.

H 90, Ch. 9, h 9
A number of our people have narrated from Ahmad ibn Muhammad ibn Khalid from his father from Fadalah ibn Ayyub from 'Umar ibn Aban from Mansur al-Sayqal who has said the following:
"I heard Imam abu Ja'far, *'Alayhi al-Salam*, saying, 'Discussing knowledge is a study and to study is (like) a good prayer.'"

Chapter 10 - Giving Knowledge as Charity

H 91, Ch. 10, h 1
Muhammad ibn Yahya has narrated from Ahmad ibn Muhammad ibn 'Isa from Muhammad ibn 'Isma'il ibn Bazi' from Mansur ibn Hazim from Talha ibn Zayd from abu 'Abd Allah, *'Alayhi al-Salam*, who has said the following:
"I read in the book of Imam Ali, *'Alayhi al-Salam*, that Allah had no commitment from and covenant with ignorant people to seek knowledge before having a

commitment from and covenant with scholars to give knowledge as charity to the ignorant ones; Knowledge existed before Ignorance."

H 92, Ch. 10, h 2

A number of our people have narrated from Ahmad ibn Muhammad al-Barqi from his father from 'Abd Allah ibn Mughirah and Muhammad ibn Sinan from Talha ibn Zayd from abu 'Abd Allah, *'Alayhi al-Salam*, who has said the following about the words of Allah:

"Do not scornfully turn your face away from people ..." (31:18) so that people would all be equal in matters of knowledge before you, said the Imam, *'Alayhi al-Salam*."

H 93, Ch. 10, h 3

Through the same chain of narrators he has narrated from his father from Ahmad ibn Nadr from 'Amr and ibn Shimr from Jabir from abu Ja'far, *'Alayhi al-Salam*, who has said the following:

"The tax (*Zakat*) on knowledge is teaching it to servants of Allah."

H 94, Ch. 10, h 4

Ali ibn Ibrahim has narrated from Muhammad ibn 'Isa ibn 'Ubayd from Yunus ibn 'Abd al-Rahman from the person who he mentioned from abu 'Abd Allah, *'Alayhi al-Salam*, who has said the following:

"Jesus son of Mary, *'Alayhi al-Salam*, once stood up to speak to the Israelites saying, 'O Israelites, do not speak the words of wisdom to ignorant people; you will be doing injustice to them (words of wisdom). Do not keep them (words of wisdom) from those who deserve them lest you will do injustice to them (deserving people).'"

Chapter 11 - Prohibition on Speaking Without Knowledge

H 95, Ch. 11, h 1

Muhammad ibn Yahya has narrated from Ahmad and 'Abd Allah (both) sons of Muhammad ibn 'Isa from Ali ibn al-Hakam from Sayf ibn 'Umayra from Mufaddal ibn Yazid who has said the following:

"Once, (Imam) abu 'Abd Allah, *'Alayhi al-Salam*, said to me, 'I like to warn you about two forms of behavior that lead a man to destruction. I prohibit you from dealing with Allah on the basis of falsehood and from giving *fatwa* (a legal opinion) to people without knowledge.'"

H 96, Ch. 11, h 2

Ali ibn Ibrahim has narrated from Muhammad ibn 'Isa ibn 'Ubayd from Yunus ibn 'Abd al-Rahman from 'Abd al-Rahman ibn al-Hajjaj who has said the following:

"Imam abu 'Abd Allah, *'Alayhi al-Salam*, once said to me, 'Beware of two forms of behavior. It is such behaviors that have led many people to their destruction. Beware of giving *fatwa* to people on the basis of your own opinion, and of following a religion without knowledge.'"

H 97, Ch. 11, h 3

Muhammad ibn Yahya has narrated from Ahmad ibn Muhammad ibn 'Isa from al-Hassan ibn Mahbub from Ali ibn al-Ri'ab from abu 'Ubayda al-Hadhdha' from abu Ja'far, *'Alayhi al-Salam*, who has said the following:

"The angels of mercy and the angels of wickedness condemn those who give to people *fatwas* without knowledge and guidance. Such people will be held responsible for the sins of all those who have followed such *fatwas*."

H 98, Ch. 11, h 4

A number of our people have narrated has narrated from Ahmad ibn Muhammad ibn Khalid from al-Hassan ibn Ali al-Washsha' from Aban al-Ahmar from Ziyad ibn abu Raja' from abu Ja'far, *'Alayhi al-Salam*, who has said the following:

"What you know you may speak about, but what you do not know say, 'Allah knows best.' A man refers to a verse in the Holy Quran and gives it a meaning that is farther from the truth than the heavens are from earth."

H 99, Ch. 11, h 5

Muhammad ibn 'Isma'il has narrated from al-Fadl ibn Shadhan from Hammad ibn 'Isa from Rib'i ibn 'Abd Allah from Muhammad ibn Muslim from abu 'Abd Allah, *'Alayhi al-Salam*, who has said the following:

"It is very proper for a scholar to say, 'Allah knows best' if he does not know. This is not proper for a non-scholar.'"

H 100, Ch. 11, h 6

Ali ibn Ibrahim has narrated from Ahmad ibn Muhammad ibn Khalid from Hammad ibn 'Isa from Hariz ibn 'Abd Allah from Muhammad ibn Muslim from abu 'Abd Allah, *'Alayhi al-Salam*, who has said the following:

"If one of you is asked about something you do not know you must say, 'I have no knowledge,' and you must not say, 'Allah knows best' because it may create doubts in the hearts of your audience. If the person questioned says, 'I do not know' his audience will not accuse him of anything."

H 101, Ch. 11, h 7

Al-Husayn ibn Muhammad has narrated from Mu'alla ibn Muhammad from Ali ibn Asbat from Ja'far ibn Sama'a from several persons, from Aban, from Zurara ibn A'yan who has said the following:

"Once I asked Imam abu Ja'far, *'Alayhi al-Salam*, 'What are of the rights of Allah on people?' The Imam, *'Alayhi al-Salam*, replied, 'They must say what they know and abstain from saying anything that they have no knowledge of.'"

H 102, Ch. 11, h 8

Ali ibn Ibrahim has narrated from his father from ibn abu 'Umayr from Yunus (ibn 'Abd al-Rahman) from abu Ya'qub Ishaq ibn 'Abd Allah from abu 'Abd Allah, *'Alayhi al-Salam*, who has said the following:

"Allah has addressed His servants in two verses of the Holy Quran very particularly: 'Did they not make a covenant (with Allah) in the Book not to speak anything other than the Truth about Allah and to study its contents well? They call a lie something that is beyond the limit of their knowledge and whose interpretation has not yet been revealed . . .'" (10:39)

H 103, Ch. 11, h 9

Ali ibn Ibrahim has narrated from Muhammad ibn 'Isa from Yunus from Dawud ibn Farqad from one he narrated from ibn Shubruma (a judge in al-Kufa during the rule of al-Mansur) who has said the following:

"I never heard anything like a statement I heard from Imam abu 'Abd Allah, *'Alayhi al-Salam*, and it almost pierced my heart. The Imam, *'Alayhi al-Salam*, said, 'My father narrated from my great-great-great-great grandfather, the Holy Prophet, *'Alayhi al-Salam*, who said, "Those who act on the basis of analogy will face their destruction and lead others to their destruction. Those who give *fatwas* (legal opinions) without knowing the abrogating and the abrogated (texts of the law), the clear text and that which requires interpretation, they will face destruction and lead others to their destruction.'"

Chapter 12 - Those Who Act Without Knowledge

H 104, Ch. 12, h 1

A number of our people have narrated from Ahmad ibn Muhammad ibn Khalid from his father from Muhammad ibn Sinan from Talha ibn Zayd who has said the following:

"I heard (Imam) abu 'Abd Allah, *'Alayhi al-Salam*, saying, 'Working without understanding and insight is like traveling in the wrong direction; it only takes one farther away from the destination.'"

H 105, Ch. 12, h 2

Muhammad ibn Yahya from Ahmad ibn Muhammad ibn 'Isa from Muhammad ibn Sinan from ibn Muskan from Hassan al-Sayqal who has said the following:

"I heard (Imam) abu 'Abd Allah, *'Alayhi al-Salam*, saying, 'Allah does not accept a deed without good understanding; and proper understanding does not come into being without work. One who achieves proper understanding, it (proper understanding) will guide him to good deeds, and one who does not work will not have any understanding. Is it not a fact that certain parts of faith come from other parts?'"

H 106, Ch. 12, h 3

It is narrated from him from Ahmad ibn Muhammad from ibn Faddal from the one he narrated from abu 'Abd Allah, *'Alayhi al-Salam*, who has said the following:

"Imam abu 'Abd Allah, *'Alayhi al-Salam*, has narrated from the Holy Prophet who has said, 'Those who work without knowledge destroy more than they gain.'"

Chapter 13 - Utilization of Knowledge

H 107, Ch. 13, h 1

Muhammad ibn Yahya has narrated from Ahmad ibn Muhammad ibn 'Isa from Hammed from 'Umar ibn 'Udhayna from Aban ibn abu 'Ayyash from Sulaym ibn Qays al-Hilali who has said the following:

"I heard Imam Ali, *'Alayhi al-Salam*, narrate from the Holy Prophet, *'Alayhi al-Salam*, who has said, 'There are two kinds of scholars: One kind consists of those who uphold their knowledge; and they gain salvation. The other kind consists of those who disregard their knowledge, and they face destruction. The people of hell will suffer from the foul smell of the scholars who do not act according to their knowledge. Of the people of hell, the one who will regret most will be the man who teaches someone and shows him the way of Allah. The student accepts and acts according to such teachings. Consequently Allah takes him to paradise, but the teacher is sent to hell for ignoring his own knowledge, following his desires and entertaining unending worldly hopes. Following one's desires bars one from the truth and cherishing unending worldly hopes causes one to forget the next life.'"

H 108, Ch. 13, h 2

Muhammad ibn Yahya from Ahmad ibn Muhammad from Muhammad ibn Sinan from 'Isma'il ibn Jabir from abu 'Abd Allah, *'Alayhi al-Salam*, who has said the following:

"Knowledge and good (virtuous) work are closely related. One who has knowledge, works; and one who performs good works, learns. Knowledge invites work and if it is not accepted knowledge departs the good deeds."

H 109, Ch. 13, h 3

A number of our people have narrated from Ahmad ibn Muhammad ibn Khalid from Ali ibn Muhammad al-Qasani from one he mentioned from 'Abd Allah ibn Qasim al-Ja'fari from abu 'Abd Allah, *'Alayhi al-Salam*, who has said the following:

"If a scholar preaches and does not practice what he preaches, his words bounce away from the hearts of the audience like rain that bounce off the rocks."

H 110, Ch. 13, h 4

Ali ibn Ibrahim has narrated from his father from al-Qasim ibn Muhammad from al-Minqari from Ali ibn Hashim ibn al-Burayd from his father who has said the following:

"Once a man came to (Imam) Ali ibn al-Husayn, *'Alayhi al-Salam*, and asked him certain questions and the Imam answered his questions. The man then wanted to ask similar questions but the Imam said, 'It is written in the Gospel, "Do not inquire to know what you do not know until you practice what you know; neglecting to practice what one knows does not increase anything but disbelief; nor does it increase anything for one's relation with Allah but alienation.'''

H 111, Ch. 13, h 5

Muhammad ibn Yahya has narrated from Ahmad ibn Muhammad ibn 'Isa from Muhammad ibn Sinan from al-Mufaddal ibn 'Umar who has said the following:

"I asked Imam abu 'Abd Allah, *'Alayhi al-Salam*, 'What are the facts that help one recognize those who have gained salvation?' The Imam replied, 'One whose words agree with his deeds, has established testimony and evidence to his gaining salvation. One whose words do not agree with his deeds, it (his belief) is temporary.'''

H 112, Ch. 13, h 6

A number of our people have narrated from Ahmad ibn Muhammad ibn Khalid from his father in a marfu' manner *(rafa'ahu)* from Amir al-Mu'minin Ali, *'Alayhi al-Salam*, who has said the following:

"Once, Imam Ali, *'Alayhi al-Salam*, said in one of his sermons, 'O people, if you learn and gain knowledge, you must act accordingly, so that you may have guidance. A learned person who disregards his knowledge is like a lost and ignorant person who never comes to the right path due to his ignorance. In fact, you will find the case against such a learned one who disregards his knowledge more severe and his regret more prolonged, compared to the ignorant person who wanders about in his ignorance. Both people stray and are devoid of goodness. Do not hesitate lest you doubt, and do not doubt lest you disbelieve. Do not be lenient with your souls to allow them become lazy. Do not trivialize the truth lest you lose badly. It is of the truth to learn *Fiqh* (proper understanding of religion). It is of *Fiqh* not to suffer deceit. The wisest among you is the one most obedient to his Lord. The most self-deceiving among you is the one disobedient to his Lord. One who obeys Allah is safe and glad news awaits him, but one who disobeys Allah loses and regrets.'''

H 113, Ch. 13, h 7

A number of our people have narrated from Ahmad ibn Muhammad ibn Khalid from his father from the one mentioned from Muhammad ibn 'Abd al-Rahman ibn abu Layla from his father who has said the following:

"I heard Imam abu Ja'far, *'Alayhi al-Salam*, saying, 'When you hear knowledge you must use it and your hearts must become more open. If knowledge increases in one's heart but one fails to exercise forbearance, Satan may overpower him. If Satan would dispute with you, move on him with whatever you know. The plots of Satan are weak.' I asked the Imam, *'Alayhi al-Salam*, 'What is it that we know?' The Imam replied, 'Fight him with whatever of the power of Allah, the Majestic, the Glorious, has come to light before you.'"

Chapter 14 - Those Who Use Their Knowledge for Personal Fulfillment and Are Boastful of It

H 114, Ch. 14, h 1

Muhammad ibn Yahya has narrated from Ahmad ibn Muhammad ibn 'Isa and Ali ibn Ibrahim from his father, both of them from Hammad ibn 'Isa from 'Umar ibn 'Udhayna from Aban ibn abu 'Ayyash from Sulaym ibn Qays who has said the following:

"I heard (Imam) Ali, *'Alayhi al-Salam*, narrating from the Holy Prophet who has said, 'Two kinds of people with great appetites do not become satisfied. There is a person of great appetite for the worldly gains, and a person with great appetite for knowledge. In the matters of the worldly gains, if one limits himself to what Allah has made lawful for him, he is saved, and if one accumulates such gains in unlawful ways, he is destroyed, unless he repents and changes his ways. In the matters of knowledge if one acquires it from people of knowledge and practices accordingly, he is saved and if one uses it for worldly gains, then that is all he gets.'"

H 115, Ch. 14, h 2

Al-Husayn ibn Muhammad ibn 'Amir has narrated from Mu'alla ibn Muhammad from al-Hassan ibn Ali al-Washsha' from Ahmad ibn 'A'idh from abu Khadija from abu 'Abd Allah, *'Alayhi al-Salam*, who has said the following:

"One who wants *al-Hadith* for worldly benefit will have no share in the next life but if one wants *al-Hadith* for the good of the next life, Allah grants him the good of both this and the next life."

H 116, Ch. 14, h 3

Ali ibn Ibrahim has narrated from his father from al-Qasim ibn Muhammad al-Isbahani from al-Minqari from Hafs ibn Ghiyath from abu 'Abd Allah, *'Alayhi al-Salam*, who has said the following:

"Whoever wants *al-Hadith* for worldly gains will have no share in the next life."

H 117, Ch. 14, h 4

Ali ibn Ibrahim has narrated from his father from al-Qasim from al-Minqari from Hafs ibn Ghiyath from abu 'Abd Allah, *'Alayhi al-Salam*, who has said the following:

"If you find a learned person who loves worldly gains you must not trust him in the matters of your religion; whoever loves something, it will encompass and entangle him. The Holy Prophet has said, 'Allah sent *wahy* (revelation) to David (peace be upon him) and told him, "Do not set between Me and yourself a learned

36

person who loves worldly gains lest he bar you from the way to My love. Such bandits ambush My servants who want Me. The least that I will do to such bandits is to take away from them the sweetness of their private conversations and prayers with Me.'"

H 118, Ch. 14, h 5
Ali from his father from al-Nawfali from al-Sakuni from abu 'Abd Allah, *'Alayhi al-Salam*, who has said the following:

"The Holy Prophet has said, '*Al-Fuqaha* (the scholars of the *Fiqh*, Islamic laws) are the trustees of the prophets as long as they are not involved in worldly matters.' People asked, 'What is meant by their "entering in the worldly matters," O Holy Prophet of Allah?' 'It is their following the kings. When they follow the kings then you must be very careful about involving them in your religion,' replied the Holy Prophet, *'Alayhi al-Salam*."

H 119, Ch. 14, h 6
Muhammad ibn 'Isma'il has narrated from al-Fadl ibn Shadhan from Hammed ibn 'Isa from Rib'i ibn 'Abd Allah from one he narrated from abu Ja'far, *'Alayhi al-Salam*, who has said the following:

"Whoever seeks knowledge to show off to the scholars or to engage in arguments with fools or to attract people to his own self should know that in so doing he has prepared his seat in the fire. Leadership does not suit anyone besides those qualified for it."

Chapter 15 - The Need for the Existence of a Divine Authority in the World and the Seriousness of This Matter

H 120, Ch. 15, h 1
Ali ibn Ibrahim ibn Hashim has narrated from his father from al-Qasim ibn Muhammad from al-Minqari from Hafs ibn Ghiyath from abu 'Abd Allah, *'Alayhi al-Salam*, who has said the following:

"O Hafs, seventy sins of an ignorant person may be forgiven before a single sin of a learned person is forgiven."

H 121, Ch. 15, h 2
Through the same chain of narrators it is narrated from abu 'Abd Allah, *'Alayhi al-Salam*, who has said the following:

"Jesus son of Mary, peace be with him, has said, 'Woe to bad scholars! Had they only realized how intense would be the raging fire that would engulf them.'"

H 122, Ch. 15, h 3
Ali ibn Ibrahim has narrated from his father and Muhammad ibn 'Isma'il from al-Fadl ibn Shadhan, both from ibn abu 'Umayr from Jamil ibn Darraj who has said the following:

"I heard (Imam) abu 'Abd Allah, *'Alayhi al-Salam*, saying, 'When the soul reaches here' - the Imam pointed to his own throat – 'there will be no chance for learned persons to repent.' He (the Imam) recited this verse: 'Allah will only accept the repentance of those who commit evil in ignorance if they repent immediately. Allah is All-knowing and All-wise (4:17)'"

H 123, Ch. 15, h 4

Muhammad ibn Yahya has narrated from Ahmad ibn Muhammad ibn 'Isa from al-Husayn ibn Sa'id from al-Nadr ibn Suwayd from Yahya al-Halabi from abu Sa'id al-Mukari from abu Basir from abu Ja'far, *'Alayhi al-Salam*, who has said the following:

"Imam abu Ja'far, *'Alayhi al-Salam*, said about the words of Allah in the Holy Quran, 'The idol worshippers, the idols, the rebellious ones (26:94) and the army of Satan will all be thrown headlong into hell,' (26:95) has said, 'They are the people who speak about justice a great deal but in their own practice they disregard it altogether.'"

Chapter 16 - Miscellaneous Issues

H 124, Ch. 16, h 1

Ali ibn Ibrahim has narrated from his father from ibn abu 'Umayr from Hafs ibn al-Bakhtari in a *marfu'* manner from Amir al-Mu'minin Ali, *'Alayhi al-Salam*, who has said the following:

"Relax your souls with new sparks of wisdom, because souls also tire as do bodies."

H 125, Ch. 16, h 2

A number of our people have narrated from Ahmad ibn Muhammad from Nuh ibn Shu'ayb al-Naysaburi from 'Ubayd Allah ibn 'Abd Allah al-Dihqan from Durust ibn abu Mansur from 'Urwa cousin of Shu'ayb al-'Aqarqi from Shu'ayb from abu Basir who has said the following:

"I heard (Imam) abu 'Abd Allah, *'Alayhi al-Salam*, saying that Imam Ali, *'Alayhi al-Salam*, would often say, 'O seekers of knowledge, you must know that knowledge (in a personified form) has a great deal of virtues. Humility is his head, freedom from jealousy forms his eyes, proper understanding shapes his ears, truthfulness constitutes his tongue, research and investigation produce his memory, optimism stands for his heart, the knowledge of facts and events strengthen his intellect. Intelligence and kindness are his hands, visitation of the scholars builds his legs, security and peace emerge from his stamina, restraint from worldly attractions (sins) develops his wisdom, salvation is his headquarters, good health and tranquility are his lead, loyalty will provide him his conveyance, politeness in communication gives him weapons, consent frames his sword, yielding to the truth stands for his bow and arrow, communication with the scholars establishes his army, proper discipline treasures his wealth, avoiding sins preserves his savings, uprightness institutes his supplies, amicable dealing provides him water, guidance determines his direction and love of virtuous people is the archetype for his friends.'"

H 126, Ch. 16, h 3

Muhammad ibn Yahya has narrated from Ahmad ibn Muhammad ibn 'Isa from Ahmad ibn Muhammad ibn abu Nasr from Hammad ibn 'Uthman from abu 'Abd Allah, *'Alayhi al-Salam*, who has said the following:

"The Holy Prophet has said, 'The best minister for faith is knowledge, the best minister for knowledge is forbearance, the best minister for forbearance is amicable dealings and the best minister for amicable dealings is patience.'"

H 127, Ch. 16, h 4

Ali ibn Muhammad from Sahl ibn Ziyad from Ja'far ibn Muhammad al-Ash'ari from 'Abd Allah ibn Maymun al-Qaddah from abu 'Abd Allah, *'Alayhi al-Salam*, from his ancestors (*'A'immah, 'Alayhim al-Salam*, who has said the following:

"Once a man came to the Messenger of Allah, *'Alayhi al-Salam*, and said, 'O messenger of Allah, what is knowledge?' The Holy Prophet replied, 'It is silence.' The man then asked, 'Then what?' The Holy Prophet said, 'It is listening.' The man asked, 'Then what?' The Holy Prophet, *'Alayhi al-Salam*, said, 'Then it is memorizing.' The man asked, 'Then what?' The Holy Prophet said, 'Then it is practice accordingly.' The man then asked, 'Then what, O messenger of Allah?' The Holy Prophet said, 'Then it is to propagate what one has learned.'"

H 128, Ch. 16, h 5

Ali ibn Ibrahim in a *marfu'* manner has narrated from abu 'Abd Allah, *'Alayhi al-Salam*, who has said the following:

"There are three kinds of seekers of knowledge. One can recognize them from their persons or characters: (a) the group who seeks knowledge for ignorance and quarreling, (b) the group who seeks knowledge to dominate and cheat others, (c) the group who seeks knowledge for proper understanding (*Fiqh*) and power of intelligence. The group whose purpose in seeking knowledge is ignorance and quarreling is a harmful and quarrelsome group. This group interrupts conversations in the gatherings of the people to speak about knowledge and the description of forbearance. Such people appear in the garb of the gentle and humble ones but, in fact, are devoid of all the qualities of the pious people. Allah has humiliated and has condemned this group. The group that seeks domination and cheating is a deceitful and flattering group. Such people try to dominate people of their kind and flatter the wealthy ones who know less than they do. Such people consume the sweet-meat of the rich people and destroy their own religion. May Allah banish the news of such people and cut off their traces from the history of the scholars.

"The group that seeks knowledge for the sake of *Fiqh* (proper understanding) and to gain the power of intelligence consists of people who are deeply concerned and stay awake very often. They pull their robe over their heads and stand up for prayer in the darkness of nights. They work hard, anxiously, with fear and pray with deep worries. They are very attentive to their affairs, knowledgeable of the people of their time and fearful even of their own trusted brothers. May Allah strengthen the pillars of the essence of such people and grant them salvation on the Day of Judgment.'"

Muhammad ibn Mahmud abu 'Abd Allah al-Qazwini narrated to me the above *Hadith* from a number of our people one of whom is Ja'far ibn Muhammad al-Sayqal of Qazwin from Ahmad ibn 'Isa al-'Alawi from 'Abbad ibn Suhayb al-Basri from abu 'Abd Allah, *'Alayhi al-Salam*.

H 129, Ch. 16, h 6

Ali ibn Ibrahim has narrated from his father from Muhammad ibn Yahya from Talha ibn Zayd who has said the following:

"I heard (Imam) abu 'Abd Allah, *'Alayhi al-Salam*, saying, 'The narrators of the Book (the Holy Quran) are a great many but those who follow proper discipline in the matters of the Book are very few. There are many who are protective of *Hadith* but do poorly with the Book. Lack of protection and discipline saddens the scholars and the task of memorizing the text saddens the ignorant ones. Thus, one group concerned about the Book seeks to preserve its life while the other group, also concerned about it, in fact, arranges for its destruction. Therefore, the two forms of concern oppose each other and the two groups differ.'"

H 130, Ch. 16, h 7

Al-Husayn ibn Muhammad al-Ash'ari from Mu'alla ibn Muhammad from Muhammad ibn Jumhur from 'Abd al-Rahman ibn abu Najran from one he mentioned from abu 'Abd Allah, *'Alayhi al-Salam*, who has said the following:

"Whoever preserves and memorizes forty of our *Hadith,* on the Day of Judgment Allah will raise him as a scholar and *Faqih* (one with proper understanding of religion)."

H 131, Ch. 16, h 8

A number of our people have narrated from Ahmad ibn Muhammad ibn Khalid from his father from one he mentioned from Zayd al-Shahham from abu Ja'far, *'Alayhi al-Salam*, who has said the following about these words of Allah:

"Let the human being think about (how We produce) his food" (80:24) I asked the Imam what is meant by 'His food'? The Imam, *'Alayhi al-Salam*, said, 'It is the knowledge he acquires from whoever he acquires it.'"

H 132, Ch. 16, h 9

Muhammad ibn Yahya has narrated from Ahmad ibn Muhammad ibn 'Isa from Ali ibn al-Nu'man from 'Abd Allah ibn Muskan from Dawud ibn Farqad from abu Sa'id al-Zuhri from abu Ja'far, *'Alayhi al-Salam*, who has said the following:

"Holding back in an uncertain condition is better than indulging in a destructive situation. Your not narrating a *Hadith* is better than narrating one that you have not verified."

H 133, Ch. 16, h 10

Muhammad has narrated from Ahmad from ibn Faddal from ibn Bukayr from Hamza ibn al-Tayyar the following:

"Once I presented to (Imam) abu 'Abd Allah, *'Alayhi al-Salam*, certain lectures of his father. In a certain passage he (the Imam) said, 'Stop there and remain silent.' He then said, 'In the case of a text that may come to you and you have no knowledge of its veracity, you can do nothing but to hold and verify and refer it to the Imam of guidance so he may show you the way of justice in it, enlighten you in the darkness and introduce to you the truth. Allah the Most High has said, "Ask about the heavenly Books, if you do not know, from those who know them."" (16:43)

H 134, Ch. 16, h 11

Ali ibn Ibrahim has narrated from his father from al-Qasim ibn Muhammad from al-Minqari from Sufyan ibn 'Uyayna who has said the following:

"I heard (Imam) abu 'Abd Allah, *'Alayhi al-Salam*, saying, 'I have found all the knowledge of people in four categories: (a) the knowledge that teaches you about your Lord, (b) the knowledge that teaches what the Lord has done for you, (c) the knowledge that teaches what the Lord wants from you and (d) the knowledge that teaches what destroys your religion.'"

H 135, Ch. 16, h 12

Ali ibn Ibrahim has narrated from his father from ibn abu 'Umayr from Hisham ibn Salim who has said the following:

"Once I asked (Imam) abu 'Abd Allah, *'Alayhi al-Salam*, 'What is of the right of Allah on His creatures?' The Imam said, 'People must say only what they know and hold back from what they do not know. If they do so, they have observed the rights of Allah upon them.'"

H 136, Ch. 16, h 13

Muhammad ibn al-Hassan from Sahl ibn Ziyad from ibn Sinan from Muhammad ibn Marwan al-'Ijli from Ali ibn Hanzala who has said the following:

"I heard (Imam) abu 'Abd Allah, *'Alayhi al-Salam*, saying, 'Find out the value of the position of the people from the degree of their narration of *Hadith* from us. '"

H 137, Ch. 16, h 14

Al-Husayn ibn al-Hassan has narrated from Muhammad ibn Zakariyya al-Ghalabi from ibn 'A'isha al-Basri in a *marfu'* manner *(rafa'ahu)* Amir al-Mu'minin Ali, *'Alayhi al-Salam*, who has said the following:

"In certain parts of his sermons he has said, 'O people, you must know that there is no man of intelligence who becomes disappointed due to a lie spoken about him. There is no man of wisdom who becomes pleased by ignorant people's praising him. People are children of what they do best and the value of a man is what he does best. Speak knowledge and it will show your value.'"

H 138, Ch. 16, h 15

Al-Husayn ibn Muhammad has narrated from Mu'alla ibn Muhammad from al-Washsha' from Aban ibn 'Uthman from 'Abd Allah ibn Sulayman who has said the following:

"Once a man from Basra, called 'Uthman al-A'ma, in the presence of abu Ja'far, said, 'Al-Hassan al-Basri believes that those who hide knowledge, the bad odor formed in their stomach due to such an undesirable deed, will cause suffering to the people of hell,' To this I heard abu Ja'far, *'Alayhi al-Salam*, say, 'The true believer of the people of Pharaoh is then destroyed (because he hid his knowledge from Pharaoh). In fact, knowledge from the time of Noah became veiled. Let Hassan go left or right. I swear by Allah, he will not find knowledge in any other place but here with us.'"

Chapter 17 - Narrating Books and Hadith (The Virtue of Writing and Its Preservation)

H 139, Ch. 17, h 1

Ali ibn Ibrahim has narrated from his father from ibn abu 'Umayr from Mansur ibn Yunus from abu Basir who has said the following:

"About the words of Allah in the Holy Quran, '. . . give the glad news to those of Our servants who listen to the words and follow only the best ones . . .' (39:18)

(Imam) abu 'Abd Allah, *'Alayhi al-Salam*, has said, 'They are those who learn *Hadith* and report it as they have learned without any additions or omissions.'"

H 140, Ch. 17, h 2

Muhammad ibn Yahya has narrated from Muhammad ibn al-Husayn from ibn abu 'Umayr from ibn 'Udhayna from Muhammad ibn Muslim who has said the following:

"Once I asked abu 'Abd Allah, *'Alayhi al-Salam*, 'Can I add to or omit from a *Hadith* that I hear from you?' He said, "It is alright, if you preserve the meaning.'"

H 141, Ch. 17, h 3

It is narrated from him from Muhammad ibn al-Husayn from ibn Sinan from Dawud ibn Farqad who has said the following:

"I asked (Imam) abu 'Abd Allah, *'Alayhi al-Salam*, 'I hear your statement and I want to narrate to others but it does not come through exactly.' The Imam asked, 'Do you do it purposely?' I said, 'No, I do not do it purposely.' The Imam asked, 'Do you keep the meaning?' I said, 'Yes, I keep the meaning.' The Imam said, 'It then is alright.'"

H 142, Ch. 17, h 4

It is narrated from him from Ahmad ibn Muhammad ibn 'Isa from al-Husayn ibn Sa'id from al-Qasim ibn Muhammad from Ali ibn abu Hamza from abu Basir who has said the following:

"Once I asked abu 'Abd Allah, *'Alayhi al-Salam*, 'Can I narrate a *Hadith* I hear from you as a *Hadith* of your father or narrate what I have heard from your father as your *Hadith*?' The Imam said, 'It is all the same. However, I would love if you narrate from my father.' Abu 'Abd Allah, *'Alayhi al-Salam*, once said to Jamil, 'What you hear from me you may narrate as a *Hadith* of my father also.'"

H 143, Ch. 17, h 5

It is narrated from him from Ahmad ibn Muhammad and Muhammad ibn al-Husayn from ibn Mahbub from 'Abd Allah ibn Sinan who has said the following:

"Once I said to (Imam) abu 'Abd Allah, *'Alayhi al-Salam*, 'People come to me and they listen to the *Ahadith* that I narrate to them from you. I become tired and weak.' The Imam said, 'Narrate to them a *Hadith* from the beginning and one from the middle and one from the end.'"

H 144, Ch. 17, h 6

It is narrated from him from Ahmad ibn 'Umar al-Hallal who has said the following:

"Once I said to (Imam) abu al-Hassan al-Rida, *'Alayhi al-Salam*, 'One of our people gives me a book but he does not say whether I can narrate anything from it or not. Can I narrate from it?' The Imam, *'Alayhi al-Salam*, said, 'Yes, you can narrate if you know it is from his book.'"

H 145, Ch. 17, h 7

Ali ibn Ibrahim has narrated from his father from Ahmad ibn Muhammad ibn Khalid from al-Nawfali from al-Sakuni from abu 'Abd Allah, *'Alayhi al-Salam*, who has said the following:

"Amir al-Mu'minin, *'Alayhi al-Salam*, has said, 'When you narrate a *Hadith* you must say who its narrator is. If it is true it will be for you and if it is false it will be his (the narrator's) responsibility.

H 146, Ch. 17, h 8

Ali ibn Muhammad ibn 'Abd Allah has narrated from Ahmad ibn Muhammad from abu Ayyub al-Madani from ibn abu 'Umayr from Husayn al-Ahmasi from abu 'Abd Allah, *'Alayhi al-Salam*, who has said the following:

"The heart relies on writing."

H 147, Ch. 17, h 9

Al-Husayn ibn Muhammad has narrated from Mu'alla ibn Muhammad from al-Hassan ibn Ali al-Washsha' from 'Asim ibn Humayd from abu Basir who has said the following:

"Once I heard (Imam) abu 'Abd Allah, *'Alayhi al-Salam*, saying, 'You must write it down; you will not memorize until you write it down.'"

H 148, Ch. 17, h 10

Muhammad ibn Yahya has narrated from Ahmad ibn Muhammad ibn 'Isa from al-Hassan ibn Ali ibn Faddal from ibn Bukayr from 'Ubayd ibn Zurara who has said the following:

"Once abu 'Abd Allah, *'Alayhi al-Salam*, said, 'You must preserve your books; you will soon need them.'"

H 149, Ch. 17, h 11

A number of our people have narrated from Ahmad ibn Muhammad ibn Khalid al-Barqi from certain persons of his people from abu Sa'id al-Khaybari from al-Mufaddal ibn 'Umar who has said the following:

"Abu 'Abd Allah, *'Alayhi al-Salam*, has said, 'You must write down (*Hadith*) and spread your knowledge among your brethren. If you die your children will inherit your books. A time will come when people will face chaos and they will find no comfort except in their books.'"

H 150, Ch. 17, h 12

It is narrated through the same chain of narrators from Muhammad ibn Ali in a marfu' manner from abu 'Abd Allah, *'Alayhi al-Salam*, who has said the following:

"Beware of the branched-out lies." They asked the Imam, 'What are branched-out lies?' The Imam replied, 'It is when a person narrates a *Hadith* to you and you ignore him and narrate it from the person from whom he had narrated the *Hadith*.'

H 151, Ch. 17, h 13

Muhammad ibn Yahya has narrated from Ahmad ibn Muhammad ibn 'Isa from Ahmad ibn Muhammad ibn abu Nasr from Jamil ibn Darraj who has said the following:

"Once, abu 'Abd Allah, *'Alayhi al-Salam*, said, 'Express our *Hadith* (statements) in a clear manner; we are an eloquent people.'"

H 152, Ch. 17, h 14

Ali ibn Muhammad has narrated from Sahl ibn Ziyad from Ahmad ibn Muhammad from 'Umar ibn 'Abd al-'Aziz from Hisham ibn Salim, Hammed ibn 'Uthman and others who have said the following.

"Once we heard abu 'Abd Allah, *'Alayhi al-Salam*, saying, 'My *Hadith* is the *Hadith* of my father. The *Hadith* of my father is the *Hadith* of my grandfather. The *Hadith* of my grandfather is the *Hadith* of Imam Husayn. The *Hadith* of Imam al-Husayn is the *Hadith* of Imam al- Hassan. The *Hadith* of Imam al-Hassan is the *Hadith* of Imam Ali, *'Alayhi al-Salam*. The *Hadith* of Imam Ali is the *Hadith* of the Holy Prophet, *'Alayhi al-Salam*. The *Hadith* of the Holy Prophet is the words of Allah, the Majestic, the Glorious.'"

H 153, Ch. 17, h 15

A number of our people have narrated from Ahmad ibn Muhammad from Muhammad ibn al-Hassan ibn abu Khalid Shaynula who has said the following:

"Once I said to abu Ja'far *al-Thani*, (the second), *'Alayhi al-Salam*, 'May Allah keep my soul in your service, our shaykhs have narrated *Hadith* from Imam abu Ja'far and from Imam abu 'Abd Allah, *'Alayhim al-Salam*. At that time *Taqiyah* (fear) was severe. They concealed their books and did not narrate from them. When they died their books came to us.' The Imam said, 'You may narrate from them; they contain the truth.'"

Chapter 18 - Taqlid, Following the Opinions of Someone in the Matters of Religious Laws

H 154, Ch. 18, h 1

A number of our people have narrated from Ahmad ibn Muhammad ibn Khalid from 'Abd Allah ibn Yahya from ibn Muskan from abu Basir who has said the following:

"Once I asked Imam abu 'Abd Allah, *'Alayhi al-Salam*, about the verse of the Holy Quran that says, 'People (unconditionally) obeyed the rabbis and the monks and worshipped the Messiah, son of Mary, as they (people) should have obeyed Allah . . .' (9:31) The Imam replied, 'By Allah they (rabbis) did not call people to worship them. If they had done so people would not have accepted it. The rabbis and monks made unlawful things lawful for them and the lawful things as unlawful. In this way they (people) worshipped (obeyed) them unintentionally.'"

H 155, Ch. 18, h 2

Ali ibn Muhammad has narrated from Sahl ibn Ziyad from Ibrahim ibn Muhammad al-Hamdani from Muhammad ibn 'Ubayda who has said the following:

"Abu al-Hassan, *'Alayhi al-Salam*, once said, 'O Muhammad, do you observe *Taqlid* more strictly than the group of *Murji'a* does? I replied, 'They observe *Taqlid* and we observe *Taqlid*.' The Imam then said, 'I did not ask you about this.' I did not have any answer other than the first one. The Imam then said, 'The group of *Murji'a* chose a man to whom obedience was not obligatory (according to the commands of Allah) but they obeyed and followed him strictly. You chose a man and considered obedience to him necessary (according to the commands of Allah) and then you did not follow him strictly. Therefore, they are stricter in *Taqlid* (following) than you are.'"

H 156 Ch. 18, h 3

Muhammad ibn 'Isma'il has narrated from al-Fadl ibn Shadhan from Hammed ibn 'Isa from Rib'i ibn 'Abd Allah from abu Basir from abu 'Abd Allah, *'Alayhi al-Salam*, who has said the following about the words of Allah, the Most Majestic, the Most Glorious:

"People (unconditionally) obeyed the rabbis and the monks and worshipped the Messiah, son of Mary, as they should have obeyed Allah . . ." (9:31) The Imam said, 'By Allah, they (the people) did not pray or fast for them (rabbis and monks) but they (rabbis and monks) made lawful for the people what was unlawful and unlawful what was lawful and people followed them accordingly.'"

Chapter 19 - Innovations, Personal Opinions and Analogies

H 157, Ch. 19, h 1

Al-Husayn ibn Muhammad al-Ash'ari has narrated from Mu'alla ibn Muhammad from al-Hassan ibn Ali al-Washsha' and a number of our people from Ahmad ibn Muhammad from ibn Faddal all from 'Asim ibn Humayd from Muhammad ibn Muslim from abu Ja'far, *'Alayhi al-Salam*, who has said the following:

"Imam Ali, *'Alayhi al-Salam*, in one of his sermons has said, 'O people, mischief begins with following certain desires and obeying certain man-made rules that are different from the rules and laws of the book of Allah. In such a case, people yield to other people as a higher authority. If falsehood had been clear it remained so to the people of intelligence. If truth had been clearly distinct differences did not emerge. But (in practical life) people mix certain parts of truth with a few things from falsehood and present them together. In such case Satan overwhelms his friends and only those who have previously received protection from Allah remain safe.'"

H 158, Ch. 19, h 2

Al-Husayn ibn Muhammad has narrated from Mu'alla ibn Muhammad from Muhammad ibn Jumhur al-'Ammi in a marfu' manner *(rafa 'ahu)*, from the Messenger of Allah who has said the following:

"When innovations (heresy) emerge it becomes necessary for scholars to make their knowledge public, otherwise Allah will condemn them."

H 159, Ch. 19, h 3

It is narrated through the same chain of narrators from Muhammad ibn Jumhur in a *marfu'* manner from the Messenger of Allah who has said the following:

"If one meets an innovator (heretic) and considers him great, such person has, in fact, sought the destruction of Islam."

H 160, Ch. 19, h 4

It is narrated through the same chain of narrators from Muhammad ibn Jumhur in a *marfu'* manner from the Messenger of Allah, *'Alayhi al-Salam*, who has said the following:

"Allah rejects the repentance of an innovator (heretic in religion)." People asked the Holy Prophet, 'Why is this?' The Holy Prophet replied, 'Because his heart is filled with the love of his heresy.'"

H 161, Ch. 19, h 5

Muhammad ibn Yahya has narrated from Ahmad ibn Muhammad ibn 'Isa from al-Hassan ibn Mahbub from Mu'awiya ibn Wahab who has said the following:

"Abu 'Abd Allah, *'Alayhi al-Salam*, has said that the Holy Prophet has said, 'It is certain that against every innovation (deviation and heresy) with plots to destroy faith after me there will be a (religious) authority from my family as guardian of faith and as its defender. (Such) authority will speak on inspiration from Allah to declare the truth and bring it to light, repulse and foil the evil plots of the agents of wickedness and speak for the weak. O intelligent people, take a lesson from it and trust Allah.'"

H 162, Ch. 19, h 6

Muhammad ibn Yahya has narrated from certain persons of his people and Ali ibn Ibrahim from his father from Harun ibn Muslim from Mas'ada ibn Sadaqa from abu 'Abd Allah, *'Alayhi al-Salam*, and

Ali ibn Ibrahim from his father from ibn Mahbub *in a marfu' manner* from Amir al-Mu'minin Ali, *'Alayhi al-Salam*, who has said the following:

"Of the most intensely disliked men in the sight of Allah, the Majestic, the Most Glorious, are two kinds of people: A man whom Allah has left all to his own soul and who deviates from the path of justice, and is extremely attracted toward the words of innovation (heresy). He seems a master at performing prayer and fasting but is a mischief-maker to deceive people; he has strayed from guidance of the people before him and misleads those who may follow him in his lifetime and after his death. He carries the responsibility for others' sins and is a hostage of his own sins.

"The other man is one who displays ignorance as knowledge among the ignorant. He receives assistance from the darkness of existing mischief. The people, who appear like people (who in fact have no intelligence), consider him a scholar, but he has not spent even a complete day with scholars. He has made an early effort to accumulate something that in its being of a smaller quantity is better than in larger quantities and in this way he has filled himself with polluted water and has treasured what is of no use. He sits among people as a judge to carry the responsibility of adjudicating what is confusing and uncertain to others. He may even oppose the ruling of the judge before him. One can never tell whether his judgment will remain valid or if a judge after him will overturn it just as he has done to the judgments of the judges before him. If he faces complex and difficult issues he comes up with a great deal of his personal opinions and shapes them up as a clear-cut judgment. In fact, he has dressed himself up with doubtful issues the way a spider weaves his fragile web. He is not sure if he has done the right thing or the wrong one. He does not consider the fact that in an unknown case to have proper knowledge is necessary, and he does not see that beyond his opinion there is a school of law. He analogizes one thing to the other but it does not matter to him if his opinion will turn out to be a lie. If an issue is dark (not known) to him he hides it to hide his own ignorance so that people will not say he does not know. He then boldly judges and thus he is the key to hazards, a storage of doubts, perplexed in ignorance, and he never regrets his lacking knowledge. The level of his knowledge never rises to absolute certainty so that he could benefit. He blows out *Hadith* like winds that blow away hay. The legacies weep because of him, the bloods (judging the case of murder) shout against him. The lawful marital relations become unlawful because of his judgment and unlawful ones become lawful. He has no confidence in the judgments he issues and he can never be trusted for judgments that he may make nor was he qualified for what he may have done in the matters in which he claimed to have true knowledge."

H 163, Ch. 19, h 7

Al-Husayn ibn Muhammad has narrated from Mu'alla ibn Muhammad from al-Hassan ibn Ali al-Washsha' from Aban ibn 'Uthman from abu Shaybah al-Khurasani who has said the following:

"I heard abu 'Abd Allah, *'Alayhi al-Salam*, saying, 'The people of analogy have sought knowledge through analogy (using analogy) and it has increased their knowledge with nothing but further remoteness. The religion of Allah is beyond the reach of analogy.'"

H 164, Ch. 19, h 8

Ali ibn Ibrahim has narrated from his father from Muhammad ibn 'Isma'il from al-Fadl ibn Shadhan in a marfu' manner *(rafa'ahu)* from abu Ja'far and abu 'Abd Allah, *'Alayhi al-Salam*, who have said the following.

"All innovations (heresy) are misguidance and all misguidance leads to hell."

H 165, Ch. 19, h 9

Ali ibn Ibrahim has narrated from his father from ibn abu 'Umayr from Muhammad ibn Hukaym who has said the following:

"Once I asked (Imam) abu al-Hassan Musa, *'Alayhi al-Salam*, 'May Allah keep my soul in your service, please make us *Faqih* (people of proper understanding in religion). Allah has granted us the blessing of your existence among us and has made us independent of other people. This blessing is so great that even if a whole group of us may come to one place, no one needs to ask another a question to prepare an answer for it. Sometimes, however, we may come across an issue for which we have heard nothing from you or from your forefathers. We then look into the best resources available and the closest to your guidance. Can we take such a finding as an authority?' 'Never, ever, by Allah, O ibn Hakim, many people have been destroyed in it,' replied the Imam, *'Alayhi al-Salam*. Ibn Hakim has said that the Imam then said, 'May Allah condemn abu Hanifa who says, "Ali said so and so, therefore, I said so and so."' Muhammad ibn Hakim has said that he told Hisham ibn al-Hakam, 'By Allah, I only wanted the Imam to give us permission to use analogy.'"

H 166, Ch. 19, h 10

Muhammad ibn abu 'Abd Allah has narrated *in a marfu'* manner from Yunus ibn 'Abd al-Rahman who has said the following:

"Once I asked (Imam) abu al-Hassan the First, 'How can I prove that Allah is one?' The Imam replied, 'O Yunus, do not be an innovator (heretic). One who depends on his personal opinion is destroyed. One who abandons the members of the family of his Prophet goes astray. Whoever abandons the book of Allah and the words of His prophet becomes an unbeliever.'"

H 167, Ch. 19, h 11

Muhammad ibn Yahya has narrated from Ahmad ibn Muhammad from al-Washsha' from Muthanna al-Hannat from abu Basir who has said the following:

"Once I asked (Imam) abu 'Abd Allah, *'Alayhi al-Salam*, saying, 'We may face an issue about which there is nothing said in the book of Allah or in the *Sunnah*, tradition of the Holy Prophet, *'Alayhi al-Salam*, can we use our own opinion in such matters?' The Imam replied, 'No, you must not do that. If you, in this way, find the truth you will receive no rewards for it, and if you missed the truth you have forged lies against Allah, the Majestic, the Glorious.'"

H 168, Ch. 19, h 12

A number of our people have narrated from Ahmad ibn Muhammad ibn 'Isa from Ali ibn al-Hakam from 'Umar ibn Aban al-Kalbi from 'Abd al-Rahim al-Qasir from abu 'Abd Allah, *'Alayhi al-Salam*, who has said the following:

"The messenger of Allah has said, 'All innovations (heresies) are misguidance and all misguidance is in hell.'"

H 169, Ch. 19, h 13

Ali ibn Ibrahim has narrated from Muhammad ibn 'Isa ibn 'Ubayd from Yunus ibn 'Abd al-Rahman from Sama'a ibn Mihran who has said the following:

"Once I said to (Imam) abu al-Hassan Musa, *'Alayhi al-Salam,* 'May Allah keep you well, in our meetings we discuss the issues and find out that for almost everything there is something in writing with us and that is all because of the blessings of your existence among us. We find only few small things for which we do not find anything in writing. We look on each other and we find certain issues similar to it, then we use analogy in its best form.' The Imam said, 'What do you have to do with analogy? Many people before have been destroyed because of analogy.' The Imam then said, 'When you face an issue and know the rule about it, deal with it accordingly, and if you would have no knowledge about its rule then this'- he pointed to his own mouth, 'This will give you the answer.' The Imam then said, 'May Allah condemn abu Hanifa who used to say, 'Ali said so and so, therefore, I said so and so. The *Sahaba* said so and so, therefore, I said so and so.' The Imam then asked me, 'Have you been sitting with him?' I then replied, 'No, I have not sat with him but such are his statements.' I then said to the Imam, *'Alayhi al-Salam,* 'May Allah keep you well, did the Messenger of Allah bring everything that people needed?' The Imam said, 'Yes, and all that they will need up to the Day of Judgment.' I then said, 'Is anything lost from it?' The Imam replied, 'No, it all is with the people to whom they belong.'"

H 170, Ch. 19, h 14

It is narrated from him from Muhammad from Yunus from Aban from abu Shaybah who has said the following:

"I heard (Imam) abu 'Abd Allah, *'Alayhi al-Salam,* saying, 'Ibn Shubrama's knowledge is lost and void before *Al-Jami'ah.* It is a large book that was dictated by the Messenger of Allah to Imam Ali, *'Alayhi al-Salam,* who wrote it with his own hands. *Al-Jami'ah* has left nothing untold. In it (*Al-Jami'ah*) is the knowledge of all lawful and unlawful matters. The people of analogy (people who consider use of analogical reasoning as an authority in the matters of Shari'a) sought knowledge through analogy and it has not added to their knowledge anything. Instead it has taken them away from knowledge. The religion of Allah is not of matters to learn through analogy.'"

H 171, Ch. 19, h 15

Muhammad ibn 'Isma'il has narrated from al-Fadl ibn Shadhan from Safwan Yahya from 'Abd al-Rahman ibn al-Hajjaj from Aban ibn Taghlib from abu 'Abd Allah, *'Alayhi al-Salam,* who has said the following:

"The *Sunnah* (tradition of the Holy Prophet, *'Alayhi al-Salam*) cannot be learned through analogy. Consider a woman has to make up for her fast missed due to menses, but she does not have to make up for the prayers that she would miss in such times. O Aban, the use of analogy destroys religion."

H 172, Ch. 19, h 16

A number of our people have narrated from Ahmad ibn Muhammad from 'Uthman ibn 'Isa who has said the following:

48

"Once I asked (Imam) abu al-Hassan Musa, *'Alayhi al-Salam*, about the use of analogy and the Imam said, 'What do you have to do with analogy? Allah will not ask how it was made lawful or unlawful.'"

H 173, Ch. 19, h 17

Ali ibn Ibrahim has narrated from Harun ibn Muslim from Mas'ada ibn Sadaqa who has said the following:

"(Imam) abu 'Abd Allah, *'Alayhi al-Salam*, has narrated from his father who said that Imam Ali, *'Alayhi al-Salam*, has said, 'Whoever decides to use analogical reasoning as a source of authority, his whole life will remain in confusion. Whoever practices the religion of Allah by means of analogical reasoning his whole life will pass in a drowning condition.' Imam abu Ja'far, *'Alayhi al-Salam*, then said, "Whoever issues *Fatwa* on the basis of his personal opinion has practiced the religion of Allah by means of what is not knowledge. Whoever practices the religion of Allah without knowledge has opposed Him by making things lawful and unlawful through things he has no knowledge of.'"

H 174, Ch. 19, h 18

Muhammad ibn Yahya has narrated from Ahmad ibn Muhammad from al-Hassan ibn Ali ibn Yaqtin from al-Husayn ibn Maya from his father from abu 'Abd Allah, *'Alayhi al-Salam*, who has said the following:

"Satan analogized himself with Adam saying, 'Lord, You have created me from fire and created him from clay,' (7:12) In an analogous explanation if the substance from which Adam was made were compared with fire, it comes to light that it has more light and value than fire."

H 175, Ch. 19, h 19

Ali ibn Ibrahim has narrated from Muhammad ibn 'Isa ibn 'Ubayd from Yunus from Hariz from Zurara who has said the following:

"Once I asked Imam abu 'Abd Allah, *'Alayhi al-Salam*, about lawful and unlawful matters and he said, 'Whatever the Holy Prophet, *'Alayhi al-Salam*, has made lawful will remain lawful forever up to the Day of Judgment, and whatever he has made unlawful will remain unlawful forever up to the Day of Judgment. There will be no one other than him and there will come no one other than him.' He said that Imam Ali has said, 'No one has established any innovation (heresy) without abandoning an established noble tradition.'"

H 176, Ch. 19, h 20

Ali ibn Ibrahim has narrated from his father from Ahmad ibn 'Abd Allah al-'Aqili from 'Isa ibn 'Abd Allah al-Qurashi who has said the following:

"Once, abu Hanifa came to see Imam abu 'Abd Allah, *'Alayhi al-Salam*, who said to abu Hanifa, 'O abu Hanifa, do you practice analogy as I hear you do'? Abu Hanifa replied, 'Yes, I do practice analogy.' The Imam then said to him, 'Do not practice it; the first person who used analogy was Satan when he said, "Lord, You have created me from fire and created him from clay." He analogized fire with clay. If he had analogized the light in the clay and fire he would have learned about the difference between the two lights and the excellence of one over the other.'"

H 177, Ch. 19, h 21

Ali has narrated from Muhammad ibn 'Isa from Yunus from Qutayba who has said the following:

"Once a man asked Imam abu 'Abd Allah, *'Alayhi al-Salam*, about an issue and the Imam replied. The man then said, 'Have you considered if it had been so and so the opinion in it would not have been as such.' The Imam then said, 'Wait; whatever I said in answer was from the Messenger of Allah, *'Alayhi al-Salam*. We are not of the people, "Have you considered" who need thinking.'"

Note: The Imam pointed out that they did not need the common reasoning process and that all they said had come to them from the Messenger of Allah, *'Alayhi al-Salam*.

H 178, Ch. 19, h 22

A number of our people have narrated from Ahmad ibn Muhammad ibn Khalid from his father in *mursal* manner (Mursalan) from abu Ja'far, *'Alayhi al-Salam*, who has said the following:

"Do not take anyone closely and intimately between yourselves and Allah; if you did so it would cause you to become unbelievers. Every means, ancestral and relative relations and intimacy, innovations (heresy) and doubts will be cut off except what is established in the Holy Quran."

Chapter 20 - The Need to Refer to the Book and Sunnah (There is Nothing About Lawful and Unlawful Matters That May Have Been Left Without a Rule in the Book and the Sunnah)

H 179, Ch. 20, h 1

Muhammad ibn Yahya has narrated from Ahmad ibn Muhammad ibn 'Isa from Ali ibn Hadid from Murazim from abu 'Abd Allah, *'Alayhi al-Salam*, who has said the following:

"Allah, the Most Holy, the Most High, has certainly revealed an explanation for all things. I swear by Allah, He has not left untold any rule that His servants would need up to the Day of Judgment. He has done so, so that people will not say, 'Would that such and such had been said in the Holy Quran.' The fact is that He has already said it in the Holy Quran."

H 180, Ch. 20, h 2

Ali ibn Ibrahim has narrated from Muhammad ibn 'Isa from Yunus from Husayn ibn al-Mundhir from 'Umar ibn Qays from abu Ja'far, *'Alayhi al-Salam*, who has said the following:

"I heard Imam abu Ja'far, *'Alayhi al-Salam*, saying, 'Allah, the Most Holy, the Most High, has not left untold any rule that the *'Umma*, nation, may need. He has revealed them in His book and has explained them to His messenger. He has made a limit for everything and an indication for it to point forward to it and He has made a limit of penalties for those who trespass those limits.'"

H 181, Ch. 20, h 3

Ali has narrated from Muhammad from Yunus from Aban from Sulayman ibn Harun who has said the following:

"I heard abu 'Abd Allah, *'Alayhi al-Salam*, saying, 'All that Allah has created has a limit like the limits of a house, which shows what is of the house, what is of the road and the walkway. There is even the law for compensation for a scratch, and a penalty in the form of a lash or half a lashing.'"

H 182, Ch. 20, h 4

Ali has narrated from Muhammad ibn "Isa from Yunus from Hammad from abu 'Abd Allah, *'Alayhi al-Salam*, who has said the following:

"I heard the Imam saying, 'There is no case for which there is not a law in the book or the *Sunnah* (the noble tradition of the Holy Prophet, *'Alayhi al-Salam*)."

H 183, Ch. 20, h 5

Ali ibn Ibrahim has narrated from his father from Muhammad ibn 'Isa from Yunus from Hammad from 'Abd Allah ibn Sinan from abu al-Jarud who has said the following:

"Abu Ja'far, *'Alayhi al-Salam*, has said, 'When you speak of anything, ask me for its law in the book of Allah.' He also has said in his *Hadith*, 'The Holy Prophet prohibited much squabbling and brawling, spoiling of property and much dispute.' A person then asked, 'O descendent of the Messenger of Allah, where is this in the Holy Quran?' The Imam, *'Alayhi al-Salam*, replied, 'Allah, the Most Glorious, the Most Majestic, says, 'There is nothing good in much of their secret talks except for that which is for charity, justice or for reconciliation among people to . . .' (4:114)

'Do not give your property, for which Allah has made you to supervise, over people weak of understanding . . .' (4:5) 'Believers, do not ask about things that if revealed to you, may disappoint you . . .'" (5:101)

H 184, Ch. 20, h 6

Muhammad ibn Yahya has narrated from Ahmad ibn Muhammad from ibn Faddal from Al-Tha'laba ibn Maymun from one he narrated from al-Mu'alla ibn Khunays who has said the following:

"Abu 'Abd Allah, *'Alayhi al-Salam*, has said, 'For every issue disputed between two people there is a principle for it in the book of Allah, the Most Majestic, the Most Glorious, however, man's power of intelligence is not able to find it.'"

H 185, Ch. 20, h 7

Muhammad ibn Yahya has narrated from certain persons of his people from Harun ibn Muslim from Mas'ada ibn Sadaqa from abu 'Abd Allah, *'Alayhi al-Salam*, who has said the following:

"Imam Ali, *'Alayhi al-Salam*, has said, 'O people, Allah, the Most Holy, the Most High, has sent to you His messenger, *'Alayhi al-Salam*, and given him the book with truth, while you all were illiterate (ignorant) about the book and the One Who revealed it and about the messenger and the One Who sent him in a period of time wherein no messenger had been sent, during a prolonged delinquency of the nations with widespread ignorance, over-looming afflictions, the crumbling of the established social order, blindness toward the truth, the practice of injustice, the destruction of religion, the raging of wars, at the time of paling away of the gardens of the worldly life, the withering away of the branches therein, the scattering away of its protectors, the loss of hope of its fruits, the drying out of its waters and during the decadence of its lighthouses. At such a period of time the elements of wickedness were manifest everywhere. The world seemed aggressive, rough and frowning at the face of its inhabitants, regressing instead of helping to progress and with wicked fruits. Its food was but carrion, its slogan fear and the swords as overall garments. You were totally crushed and the eyes of the inhabitants of the world had turned blind, and their days dark. They had boycotted their relatives, caused much bloodshed and buried their baby girls alive, expecting thereby goodness of life and worldly tranquility. They did not cherish any hope in the rewards of Allah or preserve any fear of the punishment of Allah. Their living was blind and filthy and their dead in the fire in total despair.

"At such time came to them a copy of what was in the ancient pages (of guidance) and a confirmation of what existed with them, containing a complete account of the lawful and unlawful matters. That is the Holy Quran. Ask it for the answers but it will not speak to you. I can tell you about it. In it there is the knowledge of the past and the knowledge of what comes in the future up to the Day of Judgment. Therein is the rule (needed) among you to settle disputes that may arise among you. If you ask me about it (meaning of the Holy Quran) I can certainly teach you'"

H 186, Ch. 20, h 8
Muhammad ibn Yahya has narrated from Muhammad ibn 'Abd al-Jabbar from ibn Faddal from Hammad ibn 'Uthman from 'Abd al-'Ala' ibn A'yan who has said the following:
"I heard abu 'Abd Allah, *'Alayhi al-Salam*, saying, 'I was born of the descendents of the messenger of Allah, *'Alayhim al-Salam*, and I know the book of Allah wherein is the knowledge of how the world was first created and the knowledge of all that may come up to the Day of Judgment. Therein is the news of the heavens and the earth, the news of paradise and hell, the news of things of the past, and those that will come into existence. I know all of these just as I can see in the palm of my hands. Allah says, 'In it there is an explanation of everything.'"

H 187, Ch. 20, h 9
A number of our people have narrated from Ahmad ibn Muhammad ibn 'Isa from Ali ibn Nu'man from 'Isma'il ibn Jabir from abu 'Abd Allah, *'Alayhi al-Salam*, who has said the following:
"In the Book of Allah there is the news of things before you, the reports of the matters after you and the laws to settle your disputes, and we know it all."

H 188, Ch. 20, h 10
A number of our people have narrated from Ahmad ibn Muhammad ibn Khalid from 'Isma'il ibn Mihran from Sayf ibn 'Amira from abu al-Maghra from Sama'a from abu al-Hassan Musa, *'Alayhi al-Salam*, who has said the following:
"Once I asked the Imam, 'Is everything in the Book of Allah and the *Sunnah* of His prophet or do you have a say in it also?' The Imam replied, 'As a matter of fact, everything is in the book of Allah and the *Sunnah* of His prophet, *'Alayhi al-Salam*.'"

Chapter 21 - The Differences in al-Hadith

H 189, Ch. 21, h 1
Ali ibn Ibrahim ibn Hashim has narrated from his father from Hammad ibn 'Isa from Ibrahim ibn 'Umar al-Yamani from Aban ibn abu 'Ayyash from Sulaym ibn Qays al-Hilali who has said the following:
"Once I said to Imam Ali, *'Alayhi al-Salam*, 'I have heard from Salman, al-Miqdad and abu Dhar certain matters about the interpretations of the Holy Quran and certain *Ahadith* of the Holy Prophet, *'Alayhi al-Salam*, which are different from such texts that others have. I have heard from you what confirms that which

I have heard from Salman and his friends. I have heard a great deal of *Hadith* and about the interpretations of the Holy Quran and *Ahadith* of the Holy Prophet of Allah. Do you disagree with what I have heard from other people (non-Shi'a) and consider such materials false? Do you think people ascribe lies to the Messenger of Allah, *'Alayhi al-Salam*, purposely and interpret the Holy Quran by their own personal opinions?' The Imam then said, 'You have posed a question, now listen carefully.'

"What people have consists of the truth, falsehood, lies, what is abrogating, already abrogated, facts of general nature, of particular natures, clear texts, unclear texts, facts properly memorized and matters that are conjecturally preserved. People had forged certain narrations that they called *Hadith* of the Holy Prophet. The condition was such that once the Holy Prophet addressed the people from the pulpit saying, 'O people, many lies have spread around and they are considered to be my *Hadith*. Whoever forges lies and calls them my *Hadith* has filled up his seat with fire.' After the Holy Prophet, *'Alayhi al-Salam*, there were more such lies. There are four kinds of *Hadith* only and there is no fifth kind.

"One narrator of *Hadith* is a hypocrite who only pretends to be a Muslim. He does not consider it a sin and offense to lie and calls purposely a narration a *Hadith* of the Holy Prophet while it is not a *Hadith* of the Holy Prophet in reality. If people know that he is hypocrite and a liar they will not believe him. The people say, 'He lived at the time of the Holy Prophet, saw him, has heard *Hadith* from him and has preserved those *Ahadith*' but they do not know his condition. It is certain that Allah has spoken about the hypocrites the way He has spoken about them and has described them the way He has described them. 'Their physical appearance attracts you when you see them and when they speak, you carefully listen to them. . . .' (63:4) The hypocrites then sought closeness to the misguiding leaders and those calling others to hellfire with falsehood, with lies and false accusations. The misguiding rulers assigned them for certain offices and made them to dominate people. They, with their help, devoured the world. People follow only the kings and the worldly gains except for those whom Allah has protected. This is one of the four kinds.

"Another kind is one who has heard *Hadith* from the Holy Prophet, but has not preserved it the way it should have been preserved and he is uncertain about it. He has not fabricated anything purposely and he has it with him. He speaks about it, practices accordingly and narrates it saying: 'I heard it from the Messenger of Allah, *'Alayhi al-Salam*.' If the Muslims learn about his uncertainty they do not accept it from him and if he becomes aware of such uncertainty he also rejects it.

"The third kind is one who has heard something from the Messenger of Allah, *'Alayhi al-Salam*, that contained a command but later the Holy Prophet prohibited it and the man did not have any knowledge of such prohibition. Or he heard a prohibition from the Holy Prophet and then the Holy Prophet made it a command but the man did not know of such commandment. In this way he preserved the abrogated but not the abrogating. If he had known the abrogating thereof he would have rejected it. If the Muslims had known what they had heard from him was abrogated they would also have rejected it.

"The last and fourth kind is one who has not ascribed a lie to the Messenger of Allah, who hates lies, has fear of Allah and respect for the Messenger of Allah, *'Alayhi al-Salam*. He has not forgotten anything and he has preserved it the way it should have been preserved. He speaks it just the way he has heard without any addition or omission. He knows which is abrogating and which is abrogated. He thus has practiced according to the abrogating and has rejected the abrogated. There is no doubt that the commands of the Messenger of Allah, *'Alayhi al-Salam*, like the Holy Quran are abrogating and abrogated, of general nature and of particular nature, clear text and unclear text. Oftentimes the statements of the Messenger of Allah may have two aspects: One being a general statement and a statement of a particular nature just as the Holy Quran as Allah, the Most Majestic, the Most Glorious, has said, '. . . Take only what the Messenger gives to you and desist from what he forbids you. . . .' (59:7) It may become confusing for one who does not know what exactly Allah and His messenger want people to do. All the companions of the Messenger of Allah did not clearly understand the answer to their questions. There were those who would ask a question but could not ask for explanations and rather welcomed the arrival of a Bedouin or a stranger to ask the Messenger of Allah questions so that he could also listen.

"I (Ali ibn abu Talib) would go in the presence of the Messenger of Allah once every day and once every night when he would admit me and deal with me the way he wanted. The *Sahaba* (companions of the Prophet) knew that the Messenger of Allah did not deal with others the way he dealt with me. Also, the Prophet would come to my house most of the time but whenever I went to any one of his houses he would admit me and ask his wife to leave us alone and then we would have been the only ones therein. Whenever he came to my house he would not ask *Fatimah, 'Alayha al-Salam*, or any of my children to leave the house. Then whatever I would ask he would answer me and when I had exhausted all of my questions he would begin to speak. Thus, nothing of the Holy Quran has ever been revealed to the Messenger of Allah that he did not make me read and dictate to me. I would write it down with my own handwriting. He taught me the interpretations of that verse and its explanations, its abrogating or that which was abrogated, the clear texts and the unclear statements, the ones of particular or general nature. He would pray to Allah to give me strong memory and understanding. I never forgot any of the verses of the Book of Allah or any of the knowledge that he had dictated to me, which I wrote down from the time he prayed to Allah for me. He did not leave out anything of the lawful and unlawful, commands or prohibitions that were there or that would come into being in future or any book that was revealed to anyone before him about the matters of obedience or disobedience, that he had not completely taught me and I had not memorized them all. I have not forgotten even a single letter of them. The Holy Prophet once placed his hand on my chest and prayed to Allah to fill my heart with knowledge, proper understanding, wisdom and light. I then said, 'O Prophet of Allah, may Allah keep the soul of my mother and father in service for your cause, from the time you prayed for me I have not forgotten a single matter or missed writing down anything. Do you fear that I might forget them in future?' 'I do not fear for you any forgetfulness or ignorance,' the Holy Prophet, *'Alayhi al-Salam*, replied.'"

H 190, Ch. 21, h 2
A number of our people have narrated from Ahmad ibn Muhammad from 'Uthman ibn 'Isa from abu Ayyub al-Khazzaz from Muhammad ibn Muslim who has said the following:

"Once I said to Imam abu 'Abd Allah, *'Alayhi al-Salam*, saying, 'What is the matter with people? They narrate from so and so who narrate from the Messenger of Allah, *'Alayhi al-Salam*. They do not accuse these narrators of telling lies and so forth. From you, then, facts against it come to light.' The Imam, *'Alayhi al-Salam*, said, *'Hadith* becomes abrogated just as it may happen with the Holy Quran.'"

H 191, Ch. 21, h 3
Ali ibn Ibrahim has narrated from his father from ibn abu Najran from 'Asim ibn Humayd from Mansur ibn Hazim who has said the following:

"Once, I said to (Imam) abu 'Abd Allah, *'Alayhi al-Salam*, 'It confuses me when I ask you a question and you give an answer. Then another person comes, you give a different answer for the same question.' The Imam replied, 'We answer people in a larger and reduced form.' I then asked, 'Did the *Sahaba* (companions of the Messenger of Allah) speak the truth or lies when narrating his *Hadith*?' The Imam replied, 'They spoke the truth.' I then said, 'Why then do they have differences?' The Imam then said, 'Have you not considered the fact that a man would come to the Messenger of Allah, *'Alayhi al-Salam*, and ask him a question and he would give him an answer. Then he would give an answer that abrogated the previous answer. Thus, *Ahadith* abrogated other *Ahadith*.'"

H 192, Ch. 21, h 4
Ali ibn Muhammad has narrated from Sahl ibn Ziyad from ibn Mahbub from Ali ibn Ri'ab from abu 'Ubayda who has said the following:

"Once abu Ja'far, *'Alayhi al-Salam*, said, 'O Ziyad, what would you say if we gave a *Fatwa* to one of our followers under pressure (and conceal the truth)?' I (Ziyad) said, 'You know better, may Allah keep my soul in your service.' The Imam said, 'If he would follow such *Fatwa* it would be better for him and of a greater reward.' In another *Hadith* it says, 'If he follows it, he will be rewarded and if he disregards it, I swear by Allah, he has sinned.'"

H 193, Ch. 21, h 5
Ahmad ibn Idris has narrated from Muhammad ibn 'Abd al-Jabbar from al-Hassan ibn Ali from Al-Tha'laba ibn Maymun from Zurara ibn 'A'yan who has said the following:

"Once I asked Imam abu Ja'far, *'Alayhi al-Salam*, a question and he answered me. Then another man came and asked the same question but the Imam gave a different answer. Then a third man came and asked the same question and the Imam gave him an answer that was different from both of the previous answers. When the other two men left I asked the Imam, *'Alayhi al-Salam*, 'Two of your followers from Iraq asked you the same question. How is it that you gave each one a different answer?' The Imam replied, 'O Zurara, it is better for us and it gives all of us more time. If you all say the same thing, people will know that you speak the truth from us and this will leave all of us with less time.' Zurara has said, 'I then said to Imam, abu 'Abd Allah, *'Alayhi al-Salam*, 'Your followers can walk on spears and fire if you asked them but they come out of your presence with different answers and disunited for the same question.' He gave me the same answer as his father had given.'"

H 194, Ch. 21, h 6
Muhammad ibn Yahya has narrated from Ahmad ibn Muhammad ibn 'Isa from Muhammad ibn Sinan from Nasr al-Kath'ami who has said the following:

"I heard abu 'Abd Allah, *'Alayhi al-Salam*, saying, 'Those who know that we say nothing but the truth, they should then consider what they have learned from us is sufficient for them. If they hear from us something different from the knowledge they already have learned from us they should note that it is a way we have taken to defend them.'"

H 195, Ch. 21, h 7
Ali ibn Ibrahim has narrated from his father from 'Uthman ibn 'Isa and al-Hassan ibn Mahbub both from Sama'a from 'Abd Allah who has said the following:

"Once I asked (Imam) abu 'Abd Allah, *'Alayhi al-Salam*, about, if a man faces a case in which two people of his own faith in a certain issue oppose each other about what they both have narrated. One of them says that it is obligatory and the other says it is prohibited. How can it be resolved?" The Imam replied, "He must wait until he finds one who will inform him and until then he is not under any pressure." In another *Hadith* it says, "He may follow any one of the two answers. Whichever he follows in obedience and submission it is permissible for his ease."

H 196, Ch. 21, h 8
Ali ibn Ibrahim has narrated from his father from 'Uthman ibn 'Isa from al-Husayn ibn al-Mukhtar from certain persons of our people from abu 'Abd Allah, *'Alayhi al-Salam*, who has said the following:

"If you come to me for an answer to a question and I give you an answer of a general nature and then you come again and I give you an opposite answer, which one would you follow?" I replied, "I would follow the later one." The Imam, *'Alayhi al-Salam*, said, "May Allah grant you blessings."

H 197, Ch. 21, h 9
It is narrated from him from his father from Isma'il ibn Marrar from Yunus from Dawud ibn Farqad from Mu'alla ibn Khunays who has said the following:

"Once, I asked Imam abu 'Abd Allah, *'Alayhi al-Salam*, 'If we receive a *Hadith* from the first of you (your earlier generation) and also from the members of your later generation which one should we follow?' The Imam replied, 'Follow it until you receive it from the living Imam. When it comes from a living Imam, follow his words.' The Imam then said, 'We by Allah like you to follow what is easy for you.' In another *Hadith* it says, 'Follow whichever is the newest.'"

H 198, Ch. 21, h 10
Muhammad ibn Yahya has narrated from Muhammad ibn al-Husayn from Muhammad ibn 'Isa from Safwan ibn Yahya from Dawud ibn al-Husayn from 'Umar ibn Hanzala who has said the following:

"Once I asked Imam abu 'Abd Allah, *'Alayhi al-Salam*, about two people disputing over an issue of debts or inheritance and they go to the king or the judges to settle their dispute through his or their decision. I said, 'Is it permissible to seek such a judgment?' The Imam replied, 'Going to them for a judgment in a right or wrongful matter is like seeking the judgment of the devil. Any benefit received through such judgment is like consuming filth even if it is one's firmly established right. It is like filth because it is a benefit received through the judgment of the devil and Allah has commanded to reject the devil, ' . . . yet they choose to take their affairs to Satan for judgment, even though they are commanded to reject him (the devil). Satan wants to lead them far away from the right path.' (4:60)

"I said, 'What should they do then?' The Imam replied, 'They must look for one among you who has narrated our *Hadith* and has studied what is lawful and unlawful according to our teachings and has learned our laws. They must agree to settle their dispute by his judgment; I have given him authority to settle your disputes. If he issues a judgment according to our commands but then it is not accepted, the dissenting party has ignored the commands of Allah and it is a rejection of us. Rejecting us is rejecting Allah and that is upto the level of paganism and considering things equal to Allah.'

"I said, 'What if each one of such disputing parties chooses a man from among our people and agrees to accept their judgment but these two men come up with different judgments and they have differences in your *Hadith*?'

"The Imam replied, 'The judgment will be the judgment of the one who is more just, has better understanding of the law (*Fiqh*), who is more truthful in *Hadith* and is more pious of the two. The judgment of the other one will be disregarded.'

"I said, 'What if both (judges) are just and accepted among our people and neither of them has been given any preference over the other?'

"The Imam replied, 'One must consider and study the *Hadith* that each one of them narrate from us to see which one has received the acceptance of all of your people. Such *Hadith* must be followed and the one, which is rarely accepted and is not popular in your people, must be disregarded; the one popularly accepted is free of doubts. The nature of cases is of three kinds: (a) a case that is well-known and true that must be followed; (b) a case that is well-known as false that must be avoided, (c) and a confusing case the knowledge of which must be left to Allah and His messenger for an answer. The messenger of Allah has said, "There are the clearly lawful and the clearly unlawful and the confusing cases. One who stays away from the confusing ones has protected himself against the unlawful ones. Those who follow the confusing matters indulging in unlawful matters will be destroyed unexpectedly."

"I said, 'What if both *Hadith* from you would be popular and narrated by the trustworthy people from you?'

"The Imam replied, 'One must study to find out which one agrees with the laws of the Quran and the *Sunnah* and does not agree with the laws of those who oppose us. Such *Hadith* must be accepted and the one that disagrees with the laws of the Quran and the *Sunnah* and coincides with the masses must be disregarded.

"I said, 'May Allah keep my soul in service for your cause, what if both *Faqih*, scholars of the law, would have deduced and learned their judgment from the book and the *Sunnah* and found that one of the *Hadith* agrees with the masses, and the other disagrees with the masses, which one must be followed?'

"The Imam replied, 'The one which disagrees with the masses must be followed due to its containing guidance.'

"I said, 'May Allah keep my soul in the service of your cause, what if both *Hadith* agree with the masses?'

"The Imam replied, 'One must study to find out which of the two is more agreeable to their (non-Shi'a') rulers and judges, so it must be disregarded and the other must be followed.'

"I said, 'What if both *Hadith* are agreeable to their rulers?' The Imam replied, 'If such is the case it must be suspended until you meet your Imam. Restraint in confusing cases is better than indulging in destruction.'"

Chapter 22 - Following the Sunnah and Evidence of the Book

H 199, Ch. 22, h 1

Ali ibn Ibrahim has narrated from his father from al-Nawfali from al-Sakuni from abu 'Abd Allah, *'Alayhi al-Salam*, who has said the following:

"The messenger of Allah, *'Alayhi al-Salam*, has said, 'Over every truth there is a reality and above every valid issue there is light. Whatever agrees with the Holy Quran you must follow and whatever does not agree, disregard it.'"

H 200, Ch. 22, h 2

Muhammad ibn Yahya has narrated from 'Abd Allah ibn Muhammad from Ali ibn al-Hakam from Aban ibn 'Uthman from 'Abd Allah ibn abu Ya'fur who has said the following:

"In a meeting where ibn abu Ya'fur was also present I asked Imam abu 'Abd Allah, *'Alayhi al-Salam*, about the differences in *Hadith* narrated from people whom we trust and also from people we do not trust. The Imam replied, 'If you find a *Hadith* with evidence in the Holy Quran to support it or a *Hadith* of the Messenger of Allah (you may follow it). Otherwise, you follow the one that has come to you through the trustworthy narrator.'"

H 201, Ch. 22, h 3

A number of our people have narrated from Ahmad ibn Muhammad ibn Khalid from his father from al-Nadr ibn Suwayd from Yahya al-Halab from Ayyub ibn al-Hurr who has said the following:

"I heard abu 'Abd Allah, *'Alayhi al-Salam*, saying, 'Everything must be referred to the Holy Quran and the *Sunnah* (the noble traditions of the Messenger of Allah,

'Alayhi al-Salam). Any *Hadith* that does not agree with the Holy Quran is a useless statement.'"

H 202, Ch. 22, h 4

Muhammad ibn Yahya has narrated from Ahmad ibn Muhammad ibn 'Isa from ibn Faddal from Ali ibn 'Uqba from Ayyub ibn Rashid from abu 'Abd Allah, *'Alayhi al-Salam,* who has said the following:

"Of *Hadith,* whatever does not agree with the Holy Quran is a useless statement."

H 203, Ch. 22, h 5

Muhammad ibn 'Isma'il from al-Fadl ibn Shadhan from ibn abu 'Umayr from Hisham ibn al-Hakam and others from abu 'Abd Allah, *'Alayhi al-Salam,* who has said the following:

"The Holy Prophet once addressed the people in Mina (a place in Makkahh) saying, 'O people, whatever comes to you in the form of my *Hadith,* if it agrees with the Holy Book of Allah, it is genuine, but whatever comes to you that does not agree with the book of Allah you must know that I have not said it.'"

H 204, Ch. 22, h 6

It is narrated through the same chain of narrators from ibn abu 'Umayr from certain persons of his people who have said the following:

"I heard abu 'Abd Allah, *'Alayhi al-Salam,* saying, 'Whoever disagrees with the book of Allah and the *Sunnah* of Prophet Muhammad, *'Alayhi al-Salam,* has certainly become an unbeliever.'"

H 205, Ch. 22, h 7

Ali ibn Ibrahim has narrated from Muhammad ibn 'Isa ibn 'Ubayd from Yunus in a *marfu'* manner from Ali ibn al-Husayn, *'Alayhi al-Salam,* who has said the following:

"The best deed in the sight of Allah is the one that is performed according to the *Sunnah* (the noble tradition of the Messenger of Allah, *'Alayhi al-Salam),* even if it is of a small degree."

H 206, Ch. 22, h 8

A number of our people have narrated from Ahmad ibn Muhammad ibn Khalid from 'Isma'il ibn Mihran from abu Sa'id al-Qammat and Salih ibn Sa'id from Aban ibn Taghlib who has said the following:

"Once a man asked a question from Imam abu Ja'far, *'Alayhi al-Salam,* who replied to it, and then the man said, 'The *Fuqaha* (scholars of law) do not say this.'

"The Imam then said, 'It is a pity. Have you ever seen a *Faqih* (a scholar of law)? The real *Faqih* is one who maintains restraint from worldly matters, who is deeply interested in the life hereafter and holds firmly to the *Sunnah* (noble tradition of the Holy Prophet, *'Alayhi al-Salam).*'"

H 207, Ch. 22, h 9

A number of our people have narrated from Ahmad ibn Muhammad ibn Khalid from his father from abu 'Isma'il Ibrahim ibn Ishaq al-Azdi from abu 'Uthman al-'Abdi from Ja'far from his ancestors from Amir al-Mu'minin Ali, *'Alayhi al-Salam,* who has said the following:

"The messenger of Allah has said, 'There are no words without action, there are no words or actions without intention and there are no words, actions and intentions without learning the *Sunnah* (the noble tradition of the Holy Prophet, *'Alayhi al-Salam).*'"

H 208, Ch. 22, h 10

Ali ibn Ibrahim has narrated from his father from Ahmad ibn al-Nadr from 'Amr ibn Shimr from Jabir from abu Ja'far, *'Alayhi al-Salam*, who has said the following:

"There is no one without excitement and calmness. Whoever's calmness leads him toward the *Sunnah* (noble tradition of the Holy Prophet, *'Alayhi al-Salam*), is rightly guided, but if it leads him toward innovations (heresy) then he has gone astray."

H 209, Ch. 22, h 11

Ali ibn Muhammad has narrated from Ahmad ibn Muhammad al-Barqi from Ali ibn Hassa'n and Muhammad ibn Yahya from Salama ibn al-Khattab from Ali ibn Hassa'n from Musa ibn Bakr from Zurara ibn A'yan from abu Ja'far, *'Alayhi al-Salam*, who has said the following:

"Whoever transgresses against the *Sunnah* (noble tradition of the Holy Prophet, *'Alayhi al-Salam*), must return to the *Sunnah*."

H 210, Ch. 22, h 12

Ali ibn Ibrahim has narrated from his father from al-Nawfali from al-Sakuni from abu 'Abd Allah from his ancestors (*'A'immah, 'Alayhim al-Salam*) who have said the following:

"Imam Ali, *'Alayhi al-Salam*, has said, 'There are two kinds of *Sunnah* (tradition). There is a *Sunnah* in obligations and following such *Sunnah* is guidance and its disregard is misguidance. There is a *Sunnah* (tradition) in non-obligatory issues. The following of this kind of *Sunnah* is a virtuous deed and its disregard for other matters is a sin.'"

This is the end of the Book on the virtue of knowledge. All praise belongs to Allah. May Allah send blessings upon Prophet Muhammad and his purified Family.

In the Name of Allah, the Beneficent, the Merciful

Part Three:
The Book on the Oneness of Allah

Chapter 1 - Contingency of the Universe and Proof of the Existence of Its Creator

H 211, Ch. 1, h 1

Abu Ja'far Muhammad ibn Ya'qub has narrated from Ali ibn Ibrahim ibn Hashim from his father, from al-Hassan ibn Ibrahim from Yunus ibn 'Abd al-Rahman from Ali ibn Mansur who narrated the following:

"Hisham ibn al-Hakam has reported that in Egypt there lived an atheist who had heard a great deal about (Imam) abu 'Abd Allah, *'Alayhi al-Salam*. He traveled to Madina to debate the Imam but he missed finding the Imam therein. He was told that the Imam had traveled to the city of Makkahh. He then left for Makkahh and we were with the Imam, *'Alayhi al-Salam*, when we came across him during our performing *Tawaf* (the seven times walking around the Ka'ba). The man's name was 'Abd al-Malik, also called abu 'Abd Allah as his *Kunya* in Arabic. He touched (Imam) abu 'Abd Allah's shoulder with his shoulder as he walked along. The Imam asked him, 'What is your name?' 'It is 'Abd al-Malik (meaning slave of the King),' the man replied. 'What is your Kunya?' the Imam, *'Alayhi al-Salam*, asked. 'It is abu 'Abd Allah (meaning father of slave of Allah),' he replied. The Imam then asked, 'Who is this king whose slave you are? Is he of the earthly kings or of the heavenly ones? Tell us about your son. Is he a slave of the Lord of the Heavens or a slave of the Lord of the Earth? Say whatever you may it will be against you.'

"Hisham has said that I asked him (the atheist man), 'Why do you not answer?' The man seemed to dislike my words. The Imam, *'Alayhi al-Salam*, then told him, 'Meet us when we finish our *Tawaf* (walking around the Ka'ba).'

"The atheist came to the Imam, *'Alayhi al-Salam*, later and sat in front of the Imam, and we were all gathered around him.

"The Imam, *'Alayhi al-Salam*, then asked him, 'Do you know that the earth has an underside and an upper-side?' 'Yes, I know it,' the man replied. The Imam then asked, 'Have you gone in the underside of the earth?' 'No, I have not gone there,' the man replied. The Imam, *'Alayhi al-Salam*, then asked, 'Do you know what is there?' 'I do not know but I guess there is nothing there,' he replied. The Imam then said, 'Guessing is weakness. Why do you not acquire certainty?' The Imam, *'Alayhi al-Salam*, then asked, 'Have you climbed up into the sky?' 'No, I have not done so,' the man replied. The Imam then asked, 'Do you know what is up there?' 'No, I do not know,' he replied. The Imam said, 'It is very strange. Without reaching the East or West, without going under the earth or climbing up the sky and without even having crossed anything to know what is behind there, you deny what is in them. Does any man of reason deny what he does not know?'

"The atheist man then said, 'No one has ever come up to me with such statements as you have.' The Imam, *'Alayhi al-Salam*, then said, 'So you are uncertain about Him. Perhaps He is or maybe He does not exist.' The atheist man then said, 'Perhaps He is.' The Imam then said, 'O man, one who does not know has no authority over the one who knows. O Egyptian brethren, listen carefully. We have no doubts about the existence of Allah. Think about the sun, the moon, the day and the nights that follow each other and do not miss their turns or become confused. They each have their place and do not have any choice. If they had any other choice they would not come back again. If they had a choice the day would not always end with night and the night would not always end in the day. They are forced, I swear by Allah, to continue. O Egyptian brethren, the One who has forced them is stronger than them and greater.' The atheist man then said, 'You have spoken the truth.'

"The Imam then said, 'You people speak of and guess that it is *dahr* (time) that causes people to die and brings changes. If it were so, then, when it took them away why then would it not return them, and if such form of time had returned them then why would it not be taking them away? These things, O Egyptian brethren, are compelled. Why the sky is up high and why the earth is low? Why the sky does not fall down on earth? Why the earth does not flow one layer over the other and the two do not stick to each other, and why do not those on it stick to it?' The man then said, 'Allah their Lord has made them to hold together.'

"Hisham has said, 'He professed belief in Allah in the presence of (Imam) abu 'Abd Allah, *'Alayhi al-Salam.'*

"Humran then said to the Imam, 'May Allah keep my soul in service for your cause, if atheists profess belief in Allah before you it is because the unbelievers converted to faith because of your father.' The man who had just professed belief in Allah requested (Imam) abu 'Abd Allah, *'Alayhi al-Salam*, to allow him to become one of his students. The Imam then asked Hisham to teach him. Hisham taught him well and he became a teacher for the people in Syria and Egypt. His purification was very good and the Imam, *'Alayhi al-Salam*, became happy with him."

H 212, Ch. 1, h 2

A number of our people have narrated from Ahmad ibn Muhammad ibn Khalid from Muhammad ibn Ali from 'Abd al-Rahman ibn Muhammad ibn abu Hashim from Ahmad ibn Muhsin al-Maythami. Al-Maythami has said the following:

"Once I was with abu Mansur al-Mutatabbib who said that one of his friends narrated the following: 'At a certain time with ibn abu al-'Awja', 'Abd Allah ibn al-Muqaffa' and I were in the holy Mosque of Makkah. Ibn al-Muqaffa' said, 'Do you see these creatures? (He pointed out toward the location where people walk seven times around the Ka'ba.) Of all these no one deserves to be called a human being accept that Shaykh sitting there (meaning thereby Imam abu 'Abd Allah,

'Alayhi al-Salam), the rest is garbled (people who have no meaningful opinion of life) and beasts.

"Upon this ibn abu al-'Awja' said, 'For what reason do you call him a human being and not the rest?'

"Ibn al-Muqaffa' then replied, 'Because I saw from him what I had not seen from the others.'

"Ibn abu al-'Awja' then said, 'We must test your claim.' Ibn al-Muqaffa' then said, 'I advise you not to do so or else you will lose whatever faith you have.'

"Ibn abu al-'Awja' then said, 'I do not think that is what you mean. I think you are afraid of failing to substantiate what you have just said about this man.'

"Ibn al-Muqaffa' then said, 'If that is what you think, then go to him and protect yourself as much as you can. Be strong as much as you can so you are not embarrassed, and note all points against and in your favor.'

"Ibn abu al-'Awja' then left and ibn al-Muqaffa' and I remained there. When ibn abu al-'Awja' returned he said, 'Woe is you, O ibn al-Muqaffa'. This is not a human being even though he lives in this world. He is a spiritual being but appears in the form of a man whenever he wants the outer world and turns into a spiritual being whenever he wants the inner world. That is the way he is.'

"Ibn al-Muqaffa' then asked, 'How does that happen?' Ibn abu al-'Awja' then said, 'I sat near him and when everyone had gone he turned to me and said, 'If it is the way they (people walking around the Ka'ba) say which is true, then they are saved and you are destroyed. If it is the way you say it is, in fact, it is not so, then you and they are all equal.'

"I then asked, 'May Allah be kind to you. What is it that we say and what is it that they say? We all say the same thing.' 'How can what you say be equal to what they say?' said (Imam) abu 'Abd Allah, who continued, 'They say that they will have a return, a day of receiving their rewards and penalties. They believe in a religion that says, "In the heaven is the Lord and that it is habitable" while you say that it is in ruins and there is nothing in it (heaven).'

"Ibn abu al-'Awja' has said that I then found the opportunity to speak and I asked, 'What then keeps this Lord (if it is true as they say He exists) from appearing to His creatures? (He should appear) and call them to His worship so that no two people would oppose each other. Why is He hiding from them and has only sent messengers? If He had been in direct contact with them it would be more helpful to have faith in Him.'

"Woe is you. One who has already shown His power within you, in what way is He hiding from you?" He (the Imam) responded and continued, "He brought you up. You did not even exist. He made you grow when you were so small. He gave you strength and power when you were so weak and will make you weak again after being strong. He causes you to become sick after being healthy and can give you good health after suffering sickness. He can make you happy after you experience anger and make you angry after being happy. He can make you sad after your joy and give you joy after sadness. He can give love after your experiencing hatred and hatred after enjoying love. He can give you determination after your uncertainty and uncertainty after having determination. He can give you strong desires after your experiencing dislike and dislike after having strong desires. He can give you willingness after experiencing fear and concerns and fear after having strong willingness. He can give you hope after despair and despair after having a great deal of hope. He can give you good remembrance of that of which you had no idea and remove what you may have had as a belief." He (the Imam) kept reminding and counting for me the effects of His power within my soul that I could not deny. I began to have a feeling that he would win the debate openly."

"From the same source the following is narrated from a number of our people in a *marfu'* manner as additional statements to the above discourse of ibn abu al-'Awja' with (Imam) abu 'Abd Allah, *'Alayhi al-Salam*. That ibn abu al-'Awja' came the next day to the meeting of the Imam and sat down quietly. The Imam, *'Alayhi al-Salam*, said to him, 'Would you like to review the issues we discussed yesterday'? Ibn abu al-'Awja' replied, 'I do intend to do so, O son of the Messenger of Allah.'

"The Imam then said, 'It is strange that one who does not believe in Allah acknowledges the existence of the Messenger of Allah.' Ibn abu al-'Awja then said, 'What made me say so is only a habit.' The 'Alim (the Imam) then asked, 'What is it that keeps you quiet?' He replied, 'It is your excellence and awesome spiritual ability that holds my tongue back from speaking. I have seen many scholars and have debated many theologians but I have never experienced such an awesome feeling from them as I feel in your presence.'

"The Imam then said, 'It may happen. I like to open this session with a question to you. Are you created or non-created?' 'Abd al-Karim ibn abu al-'Awja' answered, 'I am non-created.' The 'Alim (the Imam) then asked him, 'Describe for us how you might be if you were created.' 'Abd al-Karim remained quiet and confused and kept himself busy with a piece of wood, saying, 'Long, wide, deep, short, moving and motionless. All these are the qualities of His creatures.' The 'Alim (Imam) then said, 'If you do not know anything other than these as the qualities of the creation then consider yourself a creature; that is what you find within yourself that takes place and comes into existence.' 'Abd al-Karim then said, 'You have asked me a question that no one before has ever asked and no one ever will ask afterwards.' Abu 'Abd Allah, *'Alayhi al-Salam*, then said, 'It may be considered true that you may not have been asked such questions in the past but how do you know that you will not be asked anything in future? Besides, O 'Abd al-Karim, what you said is against your notion that from eternity all things are equal (a reference to the belief in the eternity of all things). How then have you made them before and after?'

"The Imam then said, 'O 'Abd al-Karim, let me explain. Suppose you had a bag with you full of pearls and someone asked you, 'Is there a Dinar in your bag?' You then denied and said, 'No, there is no Dinar in my bag.' The person then said, 'All right, then describe for me the qualities of the Dinar.' But you had no knowledge of the qualities of the Dinar. Could you deny the existence of the Dinar that was from the bag but you did not know about it?' He replied, 'No, I would not deny.' The Imam then said, 'The world is bigger, taller and wider than a bag. Perhaps in the world there is a creature that you do not know and in whose case you may not be able to tell the qualities of the created from the non-created.' 'Abd al-Karim remained quiet but certain persons among his people agreed to accept Islam and a few of them remained with him.

"He came again to the meeting of the Imam on the third day and said, 'I want to reverse the question.' The Imam replied, 'Ask whatever you like.' He then asked, 'What is the proof that bodies did not exist and then they came into existence?' The Imam then said, 'I have not seen anything small or large that on adding to it something of the same size would not make it bigger and would not cause a change and transformation from the first condition. If, however, it had been eternal, there would have been no changing and transformation. What may cease to exist or change may also come into existence and may get destroyed. Thus, its existence after its non-existence is entering into the state of coming into being. As being eternal this will take it into nothingness. However, the two qualities of being eternal and nothingness and the qualities of a contingent and something without a beginning do not come together in one thing.'

"'Abd al-Karim then said, 'Suppose I noticed that with a view to the two conditions you mentioned you considered it a proof of their contingency (being created). If, however, things remained small, despite the addition, then how can you prove their contingency?'

"The 'Alim then said, 'We speak of this universe that is already there. Were we to take it away and place another universe in its place nothingness would have certainly, a stronger proof of its contingency than its removal and its replacing with a different one. I, however, will answer you according to your assumption. Even if things remained small, it would certainly come into one's thinking that whenever something like it is added to another thing it then would be bigger. The fact that it can change is proof of its becoming temporal and in its changing condition is proof of its contingency. There is nothing beyond it for you, O 'Abd al-Karim.' 'Abd al-Karim had nothing else to say.'

"Next year he met the Imam, *'Alayhi al-Salam*, in Makkah again and people from among his followers said that 'Abd al-Karim has become a Muslim. The Imam told him that 'Abd al-Karim was blind in this matter and would not become a Muslim. He ('Abd al-Karim) saw the 'Alim and said, 'There you are, my master, my chief.' The 'Alim then asked him, 'What brings you here?' He then replied, 'It is the habits of the body and the traditions of the town. We like to see what craziness makes them shave and throw pebbles.' The 'Alim said, 'It seems that you still live in your arrogance and misguidance, O 'Abd al-Karim.' He began to speak but the Imam said, 'Disputation during Hajj is not permissible,' the Imam freed his gown from the hand of the heretic man and said, 'If it is the way you say, which in fact is not true, then we as well as you are all saved. However, if it is the way we say, which in fact, is true, we are saved but you are destroyed.' 'Abd al-Karim then turned to his people saying, 'I feel pain in my heart. Take me back.' They took him away and he died."

H 213, Ch. 1, h 3

Muhammad ibn Ja'far al-Asadi has narrated from Muhammad ibn Isma'il al-Barmaki al-Razi from al-Husayn ibn al-Hassan ibn Bard al-Daynuri from Muhammad ibn Ali from Muhammad ibn 'Abd Allah al-Khurasani the employee of (Imam) al-Rida, *'Alayhi al-Salam*, who said the following:

"Once an atheist man came to Imam abu al-Hassan, *'Alayhi al-Salam*, while a group of people was in his presence. The Imam, *'Alayhi al-Salam*, said to him, 'Consider, if what you say is true, in fact is not true, in such case, we all will be equal. However, our fasting, prayers, giving charity and belief will not harm us.' The man remained quiet. The Imam then said, 'If what we say is true, in fact is true, then you will be the one facing your destruction and we will be saved.' The man then said, 'Please help me learn where is He and how is He?' The Imam then said, 'What is the matter with you? What you say is not right. He is the 'Where' of 'Where' but without 'Where'. He is the 'How' of 'How' without 'How'. He cannot be defined with 'How' and 'Where' and cannot be comprehended with the senses or compared with anything.

"The man said, 'He then is nothing; none of the senses comprehends Him.' Abu al-Hassan, *'Alayhi al-Salam*, said, 'That is not reasonable. Weakness of your senses and their inability to comprehend Him is not proof that He does not exist and that He is not the Lord. On the other hand, when we realize the weakness of our senses and their inability to comprehend Him it gives us certainty that He is our Lord and He is different from all things.'

"The man then said, 'Tell me then when was He?' The Imam replied, 'You tell me when He was not there so that I will tell when He was there?' The man then asked, 'What is the proof for His existence?' The Imam said, 'When I look at my body I find that I cannot do any addition or alteration to it such as width and breadth or remove its sufferings and attract all its interests. I then come to understand that for this establishment there must be a founder and then I acknowledge His existence. Besides, I see all the orbiting planets and stars, the movements of the clouds and driving of the winds, the paths of the sun, the moon, the stars and other things like these marvelous clear signs, I come to believe that there is One who has designed and created all such wonderful things.'"

H 214, Ch. 1, h 4

Ali ibn Ibrahim has narrated from Muhammad ibn Ishaq al-Khaffaf or from his father from Muhammad ibn Ishaq who said the following:

"Once 'Abd Allah al-Daysani asked Hisham ibn al-Hakam, 'Do you have a creator?' He replied, 'Yes, I have a creator.' He then asked, 'Is He powerful?' Hisham then replied, 'Yes, He is powerful and the most powerful One.' The man then asked, 'Can He fit the whole world inside an egg without any change in the size of either one?' Hisham then said, 'Give me time.' The man said, 'I give you one whole year' and he left.

"Hisham then went to see (Imam) abu 'Abd Allah, *'Alayhi al-Salam*, for an answer. After asking permission that he was granted Hisham explained, 'Al-Daysani asked me a question today and I see no one except Allah and you to answer it.' The Imam then asked, 'What is the question?' Hisham restated the question that al-Daysani had asked. The Imam then said, 'O Hisham, how many are your senses?' He replied, 'They are five.' The Imam then asked, 'Which one is the smallest?' He replied, 'The seeing sense.' The Imam then asked, 'How big is its size?' He replied, 'It is about the size of the pupil or smaller.' The Imam then said, 'O Hisham, look in front of you and above you and then tell me what you have seen.' Hisham then replied, 'I can see the sky, the earth, the houses, the buildings, the land, the mountains and the water canals.' The Imam then said, 'The One who has been able to fit all that you can see in a pupil or even a smaller thing is also able to fit the whole world inside an egg without any change in the size of either one of them.' Hisham bowed down and kissed the feet, the hands and the head of the Imam, *'Alayhi al-Salam*, saying, 'This is enough for me, O descendant of the holy Prophet,' and then left for his home. The next day al-Daysani met him and said, 'I have come just to say greetings to you and not for an answer to my question' Hisham then said, 'Even if you have come for an answer it is ready.' Al-Daysani then left to meet (Imam) abu 'Abd Allah, *'Alayhi al-Salam*, and after asking permission for a meeting which was granted he sat down and said, 'O Ja'far ibn Muhammad, guide me to my Lord.' The Imam then asked, 'What is your name?' He then left without answering the Imam and his people asked him, 'Why did you not answer the Imam?' He replied, 'Were I to tell him that it is 'Abd Allah he would then ask, "Who is this Lord whose slave you are?"' They then said, 'Return to him and ask him to guide you to your Lord without asking your name.' He then returned back to the Imam and asked, 'O Ja'far ibn Muhammad, guide me to my Lord but do not ask my name.' The Imam asked him to sit down. A young boy, son of the Imam was there playing with an egg in his hand and the Imam said, 'Fetch me the egg, O young man.' The boy gave the egg to the Imam. The Imam said, 'O Daysani, this is a secure castle. It has a thicker outer shell, and inside of it there is a much finer shell inside, of which there is liquid gold and flowing silver. The liquid gold does not mix with the flowing silver, nor does the flowing silver mix the liquid gold. Such is its condition that no expert comes out from there to find out what is beneficial to it to report back all about it, nor does any corrupting agent enter therein so that its problems would be reported. No one knows if it is created for a male or a female. It will burst out with colors of a peacock. Do you think there is someone who has designed and managed it?'

"Al-Daysani thought for a while, quietly, and said, 'I testify that no one deserves to be obeyed except Allah who is the only Lord and has no partner. I testify that

Muhammad, *'Alayhi al-Salam*, is His servant and messenger and that you are the Imam and an authority from Allah over His creatures and I repent and regret because of previous beliefs."'

H 215, Ch. 1, h 5

Ali ibn Ibrahim has narrated from his father from 'Abbass ibn 'Amr al-Faqimi from Hisham ibn al-Hakam in the narration about the atheist who came to (Imam) abu 'Abd Allah, *'Alayhi al-Salam*, and the Imam had explained to him the following:

"You assume that there are two eternal and powerful powers (who control the universe) or that both are weak or only one of them is weak and the other is powerful. If they both are powerful, why then does neither one ever make an effort to remove the other one to have full control of the universe? If you assume that one is powerful and the other is weak then it is proof that there is only one, as we believe; the weakness of the other is so apparent. Besides, if you say that they are two then they either agree with each other in all matters or disagree in the same way. Since we see the creation works in an organized manner, the orbiting objects continue to do so, the organization is one, the day, the night, the sun and the moon all show that the organization is valid and correct. The harmony in the matter shows that the organizer is one. If your claim of two causes you to believe that there must be a gap (void) in between to show two things, in that case the gap will become a third one and eternal. Thus, it will involve you in three and this will involve to say what you said about the two where you needed to have a gap and in this case it will become five and so on indefinite in number and multiplicity.

"Hisham has said that of the questions of the atheist from (Imam) abu 'Abd Allah one was 'what is the evidence of His existence'? The Imam, *'Alayhi al-Salam*, answered, "The existence of the effects (activities) shows that someone has produced those effects and activities. Consider, when you see a well-constructed building, you learn that there is someone who has built it, even if you have not seen the builder with your own eyes." The atheist then asked, 'What is it then?' The Imam replied, "He is something but different from all things. I repeat my statement that speaks about Him as a *thing*. He is a thing in the sense of the reality of things except that He does not have a body and form. He does not have a feeling (like our sense of feeling) or touching and He does not comprehend with the five senses (as we do). Imaginations cannot comprehend Him and *Dahr* (times) do not reduce or change Him."'

H 216, Ch. 1, h 6

Muhammad ibn Ya'qub has said that a number of our people have narrated from Ahmad ibn Muhammad al-Barqi from his father, from Ali ibn al-Nu'man, from ibn Muskan, from Dawud ibn Farqad from abu Sa'id al-Zuhri from Imam abu Ja'far, *'Alayhi al-Salam*, who said the following:

"For the people of understanding as proof of the existence of Allah it is enough that He has created all things and has kept them under His full control. It is enough proof that He is the most powerful King. It is enough proof that His Majesty is manifest everywhere. His light is brightest; His testimony is the most truthful. There is enough proof of His existence in what the people speak and what the messengers have brought and what He has revealed to people as proof of His own existence."

68

Chapter 2 - Can Allah Be Considered a Thing?

H 217, Ch. 2, h 1
Muhammad ibn Ya'qub has narrated from Ali ibn Ibrahim, from Muhammad ibn 'Isa from 'Abd al-Rahman ibn abu Najran who said the following:
"Once I asked (Imam) abu 'Abd Allah about the Oneness of Allah, 'Can I think of Him (the Creator) as a thing?' The Imam replied, 'Yes, but not as a thing that can be well understood and clearly defined within limits. What may become a subject of your thoughts is different from Him. Nothing resembles Him and the thoughts and imaginations cannot reach Him. How could the imaginations reach Him when He is different from what can become the subject of thoughts and is different from whatever can be perceived in one's thoughts? You can think of Him as a thing that cannot be well understood and clearly defined (under certain limits).'"

H 218, Ch. 2, h 2
Muhammad ibn 'Abd Allah has narrated from Muhammad ibn Isma'il from al-Husayn ibn al-Hassan from Bakr ibn Salih from al-Husayn ibn Sa'id who said that I asked Imam abu Ja'far, the second, *'Alayhi al-Salam*, the following.
"Is it permissible to say that Allah is a thing?" The Imam replied, "Yes, because it removes two kinds of limitations, the limitation of being forgotten altogether and that of considering Him like other things."

H 219, Ch. 2, h 3
Ali ibn Ibrahim has narrated from Muhammad ibn 'Isa from Yunus from abu al-Maghra in a *marfu'* manner from (Imam) abu Ja'far, *'Alayhi al-Salam*, who said the following:
"Allah is distinct from His creatures and His creatures are different from Him and whatever is called a thing is a creature except Allah."

H 220, Ch. 2, h 4
A number of our people have narrated Ahmad ibn Muhammad ibn Khalid al-Barqi from his father from al-Nadr ibn Suwayd from Yahya al-Halabi from ibn Muskan from Zurara ibn 'Ayan who has said he heard abu 'Abd Allah, *'Alayhi al-Salam*, say the following.
"Allah is distinct from His creatures and the creatures are different from Him. Whatever could be called a thing is a creature except Allah who is the Creator of all things. Holy is He for Whom there is no similarity and He is All-hearing and All-aware."

H 221, Ch. 2, h 5
Ali ibn Ibrahim has narrated from his father from ibn abu 'Umayr from Ali ibn 'Atiyya from Khaythama from abu Ja'far, *'Alayhi al-Salam*, who said the following:
"Allah is distinct from His creatures and the creatures are different from Him and whatever could be called a thing is a creature, except Allah who is the Creator of all things."

H 222, Ch. 2, h 6
Ali ibn Ibrahim has narrated from his father from al-'Abbass ibn 'Amr al-Fuqaymi from Hisham ibn al-Hakam from abu 'Abd Allah, *'Alayhi al-Salam*, who has said the following:
Abu 'Abd Allah, *'Alayhi al-Salam*, said this to an atheist in answer to a question. 'He (Allah) is a thing but different from all other things. I repeat my statement

69

that speaks about Him as a thing. He is a thing in the sense of the reality of things except that He does not have a body and form. He cannot be felt, touched or comprehended with the five senses. Imagination cannot comprehend Him, *Dahr* (times) do not reduce Him and passing of time does not change Him.'

"The man asking questions then said, 'Do you say that He hears and sees?' The Imam said, 'He does hear and see: He hears without a hearing organ and sees without a means. He Himself hears and He Himself sees. My saying, 'He hears without a hearing organ and sees without a means, He Himself hears and He Himself sees,' does not mean that He is a thing and His-Self is another thing but only that I meant to express myself thereby as I was questioned and explained to you as you had asked a question. Thus, I say that He hears with the whole of His-Self but not in the sense that His whole self has parts. I intended only to explain it to you and to express myself. All I mean thereby is that He does hear, see and He is All-knowing and is the expert in knowing without any multiplicity in His Self or meaning.'

"The man asking questions then said, 'What then is He?' The Imam said, 'He is the Lord. He is the One who is worshipped and He is Allah. When I say Allah, it does not mean establishing the proof for these letters (of alphabet) like *Alif, Lam, Ha', al-Ra'* or *al-Ba'* but I intend thereby the meaning of a *thing* and a thing that is the Creator of all things and the Designer of all things. These letters refer only to the meaning that is called *Allah, al-Rahman* (the Beneficent), *al-Rahim* (the Merciful), *al-'Aziz* (the Majestic) and so forth, and so are other such names. He is the One who is worshipped, the Majestic, the Glorious One.'

"The man asking questions then said, 'Whatever we can think of is but a creature.' The Imam then said, 'Had it been as you said we would not have had any responsibility to believe in the Oneness of the Creator; we would not have any responsibility toward something of whose existence we cannot even think. In fact, whatever is thought of and our senses comprehend with clear limits and similarities such thing is a creature. However, complete negation is total nullification and nothingness.

'The second invalid aspect (in the matter) is similarity and analogy. If similarity is a kind of attribute of the creatures that undergoes manifest composition and assemblage, it necessitates proving the existence of the Creator. This is because the existence of the creatures and their evident dependence on Him as His creatures cannot happen without their Creator. The Creator is something other than them and He is not similar to them. Had he been something similar to them, resembled them in manifest composition and assemblage, He would then be just one of the creatures. So also is the case with other conditions of the creatures, such as coming into existence from nothing and the changing from a smaller size to a full grown size, from blackness to whiteness, from strength to weakness and so forth, or such other existing conditions that do not need explanations.'

"The man asking questions then said, 'You have already defined and limited Him in your proving His existence.' The Imam, *'Alayhi al-Salam*, then said, 'I did not limit Him. I only presented proofs of His existence; between proving and disproving no third alternative exists.'

"The man asking questions then said, 'Can His existence be proved through reasoning from the effect to the cause or the cause to the effect?'

"The Imam said, 'Yes, there is nothing whose existence can be proved without adopting either of the two above processes of reasoning.'

"The man then asked, 'Does the question *how* apply to Him?' The Imam said, 'No, this question does not apply to Him; it is the aspect of qualities and limitations. However, it is necessary to avoid abandoning or nullifying His existence (in one's belief) and analogizing Him. Negating Him is denying His existence, refusing to accept Him as the Lord and abandoning Him (in one's belief) altogether. Whoever analogizes Him with other things from His creatures has proved that qualities of creatures exist in Him. Creatures do not deserve to be called the Lord. It is necessary to believe, however, that the question *how* applies to Him only in a way that does not apply to things other than Him and things other than Him do not deserve any share Him in it. The question *how* cannot apply to Him if it limits Him or makes Him a subject of knowing for others.'

"The man then asked, 'Do things make Him tired?' The Imam then said, 'He is by far Exalted and above experiencing such conditions. Such conditions are due to coming into physical association or dealing with the creatures. They are qualities of creatures that can only associate with others through physical contact. But He is the Most High and His will and demand are effective and He does whatever He wants.'"

H 223, Ch. 2, h 7
A number of our people have narrated from Ahmad ibn Muhammad ibn Khalid from Muhammad ibn 'Isa from one he mentioned and who said the following:
"Imam abu Ja'far, *'Alayhi al-Salam*, was asked, 'Is it permissible to say Allah is a thing?' The Imam said, 'Yes, it is permissible; it excludes Him from being ignored (in one's belief) altogether and from being analogized or considered similar to the creatures.'"

Chapter 3 - (The Issue) That Only He Is Proof of His Own Existence

H 224, Ch. 3, h 1
Ali ibn Muhammad has narrated from the people he mentioned from Ahmad ibn Muhammad ibn 'Isa from Muhammad ibn Humran from al- Fadl ibn al-Sakan from (Imam) abu 'Abd Allah, *'Alayhi al-Salam*, who has narrated the following:
"Imam Ali, *'Alayhi al-Salam*, has said, 'Recognize Allah by Allah's Own Self, recognize the Messenger through the message, and the people with Divine

Authority through their commanding others to do what is obligatory, prohibiting evil, the practicing of justice and kindness.'"

The following is a comment by al-Kulayni on the above *Hadith*: 'Recognize Allah by His Own Self,' means that Allah has created the individuals, the lights, the substance and the objects. The objects are the bodies, the substance stands for the spirits and He is not similar to the bodies or spirit in any of the creatures. No one has any part or effect in the creation of the spirits that comprehend and feel. He is the only One who has created the spirits and the bodies. When one considers Him dissimilar to both kinds of creatures, spiritual and non-spiritual, then one has recognized Allah by Allah's Own Self. If one considers Him similar to the spirits, lights or bodies he has not recognized Him by His Own Self.

H 225, Ch. 3, h 2
A number of our people have narrated from Ahmad ibn Muhammad ibn Khalid from some of our people from Ali ibn Ali ibn 'Uqba ibn Qays ibn Sam'an ibn abu Rabi'a Mawla of the Messenger of Allah who said the following:

"A certain person asked Imam Ali, *'Alayhi al-Salam*, 'By what means do you recognize your Lord and acknowledge His existence'? The Imam, *'Alayhi al-Salam*, replied, "I recognize my Lord by those (of His attributes) which have made me to recognize His Own Self and acknowledge His existence.' He was asked, 'How has that happened?' The Imam, *'Alayhi al-Salam*, then replied, 'He is not similar to any form and is not felt and comprehended through any of the senses and cannot be analogized with the people. He is near in that He is far and He is far in that He is near. He is above everything but one cannot say that certain things are above Him. He is before everything but one cannot say that something is before Him. He is inside all things but not the way things are inside other things. He is outside everything but not the way things are outside other things. Glory belongs to the One who is such and nothing else other than Him is as such and for everything there is a beginner.'"

Muhammad ibn Isma'il has narrated the following from al-Fadl ibn Shadhan from Safwan ibn Yahya from Mansur ibn Hazim who said the following:

"Once I spoke to (Imam) abu 'Abd Allah, *'Alayhi al-Salam*, saying, 'I debated with certain people and said to them, 'Allah, Glory be to Him, is Glorious, Majestic and Honorable. It is not possible to define Him by means of His creatures. In fact, the existence of the creatures is proved through the existence of Allah.' The Imam, *'Alayhi al-Salam*, said, 'May Allah bestow upon you blessings.'"

Chapter 4 - The Minimum Degree of the Acknowledgement of the Existence of Allah

H 226, Ch. 4, h 1
Muhammad ibn al- Hassan has narrated from 'Abd Allah ibn al-Hassan al-'Alawi and Ali ibn Ibrahim from al-Mukhtar ibn Muhammad ibn al-Mukhtar al-Hamdani all from al- Fath ibn Yazid who said the following:

"Once, I asked (Imam) abu al-Hassan, *'Alayhi al-Salam*, 'What is the minimum required degree of acknowledgement of the existence of Allah?' The Imam said, 'To acknowledge that there is no other lord besides Him and that nothing is similar to Him or resembles Him and that He is eternal, positively existing and not absent and that nothing is like Him.'"

H 227, Ch. 4, h 2

Ali ibn Ibrahim has narrated from Sahl ibn Ziyad, from Tahir ibn Hatam when he was normal and wrote to the man (meaning thereby Imam abu al-Hassan al-Rida, *'Alayhi al-Salam*, the following:

"What is it that without which one's acknowledgement of the existence of Allah cannot be considered sufficient?" In answer the Imam, *'Alayhi al-Salam*, replied, 'That He is All-knowing, All-hearing, All-aware and that He acts as He wills.' (Imam) abu Ja'far, *'Alayhi al-Salam*, was asked about the minimum required degree of acknowledgement of the existence of Allah without which an acknowledgement would not be considered sufficient. The Imam, *'Alayhi al-Salam*, said, 'A degree of knowledge of Him must have these facts: There is nothing similar to Him or resembling Him. He is All-knowing, All-hearing and All-aware.'"

H 228, Ch. 4, h 3

Muhammad ibn Yahya has narrated from Muhammad ibn al-Hassan from al-Hassan ibn Ali ibn Yusuf ibn Baqqah from Sayf ibn 'Umayra from Ibrahim ibn 'Umar who said the following:

"Imam abu 'Abd Allah, *'Alayhi al-Salam*, has said, 'The issue about Allah is totally extraordinary. Notice that He has presented to you His arguments in proof of His existence by means of only those facts which He has made known to you.'"

Chapter 5 - The One Who is Worshipped

H 229, Ch. 5, h 1

Ali ibn Ibrahim has narrated from Muhammad ibn 'Isa ibn 'Ubayd from Hassan ibn Mahbub from ibn Ri'ab from more than one person from abu 'Abd Allah, *'Alayhi al-Salam*, who said the following:

"Whoever worships Allah on the basis of *Wahm*, (a degree of acknowledgement that in terms of knowledge about His existence is valued less than fifty percent), has certainly denied His existence. Whoever worships the names without their meaning certainly has denied His existence also. Whoever worships both the names and the meanings he certainly has become a polytheist. There are those who worship the meaning, with an understanding that names only point to the attributes that He Himself has said are His. They firmly tie this up to their hearts and make their tongues speak it up in private and in public. These are certainly of the friends of 'Amirul al- Mu'minin Ali ibn abu Talib, *'Alayhi al-Salam*."According to another *Hadith*, "They, certainly, are true believers."

H 230, Ch. 5, h 2

Ali ibn Ibrahim has narrated from his father from al-Nadr ibn Suwayd from Hisham ibn al-Hakam who has said the following:

"Once I asked Imam abu 'Abd Allah, *'Alayhi al-Salam*, about the names of Allah and about the root or derivative forms of those names, 'What is the root word for the word *Allah*?' The Imam replied, 'The word *Allah* is derived from the word *'aliha* and *'Ilah* (Lord), which requires *Ma'luh* (servant). Note that names are something other than that to which they apply. O Hisham, whoever worships the name without the fact for which the name stands he has denied the existence of Allah and has not worshipped anything. Whoever worships the name and the meaning for which the name stands he has worshipped two things. Whoever worships the meaning without the name he is a monotheist. Did you understand it, O Hisham?' Hisham then asked, 'Please explain further.' The Imam then said, 'Allah has ninety-nine names. If names were the same thing for which they stand every one of them would be a Lord. However, Allah is a meaning for which these names stand and they all are something other than Him. O Hisham, bread is the name for a certain kind of food, water is the name for a certain kind of drink, cloth is the name for a certain kind of garment and fire is the name for a thing that burns. Did you understand, O Hisham, in a manner of understanding that would help you to defend our cause against our enemies and those who worship things other than Allah?' I said, 'Yes, I have gained such understanding.' The Imam then said, 'May Allah grant you success in it and keep you steadfast (in your belief).'

"Hisham has said, 'I swear by Allah that since then, no one has been able to defeat me in an argument on the issue of the Oneness of Allah and that has made me reach this position that I hold.'"

H 231, Ch. 5, h 3
Ali ibn Ibrahim has narrated from 'Abbass al-Ma'ruf from 'Abd al-Rahman ibn abu Najran who has said the following:
"Once I wrote or said to (Imam) abu Ja'far, *'Alayhi al-Salam*, 'May Allah keep my soul in your service. We worship the Beneficent, the Merciful, the One Who is One only and Self-sufficient.' The Imam then said, 'Whoever worships the names without the meaning for which they (names) stand becomes a polytheist and denies the existence of Allah and has worshipped nothing. You must worship Allah Who is the One and only One, the Self-sufficient, Who is the meaning for these names but not these names. The names are attributes that He has said are of His attributes.'"

Chapter 6 - Being and Space (al-Kawn Wa al-Makan)

H 232, Ch. 6, h 1
Muhammad ibn Yahya from has narrated Ahmad ibn Muhammad from al-Hassan ibn Mahbub from Abu Hamza who said the following:
"Once Nafi' ibn al-Azraq (ibn Qays al-Hanafi, abu Rashid (d.65/685), the head of al-Azariqa, one of the great sects of the Kharijites) asked Imam abu Ja'far, *'Alayhi al-Salam*, 'Please tell me when did Allah come into existence?' The Imam replied, '(Tell me) when did Allah not exist, so that I can tell you when He came into existence. Glory belongs to Him, Who existed and will exist eternally. The One Self-sufficient, the Eternal, the Absolute, Who has held for Himself no female companion or any child.'"

H 233, Ch. 6, h 2
A number of our people have narrated from Ahmad ibn Muhammad ibn Khalid from Ahmad ibn Muhammad ibn Abu Nasr who said the following:

"Once a man from Ma Wara'-e Nahr of Balkh (Transoxania) came to abu al-Hassan al-Rida, *'Alayhi al-Salam*, and said, 'I have a question for you. If your answer is the same as I already know, I will accept you as my Imam (Leader with Divine Authority).' Imam abu al-Hassan, *'Alayhi al-Salam*, replied, 'Ask whatever you wish.' The man said, 'Tell me when did your Lord come into existence, how has He been and on what did He depend?'

"Imam Abu al-Hassan, *'Alayhi al-Salam*, replied, 'Allah, the Blessed, the Almighty, is the space maker for space, Who Himself is not subject to the effects of any space. He is the maker of *How* and Himself is not subject to *How*. He is Self-sufficient with His own power.' The man stood up and kissed the head of the Imam, *'Alayhi al-Salam*. He then said, 'I testify that no one other than Allah deserves to be obeyed and Muhammad, *'Alayhi al-Salam*, is the Messenger of Allah. That Imam Ali, ibn abu Talib, *'Alayhi al-Salam*, is the successor of the Messenger of Allah and the guardian and protector of what the Messenger of Allah has brought from Allah. That your ancestors are the Leaders with Divine Authority and that you are a successor to them.'"

H 234, Ch. 6, h 3

Muhammad ibn Yahya from Ahmad ibn Muhammad ibn 'Isa from al-Husayn ibn Sa'id from al-Qasim-ibn Muhammad from Ali ibn Abu Hamza from abu Basir who said the following:

"Once, a man came to (Imam) abu Ja'far, *'Alayhi al-Salam*, saying, 'Tell me about your Lord. When did He come into existence?' The Imam, *'Alayhi al-Salam*, replied, 'Woe upon you! Such a question is asked only about a thing that did not exist. My Lord, all Glory belongs to Him, exists and will exist eternally. He lives and no *How* question applies to Him. He did not have any coming into existence and nor was there any being for His coming into being. This does not apply to Him; He is not subject to the effects of space. He was not in anything or on anything nor did He invent any space for His own space. He did not become stronger after making all things nor was He weak before giving being to the beings. He was not lonely before His inventing all things. He is not similar to anything that could be called a thing. He was also not without a Kingdom before the creation nor will He be without it after all things. He lives eternally without life and was the powerful King before His invention of the things and He is an all-powerful King after the creation of all things. To His existence no *How* or *Where* question is applicable. There is no limit for Him nor is He definable by analogy. He does not become old due to eternal living. He does not become alarmed because of anything but that all things are fearful of His (disappointment). He lived without newly emerging life. He is not a describable being or that can be limited with conditions or may have a space to depend on. He does not have a place so that He can be considered as neighboring something. He is living and one can know Him. He is the eternal King. He has the power and the kingdom. He has created all that He wanted and when He decided by His will. He cannot be limited. He cannot be divided or destroyed. He was before everything but no *How* question would apply to Him. He will be the last but no *Where* will apply to Him. All things will be destroyed except He. The creation belongs to Him and His is the command. He is the Holy Lord of the worlds.

'O inquirer, imaginations cannot encompass my Lord and He does not face any confusions or bewilderment. Nothing is able to reach Him and nothing happens to Him. He cannot be held responsible for anything and He does not become regretful. Neither slumber nor sleep overcomes Him. To Him belongs all that is in the heavens and all that is in the earth and all that is between them and under the soil.'"

H 235, Ch. 6, h 4

A number of our people have narrated from Ahmad ibn Muhammad ibn Khalid from his father in a *marfu'* manner, who said the following:

"The Jews came to their chief Ra's al-Jalut and said, 'This man,' meaning Imam Ali ibn abu Talib, *'Alayhi al-Salam*, 'is a scholar. Come with us to ask him questions.' They all came to Imam Ali, *'Alayhi al-Salam*, but the Imam was in the castle (government building). They waited until the Imam, *'Alayhi al-Salam*, came out. Ra's al-Jalut, said, 'We have come to you with a question.' The Imam said, 'You may ask whatever you like, O Jewish person.' He said, 'I want to ask you about your Lord. When did He come into existence?' The Imam, *'Alayhi al-Salam*, replied, '(Allah) has always been without coming into being and without being subject to a *How* question. He is eternal without quantity and quality. He was there without a *before*. He is before every *before* without being before and without a beginning and end. The end falls short before Him and He Himself is the end of all ends.' Ra's al-Jalut then said to his people, 'Allow us to leave this place. This man knows more than what people say he knows.'"

H 236, Ch. 6, h 5

It is narrated, through the same chain of narrators and source, from Ahmad ibn Muhammad ibn Khalid from his father from Ahmad ibn Muhammad ibn Abu Nasr from abu al-Hassan al-Muwsali from (Imam) abu 'Abd Allah, *'Alayhi al-Salam*, who said the following:

"Once one of the Jewish rabbis *(hibr)* came to Imam Ali, *'Alayhi al-Salam*, and asked, 'O Amir al-Mu'minin, when did your Lord come into existence?' Imam Ali, *'Alayhi al-Salam*, replied, 'Bereft of you be your mother! When has Allah not been (in existence), so that it could be said when did He come into existence? My Lord existed before every *before* without before. He is after every *after*, without any after. There is no final destination or end for Him. All ends fall short before Him. He is the final destination of all goals.' He asked further, 'O Amir al-Mu'minin, are you a prophet?' Imam Ali, *'Alayhi al-Salam*, replied, 'Stop there. I am one of the slaves of Muhammad, *'Alayhi al-Salam*, the Messenger of Allah.'

"It has also been narrated that someone asked Imam Ali, *'Alayhi al-Salam*, this. 'Where was our Lord before the creation of the heavens and the earth?' Imam Ali, *'Alayhi al-Salam*, replied, '*Where* is a question about space. Allah has been there before there was space.'"

H 237, Ch. 6, h 6

Ali ibn Muhammad has narrated from Sahl ibn Ziyad from 'Amr ibn 'Uthman from Muhammad ibn Yahya from Muhammad ibn Sama'a from abu 'Abd Allah, *'Alayhi al-Salam*, who said the following:

"Once Ra's al-Jalut said to the Jews, 'The Muslims consider Ali ibn abu Talib excelling everyone in polemics and the most learned. Allow us go to him. I will ask him certain questions and perhaps catch him in errors.' He went to Imam Ali, *'Alayhi al-Salam*, and said, 'O Amir al-Mu'minin, I have a question about a matter.' The Imam, *'Alayhi al-Salam*, said, 'Ask whatever you like.' He then asked, 'O Amir al-Mu'minin, when did our Lord come into existence?' Imam Ali replied, 'O Jewish man, the question *When* applies to one who did not exist and (then) came into being. Allah has existed without coming into being, and without being in any becoming. Certainly, O Jewish man, most certainly, O Jewish man, how can there be any *before* for Him Who was before the *before?* He does not have any destination. He is not the end of any destination and no destination ends up to Him. All destinations fall short before Him and He is the goal of all destinations.' The Jewish man then said, 'I testify that your religion is the true religion and anything against it is false.'"

H 238, Ch. 6, h 7

Ali ibn Muhammad has narrated in a *marfu'* manner from Zurara who has said the following:

"Once I asked (Imam) abu Ja'far, *'Alayhi al-Salam*, 'Did Allah exist when there was nothing?' The Imam replied, 'Certainly, Allah existed when there was nothing.' I further inquired, 'Where did Allah exist?' The Imam was leaning; he then sat up and said, 'O Zurara, you spoke of the impossible. You ask about space where there is no space.'"

H 239, Ch. 6, h 8

Ali ibn Muhammad has narrated from Sahl ibn Ziyad from Muhammad ibn al-Walid from ibn abu Nasr from abu al-Hassan al-Muwsali who has narrated the following from abu 'Abd Allah, *'Alayhi al-Salam*:

"Once a rabbi, *hibr,* came to Imam Ali, *'Alayhi al-Salam*, and asked, 'O Amir al-Mu'minin, when did your Lord come into existence?' Imam Ali, *'Alayhi al-Salam*, replied, 'Consider carefully. The question *when* applies to one who did not exist (and then came into being). *When* does not apply to the One Who is eternal. He was before the *before* without before and after the *after* without an after. He is not the end of a certain end so that His end would also end.' He then asked, 'Are you a prophet?' Imam Ali, *'Alayhi al-Salam*, replied, 'Bereft of you be your mother! I am a slave among the slaves of the Messenger of Allah, *'Alayhi al-Salam*.'"

Note: The words 'was' 'is' and so forth do not apply in the case of the existence of Allah. The use of such words is due to shortcomings of language in which we seek to express the fact of Allah's being, to which the factor of time cannot apply.

Chapter 7 - The Relationships (Nisbah) of Allah

H 240, Ch. 7, h 1

Ahmad ibn Idris has narrated from Muhammad ibn 'Abd al-Jabbar from Safwan ibn Yahya from abu Ayyub from Muhammad ibn Muslim from abu 'Abd Allah, *'Alayhi al-Salam*, who said the following:

"The Jews asked the Messenger of Allah, *'Alayhi al-Salam*, 'Describe for us the relationship of your Lord.' The Prophet waited for three days and gave no reply.

Then the following verses were revealed to him: In the Name of Allah, the Beneficent, the Merciful: (Muhammad), say, 'He is Allah Who is One (112:1). Allah is Absolute (112:2). He neither begets nor was He begotten. (112:3) There is no one equal to and like Him.' (112:4)."

Muhammad ibn Yahya has narrated the same *Hadith* from Ahmad ibn Muhammad from Ali ibn al-Hakam from abu Ayyub.

H 241, Ch. 7, h 2

Muhammad ibn Yahya has narrated from Ahmad ibn Muhammad ibn 'Isa and Muhammad ibn al-Husayn from ibn Mahbub from Hammad ibn 'Amr al-Nusaybi who said the following:

"Once I asked Imam abu 'Abd Allah, *'Alayhi al-Salam*, about the words of Allah: 'Say, 'He is Allah, One . . .' (112:1) The Imam replied, 'These verses define Allah's relation to His creation. He is the One, Unique, Eternal and Absolute. He does not have any shadow to follow Him but it is He who holds things by their shadows. He knows the unknown and is known to every ignorant person. He is only One. He is not in His creatures and His creatures are not in Him. He does not feel nor can others feel Him (physically). Eyes cannot see Him. He is so high that He is near and is so near that He is far. Although disobeyed, yet He forgives. When obeyed, He is appreciative. His earth does not contain Him, nor do His heavens bear Him. He holds all things through His power and He is Everlasting and Eternal. He does not forget or amuse Himself. He does not make any mistakes or play. There is no lapse in His will. His judgment is rewarding and His commands are effective. He does not have a child to become His heir, nor is He begotten so His power would be shared. And there is no one like Him.'"

H 242, Ch. 7, h 3

Muhammad ibn Yahya has narrated from Ahmad ibn Muhammad from al-Husayn ibn Sa'id from al-Nadr ibn Suwayd from 'Asim ibn Humayd who said the following:

"Once I asked Imam Ali ibn al-Husayn, *'Alayhi al-Salam*, about the Oneness of Allah. The Imam replied, 'Allah, the Almighty, the Great, the Exalted knew that eventually there will be people who would investigate the issues very deeply in a hairsplitting manner. Therefore, Allah, the Glorious, has revealed Chapter 112 of the Holy Quran that speaks of the Oneness of Allah. He has also revealed the verses of the Chapter 57 of the Holy Quran:

"In the Name of Allah, the Beneficent, the Merciful: All that is in the heavens and the earth speaks of the glory of Allah. He is Majestic and All-wise (57:1). To Him belongs the Kingdom of the heavens and the earth. He gives life and causes things to die. He has power over all things (57:2). He is the First, the Last, the Manifest and the Unseen and He knows all things. (57:3)

"It is He Who created the heavens and the earth in six days and then established His dominion over the Throne. He knows whatever enters into the earth, what comes out of it, what descends from the sky, and what ascends to it. He is with you wherever you may be and He is Well-aware of what you do. (57:4)

"To Him belong the heavens and the earth and to Him all things return (57:5). He causes night to enter into day and day into night. He knows best what all hearts contain." (57:6) 'Whoever would accept anything otherwise is destroyed.'"

H 243, Ch. 7, h 4
Muhammad ibn abu 'Abd Allah in a *marfu'* manner has narrated from 'Abd al-'Aziz ibn al-Muhtadi who said the following:
"Once I asked Imam Ali al-Rida, *'Alayhi al-Salam*, about the Oneness of Allah. He replied, 'One's acknowledgement of the Oneness of Allah is considered true and meaningful if he, with belief, recites the following:

"In the Name of Allah, the Beneficent, the Merciful: (Muhammad), say, 'He is Allah the only One. (112:1) Allah is Absolute. (112:2) He neither begets nor was He begotten. (112:3) There is no one equal to Him.' (112:4)

"I asked, 'How should I recite it (the Chapter 112)?' The Imam replied, 'Recite it as the people do.' Then the Imam said, 'After reciting the chapter say "Such is Allah, my Lord. Such is Allah, my Lord."'"

Chapter 8 - Prohibition on Saying How Allah Is (al-Kayfiyyah)

H 244, Ch. 8, h 1
Muhammad ibn al-Hassan has narrated from Sahl ibn Ziyad from al-Hassan ibn Mahbub from Ali ibn Ri'ab from abu Basir from Imam abu Ja'far, *'Alayhi al-Salam*, who said the following:
"Speak about the creation of Allah and do not speak about Allah His Self. Speaking about Allah's Self does not add anything to one's knowledge but more confusion."

In another *Hadith* from Hariz it reads, "Speak about everything but do not speak about Allah's Self."

H 245, Ch. 8, h 2
Muhammad ibn Yahya has narrated from Ahmad ibn Muhammad from ibn abu 'Umayr from 'Abd al-Rahman ibn al-Hajjaj from Sulayman ibn Khalid from (Imam) abu 'Abd Allah, *'Alayhi al-Salam*, who said the following:
"The words of Allah, the Majestic, the Glorious that say, 'And that the final end is unto thy Lord' (53:42) instruct people to end a discussion that may take up Allah's Self as an object of investigation.'"

H 246, Ch. 8, h 3
Ali ibn Ibrahim has narrated from his father from ibn abu 'Umayr from abu Ayyub from Muhammad ibn Muslim from (Imam) abu 'Abd Allah, *'Alayhi al-Salam*, who said the following:
"O Muhammad, people rationalize everything. They even speak about Allah's Self. When you hear such discourses, say to them, 'No one, other than Allah, deserves to be worshipped, (Allah) the One and no one is similar to Him.'"

H 247, Ch. 8, h 4
A number of our people have narrated from Ahmad ibn Muhammad ibn Khalid from his father from ibn abu 'Umayr from Muhammad ibn Humran from abu 'Ubaydah (Ziyad ibn 'Isa) al-Hadhdha' from (Imam) abu Ja'far, *'Alayhi al-Salam*, who said the following:

"O Ziyad, beware of debates; they create doubts, invalidate one's good deeds and turn one into a complete wreck. One may say a thing and perhaps, he will not be forgiven. In the past there lived a people who ignored acquiring the necessary knowledge. Instead they sought a knowledge that was not required of them. They came to speak of Allah's Self and they became confused. Their extreme perplexity was such that if called from the front they would reply to the back and to the front if called from the back.

"In another *Hadith* it reads, 'They (confused people mentioned above) totally vanished in the land, the earth (due to confusion).'"

H 248, Ch. 8, h 5
A number of our people have narrated from Ahmad ibn Muhammad ibn Khalid from some of his people from al-Husayn ibn al-Mayyah from his father from Imam abu 'Abd Allah, *'Alayhi al-Salam*, who said the following:

"He, who thinks in terms of *how* and *when* about Allah, is destroyed."

H 249, Ch. 8, h 6
Muhammad ibn Yahya has narrated from Ahmad ibn Muhammad ibn 'Isa from ibn Faddal from ibn Bukayr from Zurara ibn A'yan from Imam abu 'Abd Allah, *'Alayhi al-Salam*, who said the following:

"A king of great splendor, once before a gathering in his court, spoke of the (Self of) Lord, the Holy, the Most High (improperly). Thereafter the monarch disappeared and no one could understand where he was."

H 250, Ch. 8, h 7
A number of our people have narrated from Ahmad ibn Muhammad ibn Khalid from Muhammad ibn 'Abd al-Hamid from al-'Ala' ibn Razin from Muhammad ibn Muslim from (Imam) abu Ja'far, *'Alayhi al-Salam*, who said the following:

"Beware of thinking about Allah's Self. If you like to think about the greatness of Allah, think about His great and wonderful creations."

H 251, Ch. 8, h 8
Muhammad ibn abu 'Abd Allah in a *marfu'* manner has narrated from (Imam) abu 'Abd Allah, *'Alayhi al-Salam*, who said the following:

"O son of Adam, if a bird were to feed upon your heart, it could not satisfy its hunger. Only the eye of a needle, if placed over your eye, can totally cover your vision. With such (insignificant) means of perception how can you comprehend (Allah's) vast dominion over the earth and the heavens? And if you think you can do so, there is the sun, one of the creatures of Allah. If your eyes can see the sun fully you then may think that you are right."

H 252, Ch. 8, h 9
Ali ibn Ibrahim has narrated from his father from al-Hassan ibn Ali from al-Ba'qubi (Dawud ibn Ali al-Hashimi) from certain persons of our people from 'Abd al-'Ala' Mawla Ala Sam from (Imam) abu 'Abd Allah, *'Alayhi al-Salam*, who said the following:

"Once a Jewish man named Sabhut came to the Prophet, *'Alayhi al-Salam*, and said, 'O Messenger of Allah, I have come to ask about your Lord. If you will answer my question it will be fine, otherwise, I will go back.' The Prophet replied, 'Ask whatever you like.' He asked, 'Where is your Lord?' The Prophet replied, 'He is everywhere, but He is not confined in any limited space.' He asked, 'How is He?' The Prophet replied, 'How can I describe my Lord by means of conditions that are created? Allah cannot be described by His creation.' The Jewish man asked further, 'What is the proof that you are the Messenger of Allah?' The Imam said, 'At this point nothing remained around him (the Jewish man), the stones and all other things, but that they spoke in clear Arabic language, 'O Sabhut he (Muhammad) is the Messenger of Allah.' Sabhut said, 'I have not seen anything so clearly as this today.' Then he declared, 'I testify that no one deserves to be obeyed except Allah and you are the Messenger of Allah.'"

H 253, Ch. 8, h 10
Ali ibn Ibrahim has narrated from his father from ibn abu 'Umayr from Muhammad ibn Yahya al-Khath'ami from 'Abd al-Rahman ibn 'Utayk al-Qasir who said the following:
"Once I asked (Imam) abu Ja'far, *'Alayhi al-Salam*, about certain attributes of Allah. The Imam raised his hand toward the heavens and said, 'High is the Almighty. High is the Almighty. One who pursues beyond this, he is destroyed.'"

Chapter 9 - The Invalidity of the Belief in the Possibility of Seeing Allah With One's Eyes (Ru'ya of Allah)

H 254, Ch. 9, h 1
Muhammad ibn abu 'Abd Allah has narrated from Ali ibn abu al-Qasim from Ya'qub ibn Ishaq who wrote to Imam abu Muhammad al-'Askari asking the following:
"I asked the Imam, 'How can a worshipper worship his Lord, Whom he does not see?' The Imam wrote in reply, 'O abu Yusuf, my Lord, my Master and my Benefactor and the Benefactor of my ancestors, is by far exalted and is above being seen.' I (Ya'qub ibn Ishaq) asked him, 'Had the Messenger of Allah, *'Alayhi al-Salam*, seen his Lord?' The Imam replied in writing and signed, 'Allah, the Most Holy, the Most High, showed His Prophet, in his heart, the light of His Greatness as much as He liked.'"

H 255, Ch. 9, h 2
Ahmad ibn Idris has narrated from Muhammad ibn 'Abd al-Jabbar from Safwan ibn Yahya who said the following:
"Abu Qurrah (Musa ibn Tariq al-Yamani al-Zabudi (died 203A.H./818A.D.)), a narrator of *Hadith*, asked me to take him to abu al-Hassan al-Rida, *'Alayhi al-Salam*. I sought permission from the Imam, *'Alayhi al-Salam*, and an audience was granted. He asked the Imam about what is lawful and unlawful and the rules in Islamic laws. His questions came to Oneness of Allah. Abu Qurrah said, 'We (the narrators of *Hadith*) narrate that Allah the Almighty has divided His being seen, *al-Ru'ya*, and His speech, *al-Kalam*, between the two prophets. He gave Musa (Moses) the opportunity to hear His speech. He granted to Prophet Muhammad, *'Alayhi al-Salam*, the opportunity to see Him.'

"Imam abu al-Hassan, *'Alayhi al-Salam*, said, 'If it is as you say then who was it that conveyed the message from Allah to the two heavy communities, namely, mankind and the Jinn in the following words of the Holy Quran: ". . . the eyes cannot comprehend Him", (6:103) "They cannot limit Him through their knowledge," (20:110) and "There is nothing similar to Him." (42:11) 'Was it not

Muhammad, *'Alayhi al-Salam*, who conveyed the above verses?' asked the Imam, *'Alayhi al-Salam.'*

"Abu Qurrah then replied, 'Yes, he was Prophet Muhammad, *'Alayhi al-Salam.'* The Imam said, 'How can a person; who brought such messages to all creatures and told them that he has brought such messages from Allah and called them to Allah by His commands and said, "The eyes cannot comprehend Him," (6:103) "They cannot limit Him through their knowledge" (20:110) and "There is nothing similar to Him;" (42:11) say, "I saw Him with my own eyes? I did limit Him in my knowledge and that He is similar to a man." Should you not be ashamed of yourselves? Even the atheist has not said that the Prophet first brought one thing from Allah and then announced from Him other things contrary to the first.'

"Abu Qurrah then said, 'Does Allah Himself not say, "Indeed he (the Prophet) saw Him in another descent?"' (53: 13) Imam abu al-Hassan, *'Alayhi al-Salam*, said, 'The other verses point out what the Prophet actually saw. Allah has said, "His heart did not lie about what he saw," (53: 11) It means that the heart of Muhammad did not belie what his eyes saw. Therefore, Allah in the subsequent verse has said, "Indeed he saw of the greatest signs of his Lord." (53:18) The signs of Allah are different from Allah Himself. Allah has also said, "They cannot limit Him in their knowledge." (20:110) If the eyes could see Him, then people might limit Him in their knowledge and He could be fully defined.'

"Abu Qurrah asked, 'Do you disregard *Hadith*?' Imam abu al-Hassan, *'Alayhi al-Salam*, replied, 'If *Ahadith* are contrary to Holy Quran, I disregard them. Besides, all Muslims believe that Allah cannot be limited by (anyone's) knowledge, that eyes cannot see Him and that nothing is similar to Him.'"

H 256, Ch. 9, h 3

Ahmad ibn Idris has narrated from Ahmad ibn Muhammad ibn 'Isa from Ali ibn Sayf from Muhammad ibn 'Ubayd who said the following:

"Once I wrote to abu al-Hassan al-Rida, *'Alayhi al-Salam*, and asked him about the belief in witnessing Allah's Self. Is it possible to see Allah's Self with one's own eyes as is traditionally narrated in the affirmative by the Sunni Muslims *(al-'Ammah)* while the Shi'a Muslims *(al-khassah)* believe in the contrary? I requested him to explain the matter. The Imam answered in his own handwriting. 'All agree and there is no dissension among the people that knowledge of things through witnessing process is knowledge of the degree of certainty without doubt. It is of the best form of knowledge (in the logical sense). If it is true that seeing Allah's Self with the eyes is possible, then it becomes a necessity to acknowledge that Allah becomes entirely known (and defined through the witnessing process). Now, can such knowledge of Allah's Self that comes through witnessing, be considered belief (*'Iman*) or not? If the knowledge of Him as such, i.e. knowledge through witnessing process (which according to Sunni Muslims will happen on the Day of resurrection only) be considered belief, then belief in Allah in this world, which comes through sources other than witnessing process, (such as through evidence from the Holy Quran, *Hadith* and logical reasoning), is not belief. It is contrary to knowledge through witnessing process. (Belief on the basis of reasoning proves that witnessing Allah is not possible, and contrary things cannot exist at the same time). Thus, there would be no one who would have belief in Allah in this world; no one sees Him in this world, Majestic is Whose name.

'If such knowledge and understanding which come from witnessing process were not considered belief then would belief, formed and acquired from sources other than knowledge through witnessing process, or would it not continue to exist (in the next world)? In fact, it would not go away in the next life and would continue to exist on the Day of Resurrection also.

'This is proof that Allah, the Majestic, the Glorious, cannot be seen; it will lead to (the kind of confusion) that we just mentioned.'"

H 257, Ch. 9, h 4

It is narrated from the same narrator (Ahmad ibn Idris) from Ahmad ibn Ishaq who said the following:
"I wrote to (Imam) abu al-Hassan the third, and asked him about witnessing Allah's Self and the differences among people on this issue. The Imam, *'Alayhi al-Salam*, answered in writing, 'Witnessing an object is not possible until there is air (a light-carrying medium) that can allow the light to reach the eye. If air is removed from space between the viewer and the object, no witnessing will take place. In this there is ground for similarity. When the viewer and the object in view have the same medium, a similarity must exist between them to make witnessing possible, such as reflecting surfaces. (When applying this to the case of Allah) it is an analogy and similarity. The means must have a connection with the source."

H 258, Ch. 9, h 5

Ali ibn Ibrahim has narrated from his father from Ali ibn Ma'bad from 'Abd Allah ibn Sinan from his father who said the following:
"Once I met (Imam) abu Ja'far, *'Alayhi al-Salam*, and at that time a man from the *Khariji* group came to see the Imam, *'Alayhi al-Salam*, and asked, 'O abu Ja'far, whom do you worship?' The Imam replied, 'I worship Allah, the Most High.' He then asked, 'Have you seen Him?' The Imam then said, 'Eyes cannot see Him in a witnessing process but the hearts can see Him through the reality of belief. Allah cannot be known by analogy or (physical) senses and He is not similar to people. He is mentioned in the verses of revelation (Holy Quran). He is known from the signs. He does not do injustice in His judgments. Thus is Allah; besides Him there is no Lord.' The narrator has said, 'The man then left the Imam, *'Alayhi al-Salam*, saying, 'Allah knows best to whom He should entrust His message to mankind.'"

H 259, Ch. 9, h 6

A number of our people have narrated from Ahmad ibn Muhammad ibn Khalid from Ahmad ibn Muhammad ibn abu Nasr from abu al-Hassan al-Muwsali from abu 'Abd Allah, *'Alayhi al-Salam*, who said the following:
"Once a rabbi *(hibr)* came to Imam Ali ibn abu Talib, *'Alayhi al-Salam*, and asked, 'O Amir al-Mu'minin, have you seen your Lord when worshipping Him?' Imam Ali, *'Alayhi al-Salam*, replied, 'This is not a proper question. I have not

worshipped a Lord whom I could not see.' He then asked, 'How did you see Him?' Imam Ali, *'Alayhi al-Salam*, said, 'This is not a proper statement. Eyes cannot see Him in a witnessing process but hearts see Him through the realities of belief.'"

H 260, Ch. 9, h 7

Ahmad ibn Idris has narrated from Muhammad ibn 'Abd al-Jabbar from Safwan ibn Yahya from 'Asim ibn Humayd who said the following:

"Once I discussed with (Imam) abu 'Abd Allah, *'Alayhi al-Salam*, about what he says on witnessing Allah's Self. The Imam said, 'The light of the sun has a ratio equal to one seventieth of the light of the *Kursi* (the Throne). The same is the ratio of the light of *Kursi* to al-*'Arsh*, the light of which is of the same ratio to that of *al-Hijab,* the light of which is of the same ratio to the light of *al-Satr* (barrier). If they (people who say that eye-witnessing Allah is possible) tell the truth, allow them to fill their eyes with the light of the sun without a curtain in between.'"

H 261, Ch. 9, h 8

Muhammad ibn Yahya and others have narrated from Ahmad ibn Muhammad ibn 'Isa from ibn abu Nasr from abu al-Hassan al-Rida, *'Alayhi al-Salam*, who has said that the Holy Prophet, *'Alayhi al-Salam*, said the following:

"When Jibril took me for a visit to the heavens we reached a place where he had never set foot before. Then it was unveiled to him and Allah showed him of the light of His greatness that which he loved."

Explanations of Certain Words of Allah

"No mortal eyes can see Him, but He can see all eyes. He is All-kind and All-aware." (6:103)

H 262, Ch. 9, h 9

Muhammad ibn Yahya has narrated from Ahmad ibn Muhammad ibn 'Isa from ibn abu Najran from 'Abd Allah ibn Sinan from (Imam) abu 'Abd Allah, *'Alayhi al-Salam*, who said the following:

"About the words of Allah, 'No mortal eyes can see Him, but He can see all eyes. He is All-kind and All-aware' (6:103), the Imam said that, 'No mortal eyes can see Him' means through guessing (*al-Wahm*), not by witnessing Him. Consider the words of Allah in, 'Clear proofs have certainly come to you from your Lord . . . (6:104)' do not mean that such 'Clear proofs' are visible to people's eyes. Also consider, 'Whosoever sees clearly, it is to his own gain . . . (6:104)' it does not mean seeing with the eyes. In 'Whosoever is blind, it is to his own loss (6:104),' 'Blindness' does not mean deprivation of eyesight. It means within the range of *Wahm* (mentioned above). It is as is commonly said, so and so is very keen-sighted in matters of poetry, and so and so is very keen-sighted in religion and jurisprudence. So and so has a keen eye for money, and so and so has an eye for clothes. Allah is by far great and above being witnessed by people.'"

H 263, Ch. 9, h 10

Muhammad ibn Yahya has narrated from Ahmad ibn Muhammad from Abu Hashim al-Ja'fari who said the following:

"I asked (Imam) abu al-Hassan al-Rida, *'Alayhi al-Salam*, about Allah if He can be described (defined in words). The Imam, *'Alayhi al-Salam*, said, 'Have you not read the Quran?' I replied, 'Yes, I do read the Quran.' He then said, 'Have you not read the words of Allah, the Most High, "No mortal eyes can see Him, but He can see all eyes. He is All-kind and All-aware."' (6:103)

"I replied, 'Yes, I have read them.' The Imam, *'Alayhi al-Salam*, said, 'Do they know the meaning of the eyes?' I replied, 'Yes, they do.' The Imam, *'Alayhi al-Salam*, said, 'What is it?' I replied, 'It means seeing with the eyes.' Then the Imam said, 'The *Awham* (plural of *wahm* defined above) of the heart is much more comprehensive in the field of knowledge than witnessing. It *(Awham)* is not able to comprehend Him but He comprehends all things.'"

H 264, Ch. 9, h 11
Muhammad ibn abu 'Abd Allah has narrated from the person he mentioned from Muhammad ibn 'Isa from Dawud ibn al-Qasim, abu Hashim al-Ja'fari who said the following:
"Once I mentioned the words of Allah, 'No mortal eyes can see Him, but He can see all eyes. He is All-kind and All-aware' (6:103) to Imam abu Ja'far, *'Alayhi al-Salam*. He said, 'O abu Hashim, *Awham* (mentioned above) of hearts are keener and sharper than the perceptions of the eyes. Through the *Awham* of the heart you can perceive countries like Sind, Hind (India) and other cities, which you have never seen with your eyes. How can your eyes see Him when the *Awham* of your heart cannot perceive Him?'"

H 265, Ch. 9, h 12
Ali ibn Ibrahim has narrated from his father from certain persons of his people from Hisham ibn al-Hakam who said the following:
"Things can be perceived by two means: (1) by the senses and (2) by the heart (intellect). Perceptions of the senses are of three kinds: (1) perception in the form of penetration, (2) perception in the form of touching, and (3) perception without penetration or touch. Perception by means of sounds, smells and tastes are formed through penetration. Perception through touching comes from the knowledge of shapes, such as rectangular or triangular and so forth, and also softness, hardness, heat and cold. Perception without touch or penetration is that of sight which is capable of perceiving things without touching or penetration in the object or means of sight. Perception through sight needs a path and medium. Its path is air and its medium is the light. If the path is continuous between the viewer and the object and the medium, then seeing takes place such as colors and persons. If light falls on something without a path, it will return reflecting what is behind (the observed), like an observer looking into a mirror. Light does not penetrate into the mirror, because it finds no path. So it returns reflecting what lies behind the observed. It is similar to looking into the clear water that returns light that reflects what is at the rear. This happens because there is no path for the penetration of light.

"Intellect dominates the air. It perceives all that is in the air and forms his *Wahm* (intuitive form of perception). If the heart will not find anything in the air it (power of *Wahm*) comes back and reflects what is in the air. A person of reason should not force his heart against what is not in the air of the issue of the Oneness of Allah, the Majestic, the Glorious, otherwise it will form his *Wahm* of what is there in the air as mentioned about the witnessing. Allah, the Most High is by far above similarities with the creatures.'"

Chapter 10 - Prohibition of Attributing to Allah What He Himself Has Not Attributed to Himself

H 266, Ch. 10, h 1

Ali ibn Ibrahim has narrated from al-'Abbass ibn Ma'ruf from ibn abu Najran from Hammad ibn 'Uthman from Abd al-Rahim ibn 'Utayk al-Qusayr who said the following:

"Once I wrote through 'Abd al-Malik ibn 'A'yan to (Imam) abu 'Abd Allah, *'Alayhi al-Salam,* 'In Iraq there are people who attribute to Allah forms and lines. If you would consider it proper, may Allah keep my soul in your service, please write for me the correct belief on the issue of the Oneness of Allah.'

"The Imam wrote for me, 'May Allah grant you blessings. You have asked about the Oneness of Allah and the belief of the group of people before you. Exalted is Allah, similar to Him is nothing. He is All-hearing and All-seeing. Allah is above what certain people attribute to Him and above their analogizing Him to His creatures. He is above the lies of those who speak lies about Him. Note that the true creed in the Oneness of Allah is what is revealed in the Quran about the attributes of Allah, the Almighty, the Exalted. Keep away from the belief in Allah, the Most High, in the form of all ideas that amount to ignoring His existence altogether and those that amount to analogizing Him to the creatures. Neither should His existence be negated nor should He be considered similar to anything. He (Allah) the Most High, exists. Exalted is He and by far above what is falsely attributed to Him. Do not exceed the limits of the Quran lest you go astray after the clear presentation of Truth.'"

H 267, Ch. 10, h 2

Muhammad ibn Isma'il has narrated from al-Fadl ibn Shadhan from ibn abu 'Umayr from Ibrahim ibn 'Abd al-Hamid from abu Hamza who said the following:

"Once Imam Ali ibn al-Husayn said to me, 'O abu Hamza, Allah cannot be defined by means of the created things. Our Lord is by far above being described through the attributes. How can the Infinite be defined with the finite? "No mortal eyes can see Him, but He can see all eyes. He is All-kind and All-aware."'" (6:103)

H 268, Ch. 10, h 3

Muhammad ibn abu 'Abd Allah has narrated from Muhammad ibn Isma'il from al-Husayn ibn al-Hassan from Bakr ibn Salih from al-Hassan ibn Sa'id from Ibrahim ibn Muhammad al-Khazzaz and Muhammad ibn al-Husayn who both have said the following:

"Once we met Imam abu al-Hassan al-Rida, *'Alayhi al-Salam,* and stated to him that Prophet Muhammad, *'Alayhi al-Salam,* saw His Lord in the fashion of a full grown young man of thirty years. We added that Hisham ibn Salim and Sahib al-Taq and al-Maythami say that He is hollow down to His navel and the rest is solid. The Imam bowed down to a prostrating position, and then said, '(O Lord), Glory belongs to You. They have not recognized You nor have they acknowledged Your Oneness, therefore, they attribute to You such things. (O Lord), Glory belongs to

You. Had they recognized You they would attribute to You what You have attributed to Yourself and they would not consider You similar to things other than You. O Lord, I do not attribute to You anything other than what You have attributed to Yourself and do not consider You similar to Your creatures. To You belongs all good. Do not place me among the unjust ones.'

"The Imam, *'Alayhi al-Salam*, then turned to us saying, 'Whatever you may imagine (make *Wahm* of) consider Allah something other than that.' He continued, 'We, people of the family of the Prophet, *'Alayhim al-Salam*, are the median type and the criterion. Those who exceed cannot catch up with us and those who follow cannot go ahead of us.'

"O Muhammad, when the Messenger of Allah looked at the greatness of his Lord, he was of the type of people as fully grown up as thirty-year old people. O Muhammad, my Lord, the Majestic, the Glorious, is far greater than to be of the qualities of the creatures.

"I (the narrator) said, 'May the Lord keep my soul in your service, who was the one with his feet in the green (refers to things the Holy Prophet saw during his night journey)?'

"The Imam said, 'He was Prophet Muhammad, *'Alayhi al-Salam*, when he looked at his Lord with his heart He placed him in the light like that of the *Hujub* (literally meaning barriers) so he could see what is inside the *Hujub*. Of the light of Allah certain phases are green, red, white and others. O Muhammad, whatever has confirmation in the book and the *Sunnah* we affirm it.'"

H 269, Ch. 10, h 4
Ali ibn Muhammad and Muhammad ibn al-Hassan have narrated from Sahl ibn Ziyad from Ahmad ibn Bashir al-Barqi who has said that 'Abbass ibn 'Amir al-Qasani has said that Harun ibn al-Juham narrated from abu Hamza from Imam Ali ibn al-Husayn, *'Alayhi al-Salam*, has reported the following:
"Even if all those in heaven and earth gather together to speak of the greatness of Allah they will not be able to do so."

H 270, Ch. 10, h 5
Sahl has narrated from Ibrahim ibn Muhammad al-Hamdani who said the following:
"Once I wrote to the man (Imam abu al-Hassan the third, *'Alayhi al-Salam*), explaining, 'Your followers in this city differ on the issue of the Oneness of Allah. There are those of them who say that Allah has a body, and others say that Allah has a form.' The Imam replied in his own handwriting, 'Glory belongs to Allah, Who cannot be defined nor described. There is nothing similar to Him. He is All-hearing, All-knowing,' or–as the Imam said -, 'All-seeing.'"

H 271, Ch. 10, h 6
Sahl has narrated from Muhammad ibn 'Isa from Ibrahim from Muhammad ibn Hakim who said the following:
"Imam abu al-Hassan Musa ibn Ja'far, *'Alayhi al-Salam*, wrote to my father, 'Allah is most High, Glorious and Great. One can never reach the essence of His

attributes. Speak of only those of His attributes of which He Himself has spoken and refrain mentioning attributes other than those ones.'"

H 272, Ch. 10, h 7

Sahl has narrated from al-Sindi ibn al-Rabi' from ibn abu 'Umayr from Hafs, brother of Marazim from al-Mufaddal who said the following:

"Once I asked Imam abu al-Hassan, *'Alayhi al-Salam*, about certain matters of the attributes (of Allah) and the Imam said, 'Do not exceed what is in the Holy Quran.'"

H 273, Ch. 10, h 8

Sahl has narrated from Muhammad ibn Ali al-Qasani (perhaps the right name is Ali ibn Muhammad, one of the companions of Imam abu al-Hassan al-Hadi, the tenth Imam, *'Alayhi al-Salam*, who said the following:

"Once I wrote to the Imam explaining that people before us had differences on the issue of the Oneness of Allah. The Imam wrote, 'Glory belongs to Allah, Who cannot be defined or described. There is nothing similar to Him. He is All-hearing, All-seeing.'"

H 274, Ch. 10, h 9

Sahl has narrated from Bishr ibn Bashshar al-Naysaburi who said the following:

"Once I wrote to the man (Imam) explaining that people of our time have differences on the issue of the Oneness of Allah. There are people who say that Allah has a body, others say He has a form. The Imam wrote for me, 'Glory belongs to Allah, Who cannot be defined or described. There is nothing similar to Him. He is All-hearing, All-seeing.'"

H 275, Ch. 10, h 10

Sahl has said that I wrote to abu Muhammad al-Hassan al-'Askari, *'Alayhi al-Salam*, in 255 AH. the following:

"Our people *(Ashabuna)* differ on the issue of the Oneness of Allah. There are those who say that He has a body and others say He has a certain form. If you consider instructing me in this matter on which I can rely without excess, it will be a great favor to your servant.

"The Imam answered in his own handwriting, 'You have asked about the Oneness of Allah. It is not your duty to find Allah's Self. Allah is One, the Only One. He has no children and is not anyone's child. There is nothing similar to Him. He is the Creator and is not created. He, the Most Holy, the Most High, creates whatever He wants of the bodies and non-bodies. He is not a body or a certain form. He gives form to whatever He wills but Himself is not a form, Majestic is His praise and Holy are His names. He is by far above being similar to other things. Only He, and not others, is the One to Whom no one is similar and He is All-hearing and All-seeing.'"

H 276, Ch. 10, h 11

Muhammad ibn Isma'il has narrated from al-Fadl ibn Shadhan from Hammad ibn 'Isa from Rabi'a ibn 'Abd Allah from al-Fudayl ibn Yasar, who said the following:

"Once I heard (Imam) abu 'Abd Allah, *'Alayhi al-Salam*, saying, 'Allah cannot be defined. How can He be defined? He Himself has said in His book, "They have not respected Allah the way He truly should have been respected." (6:91) Therefore, He cannot be described in any way but that He is Great and by far above that.'"

H 277, Ch. 10, h 12

Ali ibn Muhammad has narrated from Sahl ibn Ziyad and from others from Muhammad ibn Sulayman from Ali ibn Ibrahim from 'Abd Allah ibn Sinan from abu 'Abd Allah, *'Alayhi al-Salam*, who said the following:

"Allah is Great and High. People cannot describe Him nor can they reach up to His Greatness. 'No mortal eyes can see Him, but He can see all eyes. He is All Kind and All Aware.' (6:103) He cannot be described by means of *how* and *where*. How can I describe Him by means of any condition? He Himself has created the conditions and *how* and so it came into being. We came to know conditions because of His designing them for us. How can I describe Him by means of space? It is He, Who spaced the *space* so it became space. I, thus, came to know space by means of what He has made into space. How can I describe Him by means of *positions* when He Himself has given position to *positions* to come into position? I, thus, came to know the *position* by means of what He has made to come into position. Allah, the Holy, the Most High, is in every place but is out of everything. 'No mortal eyes can see Him, but He can see all eyes. He is All Kind and All Aware.'" (6:103)

Chapter 11 - Prohibition on Considering Allah as Having Body (Jism) and Form (Surah)

H 278, Ch. 11, h 1

Ahmad ibn Idris has narrated from Muhammad ibn 'Abd al-Jabbar from Safwan ibn Yahya from Ali ibn abu Hamza who said the following:

"Once I stated before abu 'Abd Allah, *'Alayhi al-Salam*, 'I have heard Hisham ibn al-Hakam quoting you, "Allah is a body of self-subsisting nature and is from light. He can very clearly be recognized and He bestows such knowledge to whoever among His creatures He wills."' The Imam said, 'Glorious is He, about Whom no one knows how His essence is except He Himself. There is no one similar to Him and He is All-hearing, All Seeing. He cannot be limited, nor can He be felt or touched or moved. Eyes cannot see Him nor can any of the senses comprehend Him. He cannot be contained in anything, nor has He a body or form or figure or confine.'"

H 279, Ch. 11, h 2

Muhammad ibn al-Hassan has narrated from Sahl ibn Ziyad from Hamza ibn Muhammad who said the following:

"Once I wrote to Imam abu al-Hassan (al-Thalith, 3ʳᵈ), *'Alayhi al-Salam*, asking about the body and form (of Allah). He wrote in reply, 'Glorious is He, similar to Whom there is nothing. He is not a body nor has He any form.'"

Muhammad ibn abu 'Abd Allah has also narrated this *Hadith* without giving the name of the person (from whom he has heard).

H 280, Ch. 11, h 3
Muhammad ibn al-Hassan has narrated from Sahl ibn Ziyad from Muhammad ibn Isma'il ibn Bazi' from Muhammad ibn Zayd who said the following:

"Once I went to visit (Imam) Ali al-Rida, *'Alayhi al-Salam*, and asked him about the Oneness of Allah (Allah). The Imam dictated to me this, 'All praise belongs to Allah, Who is the Originator of all things. He is the Inventor of all things, an invention that came from His power and wisdom, but not from a thing so it would invalidate the invention or from (another) cause, so it would invalidate the novelty. He created whatever He wanted and howsoever He liked. He alone did all this to manifest His Wisdom and the truth of His Providence. Intelligence cannot comprehend Him, imagination (*Awham*) cannot reach Him, and eyes cannot see Him and measurements cannot confine Him. The power of expression is unable to express Him in words. All sights are exhausted from reaching Him and the power of describing and defining has gone astray in its description and definition of His Self. He is hidden without any veil and is concealed without any covering. He is known without being seen, described without any form, and praised without any body. No one deserves to be obeyed except Allah, the Great, the Most High.'"

H 281, Ch. 11, h 4
Muhammad ibn Abu 'Abd Allah has narrated from those he mentioned from Ali ibn al-'Abbass from Ahmad ibn Muhammad ibn abu Nasr from Muhammad ibn Hakim who has said the following:

"I explained to abu Ibrahim (Musa al-Kazim, *'Alayhi al-Salam*, the words of Hisham ibn Salim al-Jawaliqi and the words of Hisham ibn al-Hakam that say Allah is a body. The Imam, *'Alayhi al-Salam*, said, 'Allah, the Most High, is not similar to any of these things. What can be more blasphemous and scandalous than to describe the Creator of all things as having a body, form, being created, having limitations, limbs, and organs? Allah, the Most High, the Great, is by far above these things.'"

H 282, Ch. 11, h 5
Ali ibn Muhammad, in a *marfu'* manner, has narrated from Muhammad ibn al-Faraj al-Rukhkhaji who said the following:

"Once I wrote to Imam abu al-Hassan, *'Alayhi al-Salam*, about the words of Hisham ibn al-Hakam, regarding the body and the words of Hisham ibn Salim in relation to the form (of Allah). He wrote in reply, 'Remove from yourself the confusion of the confounded people and seek refuge from Allah against Shaytan (Satan). What the two Hishams have said is not correct.'"

H 283, Ch. 11, h 6
Muhammad ibn Abu 'Abd Allah has narrated from Muhammad ibn Isma'il from al-Husayn ibn al-Hassan from Bakr ibn Salih from al-Hassan ibn Sa'id from 'Abd Allah ibn al-Mughirah from Muhammad ibn Ziyad who said the following:

"I heard Yunus ibn Zabyan saying, 'Once I went to meet abu 'Abd Allah, *'Alayhi al-Salam*, and said, 'Hisham ibn al-Hakam has uttered monstrous words. I will briefly mention a few of them. He thinks Allah has a body because things are of two types: (a) body and (b) acts. It is not possible for the Creator Himself to be just actions or functions. But it is possible to consider Him as the agent.' Abu 'Abd Allah, *'Alayhi al-Salam*, then said, 'That is not proper for him. Does he not know that the body has limits and the form has limits and an end? Whatever is subject to limitations is also subject to increase and reduction, and such things are created.

"I (Yunus) then asked, 'What then I should say?' He replied, 'Allah is without body and form. He is the Giver of body to all bodies and the Giver of form to all forms. He cannot be divided or limited. He does not grow or decrease. If it were as they say, then there would remain no difference between the Creator and the created, the Inventor and the invented. But He is the Creator and the Inventor. He has made the distinction and differentiation between that to which He has given body, form and that which He has invented. This is because nothing is similar to Him nor does He resemble anything.'"

H 284, Ch. 11, h 7
Muhammad ibn abu 'Abd Allah has narrated from Muhammad ibn Isma'il from Ali ibn al-'Abbass from al-Hassan ibn 'Abd al-Rahman al-Hammani who said the following:
"Once I said to abu al-Hassan Musa ibn Ja'far, *'Alayhi al-Salam*, 'Hisham ibn al-Hakam claims that Allah is a body like unto whom there is no one. He is All-knowing, All-hearing, All-seeing and All-powerful. He speaks and reasons. His word, His power, His knowledge are all in one. No one of them is created.' The Imam said, 'May Allah be his foe! Does he not know that body is limited, and that the speech is other than what the speaker is? I seek refuge from Allah and I disclaim such words. Allah does not have a body, form, or any kind of limitations. Allah has created everything. He creates things as and when He wills without any word or planning in the mind or utterance of the tongue.'"

H 285, Ch. 11, h 8
Ali ibn Ibrahim has narrated from Muhammad ibn 'Isa from Yunus from Muhammad ibn Hakim who said the following:
"I mentioned to abu al-Hassan al-Awwal (the first), *'Alayhi al-Salam*, the statements of Hisham al-Jawaliqi and what he says about fully grown up young man (see Hadith 3 Chapter 10). I also mentioned the statements of Hisham ibn al-Hakam in this matter. The Imam said, 'Allah, certainly, is not similar to anything.'"

Chapter 12 - Attribute of the Essence (Sifat al-Dhat) of Allah

H 286, Ch. 12, h 1
Ali ibn Ibrahim has narrated from Muhammad ibn Khalid al-Tayalisi from Safwan ibn Yahya from ibn Muskan from abu Basir who said the following:
"I heard abu 'Abd Allah, *'Alayhi al-Salam*, saying, 'The Exalted, the Glorious, Allah, our Lord, is eternal. Knowledge is His Self even if there is nothing to be known. Hearing is His Self even if there is nothing to be heard. Seeing is His Self even when there is nothing to be seen. Power is His Self even if there is nothing to exercise the power. When He brought things into existence, the perceptible

objects became the objects of His knowledge, His hearing applied to audible objects, His seeing to visible objects and His power to the objects that feel power.'"

Abu Basir adds, 'I further asked, 'Has Allah always been in motion?' He replied, 'Allah is by far Highly Exalted above that. Motion is an attribute that is created through action.' I then asked, 'Did Allah always have the ability to speak?' He replied, 'Speech is a created attribute and not an eternal one. Allah, the Majestic, the Glorious, existed when there was nothing speaking.'"

H 287, Ch. 12, h 2

Muhammad ibn Yahya has narrated from Muhammad ibn al-Husayn from ibn abu 'Umayr from Hisham ibn Salim from Muhammad ibn Muslim who said the following:

"I heard abu Ja'far, *'Alayhi al-Salam*, saying, 'Allah, to Whom belong Might and Majesty, existed when nothing else existed. He eternally knows whatever comes into being. His knowledge of things before their coming into existence and afterwards is exactly the same.'"

H 288, Ch. 12, h 3

Muhammad ibn Yahya has narrated from Muhammad ibn al-Husayn from Safwan ibn Yahya from al-Kahili who said the following:

"Once I wrote to abu al-Hassan (al-Kazim), *'Alayhi al-Salam*, praising Allah in my letter as, 'All praise belongs to Allah to the limit of His knowledge.' He wrote back to me, 'Do not say, 'To the limit of His knowledge;' there is no limit to His knowledge. Instead say, "All praise belongs to Allah to the limit of His pleasure.'"

H 289, Ch. 12, h 4

Muhammad ibn Yahya has narrated from Sa'd ibn 'Abd Allah from Muhammad ibn 'Isa from Ayyub ibn Nuh the following:

"He wrote to abu al-Hassan (al-Thalith 3ʳᵈ), *'Alayhi al-Salam*, asking him about Allah, the Majestic, the Glorious, 'Did He know all things before creating and giving them being, or did He not know until He brought them into existence or until He willed their creation and existence? Did Allah come to know what He created during the process of their creation and what He originated during their being originated?' The Imam wrote in reply in his own handwriting, 'Allah, eternally, has had full knowledge of all things, before as well as after their creation.'"

H 290, Ch. 12, h 5

Ali ibn Muhammad has narrated from Sahl ibn Ziyad from Ja'far ibn Muhammad ibn Hamza who said the following:

"Once I wrote to the man (Imam), *'Alayhi al-Salam*, 'Your followers differ about the knowledge of Allah. There are those who say that before creating all things Allah had eternally full knowledge of them. Others say that we should not say so; His knowing is like His action. If we prove that His knowledge is eternal, we have also established another thing eternal along with Him. May Allah keep my soul in service for your cause, if you would consider it proper, kindly enlighten me in this issue so that I have a firm stand and do not waver there onwards.'

"He wrote in his own handwriting, 'Allah, the Most Holy, the Most High, eternally, has had Knowledge of all things.'"

H 291, Ch. 12, h 6

Muhammad ibn Yahya has narrated from Ahmad ibn Muhammad from al-Husayn ibn Sa'id from al-Qasim ibn Muhammad from 'Abd al-Samad ibn Bashir from Fudayl ibn Sukkarah who said the following:

"I asked abu Ja'far, *'Alayhi al-Salam*, 'May Allah keep my soul in service for your cause, if you would consider it proper, please enlighten me about whether Allah, Majestic is Whose Face, had knowledge of His Oneness before He brought the creation into existence? Your followers differ on this issue. There are those who believe that Allah did have knowledge of His Oneness before He created anything. Others say that His knowledge is His action. Thus, now Allah has come to know that before He created things, there had been nothing besides He Himself. They say that if we believe in the eternal knowledge of Allah, of His Oneness, we have established another thing eternal along with Him. If you would consider it proper please enlighten me in this issue so I may not waver here and there.'

"He wrote, 'Allah, the Blessed and Exalted has always had the knowledge of all things.'"

Chapter 13 - Another Chapter of the Previous Chapter

H 292, Ch. 13, h 1

Ali ibn Ibrahim has narrated from Muhammad ibn 'Isa ibn 'Ubayd from Hammad from Hariz from Muhammad ibn Muslim from abu Ja'far, *'Alayhi al-Salam*, who has said the following about being eternal:

"He, Allah, is One, the Self-sufficient. He is One and only One without any multiplicity in different meaning." The narrator has said that I further inquired, 'May Allah keep my soul in your service, certain people in Iraq think, that Allah hears with something different from what He sees with, and He sees with something different from what He hears with.' The Imam replied, 'They have said a lie and have (deviated from the truth) become atheists for considering Allah similar to other things. Allah, the Most High, indeed is above all things. He is All-Hearing and All-Seeing. He hears with what He sees, and sees with what He hears.' The narrator has said, 'I further said, 'Those people are of the opinion also that Allah is All-Seeing in the same sense and in the same way, as they perceive.

"The Imam said, 'Allah is by far Highly Exalted above all such things. Only created things perceive as they do. Allah is not created.'"

H 293, Ch. 13, h 2

Ali ibn Ibrahim has narrated from his father from al-'Abbass ibn 'Amr from Hisham ibn al-Hakam, who about the debate with an atheist (see Chapter 2 Hadith 6), has said the following:

"He asked (Imam) abu 'Abd Allah, *'Alayhi al-Salam*, 'Do you say that He is All-Hearing and All-Seeing?' Abu 'Abd Allah said, 'Allah is All-Hearing, All-Seeing. He hears without any organ and sees without any instrument. He Himself hears and He Himself sees. When I say He Himself hears I do not mean thereby that He is One and His Self is something different. I only express what I have in my mind to answer a question and help you understand the answer. So I say, 'His whole Self hears. This does not mean that His whole has parts. In our perception whole consists of parts. This is to make you understand and to express my thoughts. It is to say that He is All-Hearing, All-Seeing, All-Knowing, and All-Aware, without any multiplicity in the meaning.'"

Chapter 14 - Willpower (Iradah), an Attribute of Action (Sifat al-Fi'l), and the Rest of the Attributes of Action

H 294, Ch. 14, h 1

Muhammad ibn Yahya al-'Attar has narrated from Ahmad ibn Muhammad ibn 'Isa al-Ash'ari from al-Husayn ibn Sa'id al-Ahwazi from an-Nadr ibn Suwayd from 'Asim ibn Humayd who said the following:

"Once I asked abu 'Abd Allah, *'Alayhi al-Salam*, 'Is Allah's will eternal?' He replied, 'Will is always with what is willed. Allah is eternally All-Knowing and All-Powerful and then He wills.'"

H 295, Ch. 14, h 2

Muhammad ibn abu 'Abd Allah has narrated from Muhammad ibn Isma'il from al-Husayn ibn al-Hassan from Bakr ibn Salih from Ali ibn Asbat from al-Hassan ibn al-Jahm from Bukayr ibn A'yan who said the following:

"Once I asked abu 'Abd Allah, *'Alayhi al-Salam*, 'Are the knowledge and the will of Allah different or the same?' He replied, 'His knowledge is not the same as His will. Consider when you say, "If Allah wills, I will do this," and you do not say, 'If Allah knows, I will do this.' Your own words *if Allah wills* are proof that Allah has not yet willed it. If He wills what He would do, it happens exactly as He wills. His knowledge is before His will.'"

H 296, Ch. 14, h 3

Ahmad ibn Idris has narrated from Muhammad ibn 'Abd al-Jabbar from Safwan ibn Yahya who said the following:

"I asked abu al-Hassan, *'Alayhi al-Salam*, 'Enlighten me about the will of Allah and the will of His creatures.' He said, 'The will of His creatures comes from what goes on in their minds that leads to action. The will of Allah, the Most High, is His inventing and nothing else; Allah does not need to reflect, deliberate or think. Such qualities do not exist with Him. They are the attributes of His creation. Allah's will is His acts and nothing else. He says to it: "Be" and it comes into existence, without any words or utterance of the tongue or any inclination and reflection. His will has no conditions just as His Self has no conditions.'"

H 297, Ch. 14, h 4

Ali ibn Ibrahim has narrated from his father from ibn abu 'Umayr from 'Umar ibn 'Udhayna from abu 'Abd Allah, *'Alayhi al-Salam*, who said the following:

"Allah created His will (*al-Mashiat*) by will itself. Then, He created all things by His will."

H 298, Ch. 14, h 5

A number of our people have narrated from Ahmad ibn Muhammad al-Barqi from Muhammad ibn 'Isa from al-Mashriqi, Hamza ibn al-Murtafi' from certain persons of our people who said the following:

"Once I was in the presence of abu Ja'far, *'Alayhi al-Salam*, when 'Amr ibn 'Ubayd said, 'May Allah keep my soul in your service, what is the meaning of Allah's words, "Whoever becomes subject to My anger he is destroyed." (20:84) What is this anger?'

"Abu Ja'far, *'Alayhi al-Salam*, replied, 'O 'Amr, His anger is His punishment. O 'Amr, whoever thinks Allah changes from one state to another, has ascribed to Allah the attributes of His creatures. Nothing provokes Allah, the Sublime, to make Him change.'"

H 299, Ch. 14, h 6

Ali ibn Ibrahim has narrated from his father from al-'Abbass ibn 'Amr from Hisham ibn al-Hakam who has narrated the following:

"In the debate with the atheist who asked abu 'Abd Allah, *'Alayhi al-Salam* (see *Hadith* 6 Chapter 2), 'Does Allah become pleased and displeased?' Abu 'Abd Allah, *'Alayhi al-Salam*, replied, 'Yes, but not like that which is found in His creatures. In His creatures the pleasure is a state *(hal)*, which enters into him and changes him from one state to another. The creatures are hollow, active and of compound materials with entrance to them. Nothing can enter into our Creator. He is One, a single self and a single meaning. His pleasure is His reward and His anger is His punishment without anything entering in Him to motivate and change Him from one state to another; these are attributes of His creatures who are weak and needy.'"

H 300, Ch. 14, h 7

A number of our people have narrated from Ahmad ibn Muhammad ibn Khalid from his father from ibn abu 'Umayr from ibn 'Udhayna from Muhammad ibn Muslim from abu 'Abd Allah, *'Alayhi al-Salam*, who said the following:

"The will (*al-Mashiat*) is created."

Note from al-Kulayni (May Allah grant him favors): Concise Statements on the Attributes of His Essence, Sifat al-Dhat and the Attributes of His Actions, Sifat al-Fi'l.

"If two attributes are ascribed to Allah and both can exist at the same time, such attribute is an attribute of action of Allah. To explain it consider that in the real world you find what He wants and what He does not want, what He likes and what He dislikes, what He loves and what He hates. Had 'Will' been of the attributes of His Self like knowledge and power, then what He did not want would have been contrary to His will and it could not exist with 'Will' at the same time. Had what He loved been of the attributes of His Self what He hated would have been contrary to it (contrary things do not exist together).

"Consider that in the world we do not find anything that He would not know or would not have power to control. The same is true of the attributes of His Self that are eternal. We do not attribute to Him both power and weakness [knowledge and ignorance, foolishness and wisdom, mistakes and majesty] and meanness. It is permissible to say that He loves those who obey Him and hates those who disobey Him. He is a friend of those who obey Him and He is the enemy of those who disobey Him and that He becomes pleased and disappointed.

"In prayer it is said, 'O Lord, be pleased with me and do not be angry with me. Be my friend and do not be my enemy.'

"It, however, is not permissible to say that He has power to know but He does not have power not to know. He has power to own but He does not have power not to own. He has power to be Majestic and Wise and does not have power not to be Majestic and Wise. He has the power to be generous but He does not have the power not to be generous. He has the power to be forgiving but does not have the power not to be forgiving.

"It also is not permissible to say, 'He wills to be the Lord, Eternal, Majestic, Wise, the Owner, Knowing and Powerful.' It is because these are the attributes of His Self. Will is of the attributes of His acts.

"Consider that it is said, 'He willed this and did not will that.'

The attributes of His Self negate what is contrary to them. He is called Living, Knowing, Hearing, Seeing, Majestic, Wise, Independent, Owner, Forbearing, Just and Generous. Knowledge is contrary to ignorance, power is contrary to weakness, life is contrary to death, majesty is contrary to meanness, wisdom is contrary to blunders, forbearance is contrary to lack of thoughtfulness and contrary to justice is injustice and cruelty."

Chapter 15 - The Coming into Existence of the Names of Allah

H 301, Ch. 15, h 1

Ali ibn Muhammad has narrated from Salih ibn abu Hammad from al-Husayn ibn Yazid from al-Hassan ibn Ali ibn abu Hamza from Ibrahim ibn 'Umar from abu 'Abd Allah, *'Alayhi al-Salam*, who said the following:

"Allah, the Most Holy, the Most High, created a *name* with letters that had no sound. He created it with the word that would not be spoken. He created it with a personality that had no body. It had a similarity that is not described. He created it with color that is colorless. Diameters were negated from it. Limitations were distanced away from it. The feel of all *Mutawahhim* (intuitive sense) is curtained from it. It is hidden but not covered. He placed it to be a perfect word consisting of four parts together. No one of them is before the other. From these He made public only three names; people desperately needed them. One of them is kept out of public sight. This is the protected and treasured name.

"Of the names that became public is Allah, the Most Holy, the Most High. He, the Most Glorious, for each of these made four subservient key elements that formed twelve key elements. Then for each key element He created thirty key elements to indicate an action ascribed to the four key elements.

"He, therefore, is *al-Rahman* (the Compassionate), *al-Rahim* (the Merciful), *al-Malik* (the King), *al-Quddus* (the Holy), *al-Khaliq* (the Creator), *al-Bari'* (the Maker), *al-Musawwir* (the Fashioner), *al-Hayy* (the Ever-living) and *al-Qayyum* (the Self-subsistent). Neither slumber nor sleep seizes Him. He is *al-'Alim* (the All-Knowing), *al-Khabir* (the All-aware), *al-Sami'* (the All-Hearing), *al-Basir* (the All-Seeing), *al-Hakim* (the All-Wise), *al-'Aziz* (the Majestic), *al-Jabbar* (the Compelling), *al-Mutakabbir* (the Sublime), *al-'Aliyy* (the Most High), *al-'Azim* (the Great), *al-Muqtadir* (the Dominant), *al-Qadir* (the Almighty), *al-Salam* (the Peaceable), *al-Mu'min* (the Protector), *al-Muhaymin* (the Preserver), *al-Munshi'* (the Inventor), *al-Badi'* (the Originator), *al-Rafi'* (the Exalter), *al-Jalil* (the Majestic), *al-Karim* (the Generous), *al-Raziq* (the Provider), *al-Muhyi* (the Bestower of Life), *al-Mumit* (the Inflictor of death), *al-Ba'ith* (the Resurrecting) and *al-Warith* (the Inheritor).

"These names in addition to the (*Asma' al-Husna*) beautiful names make them three hundred sixty names. Such is the ratio of these three names. These three names are key element names. Only one name is kept out of public sight, protected and treasured with these three names. Thus, Allah has said, 'Say, call Allah or *al-Rahman*. Call whichever you call. For Him there are beautiful names.'" (17:110)"Among the narrators of this *Hadith* there are unknown people. Its language is not clear. There is secrecy in its meaning. No one knows its interpretation except Allah and those whom He has given especial knowledge." (Al-Allama al-Majlisi, Mir'at al-'Uqul, vol.2, p.24)

H 302, Ch. 15, h 2
Ahmad ibn Idris has narrated from al-Husayn ibn 'Abd Allah from Muhammad ibn 'Abd Allah and Musa ibn 'Umar and al-Hassan ibn Ali ibn 'Uthman from ibn Sinan who said the following:
"Once I asked abu al-Hassan al-Rida, *'Alayhi al-Salam*, 'Did Allah, the Majestic, the Glorious, know Himself before He created the creation?' The Imam replied, 'Yes, He knew Himself.' I further asked, 'Did He see and hear His Own Self?' The Imam replied, 'Allah did not need such things; He did not ask or demand it. He is His Own Self and His Own Self is He. His power is dominant and He does not need to name His Own Self. He chose His own name for the sake of others so they can call Him. Until one is not called by means of his name he is not recognized. The first name He chose for His Own Self was al-'Aliy al-'Azim (the Most High, the Great) because He is above all things. It then means that Allah and His name al-'Aliy al-'Azim is He. The Most High, means He is above all things.'"

H 303, Ch. 15, h 3
It is narrated through the same chain of narrators (as in the above *Hadith*) from Muhammad ibn Sinan who said the following:
"I asked the Imam (perhaps abu al-Hassan al-Rida), *'Alayhi al-Salam*, about the name (of Allah), 'What is it?' The Imam replied, 'It is an attribute of the attributes (of Allah).'"

H 304, Ch. 15, h 4

Muhammad ibn abu 'Abd Allah has narrated from Muhammad ibn Isma'il from some of his people from Bakr ibn Salih from Ali ibn Salih from al-Hassan ibn Muhammad ibn Khalid ibn Yazid from 'Abd al-A'la from abu 'Abd Allah, *'Alayhi al-Salam*, who said the following:

"The name of Allah is something other than Allah Himself. Everything that is called a *thing* is created except Allah. Whatever (like the word 'Allah') is expressed by the tongue or which is worked out by hands (written down) is all created. The word *Allah* is one example of names and an end to serve the purpose of naming. The end is different from the thing for which it is. The end that is describable is created. The Maker of things is not describable by the limits of the fact behind the name. He did not become, so the maker who is other than Him would have recognized His becoming a being. Whatever end people may reach is something other than Him. Do not ever move away from understanding this rule. This is the true and pure belief in the Oneness of Allah. Observe it, acknowledge it and understand it by the permission of Allah.

"Those who think they understand Allah by means of covering, form or image become polytheists; His covering, form and depiction are not Him. He is only One and one alone. How can one form a belief in His oneness by thinking that one is able to know Him through things other than Him? One comes to know Allah only by Allah His Own Self. One who cannot know Him by His Own Self has not known Him. He only comes to know something else. There is nothing between the Creator and the created. Allah is the Creator of things but not from a thing that was there already. Allah's names are His names but He is different from His Own names and the names are other than Him."

Chapter 16 - The Meanings of the Names of Allah and Their Derivatives

H 305, Ch. 16, h 1

A number of our people have narrated from Ahmad ibn Muhammad ibn Khalid from al-Qasim ibn Yahya from his grandfather al-Hassan ibn Rashid from 'Abd Allah ibn Sinan who said the following:

"Once I asked abu 'Abd Allah, *'Alayhi al-Salam*, about the interpretation of the verse of the Holy Quran, 'In the Name of Allah, the Beneficent, the Merciful.' The Imam replied, 'The first letter *'B'* in the Arabic version signifies *Baha'u Allah* meaning beauty of Allah. The second letter *'S'* signifies *Sana'u Allah* meaning radiance of Allah. The third letter *'M'* signifies *Majdu Allah,* meaning the Grandeur of Allah.' According to other narrators, *Majdu Allah* means Kingdom of Allah. *Allah* means Lord of all things. And *al-Rahman* means the Beneficent to all of His creatures in general. *Al-Rahim* means the Most Merciful to the believers in particular."

H 306, Ch. 16, h 2

Ali ibn Ibrahim has narrated from his father from al-Nadr ibn Suwayd from Hisham ibn al-Hakam who said the following:

"Once I asked abu 'Abd Allah, *'Alayhi al-Salam*, about the names of Allah and their derivations and roots. What is the root from which the word *Allah* is derived?

"The Imam replied, 'O Hisham, the word *Allah* is derived from *'Ilah.* It means, the One Who is worshipped (obeyed) and the One who is the Lord. The Lord requires that He be worshipped (obeyed) and is worthy of worshipping. The name of Allah is different from His Own Self. Whoever worships the name not the meaning has become an atheist and, in fact, has not worshipped Allah. Whoever worships the name and its meaning jointly, he becomes a polytheist, worshipping two Lords. Whoever worships the meaning of the word Allah only he, in reality, has worshipped the One Allah. O Hisham, did you grasp it?' Hisham has said, 'I requested, "Please enlighten me more."'"

"The Imam added, 'Allah has ninety-nine names. If each name had a separate meaning then each meaning would have been a Lord. Allah is One only and all His names stand for just One reality and all these names are other than Allah Himself. O Hisham, bread is the name of something to eat. Water is the name of something to drink. Dress is the name of something to wear. Fire is the name of something that burns. O Hisham, did you fully grasp the point so you can defend your belief and contest successfully against our opponents, who, along with Allah, the Exalted, the Great, accept as their Lord, things other than Him?' Hisham replied, 'Yes, I did understand.'

"The Imam said, 'O Hisham, may Allah benefit you thereby and grant you steadfastness.'"Hisham (the narrator) says, 'I swear by Allah, no one has ever defeated me on the issue of the Oneness of Allah until now.'"

H 307, Ch. 16, h 3

A number of our people have narrated from Ahmad ibn Muhammad from al-Barqi from al-Qasim ibn Yahya from his grandfather al-Hassan ibn Rashid from abu al-Hassan Musa ibn Ja'far, *'Alayhi al-Salam,* who said the following:

"Once, a question was asked from the Imam about the meaning of the word *"Allah"*. The Imam replied, 'The word *"Allah"* stands for one who dominates all things, small or big.'"

H 308, Ch. 16, h 4

Ali ibn Muhammad has narrated from Sahl ibn Ziyad from Ya'qub ibn Yazid from al-'Abbass ibn Hilal who said the following:

"Once I asked (Imam) al-Rida, *'Alayhi al-Salam,* about the meaning of the words of Allah, 'Allah is the Light of the heavens and the earth.' (24:35) The Imam replied, 'Allah is the Guide for all that is in the heavens and the Guide for all that is on the earth.'"

According to another *Hadith* that al-Barqi has narrated (the Imam said), "Allah has guided everyone in the heavens and everyone on the earth."

H 309, Ch. 16, h 5

Ahmad ibn Idris has narrated from Muhammad ibn 'Abd al-Jabbar from Safwan ibn Yahya from Fudayl ibn 'Uthman from ibn abu Ya'fur who said the following:

"Once I said to abu 'Abd Allah, *'Alayhi al-Salam,* about the meaning of the words of Allah, the Majestic, the Glorious, 'He (Allah) is the first and the last.' (57:3)

We have understood *His being the first* but explain for us the meaning of *His being the last.*'

"The Imam said, 'There is nothing in the universe, but that is subject to annihilation, alteration, change, decay, transition from one color to another, from one shape to another and from one quality to another. All things increase, decrease and change from decrease to increase, except He, Who is the Lord of the worlds. He alone is eternal and in one state. He is the first, before everything and the last eternally. His attributes and names do not change as they do in the case of others. A man at one time is (part of) the soil and dust, at other time flesh and blood, then turns into decaying bones and finally becomes dust. A piece of date at one time is raw, at another time ripe, mature, and then it dries up. With every change, the names and attributes also change. Allah, the Majestic, the Glorious, is different from all such things.'"

H 310, Ch. 16, h 6
Ali ibn Ibrahim has narrated from his father from ibn abu 'Umayr from ibn 'Udhayna from Muhammad ibn Hakim from Maymun al-Ban who said the following:
"I heard abu 'Abd Allah, *'Alayhi al-Salam,* saying to a question about Allah being the *first* and the *last,* 'His being the *first* means there was no first before Him and no beginning preceded Him at all. His being the *last* means He has no end; it (last) is an attribute of the created and He is eternal, the first and the last. He has always been and He will always be without any beginning and any end. Nothing new happens to Him and He does not change from one state to another. He is the Creator of all things.'"

H 311, Ch. 16, h 7
Muhammad ibn abu 'Abd Allah in a *marfu'* manner, has narrated from abu Hashim al-Ja'fari who said the following:
"Once I was in the company of abu Ja'far al-Thani, the 2nd, *'Alayhi al-Salam,* when a person asked him, 'The names and attributes of the Lord, the Most Holy, the Most High, mentioned in His book (the Holy Quran): are they He Himself?'

"The Imam replied, 'Your question has two aspects. If you say that they are His Own Self, meaning that He has plurality and multiplicity, then Allah is highly exalted from being as such. If you mean that names and attributes of Allah had eternally been there, this also has a double meaning. (First) if you mean, that names and attributes have eternally been in the knowledge of Allah and He eternally deserved them, it is true and quite right. If you mean that the letters, pictures, spellings and syllables of names and attributes were eternal, then we seek refuge with Him against such belief.

"Allah existed but there were no creatures. He created names and attributes as a means between His Own Self and the creatures. Through these means they pray to Him and ask Him for help, and names are the means to speak of Him. Allah existed without being mentioned. The One mentioned through names is Allah the eternal, Who will be there eternally. Names and attributes are created and their meaning and what they indicate is Allah, Who is by far above plurality and combination, which happens only to the moving things. If you say that Allah is compiled it is a false statement and so is saying that He is a great deal or very little. He His Own Self is eternal. What is other than the Only One, it is divisible. Allah is not divisible. Not even in one's imagination can be thought of as more or less. Everything divisible or being thought of as less or more, in one's imagination, is created. All created things are signs of the existence of the Creator.

"When you say Allah has power, you in reality say that He does not become frustrated due to weakness. In this way you negate weakness from Him and consider it other than Him. The same is the meaning of your saying that He is All-Knowing. With this, you negate ignorance from Him and have considered it other than Him. When Allah will destroy all things, the form, spelling and syllables will all be destroyed. Allah is and will eternally be there.'

"The man then said, 'Why do we call our Lord *All-hearing*? The Imam said, 'It is because everything that can be heard is not hidden from Him. We do not ascribe to Him the hearing ability that exists in the head. In the same way we call Him *All-seeing*. It is because everything that can be seen like colors or individuals and so forth, is not hidden from Him. We do not call Him All-seeing because of the blinking eye. We call Him *Subtle* because of His knowledge of delicate things such as His knowledge of insects, and so forth, or even more delicate things. It is because of His knowledge of such things as their intelligence, desires for reproduction, compassion for their offspring, their guarding each other, their carrying food and drink to their offspring in the mountains, wilderness, valleys and desolate places. From this we know that their Creator is *Subtle* but without the condition of subtlety. Such conditions (and feelings) are for the creatures that are conditioned with conditions.

'We also call our Lord powerful but not because of the aggressiveness that the creatures display. If so, a similarity will exist as well as degrees of decrease that involve increases. Whatever decreases is not eternal and is weak. To our Lord, the Most Holy, the Most High, no one is similar, contrary, resembling, of the same conditions, or end or seen with eyes. It is unlawful for the hearts to analogize Him. It is unlawful for the *Awham* (intuitive power) to limit Him. It is unlawful for one's consciousness to contain Him. He is Glorious and Majestic and above coming within the reach of the means of His creatures or having the signs of His servants. He is High and Great and by far above such matters.'"

H 312, Ch. 16, h 8
Ali ibn Muhammad has narrated from Sahl ibn Ziyad from ibn Mahbub from those he mentioned from abu 'Abd Allah, *'Alayhi al-Salam*, who said the following:
"Once a man said, *Allahu Akbar* (Allah is greater) in the presence of abu 'Abd Allah, *'Alayhi al-Salam*. The Imam asked, 'Allah is greater than whom?' The man replied, 'He is greater than everything.' The Imam said, 'You have considered Him limited.' The man asked, 'Then, how should I say it?' The Imam replied, 'Say, Allah is greater than can be described.'"

H 313, Ch. 16, h 9

Muhammad ibn Yahya has narrated from Ahmad ibn Muhammad ibn 'Isa from Marwak ibn 'Ubayd from Jumay' ibn 'Umayr who said the following:

"Once (Imam) abu 'Abd Allah, *'Alayhi al-Salam*, asked me, 'What is the meaning of *Allah is greatest*?' I replied, 'Allah is the greatest of all things.' The Imam further asked, 'Were there other things so Allah could be considered the greatest of them?' I then asked, 'What then is the meaning thereof?' The Imam replied, 'Allah is by far greater. He is beyond all descriptions.'"

H 314, Ch. 16, h 10

Ali ibn Ibrahim has narrated from Muhammad ibn 'Isa ibn 'Ubayd from Yunus from Hisham ibn al-Hakam who said the following:

"Once I asked abu 'Abd Allah, *'Alayhi al-Salam*, about the meaning of the words *Glorious is Allah*. The Imam said, 'It means distinction of Allah (His being free of all shortcomings).'"

H 315, Ch. 16, h 11

Ahmad ibn Mihran has narrated from 'Abd al-'Azim ibn 'Abd Allah al-Hassani from Ali ibn Asbat. From Sulayman Mawla Tirbal from Hisham al-Jawaliqi who said the following:

"Once I asked abu 'Abd Allah, *'Alayhi al-Salam*, about the meaning of the words of Allah, the Majestic, the Glorious, *Glorious Allah* (Quran, 12:108, 23:91, 28:68, 37:159, 52:43, 59:23). The Imam replied, 'They refer to Allah's being above all things in perfection.'"

H 316, Ch. 16, h 12

Ali ibn Muhammad and Muhammad ibn al-Hassan has narrated from Sahl ibn Ziyad and Muhammad ibn Yahya from Ahmad ibn Muhammad ibn 'Isa all of them from abu Hashim al-Ja'fari who said the following:

"Once I asked abu Ja'far al-Thani, the 2nd, *'Alayhi al-Salam*, 'What is the meaning of the *One*?' The Imam replied, 'It means the unanimity of all tongues in speaking of Allah's Oneness. If you ask them about who has created them, they all say, "It is Allah, Who has created them all."'" (43:87)

Chapter 17 - Another Chapter (Related) to the Previous Chapter

With certain additions on the difference in the meanings of names of Allah, and the names and attributes of the created

H 317, Ch. 17, h 1

Ali ibn Ibrahim has narrated from al-Mukhtar ibn Muhammad ibn al-Mukhtar al-Hamadani and Muhammad ibn al-Hassan from 'Abd Allah ibn al-Hassan al-'Alawi both of them from al-Fath ibn Yazid al-Jurjani from abu al-Hassan, *'Alayhi al-Salam*, al-Thani or al-Thalith who said the following:

"I heard the Imam saying, 'He (Allah) is Subtle, All-aware, All-hearing, All-seeing, the One, the Self-sufficient, Who does not have any children. (He) is not anyone's child and there is no one similar to Him. Had Allah been as those believing in similitude *(al-Mushabbihah)* say He is, no distinction would exist between the Creator and the created, the Inventor and the invented. In reality He is the Inventor. He has made a distinction between the owner of the body and its creator, the owner of the form and its designer and the one being invented and the inventor. Nothing is similar to Him and He is not similar to anything.'

"I then said, 'Yes, may Allah keep my soul in your service, but you just said, *the One the Self-sufficient,* that no one is similar to Him. Allah is One and a man is one. Are the two not similar in oneness?' The Imam replied, 'O Fath, you said something impossible. May Allah grant you steadfastness. Similarity is in meanings. In the case of names they are all the same. The names refer to the named and designated one. When it is said a 'Man', although (commonly) he is considered one individual, he is found in the form of one individual and not two individuals. However, in fact, man is not one thing. His parts, colors and the color of his colors that consist of distinct parts are not equal. His blood is different from his flesh. His nerves are different from his veins; his hairs are different from his skin. The black things in him are different from the white things therein. The same is true of all other creatures. Human beings are one in name but not in meaning.

'Allah, Whose Majesty is Great, is only One and no one other than Him is one. There is no difference, imbalance, increase or decrease in Him. Human beings are created, designed, compounded of different parts and various substances. Only when his parts are combined man becomes one individual.'

"I then said, 'May Allah keep my soul in service for your cause, and grant you happiness, please enlighten me about the meaning of your words 'Subtle and All-Aware' Explain it as you just did with the 'One'? I know that His subtlety or kindness is different from that of His creatures but I like more clarity.' The Imam said, 'O Fath, we said, 'He is Subtle' is because of His knowledge of the delicate creatures, may Allah give you success and steadfastness, so you would think about His creation. Consider His design in delicate and not so delicate plants and other creatures like animals, small and large such as flies and crickets and smaller ones that even the eyes cannot see. It is because of their small size that one may not know which is male and which is female, which is newborn and which is old. We find tremendously delicate things as signs of His Subtlety, in their desire for reproduction, running away from death, collecting what is good for them and what is in the depth of the oceans and on the barks of trees, in the wilderness and desolate places. We find more fastidiousness in such animals. It is found in their ability to communicate with each other and in the things that their offspring understand from them. It is in their transporting food to their young and their colors, red along with yellow, white along with red so fine that our eyes are not able to catch because of their very exquisite shape. Our eyes are not able to see them and our hands are not able to feel them. All these show that the Creator of all such marvelous creatures is "Subtle" and is kind to all the creatures we mentioned. He has done the creating without instruments and means. Every designer and manufacturer builds and manufactures something from something else but Allah does it from nothing.'"

H 318, Ch. 17, h 2

It is narrated from Ali ibn Muhammad, in a *mursal* manner, from abu al-Hassan al-Rida, *'Alayhi al-Salam*, who has said the following to one of his followers:

"May Allah bestow upon you knowledge of the good, bear in mind that Allah, the Most Holy, the Most High, is eternal. Eternity is that attribute which guides the man of reason (to the fact) that there was nothing before Him in eternity nor will there be anything with Him eternally. This attribute is a miraculous one. It has come to light from the acknowledgement of the *'Ammah* (common people) that there is nothing before Allah and with Him eternally. At the same time, it invalidates the belief that there was something before or with Him. Had there been something with Him eternal He would not have been the Creator of that thing. If it had been with Him how then could He have been its creator? Had there been something before Him then that thing might have been His creator because of its existing earlier.

"Allah, the Most Holy, the Exalted, has ascribed certain names to Himself. He told His creatures when He created them, gave them the ability to worship Him and made them responsible, to call Him with those names. He called Himself All-hearing, All-seeing, All-powerful, Guarding, Rationalizing, Manifest, Hidden, Subtle, All-aware, Powerful, Majestic, Wise, All-knowing and with such other similar names. When the anger-mongers who speak lies heard us mention such names as, 'There is nothing similar to Him' and 'Nothing of the creatures is like Him,' they began to speak out. 'When you (the Imam, *'Alayhi al-Salam*) say that there is nothing like Him and no one is similar to Him then how can you also have those beautiful names for yourselves? This is proof that you are similar to Him or in certain conditions and not in other conditions because of having all those beautiful names.'

"To answer, it can be said to them that Allah, the Most Holy, the Most High, made it necessary for His servants to have certain names from among His names but with differences in the meanings. (This is true); one name may have two different meanings. One example of this is what people consider permissible and is widely used. On this basis Allah has addressed people. He has spoken to them by means of things that they understand so that they will have no excuse in their misdeeds.

"A man is sometimes called a dog, a bull, sweet, bitter and a lion. All these are different from him and his conditions. In such expressions the names are not used in their original meaning; man is not a lion or a dog and so forth. Note this carefully, may Allah grant you blessings.

"Allah is called All-knowing. It (His knowledge) is other than the created knowledge. With His knowledge of things He knows things and uses the knowledge to preserve His future commands and the process of whatever He creates of His creatures, and destroys what He destroys of His creatures. Without such knowledge He would be weak and ignorant. We know that men of knowledge among people are called knowledgeable because of the created knowledge, which they did not have at one time. Perhaps such knowledge will go away from them and they will become ignorant.

"Allah is called All-knowing; He is not ignorant of anything. Thus, the Creator and created are both called, as having knowledge but the meaning is different, as you may have noticed above. Our Lord is called All-hearing but His hearing is not through the perforated piece (of material in the ear) and with sound, so He could hear but would not see with it, which is the case with us. We do not see with what we hear but Allah has told us that from Him nothing of the sounds is hidden. His hearing is not in the way we are called hearing people. We are also called hearing but the meaning is different. In the same way is 'Seeing.' His seeing is not that He sees through a hole as we do and we cannot use it for other uses. Allah sees but not by looking to an object. We also are called 'Seeing' but the meaning is different.

"Allah is called Standing but not in the sense of standing in an upright position on the legs, as is the case with other things. It (His standing) is in the sense that He has said 'He is preserving'. It is in the sense of the saying of a man, 'Standing for our affairs.' Allah stands over every soul and what it gains. The word standing is also in the usage of people. Words like *remaining* and *standing* also mean to suffice as in the words that one may say to a man, 'Stand up over the affairs of so and so,' which means dealing with them with efficiency and an overseeing manner. We stand on our legs, thus, the name is similar but the meaning is different.

"The name, *Subtle* is not in the sense of fastidiousness or being infinitesimal but it is in the rarity and hard to perceive nature of things. An example is the expression, 'It has become very delicate for me,' 'So and so is very fine in his manners and dealings.' This 'Delicateness' and 'Fineness' means that it is profound for one's intelligence and difficult to find. It has become bottomless and delicate so much so that even imagination is not able to reach it. Allah, the Most Holy, the Most High, is highly Subtle to be comprehended through definitions or combined in an attribute or in the way we are subtle, small and delicate. Names are the same but different in meaning.

"The name *al-Khabir*, meaning All-aware, is for one who knows all things completely but not by means of experience and learning lessons from the past. Experience and learning from mistakes are the means of learning for people. Without them (experience and so forth) there no knowledge could exist. One without experience and learning lessons is an ignorant person. Allah is eternally All-aware of what He has created, but well aware and expert among people are those who ask questions and learn. Our names are the same but they, again, are different in meaning.

"The name (of Allah), *al-Zahir* means clear, or face to face or conspicuous. It does not mean that He is (physically) found over and on top of all things or sitting on them at their peak. It means that He is dominant and has power over all things.

An example of this is when a person says, 'I overcame my enemies or Allah gave me victory over my enemies,' it is the report of the failure and victory. So also is Allah's domination over all things. Another example is that His existence is clear for those who want (to know) Him. Nothing is hidden from Him and He is the guardian of all that He has carved and fashioned. Whose existence can be clearer than that of Allah, the Most Holy, the Most High? You will not live without His creatures, no matter where you may be. Within your own self alone there is enough of His creation. His existence by far is clearer than ours is. He manifests all by His Own Self and is known by His Own Self. We are of the same name but the meaning is different.

"The name *al-Batin* means something hidden or the inside of something. This is not in the sense of being inside of things by means of diving or so but is in the sense of His dealing, having knowledge, preserving and regulating the inside of all things. As one may say, 'I tried to find the inside to learn and discover the secrets.' Hidden for us is what is unseen and covered. In this case again our names are the same but different in meaning.

"The name *al-Qahir* means subduing. It is not in the sense of plotting, using certain devices and speaking attractive words or cunning means. It is not the way people subdue each other. The victorious among people may become subdued and vice versa. For Allah, the Most Holy, the Most High, all the creatures have the garment of weakness on them. Due to the absence of obstacles in what He wills about them, it only takes less than a blinking of the eye to say, 'Be' and it *is*. It comes into existence. Subduing in our case is how I mentioned and explained. Our names are alike but the meaning is different. Thus is the case for all the names although we have not mentioned all of them. For learning a lesson what we have mentioned for you is sufficient. May Allah be your and our helper in the matters of guidance and success.'"

Chapter 18 - The Interpretation of al-Samad (Self-sufficient)

H 319, Ch. 18, h 1

Ali ibn Muhammad and Muhammad ibn al-Hassan has narrated from Sahl ibn Ziyad from Muhammad ibn al-Walid, whose title was Shabab al-Sayrafi from Dawud ibn al-Qasim al-Ja'fari who said the following:

"Once I asked Imam abu Ja'far al-Thani, the 2nd, *'Alayhi al-Salam*, 'May Allah keep my soul in your service, what is the meaning of the word *al-Samad*?' The Imam replied, *'Al-Samad* means the Lord to Whom one turns for help, in a big or small matter.'"

H 320, Ch. 18, h 2

A number of our people have narrated from Ahmad ibn abu 'Abd Allah from Muhammad ibn 'Isa from Yunus ibn 'Abd al-Rahman from al-Hassan ibn al-Sari from Jabir ibn Yazid al-Ju'fi who said the following:

"I asked (Imam) abu Ja'far, *'Alayhi al-Salam*, a few things about the Oneness of Allah. The Imam replied, 'Allah, Holy are Whose names and with which He is mentioned, is Exalted and Most High by His Own Self. He is One. In Oneness He is the One and only One for His Oneness. He then made His creatures to know Him as the only One. He is One, Self-sufficient and the Holy. All things worship (obey) Him and He has the knowledge of all things.'"Al-Kulayni has said the following. "This is the correct meaning of *al-Samad*. What *al-Mushabbihah* (people who consider Allah similar to certain things) believe is not correct. *Al-Samad* literally means solid as opposed to hollow, which applies only to physical objects. Allah, the Most High, is by far highly exalted above such attributes. Had such attributes applied to Allah, the Most High, the Most Gracious, it would have contradicted His statement that says, 'There is nothing similar to Him.'

"In the *Ahadith* of the scholar (the Imam), *'Alayhi al-Salam*, the scholars know better, *al-Samad* refers to a master whom people consider a recourse or stronghold and such meaning is close to Allah's words, 'There is nothing similar to Him.' (42:11) An example of such usage is what abu Talib had expressed in praise of the Holy Prophet, *'Alayhi al-Salam*, during his performing Hajj and during throwing pebbles onto the pillars of stones that symbolically stand for Satan. He has used the word *al-Samad* to mean 'Aiming:'

"At the farthest of pillars when they (people) *Samadu* (aimed);

They followed him (the Holy Prophet),

In throwing pebbles on the head of the pillars that stand for Satan.

"A certain poet of pre-Islamic time has said, 'I did not think there was any other known house around Makkahh besides the House of Allah that people seek and *aim* for blessing.'

"Another example is found in the expression of ibn Zabarqan, 'Mr. Rahibah is but a master and (*al-Samad*) a recourse.'

"One more example can be found in the expression of Shaddad ibn Mu'awiya about Kudhayfa ibn Badr, 'Hold it O Hudhayfa, you are a master (*al-Samad*) recourse.' There are many such examples in normal usage. To Allah, the Majestic, the Most High, the Master and the Recourse, all man and Jinn turn for help in their difficulties and from Whom they expect relief.'"

Chapter 19 - Motion and Change

H 321, Ch. 19, h 1
Muhammad ibn abu 'Abd Allah has narrated from Muhammad ibn Isma'il al-Barmaki from Ali ibn 'Abbass al-Kharadhini from al-Hassan ibn Rashid from Ya'qub ibn Ja'far al-Ja'fari, from abu Ibrahim, *'Alayhi al-Salam*, who has said the following:
"A people were mentioned, before the Imam, *'Alayhi al-Salam*. They believed that Allah, the Most Holy, the Most High, comes down to the sky above the earth. The Imam (*'Alayhi al-Salam*) said, 'Allah does not come down and He does not need to come down. His sight for near and far is the same. Near does not become

far for Him and far does not become near for Him. He does not become needy for anything, but all things need Him and He is generous. There is no Lord except Him. He is Most Majestic and All-wise. The statement that says Allah, the Most Holy, the Most High, comes down to the sky over the earth can only come from those who consider Him to decrease or increase (in size). Besides, all moving objects need something to move them or move because of them. Whoever thinks of Allah as such has caused his own destruction. Be very careful about the attributes of Allah so you will not establish a belief about them that may amount to limit Him through increase or reduction, moving or being moved, removal or His coming down, standing up or sitting down. Allah, the Most Holy, the Most High, is by far above being described by those who like to describe Him, or being characterized by those who do so or pictured in imagination. Have trust in Allah, the Most Majestic, the Most Merciful, Who sees you when you get up and when you change positions during the state of prostration.'"

H 322, Ch. 19, h 2
It is narrated from him (the narrator of the above Hadith), in a *marfu'* manner, from al-Hassan ibn Rashid from Ya'qub ibn Ja'far from abu Ibrahim, *'Alayhi al-Salam*, who said the following:
"I do not say that He is standing so I remove Him from His place. I do not limit Him in a place. I do not limit Him by His moving in something with key elements of the body or body parts. I do not limit Him by ascribing the movements of mouth or tongue. The truth is what Allah, the Most Holy, the Most High, has said, 'Be' and it comes into existence through His will without any planning in a soul. He is Self-sufficient and all alone. He does not need any partner to speak of His kingdom or open the doors of His knowledge.'"

H 323, Ch. 19, h 3
It is narrated from him (the narrator of the above Hadith) from Muhammad ibn abu 'Abd Allah from Muhammad ibn Isma'il from Dawud ibn 'Abd Allah from 'Amr ibn Muhammad from 'Isa ibn Yunus who said the following:
"Once, Ibn abu al-'Awja said to (Imam) abu 'Abd Allah, *'Alayhi al-Salam*, in one of their conversations, 'You spoke of Allah and referred to an unseen.' The Imam, *'Alayhi al-Salam*, said, 'What you said is not proper. How would He be unseen when He is present with His creatures and is closer to them than their jugular vein? He hears their speeches, sees their persons and knows their secrets.'

"Ibn abu al-'Awja then said, 'Is He everywhere? If He is in the heavens, how can He, at the same time, be on earth and when He would be on earth then how can He be in the heavens at the same time?'

"The Imam, *'Alayhi al-Salam*, said, 'You spoke only of a creature with whose changing place, another place becomes occupied with it and another place is vacated from him and does not know what has happened to the place where he used to be. Allah's position is great. He is the King, Who has full account of all things. No place is without Him and He does not occupy any place. He is not nearer to one place than another place.'"

H 324, Ch. 19, h 4

Ali ibn Muhammad has narrated from Sahl ibn Ziyad from Muhammad ibn 'Isa who said the following:

"Once I wrote to Imam abu al-Hassan, Ali ibn Muhammad, *'Alayhi al-Salam*, to clarify a question, 'May Allah keep my soul in your service, O my master, it is narrated to us that Allah is in one place and not in another place on 'Arsh (the Throne), resting. He comes down to the sky above the earth every night during the last half of the night. It is narrated that He comes down at the ninth evening of the month of Dhu al-Hajj and then He returns back to His place. Certain individuals among your friends have said that if He is found in certain places and not in other places the air must have come in contact with Him and surrounded Him because air is a thin form of body that surrounds everything proportionate to its size. How then can the air surround Allah, the Most Holy and the Most High, according to this assumption?'

"The Imam replied in writing, 'He has the knowledge of this. He is the best One in having the true measurements of all things. You must, however, note that His being in the sky over the earth is just as He is on the Throne. All things to Him are the same in the matters of His knowledge and power, domination and control.'"

Muhammad ibn Ja'far al-Kufi has narrated from Muhammad ibn 'Isa a similar *Hadith.*

A Note on the Words of Allah:

"There is not a single place wherein any secret counsel can take place among any three people without Allah being the fourth . . ." (58:7)

H 325, Ch. 19, h 5

It is narrated from him (the narrator of the above *Hadith*) from a group of our people from Ahmad ibn Muhammad ibn Khalid from Ya'qub ibn Yazid from ibn abu 'Umayr from ibn 'Udhayna from (Imam) abu 'Abd Allah, *'Alayhi al-Salam*, who said the following:

"There is not a single place wherein any secret counsel can take place among any three people without Allah being the fourth, nor five people without His being the sixth . . ." (58:7) It means He is One, the One only of His Own Self. He is distinct from His creatures and as such He has said about His Own Self, 'He has control over all things through His presence, control and power. Nothing as small as an atom in the heavens or earth is absent from Him, not even things smaller or bigger.' It is all through His control and knowledge, not by His Self. It is because the places are limited by the four boundaries. If it (control) is by His Self it limits Him.'"

A Note on the Words of Allah:

"The Beneficent Allah is dominant over the Throne (of the realm)." (20:5)

H 326, Ch. 19, h 6

Ali ibn Muhammad and Muhammad ibn al-Hassan have narrated from Sahl ibn Ziyad from al-Hassan ibn Musa al-Khashshab from certain persons of his people from (Imam) abu 'Abd Allah, *'Alayhi al-Salam*, who (the narrator) has said the following:

"Once a person asked the Imam about the words of Allah, 'The Beneficent is dominant over the Throne.' (20:5)

"The Imam said, 'Allah established His control over all things. No one thing is closer to Him than any other thing.'"

H 327, Ch. 19, h 7

Sahl through the same chain of narrators has narrated from al-Hassan ibn Mahbub from Maridin the following:

"A person once asked (Imam) abu 'Abd Allah about the words of Allah, 'The Beneficent is dominant over the Throne.' (20:5) The Imam said, 'It means He established His control in all things.'"

H 328, Ch. 19, h 8

It is narrated from him (narrator of the above *Hadith*) from Muhammad ibn Yahya from Muhammad ibn al-Husayn from Safwan ibn Yahya from 'Abd al-Rahman ibn al-Hajjaj from (Imam) abu 'Abd Allah, *'Alayhi al-Salam*, the following:

"About the words of Allah, 'The Beneficent is dominant over the Throne,' (20:5) the Imam said, 'No single thing is closer to Him than any other thing. The *far* is not far for Him and the *near* is not closer to Him. All are the same to Him.'"

H 329, Ch. 19, h 9

It is narrated from him (narrator of previous *Hadith*) from Muhammad ibn Yahya from Ahmad ibn Muhammad ibn 'Isa from al-Husayn ibn Sa'id from al-Nadr ibn Suwayd from 'Asim ibn Humayd from abu Basir from (Imam) abu 'Abd Allah, *'Alayhi al-Salam*, who said the following:

"Whoever may think that Allah is from things or in things or on things has become an atheist." "I asked the Imam, *'Alayhi al-Salam*, 'Please explain to me.'" The Imam said, 'I intend thereby His being contained, held or being preceded.'"

In another *Hadith* it is said, "Whoever believes that Allah is from things has considered Him as created. Whoever thinks that He is in things has considered Him as surrounded. Whoever thinks that He is on things has considered Him as being carried."

A Note on the Words of Allah:

"*It is Allah who is the Lord of the heavens and is the Lord on earth. He is All-wise and All-knowing.*" (43:84)

H 330, Ch. 19, h 10

Ali ibn Ibrahim has narrated from his father from ibn abu 'Umayr from Hisham ibn al-Hakam who said the following:

"Abu Shakir al-Daysani once said, 'In the Quran there is a verse that says what we say.' I asked, 'What is that?' He replied, 'It is Allah who is the Lord of the heavens and is the Lord on earth. He is All-wise and All-knowing (43:84).' I did not know the answer, whether the above verse speaks of two Lords or one. During

110

Hajj I mentioned it to (Imam) abu 'Abd Allah who said, 'This is the statement of a wicked atheist. When you go back say to him, 'What is your name in Basra?' He will say so and so. Ask, 'What is your name in al-Kufa?' He will say so and so. Say to him, 'In the same way is our Lord in the heavens. He is the King in the heavens and the Lord on earth. He is the Lord in oceans and on land and in all places.'

"The narrator has said, 'I came back, went to abu Shakir and explained to him the answer.' He said, 'This (answer) is brought from al- Hijaz.'"

Chapter 20 - About al-'Arsh and al-Kursi

H 331, Ch. 20, h 1

A number of our people have narrated from Ahmad ibn Muhammad al-Barqi, in a *marfu'* manner, the following:

"Jathaliq, a Christian scholar, asked Imam Ali ibn abu Talib, *'Alayhi al-Salam*, saying, 'Tell me about Allah, the Most Holy, the Most High. Does He carry the 'Arsh or does the 'Arsh carry Him?' Imam Ali, *'Alayhi al-Salam*, replied, 'Allah, the Most Holy, the Most High, is the One Who carries and has lifted the 'Arsh, the heavens and earth and all that is between them (from banishment). Allah prevents the heavens and the earth from falling apart. If they fall apart, then no one besides Him is able to restore them. He is All-forbearing and All-forgiving.' (35:41)

"He then asked, 'Tell me about His words, "The angels will be around the heavens and on that day eight of them will carry the Throne of your Lord above all the creatures." (69:17) How has He said it? You just said that He carries the heavens, earth and all that is between them.' Amir al-Mu'minin then said, 'Allah, the Most High, created al-'Arsh (the Throne) from four lights. From a red wherefrom the redness became red, a green light from which the greenness became green and yellow light whereby the yellowness became yellow. He created it from a white light wherefrom is white and it is the knowledge which Allah has made the carriers to carry and that is the light of His greatness. With His greatness and His light He has given sight to the hearts of believers. Because of His greatness and light the ignorant ones have become His enemies. Through His greatness and light all in the heavens and on earth and all His creatures seek to reach Allah, the Most Holy, the Most High, by means of their various deeds and mixed religions. All that is carried Allah carries them with the light of His greatness and power. They are not able to do any benefit, or harm, death or life or resurrection. All things are carried. Allah, the Most Holy, the Most High, preserves them from banishment and has control over both of them (the heavens and earth). He is the life of all things and the light of all things. Glorious is He, the Most High and by far is above what they say about Him. He is very High above them with Greatness.'

"The man then said, 'Tell me about Allah, the Most Holy, the Most High, where is He?' Amir al-Mu'minin Ali, *'Alayhi al-Salam*, said, 'He is here. He is there, above, below, encompassing us and with us as He has said, "There is not a single place wherein any secret counsel can take place among any three people without Allah being the fourth, nor five people without His being the sixth nor any gathering of more or fewer people, wherever it may be, without His being with them . . ." (58:7) Al-Kursi contains the heavens and the earth and all that is between them and below the soil. If you say anything aloud, He knows the secrets and the hidden as mentioned in His words, 'The heavens and the earth are under His dominion (contained in His al-Kursi). He does not experience fatigue in preserving them both. He is the High, and the Greatest.' (2:255) Thus, those who carry al-'Arsh (the Throne) are the scholars whom Allah has made to carry His knowledge. There is nothing that Allah has created in the heavens and in the earth that is out of these four that He has shown to those whom he has chosen. He showed them to His friend Ibrahim, peace be upon him, saying, 'Also, We showed (Abraham) the kingdom of the heavens and the earth to strengthen his faith.' (6:75) How can the carriers of al-'Arsh (the Throne) carry Allah when with life from Him their hearts receive life and with His light they find guidance to know Him.'"

H 332, Ch. 20, h 2
Ahmad ibn Idris has narrated from Muhammad ibn 'Abd al-Jabbar from Safwan ibn Yahya who said the following:
"Once, abu Qurrah, the narrator of *Hadith* asked me for help to meet Imam Ali, abu al-Hassan al-Rida, *'Alayhi al-Salam*. I requested the Imam to meet him and he agreed. Abu Qurrah asked the Imam about the lawful and the unlawful matters and then said, 'Do you affirm that Allah is carried?' Imam abu al-Hassan, *'Alayhi al-Salam*, replied, 'Everything in an objective case is related to another thing and is dependent. Being carried is the name for verbal defect. On the other hand, carrier is in a subjective case and it verbally is a word to convey praises and so is the expression of one who says, "Above, below, upper and lower." Allah has said, "For Him there are beautiful names, thus, call Him through those names." He (Allah) has not said anywhere in His books that He is *al-Mahmul* (Being carried). He has, in fact, said that He is the carrier in the sea and on land and the preserver of the heavens and earth from banishment. *Al-Mahmul* (being carried) are things other than Allah. It is never heard from anyone who believed in Allah and His greatness saying in his prayers *Ya Mahmul* (O the one being carried).'

"Abu Qurrah then said, 'He Himself has said, "The angels will be around the heavens and on that day eight of them will carry the Throne of your Lord above all the creatures." (69:17) Also He has said, 'Those who carry the Throne (al-'Arsh).'

"Imam abu al-Hassan, *'Alayhi al-Salam*, then said, 'Al-'Arsh (the Throne) is not Allah. Al-'Arsh is the name of knowledge and power. In al-'Arsh there is everything. Besides, He has ascribed *carrying* to things other than His Own Self. It is ascribed to a creature among His creatures. This is because He has made His creatures to worship Him through carrying His al-'Arsh (the Throne) and they are the carriers of His knowledge. There is a creature who speaks of His praise around His al-'Arsh (the Throne) and acts according to His knowledge, and the angels write down the deeds of His servants. He has made those on earth to worship Him in the form of *Tawaf* (walking around) His house. Allah has control over al-'Arsh (the Throne) as He has said, 'Allah carries al-'Arsh, those who carry it and those around it, preserves them, keeps them together and is the guardian of all souls and above and over all things.' It is not permissible to say that He is carried. He is below. It would be the only expression that would not make any sense. Thus, both the word and the meaning are destroyed.'

"Abu Qurrah then said, 'Do you then consider a false *Hadith* the *Hadith* that says, 'When Allah becomes angry His anger becomes known to the angels who carry al-'Arsh. They at such time feel the weight of His anger on their shoulders. They then bow down in prostration. When Allah's anger goes away it becomes light and the angels return to their places'?

"Imam abu al-Hassan, *'Alayhi al-Salam*, said, 'Tell me about Allah, the Most Holy, the Most High. From the time He condemned Satan until today is He not angry with Satan? When did He become happy with Satan? As you say He is still angry with Satan, his friends and followers. How dare you speak of your Lord as undergoing changes from one condition to another condition and that what happens to the creatures happens to Him also? He is the Most Glorious, the Most High. He does not banish with those who banish and does not change with those who change. He is not replaced with those who are replaced. The creatures are under His guardianship and they all are dependent on Him. He is Self-sufficient and independent of others.'"

H 333, Ch. 20, h 3

Muhammad ibn Isma'il has narrated from Fadl ibn Shadhan from Hammad ibn 'Isa from Rabi'a ibn 'Abd Allah from Fudayl ibn Yasar who said the following:

"Once I asked (Imam) abu 'Abd Allah, *'Alayhi al-Salam*, about the words of Allah, the Most Holy, the Most High, 'His al-Kursi (the Throne) encompasses the heavens and earth.' He said, 'O Fudayl everything is in al-Kursi (the Throne), the heavens and earth everything is in al-Kursi.'"

H 334, Ch. 20, h 4

Muhammad ibn Yahya has narrated from Ahmad ibn Muhammad ibn 'Isa from al-Hajjal form Tha'laba ibn Maymun from Zurara ibn 'A'yan who said the following:

"I asked (Imam) abu 'Abd Allah, *'Alayhi al-Salam*, about the meaning of the words of Allah, 'The heavens and the earth are (contained in His al-Kursi) under His dominion . . .' (2:255), do the heavens and earth contain al-Kursi or does the latter contain the former?' He said, 'It is al-Kursi that contains the heavens and earth and all things are contained in al-Kursi.'"

H 335, Ch. 20, h 5

Muhammad ibn Yahya has narrated from Ahmad ibn Muhammad from al-Hassan ibn Sa'id from Fudala ibn Ayyub from 'Abd Allah ibn Bukayr from Zurara ibn 'Ayan who said the following:

"Once I asked (Imam) abu 'Abd Allah, *'Alayhi al-Salam*, about the words of Allah, 'The heavens and the earth are contained in His al-Kursi (under His dominion) . . .' (2:255), do the heavens and earth contain al-Kursi or does the latter contains the former?' He said, 'All things are contained in al-Kursi.'"

H 336, Ch. 20, h 6

Muhammad ibn Yahya has narrated from Ahmad ibn Muhammad ibn 'Isa from Ahmad ibn Muhammad ibn abu Nasr from Muhammad ibn al-Fudayl from abu Hamza from (Imam) abu 'Abd Allah, *'Alayhi al-Salam*, who said the following:

"The Carriers of al-'Arsh and al-'Arsh of al-'Ilm (knowledge) are eight. Four of these are from us and the rest are whoever Allah chooses."

H 337, Ch. 20, h 7

Muhammad ibn al-Hassan has narrated from Sahl ibn Ziyad from ibn Mahbub from 'Abd al-Rahman ibn Kathir from Dawud al-Riqqyy who said the following:

"Once I asked (Imam) abu 'Abd Allah, *'Alayhi al-Salam*, about the words of Allah, '. . . His Throne existed on water . . . (11:8).' The Imam asked, 'What do they say about it?' I said, 'They say that al-'Arsh (the Throne) was on the water and the Lord was on top of it.' The Imam then said, 'They have said a lie. Whoever thinks as such has considered Allah as being carried and has described Him with the qualities of the creatures which means that the thing that carries Him is stronger than Him.' I then asked, 'May Allah keep my soul in your service, please explain it to me.' The Imam then said, 'Allah made water to carry His religion and His knowledge before there were the earth, the heavens, the Jinn, the human beings, the sun and the moon. When Allah willed to create the creatures He spread them before His-Self and said to them, "Who is your Lord?" The people who spoke first were the Holy Prophet and Amir al-Mu'Minin Ali and all *'A'immah* (plural of Imam), *'Alayhim al-Salam*. They all said, 'You are our Lord.' He then made them to carry the religion and the knowledge. Then He spoke to the angels saying, 'These are the carriers of My religion and knowledge, My trustees in My people and they are the ones from whom questions will be asked.' Then Allah spoke to the children of Adam saying, 'Acknowledge that Allah is the Lord and acknowledge that these people are the Authorities (of Allah) among you and that obedience to them is obligatory.' They said, 'O our Lord, we acknowledge.'

"Allah then told the angels, 'Bear witness to this.' The angels said, 'We bear witness so that they will not say tomorrow, "We were not aware of this or say that our forefathers worshipped idols before us and we were only their offspring. Will You then destroy us just because of what the followers of falsehood have done?" O Dawud, our Divine Authority over them was strongly stressed upon at the time of the covenant.'"

Chapter 21 - Al-Ruh, the Spirit

H 338, Ch. 21, h 1

A number of our people have narrated from Ahmad ibn Muhammad ibn 'Isa from ibn abu 'Umayr from 'Udhayna from al-Ahwal who said the following:

"Once I asked (Imam) abu 'Abd Allah, *'Alayhi al-Salam*, about the spirit (Ruh) which was in Adam as mentioned in the Holy Quran, '. . . when it was properly shaped and I blew My Spirit into it' (15:29). (Imam) abu 'Abd Allah replied, 'This is a created spirit and the spirit in Jesus is created.'"

H 339, Ch. 21, h 2

It is narrated from a number of our people from Ahmad ibn Muhammad ibn 'Isa from al-Hajjal from Tha'laba from Humran who said the following:

"Once I asked (Imam) abu 'Abd Allah, *'Alayhi al-Salam*, about the words of Allah, the Most Holy, the Most High, 'The spirit from Him.' (Imam) abu 'Abd Allah replied, 'It is the spirit (Ruh) from Allah created in Adam and Jesus.'"

H 340, Ch. 21, h 3

Muhammad ibn Yahya has narrated from Ahmad ibn Muhammad from Muhammad ibn Khalid from Qasim ibn 'Urwa from 'Abd al-Hamid al- Ta'i from Muhammad ibn Muslim who said the following:

"I asked (Imam) abu 'Abd Allah, *'Alayhi al-Salam*, about the words of Allah, the Most Holy, the Most High, 'I have blown My Spirit into it.' (15:29)

"The Imam replied, 'The spirit has motion like winds. It is called spirit (Ruh) because the word is a derivative of *Rih* (wind). This derivative is selected because the spirits are similar or are of the genus of the *Rih* (wind). He has spoken about it in a possessive case that refers to His Own Self; He selected it from among the other spirits just as He has said about a house from among the houses 'My house' and to a messenger from among the messengers 'My friend' and so on. All such things are created, invented, newly produced and are cherished by the Lord.'"

H 341, Ch. 21, h 4

It is narrated from a number of our people from Ahmad ibn Muhammad ibn Khalid from his father from 'Abd Allah ibn Bahr from abu Ayyub al-Khazzaz from Muhammad ibn Muslim who said the following:

"I asked (Imam) abu 'Abd Allah, *'Alayhi al-Salam*, about what people narrate that Allah created Adam in His Own form. The Imam replied, 'It is created in a newly invented form. Allah selected and chose it over the other various forms and He has spoken about it in a possessive case that refers to His Own Self just as He has done about Ka'ba and the spirit saying, 'My Ka'ba (house),' 'I have blown 'My spirit' in Him.'"

Chapter 22 - Comprehensive (Ahadith) About the Oneness of Allah

H 342, Ch. 22, h 1

Muhammad ibn abu 'Abd Allah and Muhammad ibn Yahya both in a *marfu'* manner have narrated from (Imam) abu 'Abd Allah, *'Alayhi al-Salam*, who said the following:

"Imam Amir al-Mu'minin Ali ibn abu Talib, *'Alayhi al-Salam*, mobilized people against Mu'awiya for the second time, and when people came in multitudes he stood up to give a speech. 'All praise is due to Allah, the One, only One, the Self-sufficient, the Single One Who was not from anything nor did He create from anything that was there, from something that had come into being before. He is the power, with His power He is distinct from others and the other things became manifest through His power. There is no attribute that can reach Him and He has no limit for a definition or an analogy. All the linguistic beauty and expressions fall far short of expressing His attributes. In speaking of Him all attributes prove to be misleading. The depths of the schools of thought are perplexed and confused about the wonders of His kingdom. All the comprehensive interpretations have remained far short of establishing any ground in His knowledge. The barriers of the unseen have curtained His treasured secrets. The high-flying ambitious intelligences with the ability to reach the depth of very subtle matters lose their way at the very beginning of their journey to Him. Most Holy is Allah. To Him not even the most far-reaching ambitions can reach. No deep-diving intelligence is able to comprehend Him. Most High is He Who is not subject to the effects of any calculated time or extended period or limited attributes. Glorious is He Who has no beginning for His start, destination to approach or end to diminish. Glorious is He Who is just the way He Himself has introduced. All those who speak of His praise can never praise Him fully and duly. He designed a limit for everything at the time He created it. It is due to their dissimilarity to Him and His dissimilarity to them. He is not housed in anything so that it could be said that He is within something. He is not far from anything so that it could be said that He has nothing to do with them (the creatures). He has not distanced Himself from them so that it can be said where is He? He is Most Glorious (and above such associations). He has encompassed all things through His knowledge. He has made their design firm and has enumerated them for safe preservation. Even the unseen and hidden things in the air, are not unnoticed to Him. Things deeply hidden in the darkness of black nights, all things high above in heavens and down to the lowest earth are not unnoticed to Him. For everything therein is a protector (through Him) and a guard. Everything therein has limits within something and is a limit for a certain thing.

"He is the One, the only One, the Self-sufficient, Who is not subject to the changes due to time. The creation of things never overburdens Him. He only, when willing, commands it to exist (and it comes into existence). He invented whatever He has created without any examples to follow and without experiencing any feeling of being overburdened or exhausted. All manufacturers manufacture things from something. Allah has not created whatever He has created from a thing. Every knowledgeable person learns after being ignorant. He has not been ignorant and has not learned from anyone. He has encompassed all things through His knowledge before their coming into existence and their existence has not increased anything in His knowledge. He knew them before their coming into existence just as He knows them after their coming into existence. He did not bring them into existence to strengthen His authority or for fear of banishment or reduction. He did not bring them into existence as helpers against a competing opponent, or a peer who could be of more (power) or a partner who could show greatness. He created them as creatures that required preservation and protection as subdued servants.

"Glorious is He, Who was not made tired in the creation of what He has created or the preservation of all that He has formed into being. He did not undergo in this work any weakness or exhaustion. Whatever He has created He has deemed it sufficient. He knows what He has created and created what He knew. It did not happen as a result of a new thought that He found to be a correct one nor because of some doubts that He may have found in whatever He had not yet created. It is due to His unchangeable decree, His firm knowledge and resolute command. He is the One and Only Lord and is very special in His Oneness. He is pure in His Glory and praise. He is the only One in Oneness, the Glory, in Highness, in Oneness in Praiseworthiness and in Glory and Gloriousness. He is Most High above the need of having children. He is Most Holy and clean from involvement in touching women and Most Majestic and Glorious and free from needing association with partners. In whatever He has created there is nothing to oppose Him nor is there anything in what He created to stand parallel to Him, and no one shares with Him His kingdom. He is the One and Only, the Self-sufficient, Who brings the (timeless) time to an end. He is the owner of the extended duration of time. He is the one Who is eternal of eternal Oneness before the beginning of the times and after all the changes in the creation. He is the one who never banishes or is diminished. Thus, I speak of my Lord. There is no lord besides Allah. He is the Great and of unmatched Greatness. He is the Most Majestic and of unmatched Majesty. He is the Most Glorious and of unmatched Glory. He is by far above what the unjust think Him to be.'"

Al-kulayni has said that this sermon of Imam Ali, *'Alayhi al-Salam*, is one of his well-known sermons. It has become so common that ordinary people have almost overlooked it. This sermon is a sufficient text on the subject of Oneness of Allah if one gives it careful thought and understands its contents. All Jinn and man may come together, including the prophets, to explain the subject of the Oneness of Allah but they will not be able to do as he (Imam Ali) has done. May Allah keep my soul and the souls of my parents in service for his cause. Had his explanation of this subject not been available people could never have known how to follow the path of monotheism.

Consider his words, ". . . Who was not from anything nor did He create from anything that was there from something that had come into being before." 'Who was not from anything,' is the basis for belief that He is not created. His words like *creation* and *invention* without a substance or pattern are the negation of the belief in the eternity of the creatures that says, 'Things have come into being one from the other." They (his words) also negate the belief of the dualists who say that things must come into being from some basics and through experimentation. His words "Nor did He create from anything what was there from something that had come into being before" negate such beliefs.

It is because people who believe in dualist ideas say that the creator has created the creatures either from something or from nothing.

However, to believe that He created from something is false. To say "He created things from nothing" is a contradiction. The expression "*from*" requires something existing. The expression "*nothing*" refers to non-existence. Thus, it is a contradiction.

Amir al-Mu'minin Ali, *'Alayhi al-Salam*, has come up with an expression that is clear of such complexity in a very eloquent manner. He has said, 'Nor did He create anything that was there from something that had come into being before.' He has not mentioned the *'from'* that required something existing. He negated something in saying 'Everything is created and contingent,' not that the Creator has made them out of some existing basics as those believing in dual dogma maintain so that His would not be considered a new design.

The Imam, *'Alayhi al-Salam*, then has said, 'There is no attribute that can reach Him and He has no limit for a definition or an analogy. All the linguistic beauty and expressions fall far short of expressing His attributes.' This is a negation of those who believe in similitude and analogize Him with a crystal and so forth, such as length and balance and so on. They say, 'Until the hearts do not form something from Him with certain qualities in a certain form or shape it (the heart) will not understand anything about Him. Thus, the existence of the Creator will not be proved.'

Amir al-Mu'minin Ali, *'Alayhi al-Salam*, has explained that He is one without qualities and that hearts know Him without assigning any form or limitation for Him.

The Imam then has said, '. . . to Him not even far-reaching ambitions are able to reach. No deep diving intelligence is able to comprehend Him. Most High is He Who is not subject to the effects of any calculated time or extended period or limited attributes.' Then he has said, 'He is not housed in anything so that it could be said that He is within something. He is not far from anything so that it could be said that He has nothing to do with them (the creatures).' With these two statements he has negated from Him the characteristics of the bodies and matters related to it such as distance and contrariness and related matters such as being in something or at a distance distinctly from something.

Then the Imam has said, 'He has encompassed all things through His knowledge. He has made their design firm,' which means He has control over all things with plans and decree, not by means of physical contact and so forth.

H 343, Ch. 22, h 2

Ali ibn Muhammad has narrated from Salih ibn Hammad from al-Husayn ibn Yazid from al-Hassan ibn Ali ibn abu Hamza from Ibrahim from abu 'Abd Allah, *'Alayhi al-Salam*, who said the following:

"Allah, Most Holy is His name, the Most High is His praise and the Most Glorious are His attributes. He is the Most Sacred, the Most Holy, the only One in oneness. He is eternal ,the First and the Last, the Manifest and the Hidden. There is no beginning for Him. He is the most exalted in His highness. He is the highest in power, exalted in authority, of greatest kingdom, the most bountiful and His highness is the most high. He is the One Whom no one can completely praise or know His Lordship completely. No one is able to limit Him; it is not possible to reach His reality with qualities."

H 344, Ch. 22, h 3

Ali ibn Ibrahim has narrated from al-Mukhtar ibn Muhammad ibn al-Mukhtar and Muhammad ibn al-Hassan from 'Abd Allah ibn al-Hassan al-'Alawi all from al-Fath ibn Yazid al-Jurjani who said the following:

"Once on a road on my way back from Makkah to Khurasan I met Imam abu al-Hassan, *'Alayhi al-Salam*, the 2nd who was going to Iraq, and I heard him say, 'Whoever observes piety before Allah is protected and whoever obeys Allah he is obeyed.' I calmly walked to him and on reaching him I offered my salutation of peace and he responded likewise and said, 'O Fath, whoever pleases Allah is not worried about the anger of people. Whoever causes the Creator to become angry with him he deserves that Allah subject him to the anger of the people. One can only speak of the attributes of the Creator the way He Himself has spoken about His attributes. How can a person speak of One Whom none of the senses is able to perceive? Senses remain frustrated and even the imagination is not able to comprehend Him. No one's sharp guessing ability can reach Him in any way or manner. No eye can limit Him in any manner. He is far above the description of those who speak of His attributes. He is above the praise of those who speak of His praise. He is far in His nearness and is near in His being far. He in His farness is near and is far in His nearness. He has given condition to the conditions and has made space for the space. No one can say that He is in a condition or is somewhere. No one can say about Him 'Where' and 'How' because He is by far high above the conditions and places.'"

H 345, Ch. 22, h 4

Muhammad ibn abu 'Abd Allah in *marfu'* manner has narrated from (Imam) abu 'Abd Allah, *'Alayhi al-Salam*, who said the following:

"Once Imam Amir al-Mu'minin Ali ibn abu Talib, *'Alayhi al-Salam*, addressed the people in the Mosque of Kufa from the pulpit and a man called Dhi'lab, a very good orator and brave in heart said, 'O Amir al-Mu'minin, have you seen your Lord?' The Imam replied, 'Fie upon you, O Dhi'lab, how would I worship a lord whom I do not see?

"The man said, 'O Amir al-Mu'minin how have you seen Him?' The Imam said, 'Fie up on you, O Dhi'lab, the eyes are not able to see Him physically but it is the hearts that see Him through the reality of belief. O Dhi'lab, my Lord is Subtle in subtleties but cannot be described by means of subtle matters. My Lord is Great but cannot be described by means of greatness. His greatness surpasses all greatness but he cannot be described by means of any such greatness. He is Glorious in His Glory but He cannot be described in terms of intensity. He is before everything and it cannot be said that something was before Him. He will be after all things but it cannot be said that there will be something after Him. He willed the existence of things but not by means of first thinking about it. He comprehends things but not with a great deal of effort. He is in all things but is not mixed with them, nor is He separate from them. He is clearly manifest but not with contacts and changes. He shines but not in the form of being found out with eyesight. He is far but not in the form of distance. He is near but not in the form of nearness. He is very fine but not in the form of physical fineness. He exists but not after nothingness. He acts but not because of being forced. He measures things but not by means of movement. He wills but not by means of thinking. He hears but not with tools. He sees but not with instruments. He is not contained in place and held up in times. Attributes do not limit Him and slumber does not seize Him. His Being was before the time and His existence was before nothingness. He was before eternity. His giving the sense of awareness proves that He does not need tools of sensing. His giving substance to the substances is proof that His Self is not a substance. The existence of a contrary to everything is proof that there is nothing contrary to Him. His giving comparability to things is proof that there is nothing similar to Him. He has made the light contrary to the darkness, the wetness to the dryness, the harshness to the softness and the coldness to heat. He combines the separating ones and separates their closeness. The separation among things is evidence of the existence of the One Who causes separation in them and their combination is evidence of the existence of the One Who combines them. It is just as Allah has said; 'We have created everything in pairs so that perhaps you may take heed.' (51:49)

"He has made a distinction between the before and the after to show that there is no before and after for Him. The instincts show that the One who created the instincts Himself has no instinct. The time is evidence that there is no timing for the One Who made the time. His hiding things from each other is evidence that nothing hides them from their Creator. He was the Lord when there was nothing to enjoy His Lordship. He was to be worshipped when there was no worshipper. He had the knowledge when there was nothing to know. He was hearing when there was nothing to hear.'"

H 346, Ch. 22, h 5
Ali ibn Muhammad has narrated from Sahl ibn Ziyad from Shabab al-Sayrafi called Muhammad ibn al-Walid from Ali ibn Sayf from 'Amira who has said that Isma'il ibn Qutayba said the following:
"Once 'Isa ibn al-Shalqan and I went to see (Imam) abu 'Abd Allah, *'Alayhi al-Salam*. The Imam said, 'It is strange that a group of people ascribe to Amir al-Mu'minin Ali, *'Alayhi al-Salam*, certain things that he had never said. Amir al-Mu'minin addressed people in Kufa in the following words:

"All praise is due to Allah Who inspired His servants with His praise and designed their nature in a way that would give them the desire to acknowledge His Lordship. It is He Who guides people through His creation to His Own existence and His creatures are evidence of His eternity. The fact that His creatures are similar is evidence that there is nothing similar to Him. His signs are evidence of His great power. His Own Self prohibits acceptance of descriptions. His being seen with the eyes and His being comprehended in the imagination are prohibited as well. There is no time limit for His being in existence and there is no final destination for Him. Awareness cannot contain Him and coverings cannot cover Him. The curtain between Him and His creatures is His creating them. It (curtain) is impossibility in His case of what is possible in the essence of the creatures (such as weakness and so forth) and possibility of what is impossible in His case. It is also because of the difference between the Creator and the created, the Creator of limits and the limited and the Lord and the worshippers. He is One without being

120

a unit of a particular kind. He is the Creator but not in terms of motion. He is seeing but not by means of devices and gagets. He is hearing but not with distinguishing instruments. He observes but not by means of touching. He is hidden but not with covering. He is manifest and distinct but not due to lapse of distance. His eternity is beyond the reach of thinking and a stop for the aims of the intelligence. His reality has worn out the ability of sight and His Own Self has uprooted the fast spreading vines of imaginations. Whoever tries to describe Allah has thought of Him as limited and whoever considers Him limited has enumerated Him and whoever enumerates Him has invalidated His eternity. Whoever asks where is He, has considered Him as having an end. Whoever says on what is He, has considered Him as distanced. Whoever says wherein is He, has considered Him contained in something.'"

H 347, Ch. 22, h 6
The above text is narrated from Muhammad ibn al-Husayn from Salih ibn Hamza from Fath ibn 'Abd Allah Mawla Banu Hashim who said the following:

"Once I wrote to abu Ibrahim, *'Alayhi al-Salam*, asking him about the Oneness of Allah. He wrote back to me in his own handwriting, 'All praise is due to Allah, Who inspires His servants with His praise.' He mentioned in it facts similar to those in the *Hadith* of Sahl ibn Ziyad (No. h5 above) . . . 'His essence has uprooted the fast (spreading) vines of imagination' with the following addition, 'The first thing in His religion is to know Him. A perfect knowledge about Him is to know that He is One. A perfect belief in His Oneness is to negate all attributes from Him. Every attribute is evidence that it is different from what it is attributed to, that everything to which an attribute is ascribed is evidence that it is something other than the attribute. Both the attribute and whatever is attributed to are evidence that there are two things, which invalidate His being eternal. Whoever attributes a quality to Allah's Self, has considered Him limited. Whoever considers Him limited has enumerated Him and whoever enumerates Him has considered His eternity invalid. Whoever says, "How is He?" He has considered Him describable. Whoever says, "In what is He?" He has considered Him as contained. Whoever says, "On what is He?" He has become ignorant of Him. Whoever says. "Where is He?" He has considered a certain place without Him. Whoever says, "What is He?" He has attributed certain qualities to Him. Whoever says, "Up to what limit is He?" He has considered Him as having an end. He had knowledge before there was anything to know. He was the Creator before there were any creatures. He was the Lord before there was a worshipper. Thus is our Lord spoken of and is beyond the way others speak of Him.'"

H 348, Ch. 22, h 7
It is narrated from a number of our people from Ahmad ibn Muhammad ibn Khalid from his father from Ahmad ibn al-Nadr and others whom he mentioned from 'Amr ibn Thabit from a man whom he mentioned from abu Ishaq al-Subay'i from Harith al-A'war who said the following:

"Once Amir al-Mu'minin Ali, *'Alayhi al-Salam*, gave a speech in the afternoon and people liked it very much because of the beautiful manner in which Allah, the Most Holy, the Most High, was praised thereby. Abu Ishaq has said, 'I asked al-Harith, "Did you memorize the sermon?" Al-Harith said, 'Yes, I did write it down.' He then dictated it to us from his book. 'All praise is due to Allah, Who does not die and Whose wonders do not end. It is because everyday He has a task in the form of the invention of something that did not exist. It is He Who has no children so that He would share others in Majesty and He is not the child of others so that He would be inherited and Himself vanish. Imagination cannot comprehend Him to figure Him out in a certain form of similitude. The eyes have not perceived Him so that after changing position He would also change. It is He for Whose beginning there is no end, nor will there be any final destination for His being the last. It is He before Whom there is no time, and is not preceded by any previous era. He does not fall subject to defects of reduction or addition. Attributes for direction, place, and instruments do not apply to Him. It is He Who knows all the hidden matters and has surpassed all intelligence by what is evident in His creatures of plans and maintenance. It is He about Whom the prophets were asked and they did not speak of Him in terms of limits and parts. They spoke of His acts and showed people His signs. The intelligence of thinkers cannot deny Him; the One Who has created the heavens and earth and all that is in them and between them is the Creator and no one is able to stand up to His power. It is He, Who is different from the creatures and there is nothing similar to Him. It is He Who has created the creatures for His worship and has given them the ability to obey Him. He has removed all their excuses (by means of the capabilities that He has placed in them), and by sending His authority (in the prophets and 'A'immah (pl. of Imam)) among them (people) so that after knowing the authority whoever perishes, perish or gain salvation whoever likes to gain salvation. Benevolent is Allah to begin and to repeat.

"Then, Allah, to whom all praise is due, introduced praise for His Own Self. He ended the affairs of the world and the coming of the next life with praise for His Own Self saying, 'He has judged among them with the truth and it is said, 'All praise is due to Allah, Lord of the worlds.'

"All praise is due to Allah, Who has dressed up with greatness but without a body, Who has the gown of Majesty and Glory which has no similarity. It is He Who has control over the Throne without losing such authority. He is exalted above the creatures but without being far from them or being in touch with them (physically). He has no limit to reach nor there is anything similar to Him to help know Him better. All things are humble before His power and might. All things, although great, are small before Him. All things respect His Greatness. They obey His authority and Majesty. Glimpses of eyes are weak and exhausted in trying to comprehend Him. The imaginations of the creatures fall far short of describing Him. He is the first before all things and there was no one before Him. He is the last after all things and there is no 'After' for Him. He has control over all things with might. He observes all places without moving thereto. No touching touches Him and no sense senses Him. He is the Lord in the heavens and the Lord on earth. He is All-wise and All-knowing. He has given firm shape and form to His creatures the way He willed but not with following previous examples or experiencing any fatigue in the creation of the things that He has created. In the cases of the two great and heavy creatures, mankind and Jinn, He began what He wanted to begin and invented what He wanted to invent, and the way He willed.

He did what He did so that they would know through such evidence His Lordship. He made it possible for them to obey Him.

"We thank Him with all of His praise for all of His bounties. We ask Him for His guidance to give us wisdom in our affairs. We seek refuge with Him from the evil of our sinful deeds and ask Him to forgive our sins that we may have committed before. We testify that no one deserves to be obeyed and worshipped except Allah and that Muhammad, *'Alayhi al-Salam*, is His servant and messenger. He sent him with truth as a prophet, as a sign of His existence and a guide to Him. We found guidance through him from straying and are saved through him from ignorance. Whoever obeys Allah and His messenger has indeed gained a great success and has earned a great reward. Whoever disobeys Allah and His messenger has indeed suffered a clear loss and is subject to a painful punishment. Do your best to succeed in obedience, listening, sincerity, good advice and proper support. Be helpful to yourselves to keep on the straight path and shun the detested matters. Deal among yourselves with truth and cooperate thereby with me. Hold back the unjust and feebleminded hands. Make others do good deeds and prevent them from committing unlawful deeds. Appreciate excellence of the excelling people. May Allah protect you and us through guidance and make you and us steadfast in piety. I ask Allah for forgiveness for myself and for you."

Chapter 23 - Miscellaneous Ahadith

H 349, Ch. 23, h 1
Muhammad ibn Yahya has narrated from Ahmad ibn Muhammad ibn 'Isa from Ali ibn al-Nu'man from Sayf ibn 'Umayr from those whom he mentioned from al-Harith ibn al-Mughirah al-Nasri who said the following:
"Once a person asked (Imam) abu 'Abd Allah, *'Alayhi al-Salam*, about the meaning of the words of Allah, the Most Holy, the Most High, 'everything will be destroyed except the face of Allah . . .' (28:88)

"The Imam, *'Alayhi al-Salam*, asked, 'What do they say about it?' I replied, 'They say that everything will perish except the 'Face' of Allah.' The Imam said, 'Glory belongs to Allah. What they say is monstrous. What is meant by 'Face' is that aspect of Allah's relation with people through which they (persons of the highest degree of excellence) establish belief in Him.'"

H 350, Ch. 23, h 2
A number of our people have narrated from Ahmad ibn Muhammad ibn Khalid from Ahmad ibn Muhammad ibn abu Nasr from Safwan al-Jammal from (Imam) abu 'Abd Allah, *'Alayhi al-Salam*, the following:
"Once I asked (Imam) abu 'Abd Allah, *'Alayhi al-Salam*, about the meaning of the words of Allah, the Most Holy, the Most High, 'everything will be destroyed except the face of Allah. . . .' (28:88)

"The Imam said, 'It means whoever comes to Allah through obeying His commandments, i.e. following Prophet Muhammad, *'Alayhi al-Salam*, is the 'Face' (the aspect of Allah's relation with people) of Allah that does not perish.

So also are His words, "One who obeys the Messenger has certainly obeyed Allah. . . .'" (4:80)

H 351, Ch. 23, h 3

Muhammad ibn Yahya has narrated from Ahmad ibn Muhammad ibn 'Isa from Muhammad ibn Sinan from abu Salam al-Nakhkhas from certain persons of our people from (Imam) abu Ja'far, *'Alayhi al-Salam*, who said the following:

"We (family of Prophet Muhammad) are the *al-Mathani* (the double) that Allah gave to Prophet Muhammad, *'Alayhi al-Salam*. We are the *Wajhu Allah* (face of Allah, meaning a certain aspect of Allah's relation with people) that moves among you on earth. We are the eyes of Allah (overseers or observers from the side of Allah) in His creatures. We are the hands of Allah that are open with blessings for His servants. Those who wanted to know us have known us. There are people who are ignorant about us, they are ignorant of us and of the leadership of the pious people."

H 352, Ch. 23, h 4

Al-Husayn ibn Muhammad al-Ash'ari and Muhammad ibn Yahya both have narrated from Ahmad ibn Ishaq from Su'dan ibn Muslim from Mu'awiya ibn 'Ammar from abu 'Abd Allah, *'Alayhi al-Salam*, who said the following:

"About the words of Allah, the Majestic, the Glorious, 'Allah has the most blessed (beautiful) names, you should address Him in your worship by these names. . . .,' (7:180) the Imam said, 'We, I swear by Allah, are the most blessed names of Allah without which Allah does not accept any of the good deeds of His servants unless they know us properly.'"

H 353, Ch. 23, h 5

Muhammad ibn abu 'Abd Allah ibn Muhammad ibn Isma'il has narrated from al-Husayn ibn al-Hassan from Bakr ibn Salih from al-Hassan ibn Sa'id from al-Haytham ibn 'Abd Allah from Marwan ibn Salih who has said that (Imam) abu 'Abd Allah has said the following:

"Allah created us and made it well. He gave us our form and formed it well. He made us His eyes among His servants and His speaking tongue in His creatures. He made us His open hands over His servants with kindness and mercy. He has made us his face through which He is approached and his door that shows the way leading to Him. He made us His treasurers in the heavens and on earth. Through us the trees give fruit and the fruits ripen and the canals flow. Through us the skies send rain and plants grow on earth. Through our worship Allah is worshipped and were we not there Allah would not have been worshipped."

H 354, Ch. 23, h 6

Muhammad ibn Yahya has narrated from Muhammad ibn al-Husayn from Muhammad ibn Isma'il ibn Bazi'a from his uncle, Hamza ibn Bazi'a from abu 'Abd Allah, *'Alayhi al-Salam*, who said the following:

"About the words of Allah, the Majestic, the Glorious, 'When they invoked Our anger, We took revenge on them, . . .' (43:55) the Imam said, 'Allah, the Most Holy, the Most High, does not become frustrated the way we do. But He has created friends for His Own Self who become frustrated and at times become happy. They are created. They worship (Allah). He has designed their happiness to be His Own happiness and their anger as His Own anger. It is because He has assigned them to guide people to Him and serve as proof of His existence. For this reason such conditions belong to them. This (anger) does not reach Allah the way it reaches people. The meaning is that just mentioned. He has also said, 'Whoever humiliates My friends such people have declared war against Me with challenge.' He has also said, 'One who obeys the Messenger has certainly obeyed Allah . . .' (4:80) 'Those who pledge obedience to you are, in fact, pledging obedience to Allah.' 'The hands of Allah are above their hands. . . .' (48:10) All of these and other similar cases mean what I just said. The same is the case with anger and happiness and other such matters. Had it been possible for frustration and anger to reach Allah, one could have said that one day Allah may vanish altogether. It is because if anger and frustration reached Him, changes also could take place in Him, and thus He would not remain safe from banishment. As a result, there would exist no distinction between the being and the Designer, between the Almighty and those subject to such might and power. No distinction would exist between the created and the Creator. Allah is by far above such things, and is the Most High and Most Great. He is the Creator of all things not because He needed them. If it (the creation) would be without a need on His part then it would be impossible to limit Him with limits and conditions. Note this if Allah, the Most High, would will it to be so.'"

H 355, Ch. 23, h 7

A number of our people have narrated from Ahmad ibn Muhammad ibn abu Nasr from Muhammad ibn Humran from Aswad ibn Sa'id who said the following:

"Once I was in the presence of (Imam) abu Ja'far, *'Alayhi al-Salam*, who began to speak without any question from me. 'We are the authority of Allah. We are the doors to Allah. We are the tongues of Allah. We are the face of Allah. We are the eyes of Allah in His people. We are the authority in the commandments of Allah among His servants.'"

H 356, Ch. 23, h 8

Muhammad ibn Yahya has narrated from Muhammad ibn al-Husayn from Ahmad ibn abu Nasr from Hassan al-Jammal who said the following:

"Hashim ibn abu 'Ummarah al-Janbiy reported to him this. 'I heard Amir al-Mu'minin Ali ibn abu Talib, *'Alayhi al-Salam*, saying, "I am the eyes of Allah. I am the hand of Allah. I am the side of Allah. I am the door to Allah."'"

H 357, Ch. 23, h 9

Muhammad ibn Yahya has narrated from Muhammad ibn al-Husayn from Muhammad ibn Isma'il ibn Bazi'a from his uncle Hamza ibn Bazi'a from Ali ibn Suwayd from abu al-Hassan Musa ibn Ja'far, *'Alayhi al-Salam*, who has said the following:

"About the words of Allah, the Majestic, the Glorious, 'Woe to me because of my failure to fulfill my duties toward the side of Allah, . . .' (39:56) the Imam, *'Alayhi al-Salam*, said that *the side of Allah* is Amir al-Mu'minin Ali ibn abu Talib, *'Alayhi al-Salam*, and so are the successors to the high position (succession to the Holy Prophet) until the matters will reach to the last one among them.'"

H 358, Ch. 23, h 10

Al-Husayn ibn Muhammad has narrated from Mu'alla ibn Muhammad from Muhammad ibn Jumhur from Ali ibn al-Salt from al-Hakam and Isma'il sons of Habib from Burayd al-'Ijli who said the following:

"Once I heard (Imam) abu Ja'far, *'Alayhi al-Salam*, saying, 'Through us Allah is worshipped. Through us Allah is known. Through us belief in the Oneness of Allah, the Most Holy, the Most High, is established. Muhammad is the Hijab (curtain) of Allah, the Most Holy, the Most High.'"

H 359, Ch. 23, h 11

Certain persons of our people have narrated from Muhammad ibn 'Abd Allah from 'Abd al-Wahhab ibn Bishr from Musa ibn Qadim from Sulayman from Zurara from abu Ja'far, *'Alayhi al-Salam*, who said the following:

"Once I asked the Imam (abu Ja'far) about the meaning of the words of Allah, the Most Holy, the Most High, 'They (children of Israel) did not wrong Us but they wronged themselves.' (2:57) The Imam said, 'Allah is Most Great and Majestic and Mighty above being wronged. However, He has mixed us up with His Own Self. He has considered the wrong done to us as being done to Him and His Own authority as our authority as He has said, 'Only Allah, His Messenger, and the true believers who are steadfast in prayer and pay alms, while they kneel during prayer, are your guardians.' (5:55) It (true believers) refers to every Imam from us. Allah has also said in another passage, 'They did not wrong Us but wronged themselves.' (2:57) Then he mentioned a similar statement.'"

Chapter 24 - Al-Bada' (New Manifesto)

H 360, Ch. 24, h 1

Muhammad ibn Yahya has narrated from Ahmad ibn Muhammad ibn 'Isa from al-Hajjal from abu Ishaq Tha'laba from Zurara ibn A'yan from one of the two Imams who said the following:

"Allah is best worshipped with belief in *al-Bada'*. (This fact also is stated) in another *Hadith* narrated from ibn abu 'Umayr from Hisham ibn Salim from abu 'Abd Allah, *'Alayhi al-Salam*, who has said this: 'Allah's Greatness is not realized as admirably as it is realized with belief in *al-Bada'*.'"

H 361, Ch. 24, h 2

Ali ibn Ibrahim has narrated from his father from ibn abu 'Umayr from Hisham ibn Salim and Hafs ibn al-Bakhtari and others from abu 'Abd Allah, *'Alayhi al-Salam*, who has said the following:

"About the words of Allah, 'Allah establishes or effaces whatever He wants, . . . ' (13:39) the Imam, *'Alayhi al-Salam*, said, 'Can anything be effaced without being established? Can anything be established unless it is after its non-existence?'"

H 362, Ch. 24, h 3

Ali has narrated from his father from ibn abu 'Umayr from Hisham ibn Salim from Muhammad ibn Muslim from abu 'Abd Allah, *'Alayhi al-Salam*, who said the following:

"Allah did not send any prophet without three conditions. Acknowledgement (a) of being His servant and worshipper, (b) that there is nothing like Him and (c) that Allah may bring forward whatever He so wills and may take back whatever He so wills."

H 363, Ch. 24, h 4

Muhammad ibn Yahya has narrated from Ahmad ibn Muhammad from ibn Faddal from ibn Bukayr from Zurara from Humran from abu Ja'far, *'Alayhi al-Salam*, who has said the following:

"Once I asked the Imam about the words of Allah, the Majestic, the Glorious, 'It is He who has created you from clay to live for a life-time and the span of your life is only known to Him . . .' (6:2) The Imam said, 'There are two appointed times. One is a definite time and the other is the conditional one.'"

H 364, Ch. 24, h 5

Ahmad ibn Mihran has narrated from 'Abd al-'Azim ibn 'Abd Allah al-Hassani from Ali ibn Asbat from Khalaf ibn Hammad from ibn Muskan from Malik al-Juhanni who said the following:

"Once I asked Imam abu 'Abd Allah, *'Alayhi al-Salam*, about the words of Allah, the Most High, 'Does he not remember that We created him when he did not exist?' (19:67) The Imam said, 'It means that he did not exist in a definite or in the form of a being.' I asked the Imam about the words of Allah, 'There was certainly a time when there was no mention of the human being.' (76:1) The Imam said, 'It was definite but not mentioned.'"

H 365, Ch. 24, h 6

Muhammad ibn Isma'il has narrated from al-Fadl ibn Shadhan from Hammad ibn 'Isa from Rabi' ibn 'Abd Allah from al-Fudayl ibn Yasar who said the following:

"I heard abu Ja'far, *'Alayhi al-Salam*, saying, 'There are two kinds of knowledge. One kind is hidden with Allah of which no one of His creatures has any knowledge. The other kind of knowledge is the knowledge He has taught to His angels and His messengers. Whatever knowledge He has given to His angels and messengers it will come to pass. He will not speak a lie nor will He let His angels or messengers do so. The knowledge that is hidden with Him, of this He brings forward whatever He would will and takes back whatever would He so will and would establish whatever would He so will.'"

H 366, Ch. 24, h 7

Through the same chain of narrators it is narrated from Hammad from Rib'i from Fudayl who said the following:

"I heard abu Ja'far, *'Alayhi al-Salam*, saying, 'Of the issues there are those that Allah has withheld. He brings forward whatever He wills and withholds whatever He wills.'"

H 367, Ch. 24, h 8

A number of our people have narrated from Ahmad ibn Muhammad ibn 'Isa from ibn abu 'Umayr from Ja'far ibn 'Uthman from Sama'a from abu Basir and Wuhayb ibn Hafs from abu Basir from abu 'Abd Allah, *'Alayhi al-Salam*, who said the following:

"Allah has two kinds of knowledge. There is the hidden and treasured knowledge of which no one has any information except Allah. From this knowledge comes *al-Bada'*. There is the knowledge that Allah has given to His angels, His messengers and His prophets and we know this knowledge."

H 368, Ch. 24, h 9

Muhammad ibn Yahya has narrated from Ahmad ibn Muhammad from al-Husayn ibn Sa'id from al-Hassan ibn Mahbub from 'Abd Allah ibn Sinan from abu 'Abd Allah, *'Alayhi al-Salam*, who said the following:

"No new manifesto emerges before Allah in a thing except that He knew it before *al-Bada'* (new manifesto) would take place."

H 369, Ch. 24, h 10

It is narrated from him from Ahmad from al-Hassan ibn Ali ibn Faddal from Dawud ibn Farqad from 'Amr ibn 'Uthman al-Juhanni from abu 'Abd Allah, *'Alayhi al-Salam*, who said the following:

"*Al-Bada'* does not take place to Allah out of ignorance."

H 370, Ch. 24, h 11

Ali ibn Ibrahim has narrated from Muhammad ibn 'Isa from Yunus from Mansur ibn Hazim who said the following:

"Once I asked abu 'Abd Allah, *'Alayhi al-Salam*, 'Can anything happen today that was not in the knowledge of Allah the day before?' The Imam said, 'No, this does not happen. Whoever may say so Allah will make him to suffer a great deal.' I then said, 'Do you consider that all that were there and all that will take place up to the Day of Judgment are all in the knowledge of Allah?' The Imam said, 'Yes, it was so before He created the creatures.'"

H 371, Ch. 24, h 12

Ali ibn Muhammad has narrated from Yunus from Malik al-Juhanni who said the following:

"I heard (Imam) abu 'Abd Allah, *'Alayhi al-Salam*, saying, 'Had the people known of the reward in the belief in *al-Bada'* no weakness could appear in their words about it.'"

H 372, Ch. 24, h 13

A number of our people have narrated from Ahmad ibn Muhammad ibn Khalid from certain persons of our people from Muhammad ibn 'Amr al-Kufi brother of Yahya from Murazim ibn Hakim who said the following:

"I heard abu 'Abd Allah, *'Alayhi al-Salam*, saying, 'No prophet has ever proclaimed prophecy before acknowledging before Allah five things: Acknowledgement of *al-Bada'*, the wish of Allah, the prostration, affirmation of worshipping, and obedience.'"

H 373, Ch. 24, h 14

Through the same chain of narrators it is narrated from Ahmad ibn Muhammad from Ja'far ibn Muhammad from Yunus from Jahm ibn abu Jahm from the one he narrated from abu 'Abd Allah, *'Alayhi al-Salam*, who said the following:

"Allah, the Most Holy, the Most High, informed Prophet Muhammad, *'Alayhi al-Salam*, about all that was there from the beginning of the world and that which will be there to the end of the world. He informed him about what is definite in them and made an exception about what is otherwise."

H 374, Ch. 24, h 15

Ali ibn Ibrahim has narrated from his father from al-Rayyan ibn al-Salt who said the following:

"Once I heard (Imam) al-Rida, *'Alayhi al-Salam*, saying, 'Allah never sent a prophet without the law that prohibits the use of wine and without belief in *al-Bada.*'"

H 375, Ch. 24, h 16

Al-Husayn ibn Muhammad has narrated from Mu'alla ibn Muhammad who said the following:

"Once the 'Alim (Imam) was asked, 'How is the knowledge of Allah? He replied, 'He knew, He wanted, He willed, He measured, He decreed and He allowed it to happen. He allowed happening what He had decreed and decreed what He had measured and measured what He had willed. From His knowledge was His wish. From His wish was His will and from His will was His measuring. From His measuring was His decree and from His decree was His allowing happening. Knowledge is before the wish. The wish is the second and the will is the third. Measuring happens upon the decree to allow it to happen. For Allah, the Most Holy, the Most High, there is al-Bada' (new manifesto) in whatever He knows when He wants and in the will to measure things. When the decree is issued to allow it to happen then there is no al-Bada'. Thus, the knowledge of the object of knowledge is before it comes into existence. The wish for the object of wishing is before its substance. The will in what is willed is before it is established. The measuring of these objects of knowledge is before their details and before their reaching the stage of being manifested in their substance and time. The decree to allow it to happen is decisive in the acts with the body and what is perceived with the senses of the colored having smells and weight and measurement and things walking, crawling and creeping on earth of man, Jinn, birds, beasts and others that are comprehended with the senses.

"Al-Bada' happens with Allah in the matters that have no substance. When substance and the understood meaning appear then there is no al-Bada'. Allah does whatever He wants. With knowledge He knew things before their coming into existence. With the wish He recognized their qualities and their limits. He invented them before they became manifest. With the will He distinguished them in their colors and qualities. With measurement He measured their sustenance and made their beginning and end. With the decree He made public for people their places and guided them thereto. With allowing them to happen He explained the reasons and made the affairs public. This is how the planning and measuring of the Most Majestic, the All-knowing is.'"

Chapter 25 - There is Nothing in the Heavens and on Earth Without Seven Characteristics

H 376, Ch. 25, h 1

A number of our people have narrated from Ahmad ibn Muhammad ibn Khalid from his father and Muhammad ibn Yahya from Ahmad ibn Muhammad ibn 'Isa from al-Husayn ibn Sa'id and Muhammad ibn Khalid both from Fudala ibn Ayyub from Muhammad ibn 'Ammara from Hariz ibn 'Abd Allah and 'Abd Allah ibn Muskan both from abu 'Abd Allah, *'Alayhi al-Salam*, who said the following:

"There is nothing in the heavens and on earth without these seven characteristics: the wish, the will, the measure, the decree, the permission, the record, and the duration. Whoever thinks that he can do without any one of these has become an unbeliever."

Ali ibn Ibrahim has narrated from his father from Muhammad ibn Hafs from Muhammad ibn 'Ammara from Hariz ibn 'Abd Allah and ibn Muskan a similar *Hadith*.

H 377, Ch. 25, h 2
He (Ali) has narrated it from his father from Muhammad ibn Khalid from Zakariya ibn 'Imran from abu al-Hassan Musa ibn Ja'far, *'Alayhi al-Salam*, who said the following:
"There is nothing in the heaven or on earth without seven: the decree, the measure, the will, the wish, the record (book), the duration and the permission. Whoever thinks something else has certainly spoken a lie against Allah or has rejected Allah, the Most Holy, the Most High."

Chapter 26 - Wish and Will

H 378, Ch. 26, h 1
Ali ibn Muhammad ibn 'Abd Allah has narrated from Ahmad ibn abu 'Abd Allah from his father from Muhammad ibn Sulayman al-Daylami from Ali ibn Ibrahim al-Hashimi who said the following:
"I heard abu al-Hassan Musa ibn Ja'far, *'Alayhi al-Salam*, saying, 'There can be nothing until Allah wishes it to be, wills, measures and decrees.' I asked, 'What is the meaning of *wish* (Sha'a')?' The Imam replied, 'It is to begin the act.' I asked, 'What is the meaning of measure (Qaddara)?' The Imam replied, 'It is measuring the length and the width of something.' I asked, 'What is the meaning of decree (Qada)?' The Imam replied, 'When He decrees He lets it happen and this is when its happening becomes unavoidable.'"

H 379, Ch. 26, h 2
Ali ibn Ibrahim has narrated from Muhammad ibn 'Isa from Yunus ibn 'Abd al-Rahman from Aban from abu Basir who said the following:
"Once I asked abu 'Abd Allah, *'Alayhi al-Salam*, 'Has (Allah) Wished, Willed, Measured and Decreed?' The Imam said, 'Yes.' I asked, 'Has He loved?' The Imam said, 'No.' I asked, 'How is it that He wished, willed, measured and decreed but did not love?' The Imam said, 'This is how it has come to us.'"

H 380, Ch. 26, h 3
Ali ibn Ibrahim has narrated from his father from Ali ibn Ma'bad from Wasil ibn Sulayman from 'Abd Allah ibn Sinan who said the following:
"I heard (Imam) abu 'Abd Allah, *'Alayhi al-Salam*, saying, 'Allah commanded but did not want. He wanted but did not command. He commanded Satan to prostrate but He did not want it (Satan to prostrate). had He wanted, Satan would have prostrated. He prohibited Adam from eating of the tree and wanted him to eat. Had He not wanted, he would not eat.'"

H 381, Ch. 26, h 4
Ali ibn Ibrahim has narrated from al-Mukhtar ibn Muhammad al-Hamadani and Muhammad ibn al-Hassan from 'Abd Allah ibn al-Hassan al-'Alawi both from al-Fath ibn Yazid al-Jurjani from abu al-Hassan, *'Alayhi al-Salam*, who said the following:
"Allah has two kinds of will and wish. He has a definite will and an intended will. He prohibits but He wants it. He commands but He does not want it. Consider that He prohibited Adam and his spouse from eating of the tree but He wanted them to eat. Had He not wanted their wish would not have materialized against Allah's wish. He commanded Ibrahim to slaughter Ishaq (Isaac) but He did not want it to happen. Had He wanted it the wish of Ibrahim would not have materialized against the wish of Allah, the Most High."

H 382, Ch. 26, h 5

Ali ibn Ibrahim has narrated from his father from Ali ibn Ma'bad from Durust ibn abu Mansur from Fudayl ibn Yasar who said the following:

"I heard (Imam) abu 'Abd Allah, *'Alayhi al-Salam*, saying, 'He wanted and willed and did not love and did not agree. He wanted something not to happen except that in His knowledge it was to happen. He willed in the same way. He did not love it to be said, 'The third of the three' (Trinity) and He did not agree that His servants become unbelievers.'"

H 383, Ch. 26, h 6

Muhammad ibn Yahya has narrated from Ahmad ibn Muhammad ibn abu Nasr who said that (Imam) abu al-Hassan al-Rida has said the following:

"Allah said, 'O son of Adam through My wish you came into existence and it is you who wish for yourself whatever you wish. Through My power you fulfill your obligations and through My bounties you receive strength to disobey Me. I made you to hear and see and be strong. Whatever good you receive is from Allah and whatever evil afflicts you is from your own self. It is because I deserve credit in your good deeds and you are held responsible for your bad deeds. This is because I am not asked what I do but they are held responsible for what they do.'"

Chapter 27 - Test and Trial

H 384, Ch. 27, h 1

Ali ibn Ibrahim ibn Hashim has narrated from Muhammad ibn 'Isa from Yunus ibn 'Abd al-Rahman from Hamza ibn al-Tayyar from (Imam) abu 'Abd Allah, *'Alayhi al-Salam*, who said the following:

"There is no reduction or expansion but that Allah therein has a wish, decree and testing."

H 385, Ch. 27, h 2

A number of our people have narrated from Ahmad ibn Muhammad ibn Khalid from his father from Fadala ibn Ayyub from Hamza ibn Muhammad al-Tayyar from abu 'Abd Allah, *'Alayhi al-Salam*, who has said the following:

"There is nothing in which there is expansion or reduction of the matters that Allah has commanded or has prohibited without the fact that Allah, the Most Holy, the Most High, therein has a decree and a testing."

Chapter 28 - Happiness and Misery

H 386, Ch. 28, h 1

Muhammad ibn Isma'il has narrated from al-Fadl ibn Shadhan from Safwan ibn Yahya from Mansur ibn Hazim from Imam abu 'Abd Allah, *'Alayhi al-Salam*, who said the following:

"Allah created happiness and misery before He created the creatures. Whomever Allah has created fortunate He never becomes angry with him even though he may do bad deeds.

"He dislikes his deeds but not his own self. If he is an unfortunate one He never loves him even if he does good deeds. He loves his deeds but not his own self because of what he will end up doing. If Allah loves something He never dislikes it and if He disliked something He would never love it."

H 387, Ch. 28, h 2

Ali ibn Muhammad in a *marfu'* manner has narrated from Shu'ayb al-'Aqarqufi from abu Basir who said the following:

"Once I was in the presence of (Imam) abu 'Abd Allah, *'Alayhi al-Salam*, when a certain person asked him saying, 'May Allah keep my soul in service for your cause, O great-great-great-great-grandson of the Messenger of Allah, *'Alayhi al-Salam*, wherefrom do misery and misfortune take hold of the people committing sins? Consequently, Allah in His knowledge decrees suffering for them due to their (bad) deeds.'

"The Imam said, 'It is the judgment of Allah, the Most Holy, the Most High, and no one has the right (to oppose it). When He passed such judgment He gave the people of love the ability to know Him. He then relieved them of the hardships of deeds by means of the reality of what they are capable of. He gave the people of sins the ability to commit sins due to His early knowledge about them and His denying them the power to accept from Him. Thus, they (their condition) coincide with what is in His knowledge about them and they remain unable to do things that can save them from His punishment. It is because His knowledge is more preferred in the reality of judgment and acknowledgement and this is what is meant by 'He wanted what He wanted and it is His secret'"

H 388, Ch. 28, h 3

A number of our people have narrated from Ahmad ibn Muhammad ibn Khalid from his father from al-Nadr ibn Suwayd for Yahya ibn 'Imran al-Halabi from Mu'alla ibn 'Uthman from Ali ibn Hanzala from (Imam) abu 'Abd Allah, *'Alayhi al-Salam*, who said the following:

"The Imam, *'Alayhi al-Salam*, has said 'A fortunate person is made to walk on the path of the unfortunate ones so much so that people may say, "How similar has he become to them? In fact, he has become one of them." Then good fortune helps him compensate for his loss. Sometimes an unfortunate one is made to walk on the path of the fortunate ones and people begin to say, 'How similar has he become to them? In fact, he has become one of them.' However, misfortune takes hold of him (again). Whoever Allah has written to be of the fortunate ones, even if very little time, such as the period of time equal to that between two breast-feedings of a camel to her young, may have been left from his life in this world, Allah will make it end in good fortune.'"

Chapter 29 - Good and Evil

H 389, Ch. 29, h 1

A number of our people have narrated from Ahmad ibn Muhammad ibn Khalid from ibn Mahbub and Ali ibn al-Hakam from Mu'awiya ibn Wahab from (Imam) abu 'Abd Allah, *'Alayhi al-Salam*, who said the following:

"I heard (Imam) abu 'Abd Allah, *'Alayhi al-Salam*, saying, 'It was of the facts that Allah revealed to Moses and sent down in the Torah, 'I am Allah, no one deserves to be obeyed and worshipped besides Me. I have created the creatures and created the *Good* and made it to run through the hands of those whom I love. Fortunate are those through whose hands I have made the Good to continue. I am Allah, no one deserves to be obeyed and worshipped besides Me. I created the creatures and created *Evil* and made it to run through the hands of whomever I wanted. Unfortunate, therefore, are those through whose hands I have made evil to run.'"

H 390, Ch. 29, h 2

A number of our people have narrated from Ahmad ibn Muhammad from his father from ibn abu 'Umayr from Muhammad ibn Hakim from Muhammad ibn Muslim who has said that he heard (Imam) abu Ja'far, *'Alayhi al-Salam*, say the following:

"In certain matters that Allah has revealed through His books is, 'I am Allah. No one deserves to be obeyed and worshipped besides Me. I created the *Good* and *Evil*. Fortunate are those through whose hands I have made good to run, and unfortunate are those through whose hands I have made evil to run, and unfortunate are those who say, "How is this and how is that.'""

H 391, Ch. 29, h 3

Ali ibn Ibrahim has narrated from Muhammad ibn 'Isa from Yunus from Bakkar from Kardam, from Mufaddal ibn 'Umar and 'Abd al-Mu'min al-Ansari from (Imam) abu 'Abd Allah, *'Alayhi al-Salam*, who has said the following:

"Allah, the Most Holy, the Most High, has said, 'I am Allah. No one deserves to be obeyed and worshipped besides Me the Creator of good and evil. Fortunate are those through whose hands I have made good to run, and unfortunate are those through whose hands I have made evil to run, and unfortunate are those who say, "How is this and how is that?'"

"Yunus has said, 'It means they are those who deny this fact instead of having proper understanding of it.'"

Chapter 30 - Predestination, Fate and the Middle Road in Between

H 392, Ch. 30, h 1

Ali ibn Muhammad has narrated from Sahl ibn Ziyad and Ishaq ibn Muhammad and others, in a *marfu'* manner, who have said the following.

"Once in Kufa, after Amir al-Mu'minin Ali's, *'Alayhi al-Salam*, return from Siffin, a man came to him and sat with his legs folded underneath in front of the Imam and said, 'O Amir al-Mu'minin, tell us about our journey against the people of Sham (Syria). Was it because of Allah's decree and determination or not?' 'Amir al-Mu'minin Ali said, "Yes, O Shaykh, every hill that you climbed and every valley that you crossed was because of the decree and the determination of Allah.'" The Shaykh then said, 'Will my tiring efforts be counted in the sight of Allah, O Amir al-Mu'minin?'

"The Imam said, 'Be patient, O Shaykh. I swear by Allah that He will grant you a great reward for your journey wherever you traveled, for your stay wherever you rested and for your return when you were headed back. In none of these conditions that you went through were you coerced or compelled.' The Shaykh then said, 'How can we not be considered compelled or coerced when all of our journey, rest and return were because of the decree and determination of Allah?'

"The Imam said, 'Do you think it was all due to unavoidable decree and binding determination? Had it been so all the reward, punishment, commandments, orders and warnings from Allah would remain invalid and meaningless. The promise and warnings would fall apart. No one could blame the sinners and no one would praise the people of good deeds. The sinners could have been more deserving than the people of good deeds could, and the latter ones could have deserved more punishment. Such can only be the belief of the idol worshippers, the enemies of the Beneficent, of the party of Satan, the determinist of this *Ummah* (nation) and her Zoroastrians.

'Allah, the Most Holy, the Most High, has obligated people on the basis of their freedom and choice. His prohibitions serve as warnings. He rewards a great deal for very little of deeds. Disobedience to Him is not due to His weakness or His defeat. Obedience to Him is not due to compulsion and coercion. He has not given the power to people in the absolute sense. He has not created the heavens and the earth and all that is between them without a purpose. He has not sent the messengers and the prophets to warn and promise people just to play a trick. Such could only be the belief of the unbelievers. Woe is for the unbelievers to suffer in the fire.'

"The Shaykh then recited the following lines that he composed instantaneously:

'You are the Imam whose obedience, one day, we hope,

'Salvation it will bring and forgiveness from the Beneficent (God).

'Explain you did our issue that was vague.

'May your Lord reward (your) favor with (His) favor.'"

H 393, Ch. 30, h 2
Al-Husayn ibn Muhammad has narrated from Mu'alla ibn Muhammad from al-Husayn ibn Ali al-Washsha' from Hammad ibn 'Uthman from abu Basir from (Imam) abu 'Abd Allah, *'Alayhi al-Salam*, who said the following:
"Whoever thinks that Allah orders people to commit sins has ascribed lies to Allah, and whoever thinks that good and evil are from Allah has ascribed lies to Allah." (See also *Hadith* No. 6 below).

H 394, Ch. 30, h 3
Al-Husayn ibn Muhammad has narrated from Mu'alla ibn Muhammad from al-Husayn ibn Ali al-Washsha' the following from abu al-Hassan al-Rida, *'Alayhi al-Salam*:
"Once I asked the Imam, *'Alayhi al-Salam*, 'Has Allah left all the matters to people?' The Imam said, 'Allah, Most Exalted, is by far above and beyond such things.' I then asked, 'Has He compelled them to commit sins?' The Imam said, 'Allah's justice and His judgment are far above and beyond such things.' The Imam further said, 'Allah has said, "O sons of Adam, I have more credit in your good deeds than you yourself do and you have more responsibility for your bad deeds than I do. You commit sins with the power that I have given to you."'"

H 395, Ch. 30, h 4

Ali ibn Ibrahim has narrated from his father from Isma'il ibn Marrar from Yunus ibn 'Abd al-Rahman who has said that abu al-Hassan al-Rida, *'Alayhi al-Salam*, said to me the following:

"O Yunus, do not say what pre-determinists say. The pre-determinists do not say what people of paradise say or what people of hell say or what Satan says. The people of paradise say, '. . . all praise is due to Allah for His guiding us. We could never have been guided without Allah's guiding us.' (7:43) The people of hell say, 'Lord, our misfortune overwhelmed us and we became lost,' (23:107) and Satan said, 'My Lord for Your making me to rebel . . .' (15:39)

"I then said, 'I swear by Allah that I do not say what they say but I only say that there will be nothing unless Allah will want, will, measure and decree.' The Imam, *'Alayhi al-Salam*, said, 'O Yunus, it is not that, *'there will be nothing unless Allah will want, will, measure and decree.'* O Yunus, do you know what is *want*?' I said, 'No, I do not know.' The Imam said, 'It is the first mention of something. Do you know what is *will*?' I said, 'No, I do not know.' The Imam said, 'It is the intention to do something. Do you know what *measurement* is?' I said, 'No, I do not know.' The Imam said, 'It is the figure, the position, the limits of survival and extinction.'

"The Imam further said, 'The decree is the readiness and the production of substance.' I then asked permission to kiss his head and said, 'You just opened for me something of which I was unaware.'"

H 396, Ch. 30, h 5

Muhammad ibn Isma'il has narrated from al-Fadl ibn Shadhan from Hammad ibn 'Isa from Ibrahim ibn 'Umar al-Yamani from abu 'Abd Allah, *'Alayhi al-Salam*, who said the following:

"Allah created the creatures and He knew what they will do. He commanded and prohibited them. He has not commanded them to do anything but that He has placed there a way for them not to obey the command (if they so wanted). They do not obey or disobey except by Allah's permission."

H 397, Ch. 30, h 6

Ali ibn Ibrahim has narrated from Muhammad ibn 'Isa from Yunus ibn 'Abd al-Rahman from Hafs ibn Qirt from abu 'Abd Allah, *'Alayhi al-Salam*, who said the following:

"The messenger of Allah, *'Alayhi al-Salam*, has said, 'Whoever believes that Allah has commanded to do evil and sin has ascribed lies to Allah. Whoever thinks that good and evil are without the wish of Allah, has considered Allah without authority. Whoever thinks that sins are without the power from Allah, has ascribed lies to Allah and whoever ascribes lies to Allah, He will make him to enter the fire.'"

H 398, Ch. 30, h 7

A number of persons of our people have narrated from Ahmad ibn abu 'Abd Allah from 'Uthman ibn 'Isa from Isma'il ibn Jabir who has said the following:

"In the mosque of Madina there was a person who spoke of the issue of predetermination and people had gathered around him. I said to him, 'O you, can I ask you a question?' He said, 'Yes, you may do so.' I then said, 'Can there be a thing in the Kingdom of Allah, the Majestic, the Glorious, that He may not want?'

135

He remained thinking for a while and then said to me, 'O you, if I said that there can be something in His Kingdom He does not want it means that He is defeated. If I say that there is nothing in His Kingdom that He may not want I am giving you permission to commit sin.

"I then told the story of that determinist to abu 'Abd Allah, *'Alayhi al-Salam*, who said, 'He (the determinist man) looked for his own interest. Had he said something else he would have been destroyed.'"

H 399, Ch. 30, h 8

Muhammad ibn Yahya has narrated from Ahmad ibn Muhammad ibn al-Hassan Za'lan from abu Talib al-Qummi from a man the following from abu 'Abd Allah, *'Alayhi al-Salam*, who has said the following:

"I asked the Imam, *'Alayhi al-Salam*, 'Has Allah compelled the servants to sin?' The Imam replied, 'No, He has not compelled them.' I then said, 'Has He left all matters to them?' He replied, 'No, He has not done so.' I asked, 'Then how is it?' The Imam then said, 'It is a way of kindness from your Lord in between.'"

H 400, Ch. 30, h 9

Ali ibn Ibrahim has narrated from Muhammad ibn 'Isa from Yunus ibn 'Abd al-Rahman from more than one person from abu Ja'far, *'Alayhi al-Salam*, and abu 'Abd Allah, *'Alayhi al-Salam*, who have said the following:

"Allah is more kind to His creatures than to compel them to sin and then punish them. Allah, the Most Majestic is by far beyond willing something that cannot come into existence." The two Imam, *'Alayhim al-Salam*, were asked if there was a third reality between compulsion and predetermination. They replied, 'Yes, there is something bigger than what is between the heavens and the earth.'"

H 401 Ch. 30, h 10

Ali ibn Ibrahim has narrated from Muhammad from Yunus ibn 'Abd al-Rahman from Salih ibn Sahl from certain persons of his people from abu 'Abd Allah, *'Alayhi al-Salam*, who has said the following when asked about compulsion and predetermination:

"There is no compulsion and no predetermination. It is something between the two. In this there is the truth that is known only to a scholar or one whom the scholar has taught."

H 402, Ch. 30, h 11

Ali ibn Ibrahim has narrated from Muhammad from Yunus from 'Idda who said the following:

"Once a man said to abu 'Abd Allah, *'Alayhi al-Salam*, 'May Allah keep my soul in service for your cause, has Allah compelled people to sin?' The Imam said, 'Allah is just and by far beyond compelling people to sin and then punishing them for it.' The man then said, 'May Allah keep my soul in service for your cause, has He then left all matters to the servants?' The Imam said, 'Had He left all matters to the people He would not have restricted them with commandments and prohibitions.' The man then said, 'May Allah keep my soul in service for your cause, is there a stage between the two?' The Imam said, 'Yes, there is something bigger than what is between the heavens and the earth.'"

H 403, Ch. 30, h 12

Muhammad ibn abu 'Abd Allah and others have narrated from Sahl ibn Ziyad from Ahmad ibn Muhammad ibn abu Nasr who said the following:

"Once I asked abu al-Hassan al-Rida, *'Alayhi al-Salam*, 'Certain persons of our people believe in compulsion and others believe in people's capabilities. The Imam said, 'Write down, "In the name of Allah, the Beneficent, the Merciful, (Imam) Ali ibn al-Husayn, *'Alayhi al-Salam*, has said that Allah, the Most Majestic has said, 'O son of Adam, through My will it is you who wish. With My power you fulfill your obligations to Me. With My bounties you become strong to sin. I made you to hear and see. Whatever good you receive is from Allah. Whatever evil befalls you is from your own soul. It is because I have more credit in your good deeds than you do and you are more responsible for your bad deeds than I am. It is because I am not questioned about what I do and they are the ones who are questioned about their deeds. I have organized for you all things that you want.'""

H 404, Ch. 30, h 13

Muhammad ibn abu 'Abd Allah has narrated from Husayn ibn Muhammad from Muhammad ibn Yahya from those he has narrated from, from abu 'Abd Allah, *'Alayhi al-Salam*, who said the following:

"There is no compulsion and no total freedom but it is a matter between the two." The narrator has said, 'I asked what is, "*it is a matter between the two?*" The Imam, *'Alayhi al-Salam*, said, 'One example of this is the case of a man whom you may see that sins and you try to stop him but he does not listen. You then leave him alone and he sins. That is because he did not listen to you and you left him alone; if you were considered as ordering him to sin, it is not true.'"

H 405, Ch. 30, h 14

A number of our people have narrated from Ahmad ibn Muhammad al-Barqi from Ali ibn al-Hakam from Hisham ibn Salim from abu 'Abd Allah, *'Alayhi al-Salam*, who said the following:

"Allah is by far Gracious and beyond ordering people to do what they are not capable of doing. Allah is by far Majestic and beyond a situation wherein things may exist in His Kingdom that He does not want."

Chapter 31 - The Capabilities

H 406, Ch. 31, h 1

Ali ibn Ibrahim has narrated from al-Hassan ibn Muhammad from Ali ibn Muhammad al-Qasani from Ali ibn Asbat who said the following:

"Once I asked Imam abu al-Hassan al-Rida, *'Alayhi al-Salam*, about *capability*. The Imam said, 'A servant (of Allah) has the *capability* if four things exist. That he is free and on his own, that he is physically well and of sound limbs and that for him there is reason and means from Allah.' I asked, 'May Allah keep my soul in the service for your cause, please explain it to me.' The Imam said, 'Being free and on one's own, physically well and of sound limbs means that one is willing to commit adultery but does not find a female party and then he finds her. He may now protect his soul and stay away from sin just as Joseph (peace be upon him) did or allow his desire to act and commit adultery and in this case he is called an adulterer. He has not obeyed Allah in coercion and disobeyed Him with defeat.'"

H 407, Ch. 31, h 2

Muhammad ibn Yahya and Ali ibn Ibrahim both have narrated from Ahmad Muhammad from Ali ibn al-Hakam and 'Abd Allah ibn Yazid both from a man from Basra who said the following:

"He asked (Imam) abu 'Abd Allah, *'Alayhi al-Salam*, about *capability*. The Imam said, 'Can you do something before its existence?' He Said, 'No, I cannot do so.' The Imam said, 'Can you stop doing what has already been done?' He said, 'No, I cannot do so.' The Imam then asked, 'When then can you have the capability?' He said, 'I do not know.'

"The Imam said, 'Allah created people and placed in them the means of *capability* and then He did not leave all matters in their hands. Thus, they are capable of acting at the time of the act with the act when they do that act. If they did not act the 'Act' in His property they do not have the capability to act the 'Act' that they did not act. Allah, the Most Holy, the Most High, is by far Majestic and above being opposed by someone in His property.'

"The man from Basra then said, 'Are people, then, compelled?' The Imam said, 'Had they been compelled they would have been excused.' The man said, 'Are then all matters up to them?' The Imam said, 'No, all things are not left to them.' The man said, 'Then how is it'?

"The Imam said, 'Allah knew that they would act, thus He placed in them the means of *capability*. If they act at the time of action they are capable.' The man from Basra then said, 'I testify that this is the truth and that you are of the family of the Messenger (of Allah).'"

H 408, Ch. 31, h 3

Muhammad ibn abu 'Abd Allah has narrated from Sahl ibn Ziyad and Ali ibn Ibrahim has narrated from Ahmad ibn Muhammad and Muhammad ibn Yahya from Ahmad ibn Muhammad all from Ali ibn al-Hakam from Salih al-Nily who said the following:

"Once I asked abu 'Abd Allah, *'Alayhi al-Salam*, 'Do the servants (of Allah) have any *capability*?' The Imam said, 'When they act an act they do have the capability that Allah has placed in them.' I asked, 'What is it?' The Imam said, 'It is a means. In a sin like adultery when one commits such sins he has the capability when he is in such an act. If he however, desists from such an act he has the capability to refrain.' The Imam further said, 'Before the act he does not have the capability in a small or large measure but at the time of the act or desisting, he has the capability.'

"I asked, 'What for then are they punished?' The Imam said, 'It is because of complete justification and because of the means that are placed in them. Allah does not compel anyone into sins. Also He does not will, in a definite form of will, disbelief for anyone, but when one disbelieves it is in the will of Allah for him to disbelieve and it is in the will and knowledge of Allah that he will not turn into anything good.'

"I asked, 'Has He willed disbelief for them?' The Imam said, 'It is not quite like that but I say that Allah knew that they would disbelieve, thus He has willed it for them because of His knowledge of it. It is not a definite will. It is a will of choice.'"

H 409, Ch. 31, h 4

Muhammad ibn Yahya has narrated from Ahmad ibn Muhammad ibn 'Isa from al-Husayn ibn Sa'id from certain persons of our people from 'Ubayd ibn Zurara from Hamza ibn Humran who said the following:

"Once I asked abu 'Abd Allah, *'Alayhi al-Salam*, about *capability* but he did not reply. In another meeting I said, 'May Allah keep you well, something happens to my heart that will not go away until I will get an answer from you.' The Imam said, 'What is in your heart will not harm you.' I said, 'May Allah keep you well. I say that Allah, the Most Holy, the Most High, does not hold people responsible for what they are not capable of doing or do not have the power to act. They do not do anything except with the will of Allah, His wish, decree and determination.' The Imam said, 'This is the religion of Allah that my forefathers and I follow,' or that the Imam made a similar expression."

Chapter 32 - Declaration, Definition and the Need for Solid Proof

H 410, Ch. 32, h 1

Muhammad ibn Yahya and others have narrated from Ahmad ibn Muhammad ibn 'Isa from al-Husayn ibn Sa'id from ibn abu 'Umayr from Jamyl ibn Durraj from ibn al-Tayyar from abu 'Abd Allah who said the following:

"Allah has justified His holding people accountable with what He has made known and sent to them."

Muhammad ibn Isma'Il has narrated from al-Fadl ibn Shadhan from ibn abu 'Umayr from Jamyl ibn Durraj a similar *Hadith.*

H 411, Ch. 32, h 2

Muhammad ibn Yahya and others have narrated from Ahmad ibn Muhammad ibn 'Isa from Muhammad ibn abu 'Umayr from Muhammad ibn Hakim who said the following:

"Once I asked abu 'Abd Allah, 'Whose creation is knowing?' The Imam said, 'It is of the creation of Allah. The servants (of Allah) have no part in it.'"

H 412, Ch. 32, h 3

A number of our people have narrated from Ahmad ibn Muhammad ibn Khalid from ibn Faddal from Tha'laba ibn Maymun from Hamza ibn Muhammad al-Tayyar from abu 'Abd Allah, *'Alayhi al-Salam*, who has said the following about the words of Allah, the Majestic, the Glorious:

"Allah does not misguide a nation after having given them guidance until the means of piety are made known to them . . ." (9:115) The Imam, *'Alayhi al-Salam*, said, 'It (means of piety) means before giving the knowledge of what He is pleased with and what He is displeased with.' The Imam, *'Alayhi al-Salam*, said the words of Allah '. . . and inspired it with knowledge of evil and piety,' (91:8) convey that He has explained what people must do and what they must not do. The words of Allah, 'We showed him the right path whether he would be grateful or ungrateful' (76:3), say that Allah has given them the knowledge. They may follow or they may ignore. About the words of Allah, 'We sent guidance to the people of Thamud but they preferred blindness to guidance so a humiliating blast of torment struck them for their evil deeds.' (41:17) The Imam said, 'It means that Allah gave them the knowledge but they preferred blindness over guidance and they knew it.'"

In another Hadith it says, "We explained to them."

H 413, Ch. 32, h 4

Ali ibn Ibrahim has narrated from Muhammad ibn 'Isa from Yunus ibn 'Abd al-Rahman from ibn Bukayr from Hamza ibn Muhammad from abu 'Abd Allah, *'Alayhi al-Salam*, the following:

"Once I asked the Imam, *'Alayhi al-Salam*, about the words of Allah, the Most Holy, the Most High, 'Have We not shown him the ways of '*al-Najdayn*' ?' (90:10) The Imam said, '*al-Najdayn*' means the ways of good and evil.'"

H 414, Ch. 32, h 5

Through the chain of narrators of the previous Hadith from Yunus has narrated from Hammad from 'Abd al-A'la who has said the following:

"Once I said to (Imam) abu 'Abd Allah, *'Alayhi al-Salam*, 'May Allah keep you well, has Allah placed a means in people to know?' He replied, 'No, He has not done so.' I asked, 'Will He hold them responsible for knowing?' He said, 'No, because it is for Allah to explain.' 'Allah does not impose on any soul a responsibility beyond its ability . . .' (2:286) 'Allah does not impose on any soul that which he cannot afford . . .' (65:7)"I asked the Imam about the words of Allah in, 'Allah does not misguide a nation after having given them guidance until the means of piety are made known to them . . .' (9:115) The Imam said, 'It (means of piety) means not until He gives the knowledge of what pleases Him and what displeases Him.'"

H 415, Ch. 32, h 6

Through the above chain of narrators it is narrated from Yunus from Sa'dan, in a *marfu'* manner, from abu 'Abd Allah, *'Alayhi al-Salam*, who said the following:

"Allah has not granted any bounties to a person without holding him justifiably responsible for them. He gives them bounties and gives them power, which justifies His holding them responsible for their duties. He gives smaller degrees of responsibilities to those who are of lesser degrees of capabilities. One who has received bounties from Allah He has provided him ease, thus the justification to hold him responsible is the comfort he has received. Then it is for him to help the needy in optional ways. The one whom Allah has favored and has made noble in his house and beautiful in his form, is justifiably obligated for the duty of praising Allah, the Most Holy, the Most High, for his part as a recipient of favor. He must not boast over the others to hold back the rights of the needy because of his respectability and beauty in his form."

Chapter 33 - Differences in the Justification of Divine Authority Among People

H 416, Ch. 33, h 1
Muhammad ibn abu 'Abd Allah has narrated from Sahl ibn Ziyad from Ali ibn Asbat from al-Husayn ibn Zayd from Durust ibn abu Mansur from whoever he narrated from, from abu 'Abd Allah, *'Alayhi al-Salam*, who said the following:

"There are six things in which the people have no doing. They are knowing, ignorance, consent, anger, sleeping and waking up."

Chapter 34 - Allah's Authorities and Means of Justification of Accountability in People

H 417, Ch. 34, h 1
Muhammad ibn Yahya has narrated from Muhammad ibn al-Husayn from abu Shu'ayb al-Mahamili from Durust ibn abu Mansur from Burayd ibn Mu'awiya from abu 'Abd Allah, *'Alayhi al-Salam*, who said the following:

"People are not accountable before Allah to know. It is up to Allah to make them know. Once Allah makes them know then people are responsible for accepting (their duties)."

H 418, Ch. 34, h 2
A number of our people have narrated from Ahmad ibn Muhammad ibn 'Isa from al-Hajjal from Tha'laba ibn Maymun from 'Abd al-A'la ibn 'A'yan who said the following:

"Once I asked abu 'Abd Allah, *'Alayhi al-Salam*, 'If a person does not know, will he be held responsible?' He said, 'No, he will not be held responsible.'"

H 419, Ch. 34, h 3
Muhammad ibn Yahya has narrated from Ahmad ibn Muhammad ibn 'Isa from ibn Faddal from Dawud ibn Farqad from abu al-Hassan Zakariyya from abu 'Abd Allah, *'Alayhi al-Salam*, who said the following:

"Whatever Allah has kept hidden from people they will not be held responsible for it."

H 420, Ch. 34, h 4
A number of our people have narrated from Ahmad ibn Muhammad ibn Khalid from Ali ibn al-Hakam from Aban al-Ahmar from Hamza ibn al-Tayyar who said the following:

"Once Imam abu 'Abd Allah, *'Alayhi al-Salam*, said to me, 'Write down.' He dictated to me the following. 'It is of our *Hadith* that Allah will, justifiably, hold people accountable for what He has given and made known to them. Allah then sent His messenger to them and sent down books upon them in which He has commanded and prohibited them. He has commanded them to perform prayers and fast. The messenger of Allah, *'Alayhi al-Salam*, remained sleeping until the time for prayer expired and Allah said, 'I make you sleep and wake you up. When you wake up then perform the prayer so that they can learn if such thing happened to them what they should do.'

"It is not the way that they say, 'If one remains asleep (at the time of prayer) one is destroyed.' In the same way is fasting. 'I (Allah) cause you to become ill and when I give you good health then you will make up for the fast that you missed during your illness.' Abu 'Abd Allah, *'Alayhi al-Salam*, then said, 'So also is, if you look at all things you will find that Allah has caused no constrictions to anyone. You will not find anyone against whom Allah may not have enough justification to hold him accountable with His wish therein. I do not say that they can do whatever they wish.

"The Imam then said, 'Allah guides and misleads.' He further said, 'People are not ordered to do what they are not capable of. For everything that people are ordered to do they have the capability for it and anything of which they are not capable is removed and lifted up from them but there is not much good in people.' He (the Imam) then recited from the Holy Quran: 'People who are weak or sick and those who do not have the means to take part in the fighting are exempt from this duty . . .' (conditions of people exempt are mentioned) 'Righteous people shall not be blamed. Allah is All-forgiving and All-merciful.' (9:91) So also relieved of the duty are 'Those who come to you (Muhammad), asking to be taken to the battle . . .' (9:92) they do not have the means.'"

Chapter 35 - Guidance Is From Allah, the Most Holy, the Most High

H 421, Ch. 35, h 1
A number of our people have narrated from Ahmad ibn Muhammad ibn 'Isa from Muhammad ibn Isma'il from Isma'il al-Sarraj from ibn Muskan from Thabit in Sa'id who said the following:
"Once, abu 'Abd Allah, *'Alayhi al-Salam*, said, 'O Thabit, why do you bother about people? Leave them alone and do not call anyone to accept your belief (the belief of the Shi'a Muslims). I swear by Allah that even if all the people in the heavens and earth come together to guide a person whom Allah wants not to guide, they will never be able to guide him. If all the people in the heavens and on earth will come together to misguide a person whom Allah wants to guide, they will never be able to misguide him. Leave the people alone. No one should say, 'O my uncle, my brother, the son of my uncle and my neighbor.' When Allah wants good for a person He cleanses his spirit. He then does not hear any lawful thing but that he knows it and no unlawful thing but that he dislikes it. Then Allah places a word in his heart with which He organizes all his affairs.'"

H 422, Ch. 35, h 2
Ali ibn Ibrahim ibn Hashim has narrated from his father from ibn abu 'Umayr from Muhammad ibn Humran from Sulayman ibn Khalid from abu 'Abd Allah, *'Alayhi al-Salam*, who said the following:
"When Allah, the Most Holy, the Most High, wants good for a person He places a point of light in his heart and opens the ears of his heart and assigns an angel to support him. When He wants bad fortune for a person He places a dark black spot in his heart, closes the ears of his heart and assigns a Satan to mislead him.' The Imam, *'Alayhi al-Salam*, then recited the following verse of the Holy Quran. 'Allah will open the hearts of whomever He wants to guide to Islam, but He will constrict the chest of one whom He has led astray, as though he were climbing high up into the sky. . . .'" (6:125)

H 423, Ch. 35, h 3

A number of our people have narrated from Ahmad ibn Muhammad from ibn Faddal from Ali ibn 'Uqba from his father who said the following:

"I heard abu 'Abd Allah, *'Alayhi al-Salam*, saying, 'Leave your affairs to Allah and do not leave them to the people. Whatever is for Allah it is for Him. Whatever is for people it will not rise up to Allah. Do not quarrel with people about your belief; quarrelling sickens the heart. Allah, the Most Holy, the Most High, said to His Prophet (Muhammad), *'Alayhi al-Salam*, 'you cannot guide whomever you love, but Allah guides whomever He wants and knows best those who seek guidance.' (28:56) '(Muhammad), do you force people to have faith?' (10:99)

"Leave the people alone; people learn from people and you have learned from the Messenger of Allah, *'Alayhi al-Salam*. I heard my father, *'Alayhi al-Salam*, saying, 'When Allah, the Most Holy, the Most High, writes for a person to enter in this belief he will do so faster than the flight of a bird to its nest.'"

H 424, Ch. 35, h 4

Abu Ali al-Ash'ari has narrated from Muhammad ibn 'Abd al-Jabbar from Safwan ibn Yahya from Muhammad ibn Marwan from Fudayl ibn Yasar the following:

"Once I asked abu 'Abd Allah, *'Alayhi al-Salam*, 'Can we invite people to this belief (the belief of the Shi'a Muslims)?' He said, 'No, do not invite them, O Fudayl. When Allah wants good for a servant of His, He orders an angel to grab him by his neck and then enters him in this belief compelled or willing.'"

This is the end of the Book on the Oneness of Allah of al-Kafi. All praise belongs to Allah alone and Allah has granted blessings upon Muhammad and his family.

In the Name of Allah, the Beneficent, the Merciful

Part Four:
The Book about People with Divine Authority

Chapter 1 - The Necessity of the Presence of Divine Authority Among the People

H 425, Ch. 1, h 1

The compiler of this book, Muhammad ibn Ya'qub al-Kulayni (may Allah grant him blessings) has said that narrated to us Ali ibn Ibrahim from his father from al-'Abbass ibn 'Umar al-Faqimi from Hisham ibn al-Hakam from abu 'Abd Allah, *'Alayhi al-Salam*, the following:

"An atheist asked the Imam, *'Alayhi al-Salam*, 'How do you prove the truthfulness of the prophets and the messengers?'

"The Imam, *'Alayhi al-Salam*, said, 'It is a fact that we have established with sufficient evidence, proof of the existence of our Creator, the Most Holy, the Most High and Exalted above all creatures. It is a fact that this Creator is All-wise and Most High. His creatures cannot see, touch, associate and directly communicate with Him. It proves that His deputies must be present among His creatures. It is His deputies and ambassadors who speak to people for Him and provide them guidance to protect their interests; to tell them what is beneficial to them and what are the best means of survival and what may cause their destruction. This proves the presence among people of those who convey the commandments of the Creator, Who is All-wise, All-knowing Allah, the Most Holy, the Most High, to them. Such people are the prophets, *'Alayhim al-Salam*, the chosen ones from among His creatures. They are the people of wisdom, disciplined with wisdom and sent to people with the message of wisdom. They are different from other people - although like them in physical form and shape - in their conditions of discipline and their receiving direct support from Allah, the Most Holy, the Most High and All-wise. This also proves their presence among people in all times to ensure the availability of the people with Divine Authority on earth who have the kind of knowledge that establishes their truthfulness and proves them to be of the people who possess the noble quality of justice.'"

H 426, Ch. 1, h 2

Muhammad ibn Isma'il has narrated from al-Fadl ibn Shadhan from Safwan ibn Yahya from Mansur ibn Hazim who has said the following:

"Once I said to Imam abu 'Abd Allah, *'Alayhi al-Salam*, 'Allah by far is Majestic and Gracious to be known through His creatures. In fact, the creatures are known through Allah.' The Imam, *'Alayhi al-Salam*, said, 'You have spoken the truth.' I said, 'One who knows that he has a Lord must also learn that his Lord agrees with certain things and disagrees with certain other things. The only way one can know what He likes and dislikes, is by revelation or through a messenger. One who does not receive revelation must find the messengers and when he finds the messengers he will know that they are the Divine Authorities and that obedience to them is necessary.

"I say to people, 'Do you know that the Messenger of Allah was the Divine Authority over His creatures?' They say, 'Yes, he was the Divine Authority.' I then ask, 'After the Messenger of Allah who was the Divine Authority over His creatures?' They say, 'After the Messenger of Allah the Divine Authority is the Holy Quran.'

"I considered the Holy Quran and found out that various kinds of people consider this Holy Book as support for their beliefs. For example the Murji'a (people who say Allah has postponed punishment), the pre-determinists and the atheists who even do not believe in it but take it as the basis for their arguments against the others. I then learned that the Holy Quran cannot serve as Divine Authority without a guardian and supervisor whose words from and about the Holy Quran can reveal the truth.

"I then ask the people, 'Who is the guardian and supervisor of the Holy Quran?' They say, 'Ibn Mas'ud knew the Holy Quran, 'Umar knew it and Hudhayfa knew the Holy Quran.' I ask them, 'Did they know all of the Holy Quran?' The people say, 'No, they did not know all of it.' I have not found anyone who knows all of the Holy Quran except Ali ibn abu Talib, *'Alayhi al-Salam*. It is a fact - whenever any issue emerged that needed a Quranic solution, except for Imam Ali, *'Alayhi al-Salam* - every one of the others (in many cases), said, 'I do not know.' Only Imam Ali, *'Alayhi al-Salam*, would say, 'I know.' I then acknowledged that Imam Ali, *'Alayhi al-Salam*, is the guardian and supervisor of the Holy Quran and obedience to him is obligatory and he is the Divine Authority over the people after the Messenger of Allah, *'Alayhi al-Salam*. Whatever Imam Ali, *'Alayhi al-Salam*, has said from the Holy Quran is the truth.' The Imam, *'Alayhi al-Salam*, said, 'I pray to Allah to grant you blessing.'"

H 427, Ch. 1, h 3

Ali ibn Ibrahim has narrated from his father from al-Hassan ibn Ibrahim from Yunus ibn Ya'qub who has said the following:

"In the presence of Imam abu 'Abd Allah, *'Alayhi al-Salam*, once there was a group of his followers consisting of Humran ibn 'Ayan, Muhammad ibn al-Nu'man, Hisham ibn Salim, al-Tayyar and others among whom was also Hisham ibn al-Hakam, a young man. Imam abu 'Abd Allah, *'Alayhi al-Salam*, said, 'O Hisham, can you tell us what did you do to 'Amr ibn 'Ubayd and how did you ask him questions?'

"Hisham said, 'O descendant of the Messenger of Allah, due to your greatness I feel shy and my tongue does not work in your presence.' The Imam, *'Alayhi al-Salam*, said, 'When I order you something you should do it.' Hisham, then said, 'Once I came to learn about the gathering of 'Amr ibn 'Ubayd and his sessions of speeches for people in the Mosque of Basra. It disturbed me a great deal and I went to Basra. It was a Friday. I went to the Mosque and found a large circle of people. Among them was 'Amr ibn 'Ubayd with a black piece of woolen cloth used as a loincloth and another piece over him as a gown and people would ask him questions. I asked people for room, which they made for me. I sat in front of the people with my legs folded beneath and I said, 'O scholar, I come from out of town. Can I ask you questions?' He said, 'Yes, you may ask.' I asked, 'Do you have eyes?' He said, 'Son, what kind of question is this? Something that you can see why then do you ask?' I said, 'That is how my questions are.' He said, 'Son, you may ask your questions even if they are meaningless ones.' I asked, 'Do you have eyes?' He said, 'Yes, I have eyes.' I asked, 'What do you do with them?' He said, 'I see with them the colors and persons.' I asked, 'Do you have a nose?' He said, 'Yes, I have a nose.' I asked, 'What do you do with it?' He ('Amr ibn 'Ubayd) said, 'I use it to smell things.' I asked, 'Do you have a mouth?' He said, 'Yes, I have a mouth.' I asked, 'What do you do with it?' He said, 'I taste things with it.' I asked, 'Do you have ears?' He said, 'Yes, I have ears.' I asked, 'What do you do with them?' He said, 'I hear sounds with them.' I asked, 'Do you have a heart?' He said, 'Yes, I have a heart.' I asked, 'What do you do with it?' He said, 'I distinguish and discern things that come to it from the other senses.' I asked, 'Why are your other senses not independent of your heart and why do they need it?' He said, 'They are not independent of my heart.' I said, 'Why do they need your heart when they are all healthy and sound?' He said, 'Son, when the other senses face a doubt about something smelling, seeing, tasting or hearing, I send it to my heart and it ascertains "certainty" and discards "doubts."'

"I asked him, 'Do you mean that Allah has set up the heart to remove doubts from the other senses?' He said, 'Yes, that is true.' I asked, 'Is then the existence of the heart necessary to remove the doubts of the other senses?' He said, 'Yes, it is necessary.' I then said, 'O abu Marwan, Allah, the Most Holy, the Most High, as you say, has not left your senses without a leader (Imam). (He has created an Imam) to correct the doubts and the mistakes of the other senses in you to remove doubts therefrom. How would He leave all the people with doubts and confusions without an Imam who would remove their doubts and settle their disputes?' He remained quiet and did not say anything for a while. He then asked, 'Are you Hisham ibn al-Hakam?' I said, 'No, I am not.' He asked, 'Are you of his associates?' I said, 'No, (I am not of his associates).' He asked, 'Wherefrom are you?' I said, 'I am from Kufa.' He said, 'You then must be Hisham ibn al-Hakam.' He then embraced me and gave me room nearby. He discontinued his speech until I left.'"

"Imam abu 'Abd Allah, *'Alayhi al-Salam*, laughed (smiled) and said, 'O Hisham, who has taught you this?' I replied, 'I learned something from you and added something to it myself.' The Imam, *'Alayhi al-Salam*, said, 'This, I swear by Allah, is written in the books of Abraham and Moses.'"

H 428, Ch. 1, h 4

Ali ibn Ibrahim has narrated from his father from those he mentioned from Yunus ibn Ya'qub who has said the following:

"Once I was in the presence of Imam abu 'Abd Allah, *'Alayhi al-Salam*, when a man from Sham (Syria) came to him and said, 'I am a man of *Kalam* (meaningful words or theology), *Fiqh* (laws) and *Fara'id* (rules of obligations) and I have come to debate with your people.'

"Imam abu 'Abd Allah asked, 'Are your meaningful words those of the Messenger of Allah or your own words?' He replied, 'Something from the words of the Messenger of Allah and there is something of my own words.' The Imam said, 'Are then you a partner of the Messenger of Allah?' He said, 'No, I am not.' The Imam, *'Alayhi al-Salam*, asked, 'Have you received any revelation from Allah, the Most Holy, the Most High?' He said, 'No, I have not.' The Imam then asked, 'Is it obligatory to obey you just as it is obligatory to obey the Messenger of Allah?' He said, 'No, it is not.' The Imam, *'Alayhi al-Salam*, then turned to me and said, 'O Yunus ibn Ya'qub, this man has just defeated himself before debating others.'

"The Imam then said, 'O Yunus, why do you not speak to him if you do well in debate?' I said, 'I wish I could but, may Allah keep my soul in service for your cause, I have heard that you do not allow debating and say that *wayl* (a place in hell) is for those who debate and say, "This is accepted and that is not accepted. This is alright to say but that is not alright to say, that this we understand and that we do not understand." The Imam, *'Alayhi al-Salam*, said, 'I said so if they ignore what I say and follow what they themselves want.'

"The Imam then said, 'Find out who is outside who could debate, and bring them in.' The reporter has said, 'I then brought in Humran ibn 'Ayan who was good in debating and Ahwal who also was good in debate. I brought Hisham ibn Salim who debated well. Another person I brought was Qays ibn Masir who was the best of them to me. He had learned Kalam (theology) from Imam Ali ibn al-Husayn, *'Alayhi al-Salam*, and our gathering took place in Makkah before Hajj. Imam abu 'Abd Allah, *'Alayhi al-Salam*, would stay in mountains near the Holy Mosque for few days in a small tent. Once the Imam, *'Alayhi al-Salam*, looked outside the tent and there was a camel growling. He said, 'By the Lord of the Ka'ba, it is Hisham.' We thought it must be Hisham, the man from the family of 'Aqil who was (very) beloved to the Imam, *'Alayhi al-Salam* It was Hisham ibn al-Hakam who came in. He had just grown a small beard and all of us were older than he was. The Imam, *'Alayhi al-Salam*, made room for him and said, 'He is our supporter with his heart, tongue and hands.' The Imam then asked Humran to debate the man. Humran came out strong. The Imam then asked Ta'qiyy to debate the man. Ahwal also came out strong. The Imam then asked Hisham ibn Salim to debate the man. They both remained the same. Abu 'Abd Allah, *'Alayhi al-Salam*, then asked Qasys al-Masir to debate the man. When they debated, abu 'Abd Allah, *'Alayhi al-Salam*, laughed because the man from Sham was distressed.

"The Imam then asked the man from Syria to speak to Hisham ibn al-Hakam. The man said, 'O boy, ask me about the *Imamat* (Divine Authority and leadership) of this man.' Hisham became angry and began to shake and said, 'O you, is your

Lord more protective of His people or are people themselves?' The man said, 'It is My Lord Who is more protective of His creatures.' Hisham then asked, 'What then has He in His opinion done for them?' The Man said, 'He has established His authority and guidance so that they would not differ and disunite and be united to support each other and remind of their duties toward their Lord.' Hisham asked, 'Who is he?' The man said, 'He is the Messenger of Allah.' Hisham then asked, 'Who is the Divine Authority after the Messenger of Allah?' The man replied, 'It is the book of Allah and the *Sunnah*.' Hisham then said, 'Have the Book and *Sunnah* helped us today in removing our differences?' The man said, 'Yes, they have helped us.' Hisham then asked, 'Why then do we have differences among us. Why have you come all the way from Sham to oppose and debate with us?' The man then remained quiet. The Imam asked him, 'Why do you not speak?' The man said, 'If I were to say that we have no differences I would be speaking lies. Were I to say that the Book and *Sunnah* solve our differences it would be invalid; they can be interpreted in so many ways. Were I to say that we do have differences and each claims to be the rightful party then the Book and the *Sunnah* would have been proved of no help. However, I can ask the same question from him also.' The Imam, *'Alayhi al-Salam*, then said to the man from Sham, 'Why do you not then ask him this question? You will find him full of knowledge.'

"The man from Sham (Syria) then turned to Hisham and asked, 'O you, is your Lord more protective of His people or are people themselves?' Hisham said, 'It is My Lord Who is more protective of His creatures.' The man then asked, 'Has He then established for them a means that would remove their differences, unite them, remove their difficulties and show them the right from wrong?' Hisham asked, 'Are you asking about the time of the Messenger of Allah or about this time?'

"The man from Sham said, 'At the time of the Messenger of Allah the authority was the Messenger of Allah. Who is the (Divine) Authority at this time?' Hisham said, '(The Divine Authority) at this time is this person sitting among us. To him people journey over long distances to find answers to their questions. He tells us about the news of the heavens and the earth as he has inherited it from his father and grandfather.' The man from Sham said, 'How can I know that?' Hisham then said, 'Ask him whatever you may like.' The man from Sham said, 'You have left no excuse for me and I must ask.'

"Imam abu 'Abd Allah, *'Alayhi al-Salam*, then said, 'O man from Sham, I can tell you how your journey was and how your road was. It was so and so.' The Imam, *'Alayhi al-Salam*, informed him with details. The man agreed and acknowledged the details and said, 'Now I have become a Muslim.' The Imam, *'Alayhi al-Salam*, said, 'In fact, you have become a believer in Allah now. Islam is before *Iman* (belief). Because of Islam people inherit each other and marry. Because of belief people receive rewards.'

"The man then said, 'You have spoken the truth. At this time I testify that no one deserves to be obeyed and worshipped except Allah, and that Muhammad is His

Messenger and that you are the executor of the will of the executors of will of the Messengers of Allah.'

"The Imam, *'Alayhi al-Salam*, then turned to Humran and said, 'When you speak on the basis of *Hadith* you speak the truth.' Turning to Hisham ibn Salim the Imam, *'Alayhi al-Salam*, said, 'You want the *Hadith* but you do not know them.' About al-Ahwal the Imam said, 'You analogize and use a great deal of cunning ways and break falsehood with falsehood but your falsehood is stronger.' To Qays al-Masir the Imam, *'Alayhi al-Salam*, said, 'You speak of something very near to the *Hadith* of the Messenger of Allah, *'Alayhi al-Salam*, but use something very far from the *Hadith* of the Holy Prophet. You mix the truth with falsehood while a small degree of truth is enough to remove falsehood. You and Ahwal are experts in jumping here and there.'

"Yunus has said, 'I thought the Imam might say about Hisham something similar to what he said about the other two.' The Imam then said, 'O Hisham, you sometimes almost fall but you spring up like a bird on take-off. People like you should speak but be careful of slipping and intercession (support from *'A 'immah*, plural of Imam) will follow, Allah willing.'"

H 429, Ch. 1, h 5

A number of our people have narrated from Ahmad ibn Muhammad ibn 'Isa from Ali ibn al-Hakam from Aban who has that al-Ahwal reported to him the following:

"Zayd ibn Ali ibn al-Husayn, *'Alayhi al-Salam*, sent a message to me for a meeting with him when he was in hiding. When I met him, he said, 'O abu Ja'far, what do you say if someone from us comes to you asking to join us? Will you rise up with him (against the enemies)?' I said, 'If such a person would be your father or brother I would join him.' He then said, 'I want to rise up against these people. Come and join me.' I said, 'No, may Allah make my soul of service to you.' He then said, 'Is it that you distance yourself away from me?' I said, 'It is only one soul. If Allah's Authority on earth existed, then those keeping away from you would have saved themselves and those joining you would have faced their destruction. If no Divine Authority existed on earth then people joining and keeping away from you would be the same.' He then said, 'O abu Ja'far, I would sit with my father at the same table and he would feed me chunky morsels and cool off for me the hot ones out of kindness and diligent care. Do you think he was not afraid for me from the fire of hell? So he has informed you about religion and did not inform me?'

"I said, 'May Allah make my soul of service to you, this also is of the kindness of your father to you. To save you from the fire he did not inform you. He was concerned for you that after having the information you might ignore his guidance and become subject to fire. He informed me also. If I follow I will be safe, and I will be destroyed, if I disobeyed (him), for which (my destruction) he was not that much concerned.'

"Then I told him, 'May Allah make my soul of service to you, are you of a higher degree of excellence or the prophets?' He said, 'It is the prophets.' I said,

'Consider what Ya'qub said to Joseph, "My son, do not tell your dream to your brothers. They may plot against you." Why did he not inform the brothers so that they would not plot against Joseph? He hid it from them and so also your father has done; he was afraid for you.' He then said, 'When you say that, I swear to Allah that your friend (the Imam, *'Alayhi al-Salam)* did tell me in Madina that I will be killed and crucified in al-Kunnasa and that he has a book with him that lists the people killed and crucified.'

"I then went for Hajj and reported the story of Zayd to abu 'Abd Allah, *'Alayhi al-Salam,* and what I said to Zayd. The Imam, *'Alayhi al-Salam,* said, 'It seems you surrounded him from his front, back, left, right, above and below and did not leave for him any way out.'"

Chapter 2 - The Categories of the Prophets, the Messengers and 'A'immah, *'Alayhim al-Salam*

H 430, Ch. 2, h 1
Muhammad ibn Yahya has narrated from Ahmad ibn Muhammad from abu Yahya al-Wasiti from Hisham ibn Salim and Durust ibn abu Mansur the following:

"Abu 'Abd Allah, *'Alayhi al-Salam,* has said that the prophets and the messengers are of four categories. There were prophets who were given Divine news in their souls just for their own selves and for no one else. There were also prophets who were given Divine news in their dreams and would hear the voice, but would not see anyone when awake and they were not sent to other people with such news. They had to follow an Imam just as it happened with Lot who followed Abraham. There were prophets who would experience in their dreams, hear the voice and see the angel and were sent to a group of people, small or large, like Yunus (Jonah), as Allah has said, 'We sent him to a hundred thousand people or a few more.' (37:148). The Imam said that 'few more' were thirty thousand people led by an Imam.

"There were those who saw in their dreams, heard the voice and saw the angel when awake, and were also Imam like *'Ulul 'Azm* ones. Abraham was a prophet but not an Imam until Allah said, 'I want to appoint you as the Imam for people.' He said, 'Also, please (let there be more Imam), from my descendents,' to which He said, 'My covenant does not go to the unjust ones.' (2:124) Those who have worshipped idols or statues will not become Imam.'"

H 431, Ch. 2, h 2
Muhammad ibn al-Hassan has narrated from those he mentioned from Muhammad ibn Khalid from Muhammad ibn Sinan from Zayd al-Shahham who has said the following:

"I heard Imam abu 'Abd Allah say, 'Allah, the Most Holy, the Most High, chose Abraham as a servant before choosing him as a prophet. Allah chose him as a prophet before choosing him as a messenger. Allah chose him as a messenger before choosing him as a friend. Allah chose him as a friend before choosing him as an Imam. When all of the above conditions accumulated in Abraham, Allah said, 'I have certainly appointed you as the Imam for the people.' To Abraham, to be an Imam was so great that he asked, 'Can this Imamat (Leadership with Divine

Authority) be placed in my descendents also?' Allah said, 'My covenant will not be made available to the unjust ones.' (2:124) He said that the feeble-minded (the unjust ones) cannot become the leaders (the Imam) of the pious ones.'"

H 432, Ch. 2, h 3
A number of our people have narrated from Ahmad ibn Muhammad ibn Muhammad ibn Yahya al-Khath'ami from Hisham from abu Ya'qub who has said the following:

"I heard abu 'Abd Allah say, 'The leaders and masters of the prophets and the messengers are five who are called *'Ulul 'Azm* (people with determination) among the messengers who have the central role. They are Noah, Abraham, Moses, Jesus and Muhammad, *'Alayhi al-Salam*,'"

H 433, Ch. 2, h 4
Ali ibn Muhammad has narrated from Sahl ibn Ziyad from Muhammad ibn al-Hassan from Ishaq ibn 'Abd al-'Aziz from abu al-Safatij from Jabir who has said the following:

"I heard the Imam abu Ja'far, *'Alayhi al-Salam*, say, 'Allah chose Abraham as a servant before He chose him as a prophet. He chose him as a prophet before He chose him as a messenger. He chose him as a messenger before He chose him as a friend. He chose him as a friend before He chose him as an Imam. When all of these conditions accumulated in him,' the Imam holding his hands said, "Allah said, 'O Ibrahim I have appointed you as the Imam (leader) of the people.'" The position was so great that Abraham then asked, 'O Lord, can it be in my descendents also?' The Lord said, 'My covenant will not be made available to the unjust ones.'""

Chapter 3 - The Difference Among the Messengers, the Prophets and al-Muhaddath

H 434, Ch. 3, h 1
A number of our people have narrated from Ahmad ibn Muhammad ibn from Ahmad ibn Muhammad ibn abu Nasr from Tha'laba ibn Maymun from Zurara who has said the following:

"Once I asked abu Ja'far, *'Alayhi al-Salam*, about the words of Allah, the Most Holy, the Most High, 'He was a messenger, a prophet' (19:51) what is a messenger and what is a prophet? The Imam said, 'A prophet is one who sees things (matters of Divine guidance) in his dreams and hears the voice but does not see the angel. The messenger is one who hears the voice, in his dreams sees things (of matters of Divine guidance) and sees the angel.' I then said, 'What is the position of the Imam?' The Imam, *'Alayhi al-Salam*, said, 'He hears the voice but does not see and observe the angel.' Then he recited the following verse of the Holy Quran. 'Satan would try to tamper with the desires of every Prophet or Messenger or [*Muhaddath*] whom We sent . . .'" (22:52) (The Imam included the word *Muhaddath* in the above verse as his commentary.)

H 435 Ch. 3, h 2
Ali ibn Ibrahim has narrated from his father from Isma'il ibn Marrar who has said the following:

"Once al-Hassan ibn al-'Abbass al-Ma'rufi wrote to Imam al-Rida, *'Alayhi al-Salam*, 'May Allah keep my soul in service for your cause, explain to me the difference between the messengers, the prophets and the Imam.' The Imam said or wrote, 'The difference between the messengers, the prophets and the Imam is that a messenger is one to whom Jibril (Gabriel) comes. He sees Jibril and hears his speech and Jibril (the angel) brings him (Divine) revelation and sometimes he may see in his dream something like the dream of Abraham (peace be upon him). A prophet is one who may hear the speech (of the angel) and may see (his) person and may not hear (him). The Imam is the one who hears the speech but does not see the person (of the angel).'"

H 436, Ch. 3, h 3

Muhammad ibn Yahya has narrated from Ahmad ibn Muhammad from al-Hassan ibn Mahbub from al-Ahwal who has said the following:

"I asked abu Ja'far, *'Alayhi al-Salam*, about the messenger, the prophet and al-Muhaddath (one to whom Divine guidance is conveyed). The Imam, *'Alayhi al-Salam*, said, 'A messenger is one to whom Jibril (Gabriel) comes openly. He sees him (the angel) and speaks to him. Such person is a messenger. A prophet is one who sees in his dream something like the dream of Abraham (peace be upon him). (Of such dreams) is the dream of the Messenger of Allah, *'Alayhi al-Salam*, about reasons and signs of prophecy before the coming of revelation. (He would experience such dreams) until Jibril came from Allah to inform him that he was to be a messenger. In the case of Prophet Muhammad, *'Alayhi al-Salam*, when prophecy was established in him, then Jibril brought him the message that he was to be a messenger. Jibril would come and speak to him openly. Certain prophets, in whom prophecy had been established, saw in their dreams, the spirit who would come to them, speak and report to them but they would not see the spirit when awake.

"*Al-Muhaddath* is one to whom matters of Divine guidance are reported and he hears the reporting but does not see (the angel) openly or in his dream.'"

H 437, Ch. 3, h 4

Ahmad ibn Muhammad and Muhammad ibn Yahya have narrated from Muhammad ibn al-Husayn from Ali ibn Hassa'n from ibn Faddal from Ali ibn Ya'qub al-Hashimi from Marwan ibn Muslim from Burayd who has narrated from abu Ja'far and abu 'Abd Allah, *'Alayhi al-Salam*, the following:

"I asked abu Ja'far and abu 'Abd Allah, *'Alayhi al-Salam*, about the words of Allah, the Most Holy, the Most High, 'Satan would try to tamper with the desires of every Prophet or Messenger or *Muhaddath* whom We sent . . .' (22:52). I said, 'May Allah keep my soul in service for your cause, we do not consider the word *Muhaddath* part of the verse of the Holy Quran. What then is the meaning of 'The Messenger, Prophet and *Muhaddath*?' The Imam, *'Alayhi al-Salam*, said, 'A messenger is one to whom the angel comes openly and speaks to him. A prophet is one who sees (matters of Divine guidance) in his dreams. Sometimes prophecy and messengership may exist in one person. *Al-Muhaddath* is one who hears the voice but does not see the person (of the angel).' I then asked, 'May Allah keep you well, how can one know that what one sees in his dreams is true and that it is from the angel?' The Imam, *'Alayhi al-Salam*, said, 'He receives help for success in knowing the angel. Allah has made your book to be the last book and your Prophet the last prophet.'"

Chapter 4 - Without the Imam Allah's Holding People Accountable Remains Unjustified

H 438 Ch. 4, h 1

Muhammad ibn Yahya al-'Attar has narrated from Ahmad ibn Muhammad ibn 'Isa from ibn abu 'Umayr from al-Hassan ibn Mahbub from Dawud al-Riqqi from the pious man, 'Alayhi al-Salam, the following:

"Allah's holding people as accountable remains unjustified without the Imam who would teach people about Him."

H 439, Ch. 4, h 2

Al-Husayn ibn Muhammad has narrated from Mu'alla ibn Muhammad from al-Hassan ibn Ali al-Washsha' who has said the following:

"I heard al-Rida say that abu 'Abd Allah, 'Alayhi al-Salam, has said, 'Allah's, the Majestic, the Glorious, holding people as accountable remains unjustified without the Imam to teach people about Him.'"

H 440, Ch. 4, h 3

Ahmad ibn Muhammad has narrated from Muhammad ibn al-Hassan from 'Abbad ibn Sulayman from Sa'd ibn Sa'd from Muhammad ibn 'Ammara from abu al-Hassan al-Rida, 'Alayhi al-Salam, who has said the following:

"Allah's holding people as accountable remains unjustified without the Imam who would teach people about Him."

H 441 Ch. 4, h 4

Muhammad ibn Yahya has narrated from Ahmad ibn Muhammad from al-Barqi from Khalaf ibn Hammad from 'Aban ibn Taghlib from abu 'Abd Allah, 'Alayhi al-Salam, who has said the following:

"A person with Divine Authority is (a must to exist on earth) before the people, with the people and after the people."

Chapter 5 - The Earth at No Time is Without a Person with Divine Authority

H 442, Ch. 5, h 1

A number of our people have narrated from Ahmad ibn Muhammad ibn 'Isa from Muhammad ibn abu 'Umayr from al-Husayn ibn abu al-'Ala' who has said the following:

"Once I asked abu 'Abd Allah, 'Alayhi al-Salam, 'Can there be a time on earth without Imam?' The Imam said, 'No, it is not left without Imam.' I asked, 'Can there be two Imam at a time?' He said, 'No, unless one is quiet (not active in the task of Imamat, the leadership).'"

H 443, Ch. 5, h 2

Ali ibn Ibrahim has narrated from his father from Muhammad ibn abu 'Umayr from Mansur ibn Yunus and Su'dan ibn Muslim from Ishaq ibn 'Ammar who has said the following from abu 'Abd Allah, 'Alayhi al-Salam:

"I heard him (the Imam), 'Alayhi al-Salam, say, 'The earth is never left without an Imam so that if the believers add anything (to the laws of Shari'a) it is brought back (to the original form) and if they reduce anything it is completed for them.'"

H 444, Ch. 5, h 3

Muhammad ibn Yahya has narrated from Ahmad ibn Muhammad from Ali ibn al-Hakam from Rabi' ibn Muhammad al-Musalliy from 'Abd Allah ibn Sulayman al-'Amiriy from abu 'Abd Allah, *'Alayhi al-Salam*, who has said the following:

"The earth has never been left without a person with Divine Authority who can teach people about the lawful and the unlawful matters, and call them to the path of Allah."

H 445, Ch. 5, h 4

Ahmad ibn Mihran has narrated from Muhammad ibn Ali from al-Husayn ibn abu 'Ala' who has said the following:

"Once I asked abu 'Abd Allah, *'Alayhi al-Salam*, 'Can the earth remain without an Imam?' He (the Imam), *'Alayhi al-Salam*, said, 'No, it is not left without the presence of the Imam.'"

H 446, Ch. 5, h 5

Ali ibn Ibrahim has narrated from Muhammad ibn 'Isa from Yunus from ibn Muskan from abu Basir from one of them (the two Imam, *'Alayhi al-Salam*, who has said the following:

"Allah does not leave the earth without an 'Alim (scholar). Without this (people) cannot distinguish truth from falsehood."

H 447 Ch. 5, h 6

Muhammad ibn Yahya has narrated from Ahmad ibn Muhammad from al-Husayn ibn Sa'id from al-Qasim ibn Muhammad from Ali ibn abu Hamza from abu Basir from abu 'Abd Allah, *'Alayhi al-Salam*, who has said the following:

"Allah, the Most Holy, the Most High, is Great and Majestic and it does not befit Him to leave the earth without an Imam of justice."

H 448, Ch. 5, h 7

Ali ibn Muhammad has narrated from Sahl ibn Ziyad from al-Hassan ibn Mahbub from abu 'Usama and Ali ibn Ibrahim from his father from al-Hassan ibn Mahbub from abu 'Usama and Hisham ibn Salim from abu Hamza from abu Ishaq from those reliable among the companions of Amir al-Mu'minin, *'Alayhi al-Salam*, who has said the following:

"(Amir al-Mu'minin) Ali ibn abu Talib, *'Alayhi al-Salam*, has said, 'O Lord, You do not leave Your earth without a person who can represent Your authority among the people.'"

H 449, Ch. 5, h 8

Ali ibn Ibrahim has narrated from Muhammad ibn 'Isa from Muhammad ibn al-Fudayl from abu Hamza from abu Ja'far, *'Alayhi al-Salam*, who has said the following:

"I swear by Allah that Allah has not, from the day Adam died, left the earth without an Imam who could serve as the source of guidance for the people toward Allah. He had Divine Authority over the servants of the Lord. The earth will never be left without an Imam with Divine Authority over His servants."

H 450, Ch. 5, h 9

Al-Hassan ibn Muhammad has narrated from Muhammad ibn Mu'alla ibn Muhammad from certain persons of our people from abu Ali ibn Rashid from abu al-Hassan, *'Alayhi al-Salam*, who has said the following:

"The earth is never left without a person with Divine Authority, and I swear to Allah that I am the person with Divine Authority."

H 451 Ch. 5, h 10
Ali ibn Ibrahim has narrated from Muhammad ibn 'Isa from al-Fudayl from ibn abu Hamza who has said the following:
"Once I asked abu 'Abd Allah, *'Alayhi al-Salam*, 'Can the earth be left without the Imam?' He (the Imam), *'Alayhi al-Salam*, replied, 'Were it to remain without the Imam it would obliterate its inhabitants.'"

H 452, Ch. 5, h 11
Ali ibn Ibrahim has narrated from Muhammad ibn 'Isa from Muhammad ibn al-Fudayl who has said the following:
"Once I asked abu al-Hassan al-Rida, *'Alayhi al-Salam*, 'Can the earth remain without Imam?' He replied, 'No, it will not remain so.' I then said, 'We narrate from Imam abu 'Abd Allah, *'Alayhi al-Salam*, that the earth will not remain without Imam unless Allah, the Most High, becomes extremely angry with the people of the earth or with His servants.' He (the Imam), *'Alayhi al-Salam*, said, 'In such condition it will not remain but it will obliterate its inhabitants.'"

H 453, Ch. 5, h 12
Ali has narrated from Muhammad ibn 'Isa from abu 'Abd Allah al-Mu'min from abu Harasa from abu Ja'far, *'Alayhi al-Salam*, who has said the following:
"Were the Imam taken away from the earth, even for one hour, it would twirl against its inhabitants just like the ocean that might twirl with its inhabitants."

H 454, Ch. 5, h 13
Al-Husayn ibn Muhammad has narrated from Mu'alla ibn Muhammad from al-Washsha' who has said the following:
"Once I asked abu al-Hassan al-Rida, *'Alayhi al-Salam*, 'Can the earth remain without an Imam?' He (the Imam), *'Alayhi al-Salam*, replied, 'No, it will not remain so.' I said, 'We narrate that it will not remain without the Imam unless Allah, the Most Holy, the Most High, becomes angry with the people.' The Imam said, 'In such condition it will not remain but it will obliterate its inhabitants.'"

Chapter 6 - Divine Authority is Ever-Present

Even if only two people may remain on earth, one of them is certainly the Imam (the Person with Divine Authority)

H 455, Ch. 6, h 1
Muhammad ibn Yahya has narrated from Ahmad ibn Muhammad from Muhammad ibn Sinan from ibn al-Tayyar who has said the following:
"Once I heard abu 'Abd Allah, *'Alayhi al-Salam*, say, 'If there remains no one on earth except two persons, one of them is certainly the person with Divine Authority."

H 456, Ch. 6, h 2
Ahmad ibn Idris and Muhammad ibn Yahya both have narrated from Ahmad ibn Muhammad from Muhammad ibn 'Isa from abu 'Ubayd from Muhammad ibn Sinan from abu Hamza ibn al-Tayyar from abu 'Abd Allah, *'Alayhi al-Salam*, who has said the following:

"Were there to remain only two people on earth, one of them would be the person with Divine Authority over the other."

Muhammad ibn al-Hassan has narrated from Sahl ibn Ziyad from Muhammad ibn 'Isa a similar *Hadith*.

H 457, Ch. 6, h 3

Muhammad ibn Yahya has narrated from those he has mentioned from al-Hassan ibn Musa al-Khashshab from Ja'far ibn Muhammad from Karram from abu 'Abd Allah, *'Alayhi al-Salam*, who has said the following:

"If, of all the people, there will remain only two men, one of them will be the Imam. He also said, 'The last person to die will be the Imam, *'Alayhi al-Salam*, so that no one can complain against Allah, the Majestic, the Glorious, because of leaving him without an Imam (the person with Divine Authority over him).'"

H 458, Ch. 6, h 4

A number of our people have narrated from Ahmad ibn Muhammad al-Barqi from Ali ibn Isma'il from ibn Sinan from Hamza ibn al-Tayyar who has said the following:

"I heard Imam abu 'Abd Allah, *'Alayhi al-Salam*, say, 'Were there to remain on earth no one except two people, one of them would be the person with Divine Authority or the second one would be the person with Divine Authority.' (Uncertainty is from the narrator.)"

H 459, Ch. 6, h 5

Ahmad ibn Muhammad has narrated from Muhammad ibn al-Hassan from al-Nahdi from his father from Yunus ibn Ya'qub from abu 'Abd Allah, *'Alayhi al-Salam*, who has said the following:

"I heard the Imam say, 'Were there to remain no one except two people, one of them would certainly be the Imam.'"

Chapter 7 - Recognizing the Imam, *'Alayhi al-Salam*, and Belief in His Divine Authority

H 460, Ch. 7, h 1

Al-Husayn ibn Muhammad has narrated from Mu'alla ibn Muhammad from al-Hassan ibn Ali al-Washsha' who has said that Muhammad ibn al-Fudayl narrated to me from abu Hamza from abu Ja'far, *'Alayhi al-Salam*, who has said the following:

"Abu Ja'far, *'Alayhi al-Salam*, has said, 'Only those who know Allah worship Him. Those who do not know Allah they worship Him just like that in misguidance.' I then asked, 'May Allah keep my soul in service for your cause, what is the knowledge about Allah?' The Imam, *'Alayhi al-Salam*, said, 'Knowledge about Allah means to acknowledge the existence of Allah, the Most Holy, the Most High, to acknowledge His messenger and to love Imam Ali ibn abu Talib, *'Alayhi al-Salam*. Of such knowledge is to follow him and *'A'immah* (plural of Imam) of guidance and to denounce before Allah, the Most Holy, the Most High, their (*'A'immah*'s) enemies. This is how Allah, the Most Glorious, the Most Majestic, is recognized.'"

H 461, Ch. 7, h 2

Al-Husayn has narrated from Mu'alla from al-Hassan ibn Ali from Ahmad ibn 'A'idh from his father from 'Udhayna who has said that more than one person has narrated to us from one of the two (Imam), *'Alayhim al-Salam*, who has said the following:

"The Imam has said, 'One will not be considered a Mu'min (believing person) until he knows Allah, His Messenger and *'A'immah* (plural of Imam) and the Imam of one's time, acknowledges his Divine Authority and submits his affairs to the Imam, *'Alayhi al-Salam*,' He then said, 'How can one know the last one if he is ignorant of the first one (Imam)?'"

H 462, Ch. 7, h 3

Muhammad ibn Yahya has narrated from Ahmad ibn Muhammad from al-Hassan ibn Mahbub from Hisham ibn Salim from Zurara who has said the following:

"Once I said to abu Ja'far, *'Alayhi al-Salam*, 'Is recognizing the Imam from among you obligatory on all creatures?' The Imam, *'Alayhi al-Salam*, said, 'Allah, the Most Holy, the Most High, sent Muhammad to all people as His Messenger and as His authority over all creatures on earth. Those who believe in Allah and that Muhammad is His Messenger and who have followed him and acknowledged his message, on such people it is obligatory to recognize the Imam from us. Those who do not believe in Allah and in His messenger and who do not follow him and do not acknowledge him knowing about the rights of Allah and His messenger, then how can recognition of the Imam, *'Alayhi al-Salam*, be obligatory on them? They do not believe in Allah and in His messenger, do not follow him while they know about their rights.'

"I then asked, 'What do you say about those who believe in Allah and His messenger, who acknowledge His messenger in all the matters that Allah has sent, is it obligatory for them to recognize the Imam, *'Alayhi al-Salam*, from you?' The Imam, *'Alayhi al-Salam*, said, 'Yes, it is obligatory. Do they not recognize so and so?' I said, 'Yes, they do.' The Imam, *'Alayhi al-Salam*, then said, 'Do you think Allah is the one who has placed such recognition (of so and so) in their hearts? I swear by Allah that no one other than Satan has placed such recognition in their hearts. I swear by Allah that no one other than Allah, the Most Holy, the Most High, has inspired the hearts of the believers with (the recognition of) our rights.'"

H 463, Ch. 7, h 4

It is narrated from the narrator of the previous *Hadith* from Ahmad ibn Muhammad from al-Hassan ibn Mahbub from 'Amr ibn abu al-Miqdam from Jabir who has said the following:

"I heard Imam abu Ja'far, *'Alayhi al-Salam*, say, 'Only those people recognize Allah, the Most Holy, the Most High, and worship Him, who recognize Him and recognize their Imam from the family of the Holy Prophet, *'Alayhi al-Salam*, Those who do not recognize Allah, the Most Holy, the Most High, and do not recognize the Imam from us (*Ahlul Bayt*, family of the Holy Prophet), *'Alayhim al-Salam*, such people only recognize and worship something other than Allah just like that in error, I swear by Allah.'"

H 464, Ch. 7, h 5

Al-Husayn ibn Muhammad has narrated from Mu'alla ibn Muhammad from Muhammad ibn Jumhur from Fadala ibn Ayyub from Mu'awiya ibn Wahab from Dharih who has said the following:

"Once I asked abu 'Abd Allah, *'Alayhi al-Salam*, about *'A'immah* after the Holy Prophet, *'Alayhi al-Salam*, The Imam, *'Alayhi al-Salam*, said, 'Amir al-Mu'minin (Ali ibn abu Talib), *'Alayhi al-Salam*, was the Imam, after him al-Hassan, *'Alayhi al-Salam*, was the Imam, after him (al-Hassan) al-Husayn, *'Alayhi al-Salam*, was the Imam, after him (al-Husayn) Ali ibn Al-Husayn, *'Alayhi al-Salam*, was the Imam and after him (Ali ibn al-Husayn) Muhammad ibn Ali, *'Alayhi al-Salam*, was the Imam. One who denies this, it is as if he has denied the existence of Allah, the Most Holy, the Most High, and the truthfulness of the Messenger of Allah, *'Alayhi al-Salam*'

"I asked, 'May Allah keep my soul in service for your cause, are you then the Imam? I repeated it three times.' He (the Imam) said, 'I only said it to you so that you will be of the witnesses before Allah, the Most Holy, the Most High, on His earth.'"

H 465, Ch. 7, h 6

A number of our people have narrated from Ahmad ibn Muhammad ibn Khalid from his father from those he mentioned from Muhammad ibn 'Abd al-Rahman ibn abu Layla from his father from abu 'Abd Allah, *'Alayhi al-Salam*, who has said the following:

"You will not be of the people of good deeds until you know and recognize. You will not know and recognize until you acknowledge. You will not acknowledge until you safeguard all the four doors (being of good deeds, recognition, acknowledgement, acceptance and safeguarding) and the first of these doors will not do any good without the last. The people of the three strayed far away from the (right) path. Allah, the Most Holy, the Most High, accepts only the righteous deeds. Allah does not accept anything without one's fulfilling the conditions of the covenant. Those who remain faithful to Allah, the Most Holy, the Most High, about His condition of covenant and follow what is prescribed in the covenant they will receive blessings from Him and He will keep His promise.

"Allah, the Most Holy, the Most High, has informed the people of the path of guidance and has sanctioned for them the laws of Shari'a as beacons. He has informed them how to follow the laws. He has said, 'I am All-forgiving to the righteously striving believers who repent and follow the right guidance.' (20:82) 'Allah only accepts the offerings of the pious ones.' (5:27)

"Those who are pious before Allah about His commandments meet Allah as believers in whatever Prophet Muhammad, *'Alayhi al-Salam*, has brought to them from Allah. It is unfortunate that people died before finding guidance. They thought that they were believers but they became polytheists without realizing it.

"Those who enter the house through the door they are rightly guided. Those who go on other ways are on the path to destruction. Allah has connected the obedience to the people who possess Divine Authority with the obedience to His Messenger and the obedience to His Messenger with the obedience to His Own Self. Those who disregard the obedience to the people who possess Divine Authority they have not obeyed Allah and His Messenger. This obedience is the acknowledgment of what Allah, the Most Holy, the Most High, has said, 'Children of Adam, be well dressed with means of beauty near every mosque . . .' (7:31) that, ' . . . you should enter the doors of the houses that Allah has given permission to be uplifted wherein His name is mentioned . . .' Allah has certainly informed you that, . . . (24:36), 'There are certain men whose attentions and minds do not deviate from speaking about Allah, prayer and paying charity because of business and trade attractions. They only fear the Day in which the hearts and eyes turn upside down.' (24:37)

"Allah has appointed the messengers for His commands. He then chose them and such choice is verified in His warning that says, 'No nation who lived before was left without a Warner . . .' (35:25) Those who are ignorant stray. Those who think and understand are finders of the right guidance. Allah, the Most Holy, the Most High, has said, 'It is their hearts in the center which are blind, not their eyes.' (22:46) How can one who does not see (think) find guidance and how can one understand without thinking? Follow the Messenger of Allah and his *Ahlul Bayt* (family); acknowledge what Allah has sent and follow the traces of guidance. They (*Ahlul Bayt, 'Alayhi al-Salam*) are the signs of trust and piety. Take proper notice of the fact that if a person would deny Jesus, the son of Mary (peace be upon her) and acknowledge all the other prophets, such person would not be considered a believer. Follow the path by the help of the lighthouses and follow the signs from behind the barriers. Try to perfect the matters of your religion and believe in Allah, your Lord.'"

H 466, Ch. 7, h 7

A number of our people have narrated from Ahmad ibn Muhammad from al-Husayn ibn Sa'id from Muhammad ibn al-Husayn ibn Saghir from those he has narrated from, from Rib'i ibn 'Abd Allah from abu 'Abd Allah, *'Alayhi al-Salam*, who has said the following:

"Allah did not want to permit things to work without their means and reasons. For everything He made a cause, for every cause an explanation, for every explanation a science, for every science a speaking (door) chapter. Certain people recognize and know it (the door) and certain others do not recognize it. It (the door and chapter) is the messengers of Allah and we (*Ahl al-Bayt, 'Alayhim al-Salam*)."

H 467, Ch. 7, h 8

Muhammad ibn Yahya has narrated from Muhammad ibn al-Husayn from Safwan ibn Yahya from al-'Ala' ibn Razin from Muhammad ibn Muslim who has said the following:

"I heard abu Ja'far, *'Alayhi al-Salam*, saying, 'Whoever worships Allah, the Majestic, the Glorious, with the expectation for reward, and works hard but without having an Imam for himself, his efforts will not find acceptance. Such person is lost and is straying and Allah dislikes his deeds. The example of such person is like that of a lost sheep who strays away from the herd. She wanders around during the day and at nightfall she finds a different flock of sheep with a shepherd and she gladly and affectionately joins it thinking it to be like her own flock. She passes the night in their barn but in the morning when the shepherd allows the flock to go out she does not recognize her flock and the shepherd, and begins to wander in search for her own flock and shepherd. She finds a flock and a shepherd rushes to the flock with great interest but the shepherd shouts, 'Go to your own flock and shepherd; you are lost and wandering.' She then runs back and forth, lost and wandering without a shepherd to show her the grazing areas and the barn. At such time a wolf seizes the opportunity and kills her for food. Just the same is the case, by Allah, O Muhammad, of those people of this *'Ummah* (nation) who have no Imam from Allah, the Most Holy, the Most High, who is in public and possesses the noble quality of justice. Such people are lost and straying. If such people, in such a condition, die their death will be like that of an unbeliever and hypocrite. O Muhammad, take notice that all unjust Imam and their followers are far away from the religion of Allah. They have lost the right path and have misled the others. Their deeds are like dust blown away by the wind on a stormy day. They will remain helpless and unable to benefit from their deeds. Such is straying far away from the right path.'"

H 468, Ch. 7, h 9

Al-Husayn ibn Muhammad has narrated from Mu'alla ibn Muhammad from Muhammad ibn Jumhur from 'Abd Allah ibn 'Abd al-Rahman from al-Haytham ibn Waqid from Muqrin who has said the following:

"I heard abu 'Abd Allah, *'Alayhi al-Salam*, saying, 'Ibn al-Kawwa came to Amir al-Mu'minin, *'Alayhi al-Salam*, and asked, 'O Amir al-Mu'minin, (what do you say) about: 'There will be people on the Heights who know everyone by their faces. . . .' (7:46) The Imam said, 'We will be on the Heights. We will recognize our supporters from their faces. We are the Heights. Without knowing and recognizing us there is no other way to know Allah, the Most Holy, the Most High. We are the Heights that Allah, the Majestic, the Glorious, on the Day of Judgment will make known to everyone on the bridge. No one will enter paradise without recognizing us and our recognition of them. No one will enter hell except those who do not recognize us and whom we will ignore.'

"If Allah, the Most Holy, the Most High, wants to permit people to know Him He may do so but He has made us the doors to knowing Him, the bridge, the path and the aspect to Him. Whoever deviates from our authority and guardianship or considers others more excellent than us, such people will fall down off the bridge. People are not the same in following guidance.

"People who have found the sparkling fountains are not equal with those who have gathered around polluted waters that fall over one another. These (the latter group of) people are not equal with those who have found the sparkling fountains that flow by the order of the Lord ceaselessly and without reduction."

H 469, Ch. 7, h 10

Al-Husayn ibn Muhammad has narrated from Mu'alla ibn Muhammad from Ali ibn Muhammad from Bakr ibn Salih from al-Rayyan ibn Shabib from Yunus from abu Ayyub al-Khazzaz from abu Hamza who has narrated from Imam abu Ja'far, *'Alayhi al-Salam*, the following.

"O abu Hamza, when one of you decides to travel for just a few miles first he finds for himself a guide and direction. Your ignorance of the paths of the heavens is much more than your ignorance of the paths of earth. You must find a guide for yourself."

H 470, Ch. 7, h 11

Ali ibn Ibrahim has narrated from Muhammad ibn 'Isa from Yunus from Ayyub ibn al-Hurr from abu Basir who has said the following:

"About the words of Allah, the Majestic, the Glorious, 'Whoever is given wisdom has received a great deal of goodness' (2:273) abu 'Abd Allah, *'Alayhi al-Salam*, said, 'It means obedience to Allah and recognition as to who one's Imam is.'"

H 471, Ch. 7, h 12

Muhammad ibn Yahya has narrated from 'Abd Allah ibn Muhammad from Ali ibn al-Hakam from Aban from abu Basir saying that Imam abu Ja'far, *'Alayhi al-Salam*, once said to him the following:

"The Imam, *'Alayhi al-Salam*, asked, 'Have you found out who your Imam is?' I said, 'Yes, I swear by Allah, I did so before I left Kufa.' The Imam said, 'Then it is sufficient for you.'"

H 472, Ch. 7, h 13

Muhammad ibn Yahya has narrated from Ahmad ibn Muhammad from Muhammad ibn Isma'il from Mansur ibn Yunus from Burayd who has said that he heard Imam abu Ja'far, *'Alayhi al-Salam*, say the following:

"About the words of Allah, the Most Holy, the Most High that say, 'Can the dead to whom We have given life and light so that they may walk among the people, be considered equal to those who can never come out of darkness?' (6:122) the Imam said, the "dead" mentioned in the above verse, do not understand anything. On the other hand, "The light by the help of which they walk" mentioned in the above verse stands for the Imam that they follow. The phrase, "Be considered equal to those who can never come out of darkness" applies to those who do not know who their Imam is.'"

H 473, Ch. 7, h 14

Al-Husayn ibn Muhammad has narrated from Mu'alla ibn Muhammad from Muhammad ibn 'Urama and Muhammad ibn 'Abd Allah from Ali ibn Hassan from 'Abd al-Rahman ibn Kathir from Imam abu 'Abd Allah, *'Alayhi al-Salam*, who has said the following:

"Imam abu Ja'far, *'Alayhi al-Salam*, has said, 'Abu 'Abd Allah al-Jadali once came to Amir al-Mu'minin, *'Alayhi al-Salam*, and Amir al-Mu'minin said to him, 'O abu 'Abd Allah may I say something to you about the words of Allah, "Whoever does a good deed will receive a better reward than what he has done. He will be secure from the horror of the Day of Judgment (27:89). Those who commit evil will be thrown headlong into hell fire. (It will be said to them) can you expect any recompense other than what you deserve for your deeds?"' (27:90) The man said, 'Yes, O Amir al-Mu'minin, please tell me, may Allah keep my soul in service for your cause.' (Amir al-Mu'minin) Ali, *'Alayhi al-Salam*, said, 'A "good deed" means to acknowledge our Divine Authority and have our love in one's heart. "Evil" means denying our Divine Authority and harboring in one's heart hatred toward us, (*Ahl al-Bayt*).' Amir al-Mu'minin, *'Alayhi al-Salam*, then read the (above) verses to him."

Chapter 8 - The Obligation to Obey 'A'immah, *'Alayhim al-Salam* (plural of Imam)

H 474, Ch. 8, h 1
Ali ibn Ibrahim has narrated from his father from Hammad ibn 'Isa from Hariz from Zurara from abu Ja'far, *'Alayhi al-Salam*, who has said the following:
"The topmost matter (in religion), the most noble, the key issue, the gateway to all affairs and the pleasure of the Most Beneficent, the Most Holy, the Most High, is obedience to the Imam after finding out who he (the Imam) is." The Imam, *'Alayhi al-Salam*, then said, 'Allah, the Most Holy, the Most High, has said, "One who obeys the Messenger has certainly obeyed Allah. You have not been sent to watch over those who turn away from you. (4:80)'"

H 475, Ch. 8, h 2
Al-Husayn ibn Muhammad al-Ash'ari has narrated from Mu'alla ibn Muhammad from al-Hassan ibn Ali al-Washsha' from Aban ibn 'Uthman from abu al-Sabbah who has said the following:
"I heard Imam abu 'Abd Allah, *'Alayhi al-Salam*, saying, 'I testify that Amir al-Mu'minin, *'Alayhi al-Salam*, is the Imam, obedience to whom is obligatory by the command of Allah, that al-Hassan, *'Alayhi al-Salam*, is the Imam, obedience to whom is obligatory by the command of Allah, that al-Husayn, *'Alayhi al-Salam*, is the Imam, obedience to whom is obligatory by the command of Allah, that Ali ibn al-Husayn, *'Alayhi al-Salam*, is the Imam, obedience to whom is obligatory by the command of Allah, and that Muhammad ibn Ali (al-Baqir, *'Alayhi al-Salam*) is the Imam, obedience to whom is obligatory by the command of Allah.'"

H 476, Ch. 8, h 3
Through the same chain of narrators as that of the above *Hadith*, it is narrated from Mu'alla ibn Muhammad from al-Hassan ibn Ali who has said that Hammad ibn 'Uthman narrated to us from Bashir al-'Attar who has said the following:
"I heard Imam abu 'Abd Allah, *'Alayhi al-Salam*, saying, 'We are the people obedience to whom is obligatory by the command of Allah, and the *'A'immah* you follow are such that people's responsibility to obey them does not cease because of people's ignorance and not knowing them.'"

H 477, Ch. 8, h 4
Muhammad ibn Yahya has narrated from Ahmad ibn Muhammad from al-Husayn ibn Sa'id from Hammad ibn 'Isa from al-Husayn ibn al-Mukhtar from certain persons of our people from Imam abu Ja'far, *'Alayhi al-Salam*, who has said the following:
"Once the Imam said, 'The words of Allah, the Most Holy, the Most High, "We gave them a great kingdom," (4:58) 'great kingdom' stands for people's obligation to obey *them*.'"

H 478, Ch. 8, h 5
A number of our people have narrated from Ahmad ibn Muhammad from Muhammad ibn Sinan from abu Khalid al-Qammat from abu al-Hassan al-'Attar who has said the following:
"I heard Imam abu 'Abd Allah, *'Alayhi al-Salam*, saying, 'Of the matters common among the successors (executors of the wills) and the messengers themselves, one is the obligation to obey all of them.'"

H 479, Ch. 8, h 6

Ahmad ibn Muhammad has narrated from Muhammad ibn abu 'Umayr from Sayf ibn 'Amiyra from abu al-Sabbah al-Kinani who has said that Imam abu 'Abd Allah, *'Alayhi al-Salam*, has said the following:

"We are a people obedience to whom is obligatory by the command of Allah, the Most Holy, the Most High. The Anfal (twenty percent in tax) is for us and we have been given the authority to choose the best out of the property seized from the enemy. We are the people very firmly established in knowledge. We are the 'Certain people' who are considered as subject to envy and the jealousy of people in the following verse of the Holy Quran, 'Are they jealous of the favors that Allah has done for certain people? . . .'" (4:54)

H 480, Ch. 8, h 7

Ahmad ibn Muhammad has narrated from Ali ibn al-Hakam from al-Husayn ibn abu al-'Ala' who has said the following:

"Once I mentioned to Imam abu 'Abd Allah, *'Alayhi al-Salam*, our expression about the successors (of the prophets, *'Alayhi al-Salam*) 'Obedience to them is obligatory', he (the Imam), *'Alayhi al-Salam*, said, 'It is very true; they are the people about whom Allah, the Most Holy, the Most High, has said, "Believers, obey Allah, His Messenger, and your 'Ulu al-'Amr (Leaders who possess Divine Authority). . . ." (4:59) It is they about whom Allah, the Most Holy, the Most High, has also said, 'Only Allah, His Messenger and the true believers who are steadfast in prayer and pay alms, while they kneel during prayer, are your guardians.'" (5:55)

H 481, Ch. 8, h 8

Through the same chain of narrators, as that of the above *Hadith*, it is narrated from Ahmad ibn Muhammad from Mu'ammar ibn Khallad who has said the following:

"Once a man from Persia asked Imam abu al-Hassan, *'Alayhi al-Salam*, 'Is obedience to you obligatory?' He (the Imam), *'Alayhi al-Salam*, replied, 'Yes, it is obligatory.' The man then asked, 'Is it in the same way as obedience to (Amir al-Mu'minin) Ali ibn abu Talib, *'Alayhi al-Salam*,?' He (the Imam), *'Alayhi al-Salam*, replied, 'Yes, it is obligatory in the same way.'"

H 482, Ch. 8, h 9

Through the same chain of narrators, as that of the above *Hadith*, it is narrated from Ahmad ibn Muhammad from Ali ibn al-Hakam from Ali ibn abu Hamza from abu Basir who has said the following:

"Once I asked Imam abu 'Abd Allah, *'Alayhi al-Salam*, about *'A'immah* (plural of Imam): whether in the matters of the obligation of obedience to them they are all the same or different. He (the Imam), *'Alayhi al-Salam*, replied, 'Yes, they are all the same.'"

H 483, Ch. 8, h 10

Through the same chain of narrators, as that for the above *Hadith*, it is narrated from Marwak ibn 'Ubayd from Muhammad ibn Zayd al-Tabari who has said the following:

"Once I was in the presence of Imam al-Rida, *'Alayhi al-Salam*, in Khurasan with a group of Hashimite people among whom was Ishaq ibn Musa ibn 'Isa from the Abbasids. He (the Imam), *'Alayhi al-Salam*, said to Ishaq, 'I hear that people say we think they are our slaves. I swear upon my close relation with the Messenger of Allah, *'Alayhi al-Salam*, that I have never said such a thing. I have never heard any such thing from my father and grandfather; neither I have received any such report from my (holy and noble) ancestors who may have said any such thing. But I must say that people are our slaves in the matters of obedience to us. They are our friends in religion. Those present here must tell this to those who are not present here.'"

H 484, Ch. 8, h 11

Ali ibn Ibrahim has narrated from Salih ibn al-Sindi from Ja'far ibn Bashir from abu Salama who has said the following:

"I heard Imam abu 'Abd Allah say, 'We are the ones obedience to whom is obligatory by the commands of Allah. People have no other choice except to recognize us. They will not be excused for not recognizing us. Those who recognize us are the true believers; and those who refuse to acknowledge our Divine Authority are unbelievers. Those who do not recognize us and do not reject us are straying and lost, until they return to guidance and affirm the fact that Allah has made obedience to us obligatory. However, if they die in their straying condition, Allah will deal with them the way He would will.'"

H 485, Ch. 8, h 12

Ali has narrated from Muhammad ibn 'Isa from Yunus from Muhammad ibn Fudayl who has said the following:

"Once I asked him (the Imam), *'Alayhi al-Salam*, 'What is the best thing that can take people closer to Allah?' He (the Imam), *'Alayhi al-Salam*, said, 'Of the matters that can take people closer to Allah, the Most Holy, the Most High, the best one is to obey Him, His messenger and those who possess Divine Authority.' Imam abu Ja'far, *'Alayhi al-Salam*, has said, 'To love us is belief and to harbor hatred toward us is disbelief.'"

H 486, Ch. 8, h 13

Muhammad ibn al-Hassan has narrated from Sahl ibn Ziyad from Muhammad ibn 'Isa from Fadala ibn Ayyub from Aban from 'Abd Allah ibn Sinan from 'Isma'il ibn Jabir who has said the following:

"Once I asked Imam abu Ja'far, *'Alayhi al-Salam*, 'May I state before you my religion and belief in Allah, the Most Holy, the Most High?' He (the Imam), *'Alayhi al-Salam*, said, 'Say it and allow us hear them.' I said, 'I testify that no one deserves to be worshipped and obeyed except Allah Who is One and has no partner. I testify that Muhammad, *'Alayhi al-Salam*, is the servant and messenger of Allah. I acknowledge the truth of all that he has brought from Allah. I testify that Imam Ali, *'Alayhi al-Salam*, was the Imam and obedience to him was and is obligatory by the command of Allah, after him al-Hassan was the Imam, obedience to whom was and is obligatory by the command of Allah, after him al-Husayn was the Imam, obedience to whom was and is obligatory by the command of Allah, and after him Ali ibn al-Husayn was the Imam, obedience to whom was and is obligatory by the command of Allah'. I continued until it was the turn for him and I said, 'Then you yourself, may Allah have you in His blessings, are such Imam.' He (the Imam), *'Alayhi al-Salam*, said, 'This is the religion that belongs to Allah and it is the religion of His angels.'"

H 487, Ch. 8, h 14

Ali ibn Ibrahim has narrated from his father from ibn Mahbub from Hisham ibn Salim from abu Hamza from abu Ishaq from certain persons of the companions of (Amir al-Mu'minin) Ali, *'Alayhi al-Salam*, who has narrated the following from (Amir al-Mu'minin) Ali, *'Alayhi al-Salam*:

"You must note that to establish companionship with the scholar and to follow him is a religion on account of which Allah will grant rewards. Obedience to the scholar is the means to gain goodness and to wipe out evil deeds. It is the most valuable treasure for the believers. It is a dignifying progress in their lifetime, and after their death people will speak of him with praise and virtue because of it."

H 488, Ch. 8, h 15

Muhammad ibn 'Isma'il has narrated from al-Fadl ibn Shadhan from Safwan ibn Yahya from Mansur ibn Hazim who has said the following:

"Once I said to Imam abu 'Abd Allah, *'Alayhi al-Salam*, 'Allah is by far the Most Holy, the Most High to be recognized through His creatures. In fact, it is the creatures that are recognized through Allah.' The Imam, *'Alayhi al-Salam*, said, 'What you have said is very true.' I then said, 'One who acknowledges that he has a Creator he must also acknowledge that his Creator likes certain things and is displeased with certain other things. He must acknowledge that the only way to know what pleases the Creator and what displeases Him is through Divine revelation or the messengers. One who does not receive Divine revelation must find the messengers, and when one finds the messengers one learns that they are the Divine Authorities and obedience to them is obligatory.'

"I say it to people, 'Do you not acknowledge that the Messenger of Allah possessed Divine Authority from Allah over His creatures?' They say, 'Yes, it is true.' I then say to them, 'When the Holy Prophet left this world, who possessed Divine Authority over the people?' They say, 'The Holy Quran.' I then looked in (matters of) the Holy Quran and I found out that all kinds of people consider this Holy Book as the basis for their beliefs. The group called al-Murji'a considers it as the basis for whatever they believe. Those who believe in predestination also consider this Holy Book as the basis for whatever they believe in. Even the atheists who do not even believe in it, at all, refer to this Holy Book to defeat the others. This proves that the Holy Quran cannot be considered a Divine Authority without a guardian whose words (of explanation) about the Holy Quran are the true ones. I then ask them, 'Who is the guardian of the Holy Quran?' They reply, 'Ibn Mas'ud knew the Quran. 'Umar knew the Quran. Hudhayfa knew the Quran.' I then ask them, 'Did these people know all of the Quran?' They say, 'No, they did not know all of the Quran.'

"I do not find anyone who can say that he knows all of the Quran. The only one who says that he knows all of the Quran is Ali ibn abu Talib, *'Alayhi al-Salam*. If any question arose in these people, that one would say, 'I do not know.' The other one would say, 'I do not know,' and so on except Ali ibn abu Talib, *'Alayhi al-Salam*, who would say, 'I know.' That gives enough proof to say that Ali, *'Alayhi al-Salam*, was the guardian of the Holy Quran. Obedience to Ali ibn abu Talib, *'Alayhi al-Salam*, was obligatory by the command of Allah and he possessed

Divine Authority over the people after the Messenger of Allah, *'Alayhi al-Salam.* Whatever Ali ibn abu Talib, *'Alayhi al-Salam,* said about the Holy Quran is true.

"The Imam said, 'May Allah's blessings be with you.' I then said, 'Imam Ali, *'Alayhi al-Salam,* did not leave this world without introducing the person who possessed Divine Authority over the people after him, just as the Messenger of Allah, *'Alayhi al-Salam,* had done. The person who possessed Divine Authority over the people after Imam Ali, *'Alayhi al-Salam,* was al-Hassan ibn Ali, *'Alayhi al-Salam.* I testify that Imam al-Hassan, *'Alayhi al-Salam,* also did not leave this world without introducing the person who possessed Divine Authority over the people after him, just as his father and grandfather had done. The person, who after Imam al-Hassan, *'Alayhi al-Salam,* possessed Divine Authority over the people was Imam al-Husayn, *'Alayhi al-Salam.* Obedience to him was obligatory by the command of Allah.'

"The Imam, *'Alayhi al-Salam,* said, 'May Allah's blessings be with you.' I then kissed his head and said, 'I testify that Imam al-Husayn, *'Alayhi al-Salam,* did not leave this world without introducing the person who possessed Divine Authority over the people after him. That person was Imam Ali ibn al-Husayn, *'Alayhi al-Salam,* obedience to whom was obligatory by the command of Allah.'

"He (the Imam), *'Alayhi al-Salam,* said, 'May Allah's blessings be with you.' I then kissed his head and said, 'I testify that Imam Ali ibn al-Husayn, *'Alayhi al-Salam,* did not leave this world without introducing the person who possessed Divine Authority over the people after him. That person was Imam abu Ja'far, Muhammad ibn Ali, *'Alayhi al-Salam,* obedience to whom was obligatory by the command of Allah.'

"The Imam, *'Alayhi al-Salam,* said, 'May Allah's blessings be with you.' I then said, 'Please let me kiss your head again.' The Imam, *'Alayhi al-Salam,* smiled. I then said, 'May Allah grant you success. I know that your Holy father did not leave this world without introducing the person who possessed Divine Authority over the people after him just as his father had done. I testify that you are the person who possesses Divine Authority over the people after your Holy father and that obedience to you is obligatory by the command of Allah.'

"The Imam, *'Alayhi al-Salam,* said, 'It is true enough, He (the Imam), *'Alayhi al-Salam,* said, 'May Allah's blessings be with you.' I then asked for his permission to kiss his head and the Imam, *'Alayhi al-Salam,* smiled. I kissed his head. The Imam, *'Alayhi al-Salam,* then said, 'Ask whatever you want. I, from this day on, will never deny you anything.'"

H 489, Ch. 8, h 16

Muhammad ibn Yahya has narrated from Ahmad ibn Muhammad ibn 'Isa from Muhammad ibn Khalid al-Barqi from al-Qasim ibn Muhammad al-Jawhari from al-Husayn ibn abu al-'Ala' who has said the following:

"Once I asked Imam abu 'Abd Allah, *'Alayhi al-Salam,* 'Is obedience to the successors (of the Holy Prophet) obligatory?' He (the Imam), *'Alayhi al-Salam,* said, 'Yes, it is. They are those about whom Allah, the Most Holy, the Most High, has said, 'Believers, obey Allah, His Messenger, and your leaders who possess (Divine) Authority . . .' (4:59) It is they about whom Allah, the Most Holy, the Most High, has said, 'Only Allah, His Messenger, and the true believers who are steadfast in prayer and pay alms, while they kneel during prayer, are your guardians.'" (5:55)

H 490 Ch. 8, h 17
Ali ibn Ibrahim has narrated from Muhammad ibn 'Isa from Yunus ibn 'Abd al-Rahman from Hammad from 'Abd al-A'la' who has said the following:
"I heard Imam abu 'Abd Allah, *'Alayhi al-Salam*, saying, 'Listening and obeying are the gates to goodness. One who listens and is obedient has all the authority in his favor. One who listens but disobeys will have no authority in his favor. The leader, the Imam of the Muslims, on the Day of Judgment, in the presence of Allah, the Most Holy, the Most High, will have complete authoritative support and rightful arguments in his favor against disobedient people.' He (the Imam), *'Alayhi al-Salam*, then said, 'Allah, the Most Holy, the Most High, says, 'On the day when We call every nation with their Imam (leaders) . . .'" (17:71)

Chapter 9 - 'A'immah, *'Alayhi al-Salam*, Are Witnesses for Allah, the Majestic, the Glorious, Over His Creatures

H 491, Ch. 9, h 1
Ali ibn Muhammad has narrated from Sahl ibn Ziyad from Ya'qub ibn Yazid from Ziyad al-Qandi from Sama'a who has said the following:
"About the words of Allah, the Majestic, the Glorious, in the Holy Quran, 'How will it be when We call for a witness from every nation and have you (Muhammad) testify against them all?' (4:41) Imam abu 'Abd Allah, *'Alayhi al-Salam*, has said, 'This verse was revealed about the followers of Prophet Muhammad, *'Alayhi al-Salam*, in particular. In every generation of these people there will be an Imam from our family who would bear witness over their activities, and Prophet Muhammad, *'Alayhi al-Salam*, himself will bear witness over us.'"

H 492, Ch. 9, h 2
Al-Husayn ibn Muhammad has narrated from Mu'alla ibn Muhammad from al-Hassan ibn al-Washsha' from Ahmad ibn 'A'idh from 'Umar ibn 'Udhayna from Burayd al-'Ijli who has said the following:
"Once I asked Imam abu 'Abd Allah, *'Alayhi al-Salam*, about the meaning of the words of Allah, the Majestic, the Glorious, 'We have made you (true Muslims) a moderate nation so that you could be witness (an example) . . .' (2:143) The Imam, *'Alayhi al-Salam*, said, 'We are the moderate nation and we bear witness to the activities of the people for Allah and we possess Divine Authority on earth.' I then asked about the meaning of the following words of Allah, the Majestic, the Glorious, '. . . the noble religion of your father, Abraham. Allah named you Muslims before and in this Book, so that the Messenger will witness (your actions) . . .' (22:78) The Imam, *'Alayhi al-Salam*, said, 'The noble religion of your father, Abraham" in the above verse refers to us particularly. The phrase,

"Allah named you Muslims" means He has named us Muslims. The word "Before" refers to the heavenly books that were sent before and the phrase "as well as this Book" refers to the Holy Quran. The expression "The messenger of Allah witness" means that he bears witness over us by means of teaching us the guidance of Allah, the Majestic, the Glorious, and we bear witness over the people. Those who acknowledge our authority, we, on the Day of Judgment, will acknowledge their belief, and those who reject our Divine Authority, we, on the Day of Judgment, will refuse to acknowledge their belief.'"

H 493 Ch. 9, h 3

Through the same chain of narrators as that for the above *Hadith*, it is narrated from Mu'alla ibn Muhammad from al-Hassan ibn Ali from Ahmad ibn 'Umar al-Hallal who has said the following:

"I asked Imam abu al-Hassan, *'Alayhi al-Salam*, about the meaning of the words of Allah, the Most Holy, the Most High, 'Should they be compared with those whose Lord has given them a guidance which is testified by a witness from among their own people . . .' (11:17) He (the Imam), *'Alayhi al-Salam*, said, 'It refers to (Amir al-Mu'minin) Ali who, *'Alayhi al-Salam*, testified to support the Messenger of Allah, *'Alayhi al-Salam*, and the Messenger of Allah has supporting evidence from his Lord.'"

H 494, Ch. 9, h 4

Ali ibn Ibrahim has narrated from his father from Muhammad ibn abu 'Umayr from ibn 'Udhayna from Burayd al-'Ijli who has said the following:

"Once I asked Imam abu Ja'far, *'Alayhi al-Salam*, about the meaning of the words of Allah, the Most Holy, the Most High, 'We have made you (true Muslims) a moderate nation so that you would be witness (an example) for all people and the Messenger of Allah a witness (an example) for you . . .' (2:143) He (the Imam), *'Alayhi al-Salam*, said, 'We are the moderate nation and we are the witness for Allah, the Most Holy, the Most High, over the activities of His creatures and possess His Authority on earth.'

"I then asked about the meaning of the following words of Allah that say, 'Believers, worship your Lord, bow down and prostrate yourselves before Him and do virtuous deeds so that perhaps you will have everlasting happiness. (22:77) Strive steadfastly for the cause of Allah. He has chosen you but has not imposed on you hardship in your religion, the noble religion of your father, Abraham. Allah named you Muslims before and in this Book, so that the Messenger will witness (your actions) and you will be the witness over mankind. . . .' (22:78) He (the Imam), *'Alayhi al-Salam*, said, 'The phrase "He has chosen you" refers to us and we are the chosen ones. Allah, the Most Holy, the Most High, has not sanctioned anything in religion that is a 'constraint' upon the people. *Al-Haraj* "Hardship" mentioned in the above verse is more serious than *al-Diyq* (constraint) as Allah has said, ". . . But has not imposed on you "hardships in your religion" . . . (22:78) The Imam, *'Alayhi al-Salam*, then said the expression: "Religion of your father" also is a reference to us. Allah has called us, specially, as Muslims in the heavenly books that were revealed before and in this Holy Book (the Holy Quran). The messenger of Allah, *'Alayhi al-Salam*, has testified in our favor by conveying the message of Allah, the Most Holy, and the Most High. We bear witness to the activities of the people and on the Day of Judgment certify the belief of those who have acknowledged our Divine Authority and reject those who have rejected our Divine Authority.'"

H 495, Ch. 9, h 5
Ali ibn Ibrahim has narrated from his father from Hammad ibn 'Isa from Ibrahim ibn 'Umar al-Yamani from Sulaym ibn Qays al-Hilali from (Amir al-Mu'minin) Ali, *'Alayhi al-Salam*, who has said the following:

"Allah, the Most Holy, the Most High, cleansed us, granted us protection against sins, made us to bear witness to the activities of His creatures and granted us Divine Authority on His earth. He made us to be with the Holy Quran and the Holy Quran to be with us. We do not depart the Holy Quran and the Holy Quran does not depart us."

Chapter 10 - They ('A'immah) (Plural of Imam), *'Alayhim al-Salam*, Are the Only True Guides

H 496, Ch. 10, h 1
A number of our people have narrated from Ahmad ibn Muhammad from al-Husayn ibn Sa'id from al-Nadr ibn Suwayd and Fudala ibn Ayyub from Musa ibn Bakr from al-Fudayl who has said the following:

"Once I asked Imam abu 'Abd Allah, *'Alayhi al-Salam*, about the meaning of the words of Allah, the Majestic, the Glorious, 'For every nation there is a guide.' (13:7) He (the Imam), *'Alayhi al-Salam*, said, 'Every Imam is the guide in his own century (time).'"

H 497, Ch. 10, h 2s
Ali ibn Ibrahim has narrated from his father from Muhammad ibn abu 'Umayr from ibn 'Udhayna from Burayd al-'Ijli who has said the following:

"About the words of Allah, the Majestic, the Glorious, '(Muhammad), you are only a Warner. For every nation there is a guide' (13:7) Imam abu Ja'far, *'Alayhi al-Salam*, has said, 'The messenger of Allah is the Warner. At all times there is a guide from us who guides people to the teachings of the Holy Prophet, *'Alayhi al-Salam*. Of the guides who possess Divine Authority after the Holy Prophet, *'Alayhi al-Salam*, is Amir al-Mu'minin, Ali, *'Alayhi al-Salam*, and his successors one after the other.'"

H 498, Ch. 10, h 3
Al-Husayn ibn Muhammad al-Ash'ari has narrated from Mu'alla ibn Muhammad from Muhammad ibn Jumhur from Muhammad ibn 'Isma'il from Sa'dan from abu Basir who has said the following:

"Once I asked Imam abu 'Abd Allah, *'Alayhi al-Salam*, about the meaning of the words of Allah, the Majestic, the Glorious, '(Muhammad), you are only a Warner. For every nation there is a guide.' (13:7) The Imam, *'Alayhi al-Salam*, said, 'The messenger of Allah is the Warner and (Amir al-Mu'minin) Ali, *'Alayhi al-Salam*, is the guide. O abu Muhammad, is there a guide today?' I said, 'Yes, may Allah keep my soul in service for your cause, there has always been a guide from you one after the other until this (noble task) is being carried on by your own self.'

"The Imam, *'Alayhi al-Salam*, said, 'O abu Muhammad, may Allah grant you blessings. If a verse (guidance) comes to a man who then dies with his death the verse (guidance) also dies. Even the whole Book dies. (In our case) it (guidance) lives and it continues with new generations as it has done so with the people in the past.'"

H 499, Ch. 10, h 4

Muhammad ibn Yahya has narrated from Ahmad ibn Muhammad from al-Husayn ibn Sa'id from Safwan from Mansur from 'Abd al-Rahim al-Qasir who has said the following:

"I asked Imam abu Ja'far, *'Alayhi al-Salam*, about the meaning of the words of Allah, the Majestic, the Glorious, '. . . For every nation there is a guide.' (13:7) The Imam, *'Alayhi al-Salam*, said, 'The messenger of Allah, *'Alayhi al-Salam*, is the Warner and (Amir al-Mu'minin) Ali, *'Alayhi al-Salam*, is the guide. I swear by Allah, that guidance (and Leadership with Divine Authority) never departed us, it is with us and will always be with us until the Day of Judgment.'"

Chapter 11 - 'A'immah, *'Alayhi al-Salam*, Possess Divine Authority and the Treasure of Divine Knowledge

H 500, Ch. 11, h 1

Muhammad ibn Yahya al-'Attar has narrated from Ahmad ibn abu Zahir from al-Hassan ibn Musa from Ali ibn Hassa'n from 'Abd al-Rahman ibn Kathir who has said the following:

"I heard Imam abu 'Abd Allah, *'Alayhi al-Salam*, saying, 'We are the ones who possess Divine Authority in the matters of the command of Allah, we are the treasurers of the knowledge of Allah and the repository of the revelations of Allah.'"

H 501, Ch. 11, h 2

A number of our people have narrated from Ahmad ibn Muhammad from al-Husayn ibn Sa'id from Ali ibn Asbat from his father, Asbat from Sawra ibn Kulayb who has said the following:

"Once Imam abu Ja'far, *'Alayhi al-Salam*, said to me, 'I swear by Allah that we are the treasurers of Allah in His heavens and on His earth, not the treasurers of gold or the treasurers of silver but the treasurers of His knowledge.'"

H 502, Ch. 11, h 3

Ali ibn Musa has narrated from Ahmad ibn Muhammad from al-Husayn ibn Sa'id and Muhammad ibn Khalid al-Barqi from al-Nadr ibn Suwayd in a *marfu'* manner from Sadir who has said the following:

"I asked Imam abu Ja'far, *'Alayhi al-Salam*, saying,'May Allah keep my soul in service for your cause, what are you?' The Imam, *'Alayhi al-Salam*, said, 'We are the treasurers of the knowledge of Allah. We are the translators of the revelations of Allah. We possess well preached Divine Authority over all that is under the heavens and those on the earth.'"

H 503, Ch. 11, h 4

Muhammad ibn Yahya has narrated from Muhammad ibn al-Husayn from al-Nadr ibn Shu'ayb from Muhammad ibn al-Fudayl from abu Hamza who has said the following:

"I heard Imam abu Ja'far, *'Alayhi al-Salam*, saying, 'The messenger of Allah, *'Alayhi al-Salam*, has said that Allah, the Most Holy, the Most High, has said,

"My Authority is completely established among the unfortunate ones of your followers. Those who refuse to acknowledge the Divine Authority of (Amir al-Mu'minin) Ali, *'Alayhi al-Salam*, and his successors, (they have rejected My Authority). With (Amir al-Mu'minin) Ali, *'Alayhi al-Salam*, and his successors there are your traditions and the traditions of the prophets before you. They (Ali and his successors) are the treasurers of My knowledge after you.'" The Messenger of Allah, *'Alayhi al-Salam*, then said, 'Jibril (Gabriel) has informed me of the names of the successors of (Amir al-Mu'minin) Ali, *'Alayhi al-Salam*, and the names of their fathers.'"

H 504, Ch. 11, h 5

Ahmad ibn Idris has narrated from Muhammad ibn 'Abd al-Jabbar from Muhammad ibn Khalid from Fadala ibn Ayyub from 'Abd Allah ibn Ya'fur who has said the following:

"Once abu 'Abd Allah, *'Alayhi al-Salam*, said to me, 'O ibn abu Ya'fur, Allah is One and is the only One in His Oneness. He alone issues His command. He created a *creature* and appointed and measured it for that command (*Amr*, task). We, O ibn abu Ya'fur, are that *creature*. We are the Authority of Allah over His creatures, the treasurers and guardians of His knowledge.'"

H 505, Ch. 11, h 6

Ali ibn Muhammad has narrated from Sahl ibn Ziyad from Musa ibn al-Qasim ibn Mu'awiya and Muhammad ibn Yahya from al-'Amrakiy ibn Ali all from Ali ibn Ja'far from abu al-Hassan Musa, *'Alayhi al-Salam*, who has said the following:

"Abu 'Abd Allah, *'Alayhi al-Salam*, has said, 'Allah, the Most Holy, the Most High, created us and He made our creation the best. He formed us and made our form the best. He made us the treasurers of His heavens and His earth. For us the tree spoke and with our worship Allah, the Most Holy, the Most High, is worshipped. Had we not been in existence Allah would not have been worshipped.'"

Chapter 12 - 'A'immah, *'Alayhim al-Salam*, Are the Deputies of Allah, On Earth

'A'immah, *'Alayhim al-Salam*, are the deputies of Allah the Most Holy, the Most High, on earth and the gates through which people become nearer to Allah.

H 506, Ch. 12, h 1

Al-Husayn ibn Muhammad al-Ash'ari has narrated from Mu'alla ibn Muhammad from Ahmad ibn Muhammad from abu Mas'ud from al-Ja'fari who has said the following:

"I heard abu al-Hassan al-Rida, *'Alayhi al-Salam*, say, '*'A'immah*, *'Alayhi al-Salam*, are the deputies of Allah, the Most Holy, the Most High, on His earth.'"

H 507, Ch. 12, h 2

Mu'alla has narrated from Muhammad ibn Jumhur from Sulayman ibn Sama'a from 'Abd Allah ibn al-Qasim from abu Basir who has said the following:

"Abu 'Abd Allah, *'Alayhi al-Salam*, has said, 'The successors (of the Holy Prophet, *'Alayhi al-Salam*) are the gates to Allah, the Most Holy, the Most High, through which people go to Him. Had they not existed, Allah, the Most Holy, the Most High, would not have been recognized. Allah, the Most Holy, the Most High, will present these successors as evidence against His creatures to support His religion.'"

H 508, Ch. 12, h 3
Al-Husayn ibn Muhammad has narrated from Mu'alla ibn Muhammad from al-Washsha' from 'Abd Allah ibn Sinan who has said the following:

"I asked abu 'Abd Allah, *'Alayhi al-Salam*, about the meaning of the words of Allah, the Most Holy, the Most High, 'Allah has promised the righteously striving believers to appoint them as His deputies on earth, as He had appointed those who lived before . . .' (24:55) He (the Imam), *'Alayhi al-Salam*, said, 'The people referred to in this verse are *'A'immah, 'Alayhim al-Salam,'*"

Chapter 13 - 'A'immah (Plural of Imam), *'Alayhim al-Salam*, Are the Light of Allah, the Most Holy, the Most High

H 509, Ch. 13, h 1
Al-Husayn ibn Muhammad has narrated from Mu'alla ibn Muhammad from Ali ibn Mirdas who has said that Safwan ibn Yahya and al-Hassan ibn Mahbub have narrated from abu Ayyub from abu Khalid al-Kabuli who has said the following:

"I asked (Imam) abu Ja'far, *'Alayhi al-Salam*, about the meaning of the words of Allah, the Majestic, the Gracious, 'Those who believe in Allah and His messenger and follow the light which is sent down. . . .' (64:8)

"He (the Imam), *'Alayhi al-Salam*, said, 'O abu Khalid, I swear by Allah, it is *'A'immah* from the family of the Holy Prophet, *'Alayhi al-Salam*, up to the Day of Judgment who are called light in the above verse. They, I swear by Allah, are the light of Allah whom He sent down. It is they, I swear by Allah, who are the light of Allah in the heavens and in the earth. O abu Khalid, I swear by Allah, that the light of Imam, *'Alayhi al-Salam*, in the hearts of the true believers is brighter than the light of the sun in the midday. They, I swear by Allah, give light to the hearts of the true believers and Allah, the Most Holy, the Most High, may block such light from reaching the hearts of whoever He may will, thus their hearts remain dark. O abu Khalid, no one believes in our Divine Authority except that Allah cleanses his heart. Allah will not cleanse the heart of a person until he or she will acknowledge our Divine Authority and live in peace with us. When one lives in peace with us Allah will safeguard him against the severity of the Day of Reckoning and grant him security against the great horror on the Day of Judgment'"

H 510, Ch. 13, h 2
Ali ibn Ibrahim has narrated through his chain of narrators from abu 'Abd Allah, *'Alayhi al-Salam*, who has said the following about the words of Allah, the Most High:

"There are those who follow the Messenger, the illiterate Prophet (not conventionally educated), whose description they find written in the Torah and the Gospel. [He (the Messenger) enjoins them to do good and forbids them to do all that is unlawful, makes lawful for them all that is pure and makes unlawful all that is filthy, removes their burdens and the entanglements in which they are involved]. Those who believe in him, honor and help him, and follow the light which is sent down to him, will have everlasting happiness." (7:157) The Imam, *'Alayhi al-Salam*, said, 'It is Ali (Amir al-Mu'minin), *'Alayhi al-Salam*, and *'A'immah* (plural of Imam), *'Alayhim al-Salam*, after him who are called 'light' in the above verse of the Holy Quran.'"

H 511, Ch. 13, h 3

Ahmad ibn Idris has narrated from Muhammad ibn 'Abd al-Jabbar from ibn Fadala from Tha'laba ibn Maymun from abu al-Jarud who has said the following:

"Once I said to (Imam) abu Ja'far, *'Alayhi al-Salam*, 'Allah has given a great deal of good to the people of the heavenly books.' He (the Imam), *'Alayhi al-Salam*, then asked, 'What is it?' I then said it is said in the words of Allah, 'Of those to whom We have given the book before him (Prophet Muhammad) they believe in him . . . These will receive double reward for their forbearance. . . .' (28:54)

"He (the Imam) *'Alayhi al-Salam*, said, 'Allah has given you also a great deal of good as He has given to them,' and he recited, 'Believers, have fear of Allah and believe in His Messenger. Allah will grant you a double share of mercy, a light by which you can walk . . .' (57:28) The 'light' mentioned in this verse stands for the Imam, *'Alayhi al-Salam*, whom you follow.'"

H 512, Ch. 13, h 4

Ahmad ibn Mihran has narrated from 'Abd al-'Azim ibn 'Abd Allah al-Hassani from Ali ibn Asbat and al-Hassan ibn Mahbub from abu Ayyub from abu Khalid al-Kabuli who has said the following:

"Once I asked (Imam) abu Ja'far, *'Alayhi al-Salam*, about the meaning of the words of Allah, the Most Holy, the Most High, in the following verse of the Holy Quran. 'Those who believe in Allah and His messenger and follow the light which is sent down. . . .' (64:8) He (the Imam), *'Alayhi al-Salam*, said, 'O abu Khalid, the 'light' in this verse, I swear by Allah, stands for *'A'immah* (plural of Imam). O abu Khalid the light of the Imam, *'Alayhi al-Salam*, in the hearts of the true believers is brighter than the light of the sun in midday. It is they who brighten the hearts of the true believers, and Allah withholds their light from reaching whomever He wills not to reach, thus their hearts become dark and Allah covers them with darkness.'"

H 513, Ch. 13, h 5

Ali ibn Muhammad and Muhammad ibn al-Hassan have narrated from Sahl ibn Ziyad from Muhammad ibn al-Hassan ibn Shammun from 'Abd Allah ibn 'Abd al-Rahman al-Asamm from 'Abd Allah ibn al-Qasim from Salih ibn Sahl al-Hamadani who has said the following:

"Abu 'Abd Allah, *'Alayhi al-Salam*, has said the following about the statement of Allah, the Most High, 'Allah is the light of the heavens and the earth. A metaphor for His light is a lantern in which there is a lamp placed in a glass. The glass is like a shining star, which is lit from a blessed olive tree that is neither eastern nor western. Its oil almost lights up even though the fire has not touched it. It is light upon light. Allah guides to His light whoever He wants. Allah uses various metaphors. He has the knowledge of all things.' (24:35) The Imam said, "Lantern" metaphorically stands for the Holy lady, *Fatimah*, *'Alayha al-Salam*, the "Lamp" stands for Imam al-Hassan, *'Alayhi al-Salam*, and "the glass" stands for Imam al-Husayn, *'Alayhi al-Salam*, "The shining star" stands for the Holy lady *Fatimah, 'Alayha al-Salam*, who shines among the ladies of the world. "The blessed olive tree" stands for Prophet Abraham. "Neither eastern nor western" means neither Jewish nor Christian. The expression: "Its oil almost lights up" means that it almost bursts up with knowledge. "Light upon light" means that there will be one Imam after the other Imam, *'Alayhi al-Salam*, "Allah guides to His light whoever He wants" means that Allah guides through the *'A'immah* (plural of Imam) whoever He wants.' About the expression "Allah uses various metaphors" I then recited the following verse of the Holy Quran: 'Or they (the deeds of the unbelievers) are like the darkness of a deep, stormy sea with layers of giant waves, covered by dark clouds. It is darkness upon darkness whereby even if one stretches out his hands he cannot see them. One can have no light unless Allah gives him light.' (24:40)

"The Imam, *'Alayhi al-Salam*, said, 'The word "Darkness" refers to the first and his friend, the expression "With layers of giant waves" refers to the third, and the expression "Covered with darkness" refers to the second. The words "It is darkness upon darkness" refer to Mu'awiya (may Allah condemn him) and the disasters caused by the Amavids. The phrase "Even if one stretches out his hands" means that even if a true believer stretches out his hands in such disastrous condition "he cannot see them." The statement "One can have no light unless Allah gives him light" stands for the light from the children of the Holy lady, *Fatimah, 'Alayha al-Salam*. The phrase "Can have no light" means an Imam on the Day of Judgment. The Imam, *'Alayhi al-Salam*, said that, 'On the Day of Judgment you will see the believers with their light shining in front of them and to their right. They will be told, 'Paradise wherein streams flow is the glad news for you today. You will live therein forever. This is the greatest triumph.' (57:12) The phrase "The shining light in front . . . " is a reference to the Imam, *'Alayhi al-Salam*, who will walk in front and on the right of the true believers until they all enter paradise.'"

Ali ibn Muhammad and Muhammad ibn al-Hassan have narrated from Sahl ibn Ziyad from Musa ibn al-Qasim al-Bajali and Muhammad ibn Yahya from al-'Amrakiy ibn Ali altogether from Ali ibn Ja'far, *'Alayhi al-Salam*, from his brother a similar *Hadith*.

H 514, Ch. 13, h 6

Ahmad ibn Idris has narrated from al-Husayn ibn 'Ubayd Allah from Muhammad ibn al-Hassan and Musa ibn 'Umar from al-Hassan ibn Mahbub from Muhammad ibn al-Fudayl who has said the following:

"Once I asked abu al-Hassan, *'Alayhi al-Salam*, about the meaning of the words of Allah, the Most Holy, the Most High, in the following verse of the Holy Quran. 'They want to put out the light of Allah with their mouths, but Allah will certainly make His light shine forever, even though the unbelievers may dislike this.' (61:8) He (the Imam), *'Alayhi al-Salam*, said, 'They want to put out the Divine Authority of Amir al-Mu'minin (Ali), *'Alayhi al-Salam*, with their mouths. However, the expression "Allah completes His light" stands for the Imam, *'Alayhi al-Salam*, as mentioned in the following verse 'Those who believe in Allah, His messenger and follow the light which is sent down . . .' (64:8) "The light" stands for Imam, *'Alayhi al-Salam*,'"

Chapter 14 - 'A'immah Are as the Cornerstone of Earth

H 515, Ch. 14, h 1

Ahmad ibn Mahran from Muhammad ibn Ali and Muhammad ibn Yahya from Ahmad ibn Muhammad altogether from Muhammad ibn Sinan from al-Mufaddal ibn 'Umar from abu 'Abd Allah, *'Alayhi al-Salam*, who has said the following:

"Whatever Imam Ali, *'Alayhi al-Salam*, has brought I follow it entirely and whatever he has forbidden I desist from it altogether. Whatever excellence was found in the Holy Prophet, *'Alayhi al-Salam*, was found in Imam Ali, *'Alayhi al-Salam*, also. The Holy Prophet was more excellent than all of the creatures of Allah, the Most Holy, the Most High. Those turning away from any item of his (Imam Ali's) guidance are like one turning away from the guidance of Allah and His messenger. Rejecting him in small or great matters is like considering things similar to Allah (sharik). Amir al-Mu'minin (Ali), *'Alayhi al-Salam*, was the only gate to Allah through which people could go closer to Him. He (Imam Ali), *'Alayhi al-Salam*, was the path that if one ignored he would be destroyed. This is also true of *'A'immah* of guidance one after the other. Allah has made them as cornerstones of the earth so that people on earth are not be destroyed. They possess the doubtless Divine Authority over the inhabitants of earth and those below the earth.

"Amir al-Mu'minin (Ali), *'Alayhi al-Salam*, would very often say, 'I am the supervisor for Allah to see who should go to paradise and who should go to hell. I am the greatest criterion, the possessor of the staff (of Moses) and the Miysam (marking seal). All the angels, the spirit and the messengers have acknowledged the existence in me of all the matters that they had acknowledged in Prophet Muhammad, *'Alayhi al-Salam*, I am held responsible for all such matters for which Prophet Muhammad, *'Alayhi al-Salam*, was held responsible. Such responsibilities are the duties to Allah, the Lord. The messenger of Allah will be called upon and will be dressed up (as the Imam of people). I will be called upon and will be dressed up (as the Imam of people). The Holy Prophet will be made to speak and I will be made to speak and I will speak just the way he will speak. I have been given certain distinctions, which are given to no one before me.

"I was taught all about the deaths, the sufferings, the genealogy of people and clear speech. I have not missed any of the knowledge that has passed me by and nothing of the future is unseen or unknown to me. I give good news by the permission of Allah and do my duty towards Allah. All of this is from Allah Who has made it possible for me through His knowledge.'"

Al-Husayn ibn Muhammad al-Ash'ari has narrated from Mu'alla ibn Muhammad from Muhammad ibn Jumhur al-'Ammi from Muhammad ibn Sinan who has said that al-Mufaddal narrated to us that he heard from abu 'Abd Allah, *'Alayhi al-Salam*, he then narrated the above *Hadith*.

H 516, Ch. 14, h 2

Ali ibn Muhammad and Muhammad ibn al-Hassan have narrated from Sahl ibn Ziyad from Muhammad ibn al-Walid Shabab al-Sayrafi who has said that Sa'id' al-A'raj has said that he and Sulayman ibn Khalid once went to abu 'Abd Allah, *'Alayhi al-Salam*, and al-A'raj began the conversation as follows:

"O Sulayman, whatever Imam Ali, *'Alayhi al-Salam*, has brought is followed entirely and whatever he has forbidden is desisted from altogether. Whatever excellence was found in the Messenger of Allah, *'Alayhi al-Salam*, was found in Imam Ali, *'Alayhi al-Salam*, also. The Messenger of Allah was more excellent than all of the creatures of Allah, the Most Holy, the Most High. Those who find faults in any item of his (Imam Ali's) guidance are like one finding faults in the guidance of Allah, the Most Holy, the Most High, and His messenger. Rejecting him in small or great matters is like considering things similar (sharik) to Allah. Amir al-Mu'minin (Ali), *'Alayhi al-Salam*, was the only gate to Allah through which people could get closer to Him. Imam Ali, *'Alayhi al-Salam*, was the path. Ignoring this path leads one to destruction. This is also true of *'A'immah* of guidance one after the other. Allah has made them as the cornerstones of the earth so that people on it are not destroyed. They possess the doubtless Divine Authority over the inhabitants of earth and those below the earth.

"Amir al-Mu'minin (Ali), *'Alayhi al-Salam*, has said, 'I am the supervisor for Allah to see who should go to paradise and who should go to hell. I am the greatest decisive factor, the possessor of the staff (of Moses) and the Miysam (marking seal). All the angels, and the spirit have acknowledged the existence in me of all the matters that they had acknowledged in Prophet Muhammad, *'Alayhi al-Salam*. I am held responsible for all such matters for which Prophet Muhammad, *'Alayhi al-Salam*, was held responsible. Such responsibilities are the duties to Allah, the Lord. The Holy Prophet will be called upon and will be dressed up (as the Imam of people). I will be called upon and will be dressed up (as the Imam of people). The Holy Prophet will be made to speak, and I will be made to speak and I will speak just the way he will speak. I have been given certain distinctions, which are given to no one before me. I was taught all about the deaths, the sufferings, the genealogy of people and clear speech. I have not missed any of the knowledge that has passed by me and nothing of the future is unseen or unknown to me. I give good news by the permission of Allah and do my duty toward Allah, the Majestic, the Glorious. All of this is from Allah Who has made it possible for me through His knowledge.'"

H 517, Ch. 14, h 3

Muhammad ibn Yahya and Ahmad ibn Muhammad both have narrated from Muhammad ibn al-Hassan from Ali ibn Hassa'n who has said that abu 'Abd Allah al-Riyahi narrated to him from abu al-Samit al-Hulwani the following:

"Abu Ja'far, *'Alayhi al-Salam*, about the excellence of Amir al-Mu'minin, Ali, *'Alayhi al-Salam*, has said, 'Whatever Imam Ali, *'Alayhi al-Salam*, has brought I follow it entirely and whatever he has forbidden I desist from it altogether. All that is true of the obedience to the Messenger of Allah, *'Alayhi al-Salam*, is true of the obedience to Imam Ali, *'Alayhi al-Salam*, after the Messenger of Allah, but excellence belongs to Prophet Muhammad, *'Alayhi al-Salam*. Those who try to

177

be ahead of Imam Ali, *'Alayhi al-Salam*, are considered as trying to be ahead of Allah and His messenger, *'Alayhi al-Salam*. Those who try to show themselves more excellent than Imam Ali, *'Alayhi al-Salam*, are considered as trying to show themselves more excellent than the Messenger of Allah, *'Alayhi al-Salam*. Whoever rejects any of the small or great items of the guidance of Imam Ali, *'Alayhi al-Salam*, is like considering things as similar (sharik) to Allah. The messenger of Allah, *'Alayhi al-Salam*, is the gate through which people can go to Allah. He is the path that if chosen leads to Allah, the Most Holy, the Most High. The same was true of Imam Ali, *'Alayhi al-Salam*, after the Messenger of Allah, *'Alayhi al-Salam*. All such matters were true of *A'immah*, *'Alayhi al-Salam*, one after the other. Allah, the Most Holy, the Most High, has made them the cornerstone of the earth so that its inhabitants are not destroyed. They were the pillars of Islam and the connection in the path of guidance. No guide can be a guide without their guidance and no straying one goes astray unless he ignores the rights of *A'immah*, *'Alayhim al-Salam*. They are the trustees of Allah over whatever knowledge, warning and excuses have been revealed to them (from the heavens). They possess the doubtless Divine Authority over those on earth. Whatever (excellence and authority) is found in one of them is true of all of them and no one can reach such a stage without support from Allah.

"Amir al-Mu'minin (Ali), *'Alayhi al-Salam*, has said, 'I am the supervisor for Allah over paradise and hell. No one will go to either one without my supervision. I am the greatest criterion and the Imam for those after me, and the provider of relief for those before me. No one is permitted to be ahead of me except Ahmad, *'Alayhi al-Salam*. He and I are on the same path except that he is called Ahmed (the most praiseworthy). I have been given six things. I have been given the knowledge of deaths, of the sufferings, of the wills and the clear speech. I have been given the power to attack the enemy, and the power to subdue the adversary. I am the owner of the staff (of Moses) and Miysam (marking seal) and the being that will speak to people. (A reference to verse 82 of chapter 27 of the Holy Quran):

"When the word about them comes true We shall make a being appear to them on earth who will tell them that people had no faith in Our revelations.'" (27:82)

Chapter 15 - The Select Ahadith That Sum Up the Excellence and Qualifications of the Imam, *'Alayhi al-Salam*

H 518, Ch. 15, h 1

Abu Muhammad al-Qasim ibn al-'Ala', may Allah grant him blessings, in a *marfu'* manner (rafa'ahu), has narrated from 'Ad al-'Aziz ibn Muslim the following:

"Once we had been with al-Rida, *'Alayhi al-Salam*, at Marw. It was a Friday assembly in the central mosque and we attended the gathering. It was when we had just arrived (in Marw). People spoke and discussed the issue of Imamat (Leadership with Divine Authority). All the differing opinions among people in this matter came up. I then went to see my master, my leader, *'Alayhi al-Salam*, and informed him of the people's disagreement over the issue (of Imamat).

"He (the Imam), *'Alayhi al-Salam*, smiled and then said the following. 'O 'Abd al-'Aziz, (ibn Muslim) people are ignorant and their opinions have misled and deceived them. Allah, the Most Holy, the Most High, did not cause His Holy Prophet to leave this world before completing for him the religion. Allah sent him the Holy Quran in which all things are clearly explained. Allah has explained in the Holy Quran what is lawful and what is unlawful. He has explained totally the limits and the rules for all issues that people may face in the affairs of life. Allah, the Most Holy, the Most High, has said, "We have left nothing without mentioning it in the Book. . . ." (6:38)

'During the last visit of the Holy Prophet to Makkah for pilgrimage toward the end of his life the following verse of the Holy Quran was sent to him. "On this day I have perfected your religion, completed My favors to you, and have chosen Islam as your religion. . . ." (5:3) The issue of Imamat (Leadership with Divine Authority) is part of the completion of religion. The Holy Prophet, *'Alayhi al-Salam*, did not leave this world before explaining to his followers the principles of their religion and showing them the path clearly. He, in fact, left them on a point of a path that faced in the direction of the truth. He raised Ali, *'Alayhi al-Salam*, among them as a flag and an Imam (Leader with Divine Authority). He did not leave anything his followers needed, without full explanation. Those who think that Allah, the Most Holy, the Most High, has not completed His religion, they have rejected the Book of Allah, and those who reject the Book of Allah have become unbelievers in it.

'Do they know the value and the status of Imamat (Leadership with Divine Authority) of the 'Umma (the nation) to find out if their selecting an Imam is justifiable and permissible? Imamat, in fact, is the most sublime in values, greatest in position, highest in status and the most exclusive issue in all aspects. It is the most profound issue and much more meaningful than the extent of the intellect of the people to reach. It is beyond the grasp of their opinions to appoint an Imam or select him.

'Imamat is that particular distinction with which Allah, the Most Holy, the Most High, has distinguished Ibrahim, His very close friend (al-Khalil), after prophethood. This close friendship is the third stage (in the progression of spiritual degrees). It is a distinction with which He honored him and established his fame. He then said, "Behold! I have made you an Imam for the people." Abraham, the close friend, then out of delight pleaded, "Please let it (Imamat) be in my offspring also." Allah, the Most Holy, the Most High, said, "My covenant does not go to the unjust ones." (2:124)

'Thus, this verse has declared the leadership (Imamat) of all the unjust ones as unlawful until the Day of Judgment and it has established it for those clean and free of evil and injustice. Allah, the Most Holy, the Most High, bestowed him more honors in establishing Imamat in purified and clean persons of his offspring. Allah has said, "We granted him Isaac and Jacob as a gift and helped both of them to become righteous people (21:72). We appointed them as leaders to guide the people through Our command and sent them revelation to strive for good deeds, worship their Lord and pay religious tax. Both of them were Our worshipping servants." (21:73)

'So Imamat remained in his offspring, inheriting it from each other, generation after generation, until Allah, the Most Holy, the Most High, made Prophet Muhammad, *'Alayhi al-Salam*, to inherit it. And He, Allah, the Most Holy, the Most High, said, "The nearest people to Abraham, among mankind, are those who followed him, and this Prophet (Muhammad) and the true believers. Allah is the Guardian of the true believers." (3:68)

'Imamat belonged to him (Prophet Muhammad, *'Alayhi al-Salam*) particularly, and he, then, entrusted Imam Ali, *'Alayhi al-Salam*, with it by the command of Allah, the Most Holy, the Most High, as He had made it obligatory. It then came to be in his (Imam Ali's) purified and clean of sins offspring, to whom Allah has given knowledge and belief, as in the words of Allah, the Most High, "Those who have received knowledge and have belief will say, 'By the decree of Allah, you have remained for the exact period, which was mentioned in the Book of Allah about the Day of Resurrection. This is the Day of Resurrection, but you did not know.'" (30:56)

'Imamat will remain in the sons of Imam Ali, *'Alayhi al-Salam*, exclusively, until the Day of Judgment and there will be no prophet after Muhammad, *'Alayhi al-Salam*, wherefrom then have these ignorant people received the right to select the Imam?

'Imamat (Leadership with Divine Authority) is, certainly, the position of the prophets, and the inheritance of the successors. Imamat indeed, is the representation (khilafa) of Allah, the deputyship of the Messenger, *'Alayhi al-Salam*, of Allah, the office of Amir al-Mu'minin Ali, *'Alayhi al-Salam*, and the inheritance of Imam al-Hassan and al-Husayn, *'Alayhim al-Salam*.

'Imamat is, in fact, the reins of religion. It is the social system of the Muslims. It is best for the world, and honor for the believers. Imamat is Islam's growing root, and its towering branch. Through the Imam, *'Alayhi al-Salam*, prayers are complete, *Zakat* (charity) is paid, fasting is maintained, Hajj is performed and Jihad, proper defense is exercised, the wealth of the nation (fay') and charity (sadaqat) are increased, the laws are enforced and the frontiers are protected and defended.

'The Imam declares as lawful what Allah has done so and prohibits what Allah has prohibited. He enforces the judicial laws of Allah and defends the religion of Allah. The Imam provides guidance with wisdom, good advice and with the topmost strong evidence.

'The Imam is like the risen sun that beautifies the world with its light and is in the horizon above the harm of hands and eyes. The Imam is as the bright moon, the shining lamp, the brilliant light and the guiding star in the depth of darkness, in the middle of the towns, in the wilderness and on the high seas. The Imam is as crystal-clear water to thirst, an indicator of true guidance and the protector against destruction. The Imam is as the fire of a lighthouse that provides warmth and guidance for those who seek heat and protection against fatalities. Whoever departs him (the Imam) will perish.

'The Imam (in terms of blessings) is as the rain-bearing cloud, the drenching rainfall, the shining sun, the shadow-providing sky, the open fields, the gushingforth spring, as a pond and a garden. The Imam is as a comforting friend, a very kind father, a real brother, and a tenderhearted mother of a small child, and a refuge for people in disastrous conditions. The Imam is Allah's trustee over His creatures, His Authority over His servants, His representative in His lands, the preacher of His cause and the defender of His sanctuary.

'The Imam is clean of sins, free of faults, possesses special knowledge and is distinguished in forbearance. The Imam maintains law and order in religion. He is the might of the Muslims that enrages the hypocrites, and exterminates unbelievers. The Imam is the peerless person of his time, no one can reach even near his rank in virtue and excellence and no scholar is comparable to him. No one can become an alternative for him, nor is there anyone similar to him or just like him. His distinctions are exclusive in all virtues and excellence of which none is acquired or is sought after. In fact, his distinctions are all bestowed upon him by the source of all perfection, the Generous One (Allah).

'Who is he that can know all about the Imam, or can select him? To affirm the ability of selection is very far from the truth. (In the task of recognizing the Imam) intellects have become confused, understanding has lost the meaning, awareness is frustrated, eyes have become dull and tired, the great ones have become humble, the sagacious ones have become bewildered and people of forbearance have lost patience. (In the task of recognizing the Imam) the orators have become speechless, the intelligent ones have become ignorant and the poets have become exhausted. The men-of-letters have become helpless, people of eloquence have turned wordless to speak of any of the aspects of his status or a virtue and excellence of his merits and instead have confessed their helplessness in the matter. How can one speak of him in full, or describe him in the real sense or understand anything of his affairs or find an alternative for him to be sufficient for what he (the Imam) suffices. There is no such thing and nowhere is such a thing found. He is like a star away from the reach of those who try to reach, or those who try to describe. Where does the idea of selecting him stand in such a case? How then can reason and intellect reach him and where can one find a person like the Imam?

'Do they think that such a person can be found outside the family of the messenger (of Allah), Muhammad, *'Alayhi al-Salam*? Their souls, I swear by Allah, have told them a lie. Falsehood has induced in them evil hopes. Be on your guard against an uphill and crushing battle in which they slip back to their first foothold.

181

They intend to raise the Imam by their confused, fruitless and faulty intellects and their misleading opinions. It will do nothing good for them. Instead it will take them away from the truth, as Allah has said, "May Allah be their adversary. Where are they headed?" (9:30) They have aimed at a difficult task and have spoken something meaningless. They have strayed far away from the truth and have faced huge confusions. They have knowingly ignored the Imam, *'Alayhi al-Salam.* It is just as Allah has said; "Satan has made their deeds to seem attractive to them and has blocked them from reaching the path (of guidance) when they know it fully." (29:38)

'They have turned away from the choice that Allah and His Messenger and his family have made for them, due to their own choice. The Holy Quran calls upon them, "Your Lord creates and chooses (to grant mercy) to whoever He wants. (In matters of guidance) they (unbelievers) do not have the choice to choose whatever they want. Allah is by far exalted and cannot be considered equal to anything else." (28:68) Allah, the Most Majestic, the Most High, also has said, "The believing men and women must not feel free to do something in their affairs other than that which has been already decided for them by Allah and His Messenger. One who disobeys Allah and His Messenger is in plain error." (33:36)

'He has further said, "What is the matter with you? How could you judge this to be so? (68:36). Do you have a book from which you study (68:37) that tells you to do whatever you want? (68:38). Do you have a covenant with Us, which allows you to do whatever you want until the Day of Judgment? (68:39) (Muhammad), ask which of them can guarantee that on the Day of Judgment (68:40) they will receive the same thing that the Muslims will? Do they have any witness to such an agreement? Let them bring out such witness, if they are truthful."(68:41)

'Allah, the Most Majestic, the Most Gracious says, "Is it that they do not think about the Quran or are their hearts sealed?' (47:24) Or as He says, '. . . their hearts were sealed and they were left with no understanding." (9:87) Or, "Do not be like those who said that they have heard (the Messenger's commands) but do not pay any attention to them (8:21). The wickedest beasts in the sight of Allah are the deaf and the dumb who have no understanding (8:22). Had they possessed any virtue, Allah would certainly have made them hear. Even if Allah were to make them hear, they would still turn away from (the words of Allah)," (8:23) or, "You said that you had listened but you disobeyed." (2:93) "It is the grace from Allah and He grants grace to whoever He wills. Allah possesses great generosity." (57:21)

'How can they have any right to choose the Imam, *'Alayhi al-Salam?* The Imam, *'Alayhi al-Salam,* is a scholar who is not ignorant of anything, a shepherd who does not step back from his duty. He is the source of holiness, of purity, noble tradition, (the force) of restraint from sins, knowledge and worship. He (enjoys) the blessings of the exclusive prayers of the Messenger of Allah and of being of the progeny of the Holy lady, al-Batul (*Fatimah, 'Alayha al-Salam*). There is no question about his genealogical purity. He is of the house of Quraysh and the topmost in the clan of Hashim and of the family of the Messenger of Allah. He enjoys the prestigious position that Allah, the Most Holy, the Most High, is happy with him. He is the noblest in all nobility. He is of the offspring of 'Abd al-Manaf. He possesses (a body of) increasing knowledge. He is perfect in forbearance, the only one to qualify for the position of Imamat (Leadership with Divine Authority). He has full knowledge of politics. Obedience to him is obligatory by the command of Allah. He is appointed for Imamat by the command of Allah, the Most Holy, the Most High, to give good advice to the servants of Allah and to protect the religion of Allah.

'Allah grants success and support to the prophets and *'A'immah, 'Alayhim al-Salam*, through His treasured knowledge and command in a way that is granted to no one else. Thus, their knowledge is above the knowledge of the people of their times as mentioned in the following words of Allah. "Is the one who guides to the Truth a proper guide or one who himself cannot find guidance unless he is guided (by others)? What is wrong with you that you judge (so unjustly)?" (10:35) And as in His words, "Whoever is given wisdom, certainly, has received much good . . ." (2:269). Or as about Talut in His following words, "Allah has chosen him as your ruler and has given him physical power and knowledge. Allah grants His Authority to anyone whom He wants. Allah is Provident and All-knowing," (2:247) or as He has said to His Prophet, *'Alayhi al-Salam*, "Allah has revealed the Book to you, has given you wisdom and has taught you what you did not know. Certainly Allah's favor to you has been great." (4:113) He also has said about *'A'immah* from the family of the Holy Prophet, *'Alayhi al-Salam*, "Are they jealous of the favors that Allah has done to certain people? We have given to the family of Abraham the Book, Wisdom and a great Kingdom (4:54). Certain people have believed, others have disbelieved and tried to prevent people from believing. For these people, only the intense fire of hell is a sufficient punishment." (4:55)

'When Allah, the Most Holy, the Most High, chooses a person for the affairs of His servants, He opens his heart for the task, places in it the fountains of wisdom and inspires him with knowledge. He then never becomes tired of answering questions and never becomes confused to miss the right answer. He is infallible, divinely supported, successful and guarded. He is immune from sins and shortcomings and faults. Allah has granted him this exclusively so that he can serve as the Divine Authority over His servant, as a witness over them, and it is due to the grace of Allah that He grants to whomever He wills and Allah's grace is the greatest.

'Can one among the people have such things so they may choose him as the Imam or can their selected person have such distinctions as to be preferred over the others?

'They, I swear by the house of Allah, have transgressed against the truth and have thrown the Book of Allah behind their backs as if they do not know. In the Book of Allah there is guidance and cure but they have ignored it and have followed their own desires. For this reason Allah has criticized, expressed anger and condemned them in His words as follows: "Who strays more than one who follows his desires without guidance from Allah? Allah does not guide the unjust people." (28:50) ". . . the fate of the unbelievers will be to stumble and their deeds will have no virtuous results.' (47:8) 'This act greatly angers Allah and the believers. Thus does Allah seal the hearts of every arrogant oppressor." (40:35)

'May Allah grant blessings upon Prophet Muhammad and his family, *'Alayhim al-Salam*, and may He grant them peace, a great deal of peace.'"

H 519, Ch. 15, h 2
Muhammad ibn Yahya has narrated from Ahmad ibn Muhammad ibn 'Isa from al-Hassan ibn Mahbub from Ishaq ibn Ghalib who has said the following:

"Abu 'Abd Allah, *'Alayhi al-Salam*, describing the condition of *'A'immah*, *'Alayhi al-Salam*, and their attributes in one of his sermons has said, 'Allah, the Most Holy, the Most High, has explained His religion through *'A'immah* of (true) guidance from the family of our Prophet, *'Alayhi al-Salam*, the *Ahl al-Bayt*, *'Alayhim al-Salam*, and has cleared through them the path of His system and plan. He has opened through them the inside of the springs of His knowledge. Whoever of the followers of Muhammad, *'Alayhi al-Salam*, has recognized his obligation toward the rights of his Imam, has realized the taste of the sweetness of his belief and the superior beauty of his Islam. It is because Allah, the Most Holy, the Most High, has appointed the Imam as torchbearer for His creatures and authority over those who receive His blessings in His world. He has crowned him with dignity and has encompassed him in the light of His Omnipotence that extends for him a means to the heavens. He does not discontinue His blessings for him. None of the things with Allah is achieved except through its right means. Allah does not accept the good deeds of His servants without their recognition of the Imam, *'Alayhi al-Salam*. The Imam, *'Alayhi al-Salam*, knows how to sort out the dark confusing matters and things that may obscure the *Sunnah* (tradition of the Holy Prophet, *'Alayhi al-Salam*) and the confounding matters in mischievous conditions. Allah, the Most Holy, the Most High, has always chosen *'A'immah* from the descendents of al-Husayn, *'Alayhi al-Salam*, one after the other Imam. He would select and choose them for the leadership of His creatures delightfully and well satisfied with them. Whenever one Imam would leave this world he would appoint for His creatures his successor as a clear beacon and a shining guide, a guarding leader, and a knowledgeable one with Divine Authority. *'A'immah* from Allah guide people with the truth and with the truth they judge. They are Allah's authority calling people to Him, and shepherds of His creatures. With their guidance people follow the religion and from them the land receives light. Through their holiness the bounties increase. Allah has made them life for the people and the torches in the darkness, the keys to communication and the strongholds for Islam. Thus, have the measures of Allah continued in them toward His final decision.

'The Imam, *'Alayhi al-Salam*, is the outstanding amicable one; the most trusted guide and the guardian who can make hopes come true. Allah has chosen him with such distinctions. He selected him as such (well protected) in the realm when all things were in the form of particles in the instant that He made him. He chose him as such (well-protected) in the realm in which all things were designed as He had designed him as a shadow, before He made the organisms, on the right side of His throne, gifted him with wisdom in the unseen knowledge with Him. He chose him in His knowledge and granted him outstanding nobility for his purity.

'He is an heir of Adam, the best one among the descendents of Noah, the chosen one of the family of Abraham, a descendent of Ishmael and of the most preferred ones in the family of Prophet Muhammad, *'Alayhi al-Salam*, He has always been looked after by the watchful eyes of Allah Who provides him security and guards him with His shield, well protected against the evil nets of Satan and his armies. He is well defended against the approaching dark nights and the false accusations of the evildoers. All wickedness is kept away from him and he is kept safe against all forms of defects and flaws. He is veiled against all scourges.

'He is infallible in matters of sins. He is kept safe and sound against all indecencies. He is well known for his forbearance and virtuousness in the early days of his life. Chastity, great knowledge and excellence are ascribed to him toward the end of his life. The task of Imamat (Leadership with Divine Authority) of his father rests with him, while in the lifetime of his father he remains silent.

'When the time of the Imamat of his father ends it is the time when the measure of Allah ends up with him due to His wish. The will of Allah brings him to His love, thus, the end of the Imamat of his father comes and he passes away. The Authority from Allah shifts to him after his father. He then is made the person in charge of His religion, the Divine Authority over His servants, the guardian over His lands, he is supported with His spirit and is given of His knowledge. He raises him as a beacon for His creatures, makes him to have His Authority over the people of His world and as the light for the people of His religion and a guardian for His servants. Allah agrees to have him as Imam of the people, entrusts him with His secret, makes him a safe-keeper of His knowledge and hides His wisdom in him. He protects him for His religion, calls upon him to serve His great task, and revives through him the phases of His system (of religion) and the obligations in His laws.

'The Imam then enforces justice - when the people of ignorance are confused and the disputing and quarrelling people are frustrated - with shining light, the beneficial cure and radiant truth. He does so with clear explanations of all aspects and exactly in the manner and practice his truthful father and forefathers would do before him. No one ignores the rights of such a scholar except the wicked ones. No one refuses and denies him except those who have strayed away from the right path. No one keeps away from him except those who are aggressive against Allah, the Most Holy, the Most High.'"

Chapter 16 - 'A'immah, *'Alayhim al-Salam*, Possess Divine Authority; They are envied and Allah, the Most Holy, the Most High, has spoken of Them

H 520, Ch. 16, h 1

Al-Husayn ibn Muhammad ibn 'Amir al-Ash'ari has narrated from Mu'alla ibn Muhammad who has said that al-Hassan ibn Ali al-Washsha' narrated to him from Ahmad ibn 'A'idh from ibn 'Udhayna from Burayd al-'Ijli who said the following:

"Once I asked abu Ja'far, *'Alayhi al-Salam*, about the meaning of the following words of Allah, the Most Holy, the Most High, 'Obey Allah and obey the Messenger and those who possess (Divine) Authority among you.' (4:59) In response he read the following words of Allah. 'Have you seen how those who had been given a share of the Book believe in idols and Satan and say, "The unbelievers are better guided than the believers." (4:51) They say that the leaders of misguidance and those who call people to hell (may Allah condemn them) are better guided than the members of the family of Prophet Muhammad, *'Alayhi al-Salam.*' The Imam then read these words from the Holy Quran, 'No one can help one whom Allah has condemned. (4:52) Do they have a share in the Kingdom (Divine Authority and Imamat)? Even if they did, they would not have given the smallest thing to the people.' (4:53) The Imam, *'Alayhi al-Salam*, thereafter said, 'The word "People" is a reference to us and the word "*naqir*" means the spot at the center of a seed.' The Imam, *'Alayhi al-Salam*, explained and added, in the expression, 'Do they envy the favors that Allah has done to certain people?' We are the "certain people," who are envied because of the Divine Authority that Allah has given us exclusively,' he (the Imam), *'Alayhi al-Salam*, explained. 'In the passage, "We have given to the family of Abraham the Book, Wisdom, and a great Kingdom," (4:54) Allah says that from the descendents of Abraham He has made His Messengers, Prophets and *'A'immah*. How is it that these people acknowledge the case about the descendents of Abraham but they refuse to accept Imamat (the Leadership with Divine Authority) in the family of Muhammad?' He (the Imam), *'Alayhi al-Salam*, further explained: 'Certain people have believed, others have disbelieved and tried to prevent people from believing. For these people, only the intense fire of hell is a sufficient punishment (4:55). We will make those who reject Our revelations suffer in hell fire. As soon as the fire destroys their skins, We will give them new skins so that they may suffer more of the torment. Allah is Majestic and All-wise.'" (4:56)

H 521, Ch. 15, h 2

A number of our people have narrated from Ahmad ibn Muhammad from al-Husayn ibn Sa'id from Muhammad ibn al-Fudayl from abu al-Hassan, *'Alayhi al-Salam*, who has said the following:

"About the words of Allah, the Most Holy, the Most High, 'Or are they envious of the people whom Allah has granted of His bounties?' (4:54) the Imam, *'Alayhi al-Salam*, said, 'They refer to us. We are the envied ones.'"

H 522, Ch. 15, h 3

Muhammad ibn Yahya has narrated from Ahmad ibn Muhammad from al-Husayn ibn Sa'id from al-Nadr ibn Suwayd from Yahya al-Halabi from Muhammad al-Ahwal from Humran ibn A'yan who has said the following:

"Once I asked Imam abu 'Abd Allah, *'Alayhi al-Salam*, about the meaning of the words of Allah, the Majestic, the Glorious, 'We have given to the family of Abraham the Book, Wisdom, and a great Kingdom.' (4:54) The Imam, *'Alayhi al-Salam*, said, 'It means Prophecy.' I then asked about the meaning of 'Wisdom.' The Imam, *'Alayhi al-Salam*, said, 'It means understanding and judgment.' I then asked about the meaning of 'great kingdom.' He (the Imam), *'Alayhi al-Salam*, said, 'It means obedience.'"

H 523, Ch. 16, h 4
Al-Husayn ibn Muhammad has narrated from Mu'alla ibn Muhammad from al-Washsha' from Hammad ibn 'Uthman from abu al-Sabbah who has said the following:

"I asked Imam abu 'Abd Allah, *'Alayhi al-Salam*, about the meaning of the words of Allah, the Most Holy, the Most High, 'Or are they envious of the people whom Allah has granted of His bounties?' (4:54) The Imam, *'Alayhi al-Salam*, said, 'O abu al-Sabbah, we, I swear by Allah, are the people who are envied.'"

H 524 Ch. 16, h 5
Ali ibn Ibrahim has narrated from his father from Muhammad ibn abu 'Umayr from 'Umar ibn Udhayna from Burayd al-'IJli who has said the following:

"About the words of Allah, the Most Holy, the Most High, 'We have given to the family of Abraham the Book, wisdom, and a Great kingdom.' (4:54) Abu Ja'far, *'Alayhi al-Salam*, has said, 'He gave messengership, prophecy and Imamat (Leadership with Divine Authority). Why is it that they (certain people) acknowledge these facts in the family of Abraham but refuse to do so in the family of Prophet Muhammad, *'Alayhi al-Salam*?' I then asked, 'What does the "Great kingdom" mean'? The Imam said, 'The great kingdom is Imamat (Leadership with Divine Authority) in the descendents of Abraham. Whoever obeys them has obeyed Allah and whoever disobeys them has disobeyed Allah. 'Obedience' stands for the great kingdom.'"

Chapter 17 - 'A'immah, *'Alayhim al-Salam*, Are the Signs of Whom Allah, the Most Holy, the Most High, Has Spoken in the Holy Quran

H 525, Ch. 17, h 1
Al-Husayn ibn Muhammad al-Ash'ari from Mu'alla ibn Muhammad from abu Dawud al-Mustariqq who has said that Dawud al-Jassas has said the following:

"About the words of Allah, 'Through the signs and with the star people do find their way,' (16:16) I heard Imam abu 'Abd Allah, *'Alayhi al-Salam*, say, 'The star is the Messenger of Allah, *'Alayhi al-Salam*, and the signs are *'A'immah* (plural of Imam), *'Alayhim al-Salam*.'"

H 526 Ch. 17, h 2
Al-Husayn ibn Muhammad has narrated from Mu'alla ibn Muhammad from al-Washsha' from Asbat ibn Salim who has said that Haytham asked Imam abu 'Abd Allah, *'Alayhi al-Salam*, while I was there, about the meaning of the following words of Allah, the Majestic, the Glorious:

"Through the signs and with the star people do find their way." (16:16) He (the Imam), *'Alayhi al-Salam*, said, 'The star is the Messenger of Allah, *'Alayhi al-Salam*, and the signs are *'A'immah, 'Alayhim al-Salam.'*"

H 527, Ch. 17, h 3

Al-Husayn ibn Muhammad has narrated from Mu'alla ibn Muhammad from al-Washsha' who has said the following:

"Once I asked Imam al-Rida, *'Alayhi al-Salam*, about the meaning of the words of Allah, the Most High, 'Through the signs and with the star people do find their way.' (16:16) He (the Imam), *'Alayhi al-Salam*, said, 'We are the signs and the Messenger of Allah is the star.'"

Chapter 18 - The Signs of Which Allah, the Most Holy, the Most High, Has Spoken in the Holy Quran Are 'A'immah, *'Alayhim al-Salam*

H 528, Ch. 18, h 1

Al-Husayn ibn Muhammad has narrated from Mu'alla ibn Muhammad from Ahmad ibn Muhammad ibn 'Abd Allah from Ahmad ibn Hilal from 'Umayya ibn Ali from Dawud al-Riqqi who has said the following:

"Once, I asked abu 'Abd Allah, *'Alayhi al-Salam*, about the meaning of the words of Allah, the Most Holy, the Most High, 'The signs and warnings are of no avail to the disbelieving people.' (10:101) The Imam said, 'Signs are *'A'immah*, and warnings are the prophets, *'Alayhim al-Salam.'*"

H 529, Ch. 18, h 2

Ahmad ibn Mahran has narrated from 'Abd al-'Azim ibn 'Abd Allah al-Hassani from Musa ibn Muhammad al-'Ijli from Yunus ibn Ya'qub in a *marfu'* manner from abu Ja'far, *'Alayhi al-Salam*, who has said the following:

"In the words of Allah, the Most Holy, the Most High, 'However, they rejected all Our signs. . . .' (54:42) 'The signs' are all the successors (of the prophets, *'Alayhim al-Salam*).'"

H 530, Ch. 18, h 3

Muhammad ibn Yahya has narrated from Ahmad ibn Muhammad from Muhammad ibn abu 'Umayr or someone other than him from Muhammad ibn al-Fudayl from abu Hamza who has said the following:

"Once I said to abu Ja'far, *'Alayhi al-Salam*, 'May Allah keep my soul in service for your cause, the Shi'a (your followers) ask about the meaning of the words of Allah, 'Of what do they ask one another? (78:1). Do they ask about the great news?' The Imam, *'Alayhi al-Salam*, said, 'It is up to my decision. I may tell them or may not tell them.' Then he said: 'I want, however, to tell you the meaning thereof.' I then asked what is the meaning of, 'Of what do they ask one another?' The Imam said, 'It refers to (Amir al-Mu'minin) Ali, *'Alayhi al-Salam*. (Amir al-Mu'minin) Ali would often say, "None of the signs of Allah, the Most Holy, the Most High, is bigger than I and none of the news of Allah is greater than I."'"

Chapter 19 - Those Matters in Which Allah, the Most Holy, the Most High, and His Messenger Have Sanctioned as Obligatory for People to Be Along With 'A'immah, *'Alayhim al-Salam*

H 531, Ch. 19, h 1

Al-Husayn ibn Muhammad has narrated from Mu'alla ibn Muhammad from al-Washsha' from Ahmad ibn 'A'idh from ibn 'Udhayna from Burayd ibn Mu'awiya al-'Ijli who has said the following:

"I asked Imam abu Ja'far, *'Alayhi al-Salam*, about the meaning of the words of Allah, the Most Majestic, the Most Gracious, 'Believers, be pious before Allah and always be (friends) with the truthful ones.' (9:119) He (the Imam), *'Alayhi al-Salam*, replied, 'The "truthful ones" is a reference to us.'"

H 532, Ch. 19, h 2

Muhammad ibn Yahya has narrated from Ahmad ibn Muhammad from ibn abu Nasr who has said the following:

"I asked abu al-Hassan al-Rida, *'Alayhi al-Salam*, about the meaning of the words of Allah, the Most Holy, the Most High, in the following verse. 'Believers, be pious before Allah and always be (friends) with the truthful ones.' (9:119) The Imam said, 'The "truthful ones" are *'A'immah*, *'Alayhim al-Salam*, who are truthful in their obedience (to Allah).'"

H 533, Ch. 19, h 3

Ahmad ibn Muhammad and Muhammad ibn Yahya have narrated from Muhammad ibn al-Husayn from Muhammad ibn 'Abd al-Hamid from Mansur ibn Yunus from Sa'd ibn Tariyf from abu Ja'far, *'Alayhi al-Salam*, who has narrated the following from the Messenger of Allah, *'Alayhi al-Salam*:

"Whoever likes to live a life similar to those of the prophets, die in a similar manner as the martyrs do and live in the garden which is planted by the Beneficent, they must love Imam Ali, *'Alayhi al-Salam*, (acknowledge his Divine Authority). They must also love those who love and support him and follow *'A'immah* after him who are of my family and are created of the substance of which I was created (according to *Hadith*, Allah created the Holy Prophet and *'A'immah* from one substance). O Lord, give them my understanding and knowledge. Send those of my people to *Wayl* (a place in hell) who oppose them *('A'immah)* and do not give them the chance to benefit from my intercession on their behalf."

H 534, Ch. 19, h 4

Muhammad ibn Yahya has narrated from Muhammad ibn al-Husayn from al-Nadr ibn Shu'ayb from Muhammad ibn al-Fudayl from abu Hamza al-Thumali who has said the following:

"I heard abu Ja'far, *'Alayhi al-Salam*, say, 'The Messenger of Allah, *'Alayhi al-Salam*, has said, "Allah, the Most Holy, the Most High, says, 'The refusal of the wicked ones among your followers to acknowledge the Divine Authority of Imam Ali, *'Alayhi al-Salam*, and their becoming friends and supporters of the enemies of Ali, their refusing to acknowledge his virtuous qualities and such qualities of his successors after him (Imam Ali, *'Alayhi al-Salam*) altogether establish My argument against such wicked ones ever more strongly. Indeed your excellence and virtues are their (*'A'immah*'s) excellence and virtues, obedience to you is like obedience to them; your right is like their right and disobedience to you is disobedience to them. They will be *'A'immah* who possess the right guidance after you. Your spirit flows in them and so does the spirit of that which your Lord has made to flow in you. They are members of your family and from the substance of which you are made. They are your flesh and blood. Allah, the Most Holy, the Most High, has made your traditions and the traditions of the prophets before to continue with them (*'A'immah*). They are the treasurers of My knowledge after you. It is a right that I owe them. I have chosen them and I have given to them nobility exclusively with pleasure. Salvation will be for those who love them, acknowledge their Divine Authority and acknowledge their excellence and virtues.' The angel Jibril has brought for me their (*'A'immah*'s) names and the names of their fathers, the names of those who love them and those who acknowledge their virtues and excellence.'"

H 535 Ch. 19, h 5

A number of our people have narrated from Ahmad ibn Muhammad ibn 'Isa from al-Husayn ibn Sa'id from Fadala ibn Ayyub from abu al-Maghra from Muhammad ibn Salim from Aban ibn Taghlib from abu 'Abd Allah, *'Alayhi al-Salam*, who has said the following:

"The Messenger of Allah has said, 'Whoever wants to live like my living, die as I will die and enter the garden of Eden that my Lord has planted with His Own hands, he must love Ali ibn abu Talib, *'Alayhi al-Salam*, and acknowledge his Divine Authority. He must love his successors and acknowledge the Divine Authority of his successors and love those who love him, be the enemy of his enemies and submit in obedience to his successors; they are of my family and my flesh and blood. Allah has given them my understanding and knowledge. I appeal to Allah and complain to Him about the case of my people's dealings, their denying the virtue and excellence of *'A'immah* from my family. I complain to Allah for their disregard of my relationship with them. By Allah, they will murder my son (al-Husayn, *'Alayhi al-Salam*). May Allah deprive them of my intercession.'"

H 536, Ch. 19, h 6

Muhammad ibn Yahya has narrated from Muhammad ibn al-Husayn from Musa ibn Sa'dan from 'Abd Allah ibn al-Qasim from 'Abd al-Qahhar from Jabir al-Ju'fi from abu Ja'far, *'Alayhi al-Salam*, who has said the following:

"The Messenger of Allah has said, 'Whoever likes to live as I have lived and die as I will do and enter the garden that my Lord has promised to me and hold in his hands the stick that Allah has planted with His Own hands, he then must love Ali ibn abu Talib, *'Alayhi al-Salam*, and acknowledge his Leadership with Divine Authority. He then must love his successors after him and acknowledge their Leadership with Divine Authority. They do not lead one into the gates of misguidance or take one out of the gate of true guidance. Thus, do not try to teach them; they know more than you do. I have asked my Lord not to cause any separation between them and the Holy Quran until the time they will arrive in my presence near *al-Kawthar* (the plentifulness or the pond) in paradise like this (showing his two fingers stretched side by side). The pond of *al-Kawthar* is as big as from San'a' (in Yemen) to 'Ayla (a place between Makkah and Madina) with cups of gold and silver around it as many as the number of the stars.'"

H 537, Ch. 19, h 7

Al-Husayn ibn Muhammad has narrated from Mu'alla ibn Muhammad from Muhammad ibn Jumhur from Fadala ibn Ayyub from al-Hassan ibn Ziyad from Fudayl ibn Yasar who has said that abu Ja'far, *'Alayhi al-Salam*, has said the following.

"Tranquility, comfort, victory, support, success, blessings, honor, forgiveness, relief, ease, glad news, satisfaction, nearness, triumph, capabilities, hope and love from Allah, the Most Holy, the Most High, are for those who love Ali, *'Alayhi al-Salam*, and acknowledge his Divine Authority and follow him, disavow the enemies of Ali, *'Alayhi al-Salam*, and acknowledge in submission the virtues and excellence of (Imam) Ali, *'Alayhi al-Salam*, and his successors after him. I am obligated to include them in my task of intervention on their behalf. It will be a truth and a right before my Lord, the Most Holy and the Most High, to approve and honor my intervention on their behalf. They are my followers and those who follow me are from me.'"

Chapter 20 - The People of Dhikr (Memory and Knowledge) That Allah Has Commanded the Creatures to Ask for Their Questions Are 'A'immah, *'Alayhim al-Salam*

H 538, Ch. 20, h 1

Al-Husayn ibn Muhammad has narrated from Mu'alla ibn Muhammad from al-Washsha' from 'Abd Allah ibn 'Ajlan who has said the following:

"About the words of Allah, the Most Holy, the Most High, 'Ask the people of *Dhikr* if you do not know' (16:43, 21: 7) Abu Ja'far, *'Alayhi al-Salam*, has said that the Messenger of Allah, *'Alayhi al-Salam*, said, 'I am the *Dhikr* and *'A'immah* are the people of *Dhikr*.' About the words of Allah, the Most Holy, the Most High, 'It is a *Dhikr* for you and for your people and you all must be asked (for guidance).' (43:44) The Imam, *'Alayhi al-Salam*, said, 'We are his "people" and we must be asked (for guidance).'"

Note: Those who have considered this *Hadith* confusing may not have noted that the above *Hadith* has dealt with two different verses of the Holy Quran. It should, however, be considered that as the Holy Quran is called *Dhikr* (reminder of Allah), the Holy Prophet, *'Alayhi al-Salam*, also is *Dhikr* (the preacher for and reminder of Allah). Thus, the above passage is not confusing.

H 539, Ch. 20, h 2

Al-Husayn ibn Muhammad has narrated from Mu'alla ibn Muhammad from Muhammad ibn 'Uwarma from Ali ibn Hassa'n from his uncle 'Abd al-Rahman ibn Kathir who has said the following:

"I asked Imam abu 'Abd Allah, *'Alayhi al-Salam*, about the meaning of the words of Allah, 'Ask the people of *Dhikr* if you do not know.' (16:43, 21: 7) The Imam, *'Alayhi al-Salam*, said, 'Prophet Muhammad, *'Alayhi al-Salam*, is *Dhikr* and we are the people of *Dhikr* who must be asked (for guidance).' I also asked about, 'It is a *Dhikr* for you and for your people and you all must be asked (for guidance).' (43:44) The Imam, *'Alayhi al-Salam*, said, 'It is a reference to us. We are the people of *Dhikr* and we must be asked (for guidance).'"

H 540, Ch. 20, h 3

Al-Husayn ibn Muhammad has narrated from Mu'alla ibn Muhammad from al-Washsha' who has said the following:

"Once I said to Imam al-Rida, *'Alayhi al-Salam*, 'May Allah keep my soul in service for your cause, what is the meaning of the words of Allah, "Ask the people of *Dhikr* if you do not know"? (16:43, 21: 7) The Imam, *'Alayhi al-Salam*, said, '*Dhikr* is Prophet Muhammad, *'Alayhi al-Salam*, and we are his family (people) who must be asked (for guidance).' I further asked, 'Are you the ones who must be asked (for guidance) and we will be the one to ask questions?' The Imam, *'Alayhi al-Salam*, said, 'Yes, that is true.' I then asked, 'Will it be a right (obligation) on us to ask you?' The Imam, *'Alayhi al-Salam*, said, 'Yes, it is so.' I then asked, 'Will it be a right on you to answer us?' The Imam, *'Alayhi al-Salam*, said, 'No, we will decide. We may or may not answer. Have you not heard the words of Allah, the Most Holy, and the Most High that say, "This is a gift from us. You may (give to others and) oblige or keep without being held accountable."' (38:39)

H 541, Ch. 20, h 4

A number of our people have narrated from Ahmad ibn Muhammad from al-Husayn ibn Sa'id from al-Nadr ibn Suwayd from 'Asim ibn Humayd from abu Basir who has said the following:

"About the words of Allah, the Most Holy, the Most High, 'It is a *Dhikr* for you and for your people and you all must be asked (for guidance),' (43:44) Imam abu 'Abd Allah, *'Alayhi al-Salam*, has said, 'The Messenger of Allah is the *Dhikr* (reminder of Allah) and members of his family, *'Alayhim al-Salam*, are the ones who must be asked (for guidance) and they are the people of *Dhikr*.'"

H 542 Ch. 20, h 5

Ahmad ibn Muhammad has narrated from al-Husayn ibn Sa'id from Hammad from Rib'iy from Fudayl who has said the following:

"About the words of Allah, the Most Holy, the Most High, 'It is a *Dhikr* for you and for your people and you all must be asked (for guidance),' (43:44) abu 'Abd Allah, *'Alayhi al-Salam*, has said, 'The Holy Quran is the *Dhikr* and we are the ones who must be asked (for guidance).'"

H 543, Ch. 20, h 6

Muhammad ibn Yahya has narrated from Muhammad ibn al-Husayn from Muhammad ibn 'Isma'il from Mansur ibn Yunus from abu Bakr al-Hadrami who has said the following:

"Once I was in the presence of Imam abu Ja'far, *'Alayhi al-Salam*, and al-Ward brother of al-Kumayt came to see him. He said to the Imam, *'Alayhi al-Salam*, 'May Allah keep my soul in service for your cause, I have chosen seventy questions and I do not know the answer even for one of them.' The Imam, *'Alayhi al-Salam*, said, 'Not even one answer, O Ward?' He then said, 'Yes, I know the answer for one of them.'

"The Imam, *'Alayhi al-Salam*, asked, 'What is it then?' He replied, 'It is the words of Allah, the Most Holy, the Most High, that say, "Ask the people of *Dhikr* if you do not know." Who are they?' asked al-Ward. The Imam, *'Alayhi al-Salam*, replied, 'We are the people of *Dhikr*?' I then said, 'Must we then ask you?' The Imam, *'Alayhi al-Salam*, said, 'Yes, you must ask us for answers.' I then asked,

'Must you then give us answers?' The Imam, *'Alayhi al-Salam*, said, 'We may or may not answer.'"

H 544, Ch. 20, h 7

Muhammad ibn Yahya has narrated from Muhammad ibn al-Husayn from Safwan ibn Yahya from al-'Ala' ibn Razin from Muhammad ibn Muslim who has said the following:

"Once I said to abu Ja'far, *'Alayhi al-Salam*, 'There are people who think that the words of Allah, the Most Holy, the Most High, "Ask the people of *Dhikr* if you do not know," refer to the Jews and the Christians.' The Imam, *'Alayhi al-Salam*, said, 'So they call you to their religion.' He (Muhammad ibn Muslim) has said that the Imam, *'Alayhi al-Salam*, said, with his hand pointing to his chest, 'We are the people of *Dhikr* (reminders of Allah) and we are the ones who must be asked (for guidance).'"

H 545, Ch. 20, h 8

A number of our people have narrated from Ahmad ibn Muhammad from al-Washsha' who has said that he heard Imam al-Rida say the following:

"Imam Ali ibn al-Husayn, *'Alayhi al-Salam*, has said, 'Certain obligations for *'A'immah* are not obligatory for their followers and certain obligations of our followers are not obligatory for us. Allah, the Most Holy, the Most High, has commanded them to ask us their questions saying, "Ask the people of *Dhikr* if you do not know," thus, Allah has commanded them to ask us their questions (for guidance) but it is not obligatory for us to answer them. We may answer them or may not answer them if we may so decide.'"

H 546, Ch. 20, h 9

Ahmad ibn Muhammad has narrated from Ahmad ibn Muhammad ibn abu Nasr who has said the following:

"Once I wrote a letter to Imam al-Rida, *'Alayhi al-Salam*. The issues for which I requested explanation in the letter, one was about the words of Allah, the Most Holy, the Most High, 'Ask the people of *Dhikr* (people who remind of Allah) if you do not know.' The other question was about the words of Allah, the Most Holy, the Most High, 'Not all believers have to become specialists in religious learning. Why do not certain persons from each group of believers seek to become specialists in religious learning and, after completing their studies, guide their group so that they will have fear of Allah?' (9:122) The above passages say that it is made obligatory upon them to ask but it is not made obligatory upon you to answer.'

"The Imam, *'Alayhi al-Salam*, answered, 'Allah the Most Holy, the Most High, has said, "If they do not do what you ask them, know that they are only following their (evil) desires. Who strays more than one who follows his desires without guidance from Allah? . . ."' (28:50)

Chapter 21- Those Whom Allah Has Called People of Knowledge in His Book they Are 'A'immah, *'Alayhim al-Salam*

H 547, Ch. 21, h 1

Ali ibn Ibrahim has narrated from his father from 'Abd Allah ibn al-Mughirah from 'Abd al-Mu'min ibn al-Qasim al-Ansari from Sa'd from Jabir who has said the following:

"About the words of Allah, the Most Holy, the Most High, 'Say, are those who know equal to those who do not know? Only the people of reason take heed,' (39:9) abu Ja'far, *'Alayhi al-Salam*, has said, 'It is a reference to us. We are the people of knowledge, the people who do not know are our enemies and our followers are the people who take heed and are the people of reason.'"

H 548, Ch. 21, h 2

A number of our people have narrated from Ahmad ibn Muhammad from al-Husayn ibn Sa'id from al-Nadr ibn Suwayd from Jabir who has said the following:

"About the words of Allah, the Most Holy, the Most High: 'Are those who know equal to those who do not know? Only the people of reason take heed,' (39:9) abu Ja'far, *'Alayhi al-Salam*, has said, 'We are the people of knowledge, our enemies are those who do not know and our followers are the people who take heed and are the people of reason.'"

Chapter 22 - The People Well-Established in Knowledge Are 'A'immah, *'Alayhim al-Salam* Alone

H 549, Ch. 22, h 1

A number of our people have narrated from Ahmad ibn Muhammad from al-Husayn ibn Sa'id from al-Nadr ibn Suwayd from Ayyub ibn Hurr and 'Imran ibn Ali from abu Basir from abu 'Abd Allah, *'Alayhi al-Salam*, who has said the following:

"We are the people well-established in knowledge and we are the ones who know how to interpret it (knowledge)."

H 550, Ch. 22, h 2

Ali ibn Muhammad has narrated from 'Abd Allah ibn Ali from Ibrahim ibn Ishaq from 'Abd Allah ibn Hammad from Burayd ibn Mu'awiya who has narrated the following from either one of *'A'immah, 'Alayhi al-Salam*:

"About the words of Allah, the Most Majestic, the Most gracious, 'No one knows its true interpretations except Allah and those who are well-established in knowledge, . . .' (3:7) the Imam, *'Alayhi al-Salam*, said that the Messenger of Allah is the best established in knowledge among the people. Allah, the Most Majestic, the Most Gracious, taught him all that He had revealed to him in the form of original text and in the form of interpretations. Allah, the Most Majestic, the Most Gracious, did not reveal anything to him without teaching him the meaning thereof. The successors of the Holy Prophet, *'Alayhi al-Salam*, after him knew all Divine revelations (to the Holy Prophet). As for those who do not know the interpretations thereof, when the scholar speaks to them with knowledge, Allah on their behalf has expressed their answer, they say, 'We believe in it, for all of this is from our Lord.'(3:7) The Holy Quran consists of specific, general, clear, not so clear, abrogating and abrogated statements. The people who are well-established in knowledge know all of the Holy Quran."

H 551, Ch. 22, h 3

Al-Husayn ibn Muhammad has narrated from Mu'alla ibn Muhammad from Muhammad ibn 'Urama from Ali ibn Hassan from 'Abd al-Rahman ibn Kathir from abu 'Abd Allah, *'Alayhi al-Salam*, who has said the following:

"(The Quranic expression), 'People well-established in knowledge' stands for (Amir al-Mu'minin) Ali, *'Alayhi al-Salam*, and *'A'immah* after him."

Chapter 23 - 'A'immah Are Those Who Have Received Knowledge and It is Firmly Recorded in Their Hearts

H 552, Ch. 23, h 1

Ahmad ibn Mihran has narrated from Muhammad ibn Ali from Hammad ibn 'Isa from al-Husayn ibn al-Mukhtar from abu Basir who has said the following:

"I saw abu Ja'far, *'Alayhi al-Salam*, on reading this verse of the Holy Quran, 'In fact, the Quran consists of illustrious verses that exist in the hearts of those who have knowledge. . . .,' (29:49) point to his own heart."

H 553, Ch. 23, h 2

It is narrated from him (narrator the of above *Hadith*) from Muhammad ibn Ali from ibn Mahbub from 'Abd al-'Aziz al-'Abdi from abu 'Abd Allah, *'Alayhi al-Salam*, who has said the following:

"About the words of Allah, the Most Holy, the Most High, 'In fact, the Quran consists of illustrious verses that exist in the hearts of those who have knowledge. . . .,' (29:49) abu 'Abd Allah said that those people are *'A'immah, 'Alayhim al-Salam.'*"

H 554, Ch. 23, h 3

It is narrated from him (narrator of the above *Hadith*) from Muhammad ibn Ali from 'Uthman ibn 'Isa from Sama'a from abu Basir who has said the following:

"About this verse of the Holy Quran, 'In fact, the Quran consists of illustrious verses that exist in the hearts of those who have knowledge. . . .,' (29:49) abu Ja'far, *'Alayhi al-Salam*, said, 'O abu Muhammad, for the sake of Allah, be the judge and tell, of whom is it spoken (so often) between the two front and back covers of the Holy Quran?' I then asked, 'Who are they, may Allah keep my soul in service for your cause?'

"The Imam, *'Alayhi al-Salam*, said, 'Who else can they be other than ourselves *('A'immah)?'*"

H 555, Ch. 23, h 4

Muhammad ibn Yahya has narrated from Muhammad ibn al-Husayn from Yazid Shaghar from Harun ibn Hamza who has said the following:

"I heard abu 'Abd Allah, *'Alayhi al-Salam*, read, 'In fact, the Quran consists of illustrious verses that exist in the hearts of those who have knowledge. . . .,' (29:49) and say that "those who have knowledge" refers to *'A'immah, 'Alayhim al-Salam*, exclusive of all others."

H 556, Ch. 23, h 5

A number of our people have narrated from Ahmad ibn Muhammad from al-Husayn ibn Sa'id from Muhammad ibn al-Fudayl who has said the following:

"I asked abu 'Abd Allah, *'Alayhi al-Salam*, about the meaning of the following words of Allah, the Majestic, the Glorious, 'In fact, the Quran consists of illustrious verses that exist in the hearts of those who have knowledge. . . .' (29:49) The Imam, *'Alayhi al-Salam*, said, 'They are *'A'immah, 'Alayhim al-Salam*, exclusive of all others.'"

Chapter 24 - The People Whom Allah Has Chosen and Has Made the Heirs of His Book Are 'A'immah (Plural of Imam), *'Alayhim al-Salam*

H 557, Ch. 24, h 1

Al-Husayn ibn Muhammad has narrated from Mu'alla ibn Muhammad from Muhammad ibn Jumhur from Hammad ibn 'Isa from 'Abd al-Mu'min from Salim who has said the following:

"Once I asked abu Ja'far, *'Alayhi al-Salam*, about the meaning of the words of Allah, the Most Holy, the Most High, 'We gave the Book as an inheritance to Our chosen servants, among whom certain ones are unjust against their souls, other are moderate and still others among them are exceedingly virtuous by the permission of Allah . . .' (35:31) The Imam said, "Exceedingly virtuous" is the Imam, the moderates are those who recognize *'A'immah, 'Alayhi al-Salam* and the unjust ones are those who do not recognize *'A'immah.* '"

H 558, Ch. 24, h 2

Al-Husayn has narrated from Mu'alla from al-Washsha' from 'Abd al-Karim from Sulayman ibn Khalid who has said the following:

"Once I asked abu 'Abd Allah, *'Alayhi al-Salam*, about the meaning of the following words of Allah, the Most High, 'We gave the Book as an inheritance to Our chosen servants, among whom some are unjust against their souls, some are moderate, and some are exceedingly virtuous by the permission of Allah. This is indeed a great favor (35:32) . . .' The Imam asked, 'What do you say about it?' I said, 'We say that they (people mentioned in the above verse) are the Fatimid (descendents of *Fatimah, 'Alayha al-Salam*, Daughter of the Holy Prophet).' The Imam said, 'It is not as you say. No one who points out his sword and calls people into schism and misguidance comes in this (category of "people exceeding in virtue").' I then asked, 'Who then are the ones "unjust against their souls"?' The Imam replied, 'It is those who sit in their homes and do not recognize the rights of their Imam. The "moderate" ones are those who recognize the rights of their Imam and the ones "exceeding in virtue" are *'A'immah, 'Alayhim al-Salam.*'"

H 559, Ch. 24, h 3

Al-Husayn ibn Muhammad has narrated from Mu'alla ibn Muhammad from al-Hassan from Ahmad ibn 'Umar who has said the following:

"Once I asked abu al-Hassan al-Rida, *'Alayhi al-Salam*, about the meaning of the words of Allah, the Most Holy, the Most High, 'We gave the book as an inheritance to Our chosen servants . . .' (35:32). The Imam said, 'Such people are the children of *Fatimah, 'Alayha al-Salam*, those "exceeding in virtue" are

'A'immah, 'Alayhim al-Salam, the "moderate" ones are those who recognize the Imam and those who are "unjust against their own souls" are the ones who do not recognize their Imam.'"

H 560, Ch. 24, h 4
Muhammad ibn Yahya has narrated from Ahmad ibn Muhammad from ibn Mahbub from abu Wallad who has said the following:

"I asked abu 'Abd Allah, 'Alayhi al-Salam, about the meaning of the words of Allah, the Most Holy, the Most High, 'The people who have received Our Book (Quran), and read it thoroughly, believe in it. . . . ' (2:121) The Imam said that such people, "the believers" are 'A'immah, 'Alayhim al-Salam.'"

Chapter 25 - Two Kinds of Imam

Two kinds of Imam are mentioned in the Holy Quran: 'A'immah, 'Alayhim al-Salam, who call to Allah, and 'A'immah who call to fire.

H 561, Ch. 25, h 1
Muhammad ibn Yahya has narrated from Ahmad ibn Muhammad from al-Hassan ibn Mahbub from 'Abd Allah ibn Ghalib from Jabir from abu Ja'far, 'Alayhi al-Salam, who has said the following:

"When the following verse of the Holy Quran was revealed, 'On the day when We will call every nation with their leaders (Imam) . . .' (17:71), people asked the Messenger of Allah, 'Alayhi al-Salam, 'Are you not the Imam of all the people altogether?' The messenger of Allah, 'Alayhi al-Salam, said, 'I am the Messenger of Allah to all the people but after me there will be 'A'immah from my family for the people. They will rise among the people but they will be rejected. The leaders of the unbelievers and misguidance and their followers will do injustice to them. Those who support, love, follow, and acknowledge their authority, are from me, they are with me and will meet me. People must know that whoever will do injustice to 'A'immah, 'Alayhim al-Salam, and reject them is not from me and is not with me. I denounce them and I have no associations with them.'"

H 562, Ch. 25, h 2
Muhammad ibn Yahya has narrated from Ahmad ibn Muhammad and Muhammad ibn al-Husayn from Muhammad ibn Yahya from Talha ibn Zayd from abu 'Abd Allah, 'Alayhi al-Salam, who has said the following:

"'A'immah mentioned in the book of Allah, the Most Holy, the Most High, are of two kinds. Allah, the Most Holy, the Most High has said, (1) 'We appointed them as 'A'immah (leaders) to guide the people through Our command . . .' (21:73) They do so but not because of the commands of the people. They allow Our command to come first and before their own orders, and Our laws before their own laws and judgment. (2) Allah has also said, 'We made them the kinds of Imams (leaders) who invite people to the fire . . .' (28:41) They (this kind of Imam) make their own commands to come before the commands of Allah and their laws before the laws of Allah. They follow their desires against what the book of Allah, the Most Holy, and the Most High, requires.'"

Chapter 26 - The Holy Quran Guides People to the Imam, *'Alayhim al-Salam*

H 563, Ch. 26, h 1
Muhammad ibn Yahya has narrated from Ahmad ibn Muhammad ibn 'Isa from al-Hassan ibn Mahbub who has said the following:

"I asked abu al-Hassan al-Rida, *'Alayhi al-Salam*, about the meaning of the words of Allah, the Most Holy, the Most High: 'We have chosen heirs for every legacy that parents and relatives may leave. Let those who have been promised a bequest receive their share of the legacy. . . .' (4:33) 'It is a reference to the *'A'immah*, *'Alayhim al-Salam*. With *'A'immah* Allah, the Most Holy, the Most High, has established your covenants,' replied the Imam, *'Alayhi al-Salam*."

H 564, Ch. 26, h 2
Ali ibn Ibrahim has narrated from his father from ibn abu 'Umayr from Ibrahim ibn 'Abd al-Hamid from Musa ibn 'Ukayl al-Numayri from al-'Ala' ibn Sayyaba from abu 'Abd Allah, *'Alayhi al-Salam*, who has said the following:

"About the words of Allah, the Most High, 'This Quran shows the way to that which is the most upright. . . .,' (17:9) abu 'Abd Allah, *'Alayhi al-Salam*, said, 'It guides to the Imam, *'Alayhi al-Salam*.'"

Chapter 27 - The Bounty and Blessing That Allah, the Most Holy, the Most High Has Mentioned in His book (the Holy Quran) Are 'A'immah (Plural of Imam), *'Alayhim al-Salam*

H 565, Ch. 27, h 1
Al-Husayn ibn Muhammad has narrated from Mu'alla ibn Muhammad from Bistam ibn Murrah from Ishaq ibn Hassa'n from al-Haytham ibn Waqid from Ali ibn al-Husayn al-'Abdi from Sa'd al-'Iskaf from al-Asbagh ibn Nubatah from ('Amir al-Mu'minin) Ali, *'Alayhi al-Salam*, who has said the following:

"What is wrong with people who changed the *Sunnah* (traditions) of the Messenger of Allah and deviated from his will? Do they not fear that severe suffering may befall them?" He then recited the following verse of the Holy Quran: 'Have you not seen (considered) those who changed the blessings (word) of Allah through disbelief and led their people to destruction? (14:28) They will suffer in hell. What a terrible place to stay!' (14:29). He then said, 'We are the "blessings" of Allah which He has granted to people. Through us succeed those who will be successful on the Day of Judgment.'"

H 566, Ch. 27, h 2
Al-Husayn ibn Muhammad has narrated from Mu'alla ibn Muhammad, in a *marfu'* manner, *(rafa'ahu)* has said the following:

"About the words of Allah, the Most Holy, the Most High, '(Mankind and Jinn) which of the favors of your Lord do you deny?' (55:13) The Imam has said, 'It means: will you deny and refuse the Holy Prophet or his successor?'" (This verse has come from Chapter 55, al-Rahman.)

H 567, Ch. 27, h 3

Al-Husayn ibn Muhammad has narrated from Mu'alla ibn Muhammad from Muhammad ibn Jumhur from 'Adallah ibn 'Abd al-Rahman from al-Haytham ibn Waqid from abu Yusuf al-Bazzaz who has said the following:

"Once abu 'Abd Allah, *'Alayhi al-Salam*, recited the following verse, 'Keep in mind (speak of) the bounties of Allah, . . .' (7:69) and said, 'Do you know what the bounties of Allah are?' I said, 'No, I do not know.' He said, 'It is the greatest of the bounties of Allah to acknowledge the Divine Authority that we possess.'"

H 568, Ch. 27, h 4

Al-Husayn ibn Muhammad has narrated from Mu'alla ibn Muhammad from Muhammad ibn 'Uwarma from Ali ibn Hassa'n from 'Abd al-Rahman ibn Kathir who has said the following:

"Once I asked abu 'Abd Allah, *'Alayhi al-Salam*, about the meaning of the following words of Allah, the Majestic, the Glorious, 'Have you not seen (considered) those who changed the blessings (word) of Allah through disbelief and led their people to destruction?' (14:28) The Imam said, 'It is a reference to all of Quraysh (a tribe) who bore animosity toward the Messenger of Allah, *'Alayhi al-Salam*, waged wars against him and rejected his will about his successor.'"

Chapter 28 - The People Whom Allah, the Most Holy, the Most High, Has Called Mutawassimin (Distinguished) in His Book Are 'A'immah (Plural of Imam), *'Alayhim al-Salam*, Who Are Also the Straight Path

H 569, Ch. 28, h 1

Ahmad ibn Mahran has narrated from 'Abd al-'Azim ibn 'Abd Allah al-Hasani from ibn abu 'Umayr who has said the following:

"Asbat Bayya' al-Zuttiyy has said that once he was in the presence of abu 'Abd Allah, *'Alayhi al-Salam*, when a man asked him (the Imam) about the meaning of the following words of Allah, the Most Holy, the Most High: 'In this there is evidence (of the Truth) for the distinguished ones. (15:75) That town lies on a road, which still exists.' (15:76) The Imam, *'Alayhi al-Salam*, said, 'We are the "distinguished ones" and the (right) path is with us.'"

H 570, Ch. 28, h 2

Muhammad ibn Yahya has narrated from Salamah ibn al-Khattab that Yahya ibn Ibrahim who has said the following:

"Asbat ibn Salim has said that once he was in the presence of abu 'Abd Allah, *'Alayhi al-Salam*, when a man from the people of Hiyt (a city near the banks of upper parts of Euphrate) came and said, 'May Allah grant you well-being, what is the meaning of the words of Allah, the Most Holy, the Most High, "In this there is evidence (of the Truth) for the distinguished ones?"' (15:75) The Imam, *'Alayhi al-Salam*, said, 'We are the "distinguished ones" and the (right) path is with us.'"

H 571, Ch. 28, h 3

Muhammad ibn Isma'il has narrated from al-Fadl ibn Shadhan from Hammad ibn 'Isa from Rib'i ibn 'Abd Allah from Muhammad ibn Muslim who has said the following:

"Once abu Ja'far, *'Alayhi al-Salam*, about the words of Allah, the Most Holy, the Most High, 'In this there is evidence (of the Truth) for the distinguished ones' (15:75), said, 'The "distinguished ones" are *'A'immah*, *'Alayhim al-Salam*. The messenger of Allah has said, "Be on your guard where the intelligence of the believer is concerned. He looks through the light of Allah, the Most Holy, the Most High, as mentioned in, 'In this there is evidence (of the Truth) for the distinguished ones.'" (15:75)

H 572, Ch. 28, h 4

Muhammad ibn Yahya has narrated from al-Hasan ibn Ali al-Kufi from 'Ubays ibn Hisham from 'Adallah ibn Sulayman from abu 'Abd Allah, *'Alayhi al-Salam*, who has said the following:

"About the words of Allah, the Most Holy, the Most High, 'In this there is evidence (of the Truth) for the distinguished ones,' (15:75) abu 'Abd Allah, *'Alayhi al-Salam*, said, 'These people are *'A'immah*, *'Alayhim al-Salam*, and, 'That town lies on a road, which still exists.' (15:76) the 'path' (of guidance) (evidence in our support) will never depart us.'"

H 573, Ch. 28, h 5

Muhammad ibn Yahya has narrated from Muhammad ibn al-Husayn from Muhammad ibn Aslam from Ibrahim ibn Ayyub from 'Amr ibn Shamir from Jabir from abu Ja'far, *'Alayhi al-Salam*, who has said the following:

"(Amir al-Mu'minin) Ali, *'Alayhi al-Salam*, about the words of Allah, the Most High, 'In this there is evidence (of the Truth) for the distinguished ones (15:75),' has said, 'the Holy Prophet, *'Alayhi al-Salam*, was the "distinguished one" and I was as such after him and *'A'immah* from my children are the distinguished ones.'"

In a different copy it is narrated from Ahmad ibn Mahran from Muhammad ibn Ali from Muhammad ibn Aslam from Ibrahim ibn Ayyub through the chain of his narrators a similar *Hadith*.

Chapter 29 - The Deeds of the People Are Presented Before the Holy Prophet and 'A'immah (Plural of Imam), *'Alayhim al-Salam*

H 574, Ch. 29, h 1

Muhammad ibn Yahya has narrated from Ahmad ibn Muhammad from al-Husayn ibn Sa'id from al-Qasim ibn Muhammad from Ali ibn abu Hamza from abu Basir from abu 'Abd Allah, *'Alayhi al-Salam*, who has said the following:

"All deeds are presented before the Messenger of Allah, *'Alayhi al-Salam*. It is the deeds of all the virtuous and the evildoing servants (of Allah) that are presented every morning and evening (before the Messenger of Allah). So pay proper attention to it and be very careful. The following words of Allah are a reference to this: '(Muhammad), tell them, "Act as you wish. Allah will see your deeds and so will His Messenger . . ."' (9:106) The Imam, *'Alayhim al-Salam*, paused at this point and did not read any further."

H 575, Ch. 29, h 2

A number of our people have narrated from Ahmad ibn Muhammad from al-Husayn ibn Sa'id from al-Nadr ibn Suwayd from Yahya al-Halabi from 'Abd al-Hamid al-Ta'i from Ya'qub ibn Shu'ayb who has said the following:

"Once I asked abu 'Abd Allah, *'Alayhi al-Salam*, about the meaning of the words of Allah, the Most Holy, the Most High, 'Act as you wish. Allah will see your deeds and so will His Messenger and the believers. . . .' (9:106) The Imam said, 'They (believers) are *'A'immah, 'Alayhi al-Salam.*'"

H 576, Ch. 29, h 3

Ali ibn Ibrahim has narrated from his father from 'Uthman ibn 'Isa from Suma' who has said that he heard abu 'Abd Allah, *'Alayhi al-Salam*, say the following:

"What is wrong with you? Why do you disappoint the Messenger of Allah?" A man asked, 'How do we disappoint him?' The Imam, *'Alayhi al-Salam*, said, 'Do you not know that your deeds are presented before him? When he finds sins in them it disappoints him. Do not disappoint the Messenger of Allah. Do things that will make him happy.'"

H 577, Ch. 29, h 4

Ali has narrated from his father from al-Qasim ibn Muhammad from al-Zayyat from 'Abd Allah ibn Aban al-Zayyat who enjoyed a good position in the sight of al-Rida, *'Alayhi al-Salam*, has said the following:

"Once I asked al-Rida, *'Alayhi al-Salam*, to pray for me and for my family. The Imam said, 'Am I not praying for them? I swear by Allah that your deeds are presented before me every day and night.' He (al-Zayyat) has said that the statement of the Imam seemed to me extremely great. The Imam said to me, 'Do you not read in the words of Allah, "Act as you wish. Allah will see your deeds and so will His Messenger and the believers . . ." (9:106) The Imam then said, 'I swear by Allah that he "the believer" is Ali ibn abu Talib, *'Alayhi al-Salam.*'"

H 578, Ch. 29, h 5

Ahmad ibn Mahran has narrated from Muhammad ibn Ali from abu 'Abd Allah al-Samit from Yahya ibn Musawwir who has said the following:

"Once I mentioned this verse to abu Ja'far, *'Alayhi al-Salam*, 'Act as you wish. Allah will see your deeds and so will His Messenger and the believers . . .' (9:106) The Imam then said, 'I swear by Allah that he "the believer" is Ali ibn abu Talib, *'Alayhi al-Salam.*'"

H 579, Ch. 29, h 6

A number of our people have narrated from Ahmad ibn Muhammad from al-Washsha' who has said the following:

"I heard Imam al-Rida say, 'All the deeds, good and bad ones, are presented before the Messenger of Allah.'"

Chapter 30 - The Path, Urged to Be Maintained Steadfastly is Acknowledgement of the Divine Authority of Imam Ali, *'Alayhi al-Salam*

H 580, Ch. 30, h 1

Ahmad ibn Mahran has narrated from 'Abd al-'Azim ibn 'Abd Allah al-Hassani from Musa ibn Muhammad from Yunus ibn Ya'qub from the person whom he mentioned, has said the following:

"Abu Ja'far, *'Alayhi al-Salam*, about the words of Allah, the Most Holy, and the Most High, 'Had they (jinn and mankind) remained steadfast in their path (religion, Islam), We would certainly have given them abundant water to drink' (72:16), has said, 'It means, had people maintained steadfastness in respecting the Divine Authority of (Amir al-Mu'minin) Ali ibn abu Talib, *'Alayhi al-Salam*, and the Divine Authority of his successors from his children and agreed to obey their orders and prohibitions, He would have given them abundant water. He (Allah) says, "We would drench their hearts with belief." The path (al-Triqah) means to have belief in the Divine Authority of (Amir al-Mu'minin) Ali, *'Alayhi al-Salam*, and his successors from his children.'"

H 581, Ch. 30, h 2

Al-Husayn ibn Muhammad has narrated from Mu'alla ibn Muhammad from Muhammad ibn Jumhur from Fudala ibn Ayyub from al-Husayn ibn 'Uthman from abu Ayyub from Muhammad ibn Muslim who has said the following:

"Once I asked abu 'Abd Allah, *'Alayhi al-Salam*, about the meaning of the following words of Allah, the Most Holy, the Most High, 'To those who have said, "Allah is our Lord," and who have remained steadfast to their belief. . . .' (41:30) The Imam said, 'For those who remain steadfast in respecting the Divine Authority of (Amir al-Mu'minin) Ali and his successors, *'A'immah, 'Alayhim al-Salam*, one after the other then, the angels will descend saying, "Do not be afraid or grieved. Receive the glad news of the Paradise, which was promised to you.'" (41:30)

Chapter 31 - 'A'immah, *'Alayhim al-Salam*, Are the Mines of Knowledge, the Tree of Prophecy and a Center of Movement of the Angels

H 582, Ch. 31, h 1

Ahmad ibn Mihran has narrated from Muhammad ibn Ali from several people from Hammad ibn 'Isa from Rib'i ibn 'Abd Allah from abu Jarud who has said that Ali ibn al-Husayn, *'Alayhi al-Salam*, has said the following:

"What is it that obscures us to people? We, I swear by Allah, are the tree of the prophecy, the house of blessings, the source of knowledge and a center of movements of the angels."

H 583, Ch. 31, h 2

Muhammad ibn Yahya has narrated from 'Abd Allah ibn Muhammad ibn 'Isa from his father from 'Abd Allah ibn al-Mughirah from Isma'il ibn abu Ziyad from Ja'far ibn Muhammad) from his father) from (Amir al-Mu'minin) Ali, *'Alayhi al-Salam*, who has said the following:

"We, the *Ahl al-Bayt* (family of the Holy Prophet, *'Alayhi al-Salam*), are the tree of the prophecy, the station of the Messengership (of Allah), a center of movements of the angels, the house of blessings and the mine of knowledge."

H 584, Ch. 31, h 3

Ahmad ibn Muhammad has narrated from Muhammad ibn al-Husayn from 'Abd Allah ibn Muhammad from al-Khashshab. He has said that a number of our people have narrated from al-Khaythama who has said that abu 'Abd Allah, *'Alayhi al-Salam*, said to him the following:

"O Khaythama, we are the tree of prophecy, the house of blessings, the keys to wisdom, the mine of knowledge, the station of the Messengership (of Allah), a center of movements of the angels and the reservoir for the secrets of Allah. We are the trust of Allah among the people and we are the great sanctuaries of Allah. We are the promised responsibility of Allah and we are His covenant. Whoever remains true to our covenant has remained true to the covenant of Allah. Whoever disregards his covenant with us has disregarded his covenant and responsibility toward Allah."

Chapter 32 - 'A'immah (Plural of Imam), *'Alayhim al-Salam*, Are the Heirs of Knowledge Inherited by One from the Other

H 585, Ch. 32, h 1

A number of our people have narrated from Ahmad ibn Muhammad from al-Husayn ibn Sa'id from al-Nadr ibn Suwayd from Yahya al-Halabi from Burayd ibn Mu'awiya from Muhammad ibn Muslim from abu 'Abd Allah, *'Alayhi al-Salam*, who has said the following:

"Ali, *'Alayhi al-Salam*, was a man of knowledge: and knowledge is inherited. Whenever a man of knowledge dies he leaves another man of knowledge behind who possesses his knowledge or whatever Allah wants."

H 586, Ch. 32, h 2

Ali ibn Ibrahim has narrated from his father from Hammad ibn 'Isa from Hariz from Zurara and al-Fudayl from abu Ja'far, *'Alayhi al-Salam*) who has said the following:

"The knowledge that came with Adam was not taken away. Knowledge is inherited. Ali, *'Alayhi al-Salam*, was the knowledgeable person of this nation (Muslims). No one from us has ever left this world without leaving behind one like himself in knowledge or whatever Allah wants."

H 587, Ch. 32, h 3

Muhammad ibn Yahya has narrated from Ahmad ibn Muhammad from al-Barqi from al-Nadr ibn Suwayd from Yahya al-Halabi from 'Abd al-Hamid al-Ta'i from Muhammad ibn Muslim from abu Ja'far, *'Alayhi al-Salam*, who has said the following:

"Knowledge is inherited. No man of knowledge (Imam) dies without leaving behind one who is as knowledgeable as his predecessor or what Allah wants."

H 588, Ch. 32, h 4

Abu Ali al-Ash'ari has narrated from Muhammad ibn 'Abd al-Jabbar from Safwan from Musa ibn Bakr from al-Fudayl ibn Yasar who has said the following:

"I heard abu 'Abd Allah, *'Alayhi al-Salam*, say, 'In Imam Ali, *'Alayhi al-Salam*, there is the *Sunnah* (tradition) of a thousand prophets. The knowledge that came with Adam was not taken away. No man of knowledge (Imam) ever died along with knowledge. Knowledge is inherited.'"

H 589, Ch. 32, h 5
Muhammad ibn Yahya has narrated from Ahmad ibn Muhammad from al-Husayn ibn Sa'id from Fadala ibn Ayyub from 'Umar ibn Aban who has said that he heard abu Ja'far, *'Alayhi al-Salam*, say the following:

"The knowledge that came with Adam was not taken away. No man of knowledge (Imam) has ever died along with his knowledge."

H 590, Ch. 32, h 6
Muhammad has narrated from Ahmad from Ali ibn Nu'man, in a *marfu'* manner *(rafa'ahu)* from abu Ja'far, *'Alayhi al-Salam*, who has said the following:

"Abu Ja'far, *'Alayhi al-Salam*, has said, 'They try to absorb the little moisture but ignore the huge river.' A certain person asked him, 'What is (this) huge river?' The Imam said, 'It is the Messenger of Allah, *'Alayhi al-Salam*, and the knowledge that Allah gave to him. Allah, the Most Holy, the Most High, combined in Muhammad, *'Alayhi al-Salam*, the *Sunnah* (tradition) of all the prophets from Adam onward to Muhammad, *'Alayhi al-Salam*.' A man then asked him, 'What is the *Sunnah* (tradition)?' The Imam said, 'It is all the knowledge of all the prophets, *'Alayhim al-Salam*. The Messenger of Allah transferred all of it to (Amir al-Mu'minin) Ali, *'Alayhi al-Salam*.

"The man then said, 'O descendent of the Messenger of Allah, is (Amir al-Mu'minin) Ali more knowledgeable or certain persons of the prophets?' Abu Ja'far, *'Alayhi al-Salam*, replied, 'Everyone, listen to what he just said. Allah opens the ears of whomever He wants. I said to him that Allah combined for Muhammad, *'Alayhi al-Salam*, the knowledge of the prophets and he combined all of it and transferred to Amir al-Mu'minin (Ali), *'Alayhi al-Salam*. He now asks me, "Was he (Ali), *'Alayhi al-Salam*, more knowledgeable or certain persons of the prophets?"'"

H 591, Ch. 32, h 7
Muhammad ibn Yahya has narrated from Ahmad ibn Muhammad from al-Barqi from al-Nadr ibn Suwayd from Yahya al-Halabi from 'Abd al-Hamid al-Ta'i from Muhammad ibn Muslim from abu Ja'far, *'Alayhi al-Salam*, who has said the following:

"Knowledge is inherited. No man of knowledge (Imam) ever leaves this world without leaving behind one who has as much knowledge as he had or what Allah wants."

H 592, Ch. 32, h 8
Ali ibn Ibrahim has narrated from Muhammad ibn 'Isa from Yunus from al-Harith ibn al-Mughirah from abu 'Abd Allah, *'Alayhi al-Salam*, who has said the following:

"The Knowledge that came with Adam was not taken away. No man of knowledge (Imam) has ever died without his knowledge being inherited. The earth does not remain without a man of knowledge (Imam)."

Chapter 33 - The Imam, *'Alayhi al-Salam*, Inherited the Knowledge of the Holy Prophet, *'Alayhi al-Salam*, and All the Prophets and Their Successors Before Them

H 593, Ch. 33, h 1

Ali ibn Ibrahim has narrated from his father from 'Abd al-'Aziz ibn al-Muhtadi from 'Abd Allah ibn Jundab to who Imam al-Rida, *'Alayhi al-Salam*, wrote the following:

"Thereafter (after thanking Allah I must say), Muhammad, *'Alayhi al-Salam*, was the trustee of Allah in the matters of His creatures. When he was taken away from this world, we, *Ahl al-Bayt*, inherited him; thus, we are the trustees of Allah over His earth. With us is the knowledge of the sufferings, the death, the genealogy of the Arabs and the birth of Islam. We know the man when we see him in the truth of belief or hypocrisy. Our followers (Shi'a) are listed (with us) by their names and the names of their fathers. Allah has established a covenant with them and with us. They land wherever we do so and enter wherever we enter. No one besides our followers and us lives the Islamic culture. We are the noble saviors and the descendents of the prophets and of the children of the successors of the prophets. We are the ones to whom the Book of Allah, the Most Holy, the Most High, has come exclusively. We, of all people, have the first priority (closeness) to the Book of Allah. We, of all people, have the first priority (closeness) to the Messenger of Allah. For us He formed His religion.

"Allah has said in His book, 'He has established for you [family of Muhammad] a form of religion, just as the commands issued to Noah. [We have received the commandments that Noah had received]. It (religion) is what We have revealed to you (Muhammad), that (commands) which issued to Abraham, Moses, and Jesus to follow. [He, certainly, taught and preached to us the science of the knowledge that we have and placed with us the knowledge of the prophets. We are the heirs of the commissioned Messengers, *'Ulu al-'Azm*.] (He has explained it) so you [family of Muhammad] remain steadfast and united [all in a united group] in your religion. What you call the polytheists to [polytheists in the acknowledgement of the Divine Authority of Imam Ali, *'Alayhi al-Salam*] is extremely grave for them. Allah [O Muhammad] guides to [the religion] whomever He wants and guides to it those who turn to Him in repentance [who obey you to acknowledge the Divine Authority of Ali, *'Alayhi al-Salam*].'" (42:13)

Note: In the above *Hadith* enclosed in brackets are the explanatory words of the Imam.

H 594, Ch. 33, h 2

Muhammad ibn Yahya has narrated from Ahmad ibn Muhammad from Ali ibn al-Hakam from 'Abd al-Rahman ibn Kathir from abu Ja'far, *'Alayhi al-Salam*, who has said the following:

"The Messenger of Allah has said, 'The first successor and executor of the will on earth was Hibbatu Allah (gift from Allah), the son of Adam. No prophet has ever left this world without first leaving behind one who would execute his will. The prophets were one hundred twenty thousand persons. Five of them were commissioned Messengers *'Ulu al-'Azm*, like Noah, Abraham, Moses, Jesus and Muhammad, *'Alayhi al-Salam.*' Ali ibn abu Talib, *'Alayhi al-Salam*, was the "Hibbatu Allah" (gift from Allah) for Muhammad, *'Alayhi al-Salam*. He inherited the knowledge of the executors of the wills of the prophets and the knowledge of those who were before him. (Is not it true) that Muhammad, *'Alayhi al-Salam*, inherited the knowledge of the prophets and the messengers who lived before him? It is written on the columns of the Throne ('Arsh), "Hamza is the lion of Allah and the lion of His Messenger. He (Hamza) is the master of the martyrs." On top of the Throne is written, "Ali, *'Alayhi al-Salam*, is Amir al-Mu'minin (commander of the believers)." This is evidence against those who deny our rights and refuse to yield to us our right of inheritance. We are not forbidden to speak. Before us is all certainty. What else can serve as clearer supporting evidence than this?'"

H 595, Ch. 33, h 3
Muhammad ibn Yahya has narrated from Salama ibn al-Khattab from 'Abd Allah ibn Muhammad from 'Abd Allah ibn al-Qasim from Zur'a ibn Muhammad from al-Mufaddal ibn 'Umar who has said the following:
"Abu 'Abd Allah, *'Alayhi al-Salam*, has said, 'Solomon inherited from David. Muhammad, *'Alayhi al-Salam*, inherited from Solomon and we inherited from Muhammad, *'Alayhi al-Salam*. We have the knowledge of the Torah and the Gospel (Injil), the Psalms, (al-Zabur) and the explanation of what the Tablets contained.'

"I (the narrator) said, 'This certainly is the knowledge.' The Imam, *'Alayhi al-Salam*, said, 'This is not knowledge. Knowledge is what happens day after day and hour after hour.'"

H 596, Ch. 33, h 4
Ahmad ibn Idris has narrated from Muhammad ibn 'Abd al-Jabbar from Safwan ibn Yahya from Shu'ayb al-Haddad from Durays al-Kunasi who has said the following:
"Once I was in the presence of abu 'Abd Allah, *'Alayhi al-Salam*, and abu Basir also was there. The Imam said, 'David inherited knowledge from the prophets. Solomon inherited from David. Prophet Muhammad, *'Alayhi al-Salam*, inherited from Solomon and we inherited from Muhammad, *'Alayhi al-Salam*. With us are the books (pages) of Abraham and the tablets of Moses.' Abu Basir then said, 'This is the knowledge.' The Imam said, 'O abu Muhammad, this is not the knowledge. The knowledge is what happens in the nights and in the days, day after day and hour after hour.'"

H 597, Ch. 33, h 5
Muhammad ibn Yahya has narrated from Muhammad ibn 'Abd al-Jabbar from Muhammad ibn Isma'il from Ali ibn an-Nu'man from ibn Muskan from abu Basir who has said the following:
"Imam abu 'Abd Allah, *'Alayhi al-Salam*, once said to me, 'O abu Muhammad, whatever Allah, the Most Holy, the Most High, has given to the prophets, He has given to Prophet Muhammad, *'Alayhi al-Salam*, also.' The Imam further said, 'Allah gave to Prophet Muhammad, *'Alayhi al-Salam*, all that He had given to the

prophets. With us is the Book about which Allah, the Most Holy, the Most High, said, 'The books of Abraham and Moses.'(87:19)

"I then said, 'May Allah keep my soul in service for your cause, are they the tablets?' The Imam said, 'Yes, they are the tablets.'"

H 598, Ch. 33, h 6

Muhammad has narrated from Ahmad ibn Muhammad from al-Husayn ibn Sa'id from al-Nadr ibn Suwayd from 'Abd Allah ibn Sinan who has said the following:

"Once I mentioned before abu 'Abd Allah, *'Alayhi al-Salam*, the words of Allah, the Most Holy, the Most High. 'We have written in *al-Zabur* (the psalms), which We had revealed after *al-Dhikr* (the Torah). . . .' (21:105) and I asked, 'What is *al-Zabur* and what is *al-Dhikr*?' The Imam said, '*Al-Dhikr* is with Allah and *al-Zabur* is what He gave to David. Every book that was revealed is with the people of knowledge and we are the people of knowledge.'"

H 599, Ch. 33, h 7

Muhammad ibn Yahya has narrated from Ahmad ibn abu Zahir or another man from Muhammad ibn Hammad from his brother Ahmad ibn Hammad from Ibrahim from his father who has said the following:

"I said to abu al-Hassan al-Awwal, the 1ª, *'Alayhi al-Salam*, 'May Allah keep my soul in service for your cause, can you tell me about the Holy Prophet, *'Alayhi al-Salam*, if he received inheritance from all the prophets?' The Imam said, 'Yes, I can do so.' I asked, 'Did he inherit from Adam and all the other prophets?' The Imam said, 'Of every prophet that Allah sent, Prophet Muhammad, *'Alayhi al-Salam*, was most knowledgeable.' I then said, 'Jesus son of Mary could bring the dead to life by the permission of Allah.' The Imam said, 'You spoke the truth.' I said, 'Solomon son of David could understand the language of the birds. The messenger of Allah, *'Alayhi al-Salam*, was also capable of doing such things.' The narrator has said that the Imam then said, 'Solomon son of David said about the *Hud-Hud* (Hoopoe), when he found him missing and had doubts about the bird, "How is it that I cannot see the hoopoe? [When he did not find him present and became angry]. Is he absent? (27:20) I shall certainly punish him severely or slaughter him unless he has a good reason for his absence." (27:21) He became angry; the bird would show him how to find water. This was only a bird but had received something that was not given to Solomon. The wind, ants, man, Jinn, devils and the rebels obeyed him in submission but he did not know about the water under the space (in the surroundings), but the bird knew.

"On the other hand, Allah says in His Book, 'Even if the Quran would make mountains move, cut the earth into pieces and make the dead able to speak. . . .' (13:31) We have as inheritance this Quran which contains such things that can make the mountains move, crisscross the lands and make the dead to come to life. We know there is water under the space (in the surroundings). In the book of Allah there are verses that are indicative of certain issues only if Allah gives permission. This is along with the fact that Allah sometime grants permission to make use of the things that people of the past had written. Allah has set them for us in the origin of the Book as Allah says, 'All the secrets in heavens and earth are recorded in the illustrious Book.' (27:75) Allah has also said, 'We gave the Book as an inheritance to Our chosen servants,' (35:32) We are the ones whom Allah, the Most Holy, the Most High, has chosen and has given this (Book) which contains the explanation of all things.'"

Chapter 34 - 'A'immah (Plural of Imam), *'Alayhim al-Salam*, Have All the Books That Allah, the Most Holy, the Most High, Has Revealed and They Know Them Even though the Languages Differ

H 600, Ch. 34, h 1
Ali ibn Ibrahim has narrated from his father from al-Hassan ibn Ibrahim from Yunus from Hisham ibn al-Hakam who has said the following about the narration of Burayh:

"With Burayh I once went to see abu 'Abd Allah, *'Alayhi al-Salam*, but we met abu al-Hassan Musa ibn Ja'far, *'Alayhi al-Salam*. I (Hisham) explained to the Imam about Burayh. When I (Hisham) finished speaking, abu al-Hassan, *'Alayhi al-Salam*, asked, 'O Burayh, how is your knowledge of your book?' He replied, 'I know it.' The Imam then asked, 'What is the degree of your confidence in its interpretation?' He said, 'My knowledge of it is very reliable to me.' The narrator has said, 'Abu al-Hassan, *'Alayhi al-Salam*, then began to read (from) the Gospel. Burayh then said, 'It is you for whom I was searching for fifty years or someone like you.' He (Hisham) has said that Burayh accepted the faith and also the lady who was with him. Burayh, the lady and I (Hisham) then came to abu 'Abd Allah, *'Alayhi al-Salam*. I (Hisham) informed the Imam about what had happened between Burayh and abu al-Hassan, Musa, *'Alayhi al-Salam*. Abu 'Abd Allah, *'Alayhi al-Salam*, then read this from the Holy Quran, '. . . These are offspring one from the other, and Allah hears and knows best.' (3:34) Burayh then asked, 'How have you possessed the Torah and the Gospel and the books of the prophets?' The Imam said, 'We have received them in the form of inheritance from them (prophets). We read them as they did and speak about them, as the prophets would do. Allah does not grant Divine Authority on His earth to those who if questioned are not able to give the right answer and say. "I do not know".'"

H 601, Ch. 34, h 2
Ali ibn Muhammad and Muhammad ibn al-Hassan have narrated from Sahl ibn Ziyad from Bakr ibn Salih from Muhammad ibn Sinan from Mufaddal ibn 'Umar who has said the following:

"Once we went to abu 'Abd Allah, *'Alayhi al-Salam*, and wanted permission to visit him. We heard him speaking in a non-Arabic language and we thought it was Suryani (Syrian) language. The Imam then wept and we also did so because of his weeping. A boy then came out to give us permission for a meeting. In the meeting I asked him, 'May Allah keep you well, we came to ask permission for a meeting and we heard you speak in a non-Arabic language and we thought it was Suryani language. Then we heard you weeping and because of that we also wept.'

"The Imam said, 'Yes, I remembered prophet Ilyas, one of the Israelite prophets devoted in worship. I then said what he used to say in his prostration.' He then went into it in Suryani language. I swear by Allah, we had not seen any monk or minister as eloquent in it as he was. He then explained it to us in Arabic saying: 'Ilyas would say in his prostration, "O Lord, will I find You punish me even though I have endured so much thirst in the heat of the midday for your sake? Will I find You punish me although You know that I rub my face on earth to worship You? Will I find You punish me although You know that I give up sins for Your sake? Will I find You punish me although You know that I stay awake all night just for You?"' The Imam then said, 'Allah then told him through inspiration, "Raise your head from the earth. I will not punish you."' The Imam then said that he (Ilyas) said to Allah, 'What if You say, "I will not punish you" but then You punish me? After all, am I not your slave and You are my Lord?' The Imam said, 'Allah then spoke to him through inspiration, "Raise your head. I will not punish you because when I promise I then keep My promise."'"

Chapter 35 - No One Collected All of the Holy Quran Except 'A'immah, *'Alayhim al-Salam*, and They Have the Knowledge of All of the Quran

H 602, Ch. 35, h 1

Muhammad ibn Yahya has narrated from Ahmad ibn Muhammad from ibn Mahbub from 'Amr ibn abu al-Miqdam from Jabir who has said that he heard abu Ja'far, *'Alayhi al-Salam*, say the following:

"No one from the people has claimed to have collected the whole of the Holy Quran (in a book form) as it was revealed. If anyone comes up with such a claim, he is a liar. No one collected this Holy Book and memorized as Allah, the Most Holy, the Most High, revealed it except Ali ibn abu Talib, *'Alayhi al-Salam*, and *'A'immah* after him."

H 603, Ch. 35, h 2

Muhammad ibn al-Husayn has narrated from Muhammad ibn al-Hassan from Muhammad ibn Sinan from 'Ammar ibn Marwan from al-Munakhkhal from Jabir from abu Ja'far, *'Alayhi al-Salam*, who has said the following:

"No one is able to claim that with him is the whole of the Holy Quran, its apparent and hidden essence, except the executors of the will of the Holy Prophet, *'Alayhim al-Salam*."

H 604, Ch. 35, h 3

Ali ibn Muhammad and Muhammad ibn al-Hassan have narrated from Sahl ibn Ziyad from al-Qasim ibn al-Rabi' from 'Ubayd ibn 'Abd Allah ibn abu Hashim al-Sayrafi from 'Amr ibn Mus'ab from Salama ibn Muhriz who has said that he heard abu Ja'far, *'Alayhi al-Salam*, say the following:

"I heard abu Ja'far, *'Alayhi al-Salam*, say, 'Of the knowledge that we have received is the interpretation of the Holy Quran and its laws, the knowledge of the changes of time and the happenings therein. When Allah wants good for a people, He makes them to understand. If He would address one who does not want to understand, such a person turns away as if he has heard nothing.' The Imam, *'Alayhi al-Salam*, paused, briefly, then said, 'Had we found keepers and trusted people for our knowledge, we would have said it (all to him). Allah is the best to seek support from.'"

H 605, Ch. 35, h 4

Muhammad ibn Yahya has narrated from Muhammad ibn al-Husayn from Muhammad ibn 'Isa from abu 'Abd Allah al-Mu'min from 'Abd al-A'la Mawla 'Ala Sam who has said that he heard abu 'Abd Allah, *'Alayhi al-Salam*, say the following:

"I swear by Allah that I know the book of Allah from beginning to end as if it is in the palm of my hand. In it there is the news of the heavens and the earth, the news of what has been and the news of what will come into being. Allah, the Most Holy, the Most High, has said, 'In it there is the explanation of all things.'" (16:89)

H 606, Ch. 35, h 5

Muhammad ibn Yahya has narrated from Ahmad ibn abu Zahir from al-Khashshab from Ali ibn Hass'an from 'Abd al-Rahman ibn Kathir from abu 'Abd Allah, *'Alayhi al-Salam*, who has said the following:

"The Imam, *'Alayhi al-Salam*, reciting the following verse, 'The one who had a certain amount of knowledge from the Book said, "I can bring it to you before you even blink your eye. . . ."'" (27:40), opened his two fingers and placed them on his chest and then said, 'With us, I swear by Allah, is the knowledge of the whole Book.'"

H 607, Ch. 35, h 6

Ali ibn Ibrahim has narrated from his father and Muhammad ibn Yahya from Muhammad ibn al-Hassan from those he mentioned, both of them from ibn abu 'Umayr from ibn 'Udhayna from Burayd ibn Mu'awiya who has said the following:

"Once I asked abu Ja'far, *'Alayhi al-Salam*, about the meaning of the following verse: '. . . Say, Allah and those who have the knowledge of the Book are sufficient witness (to my prophecy).' (13:43)

"The Imam said, 'It is a reference to us. Ali (ibn abu Talib), *'Alayhi al-Salam*, is the first among us and the most excellent and the best among us after the Holy Prophet, *'Alayhi al-Salam*.'"

Chapter 36 - The Degree of the Great Names of Allah That Are Given to 'A'immah, *'Alayhim al-Salam*

H 608, Ch. 36, h 1

Muhammad ibn Yahya and others have narrated from Ahmad ibn Muhammad from Ali ibn al-Hakam from Muhammad ibn al-Fudayl who has said that Shurays al-Wabishi narrated from Jabir from abu Ja'far, *'Alayhi al-Salam*, who has said the following:

"The greatest name of Allah has seventy-three letters. There was only one of these letters with A'sif (spoken of in (27:40)) He spoke that one letter and the land between him and throne of the Queen of Sheba (Bilqis) sank down such that he could reach her throne with his hand and the land returned to the original state. This happened in a blinking of the eye. Of the greatest name of Allah there are seventy-two letters with us. Allah has kept one letter exclusively for Himself in the knowledge of the unseen. There are no means and no power except by the help of Allah, the Most High, the Most Great."

H 609, Ch. 36, h 2

Muhammad ibn Yahya has narrated from Ahmad ibn Muhammad from al-Husayn ibn Sa'id and Muhammad ibn Khalid from Zakariyya ibn 'Imran al-Qummi from Harun ibn al-Juhm that a man from the companions of abu 'Abd Allah, *'Alayhi al-Salam*, I (Harun ibn al-Jahm) have forgotten his name, has said that he heard abu 'Abd Allah, *'Alayhi al-Salam*, say the following:

"Two letters were given to Jesus and he would work with them. Four letters were given to Moses. Eight letters were given to Abraham. Fifteen letters were given to Noah. Twenty-five letters were given to Adam. Allah, the Most Holy, the Most High, has combined all of them in Muhammad, *'Alayhi al-Salam*. The greatest name of Allah has seventy-three letters. Seventy-two letters are given to Muhammad, *'Alayhi al-Salam*, and only one letter is kept hidden from him."

H 610, Ch. 36, h 3
Al-Husayn ibn Muhammad al-Ash'ari has narrated from Mu'alla ibn Muhammad from Ahmad ibn Muhammad ibn 'Abd Allah from Ali ibn Muhammad al-Nawfali who has said that he heard abu al-Hassan, *'Alayhi al-Salam*, Sahib al-'Askar say the following:

"The greatest name of Allah has seventy-three letters. There was only one letter with A'sif. He spoke with it and the land between him and the throne of the Queen of Sheba (Bilqis) sank down as such that he took her throne and placed it before Solomon. The land then came to normal state within less than a blinking of an eye. There are seventy-two of those letters with us. One letter is with Allah which He has kept exclusively in the knowledge of the unseen."

Chapter 37 - Sacred Articles of the Prophets Transferred To 'A'immah, *'Alayhim al-Salam*

H 611, Ch. 37, h 1
Muhammad ibn Yahya has narrated from Salama ibn al-Khattab from 'Abd Allah ibn Muhammad from Mani' ibn al-Hajjaj al-Basri from Majashi'i from Mu'alla from Muhammad ibn al-Fayd from abu Ja'far, *'Alayhi al-Salam*, who has said the following:

"The staff of Musa (Moses) belonged to Adam. It was passed to Shu'ayb, then to Musa (Moses) ibn 'Imran. Now it is with us. I have just, moments before, seen it. It is green just as being picked from its tree. It speaks if it is induced to do so. It is prepared for the one who will rise to establish the kingdom of Allah on earth. He will use it in the same way as Moses had done. It frightens and devours things made to trick people and it accomplishes whatever commands it receives. If it moves for a task, it devours the treacherous materials. It opens into two branches, one on earth and the other toward the ceiling with an opening of forty yards in between, and devours the deceptive materials with its tongue."

H 612, Ch. 37, h 2
Ahmad ibn Idris has narrated from 'Imran ibn Musa from Musa ibn Ja'far al-Baghdadi from Ali ibn Asbat from Muhammad ibn Fudayl from abu Hamza al-Thumali who has said that he heard abu 'Abd Allah, *'Alayhi al-Salam*, say the following:

"The Tablets of Musa (Moses) are with us. The Staff of Musa (Moses) is with us. We are the heirs of the prophets (peace be upon them)."

H 613, Ch. 37, h 3
Muhammad ibn Yahya has narrated from Muhammad ibn al-Husayn from Musa ibn Sa'dan from 'Abd Allah ibn al-Qasim from abu Sa'id al-Khurasani from abu 'Abd Allah, *'Alayhi al-Salam*, who has said that abu Ja'far, *'Alayhi al-Salam*, has said the following:

"When al-Qa'im (the one who will rise to establish the kingdom of Allah on earth) will rise in Makkah at the time of his leaving for Kufa a caller will call upon him,

'No one among you should carry any food and water for the journey. One should carry the Rock of Musa (Moses) ibn 'Imran. It is a full load for a camel. Wherever you will disembark, there will gush forth a water fountain therefrom (the Rock). Whoever will be hungry, it will satisfy him; and whoever will be thirsty, it will quench his thirst. It will be their supplies until they will arrive in Najaf behind al-Kufa, Iraq.'"

H 614, Ch. 37, h 4

Muhammad Yahya has narrated from Muhammad ibn al-Husayn from Musa ibn Sa'dan from abu al-Hassan al-'Asadi from abu Basir from abu Ja'far, *'Alayhi al-Salam*, who has said the following:

"Amir al-Mu'minin, *'Alayhi al-Salam*, once came out during the night after the 'Isha' (late evening) prayer, saying, 'Ham hama, ham hama, and it is a dark night. The Imam has come out to you and he is wearing the shirt of Adam (peace be upon him). He is wearing the ring of Solomon (peace be upon him) and in his hands he has the staff of Moses (peace be upon him).'"

H 615, Ch. 37, h 5

Muhammad has narrated from al-Husayn from Muhammad ibn Isma'il al-Sarraj from Bishr ibn Ja'far from Mufaddal ibn 'Umar who has said that he heard abu 'Abd Allah, *'Alayhi al-Salam*, say the following:

"I heard abu 'Abd Allah, *'Alayhi al-Salam*, say, 'Do you know what was the shirt of Joseph?' I said, 'I do not know.' The Imam said, 'When the fire was set for Abraham, Jibril brought him a dress from paradise and made him to wear it. With that dress on him nothing of the cold or heat could harm him. When Abraham was about to die, he placed it in a covering and affixed it upon Isaac (Ishaq) who affixed it upon Jacob (Ya'qub). When Joseph was born it was affixed upon him and he had it on his shoulder until the event of the things that happened to him. When he (Joseph) took it out of its covering in Egypt, Jacob (Ya'qub) felt its fragrance as he said, "I smell Joseph's scent. I hope that you will not accuse me of senility." (12:94) It was the same shirt that was sent from paradise.' I then said, 'May Allah keep my soul in service for your cause, to whom did that shirt go thereafter?' The Imam said, 'It went to its (people) owner.' Then he said, 'Every prophet who inherited knowledge or other things, they all ended with the family of Muhammad, *'Alayhi al-Salam*.'"

Chapter 38 - The Armaments and Sacred Articles Belonging to the Messenger of Allah, *'Alayhi al-Salam*, That Were Transferred to 'A'immah, *'Alayhim al-Salam*

H 616, Ch. 38, h 1

A number of our people have narrated from Ahmad ibn Muhammad ibn 'Isa from Ali ibn al-Hakam from Mu'awiya ibn Wahab from Sa'id al-Samman who has said the following:

"Once, I was in the presence of abu 'Abd Allah, *'Alayhi al-Salam*, when two people from the Zaydia sect came to him. They asked, 'Is there with you an Imam to whom obedience is obligatory?' The narrator has said that the Imam said, 'No, there is no one as such.' They then said, 'Reliable people have informed us about you that you issue *fatwas* (rules of Shari'a) and that you affirm and speak of it. We can point out what their names are. They are very pious and alert people. They are such that cannot be rejected.' The Imam became angry and said, 'I have not ordered them to say so.' When the two men noticed anger on the face of the Imam they left.

"The Imam then asked me, 'Do you know these two?' I said, 'Yes, I know them. They are from our *Suq* (shopping place). They belong to the Zaydia sect and they think that the sword of the Messenger of Allah, *'Alayhi al-Salam*, is with 'Abd Allah ibn al-Hassan.' The Imam said, 'They have lied, may Allah condemn them. I swear by Allah, 'Abd Allah ibn al-Hassan has not seen it with his own eyes, not even one of his eyes has seen it. Even his father had not seen it except if he might have seen it with Imam Ali ibn al-Husayn, *'Alayhi al-Salam*. If they are truthful let them explain what kind of mark does its hilt has and what the mark is on its blade. With me is the sword of the Messenger of Allah. With me is the flag of the Messenger of Allah, his coat of arms, his *Lamma* (insignia) and his helmet. If they are truthful let them say what kind of mark does the coat of arms of the Messenger of Allah has? With me is the flag of the Messenger of Allah, the victorious. With me is the staff of Moses. With me is the ring of Solomon son of David. With me is the tray on which Moses used to offer offerings. With me is the name that whenever the Messenger of Allah would place it between the Muslims and pagans, no arrow from the pagans would reach the Muslims. With me is the similar object that angels brought. (Perhaps the Imam, *'Alayhi al-Salam*, has hinted of the following verse: 'Their Prophet further told them, as the evidence of his authority, he will bring to you the Ark which will be a comfort to you from your Lord and a legacy of the household of Moses and Aaron. The angels will carry it. This is the evidence for you if you have faith.') (2:248)

"The case of the Arms with us is like the case of the Ark in the Israelites. Whichever family had the Ark at their door-front that family received prophecy. To whomever of us the Arms are transferred he receives Imamat (Leadership with Divine Authority). My father wore the coats of arms of the Messenger of Allah. It would reach the earth and leave marks. I wore it also and it reached the earth and sometimes it would not. When the one from us who will rise to establish the authority of Allah on earth will come, it will fit him perfectly, if Allah so will wish.'"

H 617, Ch. 38, h 2

Al-Husayn ibn Muhammad al-Ash'ari has narrated from Mu'alla ibn Muhammad from al-Hassan ibn Ali al-Washsha' from Hammad ibn 'Uthman from 'Abd al-'Ala' ibn A'yan who has said that he heard abu 'Abd Allah, *'Alayhi al-Salam*, say the following:

"With me is the Arms of the Messenger of Allah. It is not disputable." The Imam, *'Alayhi al-Salam*, then said, 'The Arms are well defended. If they were placed with the worst creature of Allah, he would become very good among them.' The Imam then said, 'This matter (Leadership with Divine Authority) will proceed to the one who will enjoy total obedience. When Allah grants permission he will appear in public and people will say, 'What is it that has happened?' Allah will make his hand to protect his followers and subjects.'"

H 618, Ch. 38, h 3

Muhammad ibn Yahya has narrated from Ahmad ibn Muhammad ibn 'Isa from al-Husayn ibn Sa'id from al-Nadr ibn Suwayd from Yahya al-Halabi from ibn Muskan from abu Basir from abu 'Abd Allah, *'Alayhi al-Salam*, who has said the following:

"In the legacy that the Messenger of Allah left were a sword, a coat of arms, a spear, a saddle and a grey mule. Ali ibn abu Talib, *'Alayhi al-Salam*, received all of them as his legacy.'"

H 619, Ch. 38, h 4

Al-Husayn ibn Muhammad has narrated from Mu'alla ibn Muhammad from al-Washsha' from Aban ibn 'Uthman from Fudayl ibn Yasar from abu 'Abd Allah, *'Alayhi al-Salam*, who has said the following:

"My father wore the *Dhat al-Fudul*, coat of arms of the Messenger of Allah, and being tall for him it left marks on the ground. I wore it and it was tall for me also."

H 620, Ch. 38, h 5

Ahmad ibn Muhammad and Muhammad ibn Yahya have narrated from Muhammad ibn al-Hassan from Muhammad ibn 'Isa from Ahmad ibn abu 'Abd Allah who has said the following:

"I asked abu al-Hassan al-Rida, *'Alayhi al-Salam*, about *al-Dhul faqar* (the sword of the Messenger of Allah) as to wherefrom it was. The Imam said, 'Jibril (Gabriel) came down with it from the heavens. It was decorated with gold and it is with me now.'"

H 621, Ch. 38, h 6

Ali ibn Ibrahim has narrated from his father from Muhammad ibn 'Isa from Yunus ibn 'Abd al-Raman from Muhammad ibn al-Hakim from abu Ibrahim, *'Alayhi al-Salam*, who has said the following:

"The Arms are kept with us. They are well protected. Even if they were placed with the worst of the creatures, he would be a good one among them. My father stated to me that when he was married to a lady from al-Thaqif, the house was decorated for the wedding. The next morning he found fifteen stakes fixed into that wall. He became very anxious about it and asked the bride to leave the house; he needed the repairman to do certain works therein. When he examined the wall he found that all the pegs (or large nails) had turned back from the sword and none of them had reached it."

H 622, Ch. 38, h 7

Muhammad ibn Yahya has narrated from Muhammad ibn al-Husayn from Safwan ibn Yahya from ibn Muskan from Hujr from Humran who has said the following:

"I asked abu Ja'far, *'Alayhi al-Salam*, about the truth in the matter which people relate that a sealed page (or pages) was given to 'Umm Salama. The Imam then said, 'When the Messenger of Allah passed away, Imam Ali, *'Alayhi al-Salam*, inherited from the Holy Prophet his knowledge, his Arms and whatever was therein, then they were transferred to Imam al-Hassan, then to Imam al-Husayn, *'Alayhim al-Salam*. However, then we became anxious about losing them we then decided to leave them in trust of 'Umm Salama. Afterwards Imam Ali ibn al-Husayn, *'Alayhi al-Salam*, took custody of the Arms.' I then said, 'Then is it true that they were transferred to your father and then they ended up with you?' He said, 'Yes, that is true.'"

H 623, Ch. 38, h 8

Muhammad has narrated from Ahmad ibn Muhammad from al-Husayn ibn Sa'id from Fadala from 'Umar ibn Aban who has said the following:

"I asked abu 'Abd Allah, *'Alayhi al-Salam*, 'People say that a sealed page (or pages) was given to 'Umm Salama. Is it true?' The Imam said, 'When the Messenger of Allah passed away, Ali, *'Alayhi al-Salam*, inherited his knowledge, his Armaments and whatever was with them. Then they were transferred to al-Hassan, then to al-Husayn, *'Alayhim al-Salam*.' I (the narrator) then said to the Imam, 'Then they were transferred to Ali ibn al-Husayn, *'Alayhi al-Salam*, then to his son, and then they ended up with you.' He said, 'That is true.'"

H 624, Ch. 38, h 9

Muhammad ibn al-Husayn and Ali ibn Muhammad have narrated from Sahl ibn Ziyad from Muhammad ibn al-Walid Shabab al-Sayrafi from Aban ibn 'Uthman from abu 'Abd Allah, *'Alayhi al-Salam*, who has said the following:

"When the Messenger of Allah was about to die, he called al-'Abbass ibn 'Abd al-Muttalib and (Amir al-Mu'minin) Ali, *'Alayhi al-Salam*, to meet him. He said to al-'Abbass, 'O uncle of Muhammad, will you accept the legacy of Muhammad, pay his debts and fulfill his promises and commitments?' He responded, 'O the Messenger of Allah, may Allah keep my soul and the souls of my parents in service for your cause, I am an old man with a large number of dependents and with very few belongings, while you in generosity compete with the winds.' The Imam then said, he (the Messenger of Allah) remained quiet for a moment and then said, 'O 'Abbass, will you take the legacy of Muhammad, fulfill his promises, pay off his debts?' He responded, 'O the Messenger of Allah, may Allah keep my soul and the souls of my parents in service for your cause, I am an old man with a large number of dependents and with very few belongings while you in generosity compete with the winds.'

"The Holy Prophet, *'Alayhi al-Salam*, then said, 'I will give them away to whoever would want them along with their rights and responsibilities.' Then the Holy Prophet, *'Alayhi al-Salam*, said, 'O Ali, brother of Muhammad, will you pay off the liabilities of Muhammad, pay off his debt and take possession of his legacy?' He said, 'Yes, may Allah keep my soul and the soul of my parents in service for your cause, it is my responsibility and in my favor.' Ali, *'Alayhi al-Salam*, said, 'I looked at him and saw him take off even his ring from his finger and say to me "Wear this ring in my lifetime." He (Ali), *'Alayhi al-Salam*, said, 'I looked at the ring when wearing it on my finger and wished to have it out of all his properties.' He then called upon Bilal loudly, 'Bring me my helmet, the coat of arms, the flag, the shirt, the Dhul faqar, (famous sword), al-Sahab (the turban), al-Burd (the clothing), al-Abraqa (the belt), and the staff.' Ali, *'Alayhi al-Salam*, said, 'I had never before seen that belt. When it was brought its shine almost took away one's sight. It was of the belts of paradise.' He (the Messenger of Allah) then said, 'O Ali, Jibril brought this for me and said, "O Muhammad, place it (the belt) in the ring of the coat of arms and use it as a belt around your midsection."' Then he asked that the two pairs of Arabian shoes be brought to him along with the shirt. One of them was already stitched and the other was not yet stitched. It was the shirt with which he was taken for the 'Isra' (the night journey to the heavens), the shirt while wearing it he came out on the day of 'Uhud. Three caps were brought: the cap used while on a journey, the cap used on the 'Id days and the cap used on Fridays. Also the cap that was used during his meeting with his companions was brought to him.

"Then he (the Messenger of Allah) said, 'O Bilal, bring to us the two mules, the grey one and Dul-dul and the two camels, al-'Adba' and al-Qaswa' and the two horses, al-Janah, that would have been kept near the door of the Mosque in case the Messenger of Allah needed. Whenever he would need anything he would allow a man to ride on it to go for the task and the horse would run for the needs of the Messenger of Allah. Also Hayzum (the horse) was brought to him. It was that to which he would say, 'Go on, Hayzum.' The donkey called 'Ufayr was brought to him. He then said, 'Take possession of these in my lifetime.' (Amir al-Mu'minin) Ali, *'Alayhi al-Salam*, has said, 'The first one of the animals that died was 'Ufayr which died within the hour that the Messenger of Allah died. He broke off the rope that bound him and began to run until he came to the well of banu Khatmah in Quba and threw himself into it and it became his grave.' It is narrated that (Amir al-Mu'minin) Ali, *'Alayhi al-Salam*, said, 'The donkey spoke to the Messenger of Allah saying, "May Allah keep my soul and the soul of my parents in service for your cause, my father related to me from his father from his grandfather from his father who lived with Noah in the Ark. Once Noah came to him and touched him on his back and said, "From the descendents of this donkey there will be a donkey on whose back the master and the last of the prophets will ride. I thank Allah who has made me that donkey."'"

Chapter 39 - The Case of the Arms of the Messenger of Allah is Like the Ark of Covenant Among the Israelites

H 625, Ch. 39, h 1
A number of our people have narrated from Ahmad ibn Muhammad from Ali ibn al-Hakam from Mu'awiya ibn Wahab from Sa'id al-Samman who has said that he heard abu 'Abd Allah, *'Alayhi al-Salam*, say the following:

"The case of the Armaments with us is like the case of the Ark of Covenant with the Israelites. In whichever house of the Israelites the Ark of Covenant would have been found that house would receive prophecy. Whoever among us receives the Armaments he receives also Imamat (Leadership with Divine Authority)."

H 626, Ch. 39, h 2
Ali ibn Ibrahim has narrated from his father from ibn abu 'Umayr from Muhammad ibn al-Sukayn from Nuh ibn Darraj from 'Abd Allah ibn abu Ya'fur who has said that he heard abu 'Abd Allah, *'Alayhi al-Salam*, say the following:

"The case of the Armaments with us is like the case of the Ark of Covenant with the Israelites. Wherever the Ark of Covenant would go kingdom would also follow. Wherever the Armaments are found among us knowledge (Leadership with Divine Authority) also follows them."

H 627, Ch. 39, h 3

Muhammad ibn Yahya has narrated from Muhammad ibn al-Husayn from Safwan from abu al-Hassan al-Rida, *'Alayhi al-Salam*, who has said the following:

"Abu Ja'far, *'Alayhi al-Salam*, would say, 'The case of the Armaments with us is as that of the Ark of Covenant with the Israelites. Wherever the Ark of Covenant would go prophecy would also follow. Wherever the Armaments among us are found so also is the matter (Leadership with Divine Authority) settled there.' I then asked, 'Do the Armaments ever depart knowledge?' The Imam said, 'No, they do not do so.'"

H 628, Ch. 39, h 4

A number of our people have narrated from Ahmad ibn Muhammad from ibn abu Nasr from abu al-Hassan al-Rida, *'Alayhi al-Salam*, who has said the following:

"Abu Ja'far, *'Alayhi al-Salam*, would say, 'The case of the Armaments with us is as that of the Ark of Covenant with the Israelites. Wherever the Ark of Covenant would go kingdom would also follow. Wherever the Armaments among us are found so also is knowledge.'"

Chapter 40 - Statements About al-Jafr al-Jami' and the Book of Fatimah, *'Alayha al-Salam*

H 629, Ch. 40, h 1

A number of our people have narrated from Ahmad ibn Muhammad, from 'Abd Allah ibn al-Hajjal, from Ahmad ibn 'Umar al-Halabi, from abu Basir who has said the following:

"Once I went to see abu 'Abd Allah, *'Alayhi al-Salam*, and said, 'May Allah keep my soul in service for your cause, I like to ask you a question. Is there anyone else in this house that may hear my words?' The Imam then folded the curtain between his room and the next room and looked into it. Then the Imam said, 'O abu Muhammad, ask whatever you wish.'

"I said, 'May Allah keep my soul in service for your cause, your followers say that the Messenger of Allah taught Ali, *'Alayhi al-Salam*, a chapter of knowledge. From this chapter there open a thousand chapters.' The Imam said, 'The messenger of Allah taught Imam Ali, *'Alayhi al-Salam*, a thousand chapters from each of which there open a thousand chapters.' I then said, 'This, I swear by Allah, is knowledge!' He would mark the ground with his staff for a while. He then said, 'That is knowledge but it is not that knowledge.' The narrator has said that the Imam then said, 'O abu Muhammad, with us there is *al-Jami'ah*. Do they know what *al-Jami'ah* is?'

"I then asked, 'May Allah keep my soul in service for your cause. What is *al-Jami'ah*?' The Imam said, 'It is a parchment seventy yards long by the yards of the Messenger of Allah. It contains his dictations from his very own mouth that were recorded onto it in the handwriting of Ali, *'Alayhi al-Salam*. It contains all the lawful and unlawful, and all matters that people need. Even the law of compensation for a scratch caused to a person.' He then stretched his hand toward me and asked, 'May I, O abu Muhammad?' I then replied, 'May Allah keep my soul in service for your cause, I am entirely at your disposal.' He pinched me with

217

his hand and said, 'The law of compensation for this much is also included therein.' He looked angry. I then said, 'This, I swear by Allah is knowledge.'

"The Imam said, 'It certainly is knowledge but not that one.' The Imam remained silent for a while and then said, 'With us there is *al-Jafr*. Do they know what *al-Jafr* is?' I then asked, 'What is *al-Jafr*?' The Imam said, 'It is a container made of skin that contains the knowledge of the prophets and the executors of their wills. It is the knowledge of the scholars in the past from the Israelites.'

"I then said, 'This certainly, is the knowledge.' The Imam said, 'It certainly is knowledge but not that knowledge.' The Imam remained silent for a while and then said, 'With us there is the book (Mushaf) of *Fatimah, 'Alayha al-Salam*. Do they know what Mushaf of Fatimah is?' I then asked, 'What is Mushaf of Fatimah?' The Imam said, 'Mushaf of Fatimah is three times bigger than your Quran. I swear by Allah, not even a single letter therein is from your Quran.'

"I then said, 'This, I swear by Allah, is the knowledge.' The Imam said, 'This certainly is knowledge, but it is not that knowledge.' The Imam remained silent for a while and then said, 'With us there is the knowledge of whatever has been, and the knowledge of everything that will come into being to the Day of Judgment.'

"I then said, 'May Allah keep my soul in service for your cause, this, I swear by Allah, is certainly the knowledge!' The Imam said, 'It certainly is knowledge but not that knowledge.' I then asked, 'May Allah keep my soul in service for your cause, what is the knowledge?' The Imam, *'Alayhi al-Salam*, said, 'It is whatever takes place during the night and during the day, one matter after the other matter, and one thing after the other to the Day of Judgment.'"

H 630, Ch. 40, h 2

A number of our people have narrated from Ahmad ibn Muhammad from 'Umar ibn 'Abd al-'Aziz from Hammad ibn 'Uthman who has said that he heard abu 'Abd Allah, *'Alayhi al-Salam*, say the following:

"The heretics will appear in the year 128 A.H. (745/746A.D.) because I have found it in the Mushaf of *Fatimah, 'Alayha al-Salam*." I (the narrator) then asked the Imam, "What is the Mushaf of Fatimah?"

"The Imam said, 'When Allah, the Most High, took the Holy Prophet, *'Alayhi al-Salam*, from this world, it caused such a degree of grief to *Fatimah, 'Alayha al-Salam*, that only Allah, the Most Holy, the Most High, knows its extent. Allah then sent an angel to her to offer solace and speak to her. She complained about it to (Amir al-Mu'minin) Ali, *'Alayhi al-Salam*, who asked her to inform him whenever the angel spoke to her. She then informed him when the angel came to speak. (Amir al-Mu'minin) Ali, *'Alayhi al-Salam*, then would write down all that he would hear of the conversations of the angel, so much so that his notes took the shape of a whole book.'

"The Imam then said, 'There is nothing in it of the knowledge of the lawful and unlawful matters but it has the knowledge of things that had happened and things to happen in future.'"

H 631, Ch. 40, h 3

A number of our people have narrated from Ahmad ibn Muhammad from Ali ibn al-Hakam from al-Husayn ibn abu 'Ala' who has said that he heard abu 'Abd Allah, *'Alayhi al-Salam*, say the following:

"With me is the white *Jafr*." I (the narrator) then asked the Imam, *'Alayhi al-Salam*, "What is in it?" The Imam said, "In it there are the psalms of David, the Torah of Moses, the Gospel of Jesus, the Books of Abraham, the laws that explain the lawful and unlawful matters and the Mushaf of *Fatimah, 'Alayha al-Salam*, in which I do not think there is anything from the Holy Quran. In it there is all that people need us to do for them, so that we would not need anyone else. In it there is information even about a lash, half of a lash and one-fourth of a lash and about the amount of compensation for a scratch caused to someone.

"With me there is the red *Jafr*." I (the narrator) then asked the Imam, 'What is in the red *Jafr*?' The Imam said, 'In it there are the Armaments. It is because it only is opened for bloodshed. The owner of the sword opens it (to settle cases) of murder.'

"The narrator has said that 'Abd Allah ibn abu Ya'fur asked the Imam, 'May Allah keep you well, do the descendents of al-Hassan, *'Alayhi al-Salam*, know this?' The Imam, said, 'Yes, I swear by Allah, they know it just as they know the night that it is night and the day that it is day, but jealousy and worldly gains cause them to act in denial and rejection. Had they sought the truth with the truth it would have been better for them.'"

H 632, Ch. 40, h 4

Ali ibn Ibrahim has narrated from Muhammad ibn 'Isa from Yunus from the person that he mentioned from Sulayman ibn Khalid from abu 'Abd Allah, *'Alayhi al-Salam*, who has said the following:

"The *Jafr* of which they speak certainly disappoints them because they (the Zaydis) do not speak the truth while *Jafr* does contain the truth. Allow them bring to light therefrom the judgments of Ali, *'Alayhi al-Salam*, and his rules of inheritance, if they are truthful. Ask them about (the inheritance) of paternal and maternal aunts. Allow them show the Mushaf of *Fatimah, 'Alayha al-Salam*. In it, certainly, there is the will of *Fatimah, 'Alayha al-Salam*. With it there are the Armaments of the Messenger of Allah. Allah, the Most Holy, the Most High, has said, 'Bring me a Book, revealed before this Quran, or any other proof based on knowledge to support your belief, if indeed you are truthful.'" (46:4)

H 633, Ch. 40, h 5

Muhammad ibn Yahya has narrated from Ahmad ibn Muhammad from ibn Mahbub from ibn Ri'ab from abu 'Ubayda who has said the following:

"People from our group asked abu 'Abd Allah, *'Alayhi al-Salam*, about *Jafr* and the Imam said, 'It is the skin of a bull which is full of knowledge.' They then asked the Imam about *al-Jami'ah*. The Imam replied, 'It is a parchment that is seventy yards long with the width of a hide like that of the leg of a huge camel. It contains all that people may need. There is no case for which there is not a rule in it. In it there is the law even to settle the compensation for a scratch caused to a person.'

"I (the narrator) then asked the Imam, 'What is the Mushaf of Fatimah?' The Imam waited for quite a while. Then he said, 'You ask about what you really mean and what you do not mean. *Fatimah, 'Alayha al-Salam*, lived after the Messenger of Allah for seventy-five days. She was severely depressed because of the death of her father. Jibril (peace be upon him) would come to provide her solace and condolence due to the death of her father. Jibril would comfort her soul, inform her about her father, his place, of the future events and about what would happen to her children. At the same time Ali, *'Alayhi al-Salam*, would write all of them down and thus has come to be the Mushaf of *Fatimah, 'Alayha al-Salam.*'"

H 634, Ch. 40, h 6
A number of our people have narrated from Ahmad ibn Muhammad from Salih ibn Sa'id from Ahmad ibn abu Bishr from Bakr ibn Karib al-Sayrafi who has said that he heard abu 'Abd Allah, *'Alayhi al-Salam*, say the following:

"With us there are such things because of which we do not become needy to people, instead, people need us. With us there is a book that the Messenger of Allah had dictated and Ali, *'Alayhi al-Salam*, had written it down. It is a book. In it there are all the laws of lawful and unlawful matters. You come to us with an issue and we know when you follow the guidance and when you disregard it."

H 635 Ch. 40, h 7
Ali ibn Ibrahim has narrated from his father from ibn abu 'Umayr from 'Umar ibn Udhayna from Fudayl ibn Yasar, Burayd ibn Mu'wiya and Zurara who have said that 'Abd Allah ibn 'Abd al-Malik said the following to abu 'Abd Allah, *'Alayhi al-Salam*:

"The Zaydi sect and al-Mu'tazali group circle around Muhammad ibn 'Abd Allah. Does he have any authority?" The Imam, *'Alayhi al-Salam*, said, 'I swear by Allah, with me there are two books in which there are the names of every prophet and the names of every king that will rule on earth. No, I swear by Allah, the name of Muhammad ibn 'Abd Allah is not in the list among them.'"

H 636, Ch. 40, h 8
Muhammad ibn Yahya has narrated from Ahmad ibn Muhammad from al-Husayn ibn Sa'id from al-Qasim ibn Muhammad from 'Abd al-Samad ibn Bashir from Fudayl ibn Sukkara who has said the following:

"Once I went to abu 'Abd Allah, *'Alayhi al-Salam*, and he said to me, 'O Fudayl, do you know what I looked at just a while before?' I said to the Imam, 'No, I do not know.

"The Imam said, 'I was looking at the book of *Fatimah, 'Alayha al-Salam.* There is no king who would rule on earth without being listed therein by his name and the name of his father, but I did not find the name of any of the descendents of al-Hassan therein.'"

Chapter 41 - The Issues in Chapter Ninety-Seven of the Holy Quran and Its Interpretation

H 637 Ch. 41, h 1

Muhammad ibn abu 'Abd Allah and Muhammad ibn al-Hassan have narrated from Sahl ibn Ziyad and Muhammad ibn Yahya has narrated from Ahmad ibn Muhammad, both of them from al-Hassan ibn al-'Abbass ibn al-Harish from abu Ja'far al-Thani, *'Alayhi al-Salam*, who has said the following:

"Abu 'Abd Allah, *'Alayhi al-Salam*, has said, 'Once while my father was walking around the Ka'ba for *Tawaf* (walking seven times around the Ka'bah), a man who had covered his face partially with his turban suddenly came by. He cut out (interrupted) his *Tawaf* and took him (the Imam) to a house adjacent to al-Safa (name of a place in Makkahh). He sent for me also and then we were there three of us.'

"He said to me, 'Welcome, the child of the Messenger of Allah.' He then placed his hand over my head and said, 'May Allah place blessings in you, the trustworthy one before Allah after his ancestors.' (He then said to my father), 'O abu Ja'far, *'Alayhi al-Salam*, if you like you may tell me, and if you like I can tell you. If you like you may ask me. Also if you want I will ask you. If you like, affirm what I will say, and if you want, I will affirm what you will say.'

"The Imam said, 'I like all of it.' The man then said, 'You must never permit your tongue to answer me with something that is otherwise in your conscience.' The Imam said, 'That can be the doing of one in whose heart there are two kinds of knowledge, one opposing the other. Allah, the Most Holy, the Most High, disdains to have the kind of knowledge that is not harmonious.'

"He then said, 'This is the topic of my question. You just explained one part of it. Tell me about this "knowledge" that is so harmonious and without difference. Who has (knows) it?' The Imam said, 'The whole of knowledge is before Allah, Majestic is whose name. The knowledge that people need is with the executor of the will (of prophets).

"The narrator has said that he (the man) then removed the covering from his face and sat down straight. His face looked more cheerful and he said, 'This is what I wanted and for this I have come. You think that the "knowledge" that is free of differences is with the executors of the wills of the prophets. How do they know it?' The Imam said, 'Just as the Messenger of Allah knew it except that they do not see what the Messenger of Allah would see. It is because he was a prophet and they are the *Muhaddathun* (people to whom angels speak without being visible to them). The Messenger of Allah, during his delegation before Allah, the Most Holy, the Most High, heard whatever was communicated to him Divinely (through *Wahy*, Divine inspiration) but they (executors of wills of the Holy Prophet, *'Alayhi al-Salam*) do not hear such communications.'

"He then said, 'You have spoken the truth, O child of the Messenger of Allah. I now ask you a more difficult question. Tell me, why does this "knowledge" not appear as it was with the Messenger of Allah?' 'Not all Muslims acknowledge the 'A'immah, 'Alayhi al-Salam, as Leaders with Divine Authority. (In other words, 'knowledge' discussed here refers to the domination of the religion of Allah. The man has hinted that the religion of Allah and the authority of the Holy Prophet, 'Alayhi al-Salam, were dominant in his time. Why is it that 'knowledge' and authority are not dominant in the time of 'A'immah?)

"The narrator has said that my father then smiled and said, 'Allah, the Most Holy, the Most High, disdains to allow those people whom He has not yet tested with belief to have information about His knowledge. Allah decreed on His Messenger to endure the sufferings his people caused to him so much so that he would struggle against them only with His permission. Many times he would withhold matters that might cause disappointment among his people until he was commanded sternly to convey to them the commandments that he had received and disregard the pagans. The Holy Quran says, "Preach what you have been commanded to and stay away from the pagans."' (15:94)

"I swear by Allah, had he conveyed the commandments he would have been perfectly safe. He, in fact, considered obedience (to Allah) and feared the emergence of differences (among his people). For this reason he would withhold (speaking out about the Divine Authirity of 'A'immah). I love that you keep your eye upon the advent of al-Mahdi (the guide and his rise with Divine Authority) of this nation. At such time the angels with the sword of the family of David will make the dead spirits of the unbelievers between the heavens and the earth taste the results of their evil deeds and force likewise spirits of the living ones to join the unbelievers.' He (the man) then drew a sword and said, 'Here it is. This is one of them.'

"The narrator has said, 'Then my father said, "Yes, that is very true, I swear by the One Who chose Muhammad, 'Alayhi al-Salam, from among mankind."' The narrator has said that then the man drew the cover over his face and said, 'I am Ilyas. I did not ask you those questions about your issue because I did not know them. I loved this conversation and narration only because they could strengthen your followers. I will tell you about a sign and supporting evidence (of your cause). You know if they (your followers) choose to debate others with such evidence, your followers will win.'

"The narrator has said that my father then said to him, 'If you like I can tell you about it (the sign and evidence).' The man then said, 'I wish to hear it from you.' The Imam said, 'If our followers say to those who differ from us, "Allah, the Most Holy, the Most High says to His Messenger:

"We revealed the Quran on the Night of Destiny (97:1). Would that you had known what the Night of Destiny is! (97:2). (Worship on) the Night of Destiny is better than (worship) for a thousand months (97:3). On this Night, the angels and the spirit descend by the permission of their Lord with His decree (to determine everyone's destiny) (97:4). This Night is all peace until the break of dawn." (97:5)

222

'And ask, "Did the Messenger of Allah know that (besides) the knowledge of things that would come down at that night or what Jibril would bring to him at other times there is such knowledge that he knew (from other sources)?"' The opposition will say, 'No, there was nothing the Messenger of Allah knew (from other sources).' Say to the opposition, 'Could the Messenger of Allah do anything but to express such "knowledge" that comes on the night of destiny?' The opposition will say, 'It was necessary (for the Holy Prophet) to express.' Say to them, 'Was there any difference or disharmony in the "knowledge" that the Messenger of Allah had received from Allah, the Most High?' If the opposition say, 'No, there was no disharmony,' ask them, 'If one would judge in the name of the laws of Allah with disharmony, has he not opposed the Messenger of Allah?'

"They will say, 'Yes, he has opposed the Messenger of Allah.' However, if they say, 'No, he has not opposed the Messenger of Allah,' they have invalidated their starting point (where they affirmed harmony in the "knowledge" from Allah).' Say to them, 'No one knows its (knowledge from Allah) interpretation except Allah and those who are well established in knowledge.' If they ask, 'Who are the ones well established in knowledge?' Say, 'They are those in whose knowledge there is no disharmony.' If they ask, 'Who are they?' Say, 'The Messenger of Allah was (one of) such persons' and ask them, 'Did he convey such "knowledge" to his first (Khalifa) successor?'

"If they say, 'Yes, the Messenger of Allah did convey it.' Ask, 'Did the Messenger of Allah die and the Khalifa after him have the "knowledge" free of disharmony?' If they say, 'No, there was no such Khalifa with the "knowledge" free of disharmony.' Say, '(this is not logical); the successor of the Messenger of Allah is supported (has the Divine support) and the Messenger of Allah does not appoint a Khalifa who would not judge by the laws of Allah. The Messenger of Allah will not appoint a Khalifa other than one (who possesses the noble quality of) justice like him, excluding prophet-hood. If the Messenger of Allah did not appoint anyone as Khalifa (executor of his will) for his "knowledge", he (Allah forbid) caused the people of coming generations to go astray.'

"If the opposition says, 'The "knowledge" of the Messenger of Allah was from the Holy Quran,' say, 'What about the following verses of the Holy Quran that speak about the matters after the death of the Holy Prophet, *'Alayhi al-Salam*, "I swear by the illustrious Book (44:2) that We have revealed the Quran on a blessed night to warn mankind. (44:3) On this night, every absolute command coming from Us becomes distinct (44:4). The command that We have been sending (44:5) as a mercy (for the human being) from your Lord . . "? (44:6)

"If the opposition says, 'Allah, the Most Holy, the Most High, sends (angels and the Spirit) to prophets only,' say, 'These "distinct commands" that come are from the angels and the Spirit, do they come from one heaven to the other heaven? (It is not proper); in the heavens there is no one to whom obedience (to commands) and disobedience would apply.'

"If the opposition says, 'They come from the heavens to earth and the people of earth are in dire need of such "commands",' say to them, 'Is it necessary for them (people) to have a leader who would judge among them?' If they say, 'The Khalifa will judge for them,' ask them about the meaning of the following verse of the Holy Quran: 'Allah is the Guardian of the believers and it is He who takes them out of darkness into light. The Devil is the guardian of those who deny the Truth and he leads them from light to darkness. These are the dwellers of hell wherein they will live forever.' (2:257)

"I swear by my life, all those in the heavens and on earth who are under the guardianship of Allah, the Most Holy, the Most High, are supported (Divinely) and protected. Those who are supported and protected do not make mistakes. All the enemies of Allah, the Most Holy, the Most High, in the heavens and on earth suffer defeat. Those who are defeated they do not deal in a rightful way. Just as it is necessary that the "commands" must come from the heavens for the people of earth, in the same way it is necessary to have a *Wali* (mentioned in (2:257), one who possesses perfect knowledge (and Divine Authority) to guide the people.

"If the opposition says, 'We do not know such a person,' say to them, 'Say whatever you may like. Allah, the Most Holy, the Most High, disdains to leave, after Muhammad, *'Alayhi al-Salam*, the servants without the existence of one who possesses perfect knowledge and Divine Authority.'

"The narrator has said that he (the man) then stopped and said, 'This, O child of the Messenger of Allah, is a delicate point. Consider if they (opposition) would say, 'The Holy Quran is the Divine Authority.' The Imam said, 'Then I will say, "The Holy Quran does not speak, does not issue commands or prohibitions. The people of the Quran issue commands and prohibitions." I would further say, 'Allah disdains to see a certain affliction (difficult issue) befall the people of earth, and there is no law about it in the *Sunnah* or a ruling free of differences and it is not in the Quran also to solve such difficulty. He disdains to have such a thing in His knowledge or permit it to take place on earth while there would be nothing in His judgment to stop it (misery of lawlessness) from happening or the means to provide relief.'

"He (the man) then said, 'Here you gain victory, O child of the Messenger of Allah. I testify that Allah, the Most Holy, the Most High, certainly knows what kinds of afflictions and sufferings may befall people of the earth in their lives and in their religion and so forth. He then has sent the Holy Quran as a guide.

"The narrator has said that the man then said, 'Do you, O child of the Messenger of Allah, know what kind of guide it (the Holy Quran) is?' Abu Ja'far, *'Alayhi al-Salam*, said, 'Yes, in it there are the general principles of laws and its interpretation (rests with the judge) when judgment is issued.' He said, 'Allah disdains to see His servant is afflicted with hardships in his religion, his life or his property. He disdains to see that there is no one on His earth who can judge and decide truthfully and in the right way to remove the suffering.'

"The narrator has said that the man then said, 'In this matter also you have gained victory unless your enemies falsely ascribe lies to Allah and say, "Allah, the Most Holy, the Most High, does not have anyone who possesses Divine Authority." However, tell me, about the interpretation of the words of Allah: ". . . so that you would not grieve over what you have lost nor become extremely happy about what Allah has granted to you. . . .'" (57:23)

"The Imam said, 'It refers to Abu so and so and his people. One of the verses is placed before and the other is placed afterward (two verses on two issues were placed together during the compilation of the existing copy of the Holy Quran). "Grief over the loss" refers to the case of (Amir al-Mu'minin) Ali, 'Alayhi al-Salam, and the Divine position that was particularly for him' and the words of Allah: ". . . nor become extremely happy about what Allah has granted to you. . ." refers to the mischief (the government formed) after the death of the Messenger of Allah.

"The man then said, 'I testify that you are the Divine Authority in whose judgment there is no disharmony.' The man then stood up and went and I did not see him any more."

H 638, Ch. 41, h 2

(Through the same chain of narrators) it has been narrated from Abu 'Abd Allah, 'Alayhi al-Salam, who has said the following:

"Once in a meeting, in the presence of my father and a group of people also gathered, my father smiled and (the intense feeling caused) tears to flood his eyes. He then asked, 'Do you know what made me laugh?' The narrator has said that they said, 'No, we do not know the reason.' The Imam, 'Alayhi al-Salam, said, 'Ibn 'Abbass thinks he is of the people mentioned in the following verse of the Holy Quran: "To those who have said, 'Allah is our Lord,' and who have remained steadfast in their belief, the angels will descend saying, 'Do not be afraid or grieved. Receive the glad news of the Paradise which was promised to you.'" (41:30).

"I asked him, 'Have you seen the angels, O ibn 'Abbass, telling you of the fact that they guard and protect you in this and the next world and provide you complete protection and security from fear and sadness?' The Imam then quoted ibn 'Abbass who said that Allah, the Most Holy, the Most High, says, "Believers are each other's brothers. . . ." (49:10): the whole community is included in this verse.'

"The Imam said, 'I then, almost, laughed.' Then I said, 'O ibn 'Abbass, you (perhaps) are right. However, I ask you to swear by Allah and answer me truthfully. Is there any disharmony in the judgment of Allah, Majestic is whose name?' He said, 'No, there is no disharmony in His judgment.' I then asked him, 'How would you judge the case in which a man strikes the fingers of another man with a sword until they fall off? Then another man comes and cuts off his palm. He is brought to you and you are the judge. How will you then judge?' He said, 'I will order the one who cut off the palm to pay compensation for the whole hand.

225

I will ask the affected party to reach a settlement with the defendant and for this purpose I would send them to the people of justice (arbitrator).'

"I said, '(Your judgment as such assuming to be true shows that) disharmony has come in the laws of Allah, Majestic is whose name. Thus, you invalidated what you said before (that there is no disharmony in the laws and judgment of Allah). Allah, Majestic is whose name, in fact, disdains to let a judicial case remain on earth without a clarified rule. You must order, as a judge, to cut the palm of the defendant totally and pay him compensation for the fingers. Thus, is the judgment of Allah at the "night" wherein His orders descend (the night of Destiny). If you reject the order after hearing from the Messenger of Allah then Allah will send you to fire just as He blinded you on the day you hid (the truth) that existed in support of Ali ibn abu Talib, *'Alayhi al-Salam.'*

"Ibn 'Abbass then said, 'Is that a reason that my eyes have become blind?' He further said, 'How do you know that? I swear by Allah that my eyes turned blind only because of the flapping of the wing of the angel.' The Imam said, 'It made me, almost, laugh. I left him that day because of the silliness (darkness and dullness) in his intellect and reason. I then met him later and said to him, "O ibn 'Abbass, you have never spoken as true as you did yesterday (spoke of angel flapping his wing). Ali ibn abu Talib, *'Alayhi al-Salam,* told you that the "Night of Determination and Destiny" comes every year. On that night the commands for the whole year come down. It is the people with Divine Authority who receive such matters and commands, after the Messenger of Allah. You then asked him (Imam Ali) *'Alayhi al-Salam,* 'Who are these people?' He (Ali), *'Alayhi al-Salam,* said, 'I myself and the eleven men from my descendents will be *'A'immah* (Leaders with Divine Authority) and the (people to whom angels speak) *Muhaddathun.'"*

"You then said, 'I have not seen it (Night of Determination) except with the Messenger of Allah. Then the angel appeared to you (in the form of a human being). The angel who was speaking to him (Imam Ali, *'Alayhi al-Salam,* then said, 'O 'Abd Allah ibn 'Abbas, you have lied. My eyes see it (the Night of Determination), of which Ali, *'Alayhi al-Salam,* spoke to you. [His (Ali's) eyes did not see him (the angel) but his heart understood (the presence of the angel) and his voice reverberated in his ears]. Then he (angel) flapped you with his wing and you turned blind.'"

"Ibn 'Abbass then said, 'In the matters that we dispute, it is up to Allah to judge.' I then said to him, 'Has Allah judged one case with two judgments?' He replied, 'No, Allah has not done so.' I then said, 'Here you perish and cause others to perish.'"

H 639, Ch. 41, h 3
Through the same chain of narrators it is narrated from abu Ja'far, *'Alayhi al-Salam,* who has said the following:

"Allah, the Most Holy, the Most High, has said about the Night of Determination, '. . . in this night every absolute command coming from Us becomes distinguishable.' (44:4) He has spoken of absolute and strong command. Absolute and strong command is not two things. It is only one thing. One who judges without disharmony and differences, his judgment is of the judgment of Allah, the Most Holy and the Most High. Whoever judges in a disharmonious manner, with differences, and considers it as the rightful way of judging, he has judged with the judgment of the devil.

"It is certain that on the Night of Determination the explanation and clarification of all issues of the year come to the man who possesses Divine Authority. On that Night the *Wali al-'Amr* (the man who possesses Divine Authority) receives commands about himself, for so and so, and about the affairs of the people in so and so. It also is certain that for the man with Divine Authority, besides this, there comes the knowledge of Allah, the Most Holy, the Most High. His exclusive knowledge, the hidden, the wonderful and the treasured knowledge of Allah comes to him every day just as it comes in the Night of Determination in the form of commands.' Then he recited from the Holy Quran: 'If all the trees in the earth were pens, and the ocean, with seven more oceans, were ink, still these could not suffice to record all the Words of Allah. Allah is Majestic and All-wise.'" (31:27)

H 640, Ch. 41, h 4
Through the same chain of narrators it is narrated from abu 'Abd Allah, *'Alayhi al-Salam*, who has said the following:
"Imam Ali ibn al-Husayn, *'Alayhi al-Salam*, would read, 'We revealed the Quran on the Night of Destiny,' (97:1) and say, 'Allah, the Most Holy, the Most High, has certainly said the truth. He has revealed the Holy Quran on the Night of Determination. "Would that you had known what the Night of Destiny is!" (97:2) The Messenger of Allah said, 'I do not know.' Allah, the Most Holy, the Most High, said, '(Worship) on the Night of Destiny is better than (worship) for a thousand months (that are other than the Night of Determination and Destiny).' (97:3) He asked the Messenger of Allah, 'Do you know why it is better than a thousand nights?' The Messenger of Allah said, 'No, I do not know.' He said, 'It is because "on that Night the angels and the Spirit come down by the permission of their Lord for all matters"'. When Allah, the Most Holy, the Most High, grants permission for a matter it means that He has agreed. 'This Night is all peace until the break of dawn,' (97:5) means that He says, 'O Muhammad, My angels salute you and My Spirit with peaceful greetings from the beginning of time they would come down until dawn of that night.' Then He has said in another part of His book, 'Guard yourselves against discord among yourselves so that it will not mislead any one of you, especially the unjust, and know that Allah's retribution is most severe.' (8:25) It is about the Night of Determination. He has also said in His book, 'Muhammad is only a Messenger. There lived other messengers before him. Should (Muhammad) die or be slain, would you then turn back to your pre-Islamic behavior? Whoever does so can cause no harm to Allah. Allah will reward those who give thanks.' (3:144)

227

"In the above verse He has said that when Muhammad, *'Alayhi al-Salam*, will die, those opposing the command of Allah, the Most Holy, the Most High, will say, 'The Night of Determination has gone along with the Messenger of Allah.' This will be the first calamity that will befall them exclusively. With this they return back to their old ways. Had they not said so, it would have been necessary to believe that Allah, the Most Holy, the Most High, has His commands on that Night. Once they affirm and acknowledge the command (delegation of Divine Authority), it becomes necessary to believe in the existence of the man who possesses Divine Authority.'"

H 641, Ch. 41, h 5
It is narrated from abu 'Abd Allah, *'Alayhi al-Salam*, who has said the following:
"(Imam) Ali, *'Alayhi al-Salam*, would very often say, 'Whenever al-Taymies and al-'Adawies would come together in the presence of the Messenger of Allah, *'Alayhi al-Salam*, he, the Messenger of Allah, would read, "We have revealed it on the Night of Determination" very humbly and tearfully. They (al-Taymi and al-'Adawi) would say, 'How intense is the tenderness that this chapter causes to your heart!' The Messenger of Allah would say, 'It is because of what my eyes see and my heart has stored and for what the heart of this (Ali, *'Alayhi al-Salam*) will experience after me.'

"They would ask, 'What is it that you have seen and what is it that he will experience?'

"Imam Ali, *'Alayhi al-Salam*, has said, 'He (messenger of Allah) then would write for the two on the soil, 'On this Night, the angels and the spirit descend by the permission of their Lord with His decree (to determine everyone's destiny).' (97:4) Imam Ali, *'Alayhi al-Salam*, has said, 'The Messenger of Allah then would say, "Has anything else been left (untold) after the words of Allah, the Most Holy, the Most High, "For all matters"?" The two would say, 'No, nothing is left untold.' He (the Messenger of Allah) then would ask them, 'Do the two of you know to whom it will be revealed?' The two would say, 'To you, O the Messenger of Allah.' He then would say, 'Will there be the Night of Determination after me?' The two would say, 'Yes, there will be that night.' He then would ask, 'Will then the "matters" come down in that night?' The two would say, 'Yes, it will come down?' He (the Messenger of Allah) then would ask them, 'Do the two of you know to whom the "matters" will be revealed?' The two would say, 'We do not know.' He then would hold my head in his hand and say, 'If the two of you do not know, now you must know, he (whose head is my hands now) is it after me' (to receive the "matters").

"Imam Ali, *'Alayhi al-Salam*, has said that after the Messenger of Allah whenever they experienced severe anxiety and apprehension they would realize that that night was the Night of Destiny."

H 642, Ch. 41, h 6
Through the same chain of narrators it is narrated from abu Ja'far, *'Alayhi al-Salam*, who has said the following:

"O the community of our followers, reason against the opposition by means of chapter ninety-seven of the Holy Quran, '. . . We have revealed on the Night of Determination. . . .' you will gain victory. I swear by Allah, the Most Holy, the Most High, that this is the solid evidence from Allah, the Most Holy, the Most High, against the creatures after the Messenger of Allah. This is the lead evidence in your religion. It, certainly, is the goal of our knowledge.

"O the community of our followers (the Shi'a), reason against the opposition by means of, 'I swear by the illustrious Book (44:2) that We have revealed the Quran on a blessed night to warn mankind.' (44:3) This verse is exclusively about the people who possess Divine Authority after the Messenger of Allah. O the community of our followers, Allah, the Most Holy, the Most High, has said, '. . . No nation who lived before was left without a Warner . . .'(35:24) A person then said, 'O abu Ja'far, the Warner is Muhammad, *'Alayhi al-Salam,'* The Imam said, 'What you just said is true. Had he commissioned a Warner for the different parts of the land, while he (the Messenger of Allah) was living?' The person questioning said, 'No, there was no Warner.' Abu Ja'far, *'Alayhi al-Salam,* then said, 'Consider the person he commissioned. Was he not his Warner also, just as the Messenger of Allah, in being commissioned from Allah, the Most Holy, the Most High, was a Warner?' The person said, 'Yes, it is true.' The Imam said, 'In the same way Muhammad, *'Alayhi al-Salam,* did not die without having someone as his delegate and Warner.'

"The Imam said, 'If I say, "Delegating his mission to his successor was not necessary for the Holy Prophet, *'Alayhi al-Salam,*" it would mean that the Messenger of Allah has lost and left without guidance those of his followers who are still to be born.'

"The person then said, 'Is the Holy Quran not enough for them?' The Imam said, 'It is enough only if they find an interpreter for it.' The person then asked, 'Has the Messenger of Allah not interpreted it?' The Imam said, 'Yes, he has done so just for one man and he has interpreted the conditions of that man to identify him for his followers. That man is Ali ibn abu Talib, *'Alayhi al-Salam.'*

"The man asking the question then said, 'O abu Ja'far, *'Alayhi al-Salam,* this was a special matter. Common people are not able to bear it.' The Imam said, 'Allah, disdains His not being worshipped in secrecy until the time when His religion becomes public. It is just like the case of the Messenger of Allah and Khadija who would not make their religion public until they were commanded to do so.' The man then said, 'Is it proper for the author of this religion to hide?' The Imam said, 'Did Ali ibn abu Talib, *'Alayhi al-Salam,* not hide his religion on the day he became a Muslim along with the Messenger of Allah until this matter became public?' He said, 'Yes, that was the case.' The Imam then said, 'So also is our case (the publicity of Divine Authority) until the appointed time will come.'

H 643, Ch. 41, h 7
Through the same chain of narrators it is narrated from abu Ja'far, *'Alayhi al-Salam,* who has said the following:

"Allah, Majestic is Whose name, created the Night of Determination when He first created the world and created in it (the world) the first prophet to come and the first executor of the will (of prophet) to come. He decreed that in every year there must be one night in which the interpretation and the clarification of the issues be sent until another such night in the coming year. Whoever would deny it has certainly rejected the knowledge of Allah, the Majestic, the Glorious. It is because the prophets, the Messengers and *Muhaddathun* (people to whom angels speak without being visible to them) would remain without receiving Divine command and Authority through what comes to them on that night along with the authority that Jibril brings for them.'

"I (the narrator) then asked the Imam 'Do the *Muhaddathun* also experience the coming of Jibril and other angels?' The Imam said, 'The prophets and the Messenger, *'Alayhim al-Salam*, certainly experience it. For the others, besides the prophets and the Messenger, *'Alayhim al-Salam*, from the first day the earth was created to the end and perishing of the world there must be the Divine Authority. For the people of the earth Divine commands come down on that night to the one most beloved among His servants.

'I swear by Allah, the Spirit and the angels came with the command on the "Night of Determination" to Adam. I swear by Allah, that Adam did not die until he had the executor of his will. To every prophet after Adam the command came on that night and he assigned it to the executor of his will after him. I swear by Allah, that every prophet had been commanded, on that night, from Adam to Muhammad, *'Alayhi al-Salam*, to make a will in favor of so and so. Allah, the Most Holy, the Most High, has said in His book, particularly, to the people who possess Divine Authority after Prophet Muhammad, *'Alayhi al-Salam*, 'Allah has promised the righteously striving believers to appoint them as His deputies on earth, as He had appointed those who lived before. He will make the religion that He has chosen for them to stand supreme. He will replace their fear with peace and security so that they will worship Me alone and consider no one equal to Me. Whoever becomes an unbeliever after this will be a sinful person.' (24:55)

'He says that He has made you (true successors of Muhammad) His deputies in the matter of His knowledge, religion and worship after your Prophet just as Adam made a will to appoint the executor of his will after him until the time Allah sent another prophet. He (Allah) has said, '. . . so that they will worship Me alone and consider no one equal to Me.' (24:55) He has said that you must worship Him with faith in the fact that after Muhammad, *'Alayhi al-Salam*, there is no other prophet. Those who say otherwise 'Are sinful persons.'

'He has enabled the people who possess Divine Authority with knowledge. We are such people. Ask us. If we will acknowledge you then be steadfast, but you will not do so. Our knowledge is clear. The appearance of the appointed time for us in which religion will stand supreme through us so much so that there will remain no differences among people, for such time there is an appointed time that passes through the nights and days. When that time comes, the command of Allah will be only one.

'I swear by Allah, it is already decreed that there will be no differences among the believers. For this reason they are made to witness the deeds of the people so that Muhammad, *'Alayhi al-Salam*, will be witness over us and we will be the witnesses over our followers and our followers will be witnesses over the people. Allah, the Most Holy, the Most High, disdained to allow differences take place in His judgment or contradictions to take place among those who possess His knowledge.

"Abu Ja'far, *'Alayhi al-Salam*, then said the following: 'The excellence of the faith and belief in and his acceptance of, "We have revealed it in the *Night of Determination*," and its interpretation, over those who are not like him, in the matters of faith in that Night, is like the excellence of man over the animals. Allah, the Most Holy, the Most High, defends, in this world, through those who believe in it those who disbelieve it. He, however, completes the punishment for it in the next life for those whom He knows will not repent from rejecting such belief. He defends them just as He defends through those who strive (do Jihad) for His cause those who sit comfortably. I do not know if there is any *Jihad* (striving) for His cause, these days, other than Hajj, 'Umra and to be good neighbors.'"

H 644, Ch. 41, h 8
The narrator has said that once a man said to abu Ja'far, *'Alayhi al-Salam*:
"O child of the Messenger of Allah, please do not be angry with me." The Imam, *'Alayhi al-Salam*, said, 'Why should I be angry?' The man said, 'It is because of the question that I want to ask you.' The Imam said, 'Ask your question.' He said, 'Please do not be angry.' The Imam said, 'I will not be angry.' The man said, 'Consider your words about the "Night of Determination" in which the Spirit and the angels descend to the executors of the will (of Prophet). Do they bring them the command of which the Messenger of Allah had no knowledge, or bring them the commands that the Messenger of Allah knew? As I know the Messenger of Allah died and there was nothing of his knowledge that Ali, *'Alayhi al-Salam*, had not heard (and preserved).'

"Abu Ja'far, *'Alayhi al-Salam*, said, 'Why should I bother with you and why did someone allow you come in?' He said, 'Fate has let me come in, seeking religion.' The Imam said, 'Try to understand what I will say.

'When the Messenger of Allah was taken for a trip (by the angels) he did not come back before Allah, Majestic is Whose name, taught him the knowledge of the things of the past and the things in future. A great deal of such knowledge was in a whole form the interpretation of which would have to come in the "Night of Determination." In the same way Ali ibn abu Talib, *'Alayhi al-Salam*, had learned the knowledge in a whole form, the interpretation of which had to come in the "Night of Determination" as was the case with the Messenger of Allah.'

231

"The man said, 'Was there no interpretation of the whole available?' The Imam said, 'It was available but it comes through the commands of Allah in the "Night of Determination" to the Prophet and the executors of his will telling them to do so and so. It is for the matters of which they already had knowledge, but they receive the command how to act in it.'

"The man said, 'Explain it to me.' The Imam said, 'The Messenger of Allah did not die without knowing a whole body of knowledge with its interpretation.' The man said, 'What was that which would come to him in the "Night of Determination"?'

"The Imam said, 'It was the command and ease in what he already knew.' The man said, 'What then happens to them in the "Night of Determination," is it a knowledge other than what they knew before?'

"The Imam said, 'This is what they are commanded not to tell to anyone. No one knows the interpretation of what you just asked except Allah, the Most Holy, the Most High.' The man asked, 'Do the executors of the will know what the prophets did not know?' The Imam said, 'No, because how would the executor of the will know what is other than what is willed for.'

"The man asked, 'Can we say that what one executor of the will may know, may not be known to another executor of the will?' The Imam said, 'No, because no prophet dies before his knowledge is transferred to the executor of his will. The angels and the Spirit descend in the "Night of Determination" with the judgment with which they judge among the people.' The man asked, 'Is it that they did not know that judgment?' The Imam said, 'Yes, they knew it but they could not approve anything of it until they were commanded in the "Night of Determination" how to implement and accomplish them until the next year.'

"The man said, 'O abu Ja'far, 'Alayhi al-Salam, I can not deny this.' The Imam said, 'Those who deny it are not from us.' The man asked, 'O abu Ja'far, 'Alayhi al-Salam, do you think in the "Night of Determination" there would come things to the Holy Prophet, 'Alayhi al-Salam, that he did not know?' The Imam said, 'It is not lawful for you to ask this. However, the knowledge of things of the past and the knowledge of the things in future are such that no prophet or executor of the will dies before the executor of the will after him would know it. However, this knowledge about which you ask is such that Allah, the Most Holy, the Most High, disdains that the executors of the will inform anyone of it except themselves.'

"The man asked, 'O child of the Messenger of Allah, how can I know that the "Night of Determination" takes place every year?' The Imam said, 'When the month of Ramadan comes read chapter 44 of the Holy Quran 100 times every night. In the twenty-third night you will see the confirmation of what you have asked for.'"

H 645, Ch. 41, h 9

The narrator has said that abu Ja'far, 'Alayhi al-Salam, said the following:

"You, certainly, find - those whom Allah, the Most Holy, the Most High, has sent to induce misfortune into the heretics and misleading people of the army (followers) of Satan and their companions – to be in greater numbers than the angels sent to the deputy of Allah, for justice and truth."

It was said to him, "O abu Ja'far, *'Alayhi al-Salam*, how can there be anything in greater number than the angels?" The Imam said, "It is just as Allah, the Most Holy, the Most High, has wished." The man asked, "O abu Ja'far, *'Alayhi al-Salam*, if I will narrate this *Hadith* to any of your followers they will reject it." The Imam asked, "Why will they do so?" The man said, "They will say that the angels are of greater number than the Devils." The Imam said, "What you say is true. However, try to understand what I will say. There is no day or night in which all the Devils and all Satans would not visit the heretic and misleading leaders, and of the same number the angels visit the Imam of true guidance (leaders who possess Divine Authority) until it is the "Night of Determination." On that night the angels descend to those who possess Divine Authority in a number equal to the number of the Devils and Satan that Allah has created," or as he said, "has determined."

"The Devils and Satans will come to the corrupt and misleading authorities with fabrications and lies until, perhaps, dawn, and such leader says, 'I saw, this night, such and such.' However, if he would ask about it the one who possesses Divine Authority, he would say, 'You have seen a Satan who has informed you of such and such matters.' He (the Imam who possesses Divine Authority) provides him (the heretic leader) with interpretations and informs him what misleads people and informs him of the misleading conditions in which he (the heretic) lives. I swear by Allah, those who acknowledge the "Night of Determination" will certainly know that the "Night of Determination" is exclusively for us. It is because of the words of the Messenger of Allah to people about Ali, *'Alayhi al-Salam*, when the time of his death was about to approach: 'This is your guardian who possesses Divine Authority after me. If you obey him, you will enjoy a well guided way of life.' However, those who do not acknowledge what is in the "Night of Determination" they are unbelievers in it. Those who have faith in the "Night of Determination" but do not hold the opinion that we do, for them to verify it, there is no other way but to say that the "Night of Determination" is for us. Those who do not acknowledge it they are liars. Allah, the Most Holy, the Most High, is by far more exalted than to send the angels with the Spirit to a sinful unbeliever. If such people say that they (angels with the Spirit) come to the Khalifa in whom they believe, this is of no ground. If they say, "No one descends at that night to anyone," the fact is that something does not come to nothing. If they say or will say, "This is nothing," they have, certainly, strayed far away from the truth.'"

Chapter 42 - 'A'immah (Plural of Imam), *'Alayhim al-Salam*, Receive Additional (Knowledge) Every Friday Night

H 646, Ch. 42, h 1

Ahmad ibn Idris al-Qummi and Muhammad ibn Yahya have narrated from al-Hassan ibn Ali al-Kufi from Musa ibn Sa'dan from 'Abd Allah ibn Ayyub from abu Yahya al-San'ani from abu 'Abd Allah, *'Alayhi al-Salam*, who has said the following:

"O abu Yahya, on every Friday night there is a special task for us to pursue." I (the narrator) then asked the Imam, *'Alayhi al-Salam*, "May Allah keep my soul in service for your cause, of what nature is this special task?" The Imam said, "The spirits of the deceased prophets and the spirits of the deceased executors of the will of the prophets and the spirit of the executor of the will of the Holy Prophet living with you now are all taken to the heavens until they arrive at the throne of their Lord and then walk around it seven times. They perform prayers near every column of the columns of the throne, in a two Rak'at form after which they are returned to their bodies in which they were before. The prophets and the executors of the will of the prophets become full of joy and the executor of the will of the Holy Prophet living with you receives a huge increase in his knowledge."

H 647, Ch. 42, h 2

Muhammad ibn Yahya has narrated from Ahmad ibn abu Zahir from Ja'far ibn Muhammad al-Kufi from Yusuf al-Abzari from al-Mufaddal who has said the following:

"One day abu 'Abd Allah, *'Alayhi al-Salam*, addressed me with a surname, '*O abu 'Abd Allah*,' he would not address me this way before and I responded, 'Yes, O Imam, here I am.' He said, 'Every Friday night it is a time of happiness for us.' I said, 'May Allah increase such a happiness for you. Of what nature is this happiness?' The Imam said, 'When Friday night comes the Messenger of Allah arrives at the throne of Allah and *'A'immah* (the leaders who possess Divine Authority) also arrive there with him and we also arrive with them. Our souls are returned back to our bodies only after receiving very new useful knowledge, without which there would remain a blank in our knowledge.'"

H 648, Ch. 42, h 3

Muhammad ibn Yahya has narrated from Salama ibn al-Khattab from 'Abd Allah ibn Muhammad from al-Husayn ibn Ahmad al-Minqari from Yunus or al-Mufaddal from abu 'Abd Allah, *'Alayhi al-Salam*, who has said the following:

"There is no Friday night without joy and happiness for those who possess Divine Authority." I asked, 'How is it, may Allah keep my soul in service for your cause?' The Imam, *'Alayhi al-Salam*, said, 'When Friday night comes, the Messenger of Allah arrives at the throne with *'A'immah*, *'Alayhim al-Salam*, and I also arrive there with them. I do not return before receiving new knowledge, without which I would have already been left without knowledge.'"

Chapter 43 - If 'A'immah, *'Alayhi al-Salam*, Did Not Receive New Knowledge, Their Previous Knowledge Would Be Depleted

H 649, Ch. 43, h 1

Ali ibn Muhammad and Muhammad ibn al-Hassan have narrated from Sahl ibn Ziyad from Ahmad ibn Muhammad ibn abu Nasr from Safwan ibn Yahya who has said the following:

"I heard abu al-Hassan, *'Alayhi al-Salam*, saying, 'If we did not receive (new knowledge) our knowledge would diminish.'"

Muhammad ibn Yahya has narrated from Ahmad ibn Muhammad from Muhammad ibn Khalid from Safwan from abu al-Hassan, *'Alayhi al-Salam*, a similar *Hadith*.

H 650, Ch. 43, h 2

Muhammad ibn Yabya has narrated from Ahmad ibn Muhammad from al-Husayn ibn Sa'id from an-Nadr ibn Suwayd from Yahya al-Halabi from Dharih al-Muharibi who has said the following:

"Once abu 'Abd Allah, *'Alayhi al-Salam*, said to me, 'O Dharih, if we did not receive (new knowledge) our knowledge would diminish.'"

H 651, Ch. 43, h 3

Muhammad ibn Yahya has narrated from Ahmad ibn Muhammad from abu Nasr from Tha'laba from Zurara who has said the following:

"I heard abu Ja'far, *'Alayhi al-Salam*, saying, 'If we did not receive additional (knowledge) our knowledge would diminish.' I (the narrator) then asked the Imam, 'Do you receive additional something that the Messenger of Allah did not know?' The Imam said, 'The fact of the matter is that when that happens, it is presented to the Messenger of Allah, then to the *'A'immah*, *'Alayhim al-Salam*, and then it reaches us.'"

H 652, Ch. 43, h 4

Ali ibn Ibrahim has narrated from Muhammad ibn 'Isa from Yunus ibn 'Abd al-Rahman from some of his people from abu 'Abd Allah, *'Alayhi al-Salam*, who has said the following:

"Nothing comes from Allah, the Most Holy, the Most High, except that first it begins with the Messenger of Allah, then (Amir al-Mu'minin) Ali, *'Alayhi al-Salam*, then *'A'immah*, one after the other, so that the last one of us is not more knowledgeable than the first one among us."

Chapter 44 - 'A'immah, *'Alayhim al-Salam*, Know All the Knowledge That Has Come to the Angels, the Prophets and the Messengers

H 653, Ch. 44, h 1

Ali ibn Muhammad and Muhammad ibn al-Hassan from Sahl ibn Ziyad from Muhammad ibn al-Hassan ibn Shammun from 'Abd Allah ibn 'Abd al-Rahman from 'Abd Allah ibn al-Qasim from Sama'a from abu 'Abd Allah, *'Alayhi al-Salam*, who has said the following:

"Allah, the Most Holy, the Most High, has two kinds of knowledge. One kind is that which is revealed to the angels, the prophets and the Messengers of Allah. We know whatever is revealed to the angels, the Messengers of Allah and the prophets, also. The other is the kind which is exclusively for Allah. When Allah wants to make public anything from it, it is taught to us first and it is presented to *'A'immah* before us also."

Ali ibn Muhammad and Muhammad ibn al-Hassan have narrated from Sahl ibn Ziyad from Musa ibn al-Qasim and Muhammad ibn Yahya from al-'Amrakiy ibn Ali all of them from Ali ibn Ja'far from his brother Musa ibn Ja'far, *'Alayhi al-Salam*, a similar *Hadith*.

H 654, Ch. 44, h 2
A number of our people have narrated from Ahmad ibn Muhammad from al-Husayn ibn Sa'id from al-Qasim ibn Muhammad from Ali ibn abu Hamza from abu Basir from abu 'Abd Allah, *'Alayhi al-Salam*, who has said the following:
"Allah, the Most Holy, the Most High, has two kinds of knowledge. One kind is His only, and no creature knows about it. The other kind is that with which He has inspired His angels and His Messengers. Whatever is thrown to the angels and the Messengers has reached us also."

H 655, Ch. 44, h 3
Ali ibn Ibrahim has narrated from Salih ibn al-Sindi from Ja'far ibn Bashir from Durays who has said the following:
"I heard abu Ja'far, *'Alayhi al-Salam*, saying, 'Allah, the Most Holy, the Most High, has two kinds of knowledge. One kind is that which is granted and the other kind is that which is withheld. Of the one, which is granted, all that the angels and the Messengers know and we also know it. The one withheld is the kind that is before Allah, the Most Holy, the Most High, in the original Book. When it appears it permeates.'"

H 656 Ch. 44, h 4
Abu Ali al-Ash'ari has narrated from Muhammad ibn 'Abd al-Jabber from Muhammad ibn Isma'il from Ali ibn al-Nu'man from Suwayd al-Qalla from abu Ayyub from abu Basir from abu Ja'far, *'Alayhi al-Salam*, who has said the following:
"Allah, the Most Holy, the Most High, has two kinds of knowledge. One kind of knowledge is that which no one knows except He. The other kind is that which He has taught to His angels and His Messengers. Whatever His angels and Messengers have learned we also know it."

Chapter 45 - The Unique Ahadith About the Hidden Facts

H 657, Ch. 45, h 1
A number of our people have narrated from Ahmad ibn Muhammad ibn 'Isa from Mu'ammar ibn Khallad who has said that a man from Persia asked abu al-Hassan, *'Alayhi al-Salam*, the following:
"Do you know al-Ghayb (the hidden facts)? The Imam, *'Alayhi al-Salam*, said, 'Abu Ja'far, *'Alayhi al-Salam*, has said, "If it opens to us, then we know it, and if it is withheld from us then we do not know."' The Imam then said, 'It is the secret of Allah, the Most Holy, the Most High, Who has secretly given it to Jibril and Jibril has secretly given it to Muhammad, *'Alayhi al-Salam*, and Muhammad, *'Alayhi al-Salam*, has secretly given it to whoever Allah wished.'"

H 658, Ch. 45, h 2

Muhammad ibn Yahya has narrated from 'Abd Allah ibn Muhammad ibn 'Isa from al-Hassan ibn Mahbub from Ali ibn Ri'ab from Sadir al-Sayrafi who has said the following:

"I heard Humran ibn A'yan ask abu Ja'far, *'Alayhi al-Salam*, about the words of Allah, the Most Holy, the Most High Allah, '. . . One Who is the Originator of the heavens and the earth . . .' (6:101) Abu Ja'far, *'Alayhi al-Salam*, said, 'Allah, the Most Holy, the Most High, originated all things through His knowledge. It was unprecedented. He invented the heavens and the earths and there were no heavens and earths before. Have you not considered the words of Allah, the Most High, ". . . His Throne existed on water. . . ."' (11:7)

"Humran then said, 'Have you considered His words, Majestic is Whose name, "He knows the unseen and He does not allow anyone to know His secrets. . . ."' (72:26) Abu Ja'far, *'Alayhi al-Salam*, then said, 'Except those of His Messengers whom He chooses.' (72:26) Muhammad, *'Alayhi al-Salam*, I swear by Allah, was one of those whom Allah had chosen. However, there are His words: "He knows the hidden facts." The facts that Allah, the Most Holy, the Most High, knows what is hidden from His creatures of the things that He measures and determines and decrees in His knowledge before creating it and before assigning to the angels, it is because of the following. O Humran, there is the knowledge withheld before Him in which He has a wish. He then decrees it when He wills. *Al-Bada'* may take place in it and He then will not decree it. The knowledge that, however, Allah, the Most Holy, the Most High, measures and determines and approves is the knowledge that reaches the Messenger of Allah and then it reaches us.'"

H 659, Ch. 45, h 3

Ahmad ibn Muhammad has narrated from Muhammad ibn al-Hassan from 'Abbad ibn Sulayman from Muhammad ibn Sulayman from his father from Sadir who has said the following:

"Once abu Basir, Yahya al-Bazzaz, Dawud ibn Kathir and I were in the presence of abu 'Abd Allah, *'Alayhi al-Salam*. The Imam came to us while he was angry. When he settled in his seat he then said, 'How strange it is that certain people think we know the hidden facts! No one knows the hidden things except Allah, the Most Holy, the Most High. I thought to discipline our house maid, so and so. She escaped and I could not find in which quarter she was.' Sadir has said, 'When the meeting was over and the Imam went home, abu Basir, Muyassir and I went to his house. We said to him, 'May Allah keep our souls in service for your cause, we heard you say so and so about the matter of your house maid but we know that you have a great deal of knowledge. We do not say that you possess the knowledge of (al-Ghayb) "hidden facts".' The narrator has said that the Imam said, 'O Sadir, do you not read the Holy Quran?' I said, 'Yes, I do read the Holy Quran.' The Imam then asked, 'In your reading have you found the following words of Allah, the Most Holy, the Most High: 'The one who had knowledge from the Book said, "I can bring it to you before you even blink your eye . . ."'? (27:40) I (the narrator) then said that he has read those words. The Imam asked, 'Do you know who the man is? Do you know how much knowledge of the Book he had?' I (the narrator) then asked the Imam 'Please tell me about his knowledge.' The Imam said, 'His knowledge of the Book was like one drop compared to the green ocean (Atlantic).' I (the narrator) then said, 'May Allah keep my soul in service for your cause, that

237

is very little.' The Imam then said, 'O Sadir, you may indeed say, "What a great knowledge is that!" if you hear about the knowledge of which Allah, the Most Holy, the Most High, has spoken in the Holy Quran and I am about to speak and explain to you. Have you found in the book of Allah, the Most Holy, the Most High, the following: 'Say, "Allah and those who have the knowledge of the Book are sufficient witness (to my prophet-hood)."'" (13:43)

"I (the narrator) then said to the Imam, 'Yes, may Allah keep my soul in service for your cause, I have read it.' The Imam then said, 'Is the knowledge of one who possesses the knowledge of the whole Book greater or that of the one who possesses something of the knowledge of the Book?' I said, 'The knowledge of one who possesses the knowledge of the whole Book is greater.' The narrator has said that the Imam pointing to his chest said, 'The knowledge of the whole Book, I swear by Allah, is with us. The knowledge of the whole Book, I swear by Allah, is with us.'"

H 660, Ch. 45, h 4
Ahmad ibn Muhammad has narrated from Muhammad ibn al-Hassan from Ahmad al-Hassan ibn Ali from 'Amr ibn Sa'id from Musaddiq ibn Sadaqa from 'Ammar al-Sabati who has said the following:
"Once I asked abu 'Abd Allah, *'Alayhi al-Salam*, 'Does the Imam have the knowledge of the hidden facts?' The Imam said, 'No, he does not have such knowledge but if he would like to know about a thing Allah grants him such knowledge.'"

Chapter 46 - If 'A'immah (Plural of Imam), *'Alayhim al-Salam*, Wish to Know, They Are Given Such Knowledge

H 661, Ch. 46, h 1
Ali ibn Muhammad and others have narrated from Sahl ibn Ziyad from Ayyub ibn Nuh from Safwan ibn Yahya from ibn Muskan from Badr ibn al-Walid from abu al-Rabi' al-Shami from abu 'Abd Allah, *'Alayhi al-Salam*, who has said the following:
"If the Imam, *'Alayhi al-Salam*, wishes to know, he is given such knowledge."

H 662, Ch. 46, h 2
Abu Ali al-Ash'ari has narrated from Muhammad ibn 'Abd al-Jabbar from Safwan from ibn Muskan from Badr ibn al-Walid from Abu al-Rabi' from abu 'Abd Allah, *'Alayhi al-Salam*, who has said the following:
"If the Imam, *'Alayhi al-Salam*, wants to know, he is provided such knowledge."

H 663, Ch. 46, h 3
Muhammad ibn Yahya has narrated from 'Umra ibn Musa from Musa ibn Ja'far from 'Amr ibn Sa'id al-Mada'ini from abu 'Ubayda al-Mada'ini from abu 'Abd Allah, *'Alayhi al-Salam*, who has said the following:
"If the Imam, *'Alayhi al-Salam*, wishes to know something, Allah grants him such knowledge."

Chapter 47 - 'A'immah, *'Alayhim al-Salam*, Know When They Will Die and They Die Voluntarily

H 664, Ch. 47, h 1

Muhammad ibn Yahya has narrated from Salamah ibn-al-Khattab Sulayman ibn Sama'a and 'Abd Allah ibn Muhammad from 'Abd Allah ibn al-Qasim al-Batal from abu Basir from abu 'Abd Allah, *'Alayhi al-Salam*, who has said the following:

"Whoever of *'A'immah* does not know what will happen to him and to what events he will proceed, such a person does not possess Divine Authority over His creatures."

H 665, Ch. 47, h 2

Ali ibn Ibrahim has narrated from Muhammad ibn 'Isa ibn al-Hassan ibn Muhammad ibn Bashshar from a respectable man from Qati'a al- Rabi' (a quarter in the Karkh part of Baghdad) from the general public (non-Shi'a) of Baghdad, from whom people would narrate *Hadith* has said to me the following:

"I have seen (experienced) from a member of this family (*Ahl Al-Bayt, 'Alayhim al-Salam*) of whose virtues people speak, things that I have never seen (experienced) from others. No one else is like him in his virtue and worship." I (the narrator) then asked the man. "Who is he? And how did you learn about him?" He then said, "In the days of al-Sindi ibn Shahik (a Vizier of Harun al-Rashid) we gathered eighty people of the leading personalities in goodness to meet Musa ibn Ja'far, *'Alayhi al-Salam*. Al-Sindi asked us, 'Gentlemen, please examine this man. Has anything happened to him? People think that he is tortured and they make a huge noise about it. This is his dwelling place and his bed, which has enough room and he is not constrained. Amir al-Mu'minin (Harun al-Rashid) has not done any bad things to him. He is kept here until the right time comes so he can debate Amir al-Mu'minin (Harun al-Rashid). He is quite well and comfortable from all aspects. You may ask him questions.' The narrator has said, 'We had no other intention but to see the man, to see his virtue and his excellent attitude. Musa ibn Ja'far, *'Alayhi al-Salam*, then said, "Whatever he (al-Sindi) has said about the capacity of the place and other such things is as he has said. However, O people, I should inform you that I am being poisoned with seven pieces of dates. Tomorrow my color will turn green and after tomorrow I will die."' The man has said, 'I looked at al-Sindi ibn Shahik. He shivered in horror and shook like the leaves of a branch of palm tree.'"

H 666, Ch. 47, h 3

Muhammad ibn Yahya has narrated from Ahmad ibn Muhammad from ibn Faddal from abu Jamila from 'Abd Allah ibn abu Ja'far who has said the following:

"My brother narrated from Ja'far (abu 'Abd Allah, *'Alayhi al-Salam*, from his father that he went to Ali ibn al-Husayn, *'Alayhi al-Salam*, on the night in which he passed away and offered him a drink requesting: 'Father, please drink it.' He said, 'Son, this is the night in which I will pass away and during such a night the Messenger of Allah also passed away.'" (The date of the demise of the two holy ones, as generally held, is not the same. However, being the same day is a possibility.)

H 667, Ch. 47, h 4

Ali ibn Muhammad has narrated from Sahl ibn Ziyad from Muhammad ibn 'Abd al-Hamid from al-Hassan ibn al-Jahm who has said that he said to al-Rida, *'Alayhi al-Salam*, the following:

"(Amir al-Mu'minin) Ali, *'Alayhi al-Salam*, knew his assassin, the night of being murdered and the spot where he was fatally wounded. It is his words on hearing the ducks at the house, 'These are the *ululations* that will be followed by lamentations.' Also the words of 'Umm Kulthum (his daughter), 'I wish that you pray inside the house and send someone else to lead the prayer in the Mosque.' He refused to do so and that night he went many times out of the house unarmed. He knew that ibn Muljim, may he be condemned, would hurt him with a sword. He must not expose himself to it (danger).' The Imam, *'Alayhi al-Salam*, said, 'It is true but it was chosen to be that night wherein the measure and the determination of Allah, the Most Holy, the Most High would come to pass.'"

H 668 Ch. 47, h 5

Ali ibn Ibrahim has narrated from Muhammad ibn 'Isa from some of our people from abu al-Hassan Musa, *'Alayhi al-Salam*, who has said the following:

"Allah, the Most Holy, the Most High, expressed anger at the Shi'a. He, therefore, let me choose, either them or myself (to receive protection). I swear by Allah, that I protected them with my own soul."

H 669, Ch. 47, h 6

Muhammad ibn Yahya has narrated from Ahmad ibn Muhammad from al-Washsha' from Musafir that abu al-Hassan al-Rida, *'Alayhi al-Salam*, said to him the following:

"O Musafir, in this water passage there are fish." I (the narrator) then said, "Yes, may Allah keep my soul in service for your cause, there are fish there." The Imam, *'Alayhi al-Salam*, then said, "I saw the Messenger of Allah last night while saying, 'O Ali, what is with us is better for you.'" (The mention of fish is to show equality of degree of certainty in his knowledge from observation and his knowledge from his dream.)

H 670, Ch. 47, h 7

Muhammad ibn Yahya has narrated from Ahmad ibn Muhammad from al-Washsha' from Ahmad ibn 'Aidh from abu Khadija from abu 'Abd Allah, *'Alayhi al-Salam*, who has said the following:

"Once I was in the presence of my father during the day in which he passed away. He made several recommendations to me about his funeral matters, such as washing his whole body, shrouding him and placing him in his grave. I then said to him, 'Father, I, by Allah, have not seen you in better health from the day you complained of illness than today. I do not see in you any sign of death.' The Imam, *'Alayhi al-Salam*, said, 'Son, have you not heard about Ali ibn al-Husayn, *'Alayhi al-Salam*, calling from behind the wall, "O Muhammad, come. Please be quick."'"

H 671, Ch. 47, h 8

A number of our people have narrated from Ahmad ibn Muhammad from Ali ibn al-Hakam from Sayf ibn 'Umayra from 'Abd al-Malik ibn A'yan from abu Ja'far, *'Alayhi al-Salam*, who has said the following:

"Allah, the Most High, sent support for Imam al-Husayn, *'Alayhi al-Salam*, up to the fill between the heavens and earth. Then he was left to choose either victory or meeting Allah. He, however, chose the meeting of Allah, the Most High."

Chapter 48 - 'A'immah, *'Alayhim al-Salam*, Do Have the Knowledge of What Was and Will Be, and That Nothing is Unknown to Them

H 672, Ch. 48, h 1

Ahmad ibn Muhammad and Muhammad ibn Yahya have narrated from Muhammad ibn al-Husayn from Ibrahim ibn Ishaq al-Ahmar from 'Abd Allah ibn Hammad from Sayf al-Tammar who has said the following:

"Once with a group of Shi'ah I was in the presence of abu 'Abd Allah, *'Alayhi al-Salam*, in Hijr and the Imam, *'Alayhi al-Salam*, said, 'An eye is watching over us.' We then looked right and left and did not see anyone. We said, 'No eye is watching over us.' The Imam, *'Alayhi al-Salam*, said, 'I swear by the Lord of the Ka'bah. I swear by the Lord of the House.' He said so three times. 'Had I been with Moses and al-Khidr I would have told them that I had more knowledge than they did and would have informed them of that of which they had no knowledge. This is because Moses and al-Khidr were given the knowledge of what was in the past and they were not given the knowledge of what will be in future or what will exist up to the Day of Judgment, while we have inherited all of it (knowledge) from the Messenger of Allah as heirs.'"

H 673, Ch. 48, h 2

A number of our people have narrated from Ahmad ibn Muhammad ibn Sinan from Yunus ibn Ya'qub from al-Harith ibn al-Mughirah and a group of our people, among whom were 'Abd al-A'la', abu 'Ubaydah and 'Abd Allah ibn Bishr al-Khath'ami, who have said the following:

"Once we heard abu 'Abd Allah, *'Alayhi al-Salam*, say, 'I certainly know what is in the heavens and what is in the earth. I know what is in paradise and what is in the fire. I know what was there and what will be there.' The narrator has said that the Imam paused for a while and found that what he had just said was much too heavy for the audience. He, *'Alayhi al-Salam*, then said, 'I learned all of it from the book of Allah, the Most Holy, the Most High. Allah, the Most Holy, the Most High, Who has said, 'In it there is the clarification of all things.'"

H 674, Ch. 48, h 3

Ali ibn Muhammad has narrated from Sahl from Ahmad ibn Muhammad ibn abu Nasr from 'Abd al-Karim from Jama'a ibn Sa'd al-Khath'ami who has said the following:

"Once al-Mufaddal was in the presence of abu 'Abd Allah, *'Alayhi al-Salam*. He asked the Imam, 'May Allah, keep my soul in service for your cause, does Allah command (His) servants to obey a servant and hide the news of the heavens from him?' The Imam said, 'Allah is by far more honorable, kind and caring toward His servants than to command them to obey a servant (of His) and then hide from him the news of the heavens, mornings, and evenings.'"

H 675, Ch. 48, h 4

Muhammad ibn Yahya has narrated from Ahmad ibn Muhammad from ibn Mahbub from ibn Ri'ab from Durays al-Kunasi who has said the following:

"I heard abu Ja'far, *'Alayhi al-Salam*, saying to an audience of his companions, 'What a strange case is the case with a group of people! They acknowledge us as the Divine Authority over their own selves, accept us as their Imam and say that obedience to us is obligatory just as is the case with the Messenger of Allah. They then destroy the veracity of their belief as such and dispute against themselves due to weakness of their hearts. They then diminish our right and blame those whom Allah has granted evidence to know us as it should be and the (ability) to submit themselves to our Divine Authority. Do you not consider how would Allah, the Most Holy, the Most High, make it obligatory to obey those who possess Divine Authority over His servants and then hide from them (people who possess Divine Authority) the news of the heavens and the earth? How would He cut them off of the sources of knowledge that might come to them to maintain their religion?' Humran then said to the Imam, 'May Allah keep my soul in service for your cause, how do you explain the case of the uprising of Ali ibn abu Talib, al-Hassan and al-Husayn, *'Alayhim al-Salam*? They came out and rose up for the cause of Allah, Whose name is so Majestic. How much they suffered and how mercilessly were they murdered at the hands of the rebels! They were defeated, murdered and overpowered.' Abu Ja'far, *'Alayhi al-Salam*, then said, 'O Humran, Allah, the Most Holy, the Most High, had determined it for them. He had decreed, approved and made it unavoidable in a voluntary manner. He then allowed it to take place. It thus happened with a pre-existing knowledge that had come to them from the Messenger of Allah. Ali, al-Hassan and al-Husayn, *'Alayhim al-Salam*, stood up for the cause of Allah with full knowledge of the consequences and there were those of us who remained silent. Had they, O Humran, when facing what Allah, the Most Holy, the Most High, made them to face and suffer defeat at the hands of the rebels, asked Allah, the Most Holy, the Most High, to remove their suffering and implored Him to destroy the government and kingdom of the rebels He would have answered their prayers and granted them relief. In such cases the destruction of the governments of the rebels, and the ending of their time would take place quicker than the dispersal, under a great pressure, of beads threaded together. The suffering, O Humran, that befell them, was not because of the sins that they might have committed or the punishment for their opposition to Allah. It was because of the high marvelous position that Allah had prepared and wanted them to reach. Do not allow people's opinions take you away from the right path.'"

H 676, Ch. 48, h 5

Ali ibn Ibrahim has narrated from his father from Ali ibn Ma'bad from Hisham ibn al-Hakam who has said the following:

"Once I asked abu 'Abd Allah, *'Alayhi al-Salam*, at Mina five hundred letters (questions) from al-Kalam (theology). I asked the Imam, 'They say that he has said so and so.' Then he says, 'You say so and so.' I then said to the Imam, 'May Allah keep my soul in service for your cause, this is lawful and that is not lawful. I know that you are the authority in this and you are the most knowledgeable person in it and this is al-Kalam.' The Imam said to me, 'O poor Hisham, Allah, the Most Holy, the Most High, does not impose any duty from His creatures without first providing them all that they may need to comply with the command.'"

242

H 677, Ch. 48, h 6

Muhammad ibn Yahya has narrated from Ahmad ibn Muhammad from 'Umar ibn 'Abd al-'Aziz from Muhammad ibn al-Fudayl from abu Hamza who has said the following:

"I heard abu Ja'far, *'Alayhi al-Salam*, say, 'No, I swear by Allah, the scholar (who possesses Divine Authority) is never ignorant or knowledgeable in something and ignorant of other things.' The Imam then said, 'Allah, the Most Holy, Most High and Most Gracious, is by far exalted and above imposing the obedience of a servant (of His) on the others and then hiding the knowledge of things in the heavens and on earth from him. He (Allah) does not hide knowledge from him,' the Imam added. "

Chapter 49 - Allah, the Most Holy, the Most High, Did Not Teach Anything to His Messenger But That He Commanded Him to Teach Such Knowledge to Amir Al-Mu'minin (Ali), *'Alayhi al-Salam*, and He Was His Partner in Knowledge

H 678, Ch. 49, h 1

Ali ibn Ibrahim has narrated from his father from ibn abu 'Umayr from ibn 'Udhayna from 'Abd Allah ibn Sulayman from Humran ibn A'yan from abu 'Abd Allah, *'Alayhi al-Salam*, who has said the following:

"Once Jibril came to the Messenger of Allah and brought him two pieces of pomegranate. The Messenger of Allah ate one of them and broke the other one into two pieces. He then ate one-half and fed the other half to Ali, *'Alayhi al-Salam*. The Messenger of Allah said, 'O my brother, do you know what those pieces of pomegranate were?' He said, 'No, I do not know.' He then said, 'The first one was prophecy. There is no share in it for you. The other one is knowledge in which you are my partner.' I then said, 'May Allah keep you well, how was that? He would be his partner in it?' He said, 'Allah did not teach any knowledge to Muhammad, *'Alayhi al-Salam*, but that He commanded him to teach it to Ali, *'Alayhi al-Salam*.'"

H 679, Ch. 49, h 2

Ali has narrated from his father from ibn abu 'Umayr from ibn 'Udhayna from Zurarah from abu Ja'far, *'Alayhi al-Salam*, who has said the following:

"Once, Jibril brought from Paradise two pieces of pomegranate to the Messenger of Allah. The Messenger of Allah ate one of them and broke the other one into two pieces. He then ate one-half and gave the other half to Ali, *'Alayhi al-Salam*, who also ate it. The Messenger of Allah said, 'O Ali, the first one that I ate was prophet-hood. There is no share in it for you. The other one is knowledge, in which you are my partner.'"

H 680, Ch. 49, h 3

Muhammad ibn Yahya has narrated from Muhammad ibn al-Hassan from Muhammad ibn 'Abd al-Hamid from Mansur ibn Yunus from ibn 'Udhayna from Muhammad ibn Muslim who has said that he heard abu Ja'far, *'Alayhi al-Salam*, say the following:

"Once Jibril descended to Muhammad, *'Alayhi al-Salam*, (and) brought two pieces of pomegranate from Paradise. Ali, *'Alayhi al-Salam*, met him and asked, 'What (kind of) pomegranates are those in your hands?' He replied, 'As to this one, it is the prophecy in which there is no share for you. As to this one, it is knowledge.' Then the Messenger of Allah broke it into two-halves. He then gave one-half to him (Imam Ali) and the Messenger of Allah kept the other half and then said, 'You are my partner and I am your partner in it.' The Imam then said, 'I swear by Allah that there was nothing of all the knowledge that was taught to the Messenger of Allah without his teaching them all to Ali, *'Alayhi al-Salam*, and thereafter knowledge was transferred to us.' He then placed his hand over his chest.'"

Chapter 50 - Aspects of the Knowledge of 'A'immah, *'Alayhim al-Salam*

H 681, Ch. 50, h 1
Muhammad ibn Yahya has narrated from Ahmad ibn Muhammad from Muhammad ibn Isma'il from his paternal uncle Hamza ibn Bazi' from Ali al-Sa'i from abu al-Hassan, the first, Musa, *'Alayhi al-Salam*, who has said the following:
"The totality of our knowledge is of three aspects. There is the knowledge of the past, knowledge of the future and that coming into being. The knowledge of the past is that which is interpreted. The knowledge of the future is that which is written and the knowledge of that which comes into being is the kind that is thrown into the hearts and is heard by the ears, and this is the best aspect of our knowledge, and there is no prophet after our Holy Prophet, *'Alayhi al-Salam*."

H 682, Ch. 50, h 2
Muhammad ibn Yahya has narrated Ahmad ibn abu Zahir from Ali ibn Musa from Safwan ibn Yahya from al-Harith ibn al-Mughirah who has said the following:
"Once I asked abu 'Abd Allah, *'Alayhi al-Salam*, 'Tell me about the knowledge of your scholar.' He said, 'It is inherited from the Messenger of Allah and from Ali, *'Alayhi al-Salam*.' I (the narrator) then asked the Imam, 'We narrate that it is thrown into your hearts and is resonated in your ears.' He then said, 'It sometimes is so.'"

H 683, Ch. 50, h 3
Ali ibn Ibrahim has narrated from his father from the person who narrated (it) to him from al-Mufaddal ibn 'Umar who has said the following:
"Once I said to abu al-Hassan, *'Alayhi al-Salam*, 'We narrate from abu 'Abd Allah, *'Alayhi al-Salam*, that he has said, "Our knowledge consists (of the knowledge of the things) of the past, of the written nature, that which is dotted in the hearts and that which is resonated in the ears." He then said, "Of the past it is that which we know of the past. That which is written is the kind that will come in future. That which is written in the hearts is the inspired kind and that which is resonated against the ears is the order of the angel.'"

Chapter 51 - If Secrets Would Be Kept 'A'immah, *'Alayhim al-Salam*, Can Tell everyone What is for and Against Them

H 684, Ch. 51, h 1

A number of our people have narrated from Ahmad ibn Muhammad from al-Husayn ibn Sa'id from Fadala ibn Ayyub from Aban ibn 'Uthman from 'Abd al-Wahid ibn al-Mukhtar who has said the following:

"Abu Ja'far, *'Alayhi al-Salam*, has said, 'Had there been a thing (bag) to contain (to stop) your tongues I would have spoken to everyone about what is for or against him.'"

H 685, Ch. 51, h 2

Through the same chain of narrators it is narrated from Ahmad ibn Muhammad from ibn Sinan from 'Abd Allah ibn Muskan who has said that he heard abu Basir who has said the following:

"Once I asked abu 'Abd Allah, *'Alayhi al-Salam*, 'What made the supporters of Ali, *'Alayhi al-Salam*, suffer the troubles, despite the fact that they knew about their deaths and (causes of their) suffering?' The Imam replied to me as if he were angry, 'From whom could it come except from their own selves?' I then asked, 'What prevents you, may Allah keep my soul in service for your cause, from telling it all (to your friends)?' The Imam said, 'It is a door that is closed except that al-Husayn ibn Ali, *'Alayhi al-Salam*, opened it to a small degree (told a few things about the future to his supporters just before their martyrdom).' The Imam then said, 'O abu Muhammad, those people had a restraint (a stopper) over their mouths.'"

Chapter 52 - Allah's Giving Charge of the Religious Matters to the Messenger of Allah and to the 'A'immah, *'Alayhim al-Salam*

H 686, Ch. 52, h 1

Muhammad ibn Yahya has narrated from Ahmad ibn abu Zahir from Ali ibn Isma'il from Safwan ibn Yahya from 'Asim ibn Humayd from abu Ishaq al-Nahwi who has said the following:

"Once I went to see abu 'Abd Allah, *'Alayhi al-Salam*, and I heard him saying, 'Allah, the Most Holy, the Most High, disciplined and educated His prophet upon His own love and said, "You certainly possess a high degree of moral discipline and education." (64:4) He then allowed him to be in charge as He, the Most Holy, the Most High, has said, '. . . whatever the Messenger brings to you, you must take (obey) and whatever he prohibits you, you must desist from. . . .' (59:7) Allah, the Most Holy, the Most High, has said, '. . . whoever obeys the Messenger, has obeyed Allah. . . .' (4:80)

"The narrator has said that then the Imam said, 'The Prophet of Allah then made Ali and *'A'immah*, *'Alayhim al-Salam*, in charge (of the religious matters). You then acknowledged it (the Divine Authority of *'A'immah*) while other people have denied it. I swear by Allah, we love you to speak when we speak and remain silent when we remain silent. We are between you and Allah, the Most Holy, the Most High. Allah has not placed any goodness in the opposition to us.'"

A number of our people have narrated from Ahmad ibn Muhammad from abu Najran from 'Asim ibn Humayd from abu Ishaq who has said that he heard abu Ja'far, *'Alayhi al-Salam*, say the following: He cited a *Hadith* similar to the above one.

H 687, Ch. 52, h 2

Ali ibn Ibrahim has narrated from his father from Yahya ibn abu 'Umran from Yunus from Bakkar ibn Bakr from Musa ibn 'Ushaym who has said the following:

"Once I was in the presence of abu 'Abd Allah, *'Alayhi al-Salam*, when a man asked him about a verse of the Book of Allah, the Most Holy, the Most High. The Imam explained it to him. Then another person came to see the Imam and asked him about the same verse. The Imam gave him a different explanation. This made as many things come to my mind as Allah willed. My heart felt as if it were being shredded with knives. I then said to myself, 'I left abu Qatada in Syria who did not make a mistake in even the letter 'Waw' and now I have come to this man who makes all these mistakes.' At this time another person came in to see him and asked him about the same verse. His explanation to him was completely different from what he had explained to me and to the man just before. My soul relaxed at this point and I came to know that it was because of fear. He has said that then he (the Imam) turned to me and said, 'O ibn 'Ashyama, Allah, the Most Holy, the Most High, made Solomon son of David in charge (of religious matters) and said, "This is Our gift to you, you may do with it favors to others or withhold without being held responsible for anything . . ." (38:39) He also made His Prophet the in charge person and said, ". . . what the Messenger (of Allah) gives you, you must take (obey) and what he prohibits you, you must desist from. . ." (59:7) Of whatever the Messenger of Allah is made in charge he has made us the in charge persons thereof.'"

H 688, Ch. 52, h 3

A number of our people have narrated from Ahmad ibn Muhammad from al-Hajjal from Tha'laba from Zurara who has said the following:

"I heard abu Ja'far and abu 'Abd Allah, *'Alayhim al-Salam*, say, 'Allah, the Most Holy, the Most High has made the Holy Prophet in charge of the affairs of His creatures to see how their obedience is.' He then recited this verse of Holy Quran, ". . . what the Messenger (of Allah) would give you, you must take (obey) and what he prohibits you, you must desist from. . . .""" (59:7)

H 689, Ch. 52, h 4

Ali ibn Ibrahim has narrated from his father from ibn abu 'Umayr from 'Umar ibn 'Udhayna from Fudayl ibn Yasar who has said the following:

"I heard abu 'Abd Allah saying to certain persons of the companions of Qays al-Masir, 'Allah, the Most Holy, the Most High, disciplined and educated His Messenger. He then made his discipline and education to be the best. When his discipline and education were complete He said, "O Muhammad, you certainly possess a high degree of moral discipline and education." (64:4) He then made him in charge of the affairs of the religion and the nation (Muslim) so he would manage the social matters of His servants with wisdom. Allah, the Most Holy, the Most High, said, ". . . what the Messenger (of Allah) gives you, you must take (obey) and what he prohibits you, you must desist from. . . ." (59:7) The Messenger of Allah was protected, made successful and supported by the Holy Spirit. He (the Messenger of Allah) does not slip, nor makes a mistake in any of the matters of the management of the social matters of the creatures.

'He is educated with the education of Allah. Allah, the Most Holy, the Most High, commanded him to perform the prayer in two and two Rak'at form totaling ten Rak'ats. The Messenger of Allah added two more Rak'ats to each prayer and only one Rak'at to the Maghrib prayer (the prayer at sunset), which remained obligatory at home and on a journey. Such additions became just as the obligatory ones and it is not permissible to disregard them. Allah, the Most Holy, the Most High, granted him permission in all of it. Thus, the obligatory prayers became seventeen Rak'ats. The Messenger of Allah then set up the tradition of optional prayers totaling thirty-four Rak'ats, which is twice the number of the obligatory prayers. Allah, the Most Holy, the Most High, granted him permission for this. All the optional and obligatory prayers total fifty-one Rak'ats of which there are two Rak'ats in a sitting position after al-'Atma, 'Isha (late evening prayer), which is counted as one Rak'at in place of Witr.

'Allah made fasting of the month of Ramadan obligatory. It comes only once in a year. The Messenger of Allah set up the tradition of fasting in the month of Sha'ban and three days of fasting every month and the number of days in it totals twice as much as the obligatory fast. Allah, the Most Holy, the Most High, granted him permission for all of this.

'Allah, the Most Holy, the Most High, made just the substance of wine unlawful to consume. The Messenger of Allah pronounced all intoxicating liquors unlawful. Allah, the Most Holy, the Most High, granted him permission in this case also. The Messenger of Allah pronounced certain things as permissible and pronounced other things as detestable but did not declare them prohibited and unlawful. He only pronounced them prohibited in a permissible prohibition and detestable. He then spoke of such prohibition as permissible but then such permissible matters became obligatory for the servants (of Allah) such as the obligation of abiding by what is prohibited and determined.

'The Messenger of Allah did not grant permission in the matters that were prohibited as unlawful (to violate) prohibitions or what he pronounced as an order to follow as an obligation and binding. A great deal of the intoxicating liquors he pronounced as unlawful to consume and he did not grant permission to any one to consume them. The Messenger of Allah did not grant permission to anyone to further shorten the prayers that consisted of two Rak'ats that were added to what Allah, the Most Holy, the Most High, had made obligatory. In fact, he made them binding and necessary like an obligation. He did not grant permission to anyone in this matter except those on a journey.

'No one has the right to give permission in such issues until the Messenger of Allah grants permission. Thus, the orders of the Messenger of Allah concur and

247

agree with the orders of Allah, the Most Holy, the Most High. The prohibitions of the Messenger of Allah concur and agree with the prohibition of Allah, the Most Holy, the Most High. It has become obligatory for the servants (of Allah) to submit to his commands as it is obligatory for them to submit to the commands of Allah, the Most Holy, the Most High.'"

H 690, Ch. 52, h 5

Abu Ali al-Ash'ari has narrated from Muhammad ibn 'Abd al-Jabbar from ibn Faddal from Tha'laba ibn Maymun from Zurara who has said the following:

"I heard abu Ja'far and abu 'Abd Allah, *'Alayhim al-Salam*, say, 'Allah, the Most Holy, the Most High, made His Prophet the in charge person of His creatures to see how their obedience is. They then recited the following verse of the Holy Quran. ". . . what the Messenger (of Allah) brings you, you must take (obey) and what he prohibits you, you must desist from. . . ."' (59:7)

Muhammad ibn Yahya has narrated from Ahmad ibn Muhammad from al-Hajjal from Tha'laba ibn Maymun from Zurara a similar *Hadith*.

H 691, Ch. 52, h 6

Muhammad ibn Yahya has narrated from Ahmad ibn Muhammad from Muhammad ibn Sinan from Ishaq ibn 'Ammar from abu 'Abd Allah, *'Alayhi al-Salam*, who has said the following:

"Allah, the Most Holy, the Most High, disciplined and educated His Prophet to the level that He wanted and said, 'O Muhammad, you certainly possess a high degree of moral discipline and education.' (64:4) Then He made him the in charge person of His religion and said, '. . . what the Messenger (of Allah) brings you, you must take (obey) and what he prohibits you, you must desist from. . .' (59:7) Allah, the Most Holy, the Most High, declared the laws of inheritance and did not assign any part for the grandfather. The Messenger of Allah assigned one-sixth for him. Allah, the Most Holy, the Most High, granted permission in the matter in His words as follows: 'This is our gift to you, you may grant it to others or keep it without being held responsible.'" (38:39)

H 692, Ch. 52, h 7

Al-Husayn ibn Muhammad has narrated from Mu'alla ibn Muhammad from al-Washsha' from Hammad ibn 'Uthman from Zurara from abu Ja'far, *'Alayhi al-Salam*, who has said the following:

"Abu Ja'far, *'Alayhi al-Salam*, has said, 'The Messenger of Allah sanctioned compensation for a damaged eye and blood-money for the slain person. He pronounced the consumption of *Nabidh* (a beverage from dates) and all intoxicants as unlawful.' A man asked the Imam, 'Did the Messenger of Allah sanction this law without receiving anything (from Allah)?' the Imam said, 'Yes, it was to establish who obeys the Messenger and who disobeys him.'"

H 693, Ch. 52, h 8

Muhammad ibn Yahya has narrated from Muhammad ibn al-Hassan who has said the following:

"I found in the *Nawadir* (works) of Muhammad ibn Sinan narrated from 'Abd Allah ibn Sinan who has said that abu 'Abd Allah, *'Alayhi al-Salam*, has said, 'No, I swear by Allah, that He has not made any one of His creatures the in charge person except the Messenger of Allah and *'A'immah*, *'Alayhim al-Salam*. Allah, the Most Holy, the Most High, has said, 'We have sent down to you the Book with the truth, so that you may judge among the people by that which Allah has shown you.' (4:105) It has continued to be valid and in full force with the executors of his will also.'"

H 694, Ch. 52, h 9
Muhammad ibn Yahya has narrated from Muhammad ibn al-Hassan from Ya'qub ibn Yazid from al-Hassan ibn Ziyad from Muhammad ibn al-Hassan al-Maythami from abu 'Abd Allah, *'Alayhi al-Salam*, who has said the following:

"Allah, the Most Holy, the Most High, disciplined and educated His Messenger until he was well established in whatever He wanted. Then He made him the in charge person as He, the Most Holy, the Most High, has said, '. . . what the Messenger (of Allah) brings you, you must take (obey) and what he prohibits you, you must desist from. . .' (59:7) Of whatever Allah has made His Messenger the in charge person He has made us also in charge persons thereof."

H 695, Ch. 52, h 10
Ali ibn Muhammad has narrated from certain persons of our people from al-Husayn ibn 'Abd al-Rahman from Sandal al-Khayyat from Zayd al-Shahham who has said the following:

"Once I asked abu 'Abd Allah, *'Alayhi al-Salam*, about the meaning of the words of Allah, the Most High. 'This is our gift to you, you may grant it to others or keep it without being held responsible.' (38:39) The Imam said, 'Solomon was given a great kingdom. This verse continued to apply to the Messenger of Allah. He had authority to grant whatever he wished to whomever he wished and withhold from whomever he wished. Allah granted him a favor greater than what He had granted to Solomon as He has said, '. . . what the Messenger (of Allah) brings you, you must take (obey) and what he prohibits you, you must desist therefrom. . . .'" (59:7)

Chapter 53 - 'A'immah, *'Alayhi al-Salam*, Are Similar to Those Before Them and the Incongruity of Calling Them Prophets

H 696, Ch. 53, h 1
Abu Ali al-Ash'ari has narrated from Muhammad ibn 'Abd al-Jabbar from Safwan ibn Yahya from Humran ibn A'yan who has said the following:

"Once I asked abu Ja'far, *'Alayhi al-Salam*, 'What is the position of the scholars?' The Imam said, 'It is like Dhul Qarnayn (see 18:83 – 99 Holy Quran), the companion of Solomon (see 27:40), and the companion of Moses, peace be upon them." (see 18:65)

H 697, Ch. 53, h 2
Ali ibn Ibrahim has narrated from his father from ibn abu 'Umayr from al-Husayn ibn abu al-'Ala' from abu 'Abd Allah, *'Alayhi al-Salam*, who has said the following:

"One must refer to us (as the Divine Authorities) to find the the rules of lawful and unlawful matters but considering us as having prophet-hood is not valid."

H 698, Ch. 53, h 3
Muhammad ibn Yahya al-Ash'ari has narrated from Ahmad ibn Muhammad from al-Barqi from al-Nadr ibn Suwayd from Yahya ibn 'Imran al-Halabi from Ayyub ibn al-Hurr who has said the following:

"I heard abu 'Abd Allah, *'Alayhi al-Salam*, say, 'Allah, Majestic is Whose name, ended with your prophet (the coming of) the prophets. Thus, there will never come any prophet after him. With your book He ended sending of (heavenly) books. Thus, there will never come other heavenly books. In it (your book) He has placed clarifications for all things, such as your creation and the creation of the heavens and the earth. Therein is the news of the beings before you, the laws that help settle your disputes and the news of the beings that will come into being after you, the news of the issues of paradise and fire and that to which you proceed.'"

H 699, Ch. 53, h 4

A number of our people have narrated from Ahmad ibn Muhammad from al-Husayn ibn Sa'id from Hammad ibn 'Isa from al-Husayn ibn al-Mukhtar from al-Harith ibn al-Mughirah who has said the following:

"Abu Ja'far, *'Alayhi al-Salam*, has said, 'Ali, *'Alayhi al-Salam*, was a *Muhaddath* (a person to whom angels spoke).' I (the narrator) then asked the Imam, 'What does it mean, O Imam? Do you say he was a prophet?' The narrator has said that the Imam raised his hand like this (meaning thereby, no, I did not say that). The Imam then said, 'Or he is like the companion of Solomon, or the companion of Moses or like Dhul Qarnayn. Have you not heard that he (the Holy Prophet) said, "Among you is one similar to him (Dhul Qarnayn)."'"

H 700, Ch. 53, h 5

Ali ibn Ibrahim has narrated from his father from ibn abu 'Umayr from ibn 'Udhayna from Burayd ibn Mu'awiya who has said the following:

"Once I asked abu Ja'far and abu 'Abd Allah, *'Alayhim al-Salam*, 'What is your position? Whom of the people of the past do you resemble?' The Imam said, 'I resemble the companion of Moses and Dhul Qarnayn who were two scholars but not two prophets.'"

H 701, Ch. 53, h 6

Muhammad ibn Yahya has narrated from Ahmad ibn Muhammad from al-Barqi from abu Talib from Sadir who has said the following:

"Once I asked abu 'Abd Allah, *'Alayhi al-Salam*, 'A certain group of people believes that you (*'A'immah*) are gods. They read to us from the the the Holy Quran about it such as, "And it is He Who in heaven is the Lord and on earth is the Lord." (43:84) The Imam said, 'O Sadir, my hearing, my sight, my skin, my flesh, my blood and my hair all disdain such people, and Allah also disdains them. They do not follow my religion and the religion of my ancestors. I swear by Allah, Allah will not place me with them on the Day of Resurrection. The only thing from Allah to them will be His anger.' I (the narrator) then said, 'Among us there is a group of people who believe that you are messengers and they read to us from the Holy Quran: "O messengers, eat of the good things and do righteousness; surely I know the things you do."' (23:51)

"The Imam said, 'O Sadir, my hearing, my sight, my skin, my flesh, my blood and my hair all disdain such people, and Allah and His Messenger also disdain them. They do not follow my religion and the religion of my ancestors. By Allah,

Allah will not place me with them on the Day of Judgment. The only thing from Allah toward them will be His anger.'

"I (the narrator) then asked, 'What are you then?' The Imam said, 'We are the treasuries of the knowledge of Allah. We are the translators of the commands of Allah. We are infallible people. Allah, the Most Holy, the Most High, has commanded people to obey us and prohibited them from disobeying us. We are well advocated Divine Authority over all that is below the heavens and above the earth.'"

H 702, Ch. 53, h 7

A number of our people have narrated from Ahmad ibn Muhammad from al-Husayn ibn Sa'id from 'Abd Allah ibn Bahr from ibn Muskan from 'Abd al-Rahman ibn abu 'Abd Allah from Muhammad ibn Muslim who has said the following:

"I heard abu 'Abd Allah, *'Alayhi al-Salam*, say, "'A'immah, *'Alayhim al-Salam*, possess the position of the Messenger of Allah except that they are not prophets and the number of wives permissible for the Holy Prophet is not permissible for them. In the aspects other than these they possess the same positions as the Messenger of Allah did.'"

Chapter 54 - 'A'immah, *'Alayhim al-Salam*, Hear from the Angels as Muhaddathun and Are of Perfect Understanding

H 703, Ch. 54, h 1

Muhammad ibn Yahya has narrated from Ahmad ibn Muhammad from al-Hajjal from al-Qasim ibn Muhammad from 'Ubayd ibn Zurara who has said the following:

"Once abu Ja'far, *'Alayhi al-Salam*, sent (message) to Zurara to inform al-Hakam ibn 'Utayba that the executors of the will of Muhammad, *'Alayhi al-Salam*, are *Muhaddathun* (people to whom angels speak)."

Note: Al-Hakam ibn 'Utayba (al-Kindi al-Kufi, 50A.H./670A.D.-115A.H./733A.D, was one of the *tabi'un* (those who knew the companions of the Holy Prophet and are famous narrators of *Hadith*).

H 704, Ch. 54, h 2

Muhammad has narrated from Ahmad ibn Muhammad from ibn Mahbub from Jamil ibn Salih from Ziyad ibn Suqa from al-Hakam ibn 'Utayba who has said the following:

"One day I went to see Ali ibn al-Husayn, *'Alayhi al-Salam*. He said, 'O Hakam, do you know the verse (of the Holy Quran) from which Ali ibn abu Talib, *'Alayhi al-Salam*, learned who his assassin was and the extraordinary great matters of which he would speak to people?' Al-Hakam has said that I thought, 'I have now a chance to learn of the knowledge of Ali ibn al-Husayn, *'Alayhi al-Salam*, with which I will learn of those extraordinary great matters.' I (the narrator) then replied to the Imam, 'No, by Allah, I do not know.'

"I (the narrator) then said, 'Please tell me, O child of the Messenger of Allah, which verse it is.' The Imam said, 'It, I swear by Allah, is the words of Allah, Majestic is Whose name, "We have not sent any messenger or prophet before you [or a Muhahhdath] (one to whom angels speak)." (22:52) Ali ibn abu Talib, *'Alayhi al-Salam*, was a *Muhaddath*.' At this point a man called 'Abd Allah ibn

Zayd, who was a brother of Ali ibn al-Husayn (his mother had nursed Ali ibn al-Husayn, *'Alayhi al-Salam*) from his mother's side, said, "Glory belongs to Allah, *a Muhaddath!*" It seemed as if he did not believe it. Abu Ja'far, *'Alayhi al-Salam*, (also present) then turned to us and said to him, 'Do not have any doubts, I swear by Allah, that the son of your mother did have knowledge of this fact after all.' The narrator has said that when abu Ja'far, *'Alayhi al-Salam*, said so the man kept silent. Ali ibn al-Husayn, *'Alayhi al-Salam*, then said, 'This is the issue in which abu al-Khattab perished. He never learned what was the explanation of the prophet and a *Muhaddath*.'"

H 705, Ch. 54, h 3

Ahmad ibn Muhammad and Muhammad ibn Yahya have narrated from Muhammad ibn al-Hassan from Ya'qub ibn Yazid from Muhammad ibn Isma'il who has said the following:

"I heard abu al-Hassan, *'Alayhi al-Salam*, say, ''*A'immah*, *'Alayhim al-Salam*, are scholars, are truthful people, have perfect understanding and are *Muhaddathun* (people to whom the angels speak).'"

H 706, Ch. 54, h 4

Ali ibn Ibrahim has narrated from Muhammad ibn 'Isa from Yunus from a man from Muhammad ibn Muslim who has said the following:

"Once *Muhaddath* was mentioned in the presence of abu 'Abd Allah, *'Alayhi al-Salam*, and he said, 'He, *Muhaddath*, hears the voice but does not see the persons of the angels.' I then said to him, 'May Allah keep my soul in service for your cause, how can he know that the voice and words are from the angels?' The Imam said, 'He is given the serenity and dignity to the extent that he learns about its being the speech of the angels.'"

H 707, Ch. 54, h 5

Muhammad ibn Yahya has narrated from Ahmad ibn Muhammad from al-Husayn ibn Sa'id from Hammad ibn 'Isa from al-Husayn ibn al-Mukhtar from al-Harith ibn al-Mughirah from Humran ibn A'yan who has said the following:

"Once abu Ja'far, *'Alayhi al-Salam*, said, 'Ali, *'Alayhi al-Salam*, was a *Muhaddath*.' I then returned to my associates and said, 'I have brought you very strange news.' They asked, 'What is it?' I then said that I heard abu Ja'far, *'Alayhi al-Salam*, say that Ali, *'Alayhi al-Salam*, was a *Muhaddath*. They then said, 'What did you do? Would that you had asked him about who would speak to him (Ali, *'Alayhi al-Salam*).' I then went back to abu Ja'far, *'Alayhi al-Salam*, and said to him, 'I went to my associates and told them about what you had told me and they said, 'What did you do? Would that you had asked him as to who would speak to him (Ali, *'Alayhi al-Salam*).'

"The Imam said to me, 'The angel would speak to him.' I then asked, 'Do you say that he was a prophet?' He then said, 'He (the Imam) moved his hand like this' (a certain hand gesture); '(he was) similar to the companion of Solomon or the companion of Moses or like Dhul Qarnayn. Have you not heard that he (the Messenger of Allah, *'Alayhi al-Salam*) has said, "Among you there is one like him?"'"

(A *Hadith* of the Holy Prophet, *'Alayhi al-Salam*, says that Ali, *'Alayhi al-Salam*, is the Dhul Qarnayn of this Umma.)

Chapter 55 - The Spirits That Exist in 'A'immah, *'Alayhim al-Salam*

H 708, Ch. 55, h 1

Muhammad ibn Yahya has narrated from Ahmad ibn Muhammad from al-Husayn ibn Sa'id from Hammad ibn 'Isa from Ibrahim ibn 'Umar al-Yamani from Jabir al-Ju'fi from abu 'Abd Allah, *'Alayhi al-Salam*, who has said the following:

"O Jabir, Allah, the Most Holy, the Most High has created the creatures in three categories as mentioned in the words of Allah, the Most Holy, the Most High. 'On that day, you (mankind) will be divided into three groups: (56:7) the people of the right hand (those whose books of records will be placed in their right hands). How happy they will be! (56:8) The people of the left hand (those whose books of records will be placed in their left hands). How miserable they will be! (56:9) The foremost ones (in belief and virtue) are the foremost ones in receiving their reward.' (56:10)

"The foremost group are the messengers and the people of special status with Allah among His creatures. Allah has placed in them five spirits and has supported them with the Holy Spirit. Through this (the Holy Spirit) they recognize things. He has supported them with the spirit of belief because of which they maintain fear of Allah, the Majestic, the Glorious, (in their souls). They are supported also with the spirit of power because of which they are able to obey Allah. They are also supported with the spirit of desires with which they maintain their desire of worshipping and obeying Allah, the Most Holy, the Most High, and dislike disobedience to Him. He has placed in them the social spirit to socialize and establish proper relations among people. In the believers and the people of the right hand He has placed the spirit of belief because of which they maintain fear of Allah,. He has placed in them the spirit of power. With it they obey Allah. He has placed in them the spirit of desire. With it they desire to obey Allah. He has also placed in them the social spirit and because of this they maintain social relations."

H 709, Ch. 55, h 2

Muhammad ibn Yahya has narrated from Ahmad ibn Muhammad from Musa ibn 'Umar from Muhammad ibn Sinan from 'Ammar ibn Marwan from al-Munakhkhal from Jabir who has said the following:

"Once I asked abu Ja'far, *'Alayhi al-Salam*, about the knowledge of the scholar. He said, 'O Jabir, in the prophets and in the executors of their will, there are five spirits. They are: (1) the Holy Spirit, (2) the spirit of belief, (3) the spirit of life, (4) the spirit of power and (5) the spirit of desire. Through the Holy Spirit, O Jabir, they receive the knowledge of all that is below the Throne as well as what is below the land.' He then said, 'O Jabir, these four spirits are the kind of spirits that may become affected by events that take place. Only the Holy Spirit is that which does not trifle and wander around.'"

H 710, Ch. 55, h 3

Al-Husayn ibn Muhammad has narrated from al-Mu'alla ibn Muhammad from 'Abd Allah ibn Idris from Muhammad ibn Sinan from al-Mufaddal ibn 'Umar who has said the following:

"I asked abu 'Abd Allah, *'Alayhi al-Salam*, about the knowledge of Imam about the regions of the earth, when he was in his house secluded behind the curtains. The Imam said, 'O Mufaddal, Allah, the Most Holy, the Most High, has place five spirits in the Prophet. Of such one is the spirit of life from which comes movement and activities. There is the spirit of power from which comes uprising and diligence and the spirit of desire from which comes utilization of nutrients and reproduction in lawful ways. There is the spirit of belief from which comes peace and justice. There is the Holy Spirit whereby prophet-hood is carried. When the prophet passes away the Holy Spirit transfers and comes over to the Imam, *'Alayhi al-Salam*. The Holy Spirit does not sleep or become unaware. It does not trifle or maintain false hopes. The other four spirits sleep, become unaware, may maintain false hopes or trifle. With the Holy Spirit things are seen.'"

Chapter 56 - The Spirit with Which Allah Protects 'A'immah, *'Alayhim al-Salam*

H 711, Ch. 56, h 1

A number of our people have narrated from Ahmad ibn Muhammad from al-Husayn ibn Sa'id from al-Nadr ibn Suwayd from Yahya al-Halabi from abu al-Sabah al-Kinani from abu Basir who has said the following:

"Once I asked abu 'Abd Allah, *'Alayhi al-Salam*, about the words of Allah, the Most Holy, the Most High, 'Thus, We have revealed a Spirit to you (Muhammad), by Our command. Before, you did not even know what a book or belief was. . . .' (42:52) The Imam said, 'He (the Spirit) is a creature of the creatures of Allah, the Most Holy, the Most High, greater than Jibril and Mika'il. He was with the Messenger of Allah to give him news and protected him and he is with *'A'immah*, *'Alayhim al-Salam*, after the Messenger of Allah.'"

H 712, Ch. 56, h 2

Muhammad ibn Yahya has narrated from Muhammad ibn al-Husayn from Ali ibn Asbat from Asbat ibn Salim who has said the following:

"Once a man from Hiyt (a town in Iraq) asked abu 'Abd Allah, *'Alayhi al-Salam*, when I also was present, about the words of Allah, the Most Holy, the Most High. 'Thus, We have revealed a Spirit to you (Muhammad), by Our command. Before, you did not even know what a book or belief was. . . .' (42:52) The Imam said, 'From the day Allah, the Most Holy, the Most High, sent that Spirit to Muhammad, *'Alayhi al-Salam*, he did not ever since ascend (back) and he is present with us.'"

H 713, Ch. 56, h 3

Ali ibn Ibrahim has narrated from Muhammad ibn 'Isa from Yunus from ibn Muskan from abu Basir who has said the following:

"I asked abu 'Abd Allah, *'Alayhi al-Salam*, about the words of Allah, the Most Holy, the Most High, 'They ask you about the Spirit. Say, "The Spirit comes by the command of my Lord. . . .' (17:85) The Imam said, 'He is a creature greater than Jibril and Mika'il. He was with the Messenger of Allah and he is present with the *'A'immah, 'Alayhim al-Salam*. He is from the realm of the angels.'"

H 714, Ch. 56, h 4

Ali has narrated from his father from ibn abu 'Umayr from abu Ayyub al-Khazzaz from abu Basir who has said the following:

"I heard abu 'Abd Allah, *'Alayhi al-Salam*, say, 'They ask you about the Spirit. Say, "The Spirit comes by the command of my Lord . . ."' (17:85) The Imam said, 'He is a creature greater than Jibril and Mika'il. He was not present with anyone before except Muhammad, *'Alayhi al-Salam*. He is present with *'A'immah, 'Alayhim al-Salam*. He protects them. In reality any and everything desired does not come by and is not possible for everyone to achieve.'"

H 715, Ch. 56, h 5

Muhammad ibn Yahya has narrated from 'Imran ibn Musa from Musa ibn Ja'far from Ali ibn Asbat from Muhammad ibn Fudayl from abu Hamza who has said the following:

"I asked abu 'Abd Allah, *'Alayhi al-Salam*, about the knowledge, 'Is it a knowledge that the scholar learns from the mouths of the people or is it in the book with you from which you read and then learn therefrom?' The Imam said, 'The issue is greater and more urgently needed. Have you not heard the words of Allah, the Most Holy, the Most High, "Thus, We have revealed a Spirit to you (Muhammad), by Our command. Before, you did not even know what a book or belief was. . . ." (42:52)

"The Imam said, 'What do your people say about this verse? Do they read that he was such that he did not know what the book or the belief was?' I said, 'I do not know, may Allah keep my soul in service for your cause, what they say.' The Imam then said, 'Yes, he lived in a condition wherein he did not know the book and the belief until Allah, the Most High, sent the Spirit who is mentioned in the Book. When the Spirit was sent to him he learned through him the knowledge and understanding. He is the Spirit whom Allah, the Most High, grants to whomever He wants. When He grants him to a servant he teaches him understanding.'"

H 716, Ch. 56, h 6

Muhammad ibn Yahya has narrated from Muhammad ibn al-Husayn from Ali ibn Asbat from al-Husayn ibn abu al-'Ala' from Sa'd al-Iskaf who has said the following:

"Once a man came to (Amir al-Mu'minin) Ali, *'Alayhi al-Salam*, asking him about the Spirit. 'Is he not Jibril?' (Amir al-Mu'minin) Ali, *'Alayhi al-Salam*, then said, 'Jibril is of the angels. The Spirit is not Jibril.' He repeated it to the man. The man said, 'You have said something very extraordinary. No one other than you thinks that the Spirit is someone other than Jibril.' (Amir al-Mu'minin) Ali, *'Alayhi al-Salam*, said to him, 'You are misled and narrate from the misled people. Allah, the Most High has said to His Prophet, *'Alayhi al-Salam*, "Allah's help will certainly support (the believers), so pagans do not (seek) to hasten it. Allah is Most Glorious and by far too exalted to be considered equal to idols. (16:1) He sends the angels with the Spirit."(16:2) The Spirit is (a creature) other than the angels (peace be upon them).'"

255

Chapter 57 - The Time When the Imam, *'Alayhi al-Salam*, Learns the Knowledge of the Imam Before Him

H 717, Ch. 57, h 1
Muhammad ibn Yahya has narrated from Ahmad ibn Muhammad from al-Husayn ibn Sa'id from Ali ibn Asbat from al-Hakam ibn Miskin from certain persons of our people who have said the following:
"I asked abu 'Abd Allah, *'Alayhi al-Salam*, 'When does the succeeding Imam come to know what the one preceding him knew?' The Imam said, 'At the last minute of the life of the Imam before him.'"

H 718, Ch. 57, h 2
Muhammad has narrated from Muhammad ibn al-Husayn from Ali ibn Asbat from al-Hakam ibn Miskin from 'Ubayd ibn Zurara and a group with him who have said the following:
"We heard abu 'Abd Allah, *'Alayhi al-Salam*, say, 'The succeeding Imam comes to know the knowledge in the last minute of the life of the preceding Imam.'"

H 719, Ch. 57, h 3
Muhammad ibn Yahya has narrated from Muhammad ibn al-Husayn from Ya'qub ibn Yazid from Ali ibn Asbat from certain persons of his people who have aid the following:
"Once I asked abu 'Abd Allah, *'Alayhi al-Salam*, 'When does the Imam come to know that he has become the Imam and the position (Leadership with Divine Authority) is transferred to him?' The Imam replied, 'At the last minute of the life of the preceding Imam, *'Alayhi al-Salam*.'"

Chapter 58 - 'A'immah, *'Alayhim al-Salam*, Are All Equal in Knowledge, Courage and Obedience

H 720, Ch. 58, h 1
Muhammad ibn Yahya has narrated from Ahmad ibn abu Zahir from al-Khashshab from Ali ibn Hass'an from 'Abd al-Rahman ibn Kathir from abu 'Abd Allah, *'Alayhi al-Salam*, who has said the following:
"About the words of Allah, the Most High, 'The offspring of the believers will also follow them to paradise. So we shall join their offspring to them because of their belief. We shall reduce nothing from their deeds. . . .'(52:21), the Imam, *'Alayhi al-Salam*, said, "Believers" refers to the Holy Prophet and (Amir al-Mu'minin) Ali, *'Alayhim al-Salam*, "Offspring" refers to 'A'immah and the executors of the wills, *'Alayhim al-Salam*. "We make them follow" means: Allah will not reduce anything from the Divine Authority of their offspring. It will be the same as that which Muhammad, *'Alayhi al-Salam*, had transferred to Ali, *'Alayhi al-Salam*.. Their authority is one and the same and obedience to them is of the same degree."

H 721, Ch. 58, h 2
Ali ibn Muhammad ibn 'Abd Allah has narrated from his father from Muhammad ibn 'Isa from Dawud al-Nahdi from Ali ibn Ja'far who has narrated the following from abu al-Hassan, *'Alayhi al-Salam*, who has said the following:
"In knowledge and courage we all are equal. In benefaction and grants we take part to the degree we are commanded."

H 722, Ch. 58, h 3

Ahmad ibn Muhammad has narrated from Muhammad ibn al-Hassan from Ali ibn Isma'il from Safwan ibn Yahya from ibn Muskan from al-Harith ibn al-Mughirah who has said that he heard abu 'Abd Allah, *'Alayhi al-Salam*, say the following:

"We, in the matters of commands, understanding, lawful and unlawful are all alike and the same. However, the Messenger of Allah and Ali, *'Alayhim al-Salam*, have their own additional virtue and excellence."

Chapter 59 - Every Imam Knows the Succeeding Imam, *'Alayhi al-Salam*

"The words of Allah, the Most High, 'Allah commands you to deliver the trust to its people,' (4:58) is a reference to *'A'immah*, *'Alayhim al-Salam*

H 723, Ch. 59, h 1

Al-Husayn ibn Muhammad has narrated from Mu'alla ibn Muhammad from al-Hassan ibn Ali al-Washsha' from Ahmad ibn 'A'idh from ibn 'Udhayna from Burayd al-'Ijli who has said the following:

"Once I asked abu Ja'far, *'Alayhi al-Salam*, about the words of Allah, the Majestic, the Glorious: 'Allah commands you to return that which had been entrusted to you to the rightful owners. Be just when passing judgment among people. . . .' (4:58) The Imam said, 'We are intended thereby. The preceding Imam must transfer to the succeeding Imam the books, the knowledge and the Armaments. "Be just when passing judgment among people" means (judge by) what is in your possession (in the form of laws and rules). Then Allah has said to people, 'Believers, obey Allah, His messenger, and your leaders (who possess Divine Authority). . . .' (4:59) He has intended us thereby particularly. He has commanded all believers to the Day of Judgment to obey us saying, 'If you fear disputes, then refer for a solution to Allah, the messenger and those who possess Divine Authority over you,' and this is how it was revealed. How would Allah, the Most Holy, the Most High, command them to obey the people who possess authority and then allow people to dispute them (people who possess Divine Authority)? This, (verse 59 of Chapter 4) is addressed to people who possess Divine Authority mentioned in: 'Believers, obey Allah, His Messenger, and your leaders (who possess Divine Authority). . . .'" (4:59)

H 724, Ch. 59, h 2

Al-Husayn ibn Muhammad has narrated from Mu'alla ibn Muhammad from al-Hassan ibn Ali al-Washsha' from Ahmad ibn 'Umar who has said the following:

"Once I asked abu al-Hassan al-Rida, *'Alayhi al-Salam*, about the words of Allah, the Most Holy, the Most High, 'Allah commands you to return that which had been entrusted to you to the rightful owners. Be just when passing judgment among people. . . .' (4:58)

"The Imam said, 'They are *'A'immah*, *'Alayhim al-Salam*, from the family of Muhammad, *'Alayhi al-Salam*, who are commanded to deliver the trust to the succeeding Imam exclusively and to no one else, and that the trust must not be concealed from the succeeding Imam, *'Alayhi al-Salam.'*"

H 725, Ch. 59, h 3
Muhammad ibn Yahya has narrated from Ahmad ibn Muhammad from al-Husayn ibn Sa'id from Muhammad ibn Fudayl who has said the following:
"Once I asked abu al-Hassan al-Rida, *'Alayhi al-Salam*, about the words of Allah, the Most Holy, the Most High, 'Allah commands you to return that which had been entrusted to you to the rightful owners. Be just when passing judgment among people . . .' (4:58)

"The Imam said, 'They are *A'immah, 'Alayhim al-Salam*. The Imam must deliver the trust to the succeeding Imam exclusively and to no one else, and the trust must not be concealed from succeeding Imam.'"

H 726, Ch. 59, h 4
Muhammad ibn Yahya has narrated from Ahmad ibn Muhammad from Muhammad ibn Sinan from Ishaq ibn 'Ammar from ibn abu Ya'fur from Mu'alla ibn al-Khunays who has said the following:
"I asked abu 'Abd Allah, *'Alayhi al-Salam*, about the words of Allah, the Most Holy, the Most High, 'Allah commands you to return that which had been entrusted to you to the rightful owners. . . .' (4:58)

"The Imam said, 'It is the command of Allah that the preceding Imam transfers to the succeeding Imam: everything that is with him.'"

H 727, Ch. 59, h 5
Muhammad ibn Yahya has narrated from Muhammad ibn al-Husayn from ibn Mahbub from al-'Ala' ibn Razin from 'Abd Allah ibn abu Ya'fur from abu 'Abd Allah, *'Alayhi al-Salam*, who has said the following:
"The preceding Imam, *'Alayhi al-Salam*, does not die until he learns who the succeeding Imam is, so he will deliver his "will" to him."

H 728, Ch. 59, h 6
Ahmad ibn Idris has narrated from Muhammad ibn 'Abd al-Jabbar from Safwan ibn Yahya from (ibn) abu 'Uthman from al-Mu'alla ibn Khunays from abu 'Abd Allah, *'Alayhi al-Salam*, who has said the following:
"The Imam, *'Alayhi al-Salam*, knows the succeeding Imam and delivers his will to him."

H 729, Ch. 59, h 7
Ahmad has narrated from Muhammad ibn 'Abd al-Jabbar from abu 'Abd Allah al-Barqi from Fadala ibn Ayyub from Sulayman ibn Khalid from abu 'Abd Allah, *'Alayhi al-Salam*, who has said the following:
"No scholar (Imam) has ever died before Allah, the Most Holy, the Most High, granted him the knowledge of to whom he must deliver his will."

Chapter 60 - Imamat (Leadership With Divine Authority) - A Covenant

Imamat (Leadership with Divine Authority) is a covenant from Allah, the Most Holy, the Most High, to be delivered as such by the preceding Imam to the succeeding Imam, *'Alayhi al-Salam*, one after the other.

H 730, Ch. 60, h 1

Al-Husayn ibn Muhammad has narrated from Mu'alla ibn Muhammad from al-Hassan ibn Ali al-Washsha' who has said that 'Umar ibn Aban has narrated to me from abu Basir who has said the following:

"Once I was in the presence of abu 'Abd Allah, *'Alayhi al-Salam*. People mentioned the executors of the will and I mentioned Isma'il. The Imam said, 'No, I swear by Allah. O abu Muhammad, it is not up to us. It is up to no one except Allah, the Most Holy, the Most High. He makes them descend one after the other.'"

H 731, Ch. 60, h 2

Muhammad ibn Yahya has narrated from Ahmad ibn Muhammad from al-Husayn ibn Sa'id from ibn abu 'Umayr from Hammad ibn 'Uthman from 'Amr ibn al-Ash'ath who has said the following:

"I heard abu 'Abd Allah, *'Alayhi al-Salam*, say, 'Do you think that a testator from us chooses whoever he wants as the executor of his will? No, I swear by Allah, it is not so. It is a covenant from Allah and His Messenger to a man and then to the next man until the matter is delivered to its (rightful) owner.'"

Al-Husayn ibn Muhammad has narrated from Mu'alla ibn Muhammad from Muhammad ibn Jumhur from Hammad ibn 'Isa from Minhal from 'Amr ibn al-Ash'ath from abu 'Abd Allah, *'Alayhi al-Salam*, a similar *Hadith*.

H 732, Ch. 60, h 3

Al-Husayn ibn Muhammad has narrated from Mu'alla ibn Muhammad from Ali ibn Muhammad from Bakr ibn Salih from Muhammad ibn Sulayman from 'Aytham ibn Aslama from Mu'awiya ibn 'Ammar from abu 'Abd Allah, *'Alayhi al-Salam*, who has said the following:

"Imamat (Leadership with Divine Authority) is a covenant from Allah, the Most Holy, the Most High, pledged to a particularly known man. The Imam, *'Alayhi al-Salam*, does not have the right to divert it from the succeeding Imam. Allah, the Most Holy, the Most High, sent inspiration to David to appoint the executor of his will from among the members of his family saying, 'It has occurred in My knowledge that I shall not send any prophet except that he will have the executor of his will from among the members of his family.'

"David had several children. Among the family members of David there was a son whose mother lived with David and he loved her very much. David came to her when the Divine inspiration came to him and he said to her, 'Allah, the Most Holy, the Most High, has sent me inspiration and He wants me to appoint the executor of my will from among the members of my family.' His wife asked him to appoint her son for this task. He said, 'I, also, want what you said.'

"In the foregone knowledge of Allah it already decisively existed that the executor of the will of David was Solomon. Allah, the Most Holy, the Most High, sent inspiration to David commanding him not to make hasty decisions before the coming of His order. It was not long after that two men came to David to settle a dispute over the sheep and grapes among them. Allah, the Most Holy, the Most High, sent inspiration to David to gather all of his sons together and let them judge the case. 'Whoever of your sons then can judge the case rightly he will be the executor of your will.' David gathered all his sons. When the case was stated Solomon said, 'O owner of grapes, when did the sheep of this man enter your vineyard?' He replied, 'They entered at night.' Solomon said, 'O owner of sheep, I have judged against you. You must give the young and the wool of your sheep to him this year.' David then said, 'Why did you not judge giving away the very sheep just as the Israelite scholars have already evaluated them and the price of sheep is equal to the value of grapes?' Solomon answered, 'The vines are not consumed from their roots but only the fruit is consumed. (The vine) will come back in future.' Allah, the Most Holy, the Most High, sent inspiration to David that the judgment in this case is the judgment of Solomon. O David, 'You wanted one thing and We had wanted other than that.'

"David came to his wife and said, 'We wanted one thing but Allah, the Most Holy, the Most High, wanted a thing other than that. Nothing happens other than what Allah, the Most Holy, the Most High, had wanted. We accept the command of Allah, the Most Holy, the Most High, and submit (to His will).'

"The Imam then said, 'And so are the executors of the wills. They have no right to go beyond the limit to make it available to the other people.'"

Al-Kulayni has said, "The meaning of the first *Hadith* is that had the sheep entered the vineyard during the day the owner of the sheep would not have to pay anything. The sheep owner must allow them to graze during the day and the vineyard owner must guard his vineyard. The owner of the sheep must guard his sheep at night and the owner of the vineyard can rest at home."

H 733, Ch. 60, h 4
Muhammad ibn Yahya has narrated from Ahmad ibn Muhammad from ibn abu 'Umayr from ibn Bukayr and Jamil from 'Amr ibn Mu'ab who has said the following:
"I heard abu 'Abd Allah, *'Alayhi al-Salam*, say, 'Do you think that a testator from us chooses whomever he wants as the executor of his will? No, I swear by Allah, it is not so. It (will) is a covenant of the Messenger of Allah with man and then to the next man. (The Imam mentioned all the preceeding 'A'immah, *'Alayhim al-Salam*, until the Imam (abu 'Abd Allah, *'Alayhi al-Salam*) ended up with himself.' So the Imam said six times, 'To the next man.'"

(The case with David and Solomon, peace be upon them, is mentioned in the Holy Quran. (21:78 – 79)

Chapter 61 - The Covenant of Allah, the Limit for the Activities of 'A'immah', *'Alayhim al-Salam*

'A'immah, *'Alayhim al-Salam*, never did and would not do anything except because of the covenant of Allah, the Most Holy, the Most High, and a command from Him, and they did not go beyond such limits.

H 734, Ch. 61, h 1

Muhammad ibn Yahya and al-Husayn ibn Muhammad have narrated from Ja'far ibn Muhammad from Ali ibn al-Husayn ibn Ali from Isma'il ibn Mihran from abu Jamila from Mu'adh ibn Kathir from abu 'Abd Allah, *'Alayhi al-Salam*, who has said the following:

"The will came from the heavens to Muhammad, *'Alayhi al-Salam*, in a book (written) form. Nothing came to Muhammad, *'Alayhi al-Salam*, from the heavens in a written sealed document form except the will. Jibril (Gabriel peace be on him) said, 'O Muhammad, *'Alayhi al-Salam*, this is your will to your followers about your family.' The Messenger of Allah asked, 'Which family of mine O Jibril.' Jibril replied, 'The one whom Allah has granted nobility among them (your family) and his descendents so they inherit knowledge of prophecy as Abraham left it (knowledge) as his legacy. This legacy of Abraham is for Ali, *'Alayhi al-Salam*, and your descendents from his lineage.'

"The Imam said, 'The document had several seals on it.' He further said, 'Ali, *'Alayhi al-Salam*, opened the first seal and followed the instructions therein. Then al-Hassan, *'Alayhi al-Salam*, opened the second seal and followed the commandments and instructions therein. When al-Hassan, *'Alayhi al-Salam*, passed away, then al-Husayn, *'Alayhi al-Salam*, opened the third seal and found therein instruction that said, 'Fight to do away with the enemy and be murdered and rise up (against the enemy) with a group of people for martyrdom. There will not be any martyrdom for them without you.' The Imam said, 'Al-Husayn, *'Alayhi al-Salam*, followed the instructions (entirely) and when he left this world he delivered it to Ali ibn al-Husayn, *'Alayhi al-Salam*, just before his martyrdom. Ali ibn al-Husayn, *'Alayhi al-Salam*, opened the fourth seal and found in it instruction to remain silent and gaze in front because of the concealment of knowledge (widespread injustice and ignorance). Just before his passing away he delivered it to Muhammad ibn Ali, *'Alayhi al-Salam*. He opened the fifth seal and found therein instructions that said, 'Interpret the Book of Allah, the Most High, affirm veracity of his father and leave it as his legacy for his son. Do good to the 'Umma (nation), stand up for the right of Allah, the Most Holy, the Most High, say the truth in fear and in peace and do not be afraid of anyone except Allah.' He did as he was instructed and delivered it to the succeeding Imam.'

"I (the narrator) said to the Imam, 'May Allah keep my soul in service for your cause, are you then the succeeding Imam?' He then said, 'There is nothing wrong in a positive answer to your question except if then you go, O Mu'adh, and narrate to people things that may harm me.'

"I (the narrator) then said to the Imam, 'I pray to Allah who has granted you, through your noble ancestors, this high position to grant to your successor the same high position before you will die.' The Imam said, 'Allah has already done so, O Mu'adh.'

" I (the narrator) then asked the Imam, 'Who then is he, may Allah keep my soul in service for your cause?' The Imam replied, 'This sleeping one.' He pointed with his hand to the righteous servant of Allah who was asleep (Musa ibn Ja'far), *'Alayhi al-Salam*."

H 735, Ch. 61, h 2

Ahmad ibn Muhammad and Muhammad ibn Yahya have narrated from Muhammad ibn al-Husayn from Ahmad ibn Muhammad from abu al-Hassan al-Kinani from Ja'far ibn Najih al-Kindi from Muhammad ibn Ahmad ibn 'Ubayd Allah al-'Umari from his father from his grandfather from abu 'Abd Allah, *'Alayhi al-Salam*, who has said the following:

"Allah, the Most Holy, the Most High sent a document to His prophet, *'Alayhi al-Salam*, before his death. He then said, 'O Muhammad, this is your will to the noble ones in your family.' He asked, 'Who are the noble ones in my family, O Jibril (Gabriel)?' He then said, 'They are Ali ibn abu Talib and his sons, *'Alayhim al-Salam*,' On the document there were several seals of gold. The Prophet, *'Alayhi al-Salam*, delivered it to (Amir al-Mu'minin) Ali, *'Alayhi al-Salam*, and commanded him to open one seal and follow the instructions for him therein. (Amir al-Mu'minin) Ali, *'Alayhi al-Salam*, then opened one seal and followed the instructions in it. Then he delivered it to his son al-Hassan, *'Alayhi al-Salam*. He opened a seal and followed that which was therein (to follow). He then delivered it to al-Husayn, *'Alayhi al-Salam*. He opened one seal and found therein instructions that asked him to rise for martyrdom with a group of people. That there will be no martyrdom for them except along with him (al-Husayn) and to sell himself to Allah, the Most Holy, the Most High. He followed all the instructions. Then he delivered it to Ali ibn al-Husayn, *'Alayhi al-Salam*. He opened one seal and found therein instructions that asked him to fix his gaze just before him and remain silent, secluded in his house, and worship his Lord until his death will arrive. He did as he was instructed and then delivered it (the sealed document) to his son Muhammad ibn Ali, *'Alayhi al-Salam*. He opened one seal and found therein instructions that asked him to speak to people and make them learn. That he should not fear anyone except Allah, the Most Holy, the Most High; no one can harm him. He followed the instructions and then delivered it to his son Ja'far, *'Alayhi al-Salam*. He opened one seal and found therein instructions that asked him to speak to people, make them learn, propagate the knowledge of his family (*Ahl al-Bayt*) and affirm the veracity of his righteous ancestors. That he should not be afraid of anyone except Allah, the Most Holy, the Most High; he is secure and safe. He did as was instructed and then delivered it to his son Musa, *'Alayhi al-Salam*. In the same way Musa, *'Alayhi al-Salam*, will deliver it to the succeeding Imam and so on up to the appearance of al-Mahdi, *'Alayhi al-Salam*.'"

H 736, Ch. 61, h 3

Muhammad ibn Yahya has narrated from Ahmad ibn Muhammad from ibn Mahbub from ibn Ri'ab from Durays al-Kunasi from Humran who has said the following:

"Once Humran asked abu Ja'far, *'Alayhi al-Salam*, 'May Allah keep my soul in service for your cause, why did the cases of Ali, al-Hassan and al-Husayn, *'Alayhim al-Salam*, come about the way they did? We know about their rising and coming out for the religion of Allah, the Most Holy, the Most High, about their sufferings and being murdered at the hands of the rebellious devils and their defeat until they all were murdered and defeated.'

"Abu Ja'far, *'Alayhi al-Salam*, then said, 'O Humran, Allah, the Most Holy, the Most High, had destined it for them. So it was decreed, approved and was made unavoidable. Then He executed it but it all happened with the prior knowledge of the same through the Messenger of Allah, Ali, al-Hassan and al-Husayn, *'Alayhim al-Salam*. They all stood up for the cause of Allah, with the knowledge of the consequences. There were those of us who remained silent (without armed uprising against the enemies).'"

H 737, Ch. 61, h 4

Al-Husayn ibn Muhammad al-Ash'ari has narrated from Mu'alla ibn Muhammad from Ahmad ibn Muhammad from al-Harith ibn Ja'far from Ali ibn Isma'il ibn Yaqtin from 'Isa ibn al-Mustafad, abu Musa al-Darir who has said the following:

"Musa ibn Ja'far, *'Alayhi al-Salam*, narrated to me: 'I said to abu 'Abd Allah, *'Alayhi al-Salam*, "Was (Amir al-Mu'minin) Ali, *'Alayhi al-Salam*, not the writer of the will, the Messenger of Allah dictating, Jibril and the prominent angels witnessed?"'

"The Imam (Musa ibn Ja'far, *'Alayhi al-Salam*) said that he remained silent for quite a while and then said, 'O abu al-Hassan, what you said was true, however, when the command descended upon the Messenger of Allah, the will also came in the form of a sealed document. Jibril brought it along with the trustees of Allah, the Most Holy, the Most High, from among the angels. Jibril then said, "O Muhammad, *'Alayhi al-Salam*, order every one to leave you except the executor of your will so he can take possession of the same and make us to bear witness that you delivered it to him and he (Ali, *'Alayhi al-Salam*) took charge of the same in our presence. The Holy Prophet, *'Alayhi al-Salam*, ordered everyone else to leave the house, except Ali, *'Alayhi al-Salam*. Fatimah, *'Alayha al-Salam*, was present between the door and the curtain. Jibril then said, 'O Muhammad, your Lord declares peace and safety to you and says, "This is the documentation of My covenant that I had made with you, the conditions that I had set up and I had made My angels to bear witness to it. In fact, O Muhammad, I Myself am sufficient as a witness."'"

"The Imam has said, 'At that time all the joints in the body of Muhammad began to shake and shiver. He then said, 'O Jibril, my Lord Himself is peace, from Him comes peace and to Him returns peace. He, Allah, the Most Holy, the Most High, has spoken the truth and has granted favors. Please allow me to have the document.'

'Jibril then delivered it to him and commanded him to deliver it to (Amir al-Mu'minin) Ali, *'Alayhi al-Salam*. He asked Ali, *'Alayhi al-Salam*, to read it. He then read it word by word. The Prophet, *'Alayhi al-Salam*, then said, 'O Ali, *'Alayhi al-Salam*, this is the (text of the) covenant of my Lord, the Most Holy, the Most High, to me and His conditions upon me and His trust with me. I have now delivered it, given good advice and fulfilled my responsibility.'

'Ali, *'Alayhi al-Salam*, then said, 'I testify in your favor, may Allah keep my soul and the souls of my parents in service for your cause, for delivering the trust, granting good advice and affirmation of your speaking the truth. My ears, my eyes, my flesh and my blood all bear witness to this.' Jibril then said, 'I also am of the witnesses to this fact for both of you.'

'The Messenger of Allah, *'Alayhi al-Salam*, then said, 'O Ali, have you taken possession of my will, learned its contents and offered a guarantee to Allah and to me to follow the instructions therein?'

'Ali, *'Alayhi al-Salam*, then said, 'Yes, may Allah keep my soul and the souls of my parents in service for your cause, it is my responsibility to follow the instructions therein and from Allah comes support for me and my success in the fulfillment of my responsibility.' The Messenger of Allah then said, 'O Ali, I want to ask you to bear testimony to my promise of rewarding for it (your executing my will) on the Day of Judgment.'

'Ali, *'Alayhi al-Salam*, said, 'Yes, I do bear such testimony.' The Prophet, *'Alayhi al-Salam*, then said, 'Jibril and Mika'il are between us now and with them present are the prominent angels. Would you agree if I ask them to bear testimony to this fact?' He then said, 'Yes, they may bear testimony and I, may Allah keep my soul and the souls of my parents in service for your cause, also ask them to bear testimony.' Then the Messenger of Allah made them to bear testimony. Of the matters that the Messenger of Allah set as conditions upon Ali, *'Alayhi al-Salam*, on orders from Jibril of the commands of Allah, the Most Holy, the Most High, were the following:

'O Ali, you must follow the instruction in the will about loving those who love Allah and His Messenger and to disdaining and maintaining an unfriendly attitude toward those who are enemies of Allah and His Messenger. It requires patience on your part and control over your anger for the usurpation of my right and the usurpation of one -fifth that belongs to you and for the disregard of your respect and honor."

'Ali, *'Alayhi al-Salam*, then said, 'Yes, O the Messenger of Allah, I accept it (this condition).' Ali, *'Alayhi al-Salam*, has said, 'I swear by the One Who helps the seed to burst open and shapes the fetuses that I heard Jibril say to the Prophet, *'Alayhi al-Salam*, this, "O Muhammad, explain to him that people will disregard his respect and honor which is the respect and honor of Allah and His Messenger and that his beard will be tainted with fresh blood (from his head)."

'(Amir al-Mu'minin) Ali, *'Alayhi al-Salam*, has said, 'A loud sigh came out of my mouth when I understood the very words of Jibril, the trustworthy one. I fell upon my face to the ground and I said, "Yes, I accept and agree, even if it will end up with the disregard of respect to my honor and me. (I agree) even if (people) will disregard the noble traditions, insult the Book, destroy the Ka'ba and taint my beard with fresh blood from my head. (I accept it) with patience and leave to Allah for judgment for all times until I will arrive to meet you."'

'The Messenger of Allah then called Fatimah, al-Hassan and al-Husayn, *'Alayhim al-Salam*, to his presence and informed them of what he had explained to (Amir al-Mu'minin) Ali, *'Alayhi al-Salam*. They all said just what Ali, *'Alayhi al-Salam*, had said. The will was then sealed with the seals of gold that fire had not touched. It was delivered to (Amir al-Mu'minin) Ali, *'Alayhi al-Salam*.

"I (the narrator) then asked the Imam, abu al-Hassan, *'Alayhi al-Salam*, 'May Allah take my soul and the souls of my parents in service for your cause, would you please describe what was there in the will?' The Imam said, 'It contained the traditions of Allah and the traditions of His Messenger.' I then asked, 'Was there anything about their (enemies) attacking and opposition to (Amir al-Mu'minin) Ali, *'Alayhi al-Salam*?' The Imam said, 'Yes, I swear by Allah, all and everything was there, letter by letter. Have you not heard the words of Allah, the Most Holy, the Most High, "It is We that bring the dead to life and record the deeds of human beings and their consequences (of continual effects). We keep everything recorded in an illustrious Imam (Book)." (36:12) I swear by Allah that the Messenger of Allah said to (Amir al-Mu'minin) Ali, *'Alayhi al-Salam*, and Fatimah, 'Did you understand well my presentation of the matter to you and did you agree to and accept it?' They replied, 'Yes, we did so. We will exercise patience to face what will disappoint us and cause us anger.'"

In the script of al-Safwan there is the following addition:

"Ali in Ibrahim has narrated from his father from 'Abd Allah ibn 'Abd al-Rahman al-'Assam from abu 'Abd Allah al-Bazzaz from Hariz who has said the following:

"I said to abu 'Abd Allah, *'Alayhi al-Salam*, 'May Allah keep my soul in service for your cause, why is it that you, members of the family of the Prophet, *'Alayhim al-Salam*, live such short lives? Your deaths are so close and soon after the other Imam even though people need you so much?'

"The Imam said, 'For every one of us there is a document that contains what he needs to do within his time. When his assignment according to the commandments therein is complete, he learns that his time of death has arrived. The Prophet, *'Alayhi al-Salam*, comes to him to give the news of his death and informs him of all that is for him with Allah.

'Al-Husayn, *'Alayhi al-Salam*, read the document that was given to him and the news of his death was explained to him, however, certain things were not yet complete. He came out to face the enemy, and those matters that were not yet complete were that the angels had asked Allah to grant them permission to support al-Husayn, *'Alayhi al-Salam*, against his enemies, which He granted them. In readying themselves they were delayed and when they were prepared to fight, he was murdered. They descended but his time was over and he was already killed. The angels said, 'Lord, You granted us permission to descend and to help him. We descended but You have already taken his soul away. Allah then sent them inspiration that said, 'Remain on his grave until you see him come out, then help him. Weep for him and for your loss of the opportunity to provide him help and support. You were certainly assigned for his support and help and to weep for him. The angels then wept in mourning and sadness for their loss of the opportunity to help and support to him. When he comes out they will be of his helpers.'"

Chapter 62 - Evidence of Imam's, *'Alayhi al-Salam*, Possessing Divine Authority

H 738, Ch. 62, h 1
Muhammad ibn Yahya has narrated from Ahmad ibn Muhammad from ibn abu Nasr who has said the following:

"Once I asked abu al-Hassan al-Rida, *'Alayhi al-Salam*, 'When the Imam dies, through what means can one know the succeeding Imam?' He said, 'For the Imam there are certain signs. Of such signs one is that he must be the eldest son of his father (of the living ones). The "will" and distinction in excellence must be found in him and when people come to ask who is appointed the executor of the will in answer it can be said that so and so is appointed the executor of the will. The Armament with us is like the Ark of Covenant in the Israelites. Imamat (Leadership with Divine Authority) is always with the Armament wherever it may go.'"

H 739, Ch. 62, h 2
Muhammad ibn Yahya has narrated from Muhammad ibn al-Husayn from Yazid Sha'r from Harun ibn Hamza from 'Abd al-A'la who has said the following:

"I asked abu 'Abd Allah, *'Alayhi al-Salam*, 'In the case of those who rush to hold control of this matter (leadership) and who claim to be for it, how can one verify their possessing Divine Authority?'

"The Imam said, 'They are asked about the rules of lawful and unlawful matters.'

"The Imam then turned to me and said, 'There are three forms of evidence that are not found in one person except the rightful owner of this status. He must be the closest person to the preceding Imam, the Armament must be with him and he must be appointed the executor of the will in a public manner, so much so that if one comes to the town and asks the common people, even the children, about who the executor of the will of so and so is, they say so and so is the executor of the will of so and so.'"

H 740, Ch. 62, h 3

Ali ibn Ibrahim has narrated from his father from ibn abu 'Umayr from Hisham ibn Salim and Hafs ibn al-Bakhtari who has said the following:

"Once a certain person asked abu 'Abd Allah, *'Alayhi al-Salam*, 'By what means is the Imam recognized?' He said, 'He is recognized through a publicly established will and through distinctive excellence in perfection. In the case of Imam no one must be able to raise objections against him in matters of (the words from) his mouth, his consumption of food and sexual matters. People must not be able to say, "He is a liar, usurping others' properties and such similar things."

H 741, Ch. 62, h 4

Muhammad ibn Yahya has narrated from Muhammad ibn Isma'il from Ali ibn al-Hakam from Mu'awiya ibn Wahab who has said the following:

"I asked abu Ja'far, *'Alayhi al-Salam*, 'What is the sign of being an Imam after the preceding Imam?' The Imam said, 'Being of pure birth, having good upbringing and not trifling or engaging in amusement.'"

H 742, Ch. 62, h 5

Ali ibn Ibrahim has narrated from Muhammad ibn 'Isa from Yunus from Ahmad ibn 'Umar who has said the following:

"I asked abu al-Hassan al-Rida, *'Alayhi al-Salam*, 'What is the proof that establishes one's possessing Divine Authority or being the person in charge of leadership?' 'Of such proofs are being the eldest (among the sons of the preceding Imam), possessing superior moral achievements and being appointed as the executor of the will, so much so that if people come to the town and ask who is appointed as the executor of the will of so and so, it can be said to them so and so, son of so and so, and these go along wherever the Armament go. Asking questions does not establish any authority,' said the Imam, *'Alayhi al-Salam*."

H 743, Ch. 62, h 6

Muhammad ibn Yahya has narrated from Ahmad ibn Muhammad from abu Yahya al-Wasiti from Hisham ibn Salim from abu 'Abd Allah, *'Alayhi al-Salam*, who has said the following:

"The leadership is with being the eldest (of the sons of the preceding Imam) as long as he is free of defects."

H 744, Ch. 62, h 7

Ahmad ibn Mihran has narrated from Muhammad ibn Ali from abu Basir who has said the following:

"I asked abu al-Hassan, *'Alayhi al-Salam*, 'May Allah keep my soul in service for your cause, by what proofs can one know the Imam, *'Alayhi al-Salam*?' He said, 'Through several qualities. The first thing is that his father must have spoken about him in this matter so that it could be considered a proof:. that when asked he would answer, and if one remained silent, he would begin to speak on the issue and inform of the things that would happen the next day; that he can speak to people in everyone's own language.' Then he said, 'O abu Muhammad, allow me to give you a sign before you stand up to go.' Not very long after this, a man from Khurasan came in. The man from Khurasan spoke to the Imam in Arabic but abu al-Hassan, *'Alayhi al-Salam*, answered him in Persian. The man from Khurasan said, 'I swear by Allah, may Allah keep my soul in service for your cause, the only thing that stopped me from speaking to you in Persian was I thought you might not know Persian.' He then said, 'Glory belongs to Allah, if the Imam would not be able to answer you (in Persian) then how would he have any distinctive excellence over you?' He said to me, 'O abu Muhammad, no one's language is unknown to the Imam, *'Alayhi al-Salam*, the language of birds, animals and any living thing. Whoever does not have these qualities, he is not an Imam.'"

Chapter 63 - Continuation of Leadership With Divine Authority

Proof that Imamat (Leadership with Divine Authority) continues in the descendent of the preceding Imam but not through his brother or paternal uncle or other such relatives

H 745, Ch. 63, h 1
Ali ibn Ibrahim has narrated from Muhammad ibn 'Isa from Yunus from al-Husayn ibn Thuwayr ibn abu Fakhta from abu 'Abd Allah, *'Alayhi al-Salam*, who has said the following:
"Imamat (Leadership with Divine Authority) will never go to two brothers after al-Hassan and al-Husayn, *'Alayhim al-Salam*. It has continued from Ali ibn al-Husayn, *'Alayhi al-Salam*, as Allah, the Most Holy, the Most High, has said, 'The relatives are closer to each other, according to the Book of Allah. . . .' (33:6) After Imam Ali ibn al-Husayn, *'Alayhi al-Salam*, Imamat (Leadership with Divine Authority) will only be found in the descendents one after the other.'"

H 746, Ch. 63, h 2
Ali ibn Muhammad has narrated from Sahl ibn Ziyad from Muhammad ibn Walid from Yunus ibn Ya'qub who has said the following:
"I heard abu 'Abd Allah, *'Alayhi al-Salam*, say, 'Allah has disdained to place Imamat (Leadership with Divine Authority) in two brothers after al-Hassan and al-Husayn, *'Alayhim al-Salam*.'"

H 747, Ch. 63, h 3
Muhammad ibn Yahya has narrated from Ahmad ibn Muhammad ibn 'Isa from Muhammad ibn Isma'il ibn Bazi' who has said the following:
"Abu al-Hassan al-Rida, *'Alayhi al-Salam*, was once asked, 'Can Imamat (Leadership with Divine Authority) continue in uncles?' He replied, 'No, it cannot happen.'

"I (the narrator) then asked the Imam, 'Can it continue in a brother?' He replied, 'No, it can not happen.' I then asked, 'With whom then can it continue?' He replied, 'It will continue with my children.' In those days he had no children."

H 748, Ch. 63, h 4
Muhammad ibn Yahya has narrated from Muhammad ibn al-Husayn from 'Abd al-Rahman ibn abu Najran from Sulayman ibn Ja'fari from Hammad ibn 'Isa from abu 'Abd Allah, *'Alayhi al-Salam*, who has said the following:
"Imamat (Leadership with Divine Authority) does not take place in two brothers after al-Hassan and al-Husayn, *'Alayhim al-Salam*. It only continues in the descendents of the Imam, *'Alayhi al-Salam*, generation after generation."

H 749, Ch. 63, h 5

Muhammad ibn Yahya has narrated from Muhammad ibn al-Husayn from ibn abu Najran from 'Isa ibn 'Abd Allah ibn 'Umar ibn Ali ibn abu Talib, *'Alayhi al-Salam*, who has said the following:

"I asked abu 'Abd Allah, *'Alayhi al-Salam*, 'If there happens what is to happen - I wish Allah does not show me such a day (the of the death of the Imam) - who then must I follow as my Imam?'

"The Imam pointed to his son, Musa, *'Alayhi al-Salam*. I (the narrator) then asked the Imam, 'What if something were to happen to Musa, *'Alayhi al-Salam*? Whom then must I follow?' The Imam said, 'Follow a son.' I then asked, 'What if something were to happen to the son and the Imam left behind an elder brother or a small son, then whom must I follow?' The Imam said, 'Follow his son and so on one after the other.'" In the script of Safwan it says, " . . . and so on forever."

Chapter 64 - Proof of Leadership With Divine Authority in the Words of Allah and His Messenger

The specific words of Allah, the Most Holy, the Most High, and the Messenger of Allah that grant Divine Authority to everyone of 'A'immah, *'Alayhim al-Salam*.

H 750, Ch. 64, h 1

Ali ibn Ibrahim has narrated from Muhammad ibn 'Isa from Yunus and Ali ibn Muhammad from Sahl ibn Ziyad, abu Sa'id from Muhammad ibn 'Isa from Yunus from ibn Muskan from abu Basir who has said the following:

"I asked abu 'Abd Allah, *'Alayhi al-Salam*, about the words of Allah, the Most Holy, the Most High: 'Believers, obey Allah, His Messenger, and your leaders (who possess Divine Authority). . . .' (4:59)

"The Imam said, 'This was sent from the heavens about Ali ibn abu Talib, al-Hassan and al-Husayn, *'Alayhim al-Salam*.' I then said, 'People say, "Why did He not specify Ali and his family by their names in the Book of Allah, the Most Holy, the Most High?'

"The Imam said, 'Say to them, "The command for prayer came to the Messenger of Allah but He has not specified (the number of the Rak'ats) for them as being three or four. It, in fact, was the Messenger of Allah who explained to them this matter. The command for *Zakat* (a form of income tax) came to the Messenger of Allah and there was no specific taxable figure such as one Dirham on every forty Dirham. It was the Messenger of Allah who explained it for them. The command for Hajj came to the Messenger of Allah. It did not say to walk seven times around the Ka'ba. It was the Messenger of Allah who explained it for them. The verse about obedience came, 'Believers, obey Allah, His Messenger and your leaders (who possess Divine Authority). . . .' (4:59) It came to declare that Ali, al-Hassan and al-Husayn, *'Alayhim al-Salam*, were the Leaders who possessed Divine Authority. The Messenger of Allah then said about Ali, *'Alayhi al-Salam*, 'Over whomever I have Divine Authority, Ali, *'Alayhi al-Salam*, also has Divine

Authority over him.' He also has said, 'I enjoin you to follow the Book of Allah and my family. It is because I have prayed to Allah, the Most Holy, the Most High, not to separate these two from each other until He will make them arrive at *al-Kawthar* (the pond of paradise) to join me. He has granted my prayer as such.'

"The Holy Prophet, *'Alayhi al-Salam*, has said, 'Do not try to teach them (*'A'immah*); they are far more knowledgeable than you.' The Holy Prophet has said, '*'A'immah, 'Alayhim al-Salam*, will never take you out of the gate of guidance and they will never make you enter the gate of error.' Had the Messenger of Allah remained silent and had not explained anything about his *Ahl al-Bayt* (the family) the family of so and so would have advanced their claim for Imamat (Leadership with Divine Authority). However, Allah, the Most Holy, the Most High, has revealed it in His book to confirm the explanations of His Prophet about *Ahl al-Bayt* (in the following verse): 'People of the house, Allah wants to remove all kinds of uncleanness from you and to purify you thoroughly.' (33:33) Ali, Fatimah, al-Hassan and al-Husayn, *'Alayhim al-Salam*, were there and the Holy Prophet made them to enter under *al-Kisa'* (the Cloak) in the house of 'Umm Salama and then said, 'O Lord, every prophet had a family and a heaviness and credence, and these are my family, my heaviness and credence.' 'Umm Salama at this point said, 'Am I not of your family?' The Holy Prophet said, 'You are in goodness but these are my family, my heaviness and credence.'

"When the Messenger of Allah passed away Ali, *'Alayhi al-Salam*, had the utmost priority and guardianship of the people because of what the Messenger of Allah had preached about him. It was because of raising him up for the people and holding his hand in his hand. When Ali, *'Alayhi al-Salam*, (was about to) pass away he could not (and would not) enter Muhammad ibn Ali or al-'Abbass ibn Ali or any one of his other sons in the position of Imamat (Leadership with Divine Authority). Otherwise, al-Hassan and al-Husayn, *'Alayhim al-Salam*, would have said, 'Allah, the Most Holy, the Most High, has revealed about us just as He has done so about you, and He has commanded people to obey us just as He has commanded people to obey you. The Messenger of Allah has preached to people about us just as he has done so about you. Allah has removed *al-Rijs* (uncleanness) from us just as He has done so to you.'

"When Ali, *'Alayhi al-Salam*, left this world, al-Hassan had the utmost priority for Imamat (Leadership with Divine Authority); he was the eldest. When he was about to die he could not, and would not, enter his sons in the position of Imamat. It is because Allah, the Most Holy, the Most High, says, '. . . The relatives are closer to each other, according to the Book of Allah, than the believers and the emigrants. . . .' (33:6) Had he then placed Imamat in his sons, al-Husayn, *'Alayhi al-Salam*, would have said, 'Allah has commanded people to obey me just as He has commanded people to obey you and to obey your father. The Messenger of Allah has preached to people about me just as he has preached to people about you and your father. Allah has removed *al-Rijs* (uncleanness) from me just as He has removed it from you and your father.'

"When Imamat was in full force with al-Husayn, *'Alayhi al-Salam*, there was no one in his family who could claim against him as he could claim against his brother and father. He could do so in case they had (his father and brother) wanted to divert it from him but they did not and would not do so. After them it found its place with al-Husayn, *'Alayhi al-Salam*, and the interpretation of this verse continued to remain valid, '. . . The relatives are closer to each other, according to the Book of Allah, than the believers and the emigrants. . . .' (33:6)

"After al-Husayn, *'Alayhi al-Salam*, Imamat found its place with Ali ibn al-Husayn, *'Alayhi al-Salam*. After Ali ibn al-Husayn, *'Alayhi al-Salam*, it (Leadership with Divine Authority) found its place with Muhammad ibn Ali, *'Alayhi al-Salam*.' The Imam said, *'Al-Rijs* means doubts. I swear by Allah that we never doubt in our Lord.'"

Muhammad ibn Yahya has narrated from Ahmad ibn Muhammad ibn 'Isa from Muhammad ibn Khalid and al-Husayn ibn Sa'id from al-Nadr ibn Suwayd from Yahya ibn 'Imran al-Halabi from Ayyub ibn al-Hurr and 'Imran ibn Ali al-Halabi from abu 'Abd Allah, *'Alayhi al-Salam*, a similar *Hadith*.

H 751, Ch. 64, h 2

Muhammad ibn Yahya has narrated from Ahmad ibn Muhammad ibn 'Isa from his father from 'Abd Allah ibn al-Mughira from ibn Muskan from 'Abd al-Rahim ibn Ruh al-Qasir who has said the following:

"Once I asked abu Ja'far, *'Alayhi al-Salam*, about whom this verse of the words of Allah, the Most Holy, the Most High, has come? 'The Prophet has more authority over the believers than they themselves do. His wives are their mothers. The relatives are closer to each other, according to the Book of Allah, than the believers and the emigrants. However, you may show kindness to your guardians. This also is written in the Book.' (33:6) He (the Imam) then said, 'It (the above verse) came about the governance (Leadership with Divine Authority). This verse continued to apply to people of the lineage of al-Husayn, *'Alayhi al-Salam*, after him. We, have the right to exercise governance (Leadership with Divine Authority) and we are closer to the Messenger of Allah than the believers of immigrants and the Ansar.'

"I (the narrator) then asked the Imam 'Do the sons of Ja'far have any share in it?' The Imam said, 'No, they do not have any share in it.' I asked, 'Do the sons of al-'Abbass have any share in it?' He said, 'No, they do not have any share in it.' I counted for him the people from the descendents of 'Abd al-Muttalib and in answer to all he said, 'No.'

"I (the narrator) forgot the sons of al-Hassan, *'Alayhi al-Salam*. I went to see him at another time and asked him, 'Do the sons of al-Hassan, *'Alayhi al-Salam*, have any share in it?' He replied, 'No, I swear by Allah, O 'Abd al-Rahim, no one related to Muhammad, *'Alayhi al-Salam*, has any share in it except us.'"

H 752, Ch. 64, h 3

Al-Husayn ibn Muhammad has narrated from Mu'alla ibn Muhammad from Ahmad ibn Muhammad from al-Hassan ibn Muhammad al-Hashimi from his father from Ahmad ibn 'Isa from abu 'Abd Allah, *'Alayhi al-Salam,* who has said the following:

About the words of Allah, the Most Holy, the Most High, 'Only Allah, His Messenger, and the true believers who are steadfast in prayer and pay alms, while they kneel during prayer, are your guardians,' (5:55) the Imam, *'Alayhi al-Salam,* has said, 'It means to have greater right and authority to deal with your affairs, your souls and your property. Such right, priority and authority belong to Allah, His Messenger and the believers. Thus, Ali, *'Alayhi al-Salam,* and his descendents are *'A'immah* until the Day of Judgment. Allah, the Most Holy, the Most High, has then described them saying, ". . . the true believers who are steadfast in prayer and pay alms, while they kneel during prayer. . . ." (5:55) "True believers" in the above verse stand for Amir al-Mu'minin, Ali, *'Alayhi al-Salam*; he was praying *Zuhr* prayer (early afternoon). He was in the second *Ruku'* (bowing down on his knees in prayer), wearing a gown worth a thousand Dinars (unit of money), which the Holy Prophet made him to wear and King Najashi had sent as a present to him. At such time a beggar came and said the Islamic greeting words, "Be in peace, O Allah's authority and the authority over the believers who possesses greater right and priority over them than themselves. Give charity to a destitute person." He (Imam Ali) threw the gown to the beggar and pointed with his hand to pick up and take it. About this happening Allah, the Most Holy, the Most High, sent verse 55 of Chapter 5 of the Holy Quran. He granted him His blessings in the form of his children. Whoever of his children with whom Imamat (Leadership with Divine Authority) found place, in the matters of charity was like him. They would give charity while bowed down in Ruku' of prayer. The beggar that asked (Amir al-Mu'minin) Ali, *'Alayhi al-Salam,* for charity was from the angels. Those who ask *'A'immah* from his children will also be from the angels.'"

H 753, Ch. 64, h 4

Ali ibn Ibrahim from his father from Ibn Abu 'Umayr from 'Umar ibn Udhayna from Zurara and Fudayl ibn Yasar and Bukayr ibn A'yan and Muhammad ibn Muslim and Burayd ibn Mu'awiya and abu al-Jarud, all have said that abu Ja'far, *'Alayhi al-Salam,* has said the following:

"Allah, the Most Majestic, the Most Gracious, commanded His Messenger to declare the Leadership with Divine Authority of Ali, *'Alayhi al-Salam,* and sent down to him this: 'Only Allah, His Messenger, and (also) the true believers who are steadfast in prayer and pay alms, while they kneel during prayer (in *Ruku'*), are your guardians (with Divine Authority).' (5:55) He made obedience to those in authority obligatory. The people did not know who they were. Allah commanded Muhammad, *'Alayhi al-Salam,* to interpret (and explain) the 'Authority' for them as he had interpreted (and explained) Prayer, *Zakat,* Fasting and Hajj. When this command (to obey those who possess Divine Authority) came to him from Allah, the Messenger of Allah felt pressured (and afraid of people's abandoning their religion). He prayed to Allah, the Most Majestic, the Most Gracious, about it and Allah, the Most Majestic, the Most Gracious, revealed to him this: 'O Messenger, preach what is revealed to you from your Lord. If you do not preach, it will be as though you have not conveyed My message. Allah protects you from men. He does not guide the unbelieving people.' (5:67) He executed the

272

command of Allah, Most Exalted is Whose mention, and declared that Ali, *'Alayhi al-Salam*, had received Divine Authority for leadership over His creatures. He made this declaration on the day of Ghadir-e Khumm (18ᵗʰ of Dhu al-Hajja). After the prayer in congregation he conveyed the command and asked people present to bear testimony and inform those who were absent.

"'Umar ibn 'Udhayna has said, 'All, except abu al-Jarud, have narrated this *Hadith*.'

"Abu Ja'far, *'Alayhi al-Salam*, said: 'One commandment would come after the other and the commandment about Leadership and Guardianship with Divine Authority was the last of such commandments. Allah, the Most Majestic, the Most Gracious, then sent down this: 'On this day I have perfected your religion, completed My favors to you, and chosen Islam as your religion. . . .' (5:3) Abu Ja'far, *'Alayhi al-Salam*, said, 'Allah, the Most Majestic, the Most Gracious, said, 'I will not send down any other commandments thereafter. I have completed for you the commandments.'"

H 754, Ch. 64, h 5
Ali ibn Ibrahim has narrated from Salih ibn al-Sindi from Ja'far ibn Bashir from Harun ibn Kharija from abu Basir who has said the following:
"Once I was in the presence of abu Ja'far, *'Alayhi al-Salam*, and a man asked him, 'Please speak to me about the Divine Authority of Ali, *'Alayhi al-Salam*. Is it from Allah or from His Messenger?'

"The Imam who seemed angry said, 'Fie upon you, the Messenger of Allah was the most God fearing person. He would never declare it before Allah commanded him to do so. In fact, He made it obligatory as He has made Prayer, *Zakat*, Fasting and Hajj obligatory.'"

H 755, Ch. 64, h 6
Muhammad ibn Yahya has narrated from Ahmad ibn Muhammad and Muhammad ibn al-Husayn, both of them from Muhammad ibn Isma'il ibn Bazi' from Mansur ibn Yunus from abu al-Jarud who has said the following:
"I heard abu Ja'far, *'Alayhi al-Salam*, say, 'Allah, the Most Holy, the Most High, has commanded people to fulfill five obligations. They have undertaken the responsibility for four of these obligations but they have ignored one.'

"The narrator has said, 'I asked the Imam, 'May Allah keep my soul in service for your cause, will you please, describe them for me?' The Imam said, 'The Prayer is one of such obligations. People did not know how to perform the Prayer. Jibril (Gabriel) descended and said, "O Muhammad, *'Alayhi al-Salam*, explain to them the timing for the Prayer." Then the command to pay *Zakat* came. Jibril then said, 'O Muhammad, *'Alayhi al-Salam*, explain to them how to pay *Zakat* as you have explained to them about the Prayer.' Then the command to fast came. The Messenger of Allah would send information to the nearby towns and would ask people to fast on the day of 'Ashura' (tenth of the month of Muharram) and people would fast on that day. Then the month of Ramadan came between the month of

273

Sha'ban and Shawwal. Thereafter came the command for Hajj. Jibril descended and said to the Holy Prophet, "Explain to them the rules of Hajj as you have explained to them about the Prayer, *Zakat* and Fasting."

"Thereafter came the command in the verse about the people who possess Divine Authority. It came to him on Friday, the Day of 'Arafa on the ninth of the month of Dhu al-Hajja. Allah, the Most Holy, the Most High, sent the following verse of the Holy Quran: '. . . On this day I have perfected your religion, completed My favors to you, and chosen Islam as your religion. . . .' (5:3) 'The perfection of religion came about with the declaration of the fact that Ali ibn abu Talib, *'Alayhi al-Salam*, possessed Divine Authority over the people. The Messenger of Allah then said at that time, 'My followers have lived very close to the age of darkness and ignorance. When I speak of the Divine Authority of my nephew, one says this and one says that. I say this to myself in my soul without speaking it out with my tongue. Then the decisive command of Allah, the Most Holy, the Most High, came in which He had warned me of punishment for not preaching to people about the Divine Authority (of Ali, *'Alayhi al-Salam*). And then the following verse of the Holy Quran was sent: 'O Messenger, preach what is revealed to you from your Lord. If you do not preach, it will be as though you have not conveyed My message. Allah protects you from men. He does not guide the unbelieving people.' (5:67) The Messenger of Allah then holding the hand of Ali raised it up high and said, 'O people, there had lived no prophet before me whom Allah would not cause to become old. After such age Allah would call them to die. I may be called to die any time very soon but would remain responsible as well as you. What then would you say?' They replied, 'We will testify and say that you preached, gave good advice and fulfilled your responsibilities. May Allah grant you the best of the rewards that He has granted to the messengers.' He (the Holy Prophet) then said, 'O Lord, bear testimony.' He said so three times. Then he said, 'O the community of the Muslims, this is the person who possesses Divine Authority over you after me. Those of you present here must inform about this declaration to those who are absent from here.'

"Abu Ja'far, *'Alayhi al-Salam*, has said, 'I swear by Allah, that Ali, *'Alayhi al-Salam*, was the guardian of the trust of Allah in His creatures, the guardian of His secrets and religion which He has chosen for Himself. Then the Holy Prophet experienced what is to be experienced and called Ali, *'Alayhi al-Salam*, near and said, "O Ali, I want to appoint and entrust you with that which Allah has entrusted me of His secrets, His knowledge, His creatures and His religion which He has chosen for Himself." The Imam then said, 'O Ziyad, I swear by Allah that no one besides Ali, *'Alayhi al-Salam*, had any share in it (appointed as Divine Authority over the people). Ali, *'Alayhi al-Salam*, thereafter experienced what was to be experienced (the time of his leaving this world). He then called his children who numbered twelve sons. He said to them, 'My children, Allah, the Most Holy, the Most High, has decided to place in me the noble tradition that He had placed in Jacob (Ya'qub). Jacob called all of his children who numbered twelve sons and he informed them about (the status of) their companion (brother, Joseph). Please note that I also want to inform you about your companion. These two, al-Hassan and al-Husayn, *'Alayhim al-Salam*, are the children of the Messenger of Allah. You must listen to them, obey and support them. I have entrusted them with that which the Messenger of Allah had entrusted me in the matters of the creatures of Allah, His secrets and His religion, which He has chosen for Himself. Allah has made of the responsibility of Ali toward them just like the responsibility of the Messenger of Allah toward Ali, *'Alayhi al-Salam*. All of their virtuous perfection is equal except the elderliness in age. Al-Husayn, *'Alayhi al-Salam*, would never raise his voice in a meeting in the presence of al-Hassan, *'Alayhi al-Salam*, before he would leave the place.'

"Al-Hassan, *'Alayhi al-Salam*, then experienced (the coming of the time of his death) what is to be experienced. He delivered and submitted it (the Divine trust) all to al-Husayn, *'Alayhi al-Salam*. When the time of the death of al-Husayn, *'Alayhi al-Salam*, came he called his eldest daughter, Fatimah, and gave to her a sealed document and his publicly declared will. Ali ibn al-Husayn, *'Alayhi al-Salam*, was ill with internal illness and they thought he was about to die. Fatimah gave the document to Ali ibn al-Husayn, *'Alayhi al-Salam*, and thereafter, I swear by Allah, that document came to us.'"

Al-Husayn ibn Muhammad has narrated from Mu'alla ibn Muhammad from Muhammad ibn Jumhur from Muhammad ibn Isma'il ibn Bazi' from Mansur ibn Yunus from abu al-Jarud from abu Ja'far, *'Alayhi al-Salam*, a similar *Hadith*.

H 756, Ch. 64, h 7
Muhammad ibn al-Hassan has narrated from Sahl ibn Ziyad from Muhammad ibn 'Isa from Safwan ibn Yahya from Sabbah al-Azraq from abu Basir who has said the following:
"Once I mentioned to abu Ja'far, *'Alayhi al-Salam*, 'I met a man from al-Mukhtaria (followers of al-Mukhtar) who believed that Muhammad ibn al-Hanafiya (one of the sons of Imam Ali, *'Alayhi al-Salam*, but not from *Fatimah, 'Alayha al-Salam*) is the Imam.' Abu Ja'far, *'Alayhi al-Salam*, became angry and then said, 'Did you then say anything to him?'

"I said, 'No, I swear by Allah, I did not know what to say.' The Imam then said, 'Why did you not say, "The Messenger of Allah appointed Ali, al-Hassan and al-Husayn, *'Alayhim al-Salam*, as the executors of his will. When Ali, *'Alayhi al-Salam*, was about to leave this world, he appointed al-Hassan and al-Husayn, *'Alayhim al-Salam*, as the executors of his will. Had Ali, *'Alayhi al-Salam*, appointed people other than al-Hassan and al-Husayn as the executors of his will, and he never would do so, they would have said, 'We are the executors of the will of the Messenger of Allah just as you are.'

"Al-Hassan, *'Alayhi al-Salam*, appointed al-Husayn, *'Alayhi al-Salam*, the executor of his will. Had al-Hassan, *'Alayhi al-Salam*, appointed people other than al-Husayn, *'Alayhi al-Salam*, the executor of his will, al-Husayn, *'Alayhi al-Salam*, would have said, "I am the executor of the will of the Messenger of Allah and the executor of the will of my father just as you are." In fact, al-Hassan, *'Alayhi al-Salam*, was the one who would have disdained to do so. What Allah, the Most Holy, the Most High, has said in the following verse, ". . . The relatives are closer to each other, according to the Book of Allah. . . ." (33:6) is certainly about us and our ancestors.'"""

Chapter 65 - Tacit and Explicit Testimony as Proof of (Amir Al-Mu'minin) Ali's, *'Alayhi al-Salam*, Divine Authority Over the People After the Messenger of Allah

H 757, Ch. 65, h 1

Muhammad ibn Yahya has narrated from Muhammad ibn al-Husayn from Muhammad ibn Isma'il from Mansur ibn Yunus from Zayd ibn al-Jahm al-Hilali who has said the following:

"I heard abu 'Abd Allah, *'Alayhi al-Salam*, say, 'When *Wilayah* (the declaration that) Ali ibn abu Talib has (Divine Authority over the people) descended and it was in the words of the Messenger of Allah, they all greeted and congratulated Ali, *'Alayhi al-Salam*, as the commander of the believers. Of the matters that Allah had stressed upon the two of them on that day, O Zayd, was what came through the words of the Messenger of Allah for the two of them: "The two of you stand up and congratulate him (Ali, *'Alayhi al-Salam*) as the commander of the believers." The two of them asked, 'Is it from Allah or from the Messenger of Allah, O the Messenger of Allah?' The Messenger of Allah then said to the two of them, "It is from Allah and from His Messenger." Allah, the Most Holy, the Most High, then sent the following. '. . . (He commands people) to keep their established covenants with Allah and must not disregard their firm oaths; they have already appointed Allah as their Guarantor. Allah, certainly, knows what you do.'" (16:91) The Imam then said, 'It refers to the words of the Messenger of Allah to the two of them. It also refers to their words to the Messenger of Allah that said, "Is it from Allah or from the Messenger of Allah, O the Messenger of Allah?" Allah, the Most Majestic, the Most Gracious, then said this: 'Do not be like the lady behind the spinning wheel who has broken the yarn by pulling it with unnecessary force. You must not consider your oaths as means of deceit to benefit one party and inflict loss upon the other, . . .' (16:92) just because they are such *'A'immah* who possess and maintain higher spiritual standards than your Imam does.'

"I (the narrator) then asked the Imam, 'May Allah keep my soul in service for your cause, is the word *'A'immah* (plural of Imam)? However, we read it *Arba'* (meaning more beneficial).'

"The Imam then said, 'What *Arba'* is it that you mention?' He made a gesture with his hand as an indication of throwing away something and read from the Holy Quran: 'Allah tests you through him [Ali, *'Alayhi al-Salam*]. He will, on the Day of Judgment, make clear to you who was right and who was wrong. (16:92) Had Allah wanted, He would have made you one single nation but He guides or causes whoever He wants to go astray. You will certainly be questioned about what you have done. (16:93) Do not take your oaths as a means of deceit lest you damage the firmness of your belief, [This may happen after what you have heard from the Messenger of Allah about Ali, *'Alayhi al-Salam*] and you may suffer from evil for creating obstacles in the way that leads to Allah, [a reference to Ali, *'Alayhi al-Salam*] and incur a great torment upon yourselves. '"' (16:94)

Note: along with the verse above inside brackets are explanatory words of the Imam. In verse 91 above the words of the Holy Quran are *'Ummah* and *Arba'* meaning a *party* and *beneficial*. The Imam, however, has considered them *A'immah*, plural of *Imam* and *Azka'*, purifying. For this reason the narrator asked a question and the Imam, *'Alayhi al-Salam*, explained.

H 758, Ch. 65, h 2
Muhammad ibn Yahya has narrated from Muhammad ibn al-Husayn and Ahmad ibn Muhammad from ibn Mahbub from Muhammad ibn Fudayl from abu Hamza al-Thumali who has said the following:

"I heard abu Ja'far, *'Alayhi al-Salam*, say, 'When Muhammad, *'Alayhi al-Salam*, completed his task of prophet-hood and the duration of his life was about to end, Allah, the Most High, sent him *wahy* (information through the angels). It said, "O Muhammad, your task as a prophet has come to an end and the duration of your life is about to reach a close. Therefore, you must place the knowledge with you, the belief, the great name, the legacy of knowledge and the symbols of the knowledge of the prophecy in your family with Ali ibn abu Talib, *'Alayhi al-Salam*. It is because I do not want to discontinue the knowledge, the belief, the great name, the legacy of the knowledge and the symbols of knowledge of the prophecy from your posterior descendents as I had not done so with descendents of the prophets.'"

H 759, Ch. 65, h 3
Muhammad ibn al-Husayn and others have narrated from Sahl from Muhammad ibn 'Isa, Muhammad ibn Yahya and Muhammad ibn al-Husayn all of them from Muhammad ibn Sinan from Isma'il ibn Jabir and 'Abd al-Karim ibn 'Amr from 'Abd Al-Hamid ibn abu al-Daylam from abu 'Abd Allah, *'Alayhi al-Salam*, who has said the following:

"Moses, peace be on him, prepared his will and gave it to Yusha' ibn Nun. Yusha' ibn Nun made his will to give it to the sons of Harun. He did not make a will to his own sons or to the sons of Moses. To Allah, the Most High, belong all the good choices. He chooses whomever He wants from whomever He wants. He gave the glad news about Jesus to Moses and Yusha'. When Allah, the Most Holy, the Most High, raised Jesus as His Messenger Jesus, peace be on him, said to them, 'After me there will come a prophet whose name will be 'Ahmad' from the descendents of Isma'il, peace be on him. He will come and affirm my message and your message, my excuses and your excuses.' The will continued after him in the protecting disciples. Allah, the Most High, has called them 'protectors' because they preserved the greatest name and it is the Book through which such knowledge of all things is learned that existed with the prophets, peace be on them, as Allah, the Most High, has said in the following verse: 'We sent Our messengers (before you) with clear evidence (to support their truthfulness), and sent with them the Book and the Balance. . . .' (57:25) The Book is the greatest name. Of what is known as the books are the Torah, Gospel and al-Furqan (the Holy Quran) of which also is the book of Noah, the book of Salih, Shu'ayb and Abraham. Allah, the Most Holy, the Most High, has said, 'This is what is written in the ancient heavenly books, (87:18) the Scriptures of Abraham and Moses.' (87:19) Where then is the book of Abraham? In fact, the book of Abraham is the greatest name.

The book of Moses is the greatest name. Thus, the will continued through one scholar to the next scholar until they delivered it to Muhammad, *'Alayhi al-Salam.*

"When Allah, the Most Holy, the Most High, sent Muhammad, *'Alayhi al-Salam,* the descendents of the "protecting" disciples accepted his faith but the lying ones of the Israelites refused to believe in him. He prayed to Allah, the Most Holy, the Most High, and worked hard for His cause. Thereafter Allah, Most High is Whose mention, commanded him to declare the excellence of the executor of his will and he said, 'My Lord, the Arabs are the most rude and unjust ones. They did not have any books with them, no prophet had come to them and they do not know the virtues of the prophecy of the prophets, peace be on them, and their honor. They will not believe me if I declare to them the excellence and virtues of my family.' Allah, Most Holy is the mention of Whose name, said, 'Do not be grieved about them. . . .' (16:127) '. . . We have told him, 'Ignore them and say to them "peace". They will soon know the consequences of their deeds.' (43:89) He (the Holy Prophet) mentioned the name of the executor of his will and hypocrisy crept into their (certain Arabs') hearts. The Messenger of Allah noticed it and whatever they were to say.

"Allah, the Most Holy, the Most High, said, 'O Muhammad, *'Alayhi al-Salam,* We know that what they say causes sadness to your heart. They, in fact, not only reject what you say, they refuse to accept the signs of Allah also.' (6:33) However, they refused to accept them without any good reason and authority. The Messenger of Allah would associate with them and seek the support of certain ones of them against the other ones among them. He would continue to express the excellence of the executor of his will to them from time to time until the following Chapter of the Holy Quran was revealed. He presented justifications against them when he was informed of death approaching and the news of his leaving this world. Allah, Most Holy is the mention of Whose name, said, 'When you are free from (your obligations), strive hard (to worship Allah) (94:7) and be devoted to your Lord's service.' (94:8) Allah in the above verse has said to His Messenger, 'When your duty is fulfilled then establish your mark and symbol and declare who will be the executor of the will, and speak to them of his excellence and virtues.' Thus, Muhammad, *'Alayhi al-Salam,* declared, 'Over whomever I have Divine Authority, this Ali, *'Alayhi al-Salam,* also has Divine Authority over them. O Lord, support those who will support him and be the enemy of those who are hostile to him.' He said so three times.

"He has further said, 'I will commission and send the man who loves Allah and His Messenger, and Allah and His Messenger love him. He is not the one who would run away from the battlefield.' In the above statement he points out also the one who returned from the gates of the castle (of the enemy) frightening and disheartening his own people.

"He has also said, 'Ali, *'Alayhi al-Salam,* is the leader of the believers. Ali, *'Alayhi al-Salam,* is the pillar of religion.' He has further said, 'This is the one who will strive against certain people with his sword to defend the truth, after me.'

278

The Holy Prophet has also said, 'The truth is with Ali, *'Alayhi al-Salam*, wherever he inclines.'

"The Holy Prophet has further said, 'I leave among you two facts, if you hold to them firmly, you will never be misled: the Book of Allah, the Most Holy, the Most High, and my family, my descendents. O people, listen. I have, certainly, preached the message to you. You will arrive at the pond of *al-kawthar*, (in paradise) and I will ask you about your dealings with the two illustrious matters. The two illustrious matters are the Book of Allah, the Most Holy, the Most High, and my family. Do not proceed ahead of them lest you be destroyed. Do not try to teach them; they are by far more knowledgeable than you are.'

"*Al-Hujja* (solid proof of Ali's *Wilayah*, his Divine Authority over the people after the Holy Prophet), was established through the words of the Holy Prophet and those of the Book that people read. He still continued to extol the excellence and spiritual virtues of his family in words and explain with verses of the Holy Quran such as: 'People of the house, (*Ahl AlBayt*) Allah wants to remove all kinds of uncleanness from you and to purify you thoroughly.' (33:33) 'Take notice that whatever property you may gain, one-fifth belongs to Allah, the Messenger, the kindred (his relatives). . .' (8:41) 'Give the relatives (of the Holy Prophet), the destitute and those who when on a journey have become needy, their dues.' (17:26)

"It was Ali, *'Alayhi al-Salam*, and his right was to have, as the executor in his possession, the will of the Holy Prophet that gave him the Leadership with Divine Authority. The will assigned to him the custodianship of the greatest name, the legacy of knowledge and the symbols of knowledge of the prophet-hood. He (Allah) also has said, '(Muhammad), say, "I do not ask you for any payment for my preaching to you except (your) love of (my near) relatives. . . ."' (42:23) In, '. . . questions are asked about *al-Maw'udah;* translated as (the baby girls buried alive)' (81:8) He (Allah) in fact, says, 'I question you about *al-Maw'udah,* the love. I had told you about its great virtue. It was the love of the relatives (family of the Holy Prophet) but for what reason did you murder them (members of the family of the Holy Prophet)? He, Most Exalted is Whose mention, has said, 'Ask those who know about the heavenly Books if you do not know about this.' (16:43) He (Allah) has said that the Book is the reminder and the people of this reminder (the Book) are the *Ahl al-Bayt* of Muhammad, *'Alayhim al-Salam*. Allah, the Most Holy, the Most High, has commanded them (people) to ask *Ahl al-Bayt* for guidance. He has not commanded *Ahl al-Bayt* to ask the ignorant people. Allah, the Most Holy, the Most High, has called the Holy Quran *Dhikr* (reminder), thus, He, the Most Holy, the Most High, has said, 'We have revealed the Quran to you so that you can tell the people what has been revealed to them and so that perhaps they will think.' (16:44) Allah, the Most Holy, the Most High has said, 'The Quran is a reminder to you and to your people and you will soon be asked for guidance.' (43:44) Allah, the Most Holy, the Most High, has also said, 'Believers, obey Allah, His Messenger, and your leaders (who possess Divine Authority). . . .' (4:59) He, the Majestic, the Glorious, has said, 'Had they referred it to (Allah), the Messenger of Allah or to their leaders, (who possess Divine Authority), they could have used that information more properly. Were it not for the favor and mercy of Allah, all but a few of them would have followed Satan.' (4:83)

"The words 'Had they referred' in the above verse are the command referenced to in the matter and the task mentioned. People must refer in such tasks to those who possess Divine Authority among them. They are the people that Allah has commanded to be obeyed and referred to.

"When the Messenger of Allah returned from his farewell pilgrimage to the sacred House in Makkah, Jibril descended to him and said, 'Messenger, preach what is revealed to you from your Lord. If you will not preach, it will be as though you have not conveyed My message. Allah protects you from men. He does not guide the unbelieving people.' (5:67) He (the Messenger of Allah) called the people to come together at one place and they did. He ordered that the thorns and bushes be removed from the ground to make room. He, *'Alayhi al-Salam*, then said, 'O people, who is your guardian with Divine Authority who has greater right and control over your souls than you yourselves do?' They said, 'Allah and His Messenger have such authority.' The Holy Prophet then said, 'Over whomever I have Divine Authority, this Ali, *'Alayhi al-Salam*, also has the same degree of authority. O Lord, support those who support him (Ali) and be the enemy of those who are his (Ali's) enemies.' He said this three times. This made the thorn of hypocrisy to go deeper into the hearts of a certain group of people who said, 'Allah, Most Great is His name to mention, has never said any such thing to Muhammad, *'Alayhi al-Salam*. He wants only to lift up the shoulder of His cousin to promote him.' When he arrived at Madina, the Ansar (Muslims of Madina) came to see him for a certain issue. They said, 'O Messenger of Allah, Allah, Most great is the mention of Whose name, has granted us a great deal of favors. He has granted us honor in bringing you to this town among us. In so doing He has brought joy to the hearts of our friends and sorrow to our enemies. We know that many delegates come to see you and there is not enough to give them and the enemies call it degrading. We like very much if you accept one-third of our properties so that when delegates from Makkah come to see you, you will find enough means to accommodate them.' The Messenger of Allah did not reply to them and he was waiting for Jibril to come from his Lord. Jibril descended and said, '. . .Muhammad, say, "I do not ask you for any payment for my preaching to you except (your) love of (my) near relatives. . ." (42:23) He did not accept their property. The hypocrites said, 'Allah has not said this to Muhammad. He only wants to lift up the shoulder of his cousin to promote him. He is imposing his family upon us. Yesterday he said, "Over whomever I have Divine Authority, this Ali also has the same degree of Divine Authority over them" and today he says, '(Muhammad), say, "I do not ask you for any payment for my preaching to you except (your) love of (my) near relatives. . . ."'" (42:23)

"Thereafter came the verse of the Holy Quran about *Khums* (paying one-fifth of net income as tax (see 8:41 Holy Quran). They said, 'He wants only to take away our properties and interests.' Then Jibril came and said, 'O Muhammad, *'Alayhi* al-Salam, you have completed the task of prophet-hood and the duration of your life is coming to a close. You, now, must place the greatest name, the legacy of the knowledge and the symbols of knowledge of prophet-hood with Ali, *'Alayhi al-Salam*. It is because I (Allah) do not want to leave the earth without having a scholar therein so that people will learn from him how to obey Me and know through him My guardianship and authority. The scholar will be the Divine Authority for those who come to be born at a time between the passing away of one prophet and the appearance of the next prophet.'

"The Imam said, 'He (Muhammad, *'Alayhi al-Salam*), bequeathed to him (Imam Ali) the greatest name, the legacy of the knowledge and the symbols of knowledge of the prophet-hood. He also bequeathed to him a thousand words and a thousand chapters whereby there opened a thousand chapters and a thousand words from each chapter and each word.'"

H 760, Ch. 65, h 4

Ali ibn Ibrahim has narrated from his father and Salih ibn al-Sindi from Ja'far ibn Bashir from Yahya ibn Ma'mar al-'Attar from Bashir al-Dahhan from abu 'Abd Allah, *'Alayhi al-Salam*, who has said the following:

"The Messenger of Allah during the illness from which he died said, 'Call my much cherished friend to me.' We sent to call the fathers of the two of them ('A'isha and Hafsa's fathers). When the Messenger of Allah looked at them he turned away from them. He then said again, 'Call my much cherished friend to me.' Ali, *'Alayhi al-Salam*, was then called. When the Messenger of Allah looked at him, he became engrossed in talking to him. When Ali, *'Alayhi al-Salam*, left, the two met him and asked, 'What did your much cherished friend say to you?' He (Ali) replied, 'He narrated to me a thousand chapters from each of which a thousand chapters opened.'"

H 761, Ch. 65, h 5

Ahmad ibn Idris has narrated from Muhammad ibn 'Abd al-Jabbar from Muhammad ibn Isma'il from Mansur ibn Yunus from abu Bakr al-Hadrami from abu Ja'far, *'Alayhi al-Salam*, who has said the following:

"The Messenger of Allah made Ali, *'Alayhi al-Salam*, learn a thousand letters from each of which a thousand letters (words) spread out."

H 762, Ch. 65, h 6

A number of our people have narrated from Ahmad ibn Muhammad from Ali ibn al-Hakam from Ali ibn abu Hamza from abu Basir from abu 'Abd Allah, *'Alayhi al-Salam*, who has said the following:

"In the hilt of the sword of the Messenger of Allah there was a small booklet. I (the narrator) then asked the Imam, *'Alayhi al-Salam*, 'What did that booklet contain?'

"The Imam said, 'It contained the few letters from each of which a thousand letters (words or sides) spread out.'

"Abu Basir has said that abu 'Abd Allah, *'Alayhi al-Salam*, then said, 'Until this hour not even two letters have come out (their meanings understood, utilized and practiced).'"

H 763, Ch. 65, h 7
A number of our people have narrated from Ahmad ibn Muhammad from ibn abu Nasr from Fudayl (ibn) Sukkarah who has said the following:
"Once I said to abu 'Abd Allah, *'Alayhi al-Salam*, 'May Allah keep my soul in service for your cause, is there a certain quantity of water required to give *Ghusl* (bath) to a dead person?' The Imam said, 'The Messenger of Allah said to Ali, *'Alayhi al-Salam*, "When I die draw six sacks of water from the well *Ghars* (name of the well). Then wash my body, shroud it and rub camphor on my forehead, palms, knees and toes. When you finish washing my body and shrouding, hold the ends (and sides) of the shroud and set my body in a sitting posture, then ask me whatever you like. I swear by Allah, you would not ask me anything but that I will give you an answer in it."'"

H 764, Ch. 65, h 8
Muhammad ibn Yahya has narrated from Ahmad ibn Muhammad from al-Husayn ibn Sa'id from al-Qasim ibn Muhammad from Ali ibn abu Hamza from ibn abu Sa'id from Aban ibn Taghlib from abu 'Abd Allah, *'Alayhi al-Salam*, who has said the following:
"When the Messenger of Allah was about to leave this world Ali, *'Alayhi al-Salam*, came in to see him. He (the Messenger of Allah) placed his (Ali's) head under the covering that covered his own head and said, 'O Ali, when I die, wash my body and shroud it, then place me in a sitting posture, then ask me and write down (the answers).'"

H 765, Ch. 65, h 9
Ali ibn Muhammad has narrated from Sahl ibn Ziyad from Muhammad ibn al-Walid, Shabab al-Sayrafi from Yunus ibn Ribat who has said the following:
"Once Kamil al-Tammar and I went to see abu 'Abd Allah, *'Alayhi al-Salam*. Kamil said to the Imam, 'May Allah keep my soul in service for your cause, there is a *Hadith* which so and so son of so and so has narrated.'

"The Imam said, 'State and read it.' He (Kamil) then said, 'He, so and so, narrated to me that the Holy Prophet narrated a thousand chapters to Ali, *'Alayhi al-Salam*, on the day the Messenger of Allah died. Each of those chapters opens a thousand chapters. The total becomes a million chapters.' The Imam said, 'That is how it happened.' I then said, 'May Allah keep my soul in service for your cause, has this become manifest to your followers and those who love you?' The Imam said, 'O Kamil, only one or two chapters may have become so.' I then said, 'May Allah keep my soul in service for your cause, it means not more than one or two chapters out of a milliom chapters about your merits and excellence have become known to people.' The narrator has said that the Imam then said, 'You perhaps may not be able to narrate all our excellence and virtues. You do not narrate from our excellence and virtue but only a scattered thousand (items).'"

Chapter 66 - Tacit and Explicit Testimony as Proof of Al-Hassan Ibn Ali's Divine Authority Over the People After (Amir Al-Mu'minin) Ali, *'Alayhim al-Salam*

H 766, Ch. 66, h 1

Ali ibn Ibrahim has narrated from his father from Hammad ibn 'Isa from Ibrahim ibn 'Umar al-Yamani and 'Umar ibn 'Udhayna from Aban from Sulaym ibn Qays who has said the following:

"I witnessed (Amir al-Mu'minin) Ali's, *'Alayhi al-Salam*, will made before me in which he appointed his son, al-Hassan, *'Alayhi al-Salam*, as the executor of his will. He called al-Husayn, *'Alayhi al-Salam*, Muhammad and all his other sons, all the leaders among his followers and his whole family to bear testimony to his will. He then delivered the Book and the Armament to his son al-Hassan, *'Alayhi al-Salam*, and said, 'My son, the Messenger of Allah commanded me to appoint you as the executor of my will. (He commanded me) to deliver to you my Books and my Armament just as the Messenger of Allah did. He made his will in which he appointed me as the executor, delivered to me his Books and his Armament and commanded me to command you to deliver them to al-Husayn, *'Alayhi al-Salam*, when you are about to leave this world.' Then he turned to his son, al-Husayn, *'Alayhi al-Salam*, and said, 'The Messenger of Allah has commanded you to deliver them to your son, this one.' Then he held with his hand Ali ibn al-Husayn, *'Alayhi al-Salam*, and said to him, 'The Messenger of Allah has commanded you to deliver them to your son, Muhammad ibn Ali and convey to him the greeting of the Messenger of Allah and my greeting.'"

H 767, Ch. 66, h 2

Ali ibn Ibrahim has narrated from his father from ibn abu 'Umayr from 'Abd al-Samad ibn Bashir from abu al-Jarud from abu Ja'far, *'Alayhi al-Salam*, who has said the following:

"When (Amir al-Mu'minin) Ali, *'Alayhi al-Salam*, was about to leave this world, he called his son, al-Hassan, *'Alayhi al-Salam*, saying, 'Come very close to me so I can speak to you secretly just as the Messenger of Allah did to me, and entrust you with all that he entrusted me with', and he did so.'"

H 768, Ch. 66, h 3

A number of our people have narrated from Ahmad ibn Muhammad from Ali ibn al-Hakam from Sayf ibn 'Amira from abu Bakr al-Hadrami who has said that al-Ajlah, Salama ibn Kuhayl, Dawud ibn abu Yazid and Zayd al-Yamami have narrated from Shahr ibn Hawshab who has said the following:

"When (Amir al-Mu'minin) Ali, *'Alayhi al-Salam*, was about to leave for Kufa he left in 'Umm Salama's trust his books and his will. When al-Hassan, *'Alayhi al-Salam*, returned to Madina she delivered all of them to him."

H 769, Ch. 66, h 4

The above *Hadith* is as follows in the book of al-Safwan: Ahmad ibn Muhammad has narrated from Ali ibn al-Hakam from Sayf from abu Bakr from abu 'Abd Allah, *'Alayhi al-Salam*, who has said the following:

"When (Amir al-Mu'minin) Ali, *'Alayhi al-Salam*, was about to leave for Kufa he left in 'Umm Salama's trust his books and his will. When al-Hassan, *'Alayhi al-Salam*, returned to Madina she delivered all of them to him."

H 770, Ch. 66, h 5

A number of our people have narrated from Ahmad ibn Muhammad from al-Husayn ibn Sa'id from Hammad ibn 'Isa from 'Amr ibn Shimr from Jabir from abu Ja'far, *'Alayhi al-Salam*, who has said the following:

"(Amir al-Mu'minin) Ali, *'Alayhi al-Salam*, made his directive will to al-Hassan, *'Alayhi al-Salam*, and asked al-Husayn, *'Alayhi al-Salam*, Muhammad, all his sons, the leaders among his followers and the whole of his family to bear testimony. He then delivered to him the Book and the Armament. He then said to his son, al-Hassan, *'Alayhi al-Salam*, 'My son, the Messenger of Allah commanded me to entrust you with my directive will. (He commanded me) to deliver to you my Books, and my Armament just as the Messenger of Allah entrusted me with his directive will and delivered his Books and Armament to me. He commanded me to command you to deliver them all to your brother al-Husayn, *'Alayhi al-Salam*, when time for you to leave this world will come.' Then he turned to his son al-Husayn, *'Alayhi al-Salam*, and said, 'The Messenger of Allah has commanded you to deliver it all to your son, this one.' He then held with his hand Ali ibn al-Husayn, *'Alayhi al-Salam*, and said to him, 'My son, the Messenger of Allah has commanded you to deliver it all to your son, Muhammad ibn Ali, *'Alayhi al-Salam*, and convey to him the greeting of the Messenger of Allah according to his tradition as well as my greeting of the same manner.' He then turned to his son al-Hassan, *'Alayhi al-Salam*, and said, 'My son, you are the Leader with Divine Authority and the authority in the matters of the spilled blood. Were you to forgive, it would be for you. Were you to retaliate then one strike for a strike, you would not be in sin.'"

H 771, Ch. 66, h 6

Al-Husayn ibn al-Hassan al-Hassani has narrated in a *marfu'* manner, *rafa'ahu*, and Muhammad ibn al-Hassan from Ibrahim ibn Ishaq al-Ahmari has narrated in a *marfu'* manner, *rafa'ahu*, the following:

"When (Amir al-Mu'minin) Ali, *'Alayhi al-Salam*, was injured the visitors crowded around him saying, 'O (Amir al-Mu'minin) Ali, *'Alayhi al-Salam*, (please, grant us) your directive will.'

"The Imam then said, 'You must fold the pillow for me (to help me sit so I can speak).' He then said, 'All praise belongs to Allah, as He is worthy of it. We follow (obey) His commands. I praise Him just as He has loved it. No one deserves to be worshipped and obeyed except Allah, Who is One, the only One. The Self-sufficient is His own description of His Ownself. O people, every man, in his running away, comes face to face with the very thing from which he runs away so badly (namely his death). The appointed time (to die) is the driver of the soul to such time. In other words, running away from death is rushing to find it. How many days have come and gone in which I searched for the secret in this matter, however, Allah, the Majestic, the Glorious, disdains to do anything else, but to keep it secret. It certainly is beyond comprehension; it is hidden knowledge.'

"Of my directive will to you is that you must not consider anything similar to Allah, Great is Whose praise. You must not disregard the *Sunnah* (traditions) of Prophet Muhammad, *'Alayhi al-Salam*. Keep these two pillars straight and light up these two beacons. You will not face any blame as long as you do not disperse (but remain united). Every man is held responsible for what he assiduously gains. Ignorant, (the lay) people's burden is held light and reduced. The Lord is Merciful, the Imam is knowledgeable and religion is a constructive system. Yesterday I was your companion, today (I am) a lesson (one's death is the best lesson) for you to learn and tomorrow I will depart from you. If one's feet can remain firm at this slippery position (despite the fragility of life) then that is the goal. However, if the feet wavered (and failed to hang on to life) it is because we live under the shortlived shadows of the branches, in the blowing winds, under the thin cover of dissipating clouds in the air and disappearing traces (shrinking resources) on the land.

"I was your neighbor that lived along with you with my body for a number of days. You will soon escort my dead body (to the grave). It will be a motionless body that once moved, and a silent one that once spoke (so sweetly). My silence, my closed eyes and my motionless limbs must be thought of as the best preachers. They are far better preachers to you than an eloquent orator is. I have said farewell to you as the one who expects reunion. Tomorrow you will see my days and Allah, the Most Holy, the Most High, will reveal my secrets. You will know me better when you find my place vacant and see others holding my position. If I survive I will be the authority for my own self but if I die then death is my destination. If I forgive (my assassin) then forgiveness is a means of getting closer (to Allah) and for you it is a good deed. You must forgive and ignore. Do you not like it that Allah will forgive you?

"How great is the sorrow for the neglectful one, whose life will be testimony for his own condemnation or his days lead him to misfortune. May Allah place you and us among those who do not fall short in life in matters of obedience to Allah due to their desire (to obey Him) or for fear of suffering after death. We are only for Him and with Him.'

"Then he turned to al-Hassan, *'Alayhi al-Salam*, and said, 'My son, one strike for one strike, you will not be in sin.'"

H 772, Ch. 66, h 7

Muhammad ibn Yahya has narrated from Ali ibn al-Hassan from Ali ibn Ibrahim al-'Aqili, in a *marfu'* manner, *yarfa'uhu,* who has said the following:

"When ibn Muljam injured (Amir al-Mu'minin) Ali, *'Alayhi al-Salam*, he (Ali) said to al-Hassan, *'Alayhi al-Salam*, 'My son, when I die, eliminate ibn Muljam, dig the ground for him in al-Kunasa (name of a place) and throw him therein. It is a valley of the valleys of hell.'"

(According to 'Aqili's description al-Kunas is at the gate called 'Taq al-Mahamil' where people cook animals' legs and heads for food.)

Chapter 67 - Tacit and Explicit Testimony as Proof of Al-Husayn Ibn Ali's Divine Authority Over the People After Al-Hassan, *'Alayhim al-Salam*

H 773, Ch. 67, h 1

Ali ibn Ibrahim has narrated from his father from Bakr ibn Salih (al-Kulayni has said) and a number of our people from ibn Ziyad from Muhammad ibn Sulayman al-Daylami from Harun ibn al-Jahm from Muhammad ibn Muslim who has said the following:

"I heard abu Ja'far, *'Alayhi al-Salam*, say, 'When al-Hassan ibn Ali, *'Alayhi al-Salam*, was about to leave this world he said to al-Husayn, *'Alayhi al-Salam*, 'O my brother, I want to entrust you with my directive will. (Please) safeguard and protect it. When I die prepare and help me toward (the Shrine of) the Messenger of Allah so I can renew my covenant with him, then help me toward (the grave of) my mother, *'Alayhi al-Salam*. Thereafter return me back for burial in Baqi' graveyard. You must be aware that 'A'isha will create problems for me. Allah and the people are aware of her deeds and her hostile attitude toward Allah and His Messenger and of her animosity toward us, *Ahl al-Bayt* (family) of the Holy Prophet.'

"When al-Hassan, *'Alayhi al-Salam*, passed away his body was placed on the stretcher (Sarir) and then the procession was led to the place where the Messenger of Allah prayed for the dead people readied for burial. Al-Husayn, *'Alayhi al-Salam*, performed the prayer therein and then the body was taken to the Mosque. (The procession) paused near the grave of the Messenger of Allah. At this time *Dhul 'Aynayn* (spy) went to 'A'isha and told her, 'They have brought al-Hassan's body to bury near the Holy Prophet's grave.' She then came out quickly on the mule with saddle. She was the first woman in the Muslim community to ride on the saddle. She then said, 'Take your son away from my house. He will not be buried in my house (where the Messenger of Allah is buried) to violate the privacy of the Messenger of Allah.' Al-Husayn, *'Alayhi al-Salam*, said to her, 'A long time ago you and your father had violated the privacy of the Messenger of Allah. You brought to his house those whose nearness he did not love. Allah will hold you responsible for this, O 'A'isha.'"

H 774, Ch. 67, h 2

Muhammad ibn al-Hassan and Ali ibn Muhammad have narrated from Sahl ibn Ziyad from Muhammad ibn Sulayman al-Daylami from one of our people from al-Mufaddal ibn 'Umar from abu 'Abd Allah, *'Alayhi al-Salam*, who has said the following:

"When al-Hassan ibn Ali, *'Alayhi al-Salam*, was about to leave this world he said, 'O Qanbar, see if there is any believer (in Islam) other than the members of the family of Muhammad, *'Alayhi al-Salam*, behind your door.' He (Qanbar) said, 'Allah, His Messenger and the grandson of His Messenger know better than I do.' The Imam said, 'Call to me Muhammad ibn Ali.' I (Qanbar) then went to him and when I was in his presence he said, 'I hope nothing but good has happened.' I said, 'Hurry up, abu Muhammad wants to see you.' He quickly put his shoes on and could not even wear them properly. He came out with me, running. When he arrived in the presence of al-Hassan, *'Alayhi al-Salam*, he offered his greeting.

286

Al-Hassan ibn Ali, *'Alayhi al-Salam*, said to him, 'Please, sit down. A person like you must not remain absent from hearing the words that can bring the dead to life and cause death to the living. You must be the containers of knowledge and the beacons of guidance. Certain forms of the lights of the day are brighter than others are.

"Is it not in your knowledge that Allah made the sons of Abraham *'A 'immah* and granted to a few of them more excellence than to the others? He gave psalms to David and you know what kind of preference He granted to Muhammad, *'Alayhi al-Salam*.. O Muhammad ibn Ali, I fear for you of envy. Allah has said it to be of the characteristics of the unbelievers. Thus, Allah, the Most Holy, the Most High, has said, '. . . out of envy, take you back to disbelief, even after the Truth has become evident to them. . . .' (2:109) Allah, the Most Holy, the Most High, has not given your control in the hands of Satan, O Muhammad ibn Ali. May I state what I heard your father say about you?' He said, 'Yes, I want to hear it.' The Imam said, 'I heard your father say on the day of Basra, "Whoever wants to do good to me in this life and in the next life he should do good to my son, Muhammad." O Muhammad ibn Ali if you like, I can inform you of the time you were, potentially only, a person in the back of your father. O Muhammad ibn Ali, have you come to know that al-Husayn ibn Ali, *'Alayhi al-Salam*, after I die and my spirit departs my body will be the Imam (Leader with Divine Authority) after me? There is his name before Allah, Most great is Whose name, in the Book and he is the heir of the Holy Prophet. Allah, the Most Holy, the Most High, has added it to the inheritance for him from his father and mother. You are the chosen ones from His creatures. He selected Muhammad from among you and Muhammad, *'Alayhi al-Salam*, selected Ali and Ali, *'Alayhi al-Salam*, selected me for Imamat (Leadership with Divine Authority). I have chosen al-Husayn, *'Alayhi al-Salam*, as the Imam (Leader with Divine Authority) after me.'

"Muhammad ibn Ali then said, 'You are my Imam (Leader with Divine Authority) and you are my connection to Muhammad, *'Alayhi al-Salam*. I swear by Allah, I wish I were dead before hearing these words from you. Certainly there are a great many facts in my head (about your excellence and virtues) that even with buckets cannot be drained and by the songs of the winds cannot be changed. It is like an encyclopedia with decorated pages. I am ready myself to speak them out but I find others have preceded me like the preceding of a heavenly book or what the messengers have brought. It is a book that exhausts the speaking tongue and the writing hand. I do not find enough pens to complete writing and it can turn all papers to ashes. Thus, there is no reach to your excellence and virtues. This is how Allah rewards those who do good deeds and there is no power without Allah.

'Al-Husayn, *'Alayhi al-Salam*, is the most knowledgeable among us, and his forbearance is the greatest among us in gravity. He is the closest to the Messenger of Allah among us in his relationship. He was a *Faqih* (scholar of Shari'a) before he was created. He has read the messages of the divine revelation before he would speak. Had Allah found anyone else better He would not have chosen Muhammad, *'Alayhi al-Salam*, (to receive Divine Authority). Since Allah has

287

chosen Muhammad, *'Alayhi al-Salam*, and Muhammad, *'Alayhi al-Salam*, chose Ali, *'Alayhi al-Salam*, and Ali chose you as the Imam (Leader with Divine Authority) and you have chosen al-Husayn, *'Alayhi al-Salam*, we accept and agree. Who is he that accepts a person other than him (al-Husayn, *'Alayhi al-Salam*). Who is he that seeks assistance in his difficulties from a person other than him (al-Husayn, *'Alayhi al-Salam*)?'"

H 775, Ch. 67, h 3

Through the same chain of narrators it is narrated from Sahl from Muhammad ibn Sulayman from Harun ibn al-Jahm from Muhammad ibn Muslim who has said the following:

"I heard abu Ja'far, *'Alayhi al-Salam*, say, 'When al-Hassan) ibn Ali, *'Alayhi al-Salam*, was about to leave this world he said to al-Husayn, *'Alayhi al-Salam*, 'O my brother, I want to entrust you with my will. (Please) safeguard and protect it. When I die prepare and help me toward (the Shrine of) the Messenger of Allah so I can renew my covenant with him, then help me toward (the grave of) Fatimah, my mother, *'Alayha al-Salam*. Thereafter return me back for burial in Baqi' graveyard. You must be aware that al-Humayra ('A'isha) will create problems for me. People know her deeds and her hostile attitude toward Allah and His Messenger and her animosity toward us, *Ahl al-Bayt* (family) of the Holy Prophet.' When al-Hassan, *'Alayhi al-Salam*, passed away his body was placed on the stretcher and then the procession was led to the place where the Messenger of Allah prayed for the dead people readied for burial. Al-Husayn, *'Alayhi al-Salam*, performed the prayer therein for al-Hassan and then the body was taken to the Mosque. When (the procession) paused near the grave of the Messenger of Allah, news reached 'A'isha and she was told, 'They have brought al-Hassan's body to bury near the Messenger of Allah.' She then came out quickly on the mule with saddle. She was the first woman in the Muslim community to ride on the saddle. She stood and then said, 'Take your son away from my house. Nothing will be buried in my house and the privacy of the Messenger of Allah be violated.'

"Al-Husayn, *'Alayhi al-Salam*, said to her, 'A long time ago you and your father had violated the privacy of the Messenger of Allah. You brought to his house those whose nearness the Messenger of Allah did not love. Allah will hold you responsible for this O 'A'isha. My brother commanded me to place him near his grandfather, the Messenger of Allah, so he can renew his covenant with him. You, O 'A'isha, must know that my brother is the most knowledgeable person about Allah and His messenger. He is by far the most knowledgeable one in interpreting the Book of Allah. He does not disregard the privacy of the Messenger of Allah. Allah, the Most Holy, the Most High, says, ". . . do not enter the houses of the Prophet for a meal without permission, . . ." (33:53) but you have admitted into the house of the Messenger of Allah men without his permission. Allah, the Most Holy, the Most High, has said, '. . . do not raise your voices above the voice of the Prophet. . . .' (49:2) I swear, it was you who constructed a construction and used picks for your father and his *Faruq* (discerning) near the ears of the Messenger of Allah. Allah, the Most Holy, the Most High, has said, "The hearts of those who lower their voices in the presence of the Messenger of Allah are tested by Allah through piety. . . ." (49:3) I swear, your father and his *Faruq* coming so close, (the two are buried near the grave of the Messenger of Allah), have brought trouble for the Messenger of Allah. The two of them did not maintain any respect for the Messenger of Allah, when Allah had commanded them, through the words of His Messenger, to maintain. What Allah has made unlawful about a believer who is dead He has also made unlawful about a living believer. I swear by Allah, O 'A'isha, if the burial of al-Hassan that you dislike to take place near his grandfather, the Messenger of Allah would have been permissible in our view and by Allah, you would have seen it to happen before your eyes, despite your opposition.'

"The narrator has said that Muhammad ibn al-Hanafiya then spoke and said, 'O 'A'isha, one day you ride a mule and the other day you rode a camel. You do not control yourself. You cannot own the earth to keep your animosity against banu Hashim.'

"The narrator has said that she then turned to him and said, 'O ibn al-Hanafiya, these are the sons of Fatimah, 'Alayha al-Salam, who speak. What for do you speak?'

"Al-Husayn, 'Alayhi al-Salam, then said to her, 'Which way do you want to distance Muhammad from the sons of Fatimah, 'Alayha al-Salam? I swear by Allah that he has three Fatimah in his lineage from the mother's side: (1) Fatimah daughter of 'Imran ibn 'A'idh ibn 'Amr ibn Makhdhum, (2) Fatimah daughter of Asad ibn Hashim and (3) Fatimah daughter of Za'ida ibn al-Asamm ibn Rawaha ibn Hijr ibn 'Abd Ma'is ibn 'Amir.'

"The narrator has said that she ('A'isha) then said, 'Move your son and take him away. You are a quarrelsome people.' The narrator has said that al-Husayn, 'Alayhi al-Salam, went to the grave of his mother and then took the body of al-Hassan, 'Alayhi al-Salam, out (of the shrine of the Messenger of Allah) and buried him in al-Baqi'.'"

Chapter 68 - Tacit and Explicit Testimony as Proof of Ali Ibn Al-Husayn's Divine Authority over the People After Al-Husayn, 'Alayhim al-Salam

H 776, Ch. 68, h 1
Muhammad ibn Yahya has narrated from Muhammad ibn al-Husayn and Ahmad ibn Muhammad from Muhammad ibn Isma'il from Mansur ibn Yunus from abu al-Jarud from abu Ja'far, 'Alayhi al-Salam, who has said the following:
"When al-Husayn ibn Ali, 'Alayhi al-Salam, was about to leave this world he called his eldest daughter, Fatimah, and gave her a sealed document openly before the people. It was his will. Ali ibn al-Husayn, 'Alayhi al-Salam, was ill with a certain internal illness and the people could see him about to die. Fatimah then gave the document to Ali ibn al-Husayn, 'Alayhi al-Salam. Thereafter, that document, by Allah, came to us, O Ziyad." The narrator has said, 'I asked the Imam, "What is in that document, may Allah keep my soul in service for your

cause?"' The Imam said, 'In it, by Allah, there is all that the children of Adam needed from the day Allah created Adam to the end of the world. In it, by Allah, there is the law of penalties and even the rules of compensation for a scratch on the body of the affected party.'"

H 777, Ch. 68, h 2

A number of our people have narrated from Ahmad ibn Muhammad from al-Husayn ibn Sa'id from ibn Sinan from abu al-Jarud from abu Ja'far, *'Alayhi al-Salam*, who has said the following:

"When al-Husayn, *'Alayhi al-Salam*, was about to leave this world he gave his will to his daughter, Fatimah, in a sealed document before the people openly. When what had to happen to al-Husayn, *'Alayhi al-Salam*, did happen, she gave it to Ali ibn al-Husayn, *'Alayhi al-Salam*.'"The narrator has said, 'I asked the Imam, "What was in it, may Allah grant you blessings?" The Imam said, 'It contained all that the children of Adam would need from the beginning of the world until it will end.'"

H 778, Ch. 68, h 3

A number of our people have narrated from Ahmad ibn Muhammad from Ali ibn al-Hakam from Sayf ibn 'Amira from abu Bakr al-Hadrami from abu 'Abd Allah, *'Alayhi al-Salam*, who has said the following:

"When al-Husayn, *'Alayhi al-Salam*, was about to leave for Iraq he entrusted 'Umm Salama (may Allah be pleased with her) with the Books and his will. When Ali ibn al-Husayn, *'Alayhi al-Salam*, returned (to Madina) she delivered them to him."

H 779, Ch. 68, h 4

According to the manuscript of al-Safwan, the above *Hadith* reads as follows: Ali ibn Ibrahim has narrated from his father from Hanan ibn Sadir from Falih ibn abu Bakr al-Shaybani, who has said the following:

"I swear by Allah, I was sitting in the presence of Ali ibn al-Husayn, *'Alayhi al-Salam*, whose sons also were there when Jabir ibn 'Abd Allah al-Ansari came. He offered his greeting, then he held the hand of abu Ja'far, *'Alayhi al-Salam*. He took him aside for privacy and said, 'The Messenger of Allah informed me that I will find myself with a man from *Ahl al-Bayt* (family the Holy Prophet, *'Alayhim al-Salam*) who will be called "Muhammad ibn Ali, also called abu Ja'far (father of Ja'far)." When I will meet him I must convey to him greetings from him (the Messenger of Allah).' When abu Ja'far returned to the meeting, he sat near his father, Ali ibn al-Husayn, *'Alayhi al-Salam*, and his brothers. When the Imam performed the Maghrib prayer (the prayer at sunset), Ali ibn al-Husayn asked abu Ja'far, *'Alayhi al-Salam*, 'What did Jabir ibn 'Abd Allah al-Ansari say to you?' He (abu Ja'far) said, 'Jabir said that the Messenger of Allah said to him the following, "You will soon find yourself with a man from my *Ahl al-Bayt,* (family) whose name is Muhammad ibn Ali, also called abu Ja'far (father of Ja'far). Convey my greetings of peace to him." His father (abu Ja'far's father) then said, 'Success for you, my son, for what Allah has granted to you exclusively through His messenger from among the members of your family. Do not tell it to your brothers, lest they may plan against you as the brothers of Joseph did.'"

Chapter 69 - Tacit and Explicit Testimony as Proof of abu Ja'far's Divine Authority Over the People After Ali ibn Al-Husayn, *'Alayhim al-Salam*

H 780, Ch. 69, h 1
Ahmad ibn Idris has narrated from Muhammad ibn 'Abd al-Jabbar from abu al-Qasim al-Kufi from Muhammad ibn Sahl from Ibrahim ibn abu al-Bilad from Isma'il ibn Muhammad ibn 'Abd Allah ibn Ali ibn al-Husayn from abu Ja'far, *'Alayhi al-Salam*, who has said the following:
"When Ali ibn al-Husayn, *'Alayhi al-Salam*, was about to leave this world he took out a basket or a box. He then said, 'O Muhammad, pick up this box.'

"The narrator has said, 'He (Muhammad) carried away the box with the help of four people. When the Imam died, his sons came asking for the box and said, 'Give us our share from the box.' He (Muhammad) then said to them, 'By Allah, there is nothing for you in that box. Had there been anything for you he would not have given it to me.' In the box there were the Armaments of the Messenger of Allah and his books."

H 781, Ch. 69, h 2
Muhammad ibn Yahya has narrated from 'Imran ibn Musa from Muhammad ibn al-Husayn from Muhammad ibn 'Abd Allah from 'Isa ibn 'Abd Allah from his father that his grandfather has said the following:
"Ali ibn al-Husayn, *'Alayhi al-Salam*, looked at his sons when he was about to leave this world and they all had gathered around him. He then looked at his son, Muhammad ibn Ali, and said, 'O Muhammad, carry this box to your house.' He said, 'It was not full of Dirhams and Dinars (valuable properties). It, however, was full of knowledge.'"

H 782 Ch. 69, h 3
Muhammad ibn al-Hassan has narrated from Sahl from Muhammad ibn 'Isa from Fadala ibn Ayyub from al-Husayn ibn abu al-'Ala', who has said the following:
"I heard abu 'Abd Allah, *'Alayhi al-Salam*, say, ''Umar ibn 'Abd al-'Aziz wrote ibn Hazm to send him the endowment documents of Ali, 'Umar and 'Uthman. Ibn Hazm sent a person to Zayd ibn al-Hassan, *'Alayhi al-Salam*, the eldest among them, and asked him about the documents.' Zayd has said, 'The high authority after Ali was al-Hassan, after him al-Husayn, Ali ibn al-Husayn was the high authority after al-Husayn and after Ali ibn al-Husayn, Muhammad ibn Ali was the high authority. Send someone to him (to find out about the documents).' Ibn Hazm then sent to my father (abu Ja'far, *'Alayhi al-Salam*) and my father sent me with the document to him. I went and delivered it to ibn Hazm.

"The narrator has said that certain persons of our people asked the Imam, 'Did the sons of al-Hassan, *'Alayhi al-Salam*, know this?' The Imam said, 'They knew it just as they knew this was night, but envy influenced them. Had they sought truth with truth it would have been better for them, but they sought the worldly things.'"

Note: ibn Hazm, is abu Baker ibn Muhammad ibn 'Amr ibn Hazm al-Ansari (37A.H./657A.D.–120A.H./738A.D.), the judge of Madina from 87A.H./706A.D. appointed by 'Umar ibn 'Abd al-'Aziz when he was governor of Madina, as a Caliph 'Umar appointed ibn Hazm governor of Madina. (Al-

Tabari, vol.2, pp.1191, 1255, 1305, 1346, 1372 - 1375, 1437, 1452; vol.3, p.2460; ibn al-Athir, vol.5, pp.55, 67; *Tahdhib al-Takdhib,* vol.l2, pp.38 -40.)

H 782a Ch. 69, h 4
Al-Husayn ibn Muhammad has narrated from Mu'alla ibn Muhammad from al-Hassan ibn Ali al-Washsha' from 'Abd al-Karim ibn 'Amr from ibn abu Ya'fur, who has said that he heard abu 'Abd Allah, *'Alayhi al-Salam,* say the following:

"'Umar ibn 'Abd al-'Aziz wrote ibn Hazm. . . ." He then has narrated a *Hadith* similar to the above one except that he, abu 'Abd Allah, *'Alayhi al-Salam,* has said, 'Ibn Hazm sent to Zayd ibn al-Hassan who was older than my father.'

A number of our people have narrated from Ahmad ibn Muhammad from al-Washsha' a similar *Hadith.*

Chapter 70 - Tacit and Explicit Testimony as Proof of abu 'Abd Allah Ja'far ibn Muhammad Al-Sadiq's Divine Authority Over People After Muhammad ibn Ali ibn Al-Husayn, *'Alayhim al-Salam*

H 783, Ch. 70, h 1
Al-Husayn ibn Muhammad has narrated from Mu'alla ibn Muhammad from al-Washsha' from Aban ibn 'Uthman from abu al-Sabbah al-Kinani, who has said the following:

"Once abu Ja'far, *'Alayhi al-Salam,* looked at abu 'Abd Allah, *'Alayhi al-Salam,* who was taking a walking. The Imam asked, 'Do you see this (person)? This person is of those about whom Allah, the Most Holy, the Most High, has said, "However, We have decided to grant a favor to the suppressed ones on earth by means of appointing them leaders and heirs of the land. (28:5)'"

H 784, Ch. 70, h 2
Muhammad ibn Yahya has narrated from Ahmad ibn Muhammad from ibn abu 'Umayr from Hisham ibn Salim from abu 'Abd Allah, *'Alayhi al-Salam,* who has said the following:

"When my father was about to leave this world he said, 'O Ja'far, I recommend you to be good to my companions.' I then said, 'May Allah keep my soul in service for your cause, by Allah, I will educate them so that in any city where any of them will live he will not need to ask others for knowledge (of religion).'"

H 785, Ch. 70, h 3
Ali ibn Ibrahim has narrated from his father from ibn abu 'Umayr from Hisham ibn al-Muthanna from Sadir al-Sayrafi who has said that he heard abu Ja'far, *'Alayhi al-Salam,* say the following:

"It is part of the success of a man to have a child who is similar to his father physically, ethically and in good character. I do not know anyone more similar to me physically, ethically and in good character than this son of mine (meaning thereby abu 'Abd Allah, *'Alayhi al-Salam.*"

H 786, Ch. 70, h 4
A number of our people have narrated from Ahmad ibn Muhammad from Ali ibn al-Hakam from Tahir who has said the following:

"Once I was in the presence of abu Ja'far, *'Alayhi al-Salam*, and Ja'far, *'Alayhi al-Salam*, came in. Abu Ja'far, *'Alayhi al-Salam*, said, 'This (Ja'far) is the best among the people: in fact, is of much higher position among them.'"

H 787, Ch. 70, h 5
Ahmad ibn Muhammad has narrated from Muhammad ibn Khalid from certain persons of our people from Yunus ibn Ya'qub from Tahir who has said the following:

"Once I was in the presence of abu Ja'far, *'Alayhi al-Salam*, and Ja'far, *'Alayhi al-Salam*, came in. The Imam said, 'This (Ja'far) is the best of the people.'"

H 788, Ch. 70, h 6
Ahmad ibn Mihran has narrated from Muhammad ibn Ali from Fudayl ibn 'Uthman from Tahir who has said the following:

"Once I was in the presence of abu Ja'far, *'Alayhi al-Salam*, that Ja'far, *'Alayhi al-Salam*, came in. The Imam said, 'This (Ja'far) is the best of the people.'"

H 789, Ch. 70, h 7
Muhammad ibn Yahya has narrated from Ahmad ibn Muhammad from ibn Mahbub from Hisham ibn Salim from Jabir ibn Yazid al-Ju'fi who has said the following:

"A question was asked (from abu Ja'far, *'Alayhi al-Salam*, about al-Qa'im (the twelfth Imam)). He (abu Ja'far) tapped (at the shoulder of) abu 'Abd Allah, *'Alayhi al-Salam*, and said, 'This, by Allah, is the *Qa'im* (one who will establish the kingdom of Allah) of the family of Muhammad, *'Alayhi al-Salam*.'"Anbasa has said, 'When abu Ja'far passed away, I went to see abu 'Abd Allah, *'Alayhi al-Salam*, and told him of what I had heard (from Jabir). The Imam said, 'Jabir has spoken the truth.' He then said, 'You perhaps think that every succeeding Imam after a preceding Imam is not *al-Qa'im*. (*Al-Qa'im* also refers to the one who obeys and serves Allah).'"

H 790, Ch. 70, h 8
Ali ibn Ibrahim has narrated from Muhammad ibn 'Isa from Yunus ibn 'Abd al-Rahman from 'Abd al-A'la from abu 'Abd Allah, *'Alayhi al-Salam*, who has said the following:

"My father entrusted me with all that is there (the sacred objects inherited from the prophets such as wills and so forth). When he was about to leave this world, he asked me to call for him a few people to bear testimony. I then called four people from Quraysh. Among them was Nafi' Mawla 'Abd Allah ibn 'Umar.

"He then said, 'Write down: This is (like) the will of Jacob to his sons, "My sons, Allah has chosen this religion for you. You must not leave this world unless you are a Muslim (submitted to the will of the Lord of the world)." (2:132)

"Muhammad ibn Ali has recommended Ja'far ibn Muhammad in his will, and commands him to shroud him (Muhammad ibn Ali) with the gown with which he performed his prayers on Fridays, and prepare a turban for him out of his own turban. He should shape his grave squarely and raise it four inches from the ground; he should open the knots from all ends of his shroud at the time of burial."

"Then he said to the witnesses, 'You may go now, may Allah bless you.'"

"I then asked him after they had left, 'O father, you did not need to make a will for such matters.' He said, 'My son, I do not like that you will be defeated; they will say, 'No will was made in his favor.' I just wanted to establish a defense and authority in your favor.'"

Chapter 71 - Tacit and Explicit Testimony as Proof of abu Al-Hassan Musa's Divine Authority Over the People After abu 'Abd Allah, *'Alayhim al-Salam*

H 791, Ch. 71, h 1

Ahmad ibn Mihran has narrated from Muhammad ibn Ali from 'Abd Allah al-Qalla' from al-Fayd ibn al-Mukhtar who has said the following:

"Once I said to abu 'Abd Allah, *'Alayhi al-Salam*, 'Please, take my hand out of the fire. Who will be for us after you (leave this world)?' Shortly thereafter abu Ibrahim (Musa ibn Ja'far, *'Alayhi al-Salam*) came in, and he was a young boy in those days. The Imam said, 'This is your *Sahib* (your Imam); so hold fast to him.'"

H 792, Ch. 71, h 2

A number of our people have narrated from Ahmad ibn Muhammad from Ali ibn al-Hakam from abu Ayyub al-Khazzaz from Thubayt from Mu'adh ibn Kathir who has said the following:

"Once I said to abu 'Abd Allah, *'Alayhi al-Salam*, 'I pray to Allah who granted your father such a high position, to grant you such position through your successor before you leave this world.' He then said, 'Allah has already granted such a favor.'

"I (the narrator) then asked the Imam, "Who is he, may Allah keep my soul in service for your cause?" He made a hand gesture toward the pious servant (of Allah), who was asleep, saying, 'This man who is asleep.' He was a young boy."

H 793, Ch. 71, h 3

Through the same chain of narrators it is narrated from Ahmad ibn Muhammad who has said the following:

"Abu Ali al-Arjani al-Farisi narrated to me from 'Abd al-Rahman ibn al-Hajjaj in the year (179 A.H. /795 A.D.) in which former abu al-Hassan, Imam Musa, *'Alayhi al-Salam*, was detained. I (Hajjaj) said to him ('Abd al-Rahman), 'This man (abu al-Hassan Musa) has been detained by his (Mansur, current ruler's) orders. We do not know what his condition is. Have you heard anything from him about his sons?' He ('Abd al-Rahman) said to me, 'I did not think anyone would ask me about this issue. Once I went to see Ja'far ibn Muhammad, *'Alayhi al-Salam*, in his home. He was in such and such a room at the prayer area. He was praying to Allah and on his right side was Musa ibn Ja'far, *'Alayhi al-Salam*, saying Amen for his prayer.' I said to him, 'May Allah keep my soul in service for your cause, you know I have cut myself off from all others to serve you. Who will be the *Wali* (Leader with Divine Authority) for people after you?' He replied, 'Musa has dressed up in this coat of arms and it has fit him perfectly.' I then said to him, 'I will not need anything after this.'"

H 794, Ch. 71, h 4

Ahmad ibn Mihran has narrated from Muhammad ibn Ali from Musa al-Sayqal from al-Mufaddal ibn 'Umar who has said the following:

"Once I was in the presence of abu 'Abd Allah, *'Alayhi al-Salam*, when abu Ibrahim came in; he was a young boy. He (abu 'Abd Allah) said, 'Acknowledge my will (transfer of Divine Authority to him, Musa ibn Ja'far, *'Alayhi al-Salam*) and inform of his task (Leadership with Divine Authority) your reliable companions.'"

H 795, Ch. 71, h 5

Ahmad ibn Mihran has narrated from Muhammad ibn Ali from Ya'qub ibn Ja'far al-Ja'fari who has said that Ishaq ibn Ja'far, *'Alayhi al-Salam*, said to me the following:

"One day I was in the presence of my father and Ali ibn 'Umar ibn Ali asked him this question: 'May Allah keep my soul in service for your cause, from whom should we and the people seek help and assistance after you leave this world?' He (the Imam) said, 'You must seek refuge with and guidance from the man who has two pieces of yellow clothes on him and a twined bunch of hair, who will shortly appear to you from this door, opening both halves of the door with his both hands.' We did not wait very long until there appeared two palms opening both halves of the door. The person who came in was abu Ibrahim, Musa ibn Ja'far, *'Alayhi al-Salam*."

H 796, Ch. 71, h 6

Ali ibn Ibrahim has narrated from his father from ibn abu Najran from Safwan al-Jammal from abu 'Abd Allah, *'Alayhi al-Salam*, Safwan has said the following:

"Once Mansur ibn Hazim said to him (the Imam, *'Alayhi al-Salam*), 'May Allah keep my soul in service for your cause, (human) souls pass through mornings and evenings and approach death, if that (your time to leave this world) comes then who (will be the Imam)?'

"Abu 'Abd Allah, *'Alayhi al-Salam*, then said, 'If that happens then he is your *Sahib* (Imam, Leader with Divine Authority).' He tapped, I think, the right shoulder of abu al-Hassan with his hand. He was five years old (or five feet tall) at that time and 'Abd Allah ibn Ja'far was also present with us."

H 797, Ch. 71, h 7

Muhammad ibn Yahya has narrated from Muhammad ibn al-Husayn from 'Abd al-Rahman ibn abu Najran from 'Isa ibn 'Abd Allah ibn Muhammad ibn 'Umar ibn Ali ibn abu Talib, *'Alayhi al-Salam*, who has said the following:

"Once I said to abu 'Abd Allah, *'Alayhi al-Salam*, 'If something will happen (death of Imam), may Allah not make me experience it, then whom must I follow as my Imam?' The narrator has said that he pointed to his son Musa, *'Alayhi al-Salam*. I then asked, 'What if something happens to Musa, *'Alayhi al-Salam*, then whom must I follow as my Imam?' The Imam said, 'Follow his son.' Then I asked, "What if something will happen to his son who will leave behind an elder brother and a son, then whom should I follow?' He said, 'Follow his son.' Then he said, 'In this way forever.' I then asked, 'What if I will not know him and will not know his place?' The Imam said, 'Say, "O Lord, I love and take as my guardian whoever is left (on earth) as Your Authority of the sons of the preceding Imam." This will be enough for you if Allah may so will.'"

H 798, Ch. 71, h 8
Ahmad ibn Mihran has narrated from Muhammad ibn Ali from 'Abd Allah al-Qalla' from al-Mufaddal ibn 'Umar who has said the following:
"Once abu 'Abd Allah, *'Alayhi al-Salam*, spoke of abu al-Hassan, *'Alayhi al-Salam*, and he was a young boy in those days. He said, 'This is such a child that no other child born to us has been of a greater blessing to our followers than him.' The Imam then said to me, 'Do not be harsh with Isma'il (Imam's other son).'"

H 799, Ch. 71, h 9
Muhammad ibn Yahya and Ahmad ibn Idris have narrated from Muhammad ibn 'Abd al-Jabbar from al-Hassan ibn al-Husayn from Ahmad ibn al-Hassan al-Maythami from Fayd ibn al-Mukhtar who has said the following:
"In a lengthy *Hadith* on the issues of abu al-Hassan, *'Alayhi al-Salam*, abu 'Abd Allah, *'Alayhi al-Salam*, has said to the narrator, 'He is your Master of whom you asked. Stand up for him and acknowledge his rights.' I then stood up and kissed his head and hand and prayed to Allah, the Most Holy, the Most High, for him. Abu 'Abd Allah, *'Alayhi al-Salam*, then said, 'Keep in mind that permission is not given to us to speak about him to anyone before you.'

"I (the narrator) then said to the Imam, 'May Allah keep my soul in service for your cause, can I inform anyone about him?' The Imam said, 'Yes, you may inform your family (wife) and sons.' With me there were my family (wife), sons and friends, and of my friends there was Yunus ibn al-Zabyan. When I informed them they all thanked Allah, the Most Holy, the Most High. Yunus said, 'No, by Allah, I must hear that from him.' He was in a hurry. He went and I followed him. When I reached the door I heard abu 'Abd Allah, *'Alayhi al-Salam*, saying to him, he had reached him before I did, 'What Fayd has said to you is true.' I (the narrator) then said, 'I have heard it and I obey.' Abu 'Abd Allah, *'Alayhi al-Salam*, then said, 'Take him with you, O Fayd.'"

H 800, Ch. 71, h 10
Muhammad ibn Yahya has narrated from Muhammad ibn al-Husayn from Ja'far ibn Bashir from Fudayl from Tahir from abu 'Abd Allah, *'Alayhi al-Salam*, who has said the following:
"He has said that abu 'Abd Allah, *'Alayhi al-Salam*, would blame 'Abd Allah, show him his anger and advise him asking, 'What is the matter that you are not like your brother (Musa)? By Allah, I observe light in his face.' 'Abd Allah then asked, 'Why is it? Aren't his and my father and mother the same?' Abu 'Abd Allah, *'Alayhi al-Salam*, then said, 'He is from my soul and you are my son.'"

H 801, Ch. 71, h 11
Al-Husayn ibn Muhammad has narrated from Mu'alla ibn Muhammad from al-Washsha' from Muhammad ibn Sinan from Ya'qub al-Sarraj who has said the following:
"Once I went to see abu 'Abd Allah, *'Alayhi al-Salam*, who was standing by the cradle of abu al-Hassan, Musa. He began to speak secretly to him for a long time. I sat there until he was free. I then stood for him and he said to me, 'Come close to your *Mawla* (master and Leader with Divine Authority).' I went close and said

the greetings of peace. He answered my greetings very clearly and then said to me, 'Go and change the name of your daughter whom you named just yesterday. It is a name that makes Allah angry.' A girl was born to us and I had named her al-Humayra. Abu 'Abd Allah, *'Alayhi al-Salam*, said to me, 'Follow his command and you will have the right guidance.' I then changed her name."

H 802, Ch. 71, h 12

Ahmad ibn Idris has narrated from Muhammad ibn 'Abd al-Jabbar from Safwan from ibn Muskan from Sulayman ibn Khalid who has said the following:

"Abu 'Abd Allah, *'Alayhi al-Salam*, one day called abu al-Hassan, *'Alayhi al-Salam*, while we were in his presence and said to us, 'You must take hold of this man. He, by Allah, will be your Master (Leader with Divine Authority) after me.'"

H 803, Ch. 71, h 13

Ali ibn Muhammad has narrated from Sahl or another person, from Muhammad ibn al-Walid from Yunus from Dawud ibn Zurbi from abu Ayyub al-Nahwi who has said the following:

"Abu Ja'far, al-Mansur summoned me in the middle of the night and I went to see him. When I met him he was sitting in a chair. Before him there was a candle and a letter in his hand. I (the narrator) then greeted him and he threw the letter to me while he was weeping. He said, 'This is a letter of Muhammad ibn Sulayman in which he has informed us that Ja'far ibn Muhammad, *'Alayhi al-Salam*, has died. We are for Allah and to Him we will all return.' He said it three times. 'Where can one find anyone like Ja'far, *'Alayhi al-Salam*?' Then he said to me, 'Write it down.'

"I (the narrator) then wrote down the introduction of the letter. He (Mansur) said, 'Write to ask if he has left a will to any man particularly, if so summon him and kill him.' He has said that a reply to his letter came back and it said that the Imam has in fact, left a will to five people: They are abu Ja'far al-Mansur, Muhammad ibn Sulayman, 'Abd Allah, Musa and Hamida.'"

H 804 Ch. 71, h 14

Ali ibn Ibrahim has narrated from his father from al-Nadr ibn Suwayd who has said the following:

"Ibn Suwayd has narrated a similar *Hadith* as above except that he has said, 'He has left a will to abu Ja'far, al-Mansur, 'Abd Allah, Musa, Muhammad ibn Ja'far and Mawla of abu 'Abd Allah, *'Alayhi al-Salam*.' Abu Ja'far, al-Mansur then said, 'There is no way to kill these people.'"

H 805, Ch. 71, h 15

Al-Husayn ibn Muhammad has narrated from Mu'alla ibn Muhammad from al-Washsha' from Ali ibn al-Hassan from Safwan al-Jammal who has said the following:

"I asked abu 'Abd Allah, *'Alayhi al-Salam*, about the person in charge of this matter (Leadership with Divine Authority) and he said, 'The person in charge of the task does not trifle or play.' At this time abu al-Hassan, Musa came. He was very small. With him there was a baby goat of Makkah's (goats) and he was saying to her, 'Prostrate before your Lord.' Abu 'Abd Allah then took him and hugged him and said, 'May Allah keep my soul and the souls of my parents in service for the cause of one who does not trifle or engage in amusement.'"

H 806, Ch. 71, h 16
Ali ibn Muhammad has narrated from certain ones of our people from 'Ubays ibn Hisham that 'Umar al-Rummani narrated to me from Fayd ibn al-Mukhtar the following:
"Once, when I was in the presence of abu 'Abd Allah, *'Alayhi al-Salam*, abu al-Hassan Musa, *'Alayhi al-Salam*, came and he was a young boy. I held him and kissed him. Abu 'Abd Allah, *'Alayhi al-Salam*, said, 'You (the community of our followers) are the Ark and he is the captain.'

"I (the narrator) then went to perform Hajj the next year and I had two thousand Dinars. I sent one thousand to abu 'Abd Allah, *'Alayhi al-Salam*, and one thousand to him (abu al-Hassan). I went to see abu 'Abd Allah, *'Alayhi al-Salam*, who said, 'You have considered him equal to me.' I said, 'I did so because of your words.' He then said, 'I swear by Allah, I did not do so, in fact, Allah, the Most Holy, the Most High, has done it for him (abu al-Hassan Musa, *'Alayhi al-Salam*).'"

Chapter 72 - Tacit and Explicit Testimony as Proof of abu Al-Hassan Al-Rida's Divine Authority Over the People After abu Al-Hassan Musa, *'Alayhim al-Salam*

H 807, Ch. 72, h 1
Muhammad ibn Yahya has narrated from Ahmad ibn Muhammad from ibn Mahbub from al-Husayn ibn Nu'aym al-Sahhaf who has said the following:
"Hisham ibn al-Hakam, Ali ibn Yaqtin and I were in Baghdad. Ali ibn Yaqtin said, 'I was in the presence of the pious servant (of Allah) and his son Ali came. He then said to me, "O Ali ibn Yaqtin, this is Ali, the sayyid (leader, master) of my children and I have gifted him with my own *Kunya*," (the Arabic expression used to address people, 'O father of so and so, and so forth). Hisham tapped his forehead with his palm and said, 'Fie upon you! How did you say it?' Ali ibn Yaqtin said, 'I heard, by Allah, from him just as I said.' Hisham then asked, 'Did he (Imam Musa, *'Alayhi al-Salam*) inform you that after him the task (Leadership with Divine Authority) will be with him (his son)?'"

Ahmad ibn Mihran has narrated from Muhammad ibn Ali from al-Husayn ibn Nu'aym al-Sahhaf who has said the following:
"Once I was in the presence of the pious servant (of Allah). In al-Safwani manuscript it says, 'I was' . . . then he relates the rest of the above *Hadith*."

H 808, Ch. 72, h 2
A number of our people have narrated from Ahmad ibn Muhammad from Mu'awiya ibn Hakim from Nu'aym al-Qabusi from abu al-Hassan, *'Alayhi al-Salam*, who has said the following:
"My son, Ali is the eldest of my sons, the most virtuous among them in my opinion and the most beloved of them to me. He looks (reads) into the *Jafr* (a secret source of knowledge) with me. No one looks into it except a prophet, or the executor of the will of a prophet."

H 809, Ch. 72, h 3
Ahmad ibn Mihran has narrated from Muhammad ibn Ali from Muhammad ibn Sinan and Isma'il ibn 'Abbad al-Qasri, all from Dawud al-Raqqi who has said the following:

"Once I said to abu Ibrahim, *'Alayhi al-Salam*, 'May Allah keep my soul in service for your cause, I have become old, take my hand out of the fire.' The narrator has said that the Imam pointed to his son, abu al-Hassan, *'Alayhi al-Salam*, and then said, 'This is your guardian after me.'"

H 810, Ch. 72, h 4

Al-Husayn ibn Muhammad has narrated from Mu'alla ibn Muhammad from Ahmad ibn Muhammad ibn 'Abd Allah from al-Hassan from ibn abu 'Umayr from Muhammad ibn Ishaq ibn 'Ammar who has said the following:

"Once I asked abu al-Hassan the 1st, *'Alayhi al-Salam*, 'Would you guide me to a person from whom I learn my religion?' He said, 'This is my son, Ali. My father took my hand until we were in the shrine of the Messenger of Allah and said, "My son, Allah, the Most Holy, the Most High, has said, '. . . I am appointing someone as my deputy on earth. . . .' (2:30) When Allah, the Most Holy, the Most High, says a word, He keeps His word.'"

H 811, Ch. 72, h 5

Ahmad ibn Idris has narrated from Muhammad ibn 'Abd al-Jabbar from al-Hassan ibn al-Husayn al-Lu'lu'i from Yahya ibn 'Amr from Dawud al-Raqqi who has said the following:

"Once I said to abu al-Hassan Musa, *'Alayhi al-Salam*, 'I have grown old and my bones are weakening. I asked your father, *'Alayhi al-Salam*, and he informed me about you. Would you also inform me (about the Imam after you).' The Imam said, 'This, abu al-Hassan al-Rida, *'Alayhi al-Salam*, is the one whom you are looking for.'"

H 812, Ch. 72, h 6

Ahmad ibn Mihran has narrated from Muhammad ibn Ali from Ziyad ibn Marwan al-Qandi, from the *Waqifa* sect who has said the following:

"Once I went to see abu Ibrahim, *'Alayhi al-Salam*, at that time his son abu al-Hassan al-Rida was with him. The Imam said to me, 'O Ziyad, this is my son so and so. His writing is my writing, his words are my words, and his messenger is my messenger. Whatever he may say, his words are the true words.'"

H 813, Ch. 72, h 7

Ahmad ibn Mihran has narrated from Muhammad ibn Ali from Muhammad ibn Fudayl who has said that al-Makhdhumi whose mother was one of the children of Ja'far ibn abu Talib has narrated the following:

"Abu al-Hassan Musa, *'Alayhi al-Salam*, once called all of us to see him. We all gathered and then he asked us, 'Do you know why I have called you?' We said, 'We do not know.' He then said, 'Bear testimony that this, my son, is the executor of my will, the director of my affairs, and the succeeding Imam. Whoever has a loan due me should demand from my son, this one. Whomever I may have promised anything should also acquire from him. Whoever must see me must not come to see me without written permission from him.'"

H 814, Ch. 72, h 8

Ahmad ibn Mihran has narrated from Muhammad ibn Ali from Muhammad ibn Sinan and Ali ibn al-Hakam all from al-Husayn ibn al-Mukhtar who has said the following:

"Certain tablets came out to us from abu al-Hassan, *'Alayhi al-Salam*, when he was in jail, that said, 'My instructions and directives to my eldest son to do so and so. As far as so and so is concerned, do not give him anything until I will meet you, or Allah will decree for me to leave this world.'"

H 815, Ch. 72, h 9
A number of our people have narrated from Ahmad ibn Muhammad from Ali ibn al-Hakam from 'Abd Allah ibn al-Mughira from al-Husayn ibn al-Mukhtar who has said the following:
"In Basra (where the Imam was imprisoned) certain tablets came out to us from abu al-Hassan, '*Alayhi al-Salam*, on which it was written horizontally, 'My instructions and directives to my eldest son (Ali ibn Musa al-Rida, '*Alayhi al-Salam*) who should give such and such to so and so. As far as so and so is concerned, nothing should be given to him until I will come, or Allah, the Most Holy, the Most High, will decree that I must die. Allah certainly does what He wills.'"

H 816, Ch. 72, h 10
Ahmad ibn Mihran has narrated from Muhammad ibn Ali from ibn Muhriz from Ali ibn Yaqtin who has said the following:
"Abu al-Hassan, '*Alayhi al-Salam*, wrote to me from prison that so and so, my son, is the master and guardian of my children and I have gifted him with my own Kunyah (Arabic surname)."

H 817, Ch. 72, h 11
Ahmad ibn Mihran has narrated from Muhammad ibn Ali from Abu Ali al-Khazzaz from Dawud ibn Sulayman who has said the following:
"Once I said to abu Ibrahim, '*Alayhi al-Salam*, 'I am afraid that an incident may take place and I will not be able to see you. Inform me who will be the Imam after you?' The Imam said, 'My son, so and so,' meaning thereby abu al-Hassan (al-Rida, '*Alayhi al-Salam*).'"

H 818, Ch. 72, h 12
Ahmad ibn Mihran has narrated from Muhammad ibn Ali from Sa'id ibn abu al-Jahm from al-Nasr ibn Qabus who has said the following:
"I said to abu Ibrahim, '*Alayhi al-Salam*, 'I asked your father, "Who will be (the Imam) after you?' He informed me that you would be (the Imam after him). When abu 'Abd Allah, '*Alayhi al-Salam*, left this world people went left and right and I said, 'I with my people am with you. Inform me, of your sons who will be (the Imam) after you?" He (the Imam) said, 'My son so and so.'"

H 819, Ch. 72, h 13
Ahmad ibn Mihran has narrated from Muhammad ibn Ali from al-Dahhak ibn al-Ash'ath from Dawud ibn Zurbi who has said the following:
"Once I went to deliver a certain property to abu Ibrahim, '*Alayhi al-Salam*. He accepted it partially and left the rest. I asked him, 'May Allah keep you well, why have you left it with me?' He said, 'The person in charge of this task (Leadership with Divine Authority) will demand it from you.' When we heard the news of his (abu Ibrahim's) death, abu al-Hassan, '*Alayhi al-Salam*, his son, sent for me, asking for that property, and I delivered it to him."

H 820, Ch. 72, h 14

Ahmad ibn Mihran has narrated from Muhammad ibn Ali from abu al-Hakam al-Armani who has said that 'Abd Allah ibn Ibrahim ibn Ali ibn 'Abd Allah ibn Ja'far ibn abu Talib narrated to me from Yazid ibn Salit al-Zaydi. Abu al-Hakam has said that 'Abd Allah ibn Muhammad ibn 'Ammara al-Jarmi narrated to me from Yazid ibn Salit who has said the following:

"Once I met abu Ibrahim, *'Alayhi al-Salam*, on our way to perform al-'Umra, (pilgrimage to Makkah) and I said, 'May Allah keep my soul in service for your cause, do you remember this place where we are now?' He said, 'Yes, but do you remember it?' I said, 'Yes, my father and I met you at this place with abu 'Abd Allah, *'Alayhi al-Salam*, and your brothers were also present. My father said to him, 'May Allah keep my soul and the souls of my parents in service for your cause, all of you are purified *'A'immah*. However, no one is immune from death. Instruct me with a few things that I may say to my successors so that they may not go astray.'

"The Imam said, 'Yes, O abu 'Abd Allah, I will tell you what you need. These are my sons and this one is their master. He pointed to you. He said that you have been taught laws, understanding, generosity, the knowledge of whatever people need, and how to settle their disputes in the matters of religion and worldly matters. In him there are good moral qualities and good answers. He is a gate of the gates of Allah, the Most Holy, the Most High, and in him there is another quality that is better than all of these.'

"My father asked, 'What is that quality, may Allah keep my soul and the souls of my parents in service for your cause?' The Imam said, 'Allah, the Most Holy, the Most High, will bring about from him the savior of this 'Umma and her blossom, her banner, her light, distinction in excellence and her wisdom. He will be the best child and the best flourishing. Allah, the Most Holy, the Most High, will spare through him lives, bring peace among the hostile parties, harmonize the divisiveness, fill the gap of differences, clothe the naked, feed the hungry and give protection to the frightened ones. Through him Allah will send down rain and mercy to the servants. He will be the best as an aged man and the best of the flourishing ones. His words will be rules and his silence knowledge. He will clarify for people their differences and he will administer his relative (associates) before his age of puberty.'

"My father asked, 'May Allah keep my soul and the souls of my parents in service for your cause, is he yet born?' The Imam said, 'Yes, he is born and several years have passed.' Yazid has said, 'At this point a person came and in his presence we could not speak.'

"Yazid has said that I then said to abu Ibrahim, *'Alayhi al-Salam*, 'Inform me just as your father informed you.' The Imam said, 'Yes, I can do so. My father lived in a time that was not like this time.' I said, 'Whoever contents himself with only this much (of your words) then, may Allah's condemnation be upon him.' He (Yazid) has said, 'The Imam laughed quite intensely. Then he said, "O abu 'Umara, I can inform you that when I came out of my house, I gave my will to my son, so and so. In public I allowed my other sons to take part in my instructions with him but I gave my will to him in private and wanted him to be alone. Had it been up to myself, I would have placed my will with my son al-Qasim because of my love and sympathy for him. However, it is up to Allah, the Most Holy, and the Most High, who places it (Leadership with Divine Authority) wherever He wants. The Messenger of Allah, *'Alayhi al-Salam*, has brought me this information. He showed him to me as well as the people who will be with him. Such it is with us. No one of us places his will with anyone until the Messenger of Allah brings its news, and so did my great, great, great, great grandfather Ali, *'Alayhi al-Salam*. With the Messenger of Allah I saw a ring, a sword, a staff, a book and a turban. I asked, 'What is it, O Messenger of Allah?' He replied, 'The turban is the authority of Allah, the Most Holy, the Most High. The sword is the Majesty of Allah, the Most Holy, the Most High. The Book is the light of Allah, the Most Holy, the Most High. The Staff is the power of Allah. The Ring consists of all the above matters." Then he said to me, "The task (Leadership with Divine Authority) has left you for one other than you." I then said, 'O Messenger of Allah, show me which of them is he.' The Messenger of Allah said, 'I have not seen any of *'A'immah* more impatient for the departure of this task from them more than you are. Had Imamat (Leadership with Divine Authority) been based on love, Isma'il had been more beloved to your father than you were. However, that is from Allah, the Most Holy, the Most High.'

"Then abu Ibrahim said, 'I saw all of my sons, the living and the dead. Amir al-Mu'minin, *'Alayhi al-Salam*, said to me, 'This one is their master, and he pointed to my son Ali, (al-Rida). Thus, he is from me and I am from him and Allah is with the people of good deeds.'

"Yazid has said that abu Ibrahim, *'Alayhi al-Salam*, then said, 'O Yazid, this is a trust with you. Do not inform about it to anyone other than a person of reason or a servant (of Allah) whom you know is truthful. If you will be asked to testify to it you must do so as Allah, the Most Holy, the Most High, has said, "Allah commands you to return that which had been entrusted to you, to the rightful owners. . . ." (4:58) He also has asked, "Who is more unjust than one who refuses to testify to the truth that Allah has given to him . . .?"'(2:140)

"He has said that abu Ibrahim, *'Alayhi al-Salam*, then said, 'I then went close to the Messenger of Allah and asked, 'May Allah keep my soul and the souls of my parents in service for your cause, you have mentioned them in a plural form. Which one of them is he (the Imam)?' The Messenger of Allah said, 'It is he who sees with the light of Allah, the Most Holy, the Most High, hears with His understanding and speaks with His wisdom. He finds the truth without making mistakes. He knows, thus, he is not ignorant. He is taught the rules and knowledge. He is this', and he held the hand of my son, Ali. Then he said, 'How little is (the time) you will be with him! When you will return from your journey (to Makkah), prepare your will, organize your affairs and complete whatever you intended to complete. You are about to move away from them to become the neighbors of people other than them. When you will make such a decision, call Ali (al-Rida) to give you a bath and shroud you; it will cleanse you and anything otherwise will not be acceptable (other people giving you a bath). This is a well-established tradition of the past. Thereafter lie on your back before him and line up his brothers and uncles behind him and then command him to say *Allahu Akbar* (Allah is the Most Great) nine times over you. This establishes his position as the executor of your will and as your guardian when you still are alive. Then call all of your sons after them to bear the testimony and ask Allah, the Most Holy, the Most High, to bear testimony, and Allah is a sufficient witness.'

"Yazid has said that abu Ibrahim, *'Alayhi al-Salam*, then said to me, 'In this year I will be taken (to the next life) and the task (of Leadership with Divine Authority) will rest with my son Ali synonymous with Ali and Ali, *'Alayhim al-Salam*. The first Ali is Ali ibn abu Talib and the other Ali is Ali ibn al-Husayn, *'Alayhim al-Salam*. He has received the intelligence like the first Ali, forbearance like him, a victory like him and sufferings like his sufferings. He also has received a suffering like the other Ali, a patience like him against disappointments, and he must not speak soon after the death of Harun at least for four years.'

"The Imam said, 'O Yazid, whenever you will pass through this place and meet him, and you will soon meet him, give him the glad news of the birth of a trustworthy son to him, a protected and holy one. He will inform you of your meeting with me. You then inform him that the girl from whom this boy will be born is a girl from the family of Mary (Ma'ria), the maiden girl of the Messenger of Allah, mother of Ibrahim. If you will be able to convey my greetings of peace to her, please do so.'

"Yazid has said, 'After the death of abu Ibrahim, *'Alayhi al-Salam*, I met Ali (al-Rida, *'Alayhi al-Salam*) and he began to speak to me.' He said, 'O Yazid, what do you say about performing *'Umra* (visit to Makkah out of Hajj season)?' I said, 'May Allah keep my soul and the souls of my parents in service for your cause; it will be as you will decide. I do not have the means to journey.'

"The Imam said, 'Glory belongs to Allah, we would not have asked you without first taking responsibility for your expenses.' We then left for 'Umra until we reached that place. The Imam began to speak and he said, 'This is the place wherein you meet your neighbors and uncles very often.' I said, 'Yes, it is true' and then I related to him the story (about his father).

"He then said to me, 'The girl has not come yet. When she will come I will convey his greetings to her.' Then we left for Makkah and he bought her that year (people in those days bought and sold slaves). Shortly afterwards she gave birth to that boy (the news of whose birth was given by his grandfather).

"Yazid has said, 'The brothers of Ali (al-Rida) wanted to have a part in the leadership and they became my enemies without good reason.' Ishaq ibn Ja'far told them, 'By Allah, I have seen him sit so near to abu Ibrahim, *'Alayhi al-Salam*, that even I could not sit so close.'"

H 821, Ch. 72, h 15

Ahmad ibn Mihran has narrated from Muhammad ibn Ali from abu al-Hakam who has said that 'Abd Allah ibn Ibrahim al-Ja'fari and 'Abd Allah ibn Muhammad ibn 'Umara both from Yazid ibn Salit who has said the following:

"When abu Ibrahim, *'Alayhi al-Salam*, prepared his will, he called the following people to bear testimony. They were Ibrahim ibn Muhammad (ibn Ali ibn 'Abd Allah ibn Ja'far ibn abu Talib) al-Ja'fari, (his brother) Ishaq ibn Muhammad al-Ja'fari, Ishaq ibn Ja'far ibn Muhammad (the brother of al-Imam Musa, *'Alayhi al-Salam*), Ja'far ibn Salih (ibn Mu'awiya ibn 'Abd Allah ibn Ja'far ibn abu Talib), (his brother) Mu'awiya al-Ja'fari, Yahya ibn al-Husayn ibn Zayd ibn Ali (Zayn al-'Abidin, *'Alayhi al-Salam*), Sa'd ibn 'Imran al-Ansari, Muhammad ibn al-Harith al-Ansari, Yazid ibn Salit al-Ansari, and Muhammad ibn Ja'far ibn Sa'd al-Aslami who has said the following:

"Sa'd al-Aslami recorded the text of the first will as herein below: 'I ask them to witness and bear testimony that he testifies that there is no Lord except Allah Who is the only Lord Who has no partner and that Muhammad is His servant and His Messenger. The coming of the Hour (of Judgment) after death is true. The warning is true and that all people will be held responsible for their actions is true. The decree is true and the standing of people before Allah for judgment is true. All (guidance) that Prophet Muhammad has brought is true. All that the (great) trustworthy Spirit has descended with is true. I live with such beliefs and I die with such beliefs. I will be resurrected with such beliefs if Allah so wills. I ask them (witnesses) to bear testimony to the fact that this is my will, with my own handwriting. I have copied the will of my great, great, great, great, great grandfather (Amir al-Mu'minin) Ali ibn abu Talib, *'Alayhi al-Salam*, and the will of Muhammad ibn Ali before it I had copied word for word, and the will of Ja'far ibn Muhammad, *'Alayhi al-Salam*, similarly. In my will I have directed my son Ali and, afterwards, my sons with him, if he would so agree, find understanding in them and want to confirm them for the task. It will all be upto him. However, if he would dislike them and want to remove them, it will also be upto his discretion, and they will have no say against him. In my will I have given certain instructions to him about all of my charities, properties, my *Mawali* (slaves), my children that I leave behind, and my sons, and to Ibrahim, al-'Abbass, Qasim, Isma'il, Ahmad and mother of Ahmad. Upto Ali will be the affairs of my ladies, not up to them (other people). One third of the charities of my father and two-thirds of my charities will be at his (Ali's) disposal to deal with, as he may deem proper. He, just as an owner, will deal with them in whatever way he may like. He may, if he will so decide, sell, gift, grant or give as charity to those I have specified or to others. It will all be upto him. He is just as myself in my will, property, my family and my children. He may confirm his brothers (to take part in the affairs of the will) whom I have specified in this document. However, if he dislikes he can remove them from the task without it being any offense or unacceptability on his part. If he will find any changes in their attitude, which would be other than those in which I left them, and he would want to return them as in charge persons of a certain task, it will be upto him to do so. If any one of them will want to give his sister in marriage to someone, he may not do so without his permission; he is the most knowledgeable one in the matters of the marriage of his people, his relatives. Any Sultan (ruler) or other individual who would refuse him a thing, or create an obstacle for him, in the matters that I have mentioned in this document of my will, or in the matters of any of the people I have mentioned in it, such Sultan or individual will become far away from Allah and His Messenger. The later ones will become far away from him. Such a person will be subject to the condemnation and anger of Allah, those who (have the right to) condemn, the angels close to Allah, the prophets, the messengers and all the believers.

"No Sultan will have the right to prevent him from carrying on the task of his executing my will. I neither demand anything from him nor have any complaints against him. No one of my sons has any property with me. He is the one to verify what is mentioned in the will. In all shortages and excessive matters he is the authority to judge. My including certain ones of my sons, in the matters of dealing with my will with him, is just to respect and honor them.

"The mothers of my children will be maintained just as they were in my lifetime, provided they observe *Hijab* (modest dress) and if he would consider it proper. If any of them remarries then she has no right to return to my place except if Ali decides otherwise. The same conditions apply to my daughters. No one of the brothers, real or half, will have the right to give any of my daughters in marriage. Also no Sultan or uncle will have any such right without his (Ali's) approval and agreement. If they would do otherwise, they have opposed Allah and His Messenger and they have rebelled against Him in His own dominion. He (Ali al-Rida, *'Alayhi al-Salam*), knows best about the marriage of his people, his relatives. If he will decide to give in marriage he may do so, and if he will decide to refuse he may refuse. I have recommended my daughters with similar recommendation as I have recorded in this document of my will. I have appointed Allah, the Most Holy, the Most High, as the witness to bear testimony to the facts (about my daughters). He and the mother of Ahmad are two witnesses to bear testimony to this fact. No one has the right to open the document of my will or publicize if different from what I have said and specified. Whoever does evil it is against hisown self and whoever does good deeds it is for his own good. Your Lord is not unjust to anyone. May Allah send blessings upon Muhammad and his family. A Sultan or individual must not open or tear this document of my will, which I have signed below. Whoever will do so will be subject to the condemnation and anger of Allah and those who condemn of the angels close to Allah, all the messengers of Allah, all the believers and Muslims. This applies to those who may forcefully open this document of my will. Written and sealed by abu Ibrahim, *'Alayhi al-Salam*, May Allah send His blessings upon Muhammad and his family."

Abu al-Hakam has said that abu 'Abd Allah ibn Adam al-Ja'fari narrated to me from Yazid ibn Salit the following:

"Abu 'Imran al-Talhi was a judge in Madina. When Musa, *'Alayhi al-Salam*, passed away, Ali al-Rida's brothers brought him before the judge, abu 'Imran al-Talhi. Al-'Abbass ibn Musa said, 'May Allah keep you well and allow people to benefit from you. At the bottom of this document there are (mentioned) treasures and pearls and he wants to hide and keep them for himself without us. My father, may Allah grant him blessings, has left nothing that is free from being referred to him. He has left us all poor. Had I not controlled myself I would have told you something in public.' At such time Ibrahim ibn Muhammad rushed toward him asking, 'Will you speak up about a thing that no one of us will accept or believe? You will then be blamed and defeated among us. We know that you have been lying when still young and when you grew up. Your father knew you very well. If there was anything good in you even though he knew you inside and out, he would not trust you even with two pieces of date.'

"At this time Ishaq ibn Ja'far, his uncle, rushed toward him and grabbed both sides of his collar saying, 'It shows that you are foolish and feeble-minded altogether, in addition to your poor performance yesterday,' and all others supported him. Abu 'Imran, the judge then said to Ali (al-Rida), *'Alayhi al-Salam*, 'Stand up, O abu al-Hassan, *'Alayhi al-Salam*. Your father's condemnation upon me is enough damnation for me today. He has certainly given you a wide range of authority. By Allah, no one knows a person better than his father does. By Allah, abu 'Abd Allah to us was not a light-minded person, or weak in his opinions.'

"Al-'Abbass then said to the judge, 'May Allah keep you well, open the document and read what is below therein.' Abu 'Imran said, 'I will not open it. The condemnation of your father is enough damnation for me today.' Al-'Abbass said, 'I will tear it down.' He said, 'That is upto you.'

"Al-'Abbass then removed the seal and they found themselves all removed as executors of the will and the confirmation of Ali (al-Rida), *'Alayhi al-Salam*, as the sole executor of the will. They found out therein the appointment of Ali (al-Rida), *'Alayhi al-Salam*, as their guardian (with Divine Authority), whether they liked or disliked it. They also found out therein that they were all removed from the list of the recipients of charities and other benefits. Opening the document turned out to be a misfortune, disgrace and humiliation to them. It proved to be very good for Ali (al-Rida), *'Alayhi al-Salam*. In the will from which al-'Abbass removed the seal, the following persons were the signatories:

"Ibrahim ibn Muhammad, Ishaq ibn Ja'far, Ja'far ibn Salih and Sa'id ibn 'Imran were the ones who uncovered the face of the mother of Ahmad (who was brought) in the presence of the judge, *qadi*, using as an excuse the claim that she was not mother of Ahmad, until they had uncovered her face and was recognized. Whereupon she said, 'By Allah, my master (husband) said, 'You will be compelled to go before a judge.'

"Ishaq ibn Ja'far admonished her, saying, 'Be quiet, women suffer from weakness. I do not think he has said any such thing.' Ali (al-Rida), *'Alayhi al-*

Salam, then turned to al-'Abbass and said, 'My brother, I understand that debts and liabilities upon you have forced you to this. O Sa'id, come with me so we can help. Tell me how much they owe so we can pay for them. By Allah, I will not fail to help you and cooperate with you as long as I will walk on earth. You may say whatever you like.'

"Al-'Abbass then said, 'You are not giving us anything other than the extra of our own properties which are with you. In fact, our properties with you are more than that.' He (Ali al-Rida), *'Alayhi al-Salam*, said, 'Say whatever you want. Honor is your own honor. If you do good it will be for your own selves before Allah, and if you do evil Allah is forgiving, (and) merciful. By Allah, you know that today I have no son and heir other than you. If I will keep anything that you think I might have kept away from you or stored it in hiding, it will be for you and will return to you. By Allah, from the day your father, may Allah be pleased with him, left this world, I have not owned anything but that I have disposed of it as you have seen.'

"Al-'Abbass moved forward and said, 'By Allah, it is not so. Allah has not imposed any of your opinions on us. Only our father was jealous against us. His decisions are neither justifiable before Allah nor are your decisions. You know that I know Safwan ibn Yahya who sells *al-Sabiry* (fine fabrics) in Kufa. If you admit I can make it very difficult for both of you to swallow your saliva.'

"Ali (al-Rida), *'Alayhi al-Salam*, then said, 'There is no means and no power except with Allah, the Most Holy, the Most Great. My brothers, I am very keen to see you happy. Allah knows it. O Lord, You know best that if I love to see them prosper, do good to them, maintain good relations with them, show kindness to them, then help me day and night and reward me for my efforts. Otherwise, You are the One who knows the hidden facts, then reward me for what I deserve, good for good and evil for evil. O Lord, grant them well-being and grant well-being through them. Make Satan despair about us. Help them to obey You and grant them the opportunity to learn Your guidance. My brothers, I wish and work to make you happy and strive for your well being. Allah guards whatever we say.'

"Al-'Abbass then said, 'I know your language very well. Your spade can not find any soil with me to pick up.' The people dispersed at this point. May Allah send blessings upon Muhammad and his family.'"

H 822, Ch. 72, h 16

Muhammad ibn al-Hassan has narrated from Sahl ibn Ziyad from Muhammad ibn Ali and 'Ubayd Allah ibn al-Marzuban from (Muhammad) ibn Sinan who has said the following:

"Once I went to see abu al-Hassan Musa, *'Alayhi al-Salam*, one year before he would leave for Iraq. His son Ali (al-Rida), *'Alayhi al-Salam*, was also in the meeting. He looked at me and said, 'O Muhammad, during this year a movement will take place but do not allow it to disturb you.'

"I then asked the Imam, 'May Allah keep my soul in service for your cause, what will that be? What you said has made me very anxious.' The Imam said, 'I will journey to the tyrant. From him and one after him I will not suffer any serious harm.' I then asked the Imam, 'May Allah keep my soul in service for your cause, what then will happen?' The Imam said, 'Allah causes the unjust to go astray and He does whatever He wills.'

"I then asked the Imam, 'May Allah keep my soul in service for your cause, what is it that will happen?' The Imam said, 'Whoever will do injustice to my son, (Ali al-Rida), reject his Imamat (Leadership with Divine Authority) after me, will be like doing injustice to Ali ibn abu Talib, *'Alayhi al-Salam*, and reject his Imamat (Leadership with Divine Authority) after the Messenger of Allah.'

"I then said to the Imam, 'By Allah, if Allah will grant me a long life I will acknowledge his right and affirm his Imamat (Leadership with Divine Authority).'

"The Imam said, 'You have spoken the truth, O Muhammad. Allah will grant you a long life. You will acknowledge his right and affirm his Imamat (Leadership with Divine Authority), and the Imamat of the one after him.' I then asked the Imam, 'Who will he be?' The Imam said, 'He will be Muhammad, his son.' I then said to the Imam, 'I agree and accept (his Leadership with Divine Authority).'"

Chapter 73 - Tacit and Explicit Testimony as Proof of abu Ja'far Al-Thani's (the 2nd) Divine Authority Over the People After abu Al-Hassan Al-Rida, *'Alayhi al-Salam*

H 823, Ch. 73, h 1

Ali ibn Muhammad has narrated from Sahl ibn Ziyad from Muhammad ibn al-Walid from Yahya ibn Habib al-Zayyat who has said the following:

"A man who was present in a meeting (of people) with abu al-Hassan al-Rida, *'Alayhi al-Salam*, spoke to me of the following information: 'When people readied themselves to leave the meeting, the Imam said to them, 'Meet abu Ja'far, *'Alayhi al-Salam* (before you leave), offer to him greeting of peace and renew your covenant with him.' When they left, he (the Imam) said to me, 'May Allah grant well being to al-Mufaddal. He, even without it (the command to renew their covenant), would have accepted this matter (Leadership with Divine Authority of the succeeding Imam).'"

H 824, Ch. 73, h 2

Muhammad ibn Yahya has narrated from Ahmad ibn Muhammad from Mu'ammar ibn Khallad who has said the following:

"I heard (abu al-Hassan) al-Rida, *'Alayhi al-Salam*, who said something (about Leadership with Divine Authority) and then said, 'I do not think you need what I just said. This is abu Ja'far, *'Alayhi al-Salam*. I have placed him in my own place to assume my position. We are of the family (*Ahl al-Bayt*) whose younger ones inherit from elder ones everything exactly and of equal measure.'"

H 825, Ch. 73, h 3

Muhammad ibn Yahya has narrated from Ahmad ibn Muhammad ibn 'Isa from his father, Muhammad ibn 'Isa who has said the following:

"Once I went to see abu Ja'far al-Thani, the 2ⁿᵈ, *'Alayhi al-Salam*. He debated me on several issues. He then said, 'O abu Ali, there is no (reason for) doubt; I am the only son that my father had.'"

H 826, Ch. 73, h 4

A number of our people have narrated from Ahmad ibn Muhammad from Ja'far ibn Yahya from Malik ibn Ashyam from al-Husayn ibn Bashshar who has said the following:

"Ibn Qiyaman wrote a letter to abu al-Hassan, *'Alayhi al-Salam*, in which he had asked, 'How can you be an Imam when you do not have a son?'

"Abu al-Hassan al-Rida, *'Alayhi al-Salam*, replied to him with signs of anger, 'How do you know that I will not have a son? By Allah, not many days and nights will pass before Allah will grant me a male child and through him He will make the truth distinct from falsehood.'"

H 827, Ch. 73, h 5

One of our people has narrated from Muhammad ibn Ali from Mu'awiya ibn Hakim from ibn abu Nasr who has said the following:

"Al-Najashi once asked me, 'Who will be the Imam after your master? I wish you to ask him so I will know.' I then went to see Ali al-Rida, *'Alayhi al-Salam*, and informed him (of al-Najashi's wish).

"The narrator has said that the Imam said, 'The Imam will be my son.' Then he asked, 'Can anyone say that my son will be the Imam when one has yet no son?'"

H 828, Ch. 73, h 6

Ahmad ibn Mihran has narrated from Muhammad ibn Ali from Mu'ammar ibn Khallad who has said the following:

"Once in the presence of abu al-Hassan (al-Rida), *'Alayhi al-Salam*, we spoke about an issue, *Imamat*, (Leadership with Divine Authority). It was after the birth of abu Ja'far, *'Alayhi al-Salam*. The Imam said, 'You do not need any such thing (thinking who the Imam will be). This is abu Ja'far, *'Alayhi al-Salam*. I have placed him in my own place and made him to assume my position.'"

H 829, Ch. 73, h 7

Ahmad has narrated from Muhammad ibn Ali from ibn Qiyama al-Wasiti who has said the following:

"Once I went to see Ali ibn Musa, *'Alayhi al-Salam*. (During the meeting) I asked him, 'Can there be more than one Imam, such as two, at the same time?' He replied, 'No, one of them must remain silent.' I then said to him, 'This applies to you. You are the Imam and there is no silent Imam with you.' At that time his son abu Ja'far was not yet born. He said to me, 'By Allah, Allah will make an Imam from me to establish the truth and the people of truth and banish falsehood and the people of falsehood.' One year thereafter abu Ja'far, *'Alayhi al-Salam*, was born."

Ibn Qiyaman belonged to the *Waqifi* sect.

H 830, Ch. 73, h 8

Ahmad has narrated from Muhammad ibn Ali from al-Hassan ibn al-Jahm who has said the following:

"Once I was in the presence of abu al-Hassan (al-Rida), *'Alayhi al-Salam*. He called his son who was a small (boy). The Imam placed him in my lap and said to me, 'Move his shirt aside.' When I did so, the Imam said, 'Look in between his shoulders.' I looked and I found in the skin of one shoulder something like an imprint of a seal. The Imam then asked, 'Do you see this? Similar to this there was one in the shoulder of my father.'"

H 831, Ch. 73, h 9

It is narrated from him (Ahmad ibn Mihran) from Muhammad ibn Ali from abu Yahya al-San'ani who has said the following:

"Once I was in the presence of abu al-Hassan al-Rida, *'Alayhi al-Salam*. Someone brought his son, abu Ja'far, *'Alayhi al-Salam*, to him and he was a small (child). The Imam said, 'This newborn is one the like of whom with such great holiness and blessing has not before been born for our Shi'a (followers).'"

H 832, Ch. 73, h 10

Muhammad ibn Yahya has narrated from Ahmad ibn Muhammad from Safwan ibn Yahya who has said the following:

"Once I said to al-Rida, *'Alayhi al-Salam*, before Allah's granting you the blessing of the birth of abu Ja'far, *'Alayhi al-Salam*, we would ask you and you would say, 'Allah will grant me a son,' and He has granted you one. His birth is the delight of our eyes. May Allah spare us from experiencing your (sad) day. However, if something will happen, to whom then will it (Leadership with Divine Authority) go?' The Imam pointed out with his hand toward abu Ja'far, *'Alayhi al-Salam*, and he was standing before him. I then asked, 'May Allah keep my soul in service for your cause, a child of three years?'

"The Imam said, 'That will be of no harm to him. Jesus rose with Divine Authority when he was a three year old child.'"

H 833, Ch. 73, h 11

Al-Husayn ibn Muhammad has narrated from Mu'alla ibn Muhammad from Muhammad ibn Jumhur from Mu'ammar ibn Khallad who has said the following:

"I heard 'Isma'il ibn Ibrahim say to al-Rida, *'Alayhi al-Salam*, 'My son feels heaviness in his tongue. I intend to send him tomorrow to you. Grace him with passing your hand over his head and pray for him. He is your *Mawla* (dependent).' The Imam said, 'He is a *Mawla* (dependent) of abu Ja'far, *'Alayhi al-Salam*. Send him tomorrow to him (abu Ja'far, *'Alayhi al-Salam*).'"

H 834, Ch. 73, h 12

Al-Husayn ibn Muhammad has narrated from Muhammad ibn Ahmad al-Nahdi from Muhammad ibn Khallad al-Sayqal from Muhammad ibn al-Hassan ibn 'Ammar who has said the following:

"Once I was in a meeting with Ali ibn Ja'far ibn Muhammad in Madina. I stayed with him for two years to write down what he had heard from his brother, abu al-Hassan (al-Rida), *'Alayhi al-Salam*. At such time abu Ja'far Muhammad ibn Ali al-Rida, *'Alayhim al-Salam*, came in the mosque, the mosque of the Messenger of Allah. Ali ibn Ja'far rushed toward him barefoot and without his gown. He kissed his hand and showed great respect for him. Abu Ja'far, *'Alayhi al-Salam*, said to him, 'Uncle, please sit down, may Allah grant you well being.' He asked, 'My master, how can I sit when you are standing?' When Ali ibn Ja'far returned to his place his companions began to blame him, saying, 'You are the uncle of his father, how can you act as such before him?' He said to them, 'Calm down, when Allah, the Most Majestic, the Most Gracious, has not qualified this beard,' holding his beard in his hand, 'but has qualified this young man and has given him such position, should I then deny his excellence and virtue? I seek refuge before Allah from what you say. In fact, I am a servant for him.'"

H 835, Ch. 73, h 13
Al-Husayn ibn Muhammad has narrated from al-Khayrani, from his father who has said the following:
"Once I was standing before abu al-Hassan (al-Rida), *'Alayhi al-Salam*, in Khurasan and someone asked him, 'O my master, if something will happen, to whom will it (Leadership with Divine Authority) go?' The Imam said, 'It will go to abu Ja'far, *'Alayhi al-Salam*, my son.' The person asking the question thought of abu Ja'far, *'Alayhi al-Salam*, as very young for such task. Abu al-Hassan, *'Alayhi al-Salam*, said, 'Allah, the Most Holy, the Most High, sent Jesus, son of Mary as a messenger, a prophet and the owner of a whole legal system. He began his task when he was younger in age than abu Ja'far, *'Alayhi al-Salam*.'"

H 836, Ch. 73, h 14
Ali ibn Ibrahim has narrated from his father and Ali ibn Muhammad al-Qasani all from Zakariyya ibn Yahya ibn al-Nu'man al-Sayrafi who has said the following:
"I heard Ali ibn Ja'far speaking to al-Hassan ibn al-Husayn ibn Ali ibn al-Husayn as follows, 'By Allah, Allah has supported abu al-Hassan al-Rida, *'Alayhi al-Salam*.' Al-Hassan then said, 'Yes, by Allah, may Allah keep my soul in service for your cause, his brothers have rebelled against him.' Ali ibn Ja'far then said, 'Yes, by Allah, and we, his uncles, rebelled against him.' Al-Hassan said to him, 'May Allah keep my soul in service for your cause, how did you deal with it, I was not present with you?'

"He said, 'His brothers said to him and so did we, "There has never been an Imam with a dark complexion from us."' Then al-Rida, *'Alayhi al-Salam*, said to them, 'He is my son.' They said, 'Messenger of Allah did judge on the basis of physiognomy, thus, we can also have a judgment on that basis.' The Imam said, 'You may call one who knows physiognomy, but I will not do so. You should not give information about why you have called them. You must stay home. When they will come, we should, all of us, be in the garden. His uncles, brothers and sisters should all line up.'

"They dressed al-Rida, *'Alayhi al-Salam*, in a gown made of wool with a hat of wool on his head and a spade in his hand. They asked the Imam to act as the gardener in the garden. Then abu Ja'far, *'Alayhi al-Salam*, was brought in and they asked them (physiognomists) to find his father in the people present. They said, 'His father is not present among these people, but this is his uncle, this is the uncle of his father, this is his uncle and this is his aunt. If his father is here, he is the gardener; their foot prints match.' When abu al-Hassan (al-Rida), *'Alayhi al-Salam*, returned, they said, 'This is his father.'

"Ali ibn Ja'far has said, 'I stood up and kissed abu Ja'far, *'Alayhi al-Salam*, and his saliva came in my mouth. Then I said, 'I testify that you are my Imam before Allah.' Al-Rida, *'Alayhi al-Salam*, wept and said, 'O uncle, did you not hear what my father said? 'The Messenger of Allah has said, "May Allah keep my soul and the soul of my father in service for the cause of the son of the best slave girl from *Al-Nawbiya* (a town in Sudan), a lady with a fresh smelling mouth, a lady who will give birth to a purified one.' May Allah condemn the 'U'aybiss (the 'Abbassids) and their descendents, the mischief makers, who murder them (*'A'immah*) for years, months and days, cause them great sufferings and to endure bitter frustrations. He (abu Ja'far, *'Alayhi al-Salam*) will live in exile, away from home, suffering the pain of the murder of his father and grandfather. About the one who has disappeared (from the eyes of his loved ones) it will be asked, 'Is he dead or perished? No one will know in which valleys he will travel. Can such a person, O uncle, be anyone other than my own son?'

"I then said, 'You have spoken the truth, may Allah keep my soul in service for your cause.'"

Chapter 74 - Tacit and Explicit Testimony as Proof of abu Al-Hassan's (Al-Thalith, the 3ʳᵈ) Divine Authority Over the People After Muhammad ibn Ali Al-Rida, *'Alayhi al-Salam*

H 837, Ch. 74, h 1
Ali ibn Ibrahim has narrated from his father that 'Isma'il ibn Mihran who has said the following:
"When abu Ja'far, *'Alayhi al-Salam*, left Madina for Baghdad, the first time of his two journeys, on his leaving I said to him, 'May Allah keep my soul in service for your cause, I am afraid about your condition. To whom, after you, will belong the task (Leadership with Divine Authority)?'

"He turned to me laughing and said, 'The disappearance, as you have thought, will not take place this year.' When he was about to be taken to al-Mu'tasam, (179/795-Caliph 218/833-227/841), for the second time, I went to him and said, 'May Allah keep my soul in service for your cause. You are leaving. To whom, after you, will go this task (Leadership with Divine Authority)?' He wept and tears soaked his beard. He then turned to me and said, 'This time you should be afraid for my life. The task (Leadership with Divine Authority) after me will rest with my son Ali, *'Alayhi al-Salam*.'"

H 838, Ch. 74, h 2
Al-Husayn ibn Muhammad has narrated from al-Khayrani who has narrated from his father the following:
"My father was a security guard at the door of the house of abu Ja'far, *'Alayhi al-Salam*, to serve the task for which he was assigned. Ahmad ibn Muhammad ibn

'Isa would come every day at dawn for information about the health of abu Ja'far, *'Alayhi al-Salam.*

"A messenger would come and go between abu Ja'far, *'Alayhi al-Salam,* and my father. Upon the arrival of the messenger Ahmad ibn Muhammad ibn 'Isa would leave and my father would remain with him (the messenger) privately. One night I went out and Ahmad also left the meeting. My father and the messenger remained in complete privacy. Ahmad, however, walked around the meeting place in such a way that he could hear the conversation.

"The messenger said to my father, 'Your master sends you greetings of peace and says to you, "I am leaving this world and the task (Leadership with Divine Authority) goes to my son, Ali, *'Alayhi al-Salam.* His rights upon you after me will be just as my rights upon you after my father."'

"The messenger then left and Ahmad came back to his place asking, 'What did he say to you?' My father said, 'He said good things.' Ahmad said, 'I heard what he just said to you. Why do you hide it?' He then stated all that he had heard. My father said to him, 'Allah has made it (what he just did) unlawful; Allah, the Most High, has said, "Do not spy. . . ." (49:12) However, you must keep this trust (the testimony), perhaps we will need it one day, but you must not make it public before the proper time.' In the morning my father wrote down the text of the message (and placed it) in ten sealed envelops. He sent them to the leaders of the community. He wrote to them, 'If my death may take place before I will ask you about this message, you may open to learn about it.'

"My father has mentioned that when abu Ja'far, *'Alayhi al-Salam,* left this world, he did not come out of his home until about four hundred people had expressed their belief with certainty in abu al-Hassan, Ali ibn Muhammad, *'Alayhi al-Salam,* as their Imam (Leader with Divine Authority). The leaders in the community gathered together in the house of Muhammad ibn al-Faraj consulting each other about this task (Leadership with Divine Authority). Muhammad ibn al-Faraj then wrote to my father to inform him of the gathering at his house. He said that had it not been for fear of publicity he would have personally come to my father and asked him to join (them). My father rode and went to him. He found the community gathered at his place. They asked my father, 'What do you say about this issue (of Leadership with Divine Authority)?' My father asked for a copy of the text of the message from those whom he had sent one. They were brought and he said, 'This is what I was commanded to do.'

"Certain persons of them then said, 'We would have loved if you had asked another person also to bear witness and testimony to this fact.' He (my father) then said, 'Allah, the Most Majestic, the Most Gracious, has, in fact, brought for you such witness. This is abu Ja'far al-Ash'ari (Ahmad ibn 'Isa) who can testify to my hearing this message.' He asked him to testify but Ahmad denied his hearing the message as such. My father then asked him for a *mubahala* (disputing party's pleading before Allah to condemn the untrue party). He has said that when the case was proved against Ahmad he then said, 'Yes, I did hear the message and it is an honor. I loved that it should go to an Arab man and not to a non-Arab person (al-Khayrani was a non-Arab). Upon this the people there acknowledged the truth altogether.'"

H 839, Ch. 74, h 3

In the copy of al-Safwan the above *Hadith* is recorded as follows: Muhammad ibn Ja'far al-Kufi has narrated from Muhammad ibn 'Isa ibn 'Ubayd from Muhammad ibn al-Husayn al-Wasiti who has said the following:

"I heard Ahmad ibn abu Khalid, stating that he (the Imam, *'Alayhi al-Salam*) had appointed him as witness to bear testimony to his documented will in the following words:

"'Ahmad ibn abu Khalid, the slave of abu Ja'far, bears testimony that abu Ja'far, Muhammad ibn Ali ibn Musa ibn Ja'far ibn Muhammad ibn Ali ibn al-Husayn ibn Ali ibn abu Talib, *'Alayhim al-Salam*, has appointed his son, Ali, *'Alayhi al-Salam*, the executor of his will, about himself and about his sisters and the in charge person of the affairs of Musa when he (the Imam) will attain maturity (physically). He has appointed 'Abd Allah ibn al-Musawir as the supervisor of his legacy, his estate, property, expenditures and slaves and so forth, until Ali ibn Muhammad will reach the age of maturity (physically). At such time 'Abd Allah ibn al-Musawir will transfer the overseeing position to him (Ali ibn Muhammad, *'Alayhi al-Salam*). He thereafter will take charge of his own affairs and sisters. The management of the affairs of Musa will also be left to him. Musa will take charge of his own affairs after the two (overseers), according to the conditions set forth by the father of the two, (Ali, *'Alayhi al-Salam*, and Musa) in the matters of his charities. This has been documented on Sunday 3rd Dhu al-Hijja, in the year two hundred twenty.' Ahmad ibn abu Khalid has transcribed his own testimony with his own handwriting. He has asked al-Hassan ibn Muhammad ibn 'Abd Allah ibn al-Hassan ibn Ali ibn al-Husayn ibn Ali ibn abu Talib, *'Alayhim al-Salam*, also known as al-Jawani to bear testimony to his testimony. Al-Jawani also has a testimony just like the testimony of Ahmad ibn abu Khalid at the beginning of this document. He also has written his testimony with his own handwriting and the witness to bear testimony in the document is Nasr, the servant and he has written his testimony with his own hand."

Chapter 75 - Tacit and Explicit Testimony as Proof of abu Muhammad Al-Hassan's Divine Authority Over the People After Ali ibn Muhammad, *'Alayhim al-Salam*

H 840, Ch. 75, h 1

Ali ibn Muhammad has narrated from Muhammad ibn Ahmad al-Nahdi from Yahya ibn Yasar al-Qanbariyy who has said the following:

"Abu al-Hassan, *'Alayhi al-Salam*, prepared his will to his son, al-Hassan four months before his leaving this world. He appointed me as well as a group of friends to bear testimony to his will."

H 841, Ch. 75, h 2

Ali ibn Muhammad has narrated from Ja'far ibn Muhammad al-Kufi from Bashshar ibn Ahmad al-Basri from Ali ibn 'Umar al-Nawfali who has said the following:

"Once I was with abu al-Hassan (Ali al-Hadi, *'Alayhi al-Salam*) in the compound of his house and at that time his son, Muhammad, passed by. I asked him, 'May Allah keep my soul in service for your cause, will he be our master, Imam, after you?'

"The Imam said, 'No, your master and Imam after me will be al-Hassan, *'Alayhi al-Salam*.'"

Note: This abu Ja'far Muhammad ibn Ali is the eldest son of Imam al-Hadi, *'Alayhi al-Salam*. He died before his father (230/845- 252/866). His shrine is near Balad, north of Baghdad, and the place is now known as al-Sayyid Muhammad. In the following *Ahadith* his name is frequently mentioned.

H 842, Ch. 75, h 3

It is narrated from him from Bashshar ibn Ahmad from 'Abd Allah ibn Muhammad al-Isfahani who has said the following:

"Abu al-Hassan, *'Alayhi al-Salam*, has said, 'Your master and Imam after me will be the one who will perform prayer for me (prayer for burial).'"

The narrator has said, 'We did not know abu Muhammad, *'Alayhi al-Salam*, before this. Abu Muhammad came out and prayed (for his burial).'"

H 843, Ch. 75, h 4

From him who has narrated from Musa ibn Ja'far ibn Wahab from Ali ibn Ja'far who has said the following:

"I was present with abu al-Hassan, *'Alayhi al-Salam*, when his son Muhammad died. The Imam said this to (his son) al-Hassan, *'Alayhi al-Salam*, 'My son, renew your thanks to Allah; He has just granted you the mission (Leadership with Divine Authority).'"

H 844, Ch. 75, h 5

Al-Husayn ibn Muhammad has narrated from Mu'alla ibn Muhammad, from Ahmad ibn Muhammad ibn 'Abd Allah ibn Marwan al-Anbari who has said the following:

"I was present at the time of abu Ja'far Muhammad ibn Ali's, *'Alayhi al-Salam*, (leaving this world). Abu al-Hassan, *'Alayhi al-Salam*, came and a chair was set for him. He sat on it and his family around him. Abu Muhammad was standing on one side. When he was free from the affairs (funerals) of abu Ja'far, *'Alayhi al-Salam*, he then turned to abu Muhammad, *'Alayhi al-Salam*, and said, 'My son, renew thanks to Allah, the Most Holy, the Most High; He has just granted you a mission (Leadership with Divine Authority).'"

H 845, Ch. 75, h 6

Ali ibn Muhammad has narrated from Muhammad ibn Ahmad al-Qalanisi from Ali ibn al-Husayn ibn 'Amr from Ali ibn Mahziyar who has said the following:

"Once I said to abu al-Hassan, *'Alayhi al-Salam*, 'If something will happen, and I seek refuge before Allah against such loss, to whom then will go the task (Leadership with Divine Authority)?'

"He said, 'My covenant (will) is addressed to the eldest of my sons.'"

H 846, Ch. 75, h 7

Ali ibn Muhammad has narrated from abu Muhammad al-Asbarqiniy from Ali ibn 'Amr al-'Attar who has said the following:

"Once I went to see abu al-Hassan al-'Askari (Ali al-Hadi), *'Alayhi al-Salam*, while his son abu Ja'far (Muhammad) was still alive and I thought he would be the Imam after his father. I then asked the Imam, 'May Allah keep my soul in service for your cause, which of your sons will I consider (my Imam)?' The Imam said, 'Do not consider any of them (your Imam) until my command will come to you.'

"The narrator has said, 'I wrote to him afterwards asking, 'To whom will go this task (of Leadership with Divine Authority)?' The narrator has said, 'He wrote to me, "(It will go) to my eldest son." The narrator has said, 'Abu Muhammad (al-Hassan), *'Alayhi al-Salam*, was older than abu Ja'far.'"

H 847, Ch. 75, h 8

Muhammad ibn Yahya and other people have narrated from Sa'id ibn 'Abd Allah from a group of banu Hashim, among whom was al-Hassan ibn al-Hassan al-Aftas, the following:

"They were present, on the day Muhammad ibn Ali (al-Hadi), *'Alayhi al-Salam*, ibn Muhammad (al-Jawad), *'Alayhi al-Salam*, passed away, at the door of abu al-Hassan, *'Alayhi al-Salam*, to offer condolences. A place in the compound of his (abu al-Hassan's, *'Alayhi al-Salam*) house was prepared for him and people were sitting around him. They said, 'We estimated that at that time from the descendents of abu Talib, Hashim and Quraysh there were about one hundred fifty men besides his slaves and other people. At such time he abu al-Hassan (Ali ibn Muhammad, *'Alayhi al-Salam*), looked at (his son) al-Hassan ibn Ali, *'Alayhi al-Salam*, coming and the front of his shirt was torn. He stood at the right of his father and we did not know him. Abu al-Hassan, *'Alayhi al-Salam*, looked at him after a while and said, 'My son, renew your thanks to Allah, the Most Majestic, the Most Gracious; He has granted you a new task (Leadership with Divine Authority).'

"The young man wept, praised Allah, and said, 'We are for Allah and to Him we shall return.' He then said, 'All praise belongs to Allah, Lord of the worlds. I pray to Allah to complete the blessings for us in you. We are for Allah and to Him we shall return.'

"We asked about him and it was said that he was al-Hassan, *'Alayhi al-Salam*, the son of the Imam, *'Alayhi al-Salam*. We estimated his age at that time to be around twenty years or more. On that day we learned and came to know that he had tacitly made a statement about the succeeding Imam (Leader with Divine Authority)."

H 848, Ch. 75, h 9

Ali ibn Muhammad has narrated from Ishaq ibn Muhammad from Muhammad ibn Yahya ibn Daryab who has said the following:

"Once I went to see abu al-Hassan after the death of abu Ja'far, *'Alayhim al-Salam*, and offered condolences for this reason. Abu Muhammad (al-Hassan), *'Alayhi al-Salam*, was also present. Abu Muhammad, *'Alayhi al-Salam*, wept and abu al-Hassan, *'Alayhi al-Salam*, turned to him and said, 'Allah, the Most Holy, the Most High, has made you to succeed his (Imam abu Ja'far's) successor. You must thank Allah.'"

H 849, Ch. 75, h 10

Ali ibn Muhammad has narrated from Ishaq ibn Muhammad from abu Hashim al-Ja'fari who has said the following:

"Once I was in the presence of abu al-Hassan, *'Alayhi al-Salam*, after the death of his son, abu Ja'far. I thought to myself, 'The two, abu Ja'far and abu Muhammad, at this time are like abu al-Hassan Musa and 'Isma'il, the sons of Ja'far ibn Muhammad, *'Alayhi al-Salam*.' Either one, abu Ja'far or abu Muhammad, was considered an Imam to be. At such time abu al-Hassan, *'Alayhi al-Salam*, turned to me before I would say anything and said, 'Yes, O abu Hashim, Allah applied *al-Bada'* (a special change) in the case of abu Muhammad after abu Ja'far, a fact that was not known about him. In the same way, He applied *al-Bada'* in the case of Musa, *'Alayhi al-Salam*, after the death of 'Isma'il, as an issue through which his condition came to light. That is what you thought to yourself. Even though people of falsehood may dislike, abu Muhammad, my son will be the succeeding Imam after me. With him is the knowledge that he will need and with him is the means of *Imamat* (Leadership with Divine Authority).'"

H 850, Ch. 75, h 11

Ali ibn Muhammad has narrated from Ishaq ibn Muhammad from Muhammad ibn Yahya ibn Daryab from abu Bakr al-Fahfaki who has said the following

"Once abu al-Hassan, *'Alayhi al-Salam*, wrote to me as below, 'My son, abu Muhammad, instinctively, is the most considerate in the family of Muhammad, *'Alayhi al-Salam*. He possesses the strongest authoritative supporting evidence among them (family of Muhammad) and he is the eldest of my sons. He is the succeeding Imam and to him go the rings of Imamat (Leadership with Divine Authority) and its rules. Whatever you wanted to ask me, ask him. With him is whatever he may need.'"

H 851, Ch. 75, h 12

Ali ibn Muhammad has narrated from Ishaq ibn Muhammad from Shahwayh ibn 'Abd Allah al-Jullab who has said the following:

"Once Abu al-Hassan, *'Alayhi al-Salam*, (Ali al-Hadi) wrote to me in a letter as herein below: 'You wanted to ask about the succeeding Imam after (the death of) abu Ja'far and you were anxious about it. Do not feel sad' He cited this: 'Allah, the Majestic, the Glorious, does not misguide a nation after having given them guidance until the means of piety are made known to them. . . .' (9:115)

"Your master Imam after me will be my son, abu Muhammad, *'Alayhi al-Salam*. With him there is whatever you will need. Allah allows to precede whatever He wants, and Allah allows to succeed whatever He wants as He has said, 'For whatever sign We change or eliminate or cause to recede into oblivion, We bring forth a better sign, one that is identical. . . .' (2:106) I have written enough convincing facts for the people of reason with awareness."

H 852, Ch. 75, h 13
Ali ibn Muhammad has narrated from the person he mentioned from Muhammad ibn Ahmad al-'Alawi from Dawud ibn al-Qasim who has said the following:
"Once I heard abu al-Hassan, *'Alayhi al-Salam*, (Ali al-Hadi) say, 'The succeeding Imam after me will be al-Hassan, *'Alayhi al-Salam*. How will you deal (with your difficulty) with the successor of the succeeding Imam?' I then asked, 'Why will there be difficulty, may Allah keep my soul in service for your cause?'

"He said, 'You will not see him in person. It will not be lawful for you to pronounce his name.' I then asked, 'How then will we speak of him?' He said, 'Say, "The Divine Authority from the family of Muhammad, *'Alayhi al-Salam*."'

Chapter 76 - Tacit and Explicit Testimony as Proof of the Owner of the House's Divine Authority Over the People (After abu Muhammad Al-Hassan, *'Alayhim al-Salam*)

H 853, Ch. 76, h 1
Ali ibn Muhammad has narrated from Muhammad ibn Ali ibn Bilal who has said the following:
"Two years before leaving this world, abu Muhammad (al-Hassan ibn Ali al-Hadi), *'Alayhim al-Salam*, sent out information to me about the succeeding Imam after him. Just three days before leaving this world he again sent information to me about the succeeding Imam after him."

H 854, Ch. 76, h 2
Muhammad ibn Yahya has narrated from Ahmad ibn Ishaq from abu Hashim al-Ja'fari who has said the following:
"Once I said to abu Muhammad (al-Hassan ibn Ali al-Hadi), *'Alayhim al-Salam*, 'Your grace causes shyness in me to ask you questions. May I ask you a question?' He said, 'Yes, you may ask.' I asked, 'My master, do you have a son?' He said, 'Yes, I do have a son.' I then asked, 'If anything will happen to you, where would I ask him (about my religion)?' He replied, 'Ask him in Madina.'"

H 855, Ch. 76, h 3
Ali ibn Muhammad has narrated from Ja'far ibn Muhammad al-Kufi from Ja'far ibn Muhammad al-Makfuf from 'Amr al-Ahwazi who has said the following:
"Abu Muhammad (al-Hassan ibn Ali al-Hadi), *'Alayhim al-Salam*, showed me his son and said, 'This will be your master (Leader with Divine Authority) after me.'"

H 856, Ch. 76, h 4
Ali ibn Muhammad has narrated from Hamdan al-Qalanisi who has said the following:
"The narrator has said, 'I asked al-'Amri, 'Has abu Muhammad (al-Hassan ibn Ali al-Hadi), *'Alayhim al-Salam*, left this world?' He said, 'He has left this world and he has left behind (a Leader with Divine Authority) for you, whose neck is like this,' he made a hand gesture in a certain way." (The hand gesture was an indication of Imam's good health, or perhaps age.)

(Al-'Amri was the first of the twelfth Imam's representatives).

H 857, Ch. 76, h 5
Al-Husayn ibn Muhammad al-Ash'ari has narrated from Mu'alla ibn Muhammad from Ahmad ibn Muhammad ibn 'Abd Allah who has said the following:

"(A letter) came out from abu Muhammad (al-Hassan ibn Ali al-Hadi), *'Alayhim al-Salam*, when al-Zubayri, may Allah condemn him, was killed. It said, 'This is the recompense for those who disregard Allah in the matters of the people whom He has appointed as His authority over the creatures. He (al-Zubayri) thought he could murder me, thus I could be eliminated without leaving an heir and surviving son. How did he experience the power of Allah in this matter? A boy was born to him and he named him M.H.M.D. in the year 256 A.H. (The abbreviation M.H.M.D. stands for the name of the Imam because of the prohibition against pronouncing it in a complete word).'"

H 858, Ch. 76, h 6
Ali ibn Muhammad has narrated from al-Husayn and Muhammad (sons of Ali ibn Ibrahim), from Muhammad ibn Ali ibn 'Abd al-Rahman al-'Abdi of the tribe of 'Abd Qays, from Daw' ibn Ali al-'Ijli, from a man of the people of Fars whose name he mentioned and who has said the following:

"I went to Samarra and devoted myself to the gate (of the house) of abu Muhammad (al-Hassan ibn Ali al-Hadi), *'Alayhim al-Salam*. The Imam called me. I went to him and offered greetings of peace. He asked me, 'What brings you here?'

"I (the narrator) then said, 'My wish to serve you has brought me here.' He then said, 'Help us as a devoted security guard at the gate.' I then stayed at the gate with the other servants. Thereafter I would buy the necessary items from the market, and enter the house without formal permission when men were in the house. One day I entered the house and he (the Imam) was in the men's quarters. I heard a certain movement in the house and the Imam said to me, 'Stay wherever you are and do not move.' I felt shy of going either inside or outside. A maiden came out to me with something under a cover with her. Then the Imam called me to come in. I went inside. He called the maiden and she came back to him. He said to her, 'Remove the covering from (the face of) the person with you. She removed the cover from the face of a white-complexioned beautiful boy. The Imam then removed the covering further aside. There was greenish black hair between his neck and belly. The Imam said, 'This is your master (Leader with Divine Authority)'. Then he ordered her to take him and she obeyed. After that I did not see him until abu Muhammad (al-Hassan ibn Ali al-Hadi), *'Alayhim al-Salam*, left this world.'"

Chapter 77 - List of the Names of Those Who Saw the Twelfth Imam, *'Alayhi al-Salam*

H 859, Ch. 77, h 1
Muhammad ibn 'Abd Allah and Muhammad ibn Yahya, all have narrated from 'Abd Allah ibn Ja'far al-Himyari who has said the following:

"Shaykh abu 'Amr, may Allah grant him blessings, and I met each other at the place of Ahmad ibn Ishaq. Ahmad ibn Ishaq made an eye gesture to me to ask him about the succeeding Imam. I said to him, 'O abu 'Amr, I want to ask you a question about a certain matter, although I do not have any doubts in the question I am about to ask. It is my belief and religion that the earth is not left without a Leader with Divine Authority except for the forty days just before the coming of the Day of Judgment, in which period Leadership with Divine Authority will be taken away. The door to repentance will be closed. No soul will benefit from the belief with which it has not achieved any good deeds as the Holy Quran says, '. . . the belief of any soul will be of no benefit to it unless certain good deeds have been done with it, or it has been formed before the coming of such a day. . . .' (6:158) Such people would be of the evil creatures of Allah, the Most Majestic, the Most Gracious, and it is these people on whom the Day of Judgment will be established. However, I wanted to strengthen my belief further just as Abraham, peace upon him, asked his Lord, the Most Majestic, the Most Gracious, to show him how He will bring the dead to life again. He (the Lord) asked, 'Do you not yet believe?' Abraham replied, "I believe but I want more confidence for my heart. . . ." (2:260)

"Abu Ali Ahmad ibn Ishaq has narrated to me from abu al-Hassan, *'Alayhi al-Salam*, who has said that he asked the Imam, 'With whom should I deal and ask questions about my belief and religion, and whose words should I accept (after you)?' The Imam said to him, 'Al-'Amri is trustworthy to me. Whatever he will deliver to you is from me. From me he delivers. Whatever he says is from me; from me he says it. Listen to him and obey him; he is reliable and trustworthy.'

"Abu Ali has said, 'I asked abu Muhammad, *'Alayhi al-Salam*, a similar question and he said to him, 'Al-'Amri and his son are trustworthy people; whatever they deliver to you is from me, from me they deliver. Whatever they say to you, from me they say it. Listen to them and obey them; they are trustworthy and reliable people. These are the words of the Imam spoken about you.' The narrator has said, 'Abu 'Amr fell down on his face in prostration and wept.' Then he said, 'Ask what you need to ask.' I asked, 'Did you see the succeeding Imam (Leader with Divine Authority) after abu Muhammad, *'Alayhi al-Salam*?' He said, 'Yes, by Allah, his neck was like that, making a gesture with his hand.' I then said, 'One more question is left.' He said, 'Say, whatever it is.' I asked, 'What is his (succeeding Imam's) name?' He said, 'It is unlawful for you to ask about it. I do not say this from myself. It is not up to me to make things lawful or unlawful but it is from him (the Imam). According to the Sultan (Mu'tasam of the 'Abbassid rulers) abu Muhammad, *'Alayhi al-Salam*, left this world without a surviving son. His legacy is distributed and is taken away by one who has no right in it. His family is dispersed and no one has the courage to learn about them or receive from or give anything to them. When the name is mentioned a search for him takes place. Have fear of Allah and abstain from it.'"

Al-Kulayni, may Allah grant his soul blessings, has said, "A shaykh from our people narrated this to me, his name I have forgotten, that abu 'Amr asked Ahmad ibn Ishaq a similar question and received a similar answer."

H 860, Ch. 77, h 2
Ali ibn Muhammad has narrated from Muhammad ibn 'Isma'il ibn Musa ibn Ja'far, the most senior (in his time) of the descendents of the Messenger of Allah, in Iraq has said the following:

"I saw him (the twelfth Imam, *'Alayhi al-Salam*) between the two mosques when he was a boy."

H 861, Ch. 77, h 3
Muhammad ibn Yahya has narrated from al-Husayn ibn Rizq Allah, abu 'Abd Allah who has said the following:

"Musa ibn Muhammad ibn al-Qasim ibn Hamza ibn Musa ibn Ja'far narrated to me that Hakima, the daughter of Muhammad ibn Ali, *'Alayhi al-Salam*, and paternal aunt of his (the twelfth Imam's) father, said to me that she had seen him on the night of his birth and afterwards."

H 862, Ch. 77, h 4
Ali ibn Muhammad has narrated from Hamdan al-Qalanisi who has said the following:

"I asked al-'Amri, 'Has abu Muhammad (al-Hassan ibn Ali al-Hadi), *'Alayhim al-Salam*, passed away?' He said, 'Yes, he has passed away but has left behind among you a person (the succeeding Imam) whose neck is like this.' He made a gesture with his hand (thereby meaning good health and beauty)."

H 863, Ch. 77, h 5
Ali ibn Muhammad has narrated from Fath, *Mawla* (slave) of al-Zurariyy who has said the following:

"I heard abu Ali ibn Mutahhar saying that he has seen him (the twelfth Imam) and he would describe his (Imam's) figure."

H 864, Ch. 77, h 6
Ali ibn Muhammad has narrated from Muhammad ibn Shadhan ibn Nu'aym from Ibrahim ibn 'Abdahu al-Naysaburi's housemaid who has said the following:

"I was standing with Ibrahim on al-Safa' when he (the twelfth Imam) came and stood higher than Ibrahim, took his Hajj guide book and spoke to him about a number of things."

H 865, Ch. 77, h 7
Ali ibn Muhammad has narrated from Muhammad ibn Ali ibn Ibrahim from abu 'Abd Allah ibn Salih who has said the following:

"I saw him (the twelfth Imam) near the Black Stone while people were clinging over it. The Imam, *'Alayhi al-Salam*, would say, 'They are not commanded in this condition (to kiss the Black Stone).'"

H 866, Ch. 77, h 8
Ali has narrated from abu Ali Ahmad ibn Ibrahim ibn Idris from his father who has said the following:

"I saw him (the twelfth Imam, *'Alayhi al-Salam*) after the death of abu Muhammad (al-Hassan ibn Ali al-Hadi), *'Alayhim al-Salam*, when he had reached adolescence. I kissed his hand and head."

H 867, Ch. 77, h 9

Ali has narrated from abu 'Abd Allah ibn Salih and Ahmad ibn al-Nadr from al-Qanbari, one of the descendents of Qanbar al-Kabir (great), the slave of abu al-Hassan al-Rida, *'Alayhi al-Salam*, who has said the following:

"Once Ja'far ibn Ali was mentioned and he reproached him. I said to him, 'Well, there is no one (in his family) besides him. Have you seen him?'

He said, 'I have not seen him (the twelfth Imam) but other people have seen him.' I then asked, 'Who has seen him?' He said, 'Ja'far (the impostor) has seen him twice and he has quite a story about it to tell.'"

[Note: The story is that Ja'far (the impostor) saw the twelfth Imam, *'Alayhi al-Salam*, twice: once he saw the twelfth Imam when he had disputes about the legacy of the Imam abu Muhammad al-Hassan ibn Ali al-Hadi, *'Alayhim al-Salam*. The twelfth Imam appeared to him suddenly from an unexpected direction and asked Ja'far, "Why are you meddling in my rights?" Then he, *'Alayhi al-Salam*, disappeared. The second time was when Ja'far stopped the burial of the remains of the mother of Imam al-Hassan ibn Ali al-Hadi, *'Alayhi al-Salam*, in her house saying that the house belonged to him (Ja'far). The twelfth Imam appeared to Ja'far unexpectedly and said, "O Ja'far, is this house your house?" Then the twelfth Imam, *'Alayhi al-Salam*, disappeared." (Mir'at al-'Uqul P241)]

H 868, Ch. 77, h 10

Ali ibn Muhammad has narrated from abu Muhammad al-Wajnani who has said the following:

"He narrated to me from a person who had seen him (the twelfth Imam, *'Alayhi al-Salam*) stated as follows: 'He (the twelfth Imam) came out of the house ten days before his father left this world and said, "O Lord, You know that this is the most lovely place to me, had there been no expulsion" or that he spoke a similar expression.'"

H 869, Ch. 77, h 11

Ali ibn Muhammad has narrated from Ali ibn Qays from one of the security men *jalawiza*, plural of *jilwaz*, from the (al-Sawad) rural areas of Iraq who has said the following:

"I saw Sima' (a man) soon after the death of abu Muhammad, *'Alayhi al-Salam*, in *Surra man ra'a* (a city in Iraq) who had just broken the door (of the tenth Imam, *'Alayhi al-Salam*). He (the twelfth Imam), *'Alayhi al-Salam*, came out to him with an ax in his hand and asked, 'What are you doing to my house?' Sima' said, 'Ja'far thinks that your father has passed away without leaving any sons behind. If it is your house, I then get out.' He went out of the house. Ali ibn al-Qays has said, 'One of the servants of the house came out to us and I asked about this news. He asked me, 'Who has told you such a thing.' I said, 'A security man of rural areas has told me.' He then said, 'It is so difficult, almost nothing remains hidden from people.'"

H 870, Ch. 77, h 12

Ali ibn Muhammad has narrated from Ja'far ibn Muhammad al-Kufi from Ja'far ibn Muhammad al-Makfuf from 'Amr al-Ahwazi who has said the following:

"Abu Muhammad, *'Alayhi al-Salam*, showed him (the twelfth Imam, *'Alayhi al-Salam*) to me and said, 'This is your master (Leader with Divine Authority).'"

H 871, Ch. 77, h 13

Muhammad ibn Yahya has narrated from al-Hassan ibn Ali al-Niysaburi from Ibrahim ibn Muhammad ibn 'Abd Allah ibn Musa ibn Ja'far from abu Nasr Zarif, the servant (of abu Muhammad, *'Alayhi al-Salam*, who has said the following:

"I saw him (the twelfth Imam, *'Alayhi al-Salam*)."

H 872, Ch. 77, h 14

Ali ibn Muhammad has narrated from Muhammad and al-Hassan, two sons of Ali ibn Ibrahim, narrated to him in the year two hundred seventy nine from Muhammad ibn 'Abd al-Rahman al-'Abdi from Daw' ibn Ali al-'Ijli from a man from the people of Fars whose name he mentioned has said the following:

"Once, Abu Muhammad, *'Alayhi al-Salam*, showed him (the twelfth Imam, *'Alayhi al-Salam*) to me."

H 873, Ch. 77, h 15

Ali ibn Muhammad has narrated from abu Ahmad ibn Rashid from one of the people of al-Mada'in who has said the following:

"Once a friend and I were in Makkah to perform Hajj. When we arrived in 'Arafat (a place in Makkah) we found a young man sitting on the ground. He had a piece of cloth on him for the lower part of the body called *'Izar* and another piece for the upper part of the body called *Rida'*, wearing on his feet, yellow footwear. I estimated the *'Izar* and *Rida'* (worth) about a hundred and fifty Dinars. No sign of journey was visible on him. A beggar approached us and we sent him away. He then approached the young man and asked him for help. He picked up something from the ground and gave it to him. The beggar prayed for him. He continued assiduously praying and prolonged. The young man stood up and disappeared from our sight. We went near to the beggar and said, 'fie upon you! What did he give you?' He showed us pebbles of gold with marks on them. We estimated their value at about twenty *Mithqal* (a unit of weight). I then said to my companion, 'Our master (Imam, *'Alayhi al-Salam*) was with us and we did not recognize him.' We then went to search for him in the whole of station, but we could not find him. We then asked everyone around the area where we had seen him earlier, of the people of Makkah and Madina, and they said, 'He is an *'Alawi* (descendent of Ali, *'Alayhi al-Salam*), a young man, and he performs Hajj every year on foot.'"

Chapter 78 - Prohibition of Pronouncing His (the Twelfth Imam's, *'Alayhi al-Salam*) Name

H 874, Ch. 78, h 1

Ali ibn Muhammad has narrated from the person whose name he mentioned from Muhammad ibn Ahmad al-'Alawi from Dawud ibn al-Qasim al-Ja'fari who has said the following:

"I heard abu al-Hassan al-'Askari (Ali ibn Muhammad), *'Alayhi al-Salam*, say, 'The succeeding Imam after me will be al-Hassan, *'Alayhi al-Salam*. How will you deal (with your difficulty) in the case of the succeeding Imam after the Imam succeeding myself?'

"I then asked, 'May Allah keep my soul in service for your cause, why will there be difficulty?' The Imam said, 'You will not see his person and it will not be permissible for you to mention him by his name.' I then asked, 'How then will we speak of him?' The Imam said, 'Say, al-Hujja, (the Leader with Divine Authority) from the family of Muhammad, *'Alayhi al-Salam.'*"

H 875, Ch. 78, h 2
Ali ibn Muhammad has narrated from abu 'Abd Allah al-Salihi who has said the following:
"After abu Muhammad (al-Hassan ibn Ali al-Hadi), *'Alayhim al-Salam*, had passed away certain individuals of our community asked me to ask about the name of the twelfth Imam, *'Alayhi al-Salam*, and his place. The answer came as following: 'If you tell the name they will publicize it. If they will know the place they will show it to others.'"

H 876, Ch. 78, h 3
A number of our people have narrated from Ja'far ibn Muhammad from ibn Faddal from al-Rayyan ibn al-Salt who has said the following:
"I heard abu al-Hassan al-Rida, *'Alayhi al-Salam*, say, when asked about al-Qa'im (the one who will establish the kingdom of Allah on earth), 'He will neither be seen physically nor will his very name particularly be mentioned.'"

H 877, Ch. 78, h 4
Muhammad ibn Yahya has narrated from Muhammad ibn al-Husayn from al-Hassan ibn Mahbub from ibn Ri'ab from abu 'Abd Allah, *'Alayhi al-Salam*, who has said the following:
"No one will pronounce the exact name of the person in charge of the task (the one who will establish the kingdom of Allah on earth and who possesses Leadership with Divine Authority), except an unbeliever."

Chapter 79 - Select Ahadith About al-Mahdi, *'Alayhi al-Salam*

Select Ahadith about al-Mahdi, *'Alayhi al-Salam*, on conditions of his disappearance from public sight

H 878, Ch. 79, h 1
Ali ibn Ibrahim has narrated from his father from Muhammad ibn Khalid from the person who narrated to him from al-Mufaddal ibn 'Umar, and Muhammad ibn Yahya from 'Abd Allah ibn Muhammad ibn 'Isa from his father from certain people of his friends from al-Mufaddal ibn 'Umar from abu 'Abd Allah, *'Alayhi al-Salam*, who has said the following:
"People are nearer to Allah, Majestic is His mention, and He is more pleased with them when the leader who possesses authority from Allah, Majestic is His mention, will be out of their sight. He will not publicly appear among them and they will not know his place. Despite this they will know that the leader, who possesses authority from Allah, Majestic is His mention, is not invalidated and neither is His covenant. In such a case, they expect relief and happiness, through his reappearance in public, mornings and evenings. Allah's anger for His enemies is most intense when the leadership with Allah's authority will be out of public sight and will not appear to them. He (Allah) knows that his friends do not have doubts. If it had been in His knowledge that they doubt He would not have caused the leader who possesses His authority to disappear from public sight, not even

for a blinking of an eye. That (Allah's anger) hangs only over the heads of the evil ones among the people."

H 879, Ch. 79, h 2
Al-Husayn ibn Muhammad al-Ash'ari has narrated from Mu'alla ibn Muhammad from Ali ibn Mirdas from Safwan ibn Yahya and al-Hassan ibn Mahbub from Hisham ibn Salim from 'Ammar al-Sabati who has said the following:
"Once I asked abu 'Abd Allah, *'Alayhi al-Salam,* 'Is the worship in secrecy with an Imam from you during the government of falsehood more virtuous or is the worship during the reign and government of the truth with an Imam from you in public sight, more virtuous?' The Imam said, 'O 'Ammar, charity in secrecy, I swear by Allah, is more virtuous than the charity given publicly. The same is true when you worship in secrecy with your Imam out of public sight during the government of falsehood. (Worship) with fear from your enemies during the government of falsehood in peacetime is more virtuous than worshipping Allah, Majestic is His mention, during the reign of the truth distinctly in the government of the truth. Worship with fear during the government of falsehood is not like the worship in peace under the government of the truth. You must know that if one of you performs his obligatory prayer in congregation in time and completes it, and maintains secrecy from the enemy, Allah will record it as equal to fifty obligatory prayers performed in congregation. If one of you performs an obligatory prayer individually in time and completes it, and maintains secrecy from the enemy, Allah, Majestic is His mention, will record it equal in virtue to twenty-five obligatory prayers performed individually. If one of you performs an optional prayer in time and completes it, Allah will record it as equal to ten optional prayers. If one of you will do one good deed, Allah, Majestic is His mention, will record it as equal to twenty good deeds. Allah, the Majestic, the Glorious, will grant multiple rewards for the good deeds of a believer among you who does good deeds. Allah will grant him good reward in multiples for maintaining secrecy in his religion, about his Imam and his own life and controlling his tongue. Allah, Majestic is His mention, is generous.'

"I then said, 'May Allah keep my soul in service for your cause, you have certainly given me courage to do good deeds and have given me much exhortation. However, I love to know, how can we today be of more virtuous deeds than the followers of the Imam from your family living among them in public sight under the rule of government of truth while we all have the same religion?'

"The Imam said, 'You have become the winner of this in accepting the religion of Allah, the Most Majestic, the Most Gracious, in prayer, in fasting, in performing Hajj, in every good deed, in understanding and in the worship of Allah, Majestic is His mention, in 'secrecy'. (You have maintained) secrecy from your enemies when your Imam (with full Divine reign) does not live in public sight, but you obey him with patience, waiting for and expecting the establishment of the government of truth while you are afraid for your Imam and your own lives from the unjust kings. You wait for and expect to receive your rights and the rights of your Imam that unjust ones have usurped. They have denied your rights and have forced you toward the worldly gains and means of living, but with patience you perform your religious duties, your worship, and your obedience to your Imam despite fear from your enemies. For this reason Allah, the Most Majestic, the Most Gracious, will grant you the reward for your good deeds in multiples. May it be handsome and graceful for you.'

"I then said, 'May Allah keep my soul in service for your cause, what does your holiness say in the following cases? Will our deeds as the companions of al-Qa'im (the one to establish the Kingdom of Allah), when the truth will become dominant, be more virtuous or now that we are your followers and obeying you? Are our deeds now more virtuous or those during the dominance of the government of the truth and justice?'

"The Imam said, 'Glory belongs to Allah. Do you not love to see Allah, the Most Holy, the Most High, grant dominance to the truth and justice in all lands, unite ideologies, bring together the differing hearts so no one disobeys Allah, the Most Majestic, the Most Gracious, on His earth? (Do you not love to see?) His laws are practiced among His creatures and Allah to make the rights return where they belong and overcome so nothing of the truth is kept secret for fear of any of the creatures. By Allah, O 'Ammar, no one of you will die in the condition that you live now but that is more virtuous than the conditions of the martyrs of Badr and 'Uhud. It is glad news for you all.'"

H 880, Ch. 79, h 3
Ali ibn Muhammad has narrated from Sahl ibn Ziyad from ibn Mahbub from abu 'Usamah from Hisham and Muhammad ibn Yahya from Ahmad ibn Muhammad from ibn Mahbub from Hisham ibn Salim from abu Hamza from abu Ishaq who has said the following:
"Reliable men of the companions of Amir al-Mu'minin, *'Alayhi al-Salam*, have said that they heard Amir al-Mu'minin, *'Alayhi al-Salam*, say in one of his sermons as follows: 'O Lord, I know that knowledge will not be erased and its sources will not discontinue altogether and You will not leave Your earth without a leader with Your authority over Your creatures. (He is a leader to whom You have given authority over Your creatures) who lives among the people well-known but is disobeyed or is afraid and lives in obscurity so that proofs of Your authority are not invalidated and Your friends are not misled after You have granted them guidance. Where, in fact, are they (friends of Allah) and how many are they? They are very few, but are of great respect before Allah, Majestic is His name. They follow the Imam (leader) of religion. (They follow) the guiding Imam (leader), establish in their own selves the discipline of *'A 'immah* and practice their way of life. In such conditions knowledge will lead them to the true belief and their souls then accept the call of the leaders of knowledge. Those statements of the leader (the Imam), *'Alayhi al-Salam*, that are difficult to understand for others are soft and easy for them to understand. They feel comfortable with what is frightening to those who reject (the truth) and the transgressors who have disregarded them. They are the followers of the scholars. They only accompany the worldly people in obedience to Allah, the Most Holy, the Most High, and His friends. They maintain secrecy to be part of their religion for fear from their

enemies. Thus, their souls cling to the high position (of the realm of existence). Their scholars and followers live quietly and silently, under the rule of the government of falsehood, waiting for the government of the truth. Allah will soon establish truth with His words and banish falsehood. Ha, ha, how fortunate it is for them due to their patience in the matters of their religion in their peacetime! How strong is the desire to see them in the time of the dominance of their government! Allah will soon bring us together with them in the gardens of Eden along with those of their parents, children and spouse who had been of good deeds.'"

Chapter 80 - The Disappearance (of the Twelfth Imam, *'Alayhi al-Salam*) from Public Sight

H 881, Ch. 80, h 1

Muhammad ibn Yahya and al-Hassan ibn Muhammad both have narrated from Ja'far ibn Muhammad al-Kufi from al-Hassan ibn Muhammad al-Sayrafi from Salih ibn Khalid from Yaman al-Tammar who has said the following:

"Once we were in the presence of abu 'Abd Allah, *'Alayhi al-Salam*, and he said to us, 'The person in charge of this task (Leadership with Divine Authority) will disappear from public sight. At that time following one's religion will be like wiping the thorns of a cactus plant (with one's bare hands).' The Imam made certain hand gestures. 'Who among you is ready to hold in his hands a bunch of cactus?' He then remained calm for a little while and then said, 'The person in charge of this task (Leadership with Divine Authority) will disappear from public sight. A servant (of Allah) must maintain piety before Him and hold fast to His religion.'"

H 882, Ch. 80, h 2

Ali ibn Muhammad has narrated from al-Hassan ibn 'Isa ibn Muhammad ibn Ali ibn Ja'far from his father from his grandfather from Ali ibn Ja'far from his brother, Musa ibn Ja'far, *'Alayhi al-Salam*, who has said the following:

"When the fifth descendent of the seventh (Imam) will disappear from public sight, at that time for the sake of Allah, for the sake of Allah, protect your religion so no one can strip you off of it. My son, it is necessary that the person in charge of this task (Leadership with Divine Authority) should disappear from the public sight. Even those who believe in it will turn away from their belief. It will certainly be a trial from Allah, the Most Majestic, and the Most Gracious, to test His creatures. Had your fathers and ancestors known any other religion more correct than this they would certainly have followed it."

"I then asked, 'My master, who is the fifth from the descendents of the seventh?' He said, 'My son, your intelligence falls shorter to reach it and your understanding remains narrower to accommodate it but if you live you will soon comprehend its being.'"

H 883, Ch. 80, h 3

Muhammad ibn Yahya has narrated from Ahmad ibn Muhammad from ibn abu Najran from Muhammad ibn al-Musawir from al-Mufaddal ibn 'Umar who has said the following:

"I heard abu 'Abd Allah, *'Alayhi al-Salam*, say, 'Beware of publicity. By Allah, your Imam will disappear from the public sight for (many) years of your time. You will be sifted until the only thing that can be said about him will be, "He is dead, killed, destroyed and no one will know in which of the valleys he may have traveled." The eyes of the believing ones will weep for him and you will be turned upside down just as when ships face the rough seas. No one will survive this except those from whom Allah has taken a covenant, written belief in their hearts and has supported them with a spirit from His Self. Twelve similar flags will be raised and one will not be able to distinguish which is which.' I wept and then asked, 'What shall we do?' The Imam then looked to the sun (light) on the deck and said, 'O abu 'Abd Allah, our case (Leadership with Divine Authority) is more clear than the sun (light) on the deck.'"

H 884, Ch. 80, h 4

Ali ibn Ibrahim has narrated from Muhammad ibn al-Husayn from ibn Abu Najran from Fadalah ibn Ayyub from Sadir al-Sayrafi who has said the following:

"I heard abu 'Abd Allah, *'Alayhi al-Salam*, say, 'In the case of the person in charge of this task, Leadership with Divine Authority (the case of the twelfth Imam) there is a similarity to Yusuf, peace be upon him.'

I then asked, 'Are you, O Imam, speaking of his lifetime or his disappearance?' The Imam then asked, 'What is it then that certain swine-like people of this nation refuse to acknowledge? The brothers of Yusuf were grandchildren of the prophets. They did business with Yusuf, conducted trade with him and spoke to him. They were his brothers and he was their brother but they could not recognize him until he said, "I am Yusuf and this (Benjamin) is my brother." Why should (certain people of) this condemned nation refuse to accept if Allah, the Most Majestic, the Most Gracious, in a certain time would do to the possessor of His authority what He did to Yusuf? Yusuf was the person in charge of Egypt and there was a distance of twenty-eight days of journey between him and his father. If he had wanted to inform him (his father) he could have done so. Jacob and his sons journeyed after they heard the good news, for nine days from their Bedouin home to Egypt. Why then should this nation refuse to accept if Allah, the Most Majestic, the Most Gracious, would do to the person who possesses His authority, what He did to Yusuf? That he may walk in their market place and step on their furnishings until Allah will grant him permission to reappear in public as He did to Yusuf, as they asked, "Are you really Yusuf?" He said, "Yes, I am Yusuf."'"

H 885, Ch. 80, h 5

Ali ibn Ibrahim has narrated from al-Hassan ibn Musa al-Khashshab from 'Abd Allah ibn Musa from 'Abd Allah ibn Bukayr from Zurara who has said the following:

"I heard abu 'Abd Allah, *'Alayhi al-Salam*, say, 'The young boy will disappear from the public sight before his rise (with Divine power).' I then asked, 'Why (that has to take place)?' The Imam said, 'He will be afraid.' He pointed with his hand to his midsection. Then he said, 'O Zurara, he is the one whose reappearance is expected. He is the one whose coming to this world through birth will be doubted. Certain people will say, "His father died without leaving any son behind." Certain others will say, "Just before the death of his father his mother conceived him." Still others will say, "He was born two years before the death of his father." He is the one whose reappearance is expected. The fact is that Allah, the Most Majestic, the Most Gracious, loves to test the Shi'a (his followers). It is in such a condition that people of falsehood will raise doubts, O Zurara.'

"I then said, 'May Allah keep my soul in service for your cause, if I will be alive at such time, expecting his rise with Divine power, what should I do?' The Imam said, 'O Zurara, if you will live up to such time then say the following prayer: 'O Lord, make me recognize You; if You do not make me recognize You, I cannot recognize Your prophet. O Lord, make me recognize Your Messenger; if You do not make me recognize Your Messenger, I cannot recognize the one who possesses Your authority over the creatures. O Lord, make me recognize the one who possesses Your authority over the creatures; if You do not make me recognize him I will stray from my religion.' Then he said, 'O Zurara, it is necessary that a young boy be murdered in the city of Madina.'

"I then asked, 'May Allah keep my soul in service for your cause, will he not be killed in the hands of the army of al-Sufyani?' He said, 'No, but the army of the tribe of so and so will kill him. They will come to enter Madina; thus, they take hold of the young boy and kill him. When they will murder him in transgression, animosity and injustice, then they will not be given respite. At such time you can expect good news, if Allah shall so will.'"

H 886, Ch. 80, h 6

Muhammad ibn Yahya has narrated from Ja'far ibn Muhammad from Ishaq ibn Muhammad from Yahya ibn al-Muthanna from 'Abd Allah ibn Bukayr from 'Ubayd ibn Zurara who has said the following:

"I heard abu 'Abd Allah, *'Alayhi al-Salam*, say, 'People will miss their Imam. He will attend Hajj and see them, but they will not see him.'"

H 887, Ch. 80, h 7

Ali ibn Muhammad has narrated from 'Abd Allah ibn Muhammad ibn Khalid who has said that Mundhir ibn Muhammad ibn Qabus narrated to us from Mansur ibn al-Sindi from abu Dawud al-Mustariq from Tha'laba ibn Maymun from Malik al-Juhanni from al-Harith ibn al-Mughirah from al-Asbagh ibn Nubata who has said the following:

"Once I went to see Amir al-Mu'minin Ali, *'Alayhi al-Salam*, and found him thinking and drawing lines on the ground. I then said, 'O Amir al-Mu'minin, I see you thinking and drawing lines on the ground. Have you become interested in them (worldly things)?' He said, 'No, by Allah, I have not become interested in them, and I have never been interested in the whole world, not even for a day, but I thought about a baby from my descendents, the eleventh generation. He is al-Mahdi who will fill the earth with justice and fairness after its being filled with suffering and injustice. He will disappear from public sight in confusing conditions. Certain people will deviate and others will find the path of guidance.'

"I then asked, 'O Amir al-Mu'minin, how long will be the duration of confusion and (his) disappearance?' He said, 'Six days or six months or six years.' I then asked, 'Will this really come to pass?' He said, 'Yes, just as his creation will be necessary (so also will his disappearance). However, O Asbagh, this is not your concern. Those people will be of the best in this nation with the most virtuous ones of this family (*Ahl al-Bayt*).' I then asked, 'What will happen afterwards?' He said, 'Allah will do whatever He will decide. He possesses many *al-Bada'* (certain changes) wills, goals and ends.'"

H 888, Ch. 80, h 8

Ali ibn Ibrahim has narrated from his father from Hannan ibn Sadir from Ma'ruf ibn Kharrabudh from abu Ja'far, *'Alayhi al-Salam*, who has said the following:

"We only are like the stars in heaven. Whenever one star disappears (from sight) another one comes into view and you can point to him with your fingers and make a gesture with your necks (for publicity). Allah will then cause your star to disappear from your sight. The descendents of 'Abd al-Muttalib all look similar and you will have difficulty to discern one from the other. When your star will reappear you must thank your Lord."

H 889, Ch. 80, h 9

Muhammad ibn Yahya has narrated from Ja'far ibn Muhammad from al-Hassan ibn Mu'awiya from 'Abd Allah ibn Jabala from 'Abd Allah ibn Bukayr from Zurara who has said the following:

"I heard abu 'Abd Allah, *'Alayhi al-Salam*, say, 'The person who will rise with Divine power on earth will disappear from public sight before his rise.' I then asked, 'Why will it be so?' He said, 'He will be afraid.' He then pointed to his midsection, meaning thereby being murdered."

H 890, Ch. 80, h 10

Ali ibn Ibrahim has narrated from his father from ibn abu 'Umayr from abu Ayyub al-Khazzaz from Muhammad ibn Muslim who has said the following:

"I heard abu 'Abd Allah, *'Alayhi al-Salam*, say, 'If you are told that the person in charge of establishing the Kingdom of Allah on earth and owner (of Leadership with Divine Authority) will disappear from public sight, you must not reject it.'"

H 891, Ch. 80, h 11

Al-Husayn ibn Muhammad and Muhammad ibn Yahya have narrated from Ja'far ibn Muhammad from al-Hassan ibn Mu'awiya from 'Abd Allah ibn Jabala from Ibrahim ibn Khalaf ibn 'Abbad al-Anmati from Mufaddal ibn 'Umar who has said the following:

"Once I was in the presence of abu 'Abd Allah, *'Alayhi al-Salam*, and other people also were present. I thought the Imam meant people other than me when he said, 'By Allah, those in charge of establishing the Kingdom of Allah on earth and the owner of this task (Leadership with Divine Authority) will disappear from your sight. This (case) will become so obscure that people will say, "He is dead, destroyed or no one knows in which valley he has traveled." You will be shaken just as the ship is shaken in rough seas. No one will remain safe except those with whom Allah has made a covenant, written belief in their hearts and has supported with a spirit from Him. Twelve flags will be raised. They will be identical so much so that one will not be able to distinguish one from the other.'

"I then wept. The Imam asked, 'What has caused you to weep, O abu 'Abd Allah?' I then said, 'May Allah keep my soul in service for your cause, how can I stop weeping? You say, "Twelve identical flags will be raised and one will not be able to distinguish one from the other." The narrator has said that in the place of gathering, sunlight had come in through a hole. The Imam asked, 'Is this (sun-light on the spot) clear?' I said, 'Yes, it is clear.' The Imam said, 'Our case is even clearer than this sun (light).'"

H 892, Ch. 80, h 12
Al-Husayn ibn Muhammad has narrated from Ja'far ibn Muhammad from al-Qasim ibn 'Isma'il al-Anbari from Yahya ibn al-Muthanna from 'Abd Allah ibn Bukayr from 'Ubayd ibn Zurara from abu 'Abd Allah, *'Alayhi al-Salam*, who has said the following:
"*Al-Qa'im* (the one who will rise with Divine Authority) will disappear from the public sight twice. In one of those seasons he will attend Hajj. He will see the people, but they will not see him."

H 893, Ch. 80, h 13
Ali ibn Muhammad has narrated from Sahl ibn Ziyad and Muhammad ibn Yahya and others from Ahmad ibn Muhammad and Ali ibn Ibrahim from his father. All three of them have narrated from ibn Mahbub from Hisham ibn Salim from abu Hamza from abu Ishaq al-Sabi'i from a reliable one of the companions of Amir al-Mu'minin Ali, *'Alayhi al-Salam*, who has said the following:
"Amir al-Mu'minin Ali, *'Alayhi al-Salam*, once spoke the following from the pulpit in Kufa and I memorized it. 'O Lord, it is certain that You keep certain persons with Your authority on Your earth. Such persons come one after the other with Your authority over Your creatures to guide people in Your religion and teach them; Your knowledge so that Your friends do not scatter. They may live in the public sight but people disobey them or remain out of public sight but their reappearance will be expected. Even though their persons may remain hidden from the people in peacetime, their knowledge that has spread before will not be hidden from them. Their discipline will be firmly established in the hearts of people who will act accordingly.'

"In another part of this sermon he, *'Alayhi al-Salam*, has asked, 'Who will have such discipline? For this reason knowledge becomes obscure when it does not find anyone to bear, protect and narrate it to others just as they have heard it from the scholars and speak truthfully from them. O Lord, I know that all the knowledge will not become obscure and all of its sources will not vanish. You will not leave Your earth without a person with Your authority on Your earth. He may either live in public sight but is not obeyed and followed, or is afraid and hidden from public sight so that Your authority is not invalidated and Your friends are not misled after You have granted them guidance. In fact, where are they and how many are they? They are very few in number, but of very great honor and respect before Allah.'"

H 894, Ch. 80, h 14
Ali ibn Muhammad has narrated from Sahl ibn Ziyad from Musa ibn al-Qasim ibn Mu'awiya al-Bajali from Ali ibn Ja'far from his brother, Musa ibn Ja'far, *'Alayhi al-Salam*, who has said the following about the words of Allah, the Most Majestic, the Most Gracious:
"Say, have you not thought that if your water was to dry up, who will bring you water from the spring?" (67:30)

"The Imam said, 'It means when your Imam will disappear from your sight then who will bring for you a new Imam?'"

H 895, Ch. 80, h 15

A number of our people have narrated from Ahmad ibn Muhammad from Ali ibn al-Hakam from abu Ayyub al-Khazzaz from Muhammad ibn Muslim who has said the following:

"I heard abu 'Abd Allah, *'Alayhi al-Salam*, say, 'When you hear about the disappearance of your companion (Leader with Divine Authority) from public sight, do not reject it.'"

H 896, Ch. 80, h 16

A number of our people have narrated from Ahmad ibn Muhammad from al-Hassan ibn Ali al-Washsha' from Ali ibn abu Hamza from abu Basir from abu 'Abd Allah, *'Alayhi al-Salam*, who has said the following:

"It is necessary for the person in charge of the task to establish the Kingdom of Allah on earth and owner (of Leadership with Divine Authority) to disappear from the public sight and in his disappearance from public sight he must remain away from public. How good is *Tayba* (the city of Madina), one's dwelling and living with thirty people therein is not a frightening isolation."

H 897, Ch. 80, h 17

Through the same chain of narrators it is narrated from al-Washsha' from Ali ibn al-Hassan from Aban ibn Taghlib who has said the following:

"Once abu 'Abd Allah, *'Alayhi al-Salam*, asked, 'How will you feel when a large scale attack will take place between the two mosques? Thereafter, knowledge will become as obscure as a snake that goes into its hiding place. The Shi'a (Muslims) will hold differences and one group will call the other group liars. One group will spit on the faces of the other.'

"I then said, 'May Allah keep my soul in service for your cause, there will be nothing good in such conditions.' The Imam said, 'All goodness will be there.' He said it three times."

H 898, Ch. 80, h 18

Through the same chain of narrators it is narrated from Ahmad ibn Muhammad from his father, Muhammad ibn 'Isa from ibn Bukayr from Zurara who has said the following:

"I heard abu 'Abd Allah, *'Alayhi al-Salam*, say, '*Al-Qa'im* (the one who will rise with Divine Authority) will disappear before he will rise with Divine power. He will be afraid.' The Imam pointed to his midsection, meaning thereby being murdered."

H 899, Ch. 80, h 19

Muhammad ibn Yahya has narrated from Muhammad ibn al-Husayn from ibn Mahbub from Ishaq ibn 'Ammar who has said the following:

"Abu 'Abd Allah, *'Alayhi al-Salam*, has said, '*Al-Qa'im* (the one who will rise with Divine Authority and power) will have two disappearances. One will be for a short time and the other for a longer time. No one will know his place during the shorter disappearance except the special persons from his Shi'a. During his longer disappearance no one will see him except very special persons of his friends.'"

H 900, Ch. 80, h 20

Muhammad ibn Yahya and Ahmad ibn Idris have narrated from al-Hassan ibn Ali al-Kufi from Ali ibn Hass'an from his paternal uncle, 'Abd al-Rahman ibn Kathir from Mufaddal ibn 'Umar who has said the following:

"I heard abu 'Abd Allah, *'Alayhi al-Salam*, say, 'The person in charge of the task to establish the Kingdom of Allah on earth and owner of this task (Leadership with Divine Authority) will disappear from public sight twice. From one of them he will return to his family, but in the other one it will be said that he is dead or no one knows to which of the valleys he has traveled.'

"I then asked, 'What shall we do in such conditions?' The Imam said, 'If anyone will claim to have such authority, you then should ask him about several things in which he must answer like him (Leader with Divine Authority).'"

H 901, Ch. 80, h 21

Ahmad ibn Idris has narrated from Muhammad ibn Ahmad from Ja'far ibn al-Qasim from Muhammad ibn al-Walid al-Khazzaz from al-Walid ibn 'Uqba from al-Harith ibn Ziyad from Shu'ayb from abu Hamza who has said the following:

"Once I went to see abu 'Abd Allah, *'Alayhi al-Salam*, and asked him, 'Are you the person in charge of the task to establish the Kingdom of Allah on earth and owner of this task (Leadership with Divine Authority)?'

"He said, 'No, I am not the one.' I then asked, 'Is he your son?' He said, 'No, my son will not be the one either.' I then asked, 'Will the son of your son be the one?' He said, 'No, my grandson will not be him either.' I then asked, 'Will your great grandson will be the one?' The Imam said, 'No, even my great grandson will not be that person.' I then asked, 'Who will he be then?' The Imam said, 'He will be the one who will fill the earth with justice after its being filled with injustice and cruelty. (He will come) at a time when the *'A'immah* (Leaders with Divine Authority), *'Alayhim al-Salam*, will be absent just as the Messenger of Allah was raised (to preach) when for a long time there had come no messengers.'"

H 902, Ch. 80, h 22

Ali ibn Muhammad has narrated from Ja'far ibn Muhammad from Musa ibn Ja'far al-Baghdadi from Wahab ibn Shadhan from al-Hassan ibn abu al-Rabi' from Muhammad ibn Ishaq from 'Umm Hani who has said the following:

"I asked abu Ja'far Muhammad ibn Ali, *'Alayhim al-Salam*, about the meaning of the words of Allah: 'I do not (need to) swear by the orbiting (81:15) stars which are visible during the night (81:16) and fadeaway during the day.' (81:17) She has said that then he said, 'It refers to the Imam who will disappear in the year two hundred sixty, then he will rise like a shooting star that shines during the dark night. If you will attain such a time it will brighten your eyes with happiness.'"

H 903, Ch. 80, h 23

A number of our people have narrated from Sa'd ibn 'Abd Allah from Ahmad ibn al-Hassan from 'Umar ibn Yazid from al-Hassan ibn al-Rabi ' al-Hamdani who has said that Muhammad ibn Ishaq narrated to us from 'Usayd ibn Tha'laba from 'Umm Hani who has said the following:

"Once I met abu Ja'far Muhammad ibn Ali, *'Alayhi al-Salam*, and asked him about the meaning of: 'I do not swear by the orbiting (81:15) stars which are visible during the night (81:16) and fadeaway during the day. . . .' (81:17) The Imam said, 'Al-Khunnas' refers to the Imam who will disappear in his time when his knowledge will be cut off from people in the year two hundred sixty. Then he will reappear like a shooting star in the dark night. If you will attain such a time it will give light to your eyes with delight.'"

H 904, Ch. 80, h 24

Ali ibn Muhammad has narrated from certain persons of our people from Ayyub ibn Nuh from abu al-Hassan, the third, *'Alayhi al-Salam*, who has said the following:

"When your banner (Imam) will be taken away from amongst you, expect glad news (freedom and ease) to emerge beneath your feet."

H 905, Ch. 80, h 25

A number of our people have narrated from Sa'd ibn 'Abd Allah from Ayyub ibn Nuh who has said the following:

"Once I said to abu al-Hassan al-Rida, *'Alayhi al-Salam*, 'I hope that you will become the person in charge to establish the Kingdom of Allah on earth and owner of this task (Leadership with Divine Authority). Allah will drive it in your control without the sword now that the pledge of allegiance is offered to you and currency coins are printed in your name.'

"The Imam said, 'There has been no one from us with whom letters had been exchanged, being pointed out with the gesture of fingers, questions asked and properties delivered to him, but that he was murdered or died in his bed. (It will be as such) until Allah will raise for the task of establishing His Kingdom on earth and take charge of (Leadership with Divine Authority), a young boy from us whose birth place and upbringing will be unknown, (to people) but his ancestors will be well-known.'"

H 906, Ch. 80, h 26

Al-Husayn ibn Muhammad and others have narrated from Ja'far ibn Muhammad from Ali ibn al-'Abbass ibn 'Amir from Musa ibn Hilal al-Kindi from 'Abd Allah ibn 'Ata', from abu Ja'far, *'Alayhi al-Salam*, the following:

"Once I said to abu Ja'far, *'Alayhi al-Salam*, 'Your Shi'a (followers) in Iraq are many. By Allah, there is no one like you in your family. Why do you not rise (for leadership)?'

"The Imam said, 'O 'Abd Allah ibn 'Ata', you have begun to open your ears to silliness. In fact, by Allah, I am not your *Sahib* (companion, Imam) who will rise with Divine Authority and power.' I (the narrator) then asked him, 'Who is our *Sahib* (companion) then (the one who will rise with Divine Authority and power)?' The Imam then said, 'Find out the one whose time and place of birth is unknown to people and such a person will be your companion (the one who will rise with Divine Authority and power). There is no one among us toward whom people point their fingers so much and tongues will mention him so much, but that has died in frustration or due to sorrow for being ignored and neglected.'"

H 907, Ch. 80, h 27

Muhammad ibn Yahya has narrated from Ahmad ibn Muhammad from al-Husayn ibn Sa'id from ibn abu 'Umayr from Hisham ibn Salim from abu 'Abd Allah, *'Alayhi al-Salam*, who has said the following:

"*Al-Qa'im* (the one who will rise with Divine Authority and power) will rise and he will not be obliged to anyone under any covenant, agreement or oath of allegiance."

H 908, Ch. 80, h 28

Muhammad ibn Yahya has narrated from Ahmad ibn Muhammad from ibn Faddal from al-Hassan ibn Ali al-'Attar from Ja'far ibn Muhammad from Mansur from the person he mentioned who has said the following:

"Once I asked abu 'Abd Allah, *'Alayhi al-Salam*, 'If I pass the day and night and do not find an Imam to follow then what should I do?'

"The Imam said, 'Love those whom you love and hate those whom you hate until Allah, the Most Majestic, the Most Gracious, will grant him permission to reappear.'"

H 909, Ch. 80, h 29

Al-Husayn ibn Ahmad has narrated from Ahmad ibn Hilal who has said that 'Uthman ibn 'Isa narrated to us from Khalid ibn Najih from Zurara ibn A'yan from abu 'Abd Allah, *'Alayhi al-Salam*, who has said the following:

"Abu 'Abd Allah, *'Alayhi al-Salam*, has said, 'It will be necessary for the young boy to disappear from public sight.' I then asked, 'Why it will be necessary?' He said, 'Because of fear' (he then pointed toward his midsection).' He will be the one whose reappearance will be intensely expected. It will be he in whose being born people will have doubts. Certain people will say, 'His mother has just conceived him.' Others will say, 'His father died but left no surviving son.' Certain others will say, 'He was born two years before the death of his father.' I asked him, 'What do you command me if I will live at that time?' The Imam said, 'Pray to Allah in the following words. "O Lord, make me recognize You; if you do not make me recognize You, I will not recognize You. O Lord, make me recognize Your prophet; if You do not make me recognize Your prophet I will never recognize him. O Lord, make me recognize the one who possesses Your authority over the creatures; if You do not make me recognize him I will stray away from my religion.'"

Ahmad ibn Hilal has said, "I had heard this *Hadith* fifty-six years ago."

H 910, Ch. 80, h 30

Abu Ali al-Ash'ari has narrated from Muhammad ibn Hassa'n from Muhammad ibn Ali from 'Abd Allah ibn al-Qasim from al-Mufaddal ibn 'Umar who has said the following:

"About the words of Allah, the Majestic, the Glorious, that read: 'When the trumpet is sounded,' (74:8) abu 'Abd Allah, *'Alayhi al-Salam*, has said, 'From us there will be a triumphant Imam behind a cover. When Allah, Most Majestic is His name, will want to grant him permission to rise (with Divine Authority and power) He will place a spot in his heart. He will then reappear in public sight and rise (with divine power) by the command of Allah, the Most Holy, the Most High.'"

H 911, Ch. 80, h 31
Muhammad ibn Yahya has narrated from Ja'far ibn Muhammad from Ahmad ibn al-Husayn from Muhammad ibn 'Abd Allah from Muhammad ibn al-Faraj who has said the following:
"Once abu Ja'far, *'Alayhi al-Salam*, wrote to me, 'When Allah, the Most Holy, the Most High, is angry with His creatures, He keeps us (members of *Ahl al-Bayt*) away from their neighborhood.'"

Chapter 81 - The Criterion to Discern the Truthful and False Claims of Entitlement to Imamat (Leadership with Divine Authority)

H 912, Ch. 81, h 1
Ali ibn Ibrahim ibn Hashim has narrated from his father from ibn Mahbub from Salam ibn 'Abd Allah and Muhammad ibn al-Hassan and Ali ibn Muhammad from Sahl ibn Ziyad and abu Ali al-Ash'ari from Muhammad ibn Hassa'n; all of them have narrated from Muhammad ibn Ali from Ali ibn Asbat from Salam ibn 'Abd Allah al-Hashimi who has said that Muhammad ibn Ali has said that he heard him (Salam) narrate from abu 'Abd Allah, *'Alayhi al-Salam*, who has said the following:
"Once, Talha and al-Zubayr sent a man called Khidash from the tribe of 'Abd al-Qays, to Amir al-Mu'minin Ali, *'Alayhi al-Salam*. Before he was to leave they spoke to him as follows: 'We are sending you to a man who himself, as well as his family, is known to us all the time as magicians and soothsayers. You are more trusted to us than those in our presence in not listening to any of such things from him. You must debate with him in our support until you will learn the well-known matter. Bear in mind that his claim is the greatest that people can have, and it should not discourage you. Of the ways of his deceiving people are his offering food, drinks, honey, oil and to speak with one privately. Therefore, do not eat any food that he might offer, or drink anything. Do not touch any of the honey or oil that he might present to you and do not sit with him alone. Beware of all such things that might come. Go to him with the blessings of Allah. When you see him read *'Ayat al-Sakhra,* verse fifty-four of Chapter seven and ask Allah to protect you against his plots and the plots of Satan. When you will sit near him do not make eye contact and do not become friendly with him.

'Thereafter say to him, "Two of your brethren in religion, the two sons of your uncle as relatives, urge you not to cut off (good) relations. They say to you, 'Do you not know that we left people just for you and opposed our tribe's people for your sake soon after Allah, the Most Majestic, the Most Gracious, took Muhammad, *'Alayhi al-Salam*, from this world? Now that you have achieved a little status, you have disregarded our honor and shattered our hopes. Despite this, you have already seen our ability to stay away from you and find a vast land far from you. Those who isolated you from our relationships and from us were of much less advantage to you and weaker than us to defend you. Now the dawn has made it very clear to those who have eyes. It has come to our notice that you disrespect us and pray against us. What causes you to do so? (Brave people do not do such things). We had seen you to be the bravest of the strong men of the Arabs.

Has your condemning us become part of your religion? You know well that it breaks you away from us.'"'

"When Khidash came to Amir al-Mu'minin Ali, *'Alayhi al-Salam*, he did exactly what they had told him to do. When Ali, *'Alayhi al-Salam*, looked at him, as he (Khidash) spoke under his breath, the Imam laughed and said, 'O brother, from 'Abd Qays,' pointing to him to sit closer to his place. Khidash, then responded, 'There is enough room around. I am here only to deliver a message to you.' The Imam said, 'First you must eat, drink, change your clothes and use fragrance and then deliver your message. O Qanbar, provide him accommodation.' He said, 'I do not need any of the things you mentioned.' The Imam then said, 'I want to speak to you privately.' The man said, 'All secrets are public to me.'

"The Imam said, 'I urge you, on oath by Allah, Who is closer to you than yourself, Who is between you and your heart, Who knows the stealth looks of the eyes and what the hearts hide (to tell the truth). Had al-Zubayr spoken to you of all that I just offered and said to you?' He replied, 'By the Lord, yes, he did so.' The Imam then said, 'Were you to deny what I asked you, your eyesight would not return (but be destroyed). I urge you, on oath by Allah, did he teach you certain words that you were saying when you came to me?' He replied, 'By the Lord, yes, he did so.'

"Imam Ali, *'Alayhi al-Salam*, said, 'Was it not *'Ayat al-Sakhra*, verse fifty-four of Chapter seven?' He said, 'Yes, that was it.' The Imam said, 'Read it.' He read it and Ali, *'Alayhi al-Salam*, would repeat along with him, make him read again and correct his mistakes until he read it seventy times. The man asked, 'What is the reason for Amir al-Mu'minin's ordering me to repeat them seventy times?' The Imam then asked him, 'Do you feel comfort in your heart?' He said, 'Yes, by the One in Whose hand is my soul, it is comforted.'

"The Imam then said, 'Say what they told you to say.' He then informed him of their message. The Imam said 'Say to them, what you have spoken is sufficient evidence against you; however, Allah does not guide the unjust people. You think that you are my brothers in religion and the sons of my uncles in family relations. I do not deny the family relation even though it must be disregarded unless Islam requires it to be continued. Also it is your statement that you are my brothers in religion. If it is true and you really mean it, then you must know you have already distanced yourselves from the book of Allah, the Most Majestic, the Most Gracious, and have disobeyed Him practically in the affairs of your brother in religion. Otherwise, you have just lied and have created false statements to claim that you are my brothers in religion.'

'You have also said that you did not join other people (against me) soon after Allah took Muhammad, *'Alayhi al-Salam*, out of this world. If what you did was for the sake of the truth, then you must know you have just destroyed the truth in your leaving me, lately, in disregard. If you joined the others for the sake of falsehood you will be held responsible for such (sinful) matters that you have created. Besides, the way you have mentioned your not joining others after the death of Muhammad, '*Alayhi al-Salam*, shows that you did so only with "hopes" in and for the sake of worldly gains and greed. These are your own words, 'You have shattered our "hopes".' I thank Allah, you have not blamed me in the matters of my religion. On the other hand, what has distanced me from you is what has distanced you from the truth and caused you to discard your oath of allegiance (with me) as your undertaking, just as a recalcitrant beast would discard its harness.

'He is Allah, my Lord. I do not consider anything like Him. Do not say, 'He is less advantageous and weaker to defend'; you may deserve to be called polytheists as well as hypocrites. You have also said that I am the bravest of the strong Arab men and that you run away from my prayers against you and my condemnation of you. You must consider that every event requires a certain action. When the spears crisscross, the manes of horses flutter and your lungs swell inside you at such time Allah suffices me with a calm and perfect heart. You have said that you dislike my praying to Allah against you. You should not be disturbed because of the prayers of a magician who belongs to a magician people as you think they are.

'O Lord, do away with al-Zubayr in the worst way of getting killed and make him bleed to death in misguidance. (O Lord) make Talha know he is humiliated and prepare for them even worse than this in the next life, if they have done injustice to me, accused me falsely and have withheld their testimony (in my support), disobeyed You and Your Messenger in my affairs.'

"The Imam then said, 'Say Amen!' Khidash then said, 'Amen!' Khidash then said to himself, 'I have never seen a bearded man with clearer mistakes than yours. You are like a man who carries a message, wherein one part contradicts the other part. Allah has placed nothing in it to hold it together. I, therefore, disdain both of them (Talha and Zubayr) before Allah.' Ali, '*Alayhi al-Salam*, asked him to go back and inform them of what he had said in response. He said, 'No, by Allah I will not go to them until you will ask Allah to return me back to you quickly and grant me the opportunity to please Him in matters of your support.' He did so and very soon he came back and afterwards was murdered when (supporting the Imam) on the day of Jamal. May Allah grant him blessing."

H 913, Ch. 81, h 2

Ali ibn Muhammad and Muhammad ibn al-Hassan have narrated from Sahl ibn Ziyad and abu Ali al-Ash'ari from Muhammad ibn Hassa'n, all of them from Muhammad ibn Ali from Nasr ibn Muzahim from 'Amr ibn Sa'id from Jarrah ibn 'Abd Allah from Rafi' ibn Salama who has said the following:

"On the day of al-Nahrawan (the war at al-Nahrawan) I was in the presence of Ali ibn abu Talib, '*Alayhi al-Salam*. As we were sitting with the Imam, a horseman approached and said, 'Al-Salamu 'Alayka ya Ali (peace be with you O Ali).' Ali, '*Alayhi al-Salam*, said, ''Alayka al-salam (with you also be peace).' 'May your mother weep over your dead body, why did you not address me as the Leader with Divine Authority?' He said, 'Yes, I want to inform you about it. I was present in al-Siffin when the truth was on your side. However, when you approved the arbitrator to settle the warring parties I disregarded you and I called you a polytheist. Ever since I do not know where I should turn to pledge allegiance to the Leadership of one with Divine Authority. If I can find a way to know, whether you are on the right side or on the wrong side, it will be better for me than the world and all that is therein.' Ali, *'Alayhi al-Salam*, said to him, 'May your mother weep on your dead body. Come and stand up near me: I will show the signs of the right and the signs of the wrong side.' As the man stood near him, a horseman approached running until he came to Ali, *'Alayhi al-Salam*, and said, 'O Amir al-Mu'minin, *'Alayhi al-Salam*, I have the glad news of victory. May Allah make it a delight to your eyes (out of joy). It is certain, by Allah, that all men of the enemy are killed.' Ali, *'Alayhi al-Salam*, asked him, 'Did it happen before or after their crossing the river?' He said, 'It happened after crossing.' Ali, *'Alayhi al-Salam*, said, 'You have lied. I swear by the One Who makes the seed to germinate and causes the fetuses to develop, that they (enemy) will never cross the river until they are all killed.'

"The man (first horseman) has said, 'This added to my understanding.' Another horseman came running and said just as the one before had said and Amir al-Mu'minin Ali, *'Alayhi al-Salam*, refused to accept his words as those of the one before. The man who had doubts about Ali, *'Alayhi al-Salam*, has said that he wanted to attack Ali, *'Alayhi al-Salam*, with his sword and chop his head off. Two other men came running on horses soaked in perspiration. They said, 'May Allah give delight and brightness to your eyes with the joy of victory O Amir al-Mu'minin, *'Alayhi al-Salam*. We have the glad news of victory for you. It is certain, by Allah, that all of the people (of the enemy) are killed.' Ali, *'Alayhi al-Salam*, then asked, 'Did it happen before or after their crossing the river?' They said, 'It happened before their crossing the river. When they tried to cross it and water reached up to the mane of their horses they turned back and there they all were killed.' Amir al-Mu'minin Ali, *'Alayhi al-Salam*, said, 'You have spoken the truth.' The man then climbed down from his horse and touched Amir al-Mu'minin's, *'Alayhi al-Salam*, hands and feet and kissed them.' Amir al-Mu'minin Ali, *'Alayhi al-Salam*, said, 'This is the sign and evidence for you (that I am on the right side).'"

H 914, Ch. 81, h 3

Ali ibn Muhammad has narrated from abu Ali Muhammad ibn 'Isma'il ibn Musa ibn Ja'far from Ahmad ibn al-Qasim al-'Ijli from Ahmad ibn Yahya, also known as Kurd, from Muhammad ibn Khudahi from 'Abd Allah ibn Ayyub from 'Abd Allah ibn Hashim from 'Abd al-Karim ibn 'Amr al-Khath'ami from Hababa al-Walibiyyah who has said the following:

"Once I saw Amir al-Mu'minin Ali, *'Alayhi al-Salam*, in the (market) place of the elite forces with a two-pronged whip in his hand. With it he scared the sellers of inedible fish such as eel, moray and angler and so forth, and said, 'O sellers of metamorphosed Israelites and the army of the descendents of Marwan, do not sell (inedible fishes).' At this time Frat ibn Ahnaf came to him and asked, 'O Amir al-Mu'minin, *'Alayhi al-Salam*, what is the army of the descendents of Marwan?' She has said that Ali, *'Alayhi al-Salam*, said to him, 'They are the groups of people who shaved their beards and twined their mustaches and then they were metamorphosed.' I had not heard anyone speak better than him; I followed him without losing sight of his track until he sat down at an open space of the Mosque (of Kufa). I then asked him, 'O Amir al-Mu'minin, *'Alayhi al-Salam*, what are the signs of Imamat (Leadership with Divine Authority), may Allah grant you blessings?' She has said that he said, 'Bring to me that pebble.' He pointed with his hand. I then got the pebble for him and he set for me his insignia on it (engraved on solid stone). He then said to me, 'O Hababa, if anyone claims to be the Imam (Leader with Divine Authority) and can set his insignia as you just saw, then acknowledge that he is the Imam that must be obeyed. The Imam does not miss what he wants.' She has said, 'I then left him until Amir al-Mu'minin Ali, *'Alayhi al-Salam*, was taken out of this world. Thereafter I went to al-Hassan, *'Alayhi al-Salam*, who was sitting in the place of Amir al-Mu'minin Ali, *'Alayhi al-Salam*, and people around asked him questions. He said to me, 'O Hababa al-Walibiyyah.' I said, 'Yes, my master.' He then said, 'Give to me what is with you.' I then gave it (the pebble) to him. He set on it (his insignia) just as Amir al-Mu'minin Ali, *'Alayhi al-Salam*, had done. She has said, 'Afterwards I went to al-Husayn, *'Alayhi al-Salam*. He was in the Mosque of the Messenger of Allah. He welcomed me warmly and then said to me, 'There is no doubt that in the proof (that supports the true Imam) there is already enough proof for what you want. Do you want the proof to know the Imam?' I said, 'Yes, my master.' He then said, 'Bring to me what you have with you.' I gave him the pebble and he printed (his insignia) on it. She has said, 'Afterwards I went to Ali ibn al-Husayn, *'Alayhi al-Salam*, but at that time I had become very old and my hands were shaky. I could count one hundred thirteen years of my lifetime. I found him in *Ruku'* (kneeling in prayer) and *Sajdah* (prostration) or busy in certain forms of worship. I became despaired about the proof (of Leadership with Divine Authority). He pointed out with his forefinger and my youth came back.' She has said, 'I asked, saying, "My master, how much of the world is passed and how much is left?"' He said, 'Of how much is passed yes (I can tell), but not of how much is to come.' She has said that he then said to me, 'Give to me what is with you.' I then gave him the pebble and he printed on it (his insignia) for me. Thereafter I went to abu Ja'far, *'Alayhi al-Salam*, and he printed on it (his insignia) for me. Then I went to abu 'Abd Allah, *'Alayhi al-Salam*. He printed on it (his insignia) for me. Then I went to abu al-Hassan Musa, *'Alayhi al-Salam*, and he printed (his insignia) for me. Then I went to al-Rida, *'Alayhi al-Salam*, and he printed his insignia for me.'"

According to Muhammad ibn Hisham, Hababa lived thereafter another nine months.

H 915, Ch. 81, h 4

Muhammad ibn abu 'Abd Allah and Ali ibn Muhammad have narrated from Ishaq ibn Muhammad al-Nakha'i from abu Hashim Dawud ibn al-Qasim al-Ja'fari who has said the following:

"Once I was in the presence of abu Muhammad (al-Hassan ibn Ali al-Hadi), *'Alayhi al-Salam*, when permission was requested for a man from Yemen to see the Imam, *'Alayhi al-Salam*. A chubby, tall and heavy man then came in and greeted the Imam with the greeting for *Wilayah*, (Leadership with Divine Authority) and received acceptance in response. The Imam asked him to sit and he sat just next to me. I then said to myself, 'I wish I knew who he is?' Abu Muhammad, *'Alayhi al-Salam*, then said, 'He is of the children of the Arab lady for whom my ancestors had printed their insignia on a pebble and the print took place in an engraving form. He has brought it with him and wants me to print my insignia on it also.' He then asked the man to give it to him. The man took out a pebble and on one side thereof was a smooth space. Abu Muhammad, *'Alayhi al-Salam*, then received it, took out his insignia, printed on it and the print took place. Even now it is as if I see the print of his (al-Hassan ibn Ali's) insignia on the pebble. I then asked the man from Yemen, 'Had you ever seen him (abu Muhammad, *'Alayhi al-Salam*), before?' He said, 'No, I had not seen him before, however, by Allah, I had always been anxious for this hour to see him when a young man came to me and I had not seen him before. He said, "Stand up and come in" and I came in.' The man from Yemen then left saying, 'May Allah's grace and blessings be with you people of *Ahl al-Bayt* whose generations are just like the generation before. I testify before Allah that it is obligatory to preserve your rights just as it was the case with Amir al-Mu'minin Ali, *'Alayhi al-Salam*, and the *'A'immah* (Leaders with Divine Authority) after him, may Allah grant all of them blessings.' He then left and thereafter I never saw him.

"Ibn Ishaq has said that abu Hashim al-Ja'fari has said, 'I asked him his name.' He said, 'My name is Mahja' ibn al-Salt ibn 'Aqaba ibn Sam'an ibn Ghanim ibn 'Umm Ghanim.' She was the Arab lady from Yemen who had the pebble on which Amir al-Mu'minin Ali, *'Alayhi al-Salam*, had printed his insignia and also his descendents up to the time of abu al-Hassan, *'Alayhi al-Salam*."

H 916, Ch. 81, h 5

Muhammad ibn Yahya has narrated from Ahmad ibn Muhammad from ibn Mahbub from Ali ibn Ri'ab from abu 'Ubayda and Zurara all from abu Ja'far, *'Alayhi al-Salam*, who has said the following:

"When al-Husayn, *'Alayhi al-Salam*, was martyred, Muhammad ibn al-Hanafiya asked Ali ibn al-Husayn, *'Alayhi al-Salam*, for a private meeting. In the meeting he said, 'O son of my brother, you know that the Messenger of Allah, *'Alayhi al-Salam*, delivered the task of *al-Wasiyya*, (the executorship of the will) and *al-Imamat*, (Leadership with Divine Authority) to Amir al-Mu'minin Ali, *'Alayhi al-Salam*. Thereafter it was delivered to al-Hassan, *'Alayhi al-Salam*, and then to al-Husayn, *'Alayhi al-Salam*. Your father, May Allah be pleased with him, has been murdered, may Allah grant blessing up on his soul, and he did not make any will. I am your uncle and equal in status to your father and I am a son of Ali, *'Alayhi al-Salam*. Because of being older in age I am more deserving of the position of Imamat (Leadership with Divine Authority) considering that you are younger than me. Therefore, you should not dispute me about *al-Wasiyya* (the will) and *Imamat*, (Leadership with Divine Authority) and should not argue with me about it.' Ali ibn al-Husayn, *'Alayhi al-Salam*, said, 'O uncle, be pious before Allah and do not claim in what you have no right. I advise you not to be one of the ignorant people. In fact, my father, *'Alayhi al-Salam*, O my uncle, appointed me as the executor of his will before his leaving for Iraq. He made such covenant with me just an hour before his becoming a martyr. This is the Armament of the Messenger of Allah with me. You then should not dislocate them. I am afraid for you of a shorter life and difficult conditions. Allah, the Most Majestic, the Most Gracious, has placed *al-Wasiyya*, and *Imamat*, in the descendents of al-Husayn, *'Alayhi al-Salam*. If you want to know it we can go near the Black-stone and ask it for judgment about the issue.'

"Abu Ja'far, *'Alayhi al-Salam*, has said that the issue came up between them in Makkah and they went near the Black-stone. Ali ibn al-Husayn, *'Alayhi al-Salam*, said to Muhammad al-Hanafiya, 'You begin first and pray to Allah, the Most Majestic, the Most Gracious, and ask Him to make the Black-stone speak to you and then ask your question.' Muhammad then pleaded in his prayer and asked Allah and then asked the Black-stone about the disputed issue, but there was no answer. Ali ibn al-Husayn, *'Alayhi al-Salam*, said, 'O uncle, had you been the executor of the will and the Imam, it would have answered your question.' Muhammad then said, 'Now you pray to Allah, O son of my brother, and ask your question.' Ali ibn al-Husayn, *'Alayhi al-Salam*, prayed to Allah for what he wanted. He then addressed the Black-stone and said, 'I ask you for the sake of the One Who placed the covenant of the prophets in you, as well as the covenant of the executors of the will and the covenant of all the people. You must tell us who the *Wasiyy* and *Imam* after al-Husayn ibn Ali, *'Alayhi al-Salam*, is.'

"The narrator has said that the Black-stone began to shake so much that it almost came out of its place. Allah, the Most Majestic, the Most Gracious, then made it to speak in clear Arabic language and said, 'O Lord, *al-Wasiyya* and *Imamat* after al-Husayn, *'Alayhi al-Salam*, ibn Ali is for Ali ibn al-Husayn ibn Ali ibn abu Talib and ibn *Fatimah, 'Alayha al-Salam*, daughter of the Messenger of Allah.'

"The narrator has said that Muhammad ibn Ali returned and he acknowledged Ali ibn al-Husayn, *'Alayhi al-Salam*, to be his *Wali* (Leader with Divine Authority)."

Ali ibn Ibrahim has narrated from his father from Hammad ibn 'Isa from Hariz from Zurara from abu Ja'far, *'Alayhi al-Salam*, the same *Hadith*.

H 917, Ch. 81, h 6
Al-Husayn ibn Muhammad has narrated from al-Mu'alla ibn Muhammad from Muhammad ibn Ali who has said that Sama'a ibn Mihran narrated to me that al-Kalbi al-Nassaba narrated to him the following:

"Once I went to Madina and I had no knowledge of this matter, *Imamat* (Leadership with Divine Authority). I went to the Mosque where I found a group of people of Quraysh. I asked them, 'Can you give me information about the scholar of this family (the family of the Holy Prophet)?' They said, 'Abd Allah ibn Hassan is the one.' I went to his house and asked permission to see him. A man whom I thought was his slave came out of the house. I said to him, 'Ask your master to grant me permission to meet him.' He went inside and then came out saying: 'Come in.' I entered the house and found an old man devoted to worship and hard work. I greeted him and then he asked, 'Who are you?' I then said, 'I am a Kalbi (from the tribe of Kalb) and a genealogist.' He then asked, 'What is it that you need?' I said, 'I have come to ask certain questions.' He then asked, 'Have you visited my son Muhammad?' I said, 'I have begun with you.' Then he said, 'You may ask your questions.' I then said, 'Explain to me the case of a man who says to his wife, "You are divorced as many times as the number of stars in heavens.'" He said, 'It becomes irrevocable at the beginning of the month of *Jawza'* (the third month of a particular calendar). The rest are sins and he owes penalties.' I said to myself, 'This is one.' Then I asked, 'What does the honorable Shaykh say about rubbing over the shoe for *Wuzu'* (a formal washing before prayer)?' He said, 'A virtuous group would wipe over the shoe but we, *Ahl al-Bayt* do not wipe.' I then said to myself, 'This is the second.' I then asked, 'What do you say about consuming eel for food; is it edible or not edible?' He said, 'It is lawful, but we, *Ahl al-Bayt* leave it alone.' I then said to myself, 'This is the third.' Then I said, 'What do you say about drinking *al-Nabidh*, a certain kind of drink?' He said, 'It is lawful but we, *Ahl al-Bayt* do not drink it.' I then left him saying to myself, 'This group of people lies about this *Ahl al-Bayt.*'

"I then entered the Mosque and I looked at the group of people of Quraysh (a particular tribe) and other people. I greeted them and asked them, 'Who knows this *Ahl al-Bayt*?' They said, 'Abd Allah ibn al-Hassan knows.' I then said, 'I just visited him and did not find anything with him.' One person from the people raised his head and said, 'Go to Ja'far ibn Muhammad, *'Alayhi al-Salam.* He is the most knowledgeable one in this *Ahl al-Bayt.*' Certain individuals criticized that person for what he said. I then said, 'People out of jealousy did not tell me about him when first I asked them.' I then asked, 'What is the matter with you? He is the one I want.' I then walked until I reached his house. I knocked on the door and his slave, a young man, came out and asked me, 'Come in, O brother from the tribe of Kalb.' He, by Allah, amazed me (for knowing me without any introduction). I went inside but I was shaken. Upon looking I found a gentleman on the prayer rug with no pillow or blankets. He began to talk after I saluted him with greeting of peace, 'Who are you?' I then said to myself, 'Glory to Allah, his slave at the door said to me, "O brother from the tribe of Kalb, come in" and his master asked me, "Who are you?" I then said, 'I am a Kalbi, a genealogist.''

"He then tapped his forehead and said, 'The devious people lie about Allah and they stray far away and suffer a great loss. O brother from Kalb, Allah, the Most Majestic, the Most Gracious, says, 'To each of the tribes of 'Ad, Thamud, the settlers around the well and many generations in between,' (25:38) can you tell their genealogical relations?' I said, 'No, may Allah keep my soul in service for your cause.' Then he asked, 'Can you tell your own genealogical relations?' I said, 'Yes, I am so and so son of so and so' and I went on and on. He said, 'Hold it there. It is not the way you say. What is the matter with you? Do you know who so and so, son of so and so is?' I said, 'Yes, so and so son of so and so.' He said, 'So and so son of so and so was a Kurdish shepherd. Such and such Kurdish shepherd was on the mountain of the people of so and so. He went to so and so, the wife of so and so that lived on the mountain on which he grazed his sheep. He fed her something and overwhelmed her. She gave birth to so and so and so and so son of so and so, and so and so daughter of so and so and so and so.' Then he said, 'Do you know these names?' I said, 'No, may Allah keep my soul in service for your cause, if you do not mind, allow us to disregard this.'

"He then said, 'It is because you said it (brought up the subject), I said it.' I then said, 'I will not repeat.' He said, 'Therefore, we will not repeat. Ask what you have come for.' I then said, 'Explain to me the case of the man who has said to his wife, "You are divorced as many times as the number of the stars of the heavens."'"

"He asked, 'What is the matter with you? Have you not read the chapter, *Al-Talaq* (divorce)?' I said, 'Yes, I have read it.' He then said, 'Read it.' I then read from the Holy Quran, '. . . divorce them at a time after which they can start their waiting period. Let them keep an account of the number of the days in the waiting period. . . .' (65:1) He then asked, 'Do you find any of the stars of the heavens there?'"

"I said, 'No, I do not find.' Then I said, 'A man has said to his wife, 'You are divorced three times.' He said, 'You must refer it to the book of Allah and the *Sunnah* of His Prophet, *'Alayhi al-Salam.*' Then he said, 'Divorce is only valid in a menses-free period of time in which no carnal relation may have taken place between the wife and husband, and there must be two acceptable witnesses present.' I then said to myself, 'This is one.' Then he said, 'Ask.' I then asked, 'What do you say about rubbing over the shoe for *Wuzu*'?' He smiled and said, 'On the Day of Judgment when Allah will return everything to its material being and the leather (of the shoe) is returned to the sheep, then you will see the rubbing people and where their *Wuzu*' will go.' I then said to myself, 'This is the second.' He then turned to me and said, 'Ask.' I then asked, 'Tell me about eel; is it lawful to consume it for food?' He said, 'Allah, the Most Majestic, the Most Gracious, caused a certain group of Israelites to metamorphose. Whatever from them was taken by the ocean turned into eel, such as hagfish, moray and angle-fish and so forth, and whatever from them was left on land they turned into swine, and wild cats and lizards and so forth.' I then said to myself, 'This is the third.' He then turned to me and said, 'Ask.' I asked, 'What do you say about al-Nabidh, (extracts from dates)?' He said, 'It is lawful.' I said, 'We mix with it al-'Akr (residue) and other things and drink.' He said, 'Shu shu, that is foul smelling wine.' I then asked, 'May Allah keep my soul in service for your cause, what kind of Nabidh do you mean?'"

"He then said, 'Once the people of Madina complained to the Messenger of Allah about a change in their water and their feeling ill. He ordered them to make *Nabidh* (a certain drink). Thus, a man would ask his servant to throw a handful or so of dates into their water-sack. They would then drink from it and use it for cleansing.' I then asked, 'How many pieces of date would come in a handful?' He said, 'As much as a handful could be.' I then asked, 'One handful or two?' He said, 'Perhaps one or perhaps two handfuls.' I then asked, 'How big might have been the sack?' He said, 'Big enough for forty to eighty or more.' I then asked, 'Is it in *Artal* (a certain measurement)?' He said, 'Yes, in *Artal* (about three hundred grams each) according to the measurement of Iraq.'"

"Sama'a has said that Al-Kalbi has said, 'He, *'Alayhi al-Salam,* stood up and I also came out and I would slap my one hand with the other and say to myself, 'If there is anything, he, *'Alayhi al-Salam*, is it.' Thereafter al-Kalbi followed the religion of Allah with the love of *Ahl al-Bayt* until he died."

H 918, Ch. 81, h 7

Muhammad ibn Yahya has narrated from Ahmad ibn Muhammad ibn 'Isa from abu Yahya al-Wasiti from Hisham ibn Salim who has said the following:

"We were in Madina after abu 'Abd Allah, *'Alayhi al-Salam*, left this world. People had gathered around 'Abd Allah ibn Ja'far. They thought he was the person in charge of this task (Leadership with Divine Authority) after his father. Sahib al-Taq and I went to see him while people were around him because of a *Hadith*, they narrated from abu 'Abd Allah, *'Alayhi al-Salam*, that said, 'The in charge of the task (Leadership with Divine Authority) will be the eldest son, if he did not suffer any defects.' We went to see and ask him what we used to ask his father. We asked him about *Zakat* to find out on how much property it becomes due. He said, 'It is five on every two hundred.' We asked, 'What if it (the property) was one hundred?' He said, 'It (rate of tax) is two and a half.' We then said, 'By Allah, al-Murji'a sect does not say so.'

"The narrator has said that he ('Abd Allah ibn Ja'far) then raised hands to the sky and said, 'By Allah, I do not know what al-Murji'a group says.' The narrator has said that we then left him with a feeling of loss and did not know where to go. Abu Ja'far al-Ahwal and I were together. We sat down on a street corner of the city of Madina weeping and confused and did not know where and to whom should we go, asking each other, 'Where do we go now? Should we go to al-Murji'a, al-Qadria (belief in predestination), to al-Zaydiaya sect, al-Mu'tazila or the al-Khawarij sect?' At this time I saw a gentleman whom I did not know, gesture toward me with his hand. I became afraid and thought he might be a spy of the spies of abu Ja'far al-Mansur ('Abbassid ruler). He had his spies in Madina to see who the Shi'a followed after Ja'far, *'Alayhi al-Salam*, and then they would cut his neck off. I was afraid, thinking that he might be one of them. I then said to al-Ahwal, 'Get away from here; I am afraid for both of us. He only wants me and not you. Move away from me and from destruction. I do not want to become an instrument against you.' He moved a little away and I followed the gentleman. I did so, thinking that I would not be able to set myself free from him. I continued following him. I had become certain of dying until we reached the door of abu al-Hassan, *'Alayhi al-Salam*. He then left me there and went away. At that time the servant came out of the house and said, 'Come inside. May Allah grant you blessings.' I went in and found abu al-Hassan, Musa, *'Alayhi al-Salam*, therein. He began talking to me saying: '(you do not have to go to anyone) not to al-Murji'a, or al-Qadria, or al-Zaydiya, nor to al-Mu'tazila or al-Khariji group, come to me, come to me.' I then said, 'May Allah keep my soul in service for your cause, has your father left this world?' He said, 'Yes, he has passed away.' I then asked, 'Did he die a natural death?' He said, 'Yes, he did so.' I then asked, 'Who will be for us after him?' He said, 'If Allah wills to guide you He will do so.' I then asked, 'May Allah keep my soul in service for your cause, 'Abd Allah thinks that he is the one after his father.' He said, ''Abd Allah wants people not to worship Allah.' I then asked, 'May Allah keep my soul in service for your cause, who will be for us after him?' He said, 'If Allah wills to guide you He will do so.' I then said, 'May Allah keep my soul in service for your cause, is that you?' He said, 'No, I do not say that to you.'

"He (the narrator) has said that I then said to myself, 'Perhaps I could not ask in the right way.' Then I asked, 'May Allah keep my soul in service for your cause, is there any Imam above you?' He said, 'No, there is no Imam above me.' He has said that then something struck my mind in a way that no one could know except Allah, the Most Majestic, the Most Gracious. It was a feeling of his greatness and awe, greater than what I would feel in the presence of his father. Then I said, 'May Allah keep my soul in service for your cause, may I ask what I used to ask your father?' He said, 'Ask, you will have the answers but do not make them public. If you did so it would be slaughtering.' I asked him and found him to be like an ocean of knowledge that does not diminish. I then said, 'May Allah keep my soul in service for your cause, your Shi'a, followers and the followers of your father are in loss due to false guidance. Thus, can I meet them and call them to you? I will keep it secret.' He said, 'If you can find intelligent people inform them but make them to promise secrecy. If they make it public it will be slaughter,' he pointed with his hand to his throat.

"He (the narrator) has said, 'I then left him and met abu Ja'far al-Ahwal. He asked me, "What is behind you?" I said, 'It is guidance.' I then informed him of the whole story. We then met al-Fudayl and abu Basir. They went to see him, heard his words, asked him and became certain of his Imamat (Leadership with Divine Authority). Thereafter we met people in groups. Whoever went to see him he became certain of his Imamat (Leadership with Divine Authority), except the tribe of 'Ammar and his companions. 'Abd Allah was left alone and no one would go to see him except a very few people. When he found out about the conditions he asked, 'What is the matter with the people?' They told him ('Abd Allah) that Hisham has prevented people from visiting him (Abd Allah). Hisham has said, 'He ('Abd Allah) made many people ambush and beat me (Hisham).'"

H 919, Ch. 81, h 8

Ali ibn Ibrahim has narrated from his father from Muhammad from Muhammad ibn so and so al-Waqifi (a certain sect) who has said the following:

"One of the sons of my uncle was called al-Hassan ibn 'Abd Allah. He was *Zahid* (restricted himself from worldly pleasures). He was the foremost in worship in his time. The Sultan would also observe cautions due to his assiduousness and seriousness in matters of religion. He even demanded the Sultan to respect and maintain the lawful and the unlawful rule with strictness. The Sultan exercised patience with him due to his virtuousness. It continued as such every day until one day, abu al-Hassan, Musa, *'Alayhi al-Salam*, went to him while he was in the mosque and called him with a hand gesture. When he came near, the Imam said, 'O abu Ali, I like your practice very much and it makes me happy. However, you do not have any understanding. You must seek understanding.' He said, 'May Allah keep my soul in service for your cause, what is understanding?' He said, 'Go and try to understand and learn *Hadith*.' He then asked, 'From whom must I learn *Hadith*?' The Imam said, 'Learn from the scholars of law in Madina. Then read them before me to check (for authenticity).'

"The narrator has said that he then went, wrote (a few *Hadith*), came back and read them before him. The Imam deleted all of them and said to him, 'Go and learn how to understand'. The man was very serious in his religion. He kept watching abu al-Hassan, *'Alayhi al-Salam*, until one day he went out in search of a lost property and abu al-Hassan, *'Alayhi al-Salam*, met him on the way. He said, 'May Allah keep my soul in service for your cause, I will debate you before Allah unless you teach me how to have understanding.' The Imam explained to him about Amir al-Mu'minin Ali, *'Alayhi al-Salam*, and what had happened after the Messenger of Allah. He also explained to him about the two men and he agreed. Then he asked, 'Who was the Leader with Divine Authority after Amir al-Mu'minin Ali, *'Alayhi al-Salam*?' He said, 'Al-Hassan, *'Alayhi al-Salam*, was the Leader with Divine Authority, then al-Husayn, *'Alayhi al-Salam*.' He mentioned, *'A'immah* (Leaders with Divine Authority) one after the other up to his own self and remained silent.'

"The narrator has said that the man then asked, 'May Allah keep my soul in service for your cause, who is the Leader with Divine Authority today?' The Imam asked, 'Were I to tell, would you then accept?' He said, 'May Allah keep my soul in service for your cause, yes, I would accept.' He said, 'I am the one (Leader with Divine Authority).' He then asked, 'Is there any evidence I can use as proof?' The Imam said, 'Go to that tree.' He pointed out with his hand to 'Umm Ghaylan and say to it, 'Musa ibn Ja'far says, "Come to me." He has said, 'I then went to the tree and saw it, by Allah, cutting the earth a real cut until it stood before him. Then he made a gesture and it returned.'

"The narrator said that he then acknowledged his Imamat (Leadership with Divine Authority). He remained silent and devoted himself in worship and no one thereafter saw him speak.'"

Muhammad ibn Yahya and Ahmad ibn Muhammad have narrated from Muhammad ibn al-Hassan from Ibrahim ibn Hashim a similar *Hadith*.

H 920, Ch. 81, h 9

Muhammad ibn Yahya and Ahmad ibn Muhammad have narrated from Muhammad ibn al-Hassan from Ahmad ibn al-Husayn from Muhammad ibn al-Tayyib from 'Abd al-Wahhab ibn Mansur from Muhammad ibn 'Abd al-'Ala' who has said the following:

"I heard from Yahya ibn Aktham, the judge in the city of Samarra, Iraq the following: He spoke only after serious efforts in debates, conversations, maintaining good relations and asking him about the knowledge of the members of the family of Muhammad, *'Alayhi al-Salam*. He said, 'Once when I was walking around the grave of the Messenger of Allah I saw Muhammad ibn Ali al-Rida, *'Alayhi al-Salam*, also walking around the grave of the Messenger of Allah. We debated over the issues that I needed to understand. He explained them to me. I then said, 'By Allah, I want to ask you a question, but I swear by Allah that I feel shy.' He then said, 'I can tell you what you want to ask before you will ask me about it. You want to ask me about Imamat (Leadership with Divine Authority).' I then said, 'By Allah, this is it.' He said, 'I am he.' I then asked, 'Is there any evidence and proof to support it?' He had a staff in his hand and it spoke, 'My master certainly is the Imam of this time and he is the Hujja (Leader with Divine Authority).'"

H 921, Ch. 81, h 10
Muhammad ibn Yahya has narrated from Ahmad ibn Muhammad, or a person other than him from Ali ibn al-Hakam from al-Husayn ibn 'Umar ibn Yazid who has said the following:

"Once I went to see Ali al-Rida, *'Alayhi al-Salam*. At that time I was a member of *Waqifi* sect. My father had asked his (al-Rida's) father seven questions. He had replied to six of them and had refrained from answering the seventh. I said to myself, 'By Allah, I will ask him what my father had asked his father, if his answers will be like those of his father it will serve as a good proof.' I asked him those questions and his answers were just like the answers of his father to my father in the six questions. He did not add anything in the answer to six questions, not even a letter 'W' or letter 'Y', and refrained from answering the seventh question.

"My father had said to his father, 'I will debate you before Allah on the Day of Judgment for your belief that 'Abd Allah is not an Imam.' He then had placed his hand over my father's neck and said, 'Yes, you may debate me about it before Allah, the Most Majestic, the Most Gracious. If there will be any sin in it, it will be on my neck.'

"When I said farewell to him he said, 'Whoever of our Shi'a suffers from any kind of afflictions or complaints and he bears it patiently, Allah, the Most Majestic, the Most Gracious, will record for him an entitlement to a reward equal to the rewards of a thousand martyrs.'

"I then said to myself, 'By Allah, there was no mention of this (in our conversations).' I then left and on the way a vein in my leg began to feel very sore and the pain intensified. Next year when I went for Hajj I went to see him. My leg was still slightly painful. I complained before him of the pain and requested him to say a prayer on it and I stretched it before him. He said, 'There is nothing wrong with this leg, but show me your healthy leg.' I then stretched it before him and he said a protective prayer. When I left, a little later on, my leg began to feel the pain in a vein, but it was very little."

H 922, Ch. 81, h 11
Ahmad ibn Mihran has narrated from Muhammad ibn Ali from ibn Qiyaman al-Wasiti, a member of the *waqifa* sect, who has said the following:

"Once I went to see Ali ibn Musa al-Rida, *'Alayhi al-Salam*, and I asked him, 'Can there be two Imam (Leaders with Divine Authority) at the same time?' He said, 'No, unless one of them is silent.' I then asked, 'What about yourself? There is no silent Imam with you.' His son, abu Ja'far, *'Alayhi al-Salam*, was not yet born. He said, 'By Allah, Allah will create from me someone to establish the truth and the people of truth, and banish falsehood and the people of falsehood.' After a year thereafter abu Ja'far, *'Alayhi al-Salam*, was born. It was asked of ibn Qiyaman, 'Does this sign not convince you?' He then said, 'By Allah, the sign is great, but what can I say about the words of abu 'Abd Allah, *'Alayhi al-Salam*, about his son?'" (It perhaps is a reference to *al-Bada'*).

H 923, Ch. 81, h 12

Al-Husayn ibn Muhammad has narrated from Mu'alla ibn Muhammad from (al-Hassan ibn Ali) al-Washsha' who has said the following:

"I came to Khurasan when I was a member of the *Waqifa* sect. I had certain goods with me. In these goods there was a printed piece of fabric in one of the bundles. It was misplaced and I did not know where it was. When I arrived in Marv and found lodging, a man who was born in the city of Madina came by and said to me, 'Abu al-Hassan al-Rida, *'Alayhi al-Salam*, said to you, 'Send to me the piece of printed fabric that is with you.' I then asked, 'Who has told abu al-Hassan, *'Alayhi al-Salam*, about my arrival here? I have just arrived. There is no printed fabric with me.' He went back to the Imam and returned to me saying, 'The Imam says, 'It is in such and such place and in such and such bundle.' I then looked for it as he had said and found it at the bottom of the bundle, and then I sent it to him.'"

H 924, Ch. 81, h 13

Ibn Faddal has narrated from 'Abd Allah ibn al-Mughira who has said the following:

"I was a member of *Waqifa* sect and I went to Hajj with the same belief. When I arrived in Makkah an idea began to prick my chest. I got hold of al-Multazam (the wall next to the door of Ka'ba) and said, 'O Lord, You know what I ask for and my intention. Guide me to the best of the religions.' It then occurred to me to see al-Rida, *'Alayhi al-Salam*. I went to the city of Madina and stood in front of his door and said to his slave, 'Tell your master that a man from Iraq is at the door.' He has said, 'I heard his voice saying, "O 'Abd Allah ibn Mughira, come in." I then went inside and when he looked at me he said, "Allah has answered your prayer and has guided you to His religion."' I then said, 'I testify that you possess Divine Authority and you are the trustee of Allah over His creatures.'"

H 925, Ch. 81, h 14

Al-Husayn ibn Muhammad has narrated from Mu'alla ibn Muhammad from Ahmad ibn Muhammad ibn 'Abd Allah who has said the following:

"'Abd Allah ibn Hulayl believed 'Abd Allah (ibn Ja'far, *'Alayhi al-Salam*, to be the Imam. He went to the army headquarters in Samarra, Iraq and thereafter changed his belief. I asked him about the reason for such change. He said, 'I thought (while in Samarra) I should discuss it with abu al-Hassan, *'Alayhi al-Salam*, and ask him about it. Accidentally I came across him when passing through a narrow alley. He came closer and when parallel to me, he sent (as if throwing saliva) to me something out from his mouth and it landed on my chest. I then picked it up. It was a leaf with a writing on it that said, 'He never was in it (position of Leadership with Divine Authority) and he has never been qualified for it (Leadership with Divine Authority).'"

H 926, Ch. 81, h 15

Ali ibn Muhammad has narrated from one of our people whose name he mentioned. He said that Muhammad ibn Ibrahim narrated to us, that Musa ibn Muhammad ibn 'Isma'il ibn 'Ubayd Allah ibn 'Abbass ibn Ali ibn abu Talib narrated to us from Ja'far ibn Zayd ibn Musa from his father, from his ancestors, *'Alayhim al-Salam*, the following:

"One day 'Umm Aslama came to the Holy Prophet, *'Alayhi al-Salam*, when he was in the house of 'Umm Salama. She asked about the Messenger of Allah. 'Umm Salama replied that he had just gone out for something and that he might return soon. She then waited with 'Umm Salama until he (the Messenger of Allah) came. 'Umm Aslama then said, 'May Allah keep my soul and the souls of my parents in service for your cause, Messenger of Allah, I have read the books and have learned about all the prophets and the executors of their wills. Musa (Moses) had an executor for his will even in his lifetime and an executor of the will after he died. So also was Jesus. Who then is the executor of your will, O the Messenger of Allah?' He then said to her, 'O 'Umm Aslama, the executor of my will in my lifetime and after I die is the same person.' Then he said to her, 'O 'Umm Aslama, whoever will be able to do what I intend to do just now, he is and will be the executor of my will.' He then picked up a pebble from the floor and crushed it with his fingers into something like flour. He then turned it into a piece of clay and then printed his insignia on it and said, 'Whoever can do what I just did will be the executor of my will in my lifetime and after I will die.'

"She then left him. She has said that she went to Amir al-Mu'minin Ali, *'Alayhi al-Salam*, and asked, 'May Allah keep my soul and the souls of my parents in service for your cause, are you the executor of the will of the Messenger of Allah?' He said, 'Yes, I am, O 'Umm Aslama.' He then picked up a pebble, crushed it into powder like flour, turned it into clay and printed his insignia on it. He then said, 'O 'Umm Aslama, whoever can do what I just did will be the executor of my will.' I then went to al-Hassan, *'Alayhi al-Salam*, while he was a young boy. I asked him, 'My master, are you the executor of the will of your father?' He said, 'Yes, I am, O 'Umm Aslama.' He picked up a pebble and did exactly what his father had done. I left him and went to al-Husayn, *'Alayhi al-Salam*, and considered him very little because of his young age. I said to him, 'May Allah keep my soul and the souls of my parents in service for your cause,' and I asked him, 'Are you the executor of the will of your brother?' He said, 'Yes, I am. O 'Umm Aslama bring me a pebble.' He then did exactly as they had done.

"She has said that she lived until she met Ali ibn al-Husayn, *'Alayhi al-Salam*, after the martyrdom of his father, al-Husayn, *'Alayhi al-Salam*. Upon his return from Iraq she asked him, 'Are you the executor of the will of your father?' He said, 'Yes, I am.' He then also did exactly as they, *'Alayhim al-Salam*, had done."

H 927, Ch. 81, h 16

Muhammad ibn Yahya has narrated from Ahmad ibn Muhammad from al-Husayn ibn Sa'id from al-Husayn ibn al-Jarud from Musa ibn Bakr ibn Dab from the one who narrated to him from abu Ja'far, *'Alayhi al-Salam*, who has said the following:

"Zayd, ibn Ali ibn al-Husayn, once went to see abu Ja'far, Muhammad ibn Ali, *'Alayhi al-Salam*. He carried with him letters from the people of Kufa who invited him to their (city) and informed him of their unity and collective decision to ask him to rise. Abu Ja'far, *'Alayhi al-Salam*, then asked him, 'Are these letters their initiative or a response to what you had written to them and asked them to do?' He said, 'It is their initiative; they acknowledge our rights and because of our being from the family of the Messenger of Allah. It is also because of what they read in the book of Allah, the Most Majestic, the Most Gracious, about the obligation to love and obey us. Also it is because of the suffering impediments and afflictions that we had been through.

"Abu Ja'far, *'Alayhi al-Salam*, said to him, 'Obedience is an obligation from Allah, the Most Majestic, the Most Gracious. It is a tradition, *Sunnah*, that He had established in the people of the past and in the same way it will continue in the later generations of the people. Obedience is only for one of us and to love is for all of us. The command of Allah applies to His friends because of the rules already made available and because of the decision already made distinct, because of the finalized decision and of the measurement that has already taken place and because of the appointed time on a certain date. Do not be hasty; Allah does not become hasty due to hastiness in the people. Do not try to surpass Allah; in your doing so, misfortune will defeat and destroy you.'

"The narrator has said that Zayd became angry and said, 'The Imam from us is not the one who sits in his home; draw the curtain around him and hold back from struggle (jihad). The Imam from us is the one who safeguards his dominion, fights for the cause of Allah a real fight, defends those who hold high regard for him and his rights.'

"Abu Ja'far, *'Alayhi al-Salam*, then said, 'O brother, do you really find any of the things that you mentioned about yourself? If so, then can you show supporting proof from the book of Allah or evidence from the *Sunnah* of the Messenger of Allah or give a similar example? Allah, the Most Majestic, the Most Gracious, made things lawful and unlawful. He has sanctioned the obligations, provided examples and set up traditions *Sunan*. He has not made the Imam, who rises with Divine Authority on His command, engulfed in doubts in the matters of the obligation of obedience to him. He has not made him as such that he would act upon an issue before its proper place and struggle for something before it is there yet. Allah, the Most Majestic, the Most Gracious, has said, 'Believers, do not hunt when you are in the Holy precinct. . . .' (5:95) Is hunting an animal that has been made prohibited during Hajj more serious or the killing of a person that Allah has prohibited? Allah, the Most Majestic, the Most Gracious, has assigned a place for everything. 'Once the restrictions of Hajj are over, you may hunt. . . .' (5:2) Allah, the Most Majestic, the Most Gracious, has said, 'Believers, do not disrespect the reminders of Allah, the sacred months, . . .' (5:2) He has made the number of months well-known of which four are sacred ones. He has said, '. . . during the four sacred months, they (pagans) may travel peacefully through the land. You (pagans) must know that you cannot make Allah helpless . . .' (9:2) Then Allah, the Most Holy, the Most High, has said, 'When the sacred months are over, slay the pagans wherever you find them. . . .' (9:5) He has assigned a place for it. He has also said, 'Do not decide for a marriage before the appointed time is over. . . .' (2:235) He has assigned a time for everything and for every period of time there is *Kitab* (a rule). If you may have the necessary evidence from your Lord, certainty from yourself in your affairs and you know well about it then you may act accordingly. Otherwise, do not aim at an issue in which you have doubt and uncertainty. Do not act to end a kingdom the sustenance of which is not yet exhausted; its time has not ended and its *Kitab* (rule) has not reached its time. When its time comes, its sustenance diminishes and its rule reaches its time, the gap will be removed and the system will follow and Allah will make the followers (of falsehood) and those followed to suffer humiliation.'

"O brother, do you want to revive the ways of a people who have rejected the signs of Allah, disobeyed His Messenger, followed their desires, without guidance from Allah, claimed the *Khilafa* (Leadership with Divine Authority) without authority and evidence from Allah, or a covenant from the Messenger of Allah? I pray to Allah to grant you, O brother, refuge from being crucified tomorrow in al-Kunasa.' Then his eyes became flooded with tears that flowed down and then he said, 'Allah is between us and the people who disregarded our honor, ignored our rights, made our secrets public and have ascribed us to someone other than our grandfather. They have said about us what we ourselves do not say.'"

H 928, Ch. 81, h 17

Certain persons of our people have narrated from Muhammad ibn Hassa'n from Muhammad ibn Ranjawayh from 'Abd Allah ibn al-Hakam al-Armani from 'Abd Allah ibn Ibrahim ibn Muhammad al-Ja'fari who has said the following:

"Once we went to offer our condolences to Khadijah, daughter of 'Umar ibn Ali ibn al-Husayn ibn Ali ibn abu Talib, *'Alayhi al-Salam*, for the death of the son of her daughter. We found her at the place of Musa ibn 'Abd Allah ibn al-Hassan. She was to one side near the women. We offered our condolences to all of them. We then turned to him (Musa ibn 'Abd Allah) and he asked abu Yashkur's daughter, the reader of lamentations, to recite what she wanted to recite. She then recited the following lines:

'Of our family is the Messenger of Allah, and after him, the lion of the Lord, (Hamza) and thirdly is 'Abbass,

'Of our family is Ali, *'Alayhi al-Salam*, the embodiment of goodness and Ja'far,

'Of our family is 'Aqil, after him all leaders.'

"He said, 'Very good, it was very moving. Please recite more.' She was encouraged and said:

'Of our family is the leader of the pious ones, the Holy Prophet, *'Alayhi al-Salam*,

'And the chief of his army that purified Imam, (Ali, *'Alayhi al-Salam*),

'From us is Ali, his son in-law and cousin,

'And from us is Hamza and the well disciplined Ja'far.'

"We stayed with her until it was almost night. Khadija said, 'I heard my uncle Muhammad ibn Ali, *'Alayhi al-Salam*, say that a woman's reading lines of lamentation is good only if her tears flow down. It is not proper for her to say meaningless things. When night falls then you should not disturb the angels with your lamentations.'

"We then left her and went to her house next day and discussed with her the issue of separating her residence from the house of abu 'Abd Allah, Ja'far ibn Muhammad, *'Alayhi al-Salam*. He (Musa) then said, 'This is called the stolen house.' She then said, 'This is what our *Mahdi* (meaning thereby 'Abd Allah ibn al-Hassan), has chosen.' She would say such things to him in a teasing manner.

"Musa ibn 'Abd Allah then said, 'By Allah, I can tell you a very strange matter that I experienced with my father. When my father, may Allah grant him blessings, became involved in the affairs of Muhammad ibn 'Abd Allah and gathered his companions to meet him, he decided to go and he would lean on me. I went with him until we came to abu 'Abd Allah, *'Alayhi al-Salam*. We met him outside when he wanted to go to the mosque. My father stopped him and spoke to him. Abu 'Abd Allah, *'Alayhi al-Salam*, said, 'This is not a proper place to talk. We, Allah willing, will meet again.' My father returned very happy. He waited until morning or the next day and then we went to see him (the Imam). My father and I met him and he (my father) began to speak. Among other things he said to him (the Imam) was, 'May Allah keep my soul in service for your cause, you know already that I am older than you. Among your people there are those who are older than you but Allah, the Most Majestic, the Most Gracious, has granted you extra excellence that is not found in any of your people. I have come to you, to depend on your virtue, and I know, may Allah keep my soul in service for your cause, if you agree with me others will not differ. None of your companions will disagree with me and no one from the people of Quraysh or others will dispute with me.'

"Abu 'Abd Allah, *'Alayhi al-Salam*, then said to him, 'You can certainly find other people more obedient to you than I and then you will not need me. You know that I, by Allah, want to move to an empty land or think about it but I feel heavy in doing so. I want Hajj but I cannot attain it without hard work and exhaustion and hardship for myself. You should find others to support you but do not say that you have met me.' He (my father) then said, 'The people look up to you. If you support me no one will disagree. You do not have to suffer fighting or hardships.'

"The narrator has said, 'Then people surrounded us and our talks were discontinued. My father asked, 'May Allah keep my soul in service for your cause, what do you say?' He said, 'You will meet me, Allah willing' He then asked, 'Will it be the way I love?' He (the Imam) said, 'It will, Allah willing, be the way you love in your favor.' He came home and sent a messenger to Muhammad in the mountains at Juhayna, called al-Ashqar, two nights' journey from Madina. He gave him the glad news and informed him of his success in the task that he had asked for (support from Ja'far ibn Muhammad, *'Alayhi al-Salam*, for his uprising).

"After three days we went again and stood before the door. We had not been stopped before. The messenger delayed but then gave us permission. We went inside and I sat on one side of the room. My father went close to him, kissed his head and said, 'May Allah keep my soul in service for your cause, I have come again with hopes and expectation expanding with a wish to achieve what I need.'

"Abu 'Abd Allah, *'Alayhi al-Salam*, then said, 'O son of my uncle, I beseech Allah's protection for you and ask you not to become involved in this matter (political uprising). I am afraid for you from evil.' The talks continued between them and they ended with what he (my father) did not want. He said, 'For what reason was al-Husayn, *'Alayhi al-Salam*, more deserving than al-Hassan, *'Alayhi al-Salam*, (in leaving Imamat, Leadership with Divine Authority) to his descendents?'

"Abu 'Abd Allah, *'Alayhi al-Salam*, said, 'May Allah grant blessings to al-Hassan and al-Husayn, *'Alayhim al-Salam*. How could you mention this?' He (my father) said, 'Were al-Husayn to act with justice, he should have left it (Imamat) to the eldest son of al-Hassan.' Abu 'Abd Allah, *'Alayhi al-Salam*, said, 'When Allah, the Most Holy, the Most High, sent revelations to Muhammad, *'Alayhi al-Salam*, He did so as He wanted. He did not ask anyone else for consultation. Muhammad, *'Alayhi al-Salam*, commanded Ali, *'Alayhi al-Salam*, for whatever he wanted and he obeyed the order. We say nothing else in it except what the Messenger of Allah has said in his (al-Husayn's) praise and affirmation. Had he (the Holy Prophet) commanded al-Husayn, *'Alayhi al-Salam*, to transfer it (the will) to the eldest or to the sons of both of them, he would have done so. He is not accused of anything before us such as keeping for himself. He could have done anything he wanted but he did only what he was commanded to do. He is your grandfather (from mother's side) and your uncle. It is better for you to speak good things about him. If you say meaningless things about him, then may Allah forgive you. O son of my uncle, obey me and listen to my words. By Allah, besides Whom there is no Lord, I do not refrain from giving you good advice. How is it that you do not act accordingly? There is no escape from the commands of Allah.' My father became happy at this point.

'Abu 'Abd Allah, *'Alayhi al-Salam*, then said to him, 'By Allah, you know that the oblique eyed with few hairs on his forehead will be killed at the doorway of al-Ashja', near the bottom of the water bed.' My father said, "That is not him. By Allah, he will fight them a day for a day, an hour for an hour and a year for a year. He will avenge for all of the descendents of abu Talib.'

'Abu 'Abd Allah, *'Alayhi al-Salam*, then said, 'May Allah forgive you, how much I fear the applicability of this line to him:

Your soul in private gave you false hopes.

'No, by Allah, he will not gain more than the walls of Madina and cannot reach Taef no matter how hard he may try. What must happen happens. Be pious before Allah and have mercy on yourself and on the sons of your father. By Allah, I consider him to be the most unfortunate seed that man has ever deposited in the wombs of women. By Allah, he will be killed at the doorway of al-Ashja' among their houses. By Allah, it is as if I see him. He is dropped dead and looted and a brick placed between his legs. Nothing that is said to him benefits this boy.' Musa ibn 'Abd Allah has said, 'Such words were a reference to me.'

'The Imam then said, 'He will take part in the uprising but will be defeated and his friend will be killed. He then will take part in another uprising under another banner. Their leader will be killed and their soldiers will disperse. If he will obey me, immunity for him may be achieved from the descendent of 'Abbass until Allah will grant relief. You already know that this matter will not become successful. You know and we know that your son, the oblique eyed with few hairs on his forehead, will be killed at the doorway of al-Ashja', near their house in the bottom of the water bed.'

'My father stood up saying, 'In fact, Allah will make us needless of you or you will change or He will make you come back with the others. You only in this way are keeping others from helping us or have become a reason for them not to help us.' Abu 'Abd Allah, *'Alayhi al-Salam*, then said, 'Allah knows that I only want to give you good advice and guidance and that is all I can try.'

'My father then left with his clothes dragging behind him due to anger. Abu 'Abd Allah, *'Alayhi al-Salam*, reached him out and said, 'I heard your uncle, who also is your maternal uncle, mention that you and the sons of your father will be killed. If you can obey me and do what is good then do it. By Allah besides Whom there is no Lord, Who knows the unseen and what is present, the Beneficent, the Merciful, the Most Great, the Most High, you are important to me. Nothing is more important to me than you. I love to sacrifice the most beloved of my sons and most beloved person in my family to protect you. Do not think that I have cheated you.'

'My father left with anger and regrets. Thereafter we did not wait for more than twenty nights or so. The messengers of abu Ja'far (the Abbassid ruler) came and arrested my uncles. Sulayman ibn Hassan, Hassan ibn Hassan, Ibrahim ibn Hassan, Dawud ibn Hassan, Ali ibn Hassan, Sulayman ibn Dawud, Hassan, Ali ibn Ibrahim ibn Hassan, Hassan ibn Ja'far ibn Hassan, Taba taba Ibrahim ibn 'Isma'il ibn Hassan and 'Abd Allah ibn Dawud were my uncles.

'They were tied in chains and placed on camels' backs without covering. They were placed on display in the Musalla area (open space for congregational prayer) so that people could condemn them. People did not do so. In fact, they sympathized with them because of their poor conditions. Then they were released. They stood before the door of the mosque of the Messenger of Allah.

''Abd Allah ibn Ibrahim al-Ja'fari has said that Khadija daughter of 'Umar ibn Ali said to us, 'When they were made to stand before the door of the mosque, called the Gate of Jibril, abu 'Abd Allah, *'Alayhi al-Salam*, came to them, while his gown dragged behind him in a hurry. He came out of the door of the mosque saying, 'May Allah condemn you, O people of Madina'–three times. 'The messenger of Allah did not covenant with you for this nor had you pledged allegiance to him for such things. By Allah, I was hopeful, but I am defeated and there is no escape from the decision of Allah.' He then left one shoe on his foot and one in his hand with his gown dragging behind. He went home and suffered from fever for twenty days weeping day and night and we became very afraid for his life,' narrated Khadija.

"Al-Ja'fari has said that Musa ibn 'Abd Allah ibn Hassan narrated that when they appeared on the backs of the camels abu 'Abd Allah, *'Alayhi al-Salam*, came out of the mosque and bent over 'Abd Allah ibn Hassan to speak to him. He was harshly stopped and the security man pushed him aside saying, 'Get away from him. May Allah fend off your evil intents and others' like you.' They then were taken to the streets and abu 'Abd Allah, *'Alayhi al-Salam*, went home. Before they reached the graveyard al-Baqi', the security man faced a severe misfortune. His camel hit him at his leg and crushed it and he died very soon. The people were taken away. After a while Muhammad ibn 'Abd Allah ibn Hassan came and told that his father and his uncles were killed. Abu Ja'far (the Abbassid ruler) killed them. Only Hassan ibn Ja'far, Taba taba, Ali ibn Ibrahim, Sulayman ibn Dawud, Dawud ibn Hassan, and 'Abd Allah ibn Dawud were not killed.

"At that time Muhammad ibn 'Abd Allah rose and called people for a pledge of allegiance to him. I (the narrator) was one of the three people to pledge allegiance to him. No one from Quraysh, from Ansar (people of Madina) or an Arab opposed him. He consulted 'Isa ibn Yazid, a trusted person to him and a commander of his army. He consulted with him in the matter of sending a message to the leaders of his people. 'Isa ibn Yazid said to him, 'If you just call them, they may not respond. You must become strong and strict with them. Thus, allow me to handle it for you. Muhammad agreed and said, 'Do what you like.' He then said, 'Send to their leader and the greatest among them, namely abu 'Abd Allah Ja'far ibn Muhammad, *'Alayhi al-Salam*. If you become strict with him, all will learn that they also will experience what he has been through.'

"The narrator has said, 'In very little time they brought abu 'Abd Allah, *'Alayhi al-Salam*, and made him stand up before him (Muhammad). 'Isa ibn Yazid said, 'Submit and you will be safe.' Abu 'Abd Allah, *'Alayhi al-Salam*, then asked, 'Have you invented a prophet-hood after Prophet Muhammad, *'Alayhi al-Salam*?' Muhammad then said, 'No, but pledge allegiance and your life, property and children will be protected and you will not have to fight.' Abu 'Abd Allah, *'Alayhi al-Salam*, then said, 'I have nothing to do with war and fighting. I advised your father and warned him against what he went through, but warning does not help what is already measured. Son of my brother, find the young ones and leave the elderly alone.' Muhammad said, 'There is not much difference between my and your age.' Abu 'Abd Allah, *'Alayhi al-Salam*, said, 'I am not here to defeat you or compete with you in what you do.' Muhammad said, 'By Allah, you must pledge allegiance.' Abu 'Abd Allah, *'Alayhi al-Salam*, said, 'Son of my brother, I do not want a war, or to gain any worldly thing. I want to go out in the open land, but it is heavy for me. Even my family has asked me several times to do so. Only weakness holds me back. By Allah, and for the sake of family relations, save us from misfortune through your hands.'

"He then said, 'O abu 'Abd Allah, *'Alayhi al-Salam*, by Allah, abu Dawaniq (Abbassid ruler) has died.' Abu 'Abd Allah, *'Alayhi al-Salam*, said, 'What has that to do with me?' He said, 'I wanted honor through you.' He then said, 'There is no way for you to do that. By Allah, abu Dawaniq has not died, except in (your) dreams.' He said, 'By Allah, you must pledge allegiance to me, voluntarily or by force but, then, if by force your pledge will lose its value.' He (abu 'Abd Allah, *'Alayhi al-Salam*) refused it strongly. He was sent to prison. 'Isa ibn Yazid said, 'There is not enough security in the prison and without tying him up he may run away.' Abu 'Abd Allah, *'Alayhi al-Salam*, laughed and said, 'There is no means and power without Allah, the Most High, the most Great. Will you imprison me?' He said, 'I swear by the One Who honored Muhammad, *'Alayhi al-Salam*, with prophecy that I will imprison you severely.' 'Isa ibn Yazid said, 'Keep him today in the stable that belongs to Rita.' Abu 'Abd Allah, *'Alayhi al-Salam*, then said, 'By Allah, I will soon say it and I will be confirmed.' 'Isa ibn Yazid said, 'Be quiet or I will break your mouth.' Abu 'Abd Allah, *'Alayhi al-Salam*, said, 'You who are blue eyed and bald say this? I can see you looking for a hole in which to hide. You are not even worthy to be mentioned. On meeting (the enemy) even if one would clasp his hands behind you, you will run away like an ostrich. Muhammad ordered 'Isa ibn Yazid to imprison him and be strict with him.

"Abu 'Abd Allah, *'Alayhi al-Salam*, said, 'By Allah, it is as if I see you coming out of the doorway of al-Ashja' to the bottom of the waterbed in the valley. A man on a marked horse has attacked with a spear in his hand, half white and half black, riding a brown horse with a white forehead. He hits you but it does not kill you. You hit the nose of his horse and it is injured. Another man attacks you from the alley of Ale abu 'Ammar al-Du'iliyyin. He has two bands of hair coming out of his helmet with a thick mustache. He, by Allah, is your adversary. May Allah have no mercy on his bones.'

"Muhammad said, 'O abu 'Abd Allah, *'Alayhi al-Salam*, you have calculated but you have made a mistake.' At this time Al-Suraqi ibn al-Salkh al-Hut came to him and pushed him (abu 'Abd Allah, *'Alayhi al-Salam*) into the prison. They looted his (abu 'Abd Allah's, *'Alayhi al-Salam*) properties and the properties of those of his people who did not come out with Muhammad. After this they brought 'Isma'il ibn 'Abd Allah ibn Ja'far ibn Abu Talib who was very old and weak. One of his eyes was gone and both of his legs did not work. He had to be carried. He was asked to pledge allegiance to him. He said, 'Son of my brother, I am an old man and weak. I need your kindness and support.' He (Muhammad) said, 'You must pledge allegiance.' He asked, 'What is the benefit of my pledge of allegiance? By Allah, my name will only waste the space for the name of a man.' He said, 'You must do so.' He used strong language with him. 'Isma'il then said, 'Call for me Ja'far ibn Muhammad, *'Alayhi al-Salam*, perhaps we both pledge allegiance for you.'

"The narrator has said that when Ja'far ibn Muhammad, *'Alayhi al-Salam*, was brought, 'Isma'il said to him, 'May Allah keep my soul in service for your cause, if you explain to him we perhaps will all be spared.' He said, 'I have decided not to talk to him. Let him do whatever he wants.' 'Isma'il said to abu 'Abd Allah, *'Alayhi al-Salam*, 'By Allah, tell me if you remember the day I came to see your father, Muhammad ibn Ali, *'Alayhi al-Salam*, and I had two pieces of yellow cloth on me. He looked at me for a long time and wept. I asked for the reason. He said, 'I wept because you will be killed when very old for no reason and not even two goats will fight for you (no one will ask justice for you).' I asked, 'When is that?' He said, 'It will happen when you will be called to follow falsehood and you will refuse. When you will see the abusive oblique-eyed person whose people from the family of al-Hassan, *'Alayhi al-Salam*, on the pulpit of the Messenger of Allah, call people to follow him and will give himself a name that he does not deserve. At such time you must renew your covenant, make your will; you will be murdered on that day or the next day.'

"Abu 'Abd Allah, *'Alayhi al-Salam*, said, 'Yes, by the Lord of the Ka'ba he (Muhammad ibn 'Abd Allah) does not fast in the month of Ramadan except for a few days. I leave you in the trust of Allah, O abu al-Hassan. May Allah grant us great rewards for loosing you. May He grant well-being to those whom you leave behind. We are for Allah and to Him we will return.'

"The narrator has said, "Isma'il was carried away and abu 'Abd Allah, *'Alayhi al-Salam*, was sent to prison.' He has said, 'By Allah, only that evening the sons of his brother, the sons of Mu'awiya ibn 'Abd Allah ibn Ja'far went on him and crushed (his bones) under their feet. Muhammad ibn 'Abd Allah released Ja'far, *'Alayhi al-Salam*.'

"The narrator has said, 'When it was the month of Ramadan 'Isa ibn Musa began his uprising to occupy Madina.' He has said, 'Muhammad ibn 'Abd Allah came with Yazid ibn Mu'awiya ibn 'Abd Allah ibn Ja'far leading his army. In front of the army of 'Isa ibn Musa there were the sons of al-Hassan ibn Zayd ibn al-Hassan ibn al-Hassan and al-Qasim and Muhammad ibn Zayd, Ali and Ibrahim, sons of al-Hassan ibn Zayd. Yazid ibn Mu'awiya was defeated and 'Isa ibn Musa came to Madina. Fighting took place in Madina. 'Isa camped at mount Dhubab. The blacks (army of Abbassids who wore black attire) came from behind. Muhammad with his people went up to the market place then followed them to the mosque of al-Khawamin. There he looked around. There were no blacks. There were no white soldiers (opposed to Abbassids). He advanced to Sha'b Faraza then to

Hudhayl, then he went al-Ashja'. Here a horseman about whom abu 'Abd Allah, *'Alayhi al-Salam*, had spoken came out from the doorway of Hudhayl and struck him a blow. It did not do anything to him. He attacked the horseman and cut the nose of his horse with sword. The horseman hit him and penetrated the coat of arms. Muhammad turned to him and hit and killed him. Then Humayd ibn Qahtaba came on him when he was turning away from the horseman. He was hit from the alley of al-'Ammariyyin. One hit of the spear penetrated his coat of arms, but the spear broke. He attacked Humayd and hit him with the spear. Humayd then with the iron part of the broken spear hit him fatally, he then came down and hit him until he was dead. He took his head away. The soldiers came from all sides and Madina was taken and we were exiled to different places.'

"Musa ibn 'Abd Allah has said, 'I then left until I met Ibrahim ibn 'Abd Allah. I found 'Isa ibn Zayd hiding. I told him of his bad management and journeyed with him until he died, may Allah have mercy on him. I then continued with the son of my brother, al-Ashtar 'Abd Allah ibn Muhammad ibn 'Abd Allah ibn Hassan until he also died in Sind. I then came back with no place to go to and I was afraid. I remembered what abu 'Abd Allah, *'Alayhi al-Salam*, had said. I came to al-Mahdi (an Abbassid ruler) in Hajj where he was speaking to people in the shadow of the walls of Ka'ba. He did not notice when I stood up below the pulpit. I asked, 'Can I have immunity, O Amir al-Mu'minin if I give you a good advice?' He said, 'Yes, but what is it?' I said, 'I can show you where Musa ibn 'Abd Allah ibn Hassan is.' He said, 'Yes, you will have security and protection.' I said, 'I ask for guarantees.' I then asked for covenant and affirmation until I was certain of the security. Then I said, 'I am Musa ibn 'Abd Allah.' He said, 'You are respected and you will live.' I then said, 'Show me among your people one who will support me' for living.' He said, 'Look at whoever you like.' I said, 'Your uncle, Abbass ibn Muhammad should support me. He refused. I begged him then he agreed willingly or compelled.' Al-Mahdi asked, 'Who knows you?' All or most of the people around him were, our people. I said, 'This al-Hassan ibn Zayd knows me. This Musa ibn Ja'far, *'Alayhi al-Salam*, knows me. This al-Hassan ibn 'Abd Allah ibn 'Abbass knows me.' They said, 'Yes, O Amir al-Mu'minin, we know him as if he was not absent from us.' I then said to al-Mahdi, 'O Amir al-Mu'minin, the father of this man' - I pointed out to Musa ibn Ja'far, *'Alayhi al-Salam*, - 'had told me of this position.'

"Musa ibn 'Abd Allah has said, I lied against Ja'far and I said, 'He (the Imam) asked me to convey greetings of peace to you.' He ('Abbassid ruler) said, 'He is a just and generous Imam.' He has said, 'Then the ruler ordered to give five thousand Dinars to Musa ibn Ja'far, *'Alayhi al-Salam*. Musa ibn Ja'far, *'Alayhi al-Salam*, ordered to give me two thousand out of it. He helped me and he helped his people. As the sons of Muhammad ibn Ali ibn al-Husayn are mentioned, you should say, "May Allah and His angels, the carriers of His throne, the angels writers of the deeds, send blessing upon them, especially abu 'Abd Allah, *'Alayhi al-Salam*. May Allah grant Musa ibn Ja'far, *'Alayhi al-Salam*, on my behalf good rewards. I, by Allah, am a servant of them after being the servant of Allah.""

H 929, Ch. 81, h 18

Through the same chain of narrators it is narrated from 'Abd Allah ibn Ja'far ibn Ibrahim al-Ja'fari who has said that 'Abd Allah ibn al-Mufaddal the slave of 'Abd Allah ibn Ja'far ibn abu Talib narrated the following:

"When al-Husayn ibn Ali who was killed in al-Fakh, began his uprising, he controlled the city of Madina and called Musa ibn Ja'far, *'Alayhi al-Salam*, to pledge allegiance to him. When he was brought before him (al-Husayn) he (Musa ibn Ja'far, *'Alayhi al-Salam*) said, 'Son of my uncle, do not impose on me what the son of your uncle imposed on your uncle abu 'Abd Allah (Ja'far ibn Muhammad, *'Alayhi al-Salam*) and then you will experience from me what I do not want as it happened with abu 'Abd Allah, *'Alayhi al-Salam.*'

"Al-Husayn said to him, 'I just proposed the matter to you. If you like you may take part in it, if you dislike it I will not impose on you, Allah is the supporter.' He then said farewell to him. Abu al-Hassan, Musa ibn Ja'far, *'Alayhi al-Salam*, said to him when saying farewell, 'Son of my uncle, you will be killed, fight a good fight. The people are transgressors. They call themselves believers but they hide in them atheism. We are for Allah and to Him we return. I leave my request for justice, on your behalf and my people, to Allah.' Al-Husayn then went to fight. His case took shape the way it did. All of them were killed as the Imam had informed."

H 930, Ch. 81, h 19

Through the same chain of narrators it is narrated from 'Abd Allah ibn Ibrahim al-Ja'fari who has said the following:

"Once Yahya ibn 'Abd Allah ibn al-Hassan wrote to Musa ibn Ja'far, *'Alayhi al-Salam*, 'Thereafter, I recommend myself to maintain piety before Allah as I want to recommend you also; it has been the recommendation of Allah to the people of the past as well as to the later generations. People pious before Allah and who are reliable have informed me that you express sympathy for us, but, at the same time, refuse to support us. I consulted about calling people to pledge allegiance to such person from the family of Muhammad, *'Alayhi al-Salam*, who is acceptable to people. You disagreed and your father had disagreed before you. For a long time you had claimed what was not for you. You expanded your hopes toward what Allah did not grant you. You followed your desires and strayed. I warn you of what Allah has warned about.'

"Abu al-Hassan, Musa ibn Ja'far, *'Alayhi al-Salam*, wrote to him, 'From Musa ibn abu 'Abd Allah, Ja'far and Ali (ibn abu Talib), *'Alayhim al-Salam*, who both will share the rewards for their humbleness before Allah and obedience to Him, to Yahya ibn 'Abd Allah ibn Hassan. Thereafter, I warn you of being mindless about Allah as I warn myself as such about Him. I ask you to take notice of His painful torments, severe punishments and His complete penalties. I recommend you as well as myself to be pious before Allah. Piety before Allah is the beauty in speech and the establishment of the blessings. I received your letter in which you have said that my father and I have the claim (for leadership) from long before and that you have not heard it from me (personally). The Holy Quran says, '. . . their testimony will soon be recorded and they will be questioned about it.'(43:19) The greed for worldly gains has left nothing to gain from the benefits of the next life; in fact, their gains and the benefits of the next life are destroyed because of their worldly desires. You have mentioned that I keep people from following you because of my desire to achieve what you have achieved. In fact, weakness in the (knowledge of) *Sunnah* or lack of understanding of the authoritative evidence are not holding me back from what you are involved in. The fact of the matter is that Allah, the Most Holy, the Most High, has created people different from each other in instincts. I want to ask just about two letters (words). What are called *al-'Tara and al-Sahlaj* in human body? Write your answer to me. About yourself, I warn you about disobeying the Khalifa and exhort you to be good to him and obey him. I ask you to request immunity for yourself from him before the afflictions catch you and the pressure intensifies everywhere. Then you will try to find relief but you will not find it. Try until Allah will grant you from His blessings and generosity and make Khalifa (may he live long) to sympathize with you, be kind to you and preserve in you the relation with the Messenger of Allah. With best regards and peace for those who follow guidance. To us it is revealed that punishment is for those who reject and turn away (from the truth).'"

"Al-Ja'fari has said that it has come to my knowledge that this letter of Musa ibn Ja'far, *'Alayhi al-Salam*, had reached to Harun. When he saw it he said, 'People exhort me to act against Musa ibn Ja'far, *'Alayhi al-Salam*, while he is clean of what they accuse him of.'"

The end of the second section of the book, al-Kafi followed, through the wish of Allah and his support, by the third section and that is the undesirability of setting time limits. All praise belongs to Allah, Lord of the worlds. May peace and blessing be upon Muhammad and his family and all of them.

Chapter 82 - It is Undesirable to Setup Time Limits for the Reappearance of the Twelfth Imam, *'Alayhi al-Salam*

H 931, Ch. 82, h 1

Ali ibn Muhammad and Muhammad ibn al-Hassan have narrated from Sahl ibn Ziyad and Muhammad ibn Yahya from Ahmad ibn Muhammad ibn 'Isa all from al-Hassan ibn Mahbub from abu Hamza al-Thumali who has said the following:

"I heard abu Ja'far, *'Alayhi al-Salam*, say, 'O Thabit, Allah, the Most Holy, the Most High, had set a time for it (Divine Government on earth) in the year seventy, but when al-Husayn, *'Alayhi al-Salam*, was murdered Allah's anger became more intense on the people on earth. He delayed it until one hundred forty. At that time we spoke to you about it and you publicized this *Hadith* and disclosed the secret. Allah thereafter has not set any time limit that we know of. Allah obliterates whatever He wants and establishes whatever He wants; with Him is the original book.'

"Abu Hamza has said, 'I narrated the above *Hadith* to abu 'Abd Allah, *'Alayhi al-Salam*, and he said, 'It was just as you said.'"

H 932, Ch. 82, h 2

Muhammad ibn Yahya has narrated from Salma ibn al-Khattab from Ali ibn Hassa'n from 'Abd al-Rahman ibn al-Kathir who has said the following:

"Once I was in the presence of abu 'Abd Allah, *'Alayhi al-Salam*, when Mihzam came in and said to the Imam, 'May Allah keep my soul in service for your cause, enlighten me about this matter that we wait for (the rise of al-Mahdi with Divine Authority and power). When will it take place?'

"The Imam said, 'O Mihzam, those who give it a definite time have lied, the expediting ones perish and salvation is for those who are submissive (to the words of Allah and *'A'immah*).'"

H 933, Ch. 82, h 3

A number of our people have narrated from Ahmad ibn Muhammad ibn Khalid from his father form al-Qasim ibn Muhammad from Ali ibn abu Hamza from abu Basir who has said the following:

"Once I asked abu 'Abd Allah, *'Alayhi al-Salam*, about *al-Qa'im* (the one who will rise with Divine Authority and power). He said, 'Those who give it a definite time have spoken lies. We, *Ahl al-Bayt*, do not set up a definite time for it.'"

H 934, Ch. 82, h 4

Ahmad has narrated through his chain of narrators from the Imam, *'Alayhi al-Salam*, the following:

"Allah disdains people's setting time limits (for reappearance of the one who will rise with Divine Authority) to come true."

H 935, Ch. 82, h 5

Al-Husayn ibn Muhammad has narrated from Mu'alla ibn Muhammad from al-Hassan ibn Ali al-Khazzaz from 'Abd al-Karim ibn 'Umar al-Khath'ami from al-Fudayl ibn Yasar who has said the following:

"Once I asked abu Ja'far, *'Alayhi al-Salam*, 'Is there a definite time for this matter (the rise of al-Mahdi with Divine Authority and power)?' He said, 'Those who arrange a definite time have lied, those who arrange a definite time have lied, those who arrange a definite time have lied. When Musa (Moses) came out to delegate before his Lord and gave the people a definite time for his return and Allah added another ten days his people said, "He has broken his promise." Then they did what they did. When we say a *Hadith* (a statement to you), and if our *Hadith* comes true you should say, 'Allah has spoken the truth.' If we say a *Hadith* to you and something contrary takes place, you should say, "Allah has spoken the truth." You will be rewarded twice.'"

H 936, Ch. 82, h 6

Muhammad ibn Yahya and Ahmad ibn Muhammad ibn 'Idris have narrated from Muhammad ibn Ahmad from al-Sayyari from al-Hassan ibn Ali ibn Yaqtin from his brother from his father Ali ibn Yaqtin who has said the following:

"Once abu al-Hassan, *'Alayhi al-Salam*, said to me, 'The Shi'a have lived on hopes for two hundred years.' The narrator has said that Yaqtin (Ali ibn Yaqtin) said to me, 'We did not have to worry. Why is it that what was said to us came true and what is said to you has not come true yet?'

"Ali then said to him, 'What was said to you and what is said to us all come from one source, except that good news for you has come true and you received it pure. It was just as it was said to be. The good news for us has not yet come true. We thus entertain ourselves with hopes. Were we told that it would take place after two or three hundred years, our hearts could harden and the masses might turn back from Islam. However, their saying that it will come very soon and in near future is to encourage people about the coming of relief.'"

H 937, Ch. 82, h 7
Al-Husayn ibn Muhammad has narrated from Ja'far ibn Muhammad from al-Qasim ibn 'Isma'il al-Anbari from al-Hassan ibn Ali from Ibrahim ibn Mihzam from his father who has said the following:
"Once we mentioned before abu 'Abd Allah, *'Alayhi al-Salam*, the kings from the descendents of so and so. The Imam said, 'People have perished due to their haste for this matter (the rise of al-Mahdi with Divine Authority and power). Allah does not expedite it because of the haste of people. For this matter (the rise of al-Mahdi with Divine Authority and power) there is a goal toward which it proceeds. Once they (people) will reach that goal, they then will not be able to move it forward or backwards, even by one hour.'"

Chapter 83 - Refinement and Trial

H 938, Ch. 83, h 1
Ali ibn Ibrahim has narrated from his father from al-Hassan ibn Mahbub from Ya'qub al-Sarraj and Ali ibn Ri'ab from abu 'Abd Allah, *'Alayhi al-Salam*, who has said the following:
"After the assassination of 'Uthman, when people pledged allegiance to Amir al-Mu'minin Ali, *'Alayhi al-Salam*, he addressed the people from the pulpit and delivered a sermon (that abu 'Abd Allah, *'Alayhi al-Salam*, mentioned). In this sermon he has said, 'The time for your trial has returned in the same conditions as those of the day Allah sent His Prophet, *'Alayhi al-Salam*. By the One Who has sent him with the truth that you will suffer hideous confusions. You will be sifted (examined) thoroughly and turned upside down. Of the contestants those who were behind others will overtake those who were ahead and those who were ahead of others (because of their shortcomings) will be left behind those who once were behind them. By Allah I have not concealed any of the marks therein nor have I spoken a lie. I was, certainly, told about this place and this day.'"

H 939, Ch. 83, h 2
Muhammad ibn Yahya and al-Hassan ibn Muhammad have narrated from al-Qasim ibn 'Isma'il al-Anbari from al-Husayn ibn Ali from abu al-Mighra' from abu Ya'fur who has said the following:
"I heard abu 'Abd Allah, *'Alayhi al-Salam*, saying, 'Woe to the rebellious Arabs. The matter is coming closer.' I then asked, 'May Allah keep my soul in service for your cause, how many people from the Arab nation will be there with al-Qa'im (the one who will rise with Divine Authority and power)?' The Imam said, 'Just very few.' I then said, 'By Allah, those who speak of this matter (the rise of al-Mahdi with Divine Authority and power) are quite many in number.' The Imam said, 'People must be refined, distinguished and examined. A sifting process proves a great number of people as useless.'"

H 940, Ch. 83, h 3

Muhammad ibn Yahya and al-Hassan ibn Muhammad have narrated from Ja'far ibn Muhammad from al-Hassan ibn Muhammad al-Sayrafi from Ja'far ibn Muhammad al-Sayqal from his father from Mansur who has said the following:

"Once abu 'Abd Allah, *'Alayhi al-Salam*, said to me, 'O Mansur, this matter (the rise of al-Mahdi with Divine Authority and power) will not come to you before you despair of its coming. By Allah, it will not come before your good ones are distinguished from evil ones. By Allah, it will not come before you are refined and not, by Allah, before the evildoers' ending in misfortune and before the salvation of those who seek salvation.'"

H 941, Ch. 83, h 4

A number of our people have narrated from Ahmad ibn Muhammad from Mu'ammar ibn al-Khallad who has said the following:

"I heard abu al-Hassan, *'Alayhi al-Salam*, ask, 'Do people think they will not be tested because they say, "We have believed?' (29:2) Then he asked, 'Do you know what *al-Fitna*, (trial) is?' I said, 'May Allah keep my soul in service for your cause, in our opinion it is the trial and test in religion.' The Imam said, 'They will be tested and refined as gold is tested.' He then said, 'They will be purified as gold is purified and refined.'"

H 942, Ch. 83, h 5

Ali ibn Ibrahim has narrated from Muhammad ibn 'Isa from Yunus from Sulayman ibn Salih in a *marfu'* manner from abu Ja'far, *'Alayhi al-Salam*, who has said the following:

"Abu Ja'far, *'Alayhi al-Salam*, has said, 'Your story (belief in the rise of al-Mahdi with Divine Authority and power) causes apprehension in the hearts of people. You should enlighten further those who acknowledge it (belief in the rise of al-Mahdi with Divine Authority and power) and leave alone those who deny it. There must come a period of trial in which no secret and undisclosed matters will remain secret. Even those who like to split one piece of hair into two pieces to find a better argument will fall apart, until no one will be left except our Shi'a and us, ourselves.'"

H 943, Ch. 83, h 6

Muhammad ibn al-Hassan and Ali ibn Muhammad have narrated from Sahl ibn Ziyad from Muhammad ibn Sinan from Muhammad ibn Mansur al-Sayqal from his father who has said the following:

"Once al-Harith ibn al-Mughira and a group of our people and I were in the presence of abu 'Abd Allah, *'Alayhi al-Salam*, who could hear our conversations. He asked us, 'What is the issue in your dialogue? It will not happen and it will never happen. By Allah, what you are looking to will not take place before you are examined (in righteousness). By Allah, what you are longing for will not happen until Allah refines you, what you are looking for will not happen before you are distinguished. By Allah, what you are looking for will not take place before you despair. By Allah, what you are looking to will not take place before misfortune will strike those who become unfortunate and before the fortunate ones attain salvation.'"

Chapter 84 - The Rise of Al-Mahdi With Divine Authority Earlier or Later Will Not Affect One Who Has Learned Who His Imam Is

H 944, Ch. 84, h 1
Ali ibn Ibrahim has narrated from his father from Hammad ibn 'Isa from Hariz from Zurara who has said the following:
"Abu 'Abd Allah, *'Alayhi al-Salam*, has said, 'Learn who your Imam is. When you learn who he is, then it will have no negative effect on you whether this matter (the rise of al-Mahdi with Divine Authority and power) will take place earlier or later.'"

H 945, Ch. 84, h 2
Al-Husayn ibn Muhammad has narrated from Mu'alla ibn Muhammad from Muhammad ibn Jumhur from Safwan ibn Yahya from Muhammad ibn Marwan from al-Fudayl ibn Yasar who has said the following:
"Once I asked abu 'Abd Allah, *'Alayhi al-Salam*, about the words of Allah, the Most Holy, the Most High: 'On the day when We call every nation with their leaders, *'A'immah*, . . .' (17:71) He said, 'O Fudayl, find out who your Imam is; when you find out who your Imam is, then whether this matter (the rise of al-Mahdi with Divine Authority and power) will take place earlier or later will not affect you negatively at all. One who finds out who his Imam is and then dies before the rise of al-Mahdi with Divine Authority, he will be just as those who are positioned in his army. In fact, just like those who have placed themselves under his banner.'

"The narrator has said that certain persons from his companions said, 'He will be just like the martyrs in the battle supporting the Messenger of Allah.'"

H 946, Ch. 84, h 3
Ali ibn Muhammad has narrated from in a *murfu'* manner from Ali ibn abu Hamza from abu Basir who has said the following:
"Once I asked abu 'Abd Allah, *'Alayhi al-Salam*, 'May Allah keep my soul in service for your cause, when will relief come?' The Imam said, 'O abu Basir, are you after the worldly gains? In fact, one who has established belief in this matter (the rise of al-Mahdi with Divine Authority and power) already is granted relief by means of expecting his coming (with Divine Authority).'"

H 947, Ch. 84, h 4
Ali Ibrahim has narrated from Salih ibn al-Sindi from Ja'far ibn Bashir from 'Isma'il ibn Muhammad al-Khuza''i who has said the following:
"Once abu Basir asked abu 'Abd Allah, *'Alayhi al-Salam*, and I was listening, 'Do you think I will have the opportunity to meet *Al-Qa'im*, *'Alayhi al-Salam*?' The Imam asked, 'O abu Basir, do you not know who your Imam is?' He said while holding his hand, 'By Allah, you are my Imam.' The Imam said, 'Then you must not worry about not leaning against your sword in the shadow of the tent of *al-Qa'im*, *'Alayhi al-Salam*.'"

H 948, Ch. 84, h 5

A number of our people have narrated from Ahmad ibn Muhammad from Ali ibn al-Nu'man from Muhammad ibn Marwan from al-Fudayl ibn Yasar who has said the following:

"I heard abu Ja'far, *'Alayhi al-Salam*, say, 'One who dies without having an Imam, his death is like the death in ignorance (pre-Islamic age of darkness). One who dies when he knows who his Imam is, then the coming of this matter (the rise of al-Mahdi with Divine Authority and power) earlier or later does not affect him negatively at all. One who knows who his Imam is is like the one present with *al-Qa'im*, *'Alayhi al-Salam*, in his tents.'"

H 949, Ch. 84, h 6

Al-Husayn ibn Ali al-'Alawi has narrated from Sahl ibn Jumhur from 'Abd al-'Azim ibn 'Abd Allah al-Hassani from al-Hassan ibn al-Husayn al-'Arani from Ali from Ali ibn Hashim from his father from abu Ja'far, *'Alayhi al-Salam*, who has said the following:

"One who expects the coming of our task (the rise of al-Mahdi with Divine Authority and power) has not suffered any loss of not dying in the tents of *al-Mahdi*, *'Alayhi al-Salam*, and in his army."

H 950, Ch. 84, h 7

Ali ibn Muhammad has narrated from Sahl ibn Ziyad from al-Husayn ibn Sa'id from Fadala ibn Ayyub from 'Umar ibn Aban who has said the following:

"I heard abu 'Abd Allah, *'Alayhi al-Salam*, say, 'Find out (who) the sign (of Allah, the Imam) is. When you find out and learn who he is, then it will not harm you whether this matter (the rise of al-Mahdi with Divine Authority and power) will take place earlier or later. Allah, the Most Majestic, the Most Gracious, has said, 'On the day when We call every nation with their leaders, *'A'immah . . .*' (17:71) One who knows who his Imam is, he is just like the one present in the tents of *al-Mahdi*, *'Alayhi al-Salam*.'"

Chapter 85 - Unqualified Claimant, Supporting Him or Rejecting a Certain or All the 'A'immah (Leaders with Divine Authority)

The case of those who claim to be the Imam but are not qualified, the case of those who reject all or certain ones of the 'A'immah (Leaders with Divine Authority) and the case of those who argue in support of one who is not a qualified Imam

H 951, Ch. 85, h 1

Muhammad ibn Yahya has narrated from Ahmad ibn Muhammad from Muhammad ibn Sinan from abu Salam from Sawra ibn kulayb who has said the following:

"Once I asked abu Ja'far, *'Alayhi al-Salam*, about the words of Allah, the Most Majestic, the Most Gracious: 'On the Day of Judgment you will see the faces of those who had invented falsehood against Allah blackened. . . .' (39:60) The Imam said, 'It refers to those who claim to be the Imam but in fact, are not the Imam.'

"I then asked, 'Even if he is of the descendents of Ali, *'Alayhi al-Salam*?' He replied, 'Yes, even if he is of the descendents of Ali, *'Alayhi al-Salam*.' I then asked, 'Even if he is of the sons of Ali ibn abu Talib, *'Alayhi al-Salam*?' He said, 'Yes, even if he is as such.'"

H 952, Ch. 85, h 2

Muhammad ibn Yahya has narrated from 'Abd Allah ibn Muhammad ibn 'Isa from Ali ibn al-Hakam from Aban from al-Fudayl from abu 'Abd Allah, *'Alayhi al-Salam*, who has said the following:

"Whoever claims to be the Imam and, in fact, is not the Imam is considered an unbeliever."

H 953, Ch. 85, h 3

Al-Husayn ibn Muhammad has narrated from Mu'alla ibn Muhammad from Muhammad ibn Jumhur from 'Abd Allah ibn 'Abd al-Rahman from al-Husayn ibn al-Mukhtar who has said the following:

"Once I asked abu 'Abd Allah, *'Alayhi al-Salam*, 'May Allah keep my soul in service for your cause, what is the meaning of the words of Allah: "On the Day of Judgment you will see the faces of those who had invented falsehood against Allah blackened. . . ."'? (39:60) He said, 'It refers to anyone who claims to be the Imam and, in fact, is not the Imam.' I then asked, 'Even if he is a descendent of Fatimah and Ali, *'Alayhim al-Salam*?' He said, 'Yes, even if he is a descendent of Fatimah and Ali, *'Alayhim al-Salam*.'"

H 954, Ch. 85, h 4

A number of our people have narrated from Ahmad ibn Muhammad from al-Washsha' from Dawud al-Hammar from ibn abu Ya'fur who has said the following:

"I heard abu 'Abd Allah, *'Alayhi al-Salam*, say, 'There are three kinds of people to whom, on the Day of Judgment, Allah will not speak. He will not purify them and for them there will be painful suffering.' He said, 'They are those who claim to be the Imam with Divine Authority, and, in fact, are not so, those who reject the Imam who possesses Divine Authority and those who think that the 'two' had a share in Islam.'"

H 955, Ch. 85, h 5

Muhammad ibn Yahya has narrated from Ahmad ibn Muhammad from ibn Sinan from Yahya brother of 'Udaym from al-Walid ibn Sabih who has said the following:

"I heard abu 'Abd Allah, *'Alayhi al-Salam*, say, 'No one, other than the actual Imam, claims this (Leadership with Divine Authority) except that Allah will cut his life short.'"

H 956, Ch. 85, h 6

Muhammad ibn Yahya has narrated from Muhammad ibn al-Hassan from Muhammad ibn Sinan from Talha ibn Yazid from abu 'Abd Allah, *'Alayhi al-Salam*, who has said the following:

"Whoever considers someone who has no Divine Authority as a partner in the Leadership of a Leader with Divine Authority, is considered a polytheist."

H 957, Ch. 85, h 7

Muhammad ibn Yahya has narrated from Ahmad ibn Muhammad from Muhammad ibn 'Isma'il from Mansur ibn Yunus from Muhammad ibn Muslim who has said the following:

"Once I said to abu 'Abd Allah, *'Alayhi al-Salam*, 'A man said to me, "You must know the last of the *'A'immah* (Leaders with Divine Authority) and it does not matter if you do not know the first of the *'A'immah, 'Alayhim al-Salam*.'"

"The narrator has said that the Imam said, 'May Allah condemn this. I am angry with him and I do not recognize him. How can the last Imam be recognized without knowing the first Imam?'"

H 958, Ch. 85, h 8

Al-Husayn ibn Muhammad has narrated from Mu'alla ibn Muhammad from Muhammad ibn Jumhur from Safwan from ibn Muskan who has said the following:

"Once I asked the Shaykh (Musa al-Kazim, *'Alayhi al-Salam*) about the *'A'immah* (Leaders with Divine Authority). He said, 'Whoever rejects any of the living ones (Leaders with Divine Authority) has rejected the *'A'immah* who have passed away also.'"

H 959, Ch. 85, h 9

A number of our people have narrated from Ahmad ibn Muhammad from al-Husayn ibn Sa'id from abu Wahab from Muhammad ibn Mansur who has said the following:

"Once I asked the Imam, *'Alayhi al-Salam*, about the words of Allah, the Most Majestic, the Most Gracious: 'When they (the unbelievers) commit indecent acts they say, "We found our fathers doing this and Allah has commanded us to do the same. (Muhammad), tell them that Allah does not command anyone to commit indecency. Do you speak for Allah, saying things of which you have no knowledge?"' (7:28)

"The Imam asked, 'Have you come across anyone who thinks that Allah has commanded him to commit indecent acts, drink wine or other such unlawful things?' I said, 'No, I have not done so.' He then asked, 'What is this indecent act that they claim to have committed because of the command of Allah?' I said, 'Allah knows best and His deputy also knows.' He said, 'This is found in the unjust *'A'immah* (leaders without Divine Authority). They claim that Allah has commanded them to lead the people and, in fact, Allah has not given any command to anyone to follow such Imam. Allah, thus, has refuted them and has informed (others) that they have spoken lies against Him and their act as such is called an indecent one.'"

H 960, Ch. 85, h 10

A number of our people have narrated from Ahmad ibn Muhammad from al-Husayn ibn Sa'id from abu Wahab from Muhammad ibn Mansur who has said the following:

"Once I asked the virtuous servant of the Lord (the Imam) about the words of Allah, the Most Majestic, the Most Gracious: '(Muhammad), tell them, My Lord has prohibited indecent acts only, whether committed in public or in secret. . . .' (7:33)

"The narrator has said that the Imam, *'Alayhi al-Salam*, then said, 'The Holy Quran has an apparent meaning and a hidden meaning. All that Allah has prohibited in the Holy Quran, its apparent meaning is unlawful matters, and the hidden meanings in this (category) are the unjust *'A'immah* (leaders without Divine Authority). All that Allah has made lawful in the Holy Quran, its apparent meanings refer to lawful matters and the hidden meaning in it (category) is the true *'A'immah* (Leaders with Divine Authority).'"

H 961, Ch. 85, h 11

Muhammad ibn Yahya has narrated from Ahmad ibn Muhammad ibn 'Isa from al-Hassan ibn Mahbub from 'Umar ibn Thabit from Jabir who has said the following:

"Once I asked abu Ja'far, *'Alayhi al-Salam*, about the words of Allah, the Most Majestic, the Most Gracious: '. . . Certain people consider certain things equal to Allah and love them just as one should love Allah. . . .' (2:165)

"The Imam said, 'They, by Allah, are the friends of so and so and so and so whom they have taken as their *'A'immah* (leaders without Divine Authority) instead of the *'A'immah* (Leaders with Divine Authority) who are appointed for people as such by Allah. For this reason He has said, '. . . had the unjust been able to reflect upon their condition, when facing the torment, they would have had no doubt that to Allah belongs all power and that He is stern in His retribution (2:165). When the leaders see the torment and lose all their resources, they will denounce their followers (2:166). The followers will say, "If we had the chance we also would have denounced our leaders." That is how Allah will show them their regrettable deeds. They will not be able to escape from hellfire.' (2:167)

"Then abu Ja'far, *'Alayhi al-Salam*, said, 'By Allah, O Jabir, they are the unjust *'A'immah* (leaders without Divine Authority) and their followers.'"

H 962, Ch. 85, h 12

Al-Husayn ibn Muhammad has narrated from Mu'alla ibn Muhammad from abu Dawud al-Mustariqq from Ali ibn Maymun from ibn abu Ya'fur who has said the following:

"Once I heard abu 'Abd Allah, *'Alayhi al-Salam*, say, 'There will be three kinds of people to whom Allah will not look on the Day of Judgment. He will not purify them and they will suffer painful punishments. They are those who claim to be the Imam but without authority from Allah, those who reject the Imam (Leader with Divine Authority), and those who think that for the 'two' there is a share in Islam.'"

Chapter 86 - Following a Religion in the Name of Allah Without the Imam (Leader With Divine Authority)

H 963, Ch. 86, h 1

A number of our people have narrated from Ahmad ibn Muhammad (from) ibn abu Nasr who has said the following:

"About the words of Allah, the Most Majestic, the Most Gracious: 'Who strays more than one who follows his desires without guidance from Allah? . . .' (28:50), abu al-Hassan, *'Alayhi al-Salam*, has said, 'It refers to those who consider their own opinions as their religion without a true Imam from the *'A'immah* (Leaders with Divine Authority).'"

H 964, Ch. 86, h 2

Muhammad ibn Yahya has narrated from Muhammad ibn al-Husayn from Safwan ibn Yahya from al-'Ala' ibn Razin from Muhammad ibn Muslim who has said the following:

"I heard abu Ja'far, *'Alayhi al-Salam*, say, 'One who follows a religion in the name of Allah and worships Him assiduously without acknowledging the Imam

(Leader with Divine Authority), his toiling and efforts will not be accepted. In fact, he is lost and confused and Allah disdains his deeds. Such person's case and example is like a sheep that has lost its shepherd and flock and runs back and forth the whole day. As the night falls, this sheep finds a flock of sheep with a shepherd. The (lost) sheep then joins the flock affectionately, that in fact is only a deception and not her own flock of sheep. The lost sheep passes the night in their shelter but when the shepherd leads the flock to the pasture the lost sheep feels lost and away from the flock and the shepherd, thus runs back and forth in search of the flock and the shepherd. Then it finds a flock of sheep with a shepherd and affectionately joins them but, in fact, suffers a deception. This shepherd shouts at the lost sheep saying, "Go and find your own flock and shepherd. You are lost, confused and you are without a flock and shepherd." The lost sheep then runs back and forth in confusion, fear and frustration without a shepherd to guide it to the pasture and to the shelter. While the lost sheep is caught up in such confusion a wolf seizes the opportunity and kills the lost sheep for food. So also, by Allah, O Muhammad, is the case of a person from this 'Umma (nation) who lives without an Imam (Leader) from Allah, the Most Majestic, the Most Gracious, the Imam whose Divine Authority is clearly supported with evidence and who is just in his dealings. A person without such Imam is lost and confused; and if he dies in such condition, his death is like dying in disbelief and hypocrisy. O Muhammad, bear in mind properly that the unjust 'A'immah (leaders without Divine Authority) and their followers are far away from the religion of Allah. They are lost and misleading. Their deeds that they do are like the dust blown by the winds away in a windy day, which go out of hand as useless matters. Thus is straying far away from the truth.'"

H 965, Ch. 86, h 3

A number of our people have narrated from Ahmad ibn Muhammad ibn 'Isa from ibn Mahbub from 'Abd 'Aziz al-'Abdi from 'Abd Allah ibn abu Ya'fur who has said the following:

"Once I said to abu 'Abd Allah, *'Alayhi al-Salam*, 'I meet people and it increases my wonder when I find people who do not consider you (*Ahl al-Bayt*) as their guardians and *'A'immah* (Leaders with Divine Authority) but they consider so and so as their Imam. However, they are trustworthy, truthful and loyal. I also find people who consider you as their guardians and *'A'immah* (Leaders with Divine Authority) but are not trustworthy, loyal and truthful.'

"Abu 'Abd Allah, *'Alayhi al-Salam*, then sat in an upright position and turned to me as if angered, and then said, 'One who follows the religion of Allah under the guardianship of an unjust Imam who does not possesses Divine Authority, has no religion. One who follows the religion of Allah under the guardianship of an Imam who is just in his dealings and possesses Divine Authority, will suffer no negative effect.'

"I then asked, 'Do those, in fact, have no religion, and these face no destruction?' The Imam said, 'That is correct. Those have no religion and these face no destruction.' Then the Imam said, 'Have you not heard the words of Allah, the Most Majestic, the Most Gracious: "Allah is the Guardian of the believers and it is He who takes them out of darkness into light. . . ." (2:257) It means that He takes them out of the darkness of sins to the light of repentance and forgiveness because of their love for and their being under the guardianship of the just *'A'immah* who possess Divine Authority. He has also said, "The Devil is the guardian of those who deny the Truth and he leads them from light to darkness. . . ." (2:257) It means that they were in the light of Islam but when they accepted the guardianship and the leadership of every unjust Imam who possessed no authority from Allah, the Most Majestic, the Most Gracious, their guardianship took them out of the light of Islam to the darkness of disbelief. Allah then made it necessary for them to suffer in fire along with the unbelievers, ". . . these are the dwellers of hell wherein they will live forever.""" (2:257)

H 966, Ch. 86, h 4
He has narrated from Hisham ibn Salim from Habib al-Sajistani from abu Ja'far, *'Alayhi al-Salam*, who has said the following:
"Allah, the Most Holy, the Most High, has said, 'I will cause to suffer punishment all those (citizens) who live a religious life in Islam with belief in and acknowledgement of the guardianship of unjust *'A'immah* (leaders without Divine Authority) who do not possess authority from Allah, even though such followers are (apparently) virtuous and pious in their deeds. I will forgive all those (citizens) who live a religious life in Islam with belief in and acknowledgement of the guardianship of an Imam who is just in his dealings and possesses authority from Allah, even though such followers in their dealings are unjust sinners.'"

H 967, Ch. 86, h 5
Ali ibn Muhammad has narrated from ibn Jumhur from his father from Safwan from ibn Muskan from 'Abd Allah ibn Sinan from abu 'Abd Allah, *'Alayhi al-Salam*, who has said the following:
"Allah will not be embarrassed to punish an 'Umma (nation) that lives a religious life with acknowledgement of the guardianship of an unjust Imam who does not possess authority from Allah, even though such people are virtuous and pious in their deeds. However, Allah will be embarrassed to punish a people who lives a religious life with acknowledgement of the guardianship of an Imam who is just in his dealings and possesses authority from Allah, even though they (such people) are unjust in their dealings and have committed sins."

Chapter 87 - The Case of Those Who Die Without Belief in 'A'immah (Leaders with Divine Authority) of Guidance (Part of Previous Chapter)

H 968, Ch. 87, h 1
Al-Husayn ibn Muhammad has narrated from Mu'alla ibn Muhammad from al-Hassan ibn Ali al-Washsha' from Ahmad ibn 'Aidh from ibn 'Udhayna from al-Fudayl ibn Yasar who has said the following:
"One day abu 'Abd Allah, *'Alayhi al-Salam*, commenced speaking to us and said, 'The Messenger of Allah has said, "Whoever dies and is not under (the guardianship of) the Imam, his death is like a death in ignorance.' I (the narrator) then asked, 'Is that what the Messenger of Allah has said?' The Imam said, 'Yes, by Allah, he has said so.' I then asked, 'Do all who die without acknowledging

the Imam die as if they died in ignorance (without religion)?' The Imam said, 'Yes, that is correct.'"

H 969, Ch. 87, h 2

Al-Husayn ibn Muhammad has narrated from Mu'alla ibn Muhammad from al-Washsha' who has said that 'Abd al-Karim ibn 'Amr narrated to me from ibn abu Ya'fur who has said the following:

"Once I asked abu 'Abd Allah, *'Alayhi al-Salam*, about the words of the Messenger of Allah, 'Whoever dies and is not under the guardianship of the Imam his death is like a death in ignorance.'

"The narrator has said I then asked, 'Is it death in disbelief (in religion)?' He said, 'It is death in error.' I then said, 'Thus, if one dies today and does not have an Imam is his death considered as if he has died in ignorance (without religion)?' He said, 'Yes, that is true.'"

H 970, Ch. 87, h 3

Ahmad ibn Idris has narrated from Muhammad ibn 'Abd al-Jabbar from Safwan from al-Fudayl from al-Harith ibn al-Mughira who has said the following:

"Once I said to abu 'Abd Allah, *'Alayhi al-Salam*, 'The Messenger of Allah has said, 'Whoever dies without recognizing his Imam dies as if he has died in ignorance (of religion).' The Imam said, 'That is true.' I then asked, 'Is it the ignorance of uneducated people or ignorance of one's not recognizing his Imam?' The Imam said, 'It means the ignorance that is disbelief, hypocrisy and error.'"

H 971, Ch. 87, h 4

Certain persons of our people have narrated from 'Abd al-'Azim ibn 'Abd Allah al-Hassani from Malik ibn 'Amir from al-Mufaddal ibn Za'ida from al-Mufaddal ibn 'Umar who has said the following:

"Abu 'Abd Allah, *'Alayhi al-Salam*, has said, 'Whoever follows the religion of Allah without hearing (instructions) from a truthful (Imam) person, Allah will cause him inevitably to suffer hardships. Whoever claims to have heard from a source other than the one Allah has opened for him will be considered a polytheist. The source and door that Allah has opened is the one that is trustworthy in the matters of the hidden secrets of Allah.'"

Chapter 88 - The Case of Those Who Have Recognized Ahl al-Bayt, *'Alayhim al-Salam*, and Those Who Have Ignored Them

H 972, Ch. 88, h 1

A number of our people have narrated from Ahmad ibn Muhammad ibn 'Isa from Ali ibn al-Hakam from Sulayman ibn Ja'far who has said the following:

"I heard al-Rida, *'Alayhi al-Salam*, say, 'Ali ibn 'Abd Allah ibn al-Husayn ibn Ali ibn al-Husayn ibn Ali ibn abu Talib, *'Alayhim al-Salam*, his wife and children are of the people of paradise.' He then said, 'Whoever recognizes this matter (Leadership with Divine Authority) in the descendents of Ali and Fatimah, *'Alayhim al-Salam*, is not like the (ordinary) people.'"

H 973, Ch. 88, h 2

Al-Husayn ibn Muhammad has narrated from Mu'alla ibn Muhammad who has said that al-Washsha' said Ahmad ibn 'Umar, al-Hallal has narrated to us the following:

"Once I said to abu al-Hassan, *'Alayhi al-Salam*, 'Instruct me about those who have opposed you and have ignored your rights and are of descendents of *Fatimah, 'Alayha al-Salam*, will their suffering be the same as for the other people?' He said, 'Ali ibn al-Husayn, *'Alayhi al-Salam*, would say that their (such people's) suffering will be twice as much.'"

H 974, Ch. 88, h 3

Al-Husayn ibn Muhammad has narrated from Mu'alla ibn Muhammad from al-Hassan ibn Rashid who has that reported to us Ali ibn 'Isma'il al-Maythami who has said that narrated to us Rab'i ibn 'Abd Allah who has said that said to him 'Abd al-Rahman ibn abu 'Abd Allah the following:

"Once I asked abu 'Abd Allah, *'Alayhi al-Salam*, 'Are those who are ignorant of this matter (Leadership with Divine Authority) of the descendents of Hashim and others the same?' He said to me, 'Do not say, *al-Munkir* (ignorant) but say *al-Jahid* (rejecter) who are of the descendents of Hashim and other people.' Abu al-Hassan (the narrator) has said, 'I thought about it and then I recalled the words of Allah, the Most Majestic, the Most Gracious, about the brothers of Yusuf (Joseph) ". . . He recognized them but they were ignorant about him.'" (12:58)

H 975, Ch. 88, h 4

A number of our people have narrated from Ahmad ibn Muhammad from ibn abu Nasr who has said the following:

"Once I asked al-Rida, *'Alayhi al-Salam*, 'Those from your own people, who reject you and other such people, are they the same?' He replied, 'Those of our own people who reject us (Leadership with Divine Authority) are considered as having committed twice as much sin, and the good deeds from our own people who are virtuous are also considered as of twice as much value.'"

Chapter 89 - The Obligation and Duty of the People at the Time of the Passing Away of the Imam, *'Alayhi al-Salam*

H 976, Ch. 89, h 1

Muhammad ibn Yahya has narrated from Muhammad ibn al-Husayn from Safwan from Ya'qub ibn Shu'ayb who has said the following:

"Once I asked abu 'Abd Allah, *'Alayhi al-Salam*, 'If something may happen to the Imam what should the people do?' The Imam asked, 'Where do the words of Allah, the Most Majestic, the Most Gracious, apply: "Not all believers have to become specialists in religious learning. Why do not certain people from each group of believers seek to become specialists in religious learning, and after completing their studies, guide their group so that they will have fear of Allah." (9:122) The Imam then said, 'They will have good reason to be excused as long as they are searching and learning. So also are those who wait for them until they complete their religious education and return back to them.'"

H 977, Ch. 89, h 2

Ali ibn Ibrahim has narrated from Muhammad ibn 'Isa from Yunus ibn 'Abd al-Rahman who has said that narrated to us Hammad from 'Abd al-A'la' who has said the following:

"Once I asked abu 'Abd Allah, *'Alayhi al-Salam*, about the statement of Sunni Muslims, *al-'Amma,* that says the Messenger of Allah has said, 'If a person dies without recognizing who his Imam is, his death is as if he has died the death of ignorance (pre-Islamic age of darkness).'

"The Imam said, 'That is very true, by Allah.' I then asked, 'What if the Imam passes away and a person is in Khurasan and does not know who the executor of the will of the Imam is? Is this a good excuse for him?' He (the Imam) said, 'No, that is not a good reason and an excuse. When the Imam leaves this world the authority of the executor of his will applies to those who live in the area. Also the obligation of searching to learn about one's duties applies to those who are not in the area but who have learned about the passing away of the Imam. Allah, the Most Majestic, the Most Gracious, has said, "Not all believers have to become specialists in religious learning. Why do not some people from each group of believers seek to become specialists in religious learning, and after completing their studies, guide their group so that they will have fear of Allah?"' (9:122)

"I then asked, 'What if they did go to find out but certain ones from them died before they could find out?' He said, 'Allah, the Most Majestic, the Most Gracious, has said, ". . . and one who dies, after having abandoned his home to get near to Allah and His Messenger, will receive his reward from Allah. . . ." (4:100) I asked, 'What if certain ones from them may reach your town but find out that you have closed your door and the curtains are drawn closed You would not call them to yourself and there might be no one to guide them to you. How then will they know about you?' He said, 'They can learn about me from the book that Allah has revealed.'

"I then asked, 'How has Allah, the Most Majestic, the Most Gracious, said it?' He said, 'I know that you have spoken to me about it before this day also.' I said, 'That is correct.' He then said, 'Recall what Allah has said about Ali, *'Alayhi al-Salam*, and what the Messenger of Allah said to him about al-Hassan and al-Husayn, what Allah has specially said about Ali, *'Alayhi al-Salam*, and what the Messenger of Allah has said about him, about his will to him, appointing him, about their suffering and the acknowledgements of al-Hassan and al-Husayn, *'Alayhim al-Salam*, of such facts. Recall the will of al-Hassan, *'Alayhi al-Salam*, and his delivering it to al-Husayn, *'Alayhi al-Salam*. Allah has said, "The Prophet has more authority over the believers than they themselves do. His wives are their mothers. The relatives are closer to each other, according to the Book of Allah. . . ."' (33:6)

"I then said, 'People speak about abu Ja'far, *'Alayhi al-Salam*, and ask, 'How is it that Imamat (Leadership with Divine Authority) has stepped out for him from among all the sons of his father, even though certain ones among them were closer to the Imam and older than him? The ones younger than he did not receive it just because they were younger '

"He said, 'The one who possesses this matter (Leadership with Divine Authority) can be recognized through three pieces of evidence that are not found with other people. He must have greater proximity to the preceding Imam and that must be the executor of the will of the preceding Imam. With him there must be the Armaments of the Messenger of Allah and the document of his will. This document is with me and no one disputes it.' I then asked, 'Is that kept secret and hidden for fear from the rulers?' He said, 'There is nothing secret and hidden but there is clear evidence for its existence and that it is available. What is there is what my father entrusted me with. When he was about to leave this world he asked me to call people to bear testimony for him. I then called four people from Quraysh among whom was Nafi', slave of 'Abd Allah ibn 'Umar. My father said, 'Write down, this is how the will of Jacob to his children reads, "Allah has chosen this religion for you. You must not leave this world unless you are a Muslim (submitted to the will of the Lord of the Universe)." (2:132) Muhammad ibn Ali made the same kind of will to his son, Ja'far ibn Muhammad and commanded him to shroud him in his own gown, which he would use during his Friday prayers. That his own turban must be used for him, that the surface of his grave should be given a square shape, raised by four fingers (three inches) from the ground and thereafter leave it that much only. Thereafter he wrapped up the document of the will and asked the witnesses to leave saying, "May Allah grant you blessings."' When they left I asked, 'What was in it O father, that you asked them to bear testimony to?' He said, 'I do not like that you will be defeated and people will say, "He left this world without a will." I wanted it to be a supporting authority for you. This is the fact that helps one who comes to the town and asks, "To whom did so and so make a will?" And he is answered, 'The will was made to so and so.'' I then asked, 'What if he (Imam) would be a partner in the will?' He said, 'You must ask him. He will explain it to you.'"

H 978, Ch. 89, h 3

Muhammad ibn Yahya has narrated from Ahmad ibn Muhammad ibn 'Isa from Muhammad ibn Khalid from Nadr ibn Suwayd from Yahya al-Halabi from Burayd ibn Mu'awiya from Muhammad ibn Muslim who has said the following:

"Once I said to abu 'Abd Allah, *'Alayhi al-Salam*, 'May Allah grant you good health, we heard that you were not feeling well and it caused us great anxiety. Would that you had informed or taught us about who would be the succeeding Imam.'

"The Imam said, 'Ali, *'Alayhi al-Salam*, was the scholar and knowledge is inherited. No scholar dies except that he leaves behind a scholar whose knowledge is of the same level or whatever Allah wills.'

"I then asked, 'Will people be excused for not recognizing the succeeding Imam after the death of the preceding Imam?' He then said, 'The people of this area (Madina) will not be excused. People of other areas will be dealt with according to their abilities. Allah has said, "Not all believers have to become specialists in religious learning. Why do not certain people from each group of believers seek to become specialists in religious learning, and after completing their studies, guide their group so that they will have fear of Allah?'" (9:122)

"I (the narrator) then asked the Imam, 'What if certain ones of them would die before completing their education and search?' He said, 'Such people will be of the ones mentioned in the words of Allah herein below. ". . . And one who dies, after having abandoned his home to get near to Allah and His Messenger, will receive his reward from Allah. . . .'" (4:100)

"I then asked the Imam, 'If people come to the Imam then by what means can they recognize him?' He said, 'The Imam is granted serenity, dignity and an awesome presence.'"

Chapter 90 - When Does the Imam Learn That Leadership with Divine Authority Has Come to Him?

H 979, Ch. 90, h 1
Ahmad ibn Idris has narrated from Muhammad ibn 'Abd al-Jabbar from Safwan ibn Yahya from abu Jarir al-Qummi who has said the following:
"Once I said to abu al-Hassan, *'Alayhi al-Salam*, 'May Allah keep my soul in service for your cause, you know how devoted I have been toward your father and after him to yourself.' I then swore before him by the rights of the Messenger of Allah and the rights of so and so and so and so (*'A'immah*) from Ali, al-Hassan, al-Husayn . . ., *'Alayhim al-Salam*, up to his own self. I tried to assure him that whatever he may tell me will not be made public and spread to other people. I asked him about his father to find out if he was alive or had passed away.' He said, 'By Allah, his father had passed away.' I then said, 'May Allah keep my soul in service for your cause, your followers (Shi'a) narrate that in him the traditions of four prophets are found.'

"He then said, 'In certainty, by Allah, besides whom there is no Lord, that he (my father) has passed away.' I asked, 'Is his passing away in the form of disappearance or in the form of death?' He then said, 'It is in the form of death.' I then said, 'Perhaps you are observing caution and are afraid of me.' He said, 'All glory belongs to Allah (that is not the case).' I then asked, 'Did he deliver his will to you?' He said, 'Yes, he did so.' I then asked, 'Has he made others as your partners in executing his will?' He said, 'No, he has not done so.' I then asked, 'Is there any Imam over you among your brothers?' He said, 'No, there is no one from them.' I then asked, 'Are you the Imam?' He said, 'Yes, I am the Imam (Leader with Divine Authority).'"

H 980, Ch. 90, h 2
Al-Husayn ibn Muhammad has narrated from Mu'alla ibn Muhammad from Ali ibn Asbat who has said the following:
"Once I said to al-Rida, *'Alayhi al-Salam*, 'A man troubled your brother Ibrahim and said to him, "Your father is still alive." You know of this case what he knows.' The Imam said, 'Glory belongs to Allah. The Messenger of Allah dies. How is it that Musa, *'Alayhi al-Salam*, (Imam Musa al-Kazim) does not die? Certainly, by

376

Allah, he passed away just as the Messenger of Allah passed away. However, Allah, the Most Holy, the Most High, ever since He took His Prophet from this world has continued favoring the descendents of *A 'ajim* (pl. of *'Ajam*, meaning the Persians or non-Arabs) through granting this religion to them and has held it back from the people of His Prophet. Ever since, He has continued granting such favors to these (*A 'ajim*) and withheld it from them (Arabs). In the month of Dhi al-Hajjah I paid off a thousand Dinars of his debts because of which he (his brother Ibrahim) was in great difficulties. He was about to divorce his wives, free his slaves and servants. You have heard the case of Yusuf and his brothers.'"

H 981, Ch. 90, h 3
Al-Husayn ibn Muhammad has narrated from Mu'alla ibn Muhammad from al-Washsha' who has said the following:

"Once I said to abu al-Hassan, *'Alayhi al-Salam*, 'They have narrated from you about the death of abu al-Hassan (Musa al-Kazim), *'Alayhi al-Salam*, that a man said to you, "You have learned of it (the death of your father) through the report of Sa'id.' He said, 'Sa'id came only after I had learned about it (death of my father).'

"The narrator has said, 'I asked the Imam, "I heard from him that you divorced mother of Farwa, daughter of Ishaq, in the month of Rajab, one day after the death of abu al-Hassan, *'Alayhi al-Salam*. Did you divorce her when you knew that abu al-Hassan, *'Alayhi al-Salam*, has died?"' The Imam said, 'Yes, I did so.' I asked him, 'Did you do so before Sa'id came to you?' The Imam said, 'Yes, I did so before Sa'id came.'"

H 982, Ch. 90, h 4
Muhammad ibn Yahya has narrated from al-Husayn from Safwan who has said the following:

"Once I requested abu al-Hassan al-Rida, *'Alayhi al-Salam*, 'Enlighten me, when does an Imam come to know that he is the Imam? Does it take place when the preceding Imam has already passed away or when he is about to leave this world? For example abu al-Hassan, *'Alayhi al-Salam*, passed away in Baghdad and you were here (in Madina)?' The Imam said, 'He comes to know it at the time his companion (the preceding Imam) is about to leave this world.' I then asked, 'By what means does he come to know it?' He said, 'He comes to know of it through inspiration from Allah.'"

H 983, Ch. 90, h 5
Ali ibn Ibrahim has narrated from Muhammad ibn 'Isa from abu al-Fadl al-Shahbani from Harun ibn al-Fadl who has said the following:

"Once I saw abu al-Hassan Ali ibn Muhammad, *'Alayhi al-Salam*, on the day abu Ja'far, *'Alayhi al-Salam*, passed away. He said, 'To Allah we belong and to Him we return. Abu Ja'far, *'Alayhi al-Salam*, has passed away.' He was asked, 'How do you know that he has passed away?' He said, '(I learned it from) a form of humbleness before Allah that I had never experienced. It overwhelmed me.'"

H 984, Ch. 90, h 6
Ali ibn Ibrahim has narrated from Muhammad ibn 'Isa from Musafir who has said the following:

"Abu Ibrahim commanded, at the time he was summoned to Baghdad, abu al-Hassan, *'Alayhi al-Salam*, to sleep every night at his (abu Ibrahim's) house until the family hears about him or the coming of the news of his death.

"We would prepare the bed for abu al-Hassan, *'Alayhi al-Salam*, every night in the terrace and he would come after the 'Isha (late evening) to rest and leave next morning for his own house. He has said that it continued for four years. One night he delayed and the bed was prepared for him. He did not come as he usually did. The family was alarmed and deeply saddened. His delay shocked and greatly overwhelmed us. In the morning he came to the house and went to the family room to 'Umm Ahmad (mother of Ahmad) and said to her, 'Please, bring me the things that my father had entrusted you with.' She began to cry, beat up her face and tore her cloth over her heart saying, 'My master, by Allah, has passed away.' He stopped her and said, 'Do not say anything to anyone and do not make it public before the news of his death comes to the governor.' She then brought a package, two thousand and four thousand Dinars and gave all of it to him and to no one else. She said, 'He (abu Ibrahim, *'Alayhi al-Salam*) had told me when there were only two of us (she was beloved to him), "Keep this trust well protected with you and do not allow anyone to know it before I will die. When I will die whichever of my sons will come to you and ask you to deliver this trust to him give it to him and know that I have passed away." The sign that my master had informed me of has exactly come to pass.' He took charge of the package and money from her and commanded everyone to keep it secret until the coming of the news. He left the house and thereafter did not come to rest at night as before. After a few days only the news of the passing away of abu Ibrahim, *'Alayhi al-Salam*, reached the city. We calculated the time and found out that it was exactly the time abu al-Hassan, *'Alayhi al-Salam*, had done those things: his delaying to come for rest at night and taking charge of the trust from ('Umm Ahamd)."

Chapter 91 - The Conditions of the Imam, *'Alayhi al-Salam*, in the Matters of Age

H 985, Ch. 91, h 1
A number of our people have narrated from Ahmad ibn Muhammad ibn 'Isa from ibn Mahbub from Hisham ibn Salim from Yazid al-Kunasiyy who has said the following:
"Once I asked abu Ja'far, *'Alayhi al-Salam*, 'Was Jesus at the time he spoke to people from the cradle a Divine Authority over the people of his time?' He said, 'At that time he was a prophet, a Divine Authority over the people but not a Mursal (Messenger). Have you not heard the words of Allah that say, "He said, 'I am the servant of Allah. He has given me the Book and has appointed me to be a prophet (19:30). He has blessed me no matter where I dwell, commanded me to worship Him and pay the religious tax for as long as I live.'" (19:31)

"I then asked, 'Was he the Divine Authority over Zackaria at the time that he was in the cradle?' He said, 'At that time Jesus was a sign from Allah to people and a blessing to Mary (Maryam) when he spoke on her behalf. He was a prophet and a Divine Authority over all those who heard his words at that time. Thereafter he

378

did not speak until he was two years old. At such time Zackaria was the Authority of Allah, the Most Majestic, the Most Gracious, over the people after the silence of Jesus. Zackaria then died and his son Yahya (John) inherited the book and wisdom and he was a small child. You can hear it in the words of Allah, the Most Majestic, the Most Gracious, 'We commanded John, Zachariah's son, "O John, follow the guidance of the Lord with due steadfastness. We gave knowledge and wisdom to John during his childhood."' (19:12) When Jesus was seven years old, he then spoke as a prophet and a messenger until Allah, the Most Holy sent him inspiration. Thus, Jesus was the Divine Authority over John and over all the people. The earth is never left without the presence of a Divine Authority over the people, O abu Khalid, from the day Allah created Adam and settled him on earth.'

"I then asked, 'May Allah keep my soul in service for your cause, did Ali, *'Alayhi al-Salam*, possess Divine Authority from Allah and His Messenger over this nation (Muslims) during the lifetime of the Messenger of Allah?' He said, 'Yes, he received such authority on the day the Messenger of Allah appointed him Divine Authority over the people and called upon the people to acknowledge his Divine Authority and commanded them to obey him.' I then asked, 'Was obedience to Imam Ali, *'Alayhi al-Salam*, obligatory upon people during the lifetime of the Messenger of Allah as well as after his death?' The Imam said, 'Yes, but he kept silent and did not speak along with the Messenger of Allah. At that time, during the lifetime of the Messenger of Allah, obedience was of the rights of the Messenger of Allah over the 'Umma (nation) and over Ali, *'Alayhi al-Salam*. Obedience to the authority of Allah and His Messenger over the people as a whole was also obligatory to Ali, *'Alayhi al-Salam*, after the death of the Messenger of Allah. Ali, *'Alayhi al-Salam*, was a very wise and knowledgeable person.'"

H 986, Ch. 91, h 2
Muhammad ibn Yahya has narrated from Ahmad ibn Muhammad ibn 'Isa from Safwan ibn Yahya who has said the following:

"Once I said to al-Rida, *'Alayhi al-Salam*, 'Before Allah granted you the blessed birth of abu Ja'far, *'Alayhi al-Salam*, we asked you question and you would say that Allah will soon grant you a son. Allah, now, has blessed you with such a favor and may He make him to bring joy to our heart. We wish not to experience a single day without you but, Allah forbid, if something happens to you, from whom must we seek guidance?'

"He pointed with his hand to abu Ja'far, *'Alayhi al-Salam*, and he was standing before him. I then said, 'May Allah keep my soul in service for your cause; he is only a child, three years old.' He said, 'That does not matter in his case at all. Jesus rose with Divine Authority when he was less than three years old.'"

H 987, Ch. 91, h 3
Muhammad ibn Yahya has narrated from Ahmad ibn Muhammad from Ali ibn Sayf from certain persons of our people from abu Ja'far, *'Alayhi al-Salam*, al-Thani the 2ⁿᵈ who has said the following:

"Once I said to abu Ja'far, *'Alayhi al-Salam*, 'They speak about (and question) your very young age.' He said, 'Allah informed David through inspiration to appoint Sulayman (Solomon) as the executor of his will and successor when he was just a child minding sheep. The worshippers and scholars of the Israelites disliked it. Allah then inspired David to take the staff of those who had objections and that of Sulayman, place them in a room and seal them with each one's insignia. On the next day whichever staff was to be found that had grown leaves and fruits, the owner thereof was the successor. David informed them of this matter and they all agreed.'"

H 988, Ch. 91, h 4
Ali ibn Muhammad and others have narrated from Sahl ibn Ziyad from Ya'qub ibn Yazid from Mus'ab from Mas'da from abu Basir who has said the following:
"Once I went to see abu 'Abd Allah, *'Alayhi al-Salam*. Along with me there was a five-year-old boy, a guide who had not yet attained puberty. The Imam asked, 'How will it be with you if people will debate you about the Divine Authority of someone of his (the guide boy's) age?' Or he said, 'About the Divine Authority of one that will come and will be of the same age as his.'"

(At the time when Divine Authority was transferred to Imam Muhammad Taqi, *'Alayhi al-Salam*, he was eight years old.)

H 989, Ch. 91, h 5
Sahl ibn Ziyad has narrated from Ali ibn Mahziyar from Muhammad ibn 'Isma'il ibn Bazi' who has said the following:
"Once I asked abu Ja'far, *'Alayhi al-Salam*, of an issue of the Imamat (Leadership with Divine Authority) and I asked, 'Can the Imam be a boy less than seven years old?' He said, 'Yes, he can even be less than five years old.' Sahl has said that ibn Mahziyar narrated this to me in the year two hundred twenty-one A.H."

H 990, Ch. 91, h 6
Al-Husayn ibn Muhammad has narrated from al-Khayrani from his father who has said the following:
"Once I was standing in the presence of abu al-Hassan, *'Alayhi al-Salam*, in Khurasan and someone said to him, 'O my master, if something will happen to you to whom must we then turn for guidance?' The Imam said, 'You must turn for guidance to abu Ja'far, *'Alayhi al-Salam*, my son.' The person asking the question seemed to have thought his (abu Ja'far's) age as very young. Abu al-Hassan, *'Alayhi al-Salam*, then said, 'Allah, the Most Holy, the Most High, sent Jesus, son of Mary, peace be upon them, as the Messenger and the Prophet being the author of a whole system of law. He began this task at an age much smaller than the age of abu Ja'far, *'Alayhi al-Salam*.'"

H 991, Ch. 91, h 7
Al-Husayn ibn Muhammad has narrated from Mu'alla ibn Muhammad from Ali ibn Asbat who has said the following:
"Once I saw abu Ja'far, *'Alayhi al-Salam*, who had come out to me and I began to look at him from head to toe so I could describe him to our people in Egypt. I was looking until he sat down and said, 'O Ali, Allah has supported His argument against the people in the case of Imamat (Leadership with Divine Authority) just as He has done so in the case of the prophets. He has said, "We gave authority to him (John) over the people during his childhood. (19:12) When he attained

maturity, Allah gave him strength, wisdom and knowledge. Thus, do We reward those who do good." (12:22) 'When he grew up to manhood and became forty years old . . .' (46:15) It may come to pass, wisdom comes to a prophet when he is just a child or when he is forty years old.'"

H 992, Ch. 91, h 8
Ali ibn Ibrahim has narrated from his father who has said the following:
"Once abu Ali ibn Hassa'n spoke to abu Ja'far, *'Alayhi al-Salam*, saying, 'My master, people refuse to accept your Imamat (Leadership with Divine Authority) because of your very young age.' He asked, 'Why do they not refuse to accept the words of Allah, the Most Majestic, the Most Gracious? Allah, the Most Majestic, the Most Gracious, has said to His prophet, '(Muhammad), say, "This is my way. I and all my followers invite you to Allah with proper understanding. . . ."'" (12:108). By Allah, only Ali, *'Alayhi al-Salam*, followed him at that time and he was only nine years old and I am also nine years old."

Chapter 92 - Only an Imam Has the Authority to Wash the Body of an Imam for Burial

H 993, Ch. 92, h 1
Al-Husayn ibn Muhammad has narrated from Mu'alla ibn Muhammad from al-Hassan ibn Ali al-Washsha' from Ahmad ibn 'Umar al-Hallal or someone other than him who has said the following:
"Once I said to al-Rida, *'Alayhi al-Salam*, 'They argue against us about "No one has the authority to wash the body of an Imam for burial except an Imam."' The Imam then asked, 'How do they know who has washed him for burial? What did you say to them?' I then said, 'May Allah keep my soul in service for your cause, I told them that if my Imam says that he has washed his body under the throne of the Lord, he has told the truth. If he says that he has washed it at the center of the earth he has told the truth.' The Imam said, 'It is not that way.' I then asked him, 'What then should I say to them (al-Waqifiyya sect)?' The Imam said, 'Tell them that I (al-Rida) washed his body for burial.' I then asked, 'Must I tell them that you have washed his body?' He said, 'Yes, I have done so.'"

H 994, Ch. 92, h 2
Al-Husayn ibn Muhammad has narrated from Mu'alla ibn Muhammad from Muhammad ibn Jumhur who has said that abu Mu'ammar said the following:
"Once I asked al-Rida, *'Alayhi al-Salam*, about the issue "Only Imam washes the body of the Imam for burial". He said, 'It is of the traditions of Moses, son of 'Imran, peace be upon him.'"

H 995, Ch. 92, h 3
It is narrated from him from Mu'alla ibn Muhammad from Muhammad ibn Jumhur from Yunus from Talha who has said the following:
"Once I asked al-Rida, *'Alayhi al-Salam*, 'Is it true that only an Imam has the authority to wash the body of an Imam for burial?'

"The Imam asked, 'Do you not know who came to wash his body for burial? The ones who were far more excellent than those who were absent during washing his body for burial, came to wash him for burial. They were those who came to Joseph in the well to help when his parents and family were absent from him (Jibril and angels).'"

Chapter 93 - The Birth of 'A'immah, *'Alayhim al-Salam*

H 996, Ch. 93, h 1

Ali ibn Muhammad has narrated from 'Abd Allah ibn Ishaq al-'Alawi from Muhammad ibn Zayd al-Rizami from Muhammad ibn Sulayman al-Daylami from Ali ibn Hamza from abu Basir who has said the following:

"Once we went for Hajj with abu 'Abd Allah, *'Alayhi al-Salam*, in the year that his son Musa, *'Alayhi al-Salam*, was born. When we arrived at al-Abwa lunch was served. When he would serve food to his people he served good and plentiful food. At such time the messenger of Hamida (his wife) came saying, 'Hamida says, "I have almost lost myself and I have found what I was to find; I am about to give birth. You had commanded me not to do anything to this child without you."' Abu 'Abd Allah, *'Alayhi al-Salam*, then went with the messenger. When he came back his companions congratulated him and said, 'May Allah keep our souls in service for your cause, what did you do to Hamida?' He said, 'Allah granted her good health and gifted me with a boy whom He has formed as the best in His creatures. Hamida informed me of a matter about him that she thought I did not know. I, however, knew it better than she did.' I then asked him, 'May Allah keep my soul in service for your cause, what was it that Hamida told you about the child?' He said, 'She informed me about the baby's actions as soon as his body touched the ground. The baby placed his hands on the ground and raised his head to the sky'. I explained to her that it was a sign like that of the Messenger of Allah and a sign of the executor of his will after him.

"I then said, 'May Allah keep my soul in service for your cause, what sign is the sign of the Messenger of Allah and the sign of the executor of his will after him?' He said to me, 'In the night that the mother of my grandfather conceived him, someone came to my great grandfather with a drink finer than water, softer than butter, sweeter than honey, cooler than ice and whiter than milk. He was asked to drink it and then go to bed with his wife. He went to bed with his wife and she conceived the baby. In the night that the mother of my father conceived him someone came to my grandfather with the same kind of drink as that brought to my great-grandfather. He was commanded to do as my great-grandfather had done. He then went to bed with his wife and she conceived my father. In the night that my mother conceived me someone came to my father with the same kind of drink as that brought for my great-grandfather and grandfather, and made him drink as they had done and commanded him as he had commanded them before him. He then went to bed with his wife and my mother conceived me. In the night that my wife was to conceive my son someone came to me with the same kind of drink as that for my great-grandfather, my grandfather and my father. He did to me as he had done to them. I then went with the knowledge of Allah and with joy for what Allah had granted to me to bed with my wife and she conceived the baby that was just born. The newborn is with you and he, by Allah, will be your companion (master, Imam) after me. The seed of the Imam is from what I just explained to you. When the seed is accommodated in the womb for four months and the spirit is established therein, Allah, the Most Holy, the Most High, then sends an angel. This angel is called *Haywan* (animal or living). He then writes on his right shoulder, ". . . in all truth and justice, your Lord's word has been completed. No one can change His words. He is All-hearing and All-knowing." (6:115) As soon as he is born (and his body touched the ground) he places his hands on the floor and raises his head to the sky. Placing his hands on earth is an indication of his taking possession of all the knowledge of Allah that is sent from the heavens to earth. Raising his head to the sky is that because a caller from inside the Throne calls him from the high horizon with his name and the name of his father. It is for (on behalf of) the Lord, the Most Majestic, the Most Gracious, saying, 'O so and so, son of so and so, be firm so that you are established. For the great purpose that I have created you, you are my chosen one in my creatures. You are the keeper of My secrets, the container of My knowledge, the trustee of My inspiration and My deputy and representative on My earth. I have made it necessary for My blessings and mercy to reach you and those who love you (and acknowledge your Divine Authority). I have gifted My paradise and given a place near Myself to you and to them. Also, by My Majesty and Grace, I will make your enemies feel the heat of My punishment even though I may have given them expanded prosperity in My world such as prosperity in their livelihood.'

"When the call of the caller ends he responds to it by placing his hands on the ground and raising his head to the sky, and says the following: 'Allah Himself testifies that He is the only Lord. The angels and the men of knowledge and justice testify that Allah is the only Lord, the Majestic, and All-wise.' (3:18)

"The Imam then said, 'When he says this, Allah grants him the knowledge of the first and the knowledge of the last and the qualification to be visited by the Spirit in the nights of destiny.'

"I then asked, 'May Allah keep my soul in service for your cause, is the Spirit different from Jibril?' He said, 'The Spirit is a creature greater than Jibril. Jibril is of the angels. The Spirit is a creature greater than the angels are. Is it not that Allah, the Most Holy, the Most High, has said, 'On this Night, the angels and the Spirit descend. . . .'" (97:4)

Muhammad ibn Yahya and Ahmad ibn Muhammad have narrated from Muhammad ibn al-Husayn from Ahmad ibn al-Hassan from al-Mukhtar ibn Ziyad from Muhammad ibn Sulayman from his father from abu Basir a similar *Hadith*.

H 997, Ch. 93, h 2

Muhammad ibn Yahya has narrated from Muhammad ibn al-Husayn from Musa ibn Sa'dan from 'Abd Allah ibn al-Qasim from al-Hassan ibn Rashid who has said the following:

"I heard abu 'Abd Allah, *'Alayhi al-Salam*, saying, 'When Allah, the Most Holy, the Most High, loves to create the Imam He commands an angel to take a drink of water from under the Throne to his father to drink it, and from this He creates the Imam. For the first forty days and nights in his mother's womb he does not hear anything. After that he hears the words. When he is born that angel comes and writes between his eyes, ". . . in all truth and justice, your Lord's word has been completed. No one can change His words. He is All-hearing and All-knowing." (6:115)

'When the preceding Imam passes away a lighthouse made from light is prepared for him and through this lighthouse he examines the deeds of the creatures. By this means Allah establishes His authority over (and argument against) the creatures.'"

H 998, Ch. 93, h 3
Muhammad ibn Yahya has narrated from Ahmad ibn Muhammad from Ali ibn Hadid from Mansur ibn Yunus from Yunus ibn Zabyan who has said the following:

"I heard abu 'Abd Allah, *'Alayhi al-Salam*, say, 'When Allah, the Most Majestic, the Most Gracious, decides to create the Imam from another Imam He sends an angel with a drink of water from under the Throne. The angel then asks the Imam to drink it or gives it to him to drink. For the first forty days he does not hear any words and thereafter he hears words. When his mother gives birth Allah sends the same angel who had brought the water. The angel writes on his right shoulder, ". . . in all truth and justice, your Lord's Word has been completed. No one can change His Words. He is All-hearing and All-knowing." (6:115)

'When he rises to execute the task of an Imam, Allah raises a lighthouse for him in every town through which he examines the deeds of the servants of Allah.'"

H 999, Ch. 93, h 4
A number of our people have narrated from Ahmad ibn Muhammad from ibn Mahbub from al-Rab'i ibn Muhammad al-Musalli from Muhammad ibn Marwan who has said the following:

"I heard abu 'Abd Allah, *'Alayhi al-Salam*, say, 'The Imam hears in the womb of his mother and when he is born these words of Allah will be written between his shoulders, ". . . in all truth and justice, your Lord's word has been completed. No one can change His words. He is All-hearing and All-knowing." (6:115) When the matter (Leadership with Divine Authority) is delivered to him Allah establishes a pillar of light for him through which he sees the deeds of the people of every town.'"

H 1000, Ch. 93, h 5
Al-Husayn ibn Muhammad has narrated from Mu'alla ibn Muhammad from Ahmad ibn Muhammad ibn 'Abd Allah from ibn Mas'ud from 'Abd Allah ibn Ibrahim al-Ja'fari who has said the following:

"I heard Ishaq ibn Ja'far say, 'I heard my father say, "The mothers of the executors of the will when conceiving them experience a certain condition. She feels as if fainted for the rest of the day if it takes place during the day or for the rest of the night if it takes place at night. She then sees in her dream a man congratulating her with the birth of a son, very knowledgeable and very forbearing. She becomes happy and wakes up and from her right side in the house she hears a voice. It says, 'You have conceived with goodness, you are changing into goodness and you have come up with goodness. Congratulations to you for a son who is very forbearing and knowledgeable.' She then feels light and thereafter she feels no discomfort from her sides or from her belly. After nine months she hears (something) intensely in the house. On the night of the birth of the child a light appears to her in the house that only she and the father of the child can see. When the child is born he is found in a sitting position. There is enough opening for the child to come out with both thighs and legs folded. The child turns on the ground so as not to miss facing the direction of Makkah. He sneezes three times and points with his fingers for the words of blessings said upon sneezing. When born, his umbilical cord is already cut off and he is circumcised. Both of his Ruba'ia (molar) teeth from the upper and lower jaws, both of his (Na'b) canine teeth and both of his Dahika (bicuspids) are already grown. In front of him a light shines like flowing gold. For the next day and night a golden light flows from his hands. This is how the prophets are when they are born. The executors of their will are the only ones who are the attachments of the prophets."""

H 1001, Ch. 93, h 6

A number of our people have narrated from Ahmad ibn Muhammad from Ali ibn Hadid from Jamil ibn Darraj who has said the following:

"Several persons of our people have narrated that the Imam, *'Alayhi al-Salam*, has said, 'Do not speak about the Imam. The Imam hears the words while he still is in the womb of his mother. When she gives birth the angel writes between his eyes, ". . . in all truth and justice, your Lord's word has been completed. No one can change His words. He is All-hearing and All-knowing." (6:115)

"When he takes charge of the matter (Leadership with Divine Authority) in every town a lighthouse is established for him through which he examines the deeds of the servants (of Allah).'"

H 1002, Ch. 93, h 7

Ali ibn Ibrahim has narrated from Muhammad ibn 'Isa ibn 'Ubayd who has said the following:

"Once ibn Faddal and I were sitting when Yunus came and said, 'I went to see abu al-Hassan al-Rida, *'Alayhi al-Salam*, and said to him, "May Allah keep my soul in service for your cause, people speak so much about a pillar."' He said to me, 'O Yunus, what do you see? Do you see it as a pillar of iron that you may raise for your friend?' I (the narrator) then said, 'I do not know.'

"The Imam said, 'In fact, it is an appointed angel in every town. Through him Allah raises the deeds of that town.' The narrator has said that ibn Faddal then stood up and kissed his head and said, 'May Allah grant you blessings, O abu Muhammad, you continue to bring us true *Hadith* with which Allah grants us relief and comfort.'"

H 1003, Ch. 93, h 8

Ali ibn Muhammad has narrated from a certain person of our people from ibn abu 'Umayr from Hariz from Zurara from abu Ja'far, *'Alayhi al-Salam*, who has said the following:

"Imam has ten signs. He is born clean and circumcised. When born and as soon as his body touches the earth, his palms reach the ground first while he raises his head to the sky and loudly says the two testimonies. He does not endure wetdreams. His eyes sleep but not his heart. He does not yawn or stretch. He sees behind just as he sees in front. (His vision forms a 360 degree angle). His secretion smells as musk. The earth is made to conceal and devour it. When he dresses up with coat of arms of the Messenger of Allah it precisely fits him. Yet, when other people, taller or shorter, try, it is taller on them by the span of thumb to small finger stretched a part. He is a *Muhaddath* (the one to whom angels speak) up to the time of his passing away.'"

Chapter 94 - The Creation of the Bodies, Spirit and the Heart of the Imam, *'Alayhi al-Salam*

H 1004, Ch. 94, h 1

A number of our people have narrated from Ahmad ibn Muhammad from abu Yahya al-Wasiti from certain persons of our people from abu 'Abd Allah, *'Alayhi al-Salam*, who has said the following:

"Allah has created us from *'Illiyin* (high above) and He has created our spirits from above that. He has created the spirit of our Shi'as (followers) from *'Illiyin* and their bodies from below that. For this reason there is a relationship between us and them, and their hearts are affectionate toward us.'"

H 1005, Ch. 94, h 2

Ahmad ibn Muhammad has narrated from Muhammad ibn al-Hassan from Muhammad ibn 'Isa ibn 'Ubayd from Muhammad ibn Shu'ayb from 'Imran ibn Ishaq al-Za'farani from Muhammad ibn Marwan who has said the following:

"I heard abu 'Abd Allah, *'Alayhi al-Salam*, say, 'Allah has created us from the light of His greatness. Thereafter He shaped our form from preserved and hidden clay under the Throne. Then He made that light to reside in that clay. We were then spiritual creatures of the human being species. He has not placed anything as a share from that with which we were created in anyone else. He has created the spirits of our Shi'a from our clay and their bodies from preserved and hidden clay from below that clay. Allah has not placed anything as a share of that with which they are created in anyone except the prophets. Thus, our followers and we became the people. The rest of the people became riffraff for the fire and to the fire.'"

H 1006, Ch. 94, h 3

Ali ibn Ibrahim has narrated from Ali ibn Hassa'n and Muhammad ibn Yahya from Salma ibn al-Khattab and others from Ali ibn Hassa'n from Ali ibn 'Atiyya from Ali ibn Ri'ab who has narrated the following in a *marfu'* manner:

"'Amir al-Mu'minin Ali, *'Alayhi al-Salam*, has said Allah has a canal below His Throne. Below the canal that is below His Throne is a light that brightens it up. On both edges of the canal there are two created spirits. One is the Holy Spirit and the other is the Spirit from His command. Allah has ten (kinds) of clay; five from paradise and five from earth.' He then explained the earth and the paradise. Then he said, 'There is no prophet or angel that He has formed (Jabala) but that He has blown into them from one of those spirits. He has formed the Prophet, *'Alayhi al-Salam*, from one of those clays.'"I asked abu al-Hassan, the 1ª, 'What is *Jablu*?' He said, 'It is the creatures exclusive of us *Ahl al-Bayt* (family of Prophet Muhammad). Allah, the Most Majestic, the Most Gracious, has created us from ten clays and has blown into us from both the Spirits and has added fragrance to fragrance.'"

"Others have narrated from abu al-Samit who has said the following: "He said, 'Clay of paradise is the paradise of Eden, Jannat al-Ma'wa, Jannat al-Na'im, Firdaws and al-Khuld. The clay from earth is from Makkah, al-Madina, al-Kufa, Bayt al-Maqdis and al-Ha'ir.'"

H 1007, Ch. 94, h 4
A number of our people have narrated from Ahmad ibn Muhammad from Muhammad ibn Khalid from abu Nahshal who has said that Muhammad ibn 'Isma'il narrated to me from abu Hamza al-Thumali who has said the following:

"I heard abu Ja'far, *'Alayhi al-Salam*, say, 'Allah has created us from *A 'la 'Illiyin* (above the high above). He has created the hearts of our Shi'a from what He has created us and He has created their bodies from below that, thus, their hearts incline toward us; they are created of that from which we are created.' Then he recited this verse of the Holy Quran, 'However, the records of the deeds of the virtuous ones will certainly be in *'illiyin* (83:18). Would that you had known what *'illiyin* is! (83:19) It is a comprehensive Book (of records) (83:20). The ones nearest to Allah will bring it to public.' (83:21) Our enemies are created from *Sijjin* and the hearts of their followers are created of that from which they are created and their bodies are created from below that, thus, their hearts incline to them; they are created of that from which they are created.' Then he recited this verse of the Holy Quran. 'Let them know that the records of the sinner's deeds are in *Sijjin* (83:7). If only you had known what *Sijjin* is! (83:8). It is a comprehensive Book (of records).'" (83:9)

Chapter 95 - Submission and the Excellence of the Muslims

H 1008, Ch. 95, h 1
A number of our people have narrated from Ahmad ibn Muhammad ibn 'Isa from ibn Sinan from ibn Muskan from Sadir who has said the following:

"Once I said to abu Ja'far, *'Alayhi al-Salam*, 'I just left your supporters and followers opposing and scorning each other.' The narrator has said that the Imam then asked, 'What do you have to do with their conditions? People have three obligations. They must recognize the *'A'immah* (Leaders with Divine Authority), submit to the instructions they have received from the *'A'immah, 'Alayhim al-Salam*, and refer to them in their disputes and differences.'"

H 1009, Ch. 95, h 2
A number of our people have narrated from Ahmad ibn Muhammad al-Barqi from Ahmad ibn Muhammad ibn abu Nasr from Hammad ibn 'Uthman from 'Abd Allah al-Kahili who has said the following:

"Abu 'Abd Allah, *'Alayhi al-Salam*, has said, 'If a people worship only Allah, Who has no partner, maintain the prayers, pay *Zakat*, perform Hajj of the House and fast in the month of Ramadan but speak of something that Allah or the Messenger of Allah has done, "Would that it had been done differently", or find such feelings in their hearts, in this they will be considered as polytheists.' He then recited this verse of the Holy Quran: 'I swear by your Lord that they will not be considered believers until they let you judge their disputes and then they will find nothing in their souls to prevent them from accepting your judgment, thus, submit themselves to the will of Allah.' (4:65) Abu 'Abd Allah, *'Alayhi al-Salam*, then said, 'You have to be submissive (before Allah).'"

H 1010, Ch. 95, h 3

Muhammad ibn Yahya has narrated from Ahmad ibn Muhammad from al-Husayn ibn Sa'id from Hammad ibn 'Isa from al-Husayn ibn al-Mukhtar from Zayd al-Shahham who has said the following:

"Once I said to abu 'Abd Allah, *'Alayhi al-Salam*, 'Among us there is a man called Kulayb. Nothing comes from you but that he says, "I submit to it." Thus, we call him, "Kulayb, the submissive." The narrator has said that the Imam expressed kindness toward him and prayed and then asked, 'Do you know what submission is?' We remained silent. The Imam said, 'That, by Allah, is *al-Ikhbat* in the words of Allah, the Most Majestic, the Most Gracious, "The righteously striving believers who are submissive before their Lord, will be the dwellers of paradise wherein they will live forever.'" (11:23)

H 1011, Ch. 95, h 4

Al-Husayn ibn Muhammad has narrated from Mu'alla ibn Muhammad from al-Washsha' from Aban from Muhammad ibn Muslim who has said the following:

"About the words of Allah, the Most Holy, the Most High, 'Whoever achieves virtue We will increase for him its merit. . . .' (42:23) abu Ja'far, *'Alayhi al-Salam*, has said, 'Achievement refers to one's submission to us, his speaking the truth from us and not to ascribe any lies to us.'"

H 1012, Ch. 95, h 5

Ali ibn Muhammad ibn 'Abd Allah has narrated from Ahmad ibn Muhammad al-Barqi from his father from Muhammad ibn 'Abd al-Hamid from Mansur ibn Yunus from Bashir al-Dahhan from Kamil al-Tammar who has said the following:

"Abu Ja'far, *'Alayhi al-Salam*, has said about the words of Allah: 'Triumphant indeed are the believers.' (23:1) 'Do you know who the "Triumphants" are?' I said, 'You know best.' He said, 'Triumphant indeed are the believers, who are Muslims (submissive to Allah). The Muslims are noble people. The believers are rare. Best wishes for the believers.'"

H 1013, Ch. 95, h 6

Ali ibn Muhammad has narrated from certain person of our people from al-Khashshab from al-'Abbass ibn 'Amir from Rabi' al-Musalli from Yahya ibn Zakariya al-Ansari who has said the following:

"I heard abu 'Abd Allah, *'Alayhi al-Salam*, say, 'Whoever loves to have a complete belief must say, "Everything that I say is from the family of Muhammad, *'Alayhi al-Salam*, whatever they kept secret or made public, whatever has reached me from them and that has not reached me.'"

H 1014, Ch. 95, h 7

Ali ibn Ibrahim has narrated from his father from ibn abu 'Umayr from ibn 'Udhayna from Zurara or Burayd who has said the following:

"Abu Ja'far, *'Alayhi al-Salam*, has said, 'Allah has, indeed, addressed Amir al-Mu'minin Ali, *'Alayhi al-Salam*, in His book.' I (the narrator) then asked him, 'Where and in which passage?' He said, 'It is in His words that read, "If they ever do injustice to themselves and come to you (Muhammad) asking for Allah's forgiveness, if the Messenger also was to ask Allah to forgive them, they would certainly find Allah All-forgiving and All-merciful." (4:64) "I swear by your Lord that they will not be considered believers until they allow you to judge their disputes [on the issue of their forming a pact not to allow the leadership pass to the descendents of Hashim after Muhammad, *'Alayhi al-Salam*]. And then find nothing in their souls to prevent them from accepting your judgment, [whether you condemn or forgive them] thus, submitting themselves to the will of Allah.'" (4:65)

H 1015, Ch. 95, h 8

Ahmad ibn Mihran (may Allah grant him blessings) has narrated from 'Abd al-'Azim al-Hassani from Ali ibn Asbat from Ali ibn 'Aqaba from al-Hakam ibn Ayman from abu Basir who has said the following:

"Once I asked abu 'Abd Allah, *'Alayhi al-Salam*, about the words of Allah, the Most Majestic, the Most Gracious: '. . . those of Our servants who listen to the words and follow only the best ones. . . .' (39:18) The Imam said, 'They are those who are submissive to the (commands of) *Ahl al-Bayt* of Muhammad, *'Alayhim al-Salam*. It is they who when hearing a *Hadith* do not add anything thereto or omit anything therefrom. They present it just as they have heard.'"

Chapter 96 - People's Obligation After Hajj to Meet the Imam, Ask Him Religious Instructions, Declare and Pledge Him Allegiance and Express Their Love

H 1016, Ch. 96, h 1

Ali ibn Ibrahim has narrated from his father from ibn abu 'Umayr from ibn 'Udhayna from Fudayl who has said the following:

"Abu Ja'far, *'Alayhi al-Salam*, looked at the people perform *Tawaf* (walking around the Ka'ba seven times) and said, 'This is how they used to perform *Tawaf* in the times of ignorance (pre-Islamic era). What they are required to do is to perform *Tawaf* and come to us, declare their belief in our *Wilayah* (Leadership with Divine Authority), their love for us and express their support for us.' The Imam then recited this verse of the Holy Quran:. 'Lord, fill the hearts of the people with love for them. . . .'" (14:37)

H 1017, Ch. 96, h 2

Al-Husayn ibn Muhammad has narrated from Mu'alla ibn Muhammad from Ali ibn Asbat from Dawud ibn al-Nu'man from abu 'Ubayda who has said the following:

"I heard abu Ja'far *'Alayhi al-Salam*, say, when he saw people in Makkah and what they were doing, 'Activities like those in the days of ignorance. By Allah, they are not commanded to do as such. What they are commanded to do is to complete their Hajj, relieve themselves of the obligations of vows and visit us to inform us of their belief (in our Leadership with Divine Authority) and express their support for us.'"

H 1018, Ch. 96, h 3

Ali ibn Ibrahim has narrated from Salih ibn al-Sindi from Ja'far ibn Bashir and Muhammad ibn Yahya from Ahmad ibn Muhammad ibn 'Isa from ibn al-Faddal all from abu Jamila from Khalid ibn 'Ammar from Sadir who has said the following:

"I heard abu Ja'far, *'Alayhi al-Salam*, - when he was coming in and I was going out, held my hand, then turned to *al-Bayt* (the House), and say, 'O Sadir, what people are, in fact, commanded to do is to come to these stones, perform *Tawaf* around them (walk seven times around) then come to us and declare before us their belief (in our Leadership with Divine Authority). That is what Allah has said, ". . . I am All-forgiving to the righteously striving believers who repent and follow the right guidance."' (20:82) Then he pointed his hand to his chest saying, 'To our Leadership with Divine Authority'. Then he said, 'O Sadir, do you want me to show you who creates obstacles on the way of Allah?' Then he looked at abu Hanifa and Sufyan al-Thawri. At that time they had a circle of people around them in the Mosque. He then said, 'These are the ones who create obstacles on the way of Allah without guidance from Allah and a clear book. It will be very good if these malignant ones sit in their homes. When people search around and do not find anyone to inform them of the guidance of Allah, the Most Holy, the Most High, and His Messenger, they come to us and we inform them of the guidance of Allah, the Most Holy, the Most High, and His messenger.'"

Chapter 97 - The Angels Come to the Houses of 'A'immah (Leaders with Divine Authority), Step on Their Furnishings and Bring Them News

H 1019, Ch. 97, h 1

A number of our people have narrated from Ahmad ibn Muhammad from ibn Sinan from Misma' Kirdin al-Basri who has said the following:

"I used to eat one meal in twenty four hours. Sometimes I would ask permission to see abu 'Abd Allah, *'Alayhi al-Salam*, at such time that I expected their tablecloth to be collected, so that perhaps I might not see (any food) before them (and they have finished their meal). Upon my arrival he would ask to return the tablecloth. The food in it would not harm me. If, however, I ate with others again I could not do so and it would become very difficult for me to sleep because of gases. I complained about it before the Imam and said that were I to eat from his (Imam's) table it would not harm me. He said, 'O abu Sayyar, it is because you eat from the table of the virtuous people. Angels shake hands (sit along) with them on their furnishings.' I (the narrator) then asked, 'Do they (angels) appear to you?' He has said, 'The Imam wiped his hand over one of his children and said, 'They are more kind to our children than we are.'"

H 1020, Ch. 97, h 2

Muhammad ibn Yahya has narrated from Ahmad ibn Muhammad from Muhammad ibn Khalid from Muhammad ibn al-Qasim from al-Husayn ibn abu al-'Ala' who has said the following:

"Once Abu 'Abd Allah, *'Alayhi al-Salam*, said, 'O Husayn,' tapping his hand on a cushion in the house, said, 'These are cushions on which so often angels lean and perhaps we pick up parts of their fluff around.'"

H 1021, Ch. 97, h 3

Muhammad has narrated from Ahmad ibn Muhammad from Ali ibn al-Hakam who has said that Malik ibn 'Atiyya al-Ahmasi narrated to him from abu Hamza al-Thumali who has said the following:

"Once I went to see Ali ibn al-Husayn, *'Alayhi al-Salam*, and I was confined in the room for an hour, then I went inside the house while he was picking up things and giving to someone behind the curtain. I then asked, 'May Allah keep my soul in service for your cause, what was that thing that I saw you picking up?' The Imam said, 'The fluff from the angels when they come to meet us and we use it to amuse our children.' I then said, 'May Allah keep my soul in service for your cause, do they come to you?' The Imam said, 'O abu Hamza, they form a crowd over our furnishings.'"

H 1022, Ch. 97, h 4

Muhammad has narrated from Muhammad ibn al-Hassan from Muhammad ibn Aslama from Ali ibn abu Hamza who has said the following:

"I heard abu al-Hassan, *'Alayhi al-Salam*, say, 'Every angel that Allah sends down for a task, that angel first begins with meeting the Imam to present the task to him. The presence of Imam, Leader with Divine Authority, is the scene of a great mix of the angels from Allah, the Most Holy, the Most High.'"

Chapter 98 - The Jinns Come to the Imam for Religious Instructions and for Settling Their Affairs

H 1023, Ch. 98, h 1

Certain persons of our people have narrated from Muhammad ibn Ali from Yahya ibn Musawir from Sa'd al-Askaf who has said the following:

"On one of the occasions of my meeting with abu Ja'far, *'Alayhi al-Salam*, when I went to see him he asked me to wait. I waited until the sun became very hot on me. I tried to follow the shadow for cover against the sun. Not very long thereafter a people came out of his presence that looked like locusts dressed in large gowns and very pale and slim due to extensive worshipping. Their beautiful scene made me forget my trouble. When I went in the presence of the Imam he said, 'I am afraid I caused you hardships.' I said, 'Yes, it was difficult but, by Allah, I forgot other things when I saw them. A people passed by, the like of whose beauty I had not seen before. They looked like locusts and pale and slim due to worshipping a great deal.'

"The Imam said, 'O Sa'd, did you see them?' I said, 'Yes, I saw them.' The Imam said, 'They are your brethren from Jinns.' I (the narrator) asked the Imam, 'Do they come to you?' He said, 'Yes, they come to us for religious instructions and to learn the lawful and unlawful matters.'"

H 1024, Ch. 98, h 2

Ali ibn Muhammad has narrated from Sahl ibn Ziyad from Ali ibn Hassa'n from Ibrahim ibn 'Isma'il from ibn Jabal who has said the following:

"Once we were in front of the door of the house of abu 'Abd Allah, *'Alayhi al-Salam*, when a people who looked like Indian gypsies came out with loin cloth and covering on them. We asked abu 'Abd Allah, *'Alayhi al-Salam*, about them and he said, 'They were your brethren from Jinns.'"

H 1025, Ch. 98, h 3

Ahmad ibn Idris and Muhammad ibn Yahya have narrated from al-Hassan ibn Ali al-Kufiy from ibn al-Faddal from certain persons of our people from Sa'd al-Askaf who has said the following:

"Once I went to ask permission to meet abu Ja'far, *'Alayhi al-Salam*. I found saddles of camels lined up in front of the door and noises coming very loud and then a people came out with turbans like those of the Indian gypsies. I asked abu Ja'far, *'Alayhi al-Salam*, about them and said, 'May Allah keep my soul in service for your cause; today it took a long time to receive permission to meet you. I saw a people coming out with turbans whom I could not recognize.' He asked, 'Do you know, O Sa'd, who they were?' I said, 'No, I do not know.' The Imam said, 'They were your brethren in religion from Jinns. They come to us for religious instructions, to learn the lawful and unlawful matters and the principles of their religion.'"

H 1026, Ch. 98, h 4

Muhammad ibn Yahya has narrated from Muhammad ibn al-Husayn from Ibrahim ibn abu al-Balad from Sadir al-Sayrafi, who has said the following:

"Abu Ja'far, *'Alayhi al-Salam*, asked me to help him in a few things in Madina. I left and when I reached Fajj al-Rawha' (name of a place) a man waved to me with his clothes. I (the narrator) turned to him and thought he was thirsty. I offered the cup but he declined saying, 'I do not need it.' He gave me a letter with its ink still not dried up. When I (the narrator) looked at it, it had the insignia of abu Ja'far, *'Alayhi al-Salam*, on it. I asked him, 'When were you in the presence of abu Ja'far, *'Alayhi al-Salam*?' He said, 'Just now I was in his presence.' In the letter there were a few things that he had commanded me to do. When I looked around there was no one with me.'

"I (the narrator) then went to meet abu Ja'far, *'Alayhi al-Salam*, and said, 'May Allah keep my soul in service for your cause, a man came to me with your letter the ink of which was not yet dried up.' He said, 'O Sadir, we have servants from Jinns. When we need a thing to happen quickly we send them to do it.'" In another Hadith it says, 'The Imam said, "Among Jinn we have followers just as we have followers among man. When we want something we send for them.'"

H 1027, Ch. 98, h 5

Ali ibn Muhammad and Muhammad ibn al-Hassan have narrated from Sahl ibn Ziyad from the person whom he mentioned from Muhammad ibn Jahrash who has said that Hakima daughter of Musa, *'Alayhi al-Salam*, has said the following:

"Once I saw al-Rida, *'Alayhi al-Salam*, standing at the door of the firewood room and he was whispering but I did not see anyone else around. I then asked him, 'My master, who are you talking to?' He said, 'This is 'Amir al-Zahra'i. He has come to ask a few questions and he has certain complaints.' I then asked, 'My master, I want to hear his words.' He said, 'If you heard his words you might have fever for one year.' I said, 'My master, I want to hear him.' He said, 'All right, then listen.' I listened and I heard something like a whistle. I then suffered from a fever for one whole year.'"

H 1028, Ch. 98, h 6

Muhammad ibn Yahya and Ahmad ibn Muhammad have narrated from Muhammad ibn al-Hassan from Ibrahim ibn Hashim from 'Amr ibn 'Uthman from Ibrahim ibn Ayyub from 'Amr ibn Shimr from Jabir from abu Ja'far, *'Alayhi al-Salam*, who has said the following:

"Once when Amir al-Mu'minin Ali, *'Alayhi al-Salam*, was on the pulpit, a serpent entered from one of the doors of the mosque. People wanted to kill him. Amir al-Mu'minin, *'Alayhi al-Salam*, asked them to leave him alone. They left him alone. The serpent began to crawl to the pulpit. He stretched and saluted Amir al-Mu'minin, *'Alayhi al-Salam*. Amir al-Mu'minin, *'Alayhi al-Salam*, made a gesture to him to wait until the sermon was completed. When the sermon was completed he came to him and asked, 'Who are you?' He said, 'I am 'Amr ibn 'Uthman, your deputy among the Jinns. My father has died and he has asked me in his will to come to you and find out your instructions and that is why I am here. What do you command me to do and what do you instruct me to do?' Amir al-Mu'minin, *'Alayhi al-Salam*, said, 'I ask you to be pious before Allah and go back and act as the successor of your father among the Jinns. I appoint you as my deputy over them.'

"The narrator has said that 'Amr then said farewell to the Imam Ali, *'Alayhi al-Salam*, and left ('Amr) as his deputy over the Jinns. I asked the Imam, 'May Allah keep my soul in service for your cause, does 'Amr come to you and fulfill that obligation on him?' He said, 'Yes, he does so.'"

H 1029, Ch. 98, h 7

Ali ibn Muhammad has narrated from Salih ibn abu Hammad from Muhammad ibn 'Urma from Ahmad ibn al-Nadr from al-Nu'man ibn Bashir who has said the following:

"Once I was a companion of Jabir ibn Yazid al-Ju'fi on a journey. When we reached the city, Madina, he went to meet abu Ja'far, *'Alayhi al-Salam*. He said farewell to him and came out very happily until we arrived in al-'Ukhayraja, the first length of one day's journey from Fayd to Madina. It was a Friday. We said our prayers at noon. When the camel rose to leave I saw a tall brownish man with a letter. He gave it to Jabir who kissed it and placed it over his eyes. It was from Muhammad ibn Ali, *'Alayhi al-Salam*, to Jabir ibn Yazid. It had black ink that was still wet. He asked him, 'When were you in the presence of my master?' He said, 'Just now.' He asked, 'Were you in his presence before or after the prayer?' He said, 'I was there after the prayer.' He then opened the seal and began to read the letter and his face began to look strained until he read it to the end. He held the letter and I did not see him laughing or happy until we arrived in Kufa. In Kufa I spent my night; and in the morning I went to see him out of respect for him and I found him coming out to me with a large ring made of anklebones around his neck riding on a twig of reeds saying, 'I see Mansur ibn Jumhur, a ruler, but no one obeys him' and such other rhymes. He looked at me and I looked at him and he did not say anything to me and I did not say anything to him. I began to weep when I saw him. Children, and people gathered around us. He came in al-Rahba and went in circles with the children and people said, 'Jabir has gone mad, Jabir has become insane.' By Allah, only a few days had passed when a letter from Hisham ibn 'Abd al-Malik came to the governor to look for a man called Jabir ibn Yazid al-Ju'fi. It said, 'Kill him and send his head to me.'

"The governor turned to the people in his court and asked, 'Who is this Jabir ibn Yazid al-Ju'fi?' They replied, 'May Allah grant well-being to the governor, he was a man of knowledge, excellence, *Hadith* and Hajj, but now he has become insane. He is there with the children riding on a twig of reeds. He plays with them.' He went to see him and found him playing with the children while riding a twig of reeds. He said, 'Thanks to Allah for saving me from killing him.' The narrator has said that within just few days Mansur ibn Jumhur entered Kufa and did what Jabir was speaking of before.'"

Chapter 99 - Every Imam, *'Alayhi al-Salam*, Judges Like David, Peace Be Upon Him, Did

When 'A'immah, *'Alayhim al-Salam*, will rise with Divine Authority they will judge among people as David, peace be upon him, and his people had done: they will not ask any witness to testify

H 1030, Ch. 99, h 1
Ali ibn Ibrahim has narrated from his father from ibn abu'Umayr from Mansur from al-Fadl al-A'war from abu 'Ubayda al-Hadhdha' who has said the following:
"We lived during the times of abu Ja'far, *'Alayhi al-Salam*. When he passed away we were left like sheep without a shepherd. We met Salim ibn abu Hafs and he said to me, 'O abu 'Ubayda, who is your Imam?' I said, 'My *'A'immah* (Leaders with Divine Authority) are the *Ahl al-Bayt* (family) of Muhammad, *'Alayhi al-Salam*.' He said, 'You are destroyed and have destroyed. Did you and I not hear abu Ja'far, *'Alayhi al-Salam*, say, 'Whoever dies without an Imam above him has died as the death of the age of ignorance?' I said, 'Yes, that is very true. I can swear by my own life.' It was only about three days before my meeting with abu 'Abd Allah, *'Alayhi al-Salam*, in which meeting Allah granted to me the blessing to recognize him as my Imam. I said to abu 'Abd Allah, *'Alayhi al-Salam*, 'Salim said to me so and so.'

"The Imam said, 'O abu 'Ubayda, no one of us passes away before appointing a successor that acts and behaves just as the preceding Imam and calls people to what the Imam before him did. O abu 'Ubayda, what was given to David did not bar Sulayman from receiving (Allah's blessings).' Then he said, 'O abu 'Ubayda, when *Al-Qa'im* (the one who will rise with Divine Authority and power) will rise he will judge among people the way David and Sulayman (Solomon) had been judging among people. He will not call any witness to testify in a case.'"

H 1031, Ch. 99, h 2
Muhammad ibn Yahya has narrated from Ahmad ibn Muhammad from Muhammad ibn Sinan from Aban from abu 'Abd Allah, *'Alayhi al-Salam*, who has said the following:

"The world will not end before the rise of a man from us who will judge among people the way the family of David had been judging them. He will not ask any witness to testify. He will make every soul enjoy exercising its rights."

H 1032, Ch. 99, h 3

Muhammad has narrated from Ahmad ibn Muhammad from ibn Mahbub from Hisham ibn Salim from 'Ammar al-Sabati who has said the following:

"Once I asked abu 'Abd Allah, *'Alayhi al-Salam*, 'By what means do you judge when you judge?' He said, 'We judge by the laws of Allah and in the manner of David. If a case comes before us to which there is no solution with us, the Holy Spirit provides us inspiration.'"

H 1033, Ch. 99, h 4

Muhammad ibn Ahmad has narrated from Muhammad ibn Khalid from al-Nadr ibn Suwayd from Yahya al-Halabi from 'Imran ibn A'yan from Ju'ayd al-Hamadani who has said the following:

"Once I asked Ali ibn al-Husayn, *'Alayhi al-Salam*, 'On what basis do you issue judgments?' The Imam said, 'We judge by the laws of Allah and the judgment of the family of David. If a case frustrates us the Holy Spirit inspires us with its laws.'"

H 1034, Ch. 99, h 5

Ahmad ibn Mihran, may Allah grant him blessings, has narrated from Muhammad ibn Ali from ibn Mahbub from Hisham ibn Salim from 'Ammar al-Sabati who has said the following:

"Once I asked abu 'Abd Allah, *'Alayhi al-Salam*, 'What is the degree of the excellence of *'A'immah* (Leaders with Divine Authority)?' He said, 'It is like that of Dhu al-Qarnayn and like that of Yusha' and like that of Asaf, the companion of Sulayman (Solomon).' I asked, 'On what basis do you issue judgments?' The Imam said, 'We issue judgments according to the laws of Allah, the judgments of the family of David and according to the judgment of Muhammad, *'Alayhi al-Salam*. The Holy Spirit inspires us with it.'"

Chapter 100 - The Fountainhead of Knowledge is A'le Muhammad, *'Alayhi al-Salam*

H 1035, Ch. 100, h 1

A number of our people have narrated from Ahmad ibn Muhammad from ibn Mahbub who has said that Yahya ibn 'Abd Allah, abu al-Hassan the companion of al-Daylam narrated to us and has said the following:

"Once I heard Ja'far ibn Muhammad, *'Alayhi al-Salam*, say, while a group of people of Kufa was present before him, 'People are very strange. They have received their knowledge from the Messenger of Allah. They have followed such knowledge and found guidance but they think that his *Ahl al-Bayt* (family) have not received his knowledge. We are his *Ahl al-Bayt* and his descendents. In our house Divine inspiration came down and from us knowledge came out to them. Do they think that they have learned and found guidance but we remained ignorant and lost? This, certainly, is not possible.'"

H 1036, Ch. 100, h 2

Ali ibn Muhammad ibn 'Abd Allah has narrated from Ibrahim ibn Ishaq al-Ahmar from 'Abd Allah ibn Hammad from Sabbah al-Muzanni from al-Harith ibn Husayra from al-Hakam ibn 'Utayba who has said the following:

"A man met al-Husayn ibn Ali, *'Alayhi al-Salam*, at al-Tha'laba, on his way to Karbala, Iraq. He came in his presence and offered greetings of peace to him. Al-Husayn, *'Alayhi al-Salam*, asked, 'Where are you from?' He replied, 'I am from Kufa.' The Imam said, 'By Allah, O brethren from Kufa, if only I had a meeting with you in Madina, I could have shown you the marks of Jibril in and around our house and his coming with Divine message to my grandfather. O brethren from Kufa, how can it be true that we are the ones to make people quench their thirst from our knowledge and they learn, but we remain ignorant? This is of the things that cannot happen.'"

Chapter 101 - The 'A'immah (Leaders with Divine Authority), *'Alayhim al-Salam*, Are the Source of the Law and Guidance

There is nothing true with people unless it has come from 'A'immah, *'Alayhim al-Salam*, and whatever has not come from them is false

H 1037, Ch. 101, h 1

Ali ibn Ibrahim ibn Hashim has narrated from Muhammad ibn 'Isa from Yunus from ibn Muskan from Muhammad ibn Muslim who has said the following:

"I heard abu Ja'far, *'Alayhi al-Salam*, say, 'No one of the people has anything true with him, or correct, nor does anyone of the people judge with truth except by means of what is made available from *Ahl al-Bayt* (family of Prophet Muhammad, *'Alayhi al-Salam*). When the affairs grew branches and scattered chaotically, the mistake was from them and the correct solution from Ali, *'Alayhi al-Salam*.'"

H 1038, Ch. 101, h 2

A number of our people have narrated from Ahmad ibn Muhammad from ibn abu Nasr from Muthanna from Zurara who has said the following:

"Once I was in the presence of abu Ja'far, *'Alayhi al-Salam*. A man from Kufa asked him about the words of Amir al-Mu'minin Ali, *'Alayhi al-Salam*: 'Ask me whatever you like. I will give you the answer to whatever you ask.' The Imam said, 'No one has any piece of knowledge of anything that has not come through Amir al-Mu'minin Ali, *'Alayhi al-Salam*. People may go wherever they may like, however, by Allah, the truth comes from nowhere else except from here,' he pointed out with his hand toward his house.'"

H 1039, Ch. 101, h 3

A number of our people have narrated from Ahmad ibn Muhammad from al-Washsha' from Tha'laba ibn Maymun from ibn abu Maryam who has said the following:

"Abu Ja'far, *'Alayhi al-Salam*, said to Salama ibn Kuhayl and al-Hakam ibn 'Utayba, 'Easternize or westernize, you two will not find correct knowledge except that which has come to light through *Ahl al-Bayt* (the family of Prophet Muhammad, *'Alayhim al-Salam*).'"

H 1040, Ch. 101, h 4

Muhammad ibn Yahya has narrated from Ahmad ibn Muhammad from al-Husayn ibn Sa'id from al-Nadr ibn Suwayd from Yahya al-Halabi from Mu'alla ibn 'Uthman who has said the following:

"Once abu Basir said to me, 'Al-Hakam ibn 'Utayba is of those people about whom Allah has said, "Certain people say, 'We believe in Allah and the Day of Judgment, but they are not true believers.'" (2:8) 'Al-Hakam may easternize or westernize; he, by Allah, will not find the true knowledge in any other source except *Ahl al-Bayt* to whom Jibril comes (with knowledge).'"

H 1041, Ch. 101, h 5

Ali ibn Ibrahim has narrated from Salih ibn al-Sindi from Ja'far ibn Bashir from Aban ibn 'Uthman from abu Basir who has said the following:

"I asked abu Ja'far, *'Alayhi al-Salam*, about the admissibility of the testimony of a person born out of wedlock. He said, 'No, it is not admissible.' I then said, 'Al-Hakam ibn 'Utayba believes it is admissible.' The Imam said, 'O Lord, do not forgive his sin. Allah has not said to al-Hakam, "It (the Holy Quran) is a reminder to you and to your people. . . ." (43:44) Al-Hakam may go right or left, by Allah, the knowledge worthwhile to learn comes only from *Ahl al-Bayt* (the members of the family of Prophet Muhammad, *'Alayhim al-Salam*), to whom Jibril comes down.'"

H 1042, Ch. 101, h 6

A number of our people have narrated from al-Husayn ibn al-Hassan ibn Yazid from Badr from his father who has said that Salam abu Ali al-Khurasani narrated to me from Salam ibn Sa'id al-Makhzumi who has said the following:

"Once I was in the presence of abu 'Abd Allah, *'Alayhi al-Salam*, when 'Abbad ibn Kathir, the devoted worshipper of Basra, and Shurayh, the Faqih, (scholar of law) of the people of Makkah came to see the Imam. In the presence of abu 'Abd Allah, *'Alayhi al-Salam*, already there was Maymun al-Qaddah, the slave of abu Ja'far, *'Alayhi al-Salam*. 'Abbad ibn Kathir then asked abu 'Abd Allah, *'Alayhi al-Salam*, 'O abu 'Abd Allah, how many pieces of cloth were used to shroud the Messenger of Allah, *'Alayhi al-Salam*?' The Imam said, 'Three pieces were used. Two of them were Suhari (made in Suhar, Yemen) and one Hibara (made in Hibara, Yemen). Burd (fabric made in Yemen) was rare to find.' 'Abbad seemed to frown at this (as if he did not believe in the rarity of the fabric).

"The Imam said, 'The palm tree of Mary was *'Ajwa* (a certain kind of palm tree) and it had come from the heavens. Whatever grew from its roots were also *'Ajwa* and whatever grew from pits of dates became of lower quality.' When they left the house of the Imam, 'Abbad ibn Kathir said to ibn Shurayh, 'By Allah, I did not understand the simile that abu 'Abd Allah, *'Alayhi al-Salam*, put forward to me.' Ibn Shurayh then said, 'Ask this boy (Maymun al-Qaddah). He will explain it to you because he is from them (people of the house of the Imam).' He then asked the boy and he asked, 'Is it true that you did not understand what he said to you?' He ('Abbad) said, 'Yes, by Allah, I did not understand.' The boy, Maymun al-Qaddah, then said, 'The Imam refers to his own self. He informed you that he is one of the children of the Messenger of Allah and the knowledge of the

397

Messenger of Allah is with them. Whatever knowledge comes from them is true and correct and whatever comes from other sources is not genuine.'"

Chapter 102 - The Ahadith (Statements) That Say, Ahadith of Ahl al-Bayt (Members of the Family of Prophet Muhammad) Are Difficult, and They Become Difficult

H 1043, Ch. 102, h 1
Muhammad ibn Yahya has narrated from Muhammad ibn al-Husayn from Muhammad ibn Sinan from 'Ammar ibn Marwan from Jabir who has said the following:

"Abu Ja'far, *'Alayhi al-Salam*, has said that the Messenger of Allah has said, '*Hadith* (statement) of *Ahl al-Bayt* (the family of Prophet Muhammad, *'Alayhi al-Salam*) are difficult and they become difficult. No one believes in them except the angels who are close to Allah or the Prophets, who are Messengers also, and a servant of Allah whose heart Allah has tested for faith. Whatever comes to you of *Hadith* (statement) of *Ahl al-Bayt* of Muhammad, *'Alayhi al-Salam*, if your heart feels relief and you recognized them accept them. Whatever causes antipathy in your hearts and you cannot recognize, leave them to Allah, to the Messenger of Allah and the scholar from *Ahl al-Bayt* of Muhammad, *'Alayhi al-Salam*. The ones to perish are those who do not accept *Hadith* of *Ahl al-Bayt, 'Alayhim al-Salam*. Whenever one is narrated to them they say, "By Allah, this was not and that was not." Denial is disbelief.'"

H 1044, Ch. 102, h 2
Ahmad ibn 'Idris has narrated from 'Imran ibn Musa from Harun ibn Muslim from Mas'ada ibn Sadaqa who has said the following:

"Once I said to abu 'Abd Allah, *'Alayhi al-Salam*, that I one day spoke of *Taqiya* (hiding something for fear) before Ali ibn al-Husayn, *'Alayhi al-Salam*. He said, 'By Allah, if abu Dhar knew what was in the heart of Salman he would have killed him even though the Messenger of Allah had established brotherhood between them. What then do you think of the rest of the people? The knowledge of the scholars is difficult and it becomes difficult. No one is capable of bearing it except a prophet who is a messenger also, or an angel who is close to Allah, or a believer whose heart Allah has tested for belief.' The Imam then said, 'The only reason that Salman became of the scholars is that he is a man from us (*Ahl al-Bayt*). For this reason I ascribed him to the scholars.'"

H 1045, Ch. 102, h 3
Ali ibn Ibrahim has narrated from his father from al-Barqi from ibn Sinan or others in a *marfu'* manner from abu 'Abd Allah, *'Alayhi al-Salam*, who has said the following:

"Our *Ahadith* (statements) are difficult and they become difficult. Only well-brightened chests, the well-protected hearts or virtuous moral abilities are able to accept them. Allah has taken a pledge from our Shi'a (followers) just as He has taken such pledge from the children of Adam, 'Am I not Your Lord?' Whoever remains loyal to us, Allah will grant paradise. Whoever dislikes us and does not deliver our rights to us will live in fire forever."

H 1046, Ch. 102, h 4

Muhammad ibn Yahya and others have narrated from Muhammad ibn Ahmad from one of our people the following:

"Once I wrote to Imam al-Hassan al-'Askari, *'Alayhi al-Salam*, asking, 'May Allah keep my soul in service for your cause, what is the meaning of the following *Hadith* of Imam Ja'far al-Sadiq, *'Alayhi al-Salam*: 'Our *Hadith* (statements) are difficult and they become difficult. No one is capable of bearing them, not even an angel or a prophet who is also a messenger, or a believer whose heart Allah has tested for belief'? The answer came as follows, 'The meaning of the words of the truthful one, "No angel, prophet or any believer is capable of bearing," is that the angel is not able to wait without disclosing such knowledge before another angel. A prophet does not bear it" means that he is not able to wait without allowing it out before another prophet. The "believer does not bear it" means that he is not able to wait to tell another believer about it. This is the meaning of the words of my grandfather.'"

H 1047, Ch. 102, h 5

Ahmad ibn Muhammad has narrated from Muhammad ibn al-Husayn from Mansur ibn al-'Abbass from Safwan ibn Yahya from 'Abd Allah ibn Muskan from Muhammad ibn 'Abd al-Khaliq and abu Basir who has said the following:

"Once abu 'Abd Allah, *'Alayhi al-Salam*, said, 'O abu Muhammad, with us there is a secret of the secrets of Allah and a knowledge of the knowledge of Allah. No angel near to Allah or a prophet who is a messenger also, and no believer whose heart Allah has tested for belief is capable of keeping them. By Allah, Allah has not required anyone to bear it except us, nor has He required anyone to worship Him in that way except us. With us there is a secret of the secrets of Allah and knowledge of the knowledge of Allah. Allah has commanded us to preach it. We then preached what Allah, the Most Majestic, the Most Gracious, had commanded us to preach. However, we did not find a proper place for it or a people or bearers who could accept it until Allah created certain tribes. These people were created from the clay out of which Muhammad, *'Alayhi al-Salam*, and his descendents were created and from a light from which Allah had created Muhammad, *'Alayhi al-Salam*, and his descendents. He made them from the excess of His blessings out of which He had made Muhammad, *'Alayhi al-Salam*, and his descendents. We then preached what Allah had commanded us to preach and these people then accepted and acknowledged it [it reached them from us and they accepted and acknowledged it]. Our mention reached them and their hearts inclined toward us. They recognized our *Hadith* and our selves. Had they not been created from this they would not have been such. No, by Allah, they were not to acknowledge.'

"Then the Imam said, 'Allah created certain tribes for hell and fire. He then commanded us to preach to them as we had preached to those, but to them it seemed repugnant and their hearts felt hatred and they rejected it from us, did not acknowledge it and considered it as lies and they said, "Magicians and liars." Allah then placed a seal on their hearts and made them to forget. Allah then opened their tongue with certain items of the truth. Thus, they speak of it but their hearts are in denial. He uses it in defense of His friends and those who obey Him. Had it (such defense) not been there, no one would have worshipped Allah on earth. He commanded us to withhold it from them, hide and conceal. You must also hide it from those Allah has commanded to withhold from and hide from those Allah has commanded to hide and keep back from.'

"The Imam then raised his hands and wept and said, 'O Lord, this is a very small group. Make our way of living their way of living and our manner of death their manner of death. Do not make dominant over them any of Your enemies that might cause us to suffer pain for their suffering. If You allow it to cause pain to us because of their suffering no one will ever worship You on earth. May Allah send blessing upon Muhammad, *'Alayhi al-Salam*, and his *Ahl al-Bayt* and may (Your) peace and more peace be with them.'"

Chapter 103 - The Commands of the Holy Prophet to Wish Well for the Imam, *'Alayhi al-Salam*, of Muslims of One's Time, Remain Close to Their Group and Find Out Who They Are

Note: in the following passages what is inside brackets are the words of the Imam and the rest are the words of the Holy Quran.

H 1048, Ch. 103, h 1

A number of our people have narrated from Ahmad ibn Muhammad ibn 'Isa from Ahmad ibn Muhammad ibn abu Nasr from Aban ibn 'Uthman from ibn abu Ya'fur from abu 'Abd Allah, *'Alayhi al-Salam*, who has said the following:

"Once the Messenger of Allah addressed people in the mosque of Khif and said, 'May Allah grant joy and happiness to those of His servants who on hearing my words understand them, memorize them and preach them to those who have not heard them. There can be such bearers of *Fiqh* (law) who do not have understanding. There can be many carriers of *Fiqh* to those who have better understanding of *Fiqh* than the carrier. There are three things in which the heart of a Muslim does not feel greed and treachery: Sincerity in deeds for Allah, wishing well for the leaders of the Muslims and to stay close to the group of the Muslims; their prayer encompasses those behind them also and the Muslims are each other's brothers. Their lives equally match each other's lives and the least important among them strive to fulfill their responsibilities.'"

Hammad ibn 'Uthman from Aban from ibn abu Ya'fur has narrated a similar *Hadith* with an addition of "They are as one hand to face their enemies."

In his *Hadith* he has mentioned that the Holy Prophet, *'Alayhi al-Salam*, made his speech during his farewell pilgrimage in the mosque of Khif (a place in Mina, Makkah).

H 1049, Ch. 103, h 2

Muhammad ibn al-Hassan has narrated from certain persons of our people from Ali ibn al-Hakam from Hakam ibn Miskin from a man, from Quraysh from the people of Makkah, who has said the following:

"Once Sufyan al-Thawri said to me (the man from people of Makkahh), 'Come with me to meet Ja'far ibn Muhammad, *'Alayhi al-Salam*.' I went with him and we found Ja'far ibn Muhammad, *'Alayhi al-Salam*, had already mounted his horse. Sufyan said to him, 'O abu 'Abd Allah, narrate to us the text of the sermon of the Messenger of Allah in the Mosque of al-Khif.' He said, 'Allow me to attend my appoinment; I am already on horseback and when I return, then I will narrate to you the text of the sermon.' He said, 'I swear you by your close relation to the Messenger of Allah, you must narrate the sermon first.' The narrator has said that the Imam then dismounted his horse. Sufyan said to him, 'Ask someone to bring me ink and paper so I can write it down.' He asked for ink and paper and it was brought for him. Then he said, 'Write down:

"In the name of Allah, the Beneficent, the Merciful

The sermon of the Messenger of Allah in the Mosque of al-Khif:

"May Allah grant joy and happiness to a servant who listens to my words, then understands them and delivers them to those who have not heard them. O people, those of you present here must deliver them to those absent. There can be many bearers of *Fiqh* (law) who do not have understanding, as there can be many carriers of *Fiqh* to those who have better understating of *Fiqh* than the carrier.

"There are three things in which the heart of a Muslim does not feel greed and treachery. (a) Sincerity in deeds for Allah, (b) wishing well for *'A'immah*, the leaders (with Divine Authority) of the Muslims and (c) to stay close to the group of the Muslims; their call (prayer) encompasses those behind them and the believers are each other's brothers. Their lives equally match each other's lives and they act as one hand against their enemies and the least important among them strive to fulfill their responsibilities.'"

"Sufyan wrote it down and proofread before him. Abu 'Abd Allah, *'Alayhi al-Salam*, then mounted his horse. Sufyan and I came back. Somewhere on the way he said, 'Stay where you are. I want to look at this *Hadith*.' I then said to him, 'There is no doubt, by Allah, that abu 'Abd Allah, *'Alayhi al-Salam*, has tied something to your neck as such that it will never go away.' He asked, 'What is that thing?' I then said, 'There are three things in which the heart of a Muslim does not feel greed and treachery. "Sincerity in deeds for Allah," is one that we know. The other one is "wishing well for *'A'immah*, the leaders (with Divine Authority) of the Muslims." Who are these *'A'immah* for whom we must wish well? Are they Mu'awiya ibn abu Sufyan and Yazid ibn Mu'awiya and Marwan ibn al-Hakam? (They are such disqualified people that) the testimony of no one of them is acceptable to us and it is not permissible to pray behind them. Also his words, "Stay close to their group," which group is it? Is it the Murji'a group that says, 'Those who do not perform prayers, do not fast, do not clean and wash themselves after carnal relations, cause the destruction of the Ka'ba or marry their own mother have the same degree of belief as those of angel Jibril and Mika'il.' Is it the Qadri (people believing in pre-destination) who say, 'What Allah, the Most Majestic, the Most Gracious, says will not happen but what Satan says will happen?' Is it the Harawri group who is the enemy of Ali ibn abu Talib, *'Alayhi*

401

al-Salam, and calls him an unbeliever? Is it the Jahmiy group who says that the only thing needed is only to know Allah; belief is no more than this?

"He then asked, 'Woe is you, what then they say?' I said, 'They say, "Ali ibn abu Talib, by Allah, is the Imam for whom we must wish well. It is necessary to stay close to their group means his *Ahl al-Bayt* (family of Prophet Muhammad, *'Alayhi al-Salam.*'" The narrator has said that Sufyan al-Thawri then tore the document of *Hadith* and said, 'Do not tell it to anyone.'"

H 1050, Ch. 103, h 3
Ali ibn Ibrahim has narrated from his father and Muhammad ibn Yahya from Ahmad ibn Muhammad all of them from Hammad ibn 'Isa from Hariz from Burayd ibn Mu'awiya from abu Ja'far, *'Alayhi al-Salam*, who has said the following:
"The Messenger of Allah has said, 'Allah, the Most Majestic, the Most Gracious, continues looking to a friend of His, who strives and pressures his soul in obedience to his Imam and wishes well for him until he will find himself with us in the high position in paradise.'"

H 1051, Ch. 103, h 4
A number of our people have narrated from Ahmad ibn Muhammad from ibn al-Faddal from abu Jamila from Muhammad al-Halabi from abu 'Abd Allah, *'Alayhi al-Salam*, who has said the following:
"Whoever distances himself from the company of the Muslims, even by one Shibr (foot), has removed the bond of allegiance with Islam from his neck."

H 1052, Ch. 103, h 5
Through the same chain of narrators it is narrated from abu 'Abd Allah, *'Alayhi al-Salam*, who has said the following:
"Whoever distances himself from the company of Muslims and disregards the pledge of allegiance with the Imam will come before Allah with his hand cut off."

Chapter 104 - The Mutual Rights Between the Imam, *'Alayhi al-Salam*, and His Followers

H 1053, Ch. 104, h 1
Al-Husayn ibn Muhammad has narrated from Mu'alla ibn Muhammad from Muhammad ibn Jumhur from Hammad ibn 'Uthman from abu Hamza who has said the following:
"Once I asked abu 'Abd Allah, *'Alayhi al-Salam*, 'What are the rights of the Imam over the people?' He replied, 'Of his rights over them is that they must listen to him and obey him.'

"I then asked, 'What are their rights on him?' He replied, 'Maintain equality and justice among the followers. When this prevails among the people then no one will fear who has taken this or that.'"

H 1054, Ch. 104, h 2
Muhammad ibn Yahya has narrated from Muhammad ibn al-Husayn from Muhammad ibn 'Isma'il ibn Bazi' from Mansur ibn Yunus from abu Hamza from abu Ja'far, *'Alayhi al-Salam*, a similar *Hadith* except that he has said:

"This way, this way, this way and this way, meaning thereby front, back, right and left."

H 1055, Ch. 104, h 3

Muhammad ibn Yahya al-'Attar has narrated from certain members of our people from Harun ibn Muslim from Mas'ada ibn Sadaqa from abu 'Abd Allah, *'Alayhi al-Salam*, who has said the following:

"Amir al-Mu'minin Ali, *'Alayhi al-Salam*, has said, 'Do not be deceitful to your leaders, do not confuse your guides, do not be ignorant of your *'A'immah* (Leaders with Divine Authority) and do not cut off the rope of your unity, or you will fail and be disgraced. On such foundation your affairs must be based and you must strictly live within such system. Were you able to observe what those who lived before might observe (the consequences of) that they had disregarded and which you might be called to accept you would have acted fast, come out and listened. However, you can not observe what they observe (after their death), but the curtain will soon be removed.'"

H 1056, Ch. 104, h 4

A number of our people have narrated from Ahmad ibn Muhammad from 'Abd al-Rahman ibn Hammad and others from Hanan ibn Sadir al-Sayrafi who has said the following:

"I heard abu 'Abd Allah, *'Alayhi al-Salam*, say, 'The Holy Prophet, *'Alayhi al-Salam*, was given the news of his own death while he was in a good health and he did not suffer any pain.' He said, 'The trusted Spirit came to him.' He said, 'The Holy Prophet called for prayer in congregation. He then ordered the Muhajir and Ansar (people from Makkah and the people of Madina) to arm themselves. The people all came and the Holy Prophet climbed the platform, the pulpit, and gave out the news of his own death and then said, 'I remind and caution of Allah the ruler after me over my followers for not being kind to the community of the Muslims. He must honor the elders among them and be kind to their weak, treat their scholars with dignity, must not harm and humiliate them. He must not allow them to suffer poverty that would turn them to disbelief, must not close his door to them to let their strong overrun the weak ones. He must not use them in the (armed) campaigns as such that would banish the offspring of my followers.' Then he said, 'I have (certainly) delivered to you the message, given you good advice, so you must preserve this testimony.'

"Abu 'Abd Allah, *'Alayhi al-Salam*, has said that these were the last words of the Messenger of Allah from the pulpit.'"

H 1057, Ch. 104, h 5

Muhammad ibn Ali and others have narrated from Ahmad ibn Muhammad ibn 'Isa from Ali ibn al-Hakam from a man from Habib ibn abu Thabit who has said the following:

"Once honey and figs were brought to Amir al-Mu'minin Ali, *'Alayhi al-Salam*, from Hamadhan and al-Hulwan (places near Baghdad). He asked his officers to call in the orphans. They were allowed (*yal'aqu*) to test honey from the containers while he himself distributed them among people. People asked, 'Why should they be allowed to test honey (before others)?' He said, 'The Imam is the father of the orphans. I just wanted to give them a fatherly treat.'"

H 1058, Ch. 104, h 6

A number of our people have narrated from Ahmad ibn Muhammad al-Barqi and Ali ibn Ibrahim from his father all of them from al-Qasim ibn Muhammad al-Asbahani from Sulayman ibn Dawud al-Manqari from Sufyan ibn 'Uyayna from abu 'Abd Allah, *'Alayhi al-Salam*, who has said the following:

"The Holy Prophet has said, 'I have more authority over every believer than they themselves do, and after me Ali, *'Alayhi al-Salam*, will have such degree of authority.' He (abu 'Abd Allah, *'Alayhi al-Salam*) was asked, 'What is the meaning of that?' He said, 'These are the words of the Holy Prophet, "One who passes away, his debts and liabilities becomes my responsibility. If one leaves a legacy I am the heir thereof. A man will have no authority over himself if he has no property and one has no authority over his dependents if he does not provide for their expenses. The Holy Prophet and Amir al-Mu'minin Ali, *'Alayhim al-Salam*, and their successors have made it (providing maintenance) binding upon themselves. For this reason they have greater authority over them than their own selves. The general masses of the Jews accepted Islam only after these words of the Messenger of Allah. They found peace for themselves and for their dependents.""""

H 1059, Ch. 104, h 7

A number of our people have narrated from Ahmad ibn Muhammad from Ali ibn al-Hakam from Aban ibn 'Uthman from Sabbah ibn Sayyaba from abu 'Abd Allah, *'Alayhi al-Salam*, who has said the following:

"The messenger of Allah, *'Alayhi al-Salam*, has said, 'Whoever of the believers or Muslims dies and on him there is a debt, not for unlawful or extravagant reasons, it then is the responsibility of the Imam to pay it off, otherwise, he has sinned. Allah, the Most Holy, the Most High, says, "Welfare funds (*Zakat*) are only for the poor, the destitute . . . the debtors . . ." (9:60) For such persons (debtors) there is a share with the Imam. If he withholds it, he has sinned.'"

H 1060, Ch. 104, h 8

Ali ibn Ibrahim has narrated from Salih ibn al-Sindi from Ja'far ibn Bashir from Hanan from his father from abu Ja'far, *'Alayhi al-Salam*, who has said the following:

"The Messenger of Allah has said, 'Imamat (Leadership with Divine Authority) is not proper for one without the following qualities: (a) Chastity that keeps him away from disobeying Allah, (b) forbearance that gives him self-control against anger and (c) good guardianship over his dependents like a kind hearted father toward his children.'"

In another *Hadith* it is said, ". . . so that he would be like a loving father of the followers."

H 1061, Ch. 104, h 9

Ali ibn Muhammad has narrated from Sahl ibn Ziyad from Mu'awiya ibn Hakim from Muhammad ibn Aslam from a man from Tabaristan called Muhammad Qal. Mu'awiya has said that he met this man from Tabaristan who has said the following:

"I heard Ali ibn Musa (al-Rida), *'Alayhi al-Salam*, say, 'A debtor who lends or borrows' - uncertainty is from Mu'awiya – 'will be given one year's time to pay. If he still can not pay, the Imam will pay it off from public treasury.'"

Chapter 105 - The Whole Earth Belongs to the Imam, *'Alayhi al-Salam*

H 1062, Ch. 105, h 1

Muhammad ibn Yahya has narrated from Ahmad ibn Muhammad ibn 'Isa from ibn Mahbub from Hisham ibn Salim from abu Khalid al-Kabuli from abu Ja'far, *'Alayhi al-Salam*, who has said the following:

"We found this in the book of Amir al-Mu'minin Ali, *'Alayhi al-Salam*: 'The earth belongs to Allah and He gives it in inheritance to whomever of His servants that He wishes. The good end is for those who are pious before Allah, my *Ahl al-Bayt* and I are the people to whom Allah has given the earth in inheritance and we are the ones who are pious before Allah. The whole earth belongs to us. Thus, whoever of the Muslims revives a land, he must establish it and pay taxes to the Imam from my *Ahl al-Bayt*. Whatever he has used is his. If he abandons or allows it to become barren and another Muslim revives and re-establishes it, he has more right to it than the one who has abandoned. This person will now pay the taxes to the Imam from my *Ahl al-Bayt* and whatever he uses thereafter is his until *al-Qa'im* from my *Ahl al-Bayt* will rise with Divine Authority, power and with the sword. He will control and protect them and will remove them from such land just as the Messenger of Allah had controlled and protected it, except, however, for whatever is in the hands of our followers. He will form a contract with them and to them he will leave the land.'"

H 1063, Ch. 105, h 2

Al-Husayn ibn Muhammad has narrated from Mu'alla ibn Muhammad who has said that narrated to him Ahmad ibn Muhammad ibn 'Abd Allah from his narrator (one of the *'A'immah*, *'Alayhi al-Salam*, reported to me the following:

"The world and all that is therein belongs to Allah, the Most Holy, the Most High, to His Messenger and to us. If one controls a part of it he must maintain piety before Allah. He must pay the share of Allah, the Most Holy, the Most High, and be generous to his brethren, otherwise, Allah, the Messenger of Allah and we will have no responsibility toward him."

H 1064, Ch. 105, h 3

Muhammad ibn Yahya has narrated from Ahmad ibn Muhammad from ibn Mahbub from 'Umar ibn Yazid who has said the following:

"I saw Misma' in Madina. In that year he had tried to deliver a certain amount of property to abu 'Abd Allah, *'Alayhi al-Salam*, who returned the property to him. I ('Uram) asked him (Mism'a) about the reason for the return. He (Mism'a) said, "When I took the property to him (the Imam) I said, 'I had become the person in charge of the pearls in Bahrayn and I have made a four hundred thousand Dirham profit. I have brought eighty thousand Dinars as your share. I did not want to keep your share and disregard what Allah, the Most Holy, the Most High, has decreed to be for you in our properties.' The Imam said, 'Is there no more from earth and what Allah takes out of it besides one-fifth (of people's net savings) for us, O abu Sayyar? The whole earth belongs to us. Whatever Allah causes to come out therefrom belongs to us.' I then said, 'I will bring all the property to you.' He said, 'O abu Sayyar, we have made it a gift for you and relieved you of its liabilities.

Take your property with you. Whatever land is in the hands of our Shi'a, it is lawful for them until *al-Qa'im* will rise with Divine Authority and power. He will make an agreement with them about whatever land is in their hands and will give them permission to use. Whatever land is in the hands of others, their earning from it is not lawful until *al-Qa'im* will rise with Divine Authority and power. He will take such lands away from them and will remove them humiliated.'

"'Umar ibn Yazid has said, 'Abu Sayyar said to me, "I do not find anyone doing business or people as in charge persons of certain tasks, who earn their living lawfully except myself and those for whom they (*'A'immah*) have made it lawful."'"

H 1065, Ch. 105, h 4
Muhammad ibn Yahya has narrated from Ahmad ibn Muhammad from abu 'Abd Allah al-Razi from al-Hassan ibn Ali ibn abu Hamza from his father from abu Basir who has said the following:
"Once I asked abu 'Abd Allah, *'Alayhi al-Salam*, 'Is there any *Zakat* (a form of income tax) on Imam?' He said, 'O abu Muhammad, you have spoken an impossible word. Do you not know that both this and the next world belong to the Imam? He can place them as he may want, or give them to whomever he may want. Allah has granted us such permission.' The Imam said, 'O abu Muhammad, the Imam never spends a night without Allah's asking for His right due on him (the Imam).'"

H 1066, Ch. 105, h 5
Muhammad ibn Yahya has narrated from Ahmad ibn Muhammad from 'Abd Allah ibn Ahmad from Ali ibn al-Nu'man from Salih ibn Hamza from Aban ibn Mus'ab from Yunus ibn Zabyan or al-Mu'alla ibn al-Khnith who has said the following:
"Once I asked abu 'Abd Allah, *'Alayhi al-Salam*, 'What is for you from this earth?' He smiled and then said, 'Allah, the Most Holy, the Most High, sent Jibril and commanded him to dig with his toe eight rivers on earth. Of these are the River Sayhan and Jayhan, which are the Rivers in Balkh (Central Asia). Of such Rivers al-Khshu', which is the River al-Shash, River Mihran which is in India, River Nile in Egypt, Tigris and Euphrates. All that these rivers provide water and all that take water from them belong to us, and whatever is for us is for our Shi'a. There is nothing for our enemies except what they have usurped. Our friends and supporters will be in a place bigger than this and this, the sky and earth.' The Imam then recited the words of Allah. 'They are made for the believers in this world [but others have usurped it from them], and are exclusively for them in the life hereafter [no one will usurp from them].'" (7:32)

H 1067, Ch. 105, h 6
Ali ibn Muhammad has narrated from Sahl ibn Ziyad from Muhammad ibn 'Isa from Muhammad ibn al-Rayyan who has said the following:
"Once I wrote to abu Muhammad, al-Hassan, al-'Askari, *'Alayhi al-Salam*, 'May Allah keep my soul in service for your cause, it is narrated to us that nothing else from this world belongs to the Messenger of Allah except one-fifth of (people's) net savings.' The answer that came said, 'Certainly, the world and all that is in it belongs to the Messenger of Allah.'"

H 1068, Ch. 105, h 7

Muhammad ibn Yahya has narrated from Ahmad ibn Muhammad who has narrated it in a *marfu'* manner from 'Amr ibn Shimr from Jabir from abu Ja'far, *'Alayhi al-Salam*, who has said the following:

"The Messenger of Allah has said, 'Allah created Adam and granted the world to him. Whatever belonged to Adam belongs to the Messenger of Allah and whatever belonged to the Messenger of Allah, belongs to *'A'immah* (Leaders with Divine Authority), *'Alayhim al-Salam*, from *Ahl al-Bayt* of Muhammad, *'Alayhi al-Salam.'*"

H 1069, Ch. 105, h 8

Muhammad ibn 'Isma'il has narrated from al-Fadl ibn Shadhan and Ali ibn Ibrahim from his father all from ibn abu 'Umayr from Hafs ibn al-Bakhtari from abu 'Abd Allah, *'Alayhi al-Salam*, who has said the following:

"Jibril dug with his foot five rivers and the flank of water followed his foot. These rivers were Euphrates, Tigris, Nile, Mihran and the River of Balkh. Whatever these rivers provide water for or whatever that takes water from them are the properties of the Imam. The ocean that has circled the land belongs to the (Imam)."

Ali ibn Ibrahim has narrated from al-Sarriy ibn al-Rabi', who has said the following:

"Ibn abu 'Umayr did not consider anyone a match of Hisham ibn al-Hakam in anything. He would not miss meeting him. However, their relations at a time stood at a distance. The reason for this was the emergence of differences between ibn abu 'Umayr and abu Malik al-Hadrami, a friend of Hisham, over the issue of Imamat. Ibn abu 'Umayr had said that the whole world belongs to the Imam in the form of property and ownership and that he has more authority over it than those who have certain parts of it in their possession. Abu Malik had said that it is not as such. The people's properties belong to them except what Allah has given to the Imam in the form of properties captured from the enemy during a war (*al-fay'*) and one-fifth taxes or income. Such properties belong to the Imam and Allah has instructed him how to spend them and what to do with them. They agreed to ask Hisham to settle the differences. They went to Hisham but he supported the idea of abu Malik. Ibn abu 'Umayr became angry and distanced himself from Hisham thereafter."

Chapter 106 - Manners of the Imam, *'Alayhi al-Salam*, in the Matters of Food and Clothes as Leader With Divine Authority

H 1070, Ch. 106, h 1

Muhammad ibn Yahya has narrated from Ahmad ibn Muhammad ibn 'Isa from ibn Mahbub from Hammad from Humayd and Jabir al-'Abdi who has said the following:

"Amir al-Mu'minin Ali, *'Alayhi al-Salam*, has said, 'Allah has appointed me the Imam for His creation. Therefore, He made it obligatory for me to discipline myself in the matters of food, drinks and clothes to the level of the very weak ones of the people, so that poor people follow in my poverty and the rich do not become rebellious because of their riches.'"

H 1071, Ch. 106, h 2

Ali ibn Ibrahim has narrated from his father from ibn abu 'Umayr from Hammad ibn 'Uthman from Mu'alla ibn Khunays who has said the following:

"One day I said to abu 'Abd Allah, *'Alayhi al-Salam,* 'May Allah keep my soul in service for your cause, I thought of the descendents of so and so ('Abbassids) and the wealth they have at their disposal. Then I wished that had such wealth been at your disposal, we would have prosperously lived with you.'

"The Imam said, 'Never, O Mu'alla, by Allah, were it as you wished, there would have been nothing but hard labor of protection at nights and strenuous work during the days, coarse garments and tasteless food. Thus, it is kept away from us. Have you ever seen a looted property Allah, the Most High, has turned into a blessing except this one (usurpation of our leadership)?'"

H 1072, Ch. 106, h 3

Ali ibn Muhammad has narrated from Salih ibn abu Hammad and a number of our people have narrated from Ahmad ibn Muhammad and others through different chains of narrators the following:

It (*Hadith*) is about the protest of Amir al-Mu'minin Ali, *'Alayhi al-Salam,* against 'Asim ibn Ziyad who had confined himself with a cloak away from the people. His brother, al-Rabi' ibn Ziyad complained before Amir al-Mu'minin Ali, *'Alayhi al-Salam.* He complained that his ('Asim's) family had become depressed and his sons had been saddened because of his behavior. Amir al-Mu'minin Ali, *'Alayhi al-Salam,* had summoned 'Asim ibn Ziyad and he was brought before him.

"When Amir al-Mu'minin Ali, *'Alayhi al-Salam,* saw him, he frowned at him and asked, 'Why did you not feel ashamed before your wife? Why did you not show kindness to your sons? Do you think Allah had made good things lawful to you and then He disliked if you used them? You are less significant to Allah than such a thing. Is it not Allah Who has said, "He spread out the earth for the people (55:10)? There exist all kinds of fruits, palm-trees with sheathed blossoms, (55:11) grain with its husk and aromatic herbs." (55:12) Is it not Allah Who has said, 'He has made the two oceans meet each other, (55:19) but has created a barrier between them so that they will not merge totally. (55:20) (Jinn and mankind), which of the favors of your Lord do you, then deny? (55:21) From the two oceans come pearls and coral.'"" (55:22)

"I swear by Allah, the use of the bounties of Allah indeed is more preferred by Him than in mere words (thanking Allah for His bounties merely in words without the use of practical benefits). Allah, the Most Majestic, the Most Gracious, has said, '. . . and proclaim the bounties of your Lord.' (93:11)

"'Asim asked, 'O Amir al-Mu'minin, *'Alayhi al-Salam,* why have you confined yourself to tasteless food and harsh garments?' He said, 'How inconsiderate of you! Allah, the Most Majestic, the Most Gracious, has made obligatory for the *'A'immah* (Leaders with Divine Authority) of justice to measure themselves with the people of lowest standard of living so that the poverty of the poor does not plunge them into despair.' 'Asim then abandoned the gown and began to live a normal life.'"

H 1073, Ch. 106, h 4

A number of our people have narrated from Ahmad ibn Muhammad al-Barqi from his father from Muhammad ibn Yahya al-Khazzaz from Hammad ibn 'Uthman who has said the following:

"Once I was in the presence of abu 'Abd Allah, *'Alayhi al-Salam*, when a man said to him, 'May Allah grant you well being, you have mentioned that Ali ibn abu Talib, *'Alayhi al-Salam*, wore rough garments. He would buy a shirt worth four Dirhams only and so on. However, we see that you have new garments.' The Imam said, 'Ali ibn abu Talib, *'Alayhi al-Salam*, did so at a time when people disliked it. Were he to wear such garments today they might only defame him. The best garment for a given time is the garment that people of that time use. However, when our *al-Qa'im* will rise with Divine Authority and power, he will wear the kind of garment that Ali, *'Alayhi al-Salam*, did and he will live just as Ali, *'Alayhi al-Salam*, lived.'"

Chapter 107 - The Select Ahadith in This Context

H 1074, Ch. 107, h 1

Al-Husayn ibn Muhammad has narrated from Mu'alla ibn Muhammad from Ahmad ibn Muhammad ibn 'Abd Allah from Ayyub ibn Nuh who has said the following:

"Once I was in the presence of the Imam, *'Alayhi al-Salam*, and he sneezed. I then asked him, 'May Allah keep my soul in service for your cause, what should one say when the Imam sneezes?' The Imam said, 'One should say, 'May Allah grant blessings to you.'"

H 1075, Ch. 107, h 2

Muhammad ibn Yahya has narrated from Ja'far ibn Muhammad who has said that Ishaq ibn Ibrahim al-Daynuri narrated to me from 'Umar ibn Zahir from abu 'Abd Allah, *'Alayhi al-Salam*:

"He (the narrator) has said that a man asked, 'Is *al-Qa'im* (the one who will rise with Divine Authority and power) offered the greeting of peace as the commander of the believers?' The Imam said, 'No, because that is the title that Allah had given to Ali ibn abu Talib, *'Alayhi al-Salam*. Allah had not given this title to anyone before him. No one will be called by this title except an unbeliever.'

"I then said, 'May Allah keep my soul in service for your cause, what form of greeting of peace will be offered to him?' The Imam said, 'They will say, "Peace be upon you, O Baqiyyat Allah (Allah's reserved power to establish His authority on earth)."' He then recited from the Holy Quran: 'If you are true believers then know that the profit which Allah has left for you is better for you (than what you may gain through deceitful ways). I am not responsible for your deeds.'" (11:86)

H 1076, Ch. 107, h 3

Al-Husayn ibn Muhammad has narrated from Mu'alla ibn Muhammad from al-Washsha' from Ahmad ibn 'Umar who has said the following:

"Once I asked abu al-Hassan, *'Alayhi al-Salam*, 'Why is he (Ali ibn abu Talib, *'Alayhi al-Salam*) called *Amir al-Mu'minin* (commander of the believers)?' He said, 'Because he fed them knowledge. Have you not read in the book of Allah: 'We can buy more provisions with this for our family. . . .' (12:65)

"In another *Hadith* it is said, 'Because Amir al-Mu'minin Ali, *'Alayhi al-Salam*, from his own resources, fed them knowledge.'"

H 1077, Ch. 107, h 4
Ali ibn Ibrahim has narrated from Ya'qub ibn Yazid from ibn abu 'Umayr from abu al-Rabi' al-Qazzaz from Jabir who has said the following:
"Once I asked abu Ja'far, *'Alayhi al-Salam*, 'Why is he (Ali ibn abu Talib, *'Alayhi al-Salam*) called Amir al-Mu'minin?' He said, 'Allah has given him this name and as such it has come in His book: "When our Lord asked all the offspring of Adam (before their birth), 'Am I not your Lord'? All of them testified and bore witness to their testimony that on the Day of Judgment they would not say, 'We were not aware of this (fact)', (7:172) [and that Muhammad is My messenger and Ali is Amir al-Mu'minin] (commander of the believers).'"

Chapter 108 - Enlightening Points Inferred From the Holy Quran About Leadership With Divine Authority

H 1078, Ch. 108, h 1
A number of our people have narrated from Ahmad ibn Muhammad from al-Husayn ibn Sa'id from certain persons of our people from Hanan ibn Sadir from Salim al-Hannat who has said the following:
"Once I asked abu Ja'far, *'Alayhi al-Salam*, 'Explain to me the meaning of the words of Allah, the Most Holy, the Most High, "This, (Quran), is certainly the revelation from the Lord of the Universe (26:192). It has been revealed through the trustworthy Spirit (26:193) to your heart, so that you will warn (the people of the dangers of disobeying Allah). (26:194) It has been revealed in plain Arabic." (26:195)

"The Imam said, 'It (the revelation) refers to Leadership with Divine Authority of Amir al-Mu'minin Ali, *'Alayhi al-Salam*.'"

H 1079, Ch. 108, h 2
Muhammad ibn Yahya has narrated from Muhammad ibn al-Husayn from al-Hakam ibn Miskin from Ishaq ibn 'Ammara from a man who has said the following:
"About the words of Allah, the Most Majestic, the Most Gracious, 'We offered Our Trust (Our deputation) to the heavens, to the earth, and to the mountains, but they could not bear this burden and were afraid to accept it. Man (mankind) was able to accept this offer but he was unjust to himself and ignorant of the significance of this Trust.' (33:72). The Imam said, 'It (trust) is a reference to Leadership with Divine Authority of Amir al-Mu'minin Ali, *'Alayhi al-Salam*.'"

H 1080, Ch. 108, h 3
Muhammad ibn Yahya has narrated from abu Zahir from al-Hassan ibn Musa al-Khashshab from Ali ibn Hassa'n from 'Abd al-Rahman ibn Kathir who has said the following:
"About the words of Allah, the Most Majestic, the Most Gracious, 'Those who have accepted the faith and have kept it pure from injustice, have achieved security and guidance,' (6:82) the Imam said, 'It (faith) refers to belief in all that Prophet Muhammad, *'Alayhi al-Salam*, has brought from Allah about *Wilayah*,

(Leadership with Divine Authority) and has not mixed it with the authority of so and so that is mixed with injustice.'"

H 1081, Ch. 108, h 4

Muhammad ibn Yahya has narrated from Ahmad ibn Muhammad from ibn Mahbub from al-Hassan ibn Nu'aym al-Sahhaf who has said the following:

"Once I asked abu 'Abd Allah, *'Alayhi al-Salam*, about the words of Allah, the Most Majestic, the Most Gracious: '. . . certain persons of you have accepted the faith and others of you have not. . . .'(64:2) The Imam said, 'On the day that Allah made all the offspring of Adam to form a covenant with Him when they were just small particles, He established belief in our *Wilayah* (Leadership with Divine Authority), the standard for belief and disbelief.'"

H 1082, Ch. 108, h 5

Ahmad ibn Idris has narrated from Muhammad ibn Ahmad from Ya'qub ibn Yazid from ibn Mahbub from Muhammad ibn al-Fudayl who has said the following:

"About the words of Allah, the Most Majestic, the Most Gracious, '. . . fulfill their vows . . .,' (76:7) abu al-Hassan, *'Alayhi al-Salam*, has said, 'They (vows) refer to one's acknowledgement of our *Wilayah* (Leadership with Divine Authority).'"

H 1083, Ch. 108, h 6

Muhammad ibn Isma'il has narrated from al-Fadl ibn Shadhan from Hammad ibn 'Isa from Rib'i ibn 'Abd Allah from abu Ja'far, *'Alayhi al-Salam*, who has said the following:

"About the words of Allah, the Most Majestic, the Most Gracious: 'Had they followed the Laws of the Old and New Testaments and what was revealed to them from their Lord,' (5:66) abu Ja'far, *'Alayhi al-Salam*, has said, 'It (revelation) refers to *Wilayah*, (Leadership with Divine Authority).'"

H 1084, Ch. 108, h 7

Al-Husayn ibn Muhammad al-Asha'ari has narrated from Mu'alla ibn Muhammad from al-Washsha' from al-Muthanna from Zurara from 'Abd Allah ibn al-'Ajlan from abu Ja'far, *'Alayhi al-Salam*, who has said the following:

"About the words of Allah, the most High: '(Muhammad), say, "I do not ask you for any payment for my preaching to you except (your) love of (my near) relatives."' (42:23) The Imam said, 'They (the relatives) are the *'A'immah* (Leaders with Divine Authority).'"

H 1085, Ch. 108, h 8

Al-Husayn ibn Muhammad has narrated from Mu'alla ibn Muhammad from Ali ibn Asbat from Ali ibn abu Hamza from abu Basir from abu 'Abd Allah, *'Alayhi al-Salam*, who has said the following:

"About the words of Allah, the Most Majestic, the Most Gracious: 'One who obeys Allah and His Messenger [to acknowledge *Wilayah*, Leadership with Divine Authority of Ali and the *'A'immah* (Leaders with Divine Authority), *'Alayhim al-Salam*, after him] will certainly achieve a great success,' (33:71) the Imam said, 'This is how it was revealed.'"

H 1086, Ch. 108, h 9

Al-Husayn ibn Muhammad has narrated from Mu'alla ibn Muhammad from Ahmad ibn al-Nadr from Muhammad ibn Marwan in a *marfu'* manner from them (*'A'immah*, *'Alayhim al-Salam*) has said the following:

"About the words of Allah, the Most Majestic, the Most Gracious: 'You must not trouble the Prophet. . . .,' [the Imam said, 'In the matters of Ali and the *'A'immah, 'Alayhim al-Salam*], (33:53) '. . . like those who annoyed Moses. Allah proved him to be innocent of what they had said about him. . . .'" (33:70)

H 1087, Ch. 108, h 10
Al-Husayn ibn Muhammad has narrated from Mu'alla ibn Muhammad from al-Sayyariy from Ali ibn 'Abd Allah who has said the following:
"Once a man asked the Imam, *'Alayhi al-Salam*, about the words of Allah, the Most High. '. . . those who follow it (My guidance) will neither go astray nor will they endure any misery.' (20:123) The Imam said, 'It refers to those who acknowledge *'A'immah* (Leaders with Divine Authority), follow their commands and do not act disobediently.'"

H 1088, Ch. 108, h 11
Al-Husayn ibn Muhammad has narrated from Ali ibn Muhammad from Ahmad ibn Muhammad ibn 'Abd Allah in a *marfu'* manner who has said the following:
"About the words of Allah, the Most High, 'I do not (need to) swear by this town (Makkah) (90:1) in which you are now living (90:2) or by the great father and his wonderful son. . . .,' (90:3) the Imam said, 'It refers to Amir al-Mu'minin Ali, *'Alayhi al-Salam*, and *'A'immah* (Leaders with Divine Authority) from his descendents.'"

H 1089, Ch. 108, h 12
Al-Husayn ibn Muhammad has narrated from Mu'alla ibn Muhammad from Muhammad ibn 'Urama and Muhammad ibn 'Abd Allah from Ali ibn Hassa'n from 'Abd al-Rahman ibn Kathir from abu 'Abd Allah, *'Alayhi al-Salam*, who has said the following:
"About the words of Allah, the Most High, 'You must know that whatever property you may gain, one-fifth belongs to Allah, the Messenger, the kindred. . . .,' (8:41) the Imam, *'Alayhi al-Salam*, said, 'It (the kindred) refers to Amir al-Mu'minin Ali and *'A'immah* (Leaders with Divine Authority), *'Alayhim al-Salam*.'"

H 1090, Ch. 108, h 13
Al-Husayn ibn Muhammad has narrated from Mu'alla ibn Muhammad from al-Washsha' from 'Abd Allah ibn Sinan who has said the following:
"Once I asked abu 'Abd Allah, *'Alayhi al-Salam*, about the words of Allah, the Most Majestic, the Most Gracious, 'Among Our creatures are a group who guide and judge with the Truth.' (7:181) The Imam said, 'Such people are *'A'immah* (Leaders with Divine Authority), *'Alayhim al-Salam*.'"

H 1091, Ch. 108, h 14
Al-Husayn ibn Muhammad has narrated from Mu'alla ibn Muhammad from Muhammad ibn 'Urama from Ali ibn Hassa'n from 'Abd al-Rahman ibn Kathir from abu 'Abd Allah, *'Alayhi al-Salam*, who has said the following:
"About the words of Allah, the Most High, 'It is Allah Who has revealed the Book to you in which certain verses are clear statements (which accept no interpretation) and these are the fundamental ideas of the Book. . . .,' [the Imam said that they stand for Amir al-Mu'minin Ali, *'Alayhi al-Salam*, and *'A'immah* (Leaders with Divine Authority)], '. . . while other verses may have several

possibilities [they stand for so and so]. Those whose hearts are perverse, [it refers to their companions and followers], follow the unclear statements in pursuit of their own mischievous goals by interpreting them in a way that will suit their own purpose. No one knows its true interpretations except Allah and those who are firmly established in knowledge [such people are Amir al-Mu'minin Ali, *'Alayhi al-Salam*, and *'A'immah* (Leaders with Divine Authority)] . . .'" (3:7)

Note: In the above *Hadith* whatever is inside brackets are the words of the Imam, *'Alayhi al-Salam*.

H 1092, Ch. 108, h 15
Al-Husayn ibn Muhammad has narrated from Mu'alla ibn Muhammad from al-Washsha' from Muthanna from 'Abd Allah ibn 'Ajlan from abu Ja'far, *'Alayhi al-Salam*, who has said the following:
"About the words of Allah, the Most High, 'Do you think that Allah will not make any distinction between those of you who have fought for His cause and have relied on no one other than Allah, His Messenger, and the believers, and other people?' (9:16) The Imam said, 'The word "Believers" stands for Amir al-Mu'minin Ali, *'Alayhi al-Salam*, and *'A'immah* (Leaders with Divine Authority) who have not relied on any one except Allah, the Messenger of Allah and the believers.'"

H 1093, Ch. 108, h 16
Al-Husayn ibn Muhammad has narrated from Mu'alla ibn Muhammad from Muhammad ibn Jumhur from Safwan from ibn Muskan from al-Halabi from abu 'Abd Allah, *'Alayhi al-Salam*, who has said the following:
"About the words of Allah, the Most Majestic, the Most Gracious, 'If they (the unbelievers) propose peace, accept it and trust in Allah. Allah is All-hearing and All-knowing.' (8:61) I asked the Imam, *'Alayhi al-Salam*, 'What is the meaning of *al-salam* (peace)?' The Imam said, 'It is the acknowledgment of our Leadership with Divine Authority.'"

H 1094, Ch. 108, h 17
Muhammad ibn Yahya has narrated from Ahmad ibn Muhammad from ibn Mahbub from Jamil ibn Salih from Zurara from abu Ja'far, *'Alayhi al-Salam*, who has said the following:
"About the words of Allah, the Most High, '. . . You will certainly pass through one stage after another,' (84:19) the Imam, *'Alayhi al-Salam*, said, 'O Zurara, has this 'Umma (nation) not passed through stages after the Holy Prophet, *'Alayhi al-Salam*, and the affairs of three so and so ones?'"

H 1095, Ch. 108, h 18
Al-Husayn ibn Muhammad has narrated from Mu'alla ibn Muhammad from Muhammad ibn Jumhur from Hammad ibn 'Isa from 'Abd Allah ibn Jundab who has said the following:
"Once I asked abu al-Hassan, *'Alayhi al-Salam*, about the words of Allah, the Most Majestic, and the Most Gracious, 'We sent Our guidance to them so that perhaps they might take heed.' (28:51) The Imam said, 'It (guidance) refers to *'A'immah* (Leaders with Divine Authority), *'Alayhim al-Salam*, one after the other.'"

H 1096, Ch. 108, h 19

Muhammad ibn Yahya has narrated from Ahmad ibn Muhammad from al-Hassan ibn Mahbub from Muhammad ibn al-Nu'man from Salam from abu Ja'far, *'Alayhi al-Salam*, who has said the following about the words of Allah, the Most High:

"About the words of Allah, '(Muslims) say, "We believe in Allah and what He has revealed to us. . . .,"' (2:136) the Imam said, 'This is primarily addressed to Ali, Fatimah, al-Hassan and al-Husayn, *'Alayhim al-Salam*, and thereafter to *'A'immah* (Leaders with Divine Authority), *'Alayhim al-Salam*. Then the words of Allah ". . . if they [refers to people] believe, in all that you, [Ali, Fatimah, al-Hassan and al-Husayn, *'Alayhim al-Salam*] believe, they will have the right guidance, but if they turn away, it will be for no reason other than their own malice. . . ."' (2:137)

H 1097, Ch. 108, h 20

Al-Husayn ibn Muhammad has narrated from Mu'alla ibn Muhammad from al-Washsha' from Muthanna from 'Abd Allah ibn 'Ajlan from abu Ja'far, *'Alayhi al-Salam*, who has said the following:

"About the words of Allah, the Most High, 'The nearest people to Abraham, among mankind, are those who followed him, this Prophet (Muhammad) and the true believers . . .,' (3:68) the Imam said, 'They (nearest people) are *'A'immah* (Leaders with Divine Authority) and those who follow them.'"

H 1098, Ch. 108, h 21

Al-Husayn ibn Muhammad has narrated from Mu'alla ibn Muhammad 'from al-Washsha' from Ahmad ibn al-'A'idh from 'Udhayna from Malik al-Juhanni who has said the following:

"I asked abu 'Abd Allah, *'Alayhi al-Salam*, about the words of Allah, the Most Majestic, the Most Gracious, 'He has revealed this Quran to me to warn you and the coming generations (against disobeying Allah). . . .' (6:19) The Imam said, 'Whoever from the family of Muhammad, *'Alayhi al-Salam*, becomes an Imam will warn people by means of the Holy Quran just as the Messenger of Allah had done.'"

H 1099, Ch. 108, h 22

A number of our people have narrated from Ahmad ibn Muhammad from Ali ibn al-Hakam from Mufaddal ibn Salih from Jabir from abu Ja'far, *'Alayhi al-Salam*, who has said the following:

"About the words of Allah, the Most Majestic, the Most Gracious, 'We had commanded Adam (certain matters). He forgot Our commandment and We did not find in him the determination to fulfill Our commandments,' (20:115) the Imam said, 'It means that Allah commanded Adam about Muhammad, *'Alayhi al-Salam*, and *'A'immah* (Leaders with Divine Authority) after him. He did not acknowledge it *Wilayah* (Leadership with Divine Authority of *'A'immah*) and he was not an 'Ulu al-'Azm (a prophet who is granted greater determination). They are called 'Ulu al-'Azm because with them a covenant was established to acknowledge *Wilayah* of Muhammad, *'Alayhi al-Salam*, and the executors of his will after him and *al-Mahdi* and his discipline. They established their determination to acknowledge *Wilayah* of Muhammad and the executors of his will about *al-Mahdi* and his discipline.'"

H 1100, Ch. 108, h 23

Al-Husayn ibn Muhammad has narrated from Mu'alla ibn Muhammad from Ja'far ibn Muhammad ibn 'Ubayd Allah from Muhammad ibn 'Isa al-Qummi from Muhammad ibn Sulayman from 'Abd Allah ibn Sinan from abu 'Abd Allah, *'Alayhi al-Salam*, who has said the following:

"About the words of Allah, 'We had commanded Adam (certain matters) before. . . ., [the commands consisted of certain words about Ali, Fatimah, al-Hassan, al-Husayn and *'A'immah* (Leaders with Divine Authority) from their descendents, *'Alayhim al-Salam*]. '. . . He (Adam) forgot Our commandment. . . .,' (20:115) the Imam said, 'This, by Allah, is how it was revealed, about Muhammad and his family, *'Alayhim al-Salam*. That is, the material inside bracket is part of 20:115.'"

H 1101, Ch. 108, h 24

Muhammad ibn Yahya has narrated from Muhammad ibn al-Husayn from Nadr ibn Shu'ayb from Khalid ibn Ma'dd from Muhammad ibn al-Fudayl from al-Thumali from abu Ja'far, *'Alayhi al-Salam*, who has said the following:

"Allah sent revelation to His Prophet, *'Alayhi al-Salam*, in which He has said, 'Follow devotedly that which is revealed to you. You are certainly on the right path.' (43:43) Imam, *'Alayhi al-Salam*, said, 'It is just as saying, "You have acknowledged the Leadership with Divine Authority of Ali, *'Alayhi al-Salam*, and Ali is on the right path."'"

H 1102, Ch. 108, h 25

Ali ibn Ibrahim has narrated from Ahmad ibn Muhammad al-Barqi from his father Muhammad ibn Sinan from 'Ammar ibn Marwan from Munakhkhal from Jabir from abu Ja'far, *'Alayhi al-Salam*, who has said the following:

"Jibril brought this verse to Muhammad, *'Alayhi al-Salam*, 'Evil is that for which they have sold their souls: They have refused to accept Allah's revelations [about Leadership with Divine Authority of Ali, *'Alayhi al-Salam*] in rebellion. . . .'" (2:90)

H 1103, Ch. 108, h 26

Through the same chain of narrators it is narrated from Muhammad ibn Sinan from 'Ammar ibn Marwan from Munakhkhal from Jabir who has said the following:

"Jibril brought this verse of the Holy Quran to Prophet Muhammad, *'Alayhi al-Salam*: 'Should you have any doubt about what We have revealed to Our servant, [about Leadership with Divine Authority of Ali, *'Alayhi al-Salam*] present one chapter comparable to it. . . .'" (2:23)

H 1104, Ch. 108, h 27

Through the same chain of narrators it is narrated from Muhammad ibn Sinan from 'Ammar ibn Marwan from Munakhkhal from abu 'Abd Allah, *'Alayhi al-Salam*, who has said the following:

"Jibril brought the following verse to Prophet Muhammad, *'Alayhi al-Salam*, as this: 'People of the Book, you must believe in what We have revealed [about Ali's Leadership with Divine Authority] as shining light. . . .'" (4:47)

H 1105, Ch. 108, h 28

Ali ibn Muhammad has narrated from Ahmad ibn Muhammad ibn Khalid from his father from abu Talib from Yunus ibn Bakkar from his father from Jabir from abu Ja'far, *'Alayhi al-Salam*, who has said the following:

"About the words of Allah: 'If they had done what they had been advised to do, [the Imam said that it was to acknowledge Ali's Leadership with Divine Authority], it would have been for their good and to strengthen their faith." (4:66)

H 1106, Ch. 108, h 29

Al-Husayn ibn Muhammad has narrated from Mu'alla ibn Muhammad from al-Hassan ibn Ali al-Washsha' from Muthanna al-Hannat from 'Abd Allah ibn 'Ajlan from abu Ja'far, *'Alayhi al-Salam*, who has said the following:

"About the words of Allah, the Most Majestic, the Most Gracious, 'Believers, submit yourselves to the will of Allah as a whole. Do not follow the footsteps of Satan; he is your sworn enemy,' (2:208) the Imam, *'Alayhi al-Salam*, said, 'It means submit yourselves to our Leadership with Divine Authority.'"

H 1107, Ch. 108, h 30

Al-Husayn ibn Muhammad has narrated from Mu'alla ibn Muhammad from 'Abd Allah ibn Idris from Muhammad ibn Sinan from al-Mufaddl ibn 'Umar who has said the following:

"Once I asked abu 'Abd Allah, *'Alayhi al-Salam*, about the meaning of the words of Allah, the Most Majestic, the Most Gracious: 'However, (the unbelievers) prefer the worldly life. . . .' (87:16) The Imam said, 'They have preferred their (evil doer) friendship, and ". . . even though the life hereafter will be better and will last forever. . . ." (87:17) refers to the friendship of Amir al-Mu'minin Ali, *'Alayhi al-Salam*, ". . . this is what is written in the ancient heavenly Books, (87:18) the Scriptures of Abraham and Moses (87:19).'"

H 1108, Ch. 108, h 31

Ahmad ibn Idris has narrated from Muhammad ibn Hassa'n from Muhammad ibn Ali from 'Ammar ibn Marwan from Munakhkhal from Jabir from abu Ja'far, *'Alayhi al-Salam*, who has said the following:

"About the words of Allah: 'Why do you arrogantly belie certain people of them, [the Imam said that it refers to family of Muhammad, *'Alayhi al-Salam*] and murder others whenever he [Muhammad, *'Alayhi al-Salam*] brings you messages [proof of Imam Ali's Leadership with Divine Authority] which you dislike?'" (2:87)

H 1109, Ch. 108, h 32

Al-Husayn ibn Muhammad has narrated from Mu'alla ibn Muhammad from 'Abd Allah ibn Idris from Muhammad ibn Sinan from al-Rida, *'Alayhi al-Salam*, who has said the following

"About the words of Allah, the Most Majestic, the Most Gracious: 'A grave concern it [Leadership with Divine Authority of Ali, *'Alayhi al-Salam*] has become for the pagans whom you [O Muhammad] call to acknowledge,' (42:13) this is how it (Leadership with Divine Authority of Ali, *'Alayhi al-Salam*) is (mentioned) in the written book,' said the Imam, *'Alayhi al-Salam*."

H 1110, Ch. 108, h 33

Al-Husayn ibn Muhammad has narrated from Mu'alla ibn Muhammad from Ahmad ibn Muhammad from ibn Hilal from his father from abu al-Safatij from abu Basir from abu 'Abd Allah, *'Alayhi al-Salam*, who has said the following:

"About the words of Allah, the Most Majestic, the Most Gracious, 'Allah Who guided us to this, deserves all praise. Had He not guided us, we would never have been able to find the right direction. . . .' (7:43) The Imam, *'Alayhi al-Salam*, said,

'On the Day of Judgment the Holy Prophet, Amir al-Mu'minin Ali, *'Alayhim al-Salam*, and *'A'immah* (Leaders with Divine Authority) from his descendents will be brought into public sight. When their followers will see them they will say, "Allah, Who guided us to this, deserves all praise. Had He not guided us, we would have never been able to find the right direction. He guided us to acknowledge Imam Ali's Leadership with Divine Authority and *'A'immah* from his descendents.'"'

H 1111, Ch. 108, h 34
Al-Husayn ibn Muhammad has narrated from Mu'alla ibn Muhammad from Muhammad ibn 'Urama and Muhammad ibn 'Abd Allah from Ali ibn Hassa'n from 'Abd Allah ibn Kathir from abu 'Abd Allah, *'Alayhi al-Salam*, who has said the following:

"About the words of Allah, the Most High: 'What do they quarrel about? (78:1) They quarrel about the great news,' (78:2) the Imam, *'Alayhi al-Salam*, said, 'The great news stands for Leadership with Divine Authority of *'A'immah* (Leaders with Divine Authority).' I asked him about the meaning of, '. . . in such helplessness, human beings realize that it is Allah who is the true Guardian. . . .' (18:44) The Imam, *'Alayhi al-Salam*, said, 'It refers to the guardianship and Leadership with Divine Authority of Amir al-Mu'minin Ali, *'Alayhi al-Salam*.'"

H 1112, Ch. 108, h 35
Ali ibn Ibrahim has narrated from Salih ibn al-Sindi from Ja'far ibn Bashir from Ali ibn abu Hamza from abu Basir from abu Ja'far, *'Alayhi al-Salam*, who has said the following:

"About the words of Allah, the Most High, '(Muhammad) be devoted to the upright religion. It is harmonious with the nature which Allah has designed for people. . . .,' (30:30) the Imam, *'Alayhi al-Salam*, said, 'It (upright religion) is Leadership with Divine Authority.'"

H 1113, Ch. 108, h 36
A number of our people have narrated from Ahmad ibn Muhammad from Ibrahim al-Hamadani in a *marfu'* manner from abu 'Abd Allah, *'Alayhi al-Salam*, who has said the following:

"About the words of Allah, the Most High, 'We shall set up the balances to maintain proper justice on the Day of Judgment. . . .," (21:47) the Imam, *'Alayhi al-Salam*, said, "Balances are the prophets and the executors of their wills.'"

H 1114, Ch. 108, h 37
Ali ibn Muhammad has narrated from Sahl ibn Ziyad from Ahmad ibn al-Husayn ibn 'Umar ibn Yazid from Muhammad ibn Jumhur from Muhammad ibn Sinan from al-Mufaddal ibn 'Umar who has said the following:

"I asked abu 'Abd Allah, *'Alayhi al-Salam*, about the words of Allah, the Most High, '. . . those who do not wish to meet Us in the life hereafter say, "Bring us another book besides this one or change it . . .,"' (10:15) the Imam said, 'They said, "Replace Ali, *'Alayhi al-Salam*."'"

H 1115, Ch. 108, h 38
Ali ibn Muhammad has narrated from Sahl ibn Ziyad from 'Isma'il ibn Mihran from al-Hassan al-Qummi from Idris ibn 'Abd Allah who has said the following:

"Once I asked abu 'Abd Allah, *'Alayhi al-Salam*, about the interpretation of this verse of the Holy Quran, 'What has led you to Saqar' (a place in hell)? They will reply, 'We did not pray.' (74:43)

"The Imam said, 'Such people will be those who did not believe in *'A'immah* (Leaders with Divine Authority) about whom Allah, the Most Holy, the Most High, has said, "The foremost ones will be the nearest ones to Allah." (56:11) Have you not noticed that people call the one second to the lead in horseracing 'Al-Musalli' (also means the praying)? This is what is meant therein. "We did not pray" (74:43), means 'We did not follow the lead.'"

H 1116, Ch. 108, h 39

Ahmad ibn Mihran has narrated from 'Abd al-'Azim ibn 'Abd Allah al-Hassani from Musa ibn Muhammad from Yunus ibn Ya'qub from the one he mentioned from abu Ja'far, *'Alayhi al-Salam*, who has said the following:

"About the words of Allah, the Most Majestic, the Most Gracious, 'Had they (jinn and mankind) remained steadfast in their religion (Islam), We would certainly have given them abundant water to drink' (72:16) the Imam said, 'Allah says that He would quench their hearts with belief. "Religion" is a reference to Leadership of Ali ibn abu Talib, *'Alayhi al-Salam*, and the executors of his will with Divine Authority.'"

H 1117, Ch. 108, h 40

Al-Husayn ibn Muhammad has narrated from Mu'alla ibn Muhammad from Muhammad ibn Jumhur from al-Fadala ibn Ayyub from al-Husayn ibn 'Uthman from abu Ayyub from Muhammad ibn Muslim who has said the following:

"I asked abu 'Abd Allah, *'Alayhi al-Salam*, about the words of Allah, the Most Majestic, the Most Gracious, "To those who have said, 'Allah is our Lord,' and who have remained steadfast to their belief. . . ." (41:30)

"The Imam, *'Alayhi al-Salam*, said, 'It refers to those who remained steadfast in their belief in the Leadership with Divine Authority of *'A'immah* (Leaders with Divine Authority), *'Alayhim al-Salam*, one after the other, ". . . the angels will descend saying, 'Do not be afraid or grieved. Receive the glad news of the Paradise, which was promised to you.'"" (41:30)

H 1118, Ch. 108, h 41

Al-Husayn ibn Muhammad has narrated from Mu'alla ibn Muhammad from al-Washsha' from Muhammad ibn Fudayl from abu Hamza who has said the following:

"Once I asked abu Ja'far, *'Alayhi al-Salam*, about the words of Allah, the Most High, 'Say, I advise you to believe only in one. . . .' (34:46)

"The Imam said that Allah has said, 'I advise you to acknowledge Imam Ali's Leadership with Divine Authority. It is the "one" that Allah, the Most Holy, the Most High, has called, 'I advise you to believe only in "one".'"

H 1119, Ch. 108, h 42

Al-Husayn ibn Muhammad has narrated from Mu'alla ibn Muhammad from Muhammad ibn 'Urama and Ali ibn 'Abd Allah from Ali ibn Hassa'n from 'Abd al-Rahman ibn Kathir from abu 'Abd Allah, *'Alayhi al-Salam*, who has said the following:

"About the words of Allah, the Most Majestic, the Most Gracious, 'Allah will not forgive or guide to the right path those who first believe, then disbelieve, again believe and disbelieve, and then increase their disbelief,' (4:137) the Imam,

'Alayhi al-Salam, said, 'It was revealed about so and so and so and so who believed in the Holy Prophet, *'Alayhi al-Salam*, in the beginning. They turned to disbelief when Leadership with Divine Authority of Ali, *'Alayhi al-Salam*, was made known to them when the Holy Prophet, *'Alayhi al-Salam*, said, "Over whoever I have Divine Authority, Ali, *'Alayhi al-Salam*, also has Divine Authority." When the Messenger of Allah passed away they turned to disbelief. They did not remain steadfast in their oath of allegiance. They increased in their disbelief through making people pledge allegiance to them. They were left with nothing of the belief that once they had.'"

H 1120, Ch. 108, h 43

Through the same chain of narrators it is narrated from abu 'Abd Allah, *'Alayhi al-Salam*, who has said the following:

"About the words of Allah, the Most High, 'Those who have reverted to disbelief after guidance have become manifest to them. . . .,' (47:25) the Imam, *'Alayhi al-Salam*, said, 'They are so and so and so and so who reverted from the faith in rejecting Leadership with Divine Authority of Amir al-Mu'minin Ali, *'Alayhi al-Salam*.' I then asked about the words of Allah, the Most High, '. . . this is because they have said to those who hate Allah's revelation, "We shall obey you in certain matters. . . ."'" (47:26) The Imam said, 'By Allah, it was revealed about the two of them and their followers. To this the words of Allah, the Most Majestic, the Most Gracious, that Jibril brought to Muhammad, *'Alayhi al-Salam*, refer, "This is because they have said to those who hate Allah's revelation, [about Leadership with Divine Authority of Ali, *'Alayhi al-Salam*] and say, 'We shall obey you in certain matters. . . .'"'" (47:26)

"The Imam further said, 'They made an agreement with the Amawids not to allow the leadership come to us, *Ahl al-Bayt*, after the Holy Prophet, *'Alayhi al-Salam*, not to pay us anything of one-fifth taxes. They said, "If we pay to them, *Ahl al-Bayt*, the one-fifth taxes, their needs will be met and they, *Ahl al-Bayt*, then will not think of their leadership as threatened." They (the other party, Amawids) said, "We will obey you in certain matters" (47:26) that you want us to obey, such as the one-fifth taxes. We will not pay it to them.'

'Allah's words that read, '. . . who hate Allah's revelation, . . .' (47:26) refer to Amir al-Mu'minin Ali's Leadership with Divine Authority over the creatures. With them was abu 'Ubayda, their scribe. Allah has said, 'If the unbelievers persist in their disbelief, We shall also persist in punishing them (43:79). Do they think that We do not hear their secrets and whispers. . . . ?'" (43:80)

H 1121, Ch. 108, h 44

Through the same chain of narrators it is narrated from abu 'Abd Allah, *'Alayhi al-Salam*, who has said the following:

"About the words of Allah, the Most Majestic, the Most Gracious, '. . . and those who commit evil and injustice therein,' (22:25) the Imam said, 'It was revealed about them as they entered the Ka'ba and made an agreement and commitment to continue in disbelief and denial of the Divine revelation about Amir al-Mu'minin Ali, *'Alayhi al-Salam*. They, thus, committed evil and injustice toward the

Messenger of Allah about the executor of his will. May Allah do away with the unjust people.'"

H 1122, Ch. 108, h 45

Al-Husayn ibn Muhammad has narrated from Mu'alla ibn Muhammad from Ali ibn Asbat from Ali ibn abu Hamza from abu Basir from abu 'Abd Allah, *'Alayhi al-Salam*, who has said the following:

"About the words of Allah, the Most Majestic, the Most Gracious, 'You will soon know who is in manifest error . . .,' (67:29) the Messenger of Allah said, 'O you people who reject Leadership with Divine Authority of Ali, *'Alayhi al-Salam*, and *'A'immah* (Leaders with Divine Authority) after him, I have conveyed to you, as part of the message of Allah, '. . . then who is in manifest error?' (67:29) Similarly they are addressed in this verse: 'If you deviate from the truth in your testimony, or decline to present your testimony at all . . ., [should you deviate from the command or decline to obey the command] you must know that Allah is Well Aware of what you do.'" (4:135)"In the words of Allah, '. . . We shall certainly make the unbelievers, [in Leadership with Divine Authority of Imam Ali, *'Alayhi al-Salam*] suffer severe torment [in this world] and will punish them for their worst deeds,' (41:27) this is how the above were revealed to the Holy Prophet,' the Imam explained."

H 1123, Ch. 108, h 46

Al-Husayn ibn Muhammad has narrated from Mu'alla ibn Muhammad from Ali ibn Asbat from Ali ibn Mansur from Ibrahim ibn 'Abd al-Hamid from al-Walid ibn Sabih from abu 'Abd Allah, *'Alayhi al-Salam*, who has said the following:

"About the words of Allah, '. . . your suffering is only because you disbelieved when One Allah, [and the people who possess Leadership with Divine Authority] were mentioned. . . .' (40:12) the Imam explained (by his words in brakets)."

H 1124, Ch. 108, h 47

Ali ibn Ibrahim has narrated from Ahmad ibn Muhammad from Muhammad ibn Khalid from Muhammad ibn Sulayman from his father from abu Basir from abu 'Abd Allah, *'Alayhi al-Salam*, who has said the following:

"About the words of Allah, the Most High, 'Someone (needlessly) demanded to experience the torment (of Allah) (70:1), which will inevitably seize the unbelievers [in Imam Ali's Leadership with Divine Authority],' (70:2) the Imam, *'Alayhi al-Salam*, then said, 'This, by Allah, is how Jibril brought it to the Holy Prophet, *'Alayhi al-Salam*.'"

H 1125, Ch. 108, h 48

Muhammad ibn Yahya has narrated from Ahmad ibn Muhammad ibn 'Isa from al-Hassan ibn Sayf from his brother from his father from abu Hamza from abu Ja'far, *'Alayhi al-Salam*, who has said the following:

"About the words of Allah, the Most High, '. . . Your ideas are confused (51:8). Allow whoever wishes to turn away, turn away from it [*Wilayah*, Leadership with Divine Authority],' (51:9) the Imam said, 'Whoever turns away from *Wilayah*, of *'A'immah*, *'Alayhim al-Salam*, has turned away from paradise.'"

H 1126, Ch. 108, h 49

Al-Husayn ibn Muhammad has narrated from Mu'alla ibn Muhammad from Muhammad ibn Jumhur from Yunus who has said that a person in a *marfu'* manner narrated the following to me from abu 'Abd Allah, *'Alayhi al-Salam*:

"About the words of Allah, the Most Majestic, the Most Gracious: 'Yet, he has not entered into Aqaba (90:11). If only you knew what Aqaba is! (90:12). It is the setting free of a slave,' (90:13) the Imam said, 'Setting free of a slave is acknowledgment of the *Wilayah,* Leadership with Divine Authority of Amir al-Mu'minin Ali, *'Alayhi al-Salam.'*"

H 1127, Ch. 108, h 50

Through the same chain of narrators it is from abu 'Abd Allah, *'Alayhi al-Salam,* who has said the following:

"About the words of Allah, the Most High, '. . . give to the believers the glad news of their high rank in the sight of Allah. . . .' (10:2) the Imam said, 'It (glad news) is the *Wilayah* (Leadership with Divine Authority) of Imam Ali, *'Alayhi al-Salam.'*"

H 1128, Ch. 108, h 51

Ali ibn Ibrahim has narrated from Ahmad ibn Muhammad al-Barqi from his father from Muhammad ibn al-Fudayl from abu Hamza from abu Ja'far, *'Alayhi al-Salam,* who has said the following:

"About the words of Allah, the Most High: '. . . two groups who dispute with each other about their Lord. For the unbelievers [in *Wilayah,* Leadership with Divine Authority of Imam Ali], the garment of fire has already been prepared. . . .,' (22:19) the Imam explained (through his words in brackets)."

H 1129, Ch. 108, h 52

Al-Husayn ibn Muhammad has narrated from Mu'alla ibn Muhammad from Muhammad ibn 'Urama from Ali ibn Hassa'n from 'Abd al-Rahman ibn Kathir who has said the following:

"I asked abu 'Abd Allah, *'Alayhi al-Salam,* about the words of Allah, the Most High, '. . . human beings realize that the true guardianship is that of (Allah). . . .' (18:44)

The Imam said, 'It (guardianship) is the *Wilayah* (Leadership with Divine Authority) of Amir al-Mu'minin, *'Alayhi al-Salam.'*"

H 1130, Ch. 108, h 53

Muhammad ibn Yahya has narrated from Salama ibn al-Khattab from Ali ibn Hassa'n from 'Abd al-Rahman ibn Kathir from abu 'Abd Allah, *'Alayhi al-Salam,* who has said the following:

"About the words of Allah, the Most Majestic, the Most Gracious: 'It is Allah's (means of purification and His) coloring. No coloring (purification) is better than that of Allah and we (Muslims) worship Him,' (2:138) the Imam said, 'Allah had colored the believers with *Wilayah* (Leadership with Divine Authority) of Imam Ali, *'Alayhi al-Salam,* at the time He made them make the covenant.'"

H 1131, Ch. 108, h 54

A number of our people have narrated from Ahmad ibn Muhammad ibn 'Isa from ibn Faddal from al-Mufaddal ibn Salih from Muhammad ibn Ali al-Halabi from abu 'Abd Allah, *'Alayhi al-Salam,* who has said the following:

"About the words of Allah, the Most Majestic, and the Most Gracious: 'Lord, forgive me, my parents, the believers who have entered my home and all believing. . . .,' (71:28) the Imam said, "Home" means *Wilayah* (Leadership with Divine Authority) of Imam Ali, *'Alayhi al-Salam*. Whoever acknowledges *Wilayah* has entered the home of the prophets. The "house" (Bayt) mentioned in verse (33:33) also refers to *Wilayah*. "People of the house, Allah wants to remove all kinds of uncleanliness from you and to purify you thoroughly." (33:33) It stands for *'A'immah* (Leaders with Divine Authority), *'Alayhim al-Salam*, and for their *Wilayah*. Whoever acknowledges it has found a place in the house of the Holy Prophet, *'Alayhi al-Salam.*'"

H 1132, Ch. 108, h 55

Through the same chain of narrators it is narrated from Ahmad ibn Muhammad from 'Umar ibn 'Abd al-'Aziz from Muhammad ibn al-Fudayl who has said the following:

"Once I asked al-Rida, *'Alayhi al-Salam*, about the words of Allah: '(Muhammad), tell them to be happy with the favors and the mercy of Allah is better than whatever you accumulate.' (10:58)

"The Imam said, 'To acknowledge the *Wilayah* (Leadership with Divine Authority) of Muhammad and the family of Muhammad, *'Alayhim al-Salam*, is better than all that they accumulate of the worldly gains.'"

H 1133, Ch. 108, h 56

Ahmad ibn Mihran has narrated from 'Abd al-'Azim al-Hassani from Ali ibn Asbat from Ibrahim ibn 'Abd al-Hamid from Zayd al-Shahham who has said the following:

"Once abu 'Abd Allah, *'Alayhi al-Salam*, said to me on the way home on Friday night, 'Read from the Holy Quran. It is a Friday night.' I then read, 'The fixed time for all of them will be the Day of Judgment (44:40) (when wrong will be discerned from right). On this day friends will be of no benefit to one another, nor will they receive any help (44:41) except for those to whom Allah grants mercy. . . .' (44:42)

"The Imam said, 'We, by Allah, are 'Those whom He has granted mercy'. We, by Allah, are the ones whom Allah has made exceptional and we will support them (our followers) sufficiently.'"

H 1134, Ch. 108, h 57

Ahmad ibn Mihran has narrated from 'Abd al-'Azim from 'Abd Allah from Yahya ibn Salim from abu 'Abd Allah, *'Alayhi al-Salam*, who has said the following:

"When this verse, '. . . but only attentive ears will retain it. . . .' (69:12) was revealed, the Messenger of Allah said, 'They are your ears, O Ali ibn abu Talib, *'Alayhi al-Salam*,' the Imam explained."

H 1135, Ch. 108, h 58

Ahmad ibn Mihran has narrated from 'Abd al-'Azim from Muhammad ibn al-Fudayl from abu Hamza from abu Ja'far, *'Alayhi al-Salam*, who has said the following:

"Once Jibril brought the following verse to Prophet Muhammad, *'Alayhi al-Salam*, 'The unjust ones [against the rights of the family of Muhammad] (among you) changed what they were told to say. Then, We afflicted them [the unjust against the rights of the family of Muhammad, *'Alayhi al-Salam*] with a torment from the heavens for their evil deeds,' (2:59) the Imam explained."

H 1136, Ch. 108, h 59

Through the same chain of narrators it is narrated from 'Abd al-'Azim ibn 'Abd Allah al-Hassani from Muhammad ibn al-Fudayl from abu Hamza from abu Ja'far, *'Alayhi al-Salam*, who has said the following:

"Jibril brought this verse as this: 'Those who have done injustice [against the rights of the family of Muhammad, *'Alayhi al-Salam*] will not receive forgiveness from Allah or guidance to any other path but that to hell wherein they will remain forever, and that is a very easy thing for Allah to do.' (4:169) Then he recited, 'O people, the Messenger has come to you with the truth [*Wilayah,* Leadership with Divine Authority of Imam Ali, *'Alayhi al-Salam*] from your Lord, thus, you must believe in it, it will be better for you. If you reject [*Wilayah* of Imam Ali, *'Alayhi al-Salam*] (you must know) that to Allah belongs all that is in the heavens and in the earth. . . .,' (4:170) the Imam explained."

H 1137, Ch. 108, h 60

Ahmad Mihran has narrated –may Allah grant him blessings- from 'Abd al-'Azim from Bakkar from Jabir from abu Ja'far, *'Alayhi al-Salam*, who has said the following:

"This verse of the Holy Quran was revealed as, 'If they had done what they had been advised to do [about Ali, *'Alayhi al-Salam*], it would have been for their own good. . . .,' (4:66) explained the Imam."

H 1138, Ch. 108, h 61

Ahmad has narrated from 'Abd al-'Azim from ibn 'Udhayna from Malik al-Juhanni who has said the following:

"Once I asked abu 'Abd Allah, *'Alayhi al-Salam*, about the meaning of the words of Allah: '. . . He has revealed this Quran to me to warn you and those who will receive it. . . .' (6:19)

"The Imam said, 'It means, whoever of the family of Muhammad, *'Alayhi al-Salam*, will be the Imam (Leader with Divine Authority), will warn people by means of the Holy Quran, just as the Messenger of Allah did.'"

H 1139, Ch. 108, h 62

Ahmad has narrated from 'Abd al-'Azim from al-Husayn ibn Mayyah from those who informed him and has said the following:

"Once a man read this verse before abu 'Abd Allah, *'Alayhi al-Salam*, '(Muhammad), tell them, "Act as you wish. Allah, His Messenger and the believers will see your deeds. . . ."' (9:105)

"The Imam said, 'It is not all believers. It refers to the infallible ones among them. We are the infallible ones.'"

H 1140, Ch. 108, h 63

Ahmad has narrated from 'Abd al-'Azim from Hisham ibn al-Hakam from abu 'Abd Allah, *'Alayhi al-Salam*, who has said the following:

"In the Holy Quran, 'This is the path which leads straight to Me [the path of Ali leads straight to Me],' (15:41) the word is *Aliy*, the name of Imam Ali not *'Alayya* which means 'upon me' or 'to me,' the Imam, *'Alayhi al-Salam*, explained."

H 1141, Ch. 108, h 64

Ahmad has narrated from 'Abd al-'Azim from Muhammad ibn al-Fudayl from abu Hamza from abu Ja'far, *'Alayhi al-Salam*, who has said the following:

"Jibril brought this verse as: '. . . but most human beings turn away [from *Wilayah*, Leadership with Divine Authority of Ali, *'Alayhi al-Salam*] in disbelief.' (17:89)

"Jibril also brought this verse as: 'Say, Truth comes from your Lord, [About *Wilayah*, Leadership with Divine Authority of Ali, *'Alayhi al-Salam*]. Allow people to believe or disbelieve it as they choose. For the unjust [to the family of Muhammad, *'Alayhi al-Salam*] We have prepared a fire. . . .,' (18:29) the Imam explained."

H 1142, Ch. 108, h 65

A number of our people have narrated from Ahmad ibn Muhammad from Muhammad ibn 'Isma'il from Muhammad ibn al-Fudayl from abu al-Hassan, *'Alayhi al-Salam*, who has said the following:

"About the words of Allah, 'All the places for prostration, mosques (or parts of the body to be placed on the ground during prostration) belong to Allah,' (72:18) the Imam, *'Alayhi al-Salam*, said, 'They (mosques) stand for the executors of the will of the Holy Prophet, *'Alayhi al-Salam*.'"

H 1143, Ch. 108, h 66

Muhammad ibn Yahya has narrated from Ahmad ibn Muhammad ibn 'Isa from ibn Mahbub from al-Ahwal from Salam ibn al-Mustanir from abu Ja'far, *'Alayhi al-Salam*, who has said the following:

"About the words of Allah, the Most High, '(Muhammad), say, 'This is my way. I and all my followers invite you to Allah with proper understanding. . . .,' (12:108) the Imam said, 'It applies to the Messenger of Allah and Amir al-Mu'minin Ali and the executors of his will after them, *'Alayhim al-Salam*.'"

H 1144, Ch. 108, h 67

Muhammad ibn Yahya has narrated from Ahmad ibn Muhammad from Muhammad ibn 'Isma'il from Hanan from Salim al-Hannat who has said the following:

"Once I asked abu Ja'far, *'Alayhi al-Salam*, about the meaning of the words of Allah, the Most Majestic, the Most Gracious, 'We saved the believers among them, (51:35) but We found only one Muslim house.' (51:36)

"The Imam said, 'That family is the family of Muhammad, *'Alayhi al-Salam*, besides whom no one else remained.'"

H 1145, Ch. 108, h 68

Al-Husayn ibn Muhammad has narrated from Mu'alla ibn Muhammad from Muhammad ibn Jumhur from 'Isma'il ibn Sahl from al-Qasim ibn 'Urwa from abu al-Safatij from Zurara from abu Ja'far, *'Alayhi al-Salam*, who has said the following:

"About the words of Allah, the Most High, 'When they see the torment approaching, the faces of the unbelievers will blacken and they will be told, "This is what you were called,"' (67:27) the Imam said, 'This was revealed about Amir al-Mu'minin Ali, *'Alayhi al-Salam*, and his contemporaries who did what they did to him. They will see Amir al-Mu'minin Ali, *'Alayhi al-Salam*, in such a position that it will make them envious. This will cause their faces to show misery. It will be said to them, "This is what you were 'called with', meaning the title *'Amir al-Mu'minin'* that you had assumed."'"

H 1146, Ch. 108, h 69

Muhammad ibn Yahya has narrated from Salama ibn al-Khattab from Ali ibn Hassa'n from 'Abd al-Rahman ibn Kathir from abu 'Abd Allah, *'Alayhi al-Salam*, who has said the following:

"About the words of Allah, the Most High, '. . . And by the witness and that which is witnessed. . . .,' (85:3) the Imam said, 'They are the Holy Prophet and Amir al-Mu'minin Ali, *'Alayhim al-Salam*.'"

H 1147, Ch. 108, h 70

Al-Husayn ibn Muhammad from Mu'alla ibn Muhammad from al-Washsha' from Ahmad ibn 'Umar al-Hallal who has said the following:

"Once I asked abu al-Hassan, *'Alayhi al-Salam*, about the words of Allah, the Most High: '. . . someone will cry out, "Allah has condemned the unjust."' (7:44)

"The Imam said, 'The caller will be Amir al-Mu'minin Ali, *'Alayhi al-Salam*.'"

H 1148, Ch. 108, h 71

Al-Husayn ibn Muhammad from Mu'alla ibn Muhammad ibn 'Urama from Ali ibn Hassa'n from 'Abd al-Rahman ibn Kathir from abu 'Abd Allah, *'Alayhi al-Salam*, who has said the following:

"About the words of Allah, the Most High, '. . . for they were guided to speak the noblest words and follow the praiseworthy path,' (22:24) the Imam said, 'They were Hamza, Ja'far, 'Ubayda, Salman, abu Dhar, al-Miqdad ibn al-Aswad and 'Ammar who "were guided" to Amir al-Mu'minin Ali, *'Alayhi al-Salam*. 'However, Allah has endeared belief to you and has made it attractive to your hearts' [refers to Amir al-Mu'minin Ali, *'Alayhi al-Salam*]. 'He has made disbelief, evil deeds and disobedience hateful to you. . . .' (49:7) [the first, the second and the third are meant thereby], the Imam explained.'"

H 1149, Ch. 108, h 72

Muhammad ibn Yahya has narrated from ibn Mahbub from Jamil ibn Salih from abu 'Ubayda who has said the following:

"Once I asked abu Ja'far, *'Alayhi al-Salam*, about the meaning of the words of Allah, the Most High: '. . . bring me a Book, revealed before this Quran, or anything remaining of knowledge to support your belief, if indeed you are truthful.' (46:4)

"The Imam said, 'Book refers to the Tora and the Gospel and the remaining knowledge refers to the knowledge of the executors of the wills of the prophets.'"

H 1150, Ch. 108, h 73

Al-Husayn ibn Muhammad has narrated from Mu'alla ibn Muhammad from the one who had narrated to him from Ali ibn Ja'far who has said the following:

"I heard abu al-Hassan, *'Alayhi al-Salam*, say, 'When the Messenger of Allah saw (in his dream) Taym, 'Adi and Amawids climb his pulpit he was severely frightened. Allah, the Most Holy, the Most High, sent him a reading to comfort him: "When We told the angels to prostrate before Adam they all obeyed except Iblis (Satan), who refused." (20:116) Then Allah sent him a message that said, 'O Muhammad, I commanded them and they disobeyed. Do not despair if you will command them and they will disobey you in the matters of the executor of your will.'"

H 1151, Ch. 108, h 74
Muhammad in Yahya has narrated from Ahmad ibn Muhammad from ibn Mahbub from al-Husayn ibn Nu'im al-Sahhaf who has said the following:
"Once I asked abu 'Abd Allah, *'Alayhi al-Salam*, about the words of Allah: '. . . certain persons of you have believed and others of you have not . . .' (64:2)

"The Imam said, 'Allah, the Most Majestic, the Most Gracious, has defined their belief by means of their love for us. He has defined their disbelief, in the same way, by the same fact. This took place on the day He asked all the offspring of Adam (in the form of minute beings) to make a covenant.'

"I then asked him about the words of Allah, the Most Majestic, the Most Gracious: 'Obey Allah and the Messenger, but if you turn away, you must know that the only duty of Our Messenger is to clearly preach.' (64:12)

"The Imam said, 'By Allah, no one of those who were destroyed before or those who will be destroyed up to the time of the rise of al-Mahdi with Divine Authority were or will be destroyed only because of their disregarding our *Wilayah* (Leadership with Divine Authority) and the denial of our rights. The Messenger of Allah did not leave this world before establishing the great responsibility on this 'Umma to observe our rights. Allah guides to the right path whomever he wants.'"

H 1152, Ch. 108, h 75
Muhammad ibn al-Hassan and Ali ibn Muhammad have narrated from Sahl ibn Ziyad from Musa ibn al-Qasim al-Bajaliy from Ali ibn Ja'far from his brother Musa, *'Alayhi al-Salam*, who has said the following:
"About the words of Allah, the Most High, '. . . Their lofty mansions and their wells were left idle,' (22:45) the Imam said, 'The abandoned well and idle well refers to the silent Imam and lofty mansion refers to the speaking Imam.'"

Muhammad ibn Yahya has narrated a similar *Hadith* from al-'Amraki from Ali ibn Ja'far from abu al-Hassan, *'Alayhi al-Salam*.

H 1153, Ch. 108, h 76
Ali ibn Ibrahim has narrated from his father from al-Hakam ibn al-Buhlul from a man from abu 'Abd Allah, *'Alayhi al-Salam*, who has said the following:
"About the words of Allah, the Most High, 'It has been revealed to you and to those who lived before you that if you consider other things equal to Allah, your deeds will be made devoid of all virtue. . . .,' (39:65) the Imam said, 'It means equal in *Wilayah* (Leadership with Divine Authority). "(Muhammad, you must worship Allah alone and give Him thanks,"' (39:66) the Imam said, 'It means

worship Allah through obedience and be thankful that I (Allah) have provided you support through your brother, your cousin.'"

H 1154, Ch. 108, h 77

Al-Husayn ibn Muhammad has narrated from Mu'alla ibn Muhammad from Ahmad ibn Muhammad from al-Hassan ibn Muhammad al-Hashimi who has said that his father narrated to him from Ahmad ibn 'Isa who has said that Ja'far ibn Muhammad, *'Alayhi al-Salam*, narrated to me from his father and from his grand father who has said the following:

"About the words of Allah, the Most Majestic, the Most Gracious, 'They know the bounties of Allah but they deny them. . . .,' (16:83) the Imam said that when this verse was revealed, 'Only Allah, His Messenger, and the true believers who are steadfast in prayer and pay alms, while they kneel during prayer, are your guardians,' (5:55) certain persons of the companions of the Messenger of Allah, gathered in the Mosque of Madina. They said, 'If we reject this verse we have rejected the rest of them. However, if we accept, it will be humiliating for us when Ali ibn abu Talib, *'Alayhi al-Salam*, will take control.' They said, 'We have learned that Muhammad, *'Alayhi al-Salam*, is truthful in all that he has said but we turned away in disobedience of his command to obey Ali, *'Alayhi al-Salam*.' The Imam said that upon this, a verse was revealed that reads: 'They do have knowledge of the bounties of Allah but they deny them. . . .' (16:83) It means that they know about the *Wilayah* (Leadership with Divine Authority) of Ali ibn abu Talib, *'Alayhi al-Salam*, but many of them have refused to acknowledge it.'"

H 1155, Ch. 108, h 78

Muhammad ibn Yahya has narrated from Ahmad ibn Muhammad ibn 'Isa from ibn Mahbub from Muhammad ibn al-Nu'man from Salam who has said the following:

"Once I asked abu Ja'far, *'Alayhi al-Salam*, about the words of Allah, the Most High: '(Among) the servants of the Beneficent are those who walk gently on the earth. . . .' (25:63)

"The Imam said, 'They are the executors of the will (of the Holy Prophet, *'Alayhi al-Salam*) who are afraid of their enemies.'"

H 1156, Ch. 108, h 79

Al-Husayn ibn Muhammad has narrated from Mu'alla ibn Muhammad from Bastam ibn Murra from Ishaq ibn Hassa'n from al-Haytham ibn Waqid from Ali ibn al-Husayn al-'Abdi from Sa'd al-'Iskaf from Asbagh ibn Nubata that he asked Amir al-Mu'minin Ali, *'Alayhi al-Salam*, who has said the following:

"About the words of Allah, the Most High: '. . . To give thanks to Me first and then your parents, to Me all things proceed,' (31:14) the Imam said, 'The parents who must be thanked are the ones who provide knowledge, and leave wisdom as their legacy and people are commanded to obey them. Allah then has said, ' . . to Me all things proceed.' (31:14) People proceed to Allah and the parents are the guides to such goal. Allah then has addressed ibn Hantama and his friend saying in particular and in general, 'If they try to force you to consider things as My partners, . . .' (31:15) [meaning partners with the executor of the will of the Holy Prophet, *'Alayhi al-Salam*], or try to make you deviate from the command to obey him (Ali, *'Alayhi al-Salam*), then do not obey them (parents in general, ibn Hantamah and friends in particular) and do not listen to them. Then Allah directed

His words to the case of the parents: 'Maintain lawful relations with them in this world. . . . .' (31:15) It says to propagate the virtue and excellence of the (spiritual) parents and call people to their guidance which is also mentioned in these words of Allah, '. . . and follow the path of those who turn in repentance to Me. To Me you will all return. . . .' (31:15)

"The Imam said, 'To Allah then to us. You must be pious before Allah and do not disobey the parents. To please them is to please Allah and to cause them anger is to cause anger to Allah.'"

H 1157, Ch. 108, h 80

A number of our people have narrated from Ahmad ibn Muhammad from Ali ibn Sayf from his father from 'Amr ibn Harith who has said the following:

"Once I asked abu 'Abd Allah, *'Alayhi al-Salam*, about the words of Allah, the Most High: '. . . a blessed tree which has firm roots and branches rising up into the sky.' (14:24)

"The Imam said that the Messenger of Allah, *'Alayhi al-Salam*, said, 'The root is Amir al-Mu'minin Ali and the branches are *'A'immah* (Leaders with Divine Authority), *'Alayhim al-Salam*, from their (Amir al-Mu'minin Ali and the Holy Prophet's, *'Alayhim al-Salam*) descendents and the knowledge of *'A'immah* stand for the fruits. Their faithful followers represent the leaves of such tree.' The Imam then asked, 'Is there anything else in the tree?' I said, 'No, there is nothing else there.' The Imam then said, 'By Allah, when a believer gives birth to a child a leaf grows in the tree and when a believer dies a leaf falls off the tree.'"

H 1158, Ch. 108, h 81

Muhammad ibn Yahya has narrated from Hamdan ibn Sulayman from 'Abd Allah ibn Muhammad al-Yamani from Mani' ibn al-Hajjaj from Yunus from Hisham ibn al-Hakam from abu 'Abd Allah, *'Alayhi al-Salam*, who has said the following:

"About the words of Allah, the Most Majestic, the Most Gracious, '. . . The belief of any soul will be of no avail to it unless it was formed before [when Allah asked all people for a covenant] or has earned good deeds with it. . . .,' (6:158) the Imam said, 'It (earned good deeds) means to acknowledge the prophets and the executors of their wills especially Amir al-Mu'minin Ali, *'Alayhi al-Salam.*' The Imam also said, 'The belief of a soul will not be of any benefit; it will be removed.'"

H 1159, Ch. 108, h 82

Through the same chain of narrators it is narrated from Yunus from Sabah al-Muzniy from abu Hamza from one of them, *'Alayhi al-Salam*, who has said the following:

"About the words of Allah, the Most Majestic, the Most Gracious, 'There is no doubt that evil doers who are engulfed in sins, [when one rejects *Wilayah* of Amir al-Mu'minin Ali, *'Alayhi al-Salam*] are the companions of hellfire wherein they will live forever,' (2:81) the Imam explained."

H 1160, Ch. 108, h 83

A number of our people have narrated from Ahmad ibn Muhammad ibn abu Nasr from Hammad ibn 'Uthman from abu 'Ubayda al-Hadhdha' who has said the following:

"Once I asked abu Ja'far, *'Alayhi al-Salam*, about the capability and the words of people. The Imam recited this verse of the Holy Quran: '. . . they still have different beliefs (11:118) except those upon whom Allah has granted His mercy. For this reason He has created them. . . .' (11:119) 'O abu 'Ubayda, people face differences in search for truth and all of them will be destroyed,' said the Imam.

'I (the narrator) then asked, "What about the words of Allah: '. . . except those who receive mercy from your Lord. . . .?'" (11:119)

'The Imam said, "Such people are our followers whom He has created for His mercy. '. . . For this reason He has created them. . . .'" (11:119)

Note: in the following passage, as the previous ones, what is inside brackets is the words of the Imam and the rest are the words of the Holy Quran.

'[He (Allah) has said that they are created to obey the Imam of 'Blessings' that He has mentioned in His words]: ". . . My mercy and blessings have encompassed all things. . . ." (7:156) [Such 'Blessing' is the knowledge of Imam. The knowledge of *'A'immah* (Leaders with Divine Authority) is from His knowledge, which has encompassed all things. They (all things) stand for our Shi'a, followers].

'[Then He has said], ". . . I shall grant mercy to those who maintain piety [do not acknowledge the authority of and obedience to those who are not of *'A'immah*] . . ." (7:156)

'[Then Allah has said], ". . . whose description they find written in the Torah and the Gospel, . . . [the Holy Prophet, the executor of his will and *al-Qa'im* (the one who will rise with Divine Authority)] . . . enjoins them to do good [when he will rise with Divine Authority and power] . . . and forbids them to do all that is unlawful . . . [*Munkar*, unlawful, is one who does not acknowledge the *Wilayah* of Imam and denies it] . . . He makes lawful for them all that is pure . . . [he receives knowledge from its proper source] . . . and unlawful all that is filthy. . . . [The words of those who oppose the Imam are filthy] . . . He removes their burdens . . . [the sins that they had before acknowledging *Wilayah* of the Imam] . . . and the entanglements in which they are involved . . . [the entanglements are the words that they were not commanded to express. Such words were not in praise and virtue of the Imam, *'Alayhi al-Salam*. When they recognized the excellence of the Imam, He removed their burden. Such burden is the sin. Then He further has explained about them], '. . . those who believe in him [the Imam] . . . honor and help him, and follow the light which is sent down to him, will have everlasting happiness.'" (7:157) [Such people are those who kept away from the worship of the Devil and Satan. So and so and so ones are Devil and Satan. 'Worship' means people's obeying them. Allah then has said], 'Turn to your Lord in repentance and submit to Him. . . .,' (39:54) [then He has granted them rewards], '. . . will receive glad news both in this life and in the life hereafter. . . .' (10:64) [Imam gives them the glad news of the rise of *al-Mahdi* with Divine Authority, the news of the destruction of their enemies and salvation in the hereafter and their meeting Imam Ali and Prophet Muhammad, *'Alayhim al-Salam*, and their truthful family at the pond of al-Kawthar in paradise].'"

H 1161, Ch. 108, h 84

Ali ibn Muhammad has narrated from Sahl ibn Ziyad from ibn Mahbub from Hisham ibn Salim from 'Ammar al-Sabati who has said the following:

"Once I asked abu 'Abd Allah, *'Alayhi al-Salam*, about the words of Allah, the Most Majestic, the Most Gracious: 'Are those who seek Allah's pleasure equal to those who incur His wrath, and whose dwelling will be hell, the terrible destination? (3:162) People are of varying status in the sight of Allah. . . .' (3:163)

"The Imam said, 'Those who follow the pleasure of Allah are *'A'immah* (Leaders with Divine Authority), *'Alayhim al-Salam*. They, by Allah, O 'Ammar, grade and qualify the true believers. By means of our *Wilayah* (Leadership and Guardianship with Divine Authority) and their acknowledging us, Allah increases the reward for their good deeds and raises them to higher positions.'"

H 1162, Ch. 108, h 85

Ali ibn Muhammad and others have narrated from Sahl ibn Ziyad from Ya'qub ibn Yazid from Ziyad al-Qandi from 'Ammar al-'Asadi from abu 'Abd Allah, *'Alayhi al-Salam*, who has said the following:

"About the words of Allah, the Most Majestic, the Most Gracious, '. . . good words will be presented before Him and He will accept good deeds. . . .,' (35:10) the Imam said, 'It (good words) is our *Wilayah* (Leadership and Guardianship with Divine Authority).' He made a gesture with his hands to his own chest saying, 'Allah will not raise the deeds of those who do not acknowledge our *Wilayah*.'"

H 1163, Ch. 108, h 86

A number of our people have narrated from Ahmad ibn Muhammad from al-Husayn ibn Sa'id from al-Nadr ibn Suwayd from al-Qasim ibn Sulayman from Sama'a from abu 'Abd Allah, *'Alayhi al-Salam*, who has said the following:

"About the words of Allah, the Most Majestic, the Most Gracious, '. . . Allah will grant you *kiflayn* (two shares, guradians) of mercy, [al-Hassan and al-Husayn, *'Alayhi al-Salam*] a light by which you can walk. . . .' (57:28) the Imam said, 'Light' stands for the Imam you follow.'"

H 1164, Ch. 108, h 87

Ali ibn Ibrahim has narrated from his father from al-Qasim ibn Muhammad al-Jawhari from certain persons of his people from abu 'Abd Allah, *'Alayhi al-Salam*, who has said the following:

"About the words of Allah, 'They ask you, is He real . . .?' The Imam said, 'They ask, "What do you say about Ali, *'Alayhi al-Salam*?" '. . . Tell them, it certainly is true. I swear by my Lord. You cannot escape from Allah's (retribution).'" (10:53)

H 1165, Ch. 108, h 88

Ali ibn Muhammad has narrated from Sahl ibn Ziyad from Muhammad ibn Sulayman al-Daylami from his father from Aban ibn Taghlib who has said the following:

"Once I asked abu 'Abd Allah, *'Alayhi al-Salam*, 'May Allah keep my soul in service for your cause, what is the meaning of the words of Allah: "Yet, he has not entered into 'Aqaba." (90:11)

'The Imam said, "To whomever Allah has granted honor through our *Wilayah* (Leadership with Divine Authority) he has crossed the *'Aqaba* (stage). We are the *'Aqaba*. Whoever reaches us gains his salvation."

'He (the Imam) remained calm for a while and then asked me, "Do you want to learn a letter (word, a fact) from that which is better for you than the whole world and all that is therein?" I said, "Yes, may Allah keep my soul in service for your cause." He then recited, ". . . It is the setting free of a slave." (90:13) Then he (the Imam) said, "All people are slaves of fire, except you and your people. Allah has set you free from fire through our (*Ahl al-Bayt*'s) *Wilayah* (Leadership and Guardianship with Divine Authority)." ' "

H 1166, Ch. 108, h 89

Ali ibn Ibrahim has narrated from his father from ibn abu 'Umayr from Sama'a from abu 'Abd Allah, *'Alayhi al-Salam*, who has said the following:

"About the words of Allah, the Most Majestic, the Most Gracious, '. . . fulfill your covenant with Me. . . .,' the Imam said that it is [the covenant to acknowledge *Wilayah* of Ali, *'Alayhi al-Salam*] . . . and I shall fulfill Mine . . .' [Admit you in paradise]." (2:40)

H 1167, Ch. 108, h 90

Muhammad ibn Yahya has narrated from Salma ibn al-Khattab from al-Hassan ibn 'Abd al-Rahman from Ali ibn abu Hamza from abu Basir from abu 'Abd Allah, *'Alayhi al-Salam*, who has said the following:

"About the words of Allah, the Most Majestic, the Most Gracious, 'When Our clear revelations are recited to them, the unbelievers ask the believers, "Which of us has a better position and is more prosperous?"' (19:73), the Imam said, 'The Messenger of Allah once asked Quraysh (the powerful tribe in Makkah) to acknowledge our *Wilayah*, (Leadership with Divine Authority). They turned away and refused. The unbelievers of Quraysh asked the true believers of Quraysh (those who acknowledged our *Wilayah*), "Which group among us has a better position and is more prosperous?" This was to humiliate the true believers. Allah then asked, "How many generations [people of the past] of greater prosperity and splendor have We destroyed before them?"' (19:74)

"I then asked the meaning of: '(Muhammad), tell them, "The Beneficent gives respite to those who have gone astray. . . ."' (19:75)

"The Imam said, 'All of them lived a life in error and did not acknowledge *Wilayah* of Amir al-Mu'minin Ali, *'Alayhi al-Salam*, and our *Wilayah*. They lived in error and led others to error. Allah gives them time in their error and rebellion until they die. He then causes them to have the worst of dwellings and be of the weakest parties.'

"I then asked him about the meaning of: '. . . until they face the torment of which they were warned or the Day of Judgment. Then they will find out who will have the most miserable place and the weakest forces.' (19:75)

431

"The Imam said, '. . . until they face the torment of which they were warned . . .,' is the time of the rise of al-Mahdi with Divine Authority and power. That is the time when they will find out what Allah will send to them through the hands of al-Mahdi, *'Alayhi al-Salam*, and thus, are His words: '. . . who will have the most miserable place . . . [at the time of the rise of al-Mahdi with Divine Authority and power] . . . and the weakest forces.' (19:75)

"I then asked about the words of Allah: '. . . Allah further enlightens those who seek guidance. . . .' (19:76)

"The Imam said, 'Allah will grant them more guidance and certainty to follow *al-Qa'im* (the one who will rise with Divine Authority and power) so that they will not reject or refuse his authority.'

"I then asked about the words of Allah: 'No one will be able to intercede for the others except those whom the Beneficent has given authority (due to His covenant).' (19:87)

"The Imam said, 'The acknowledgment of *Wilayah* of Amir al-Mu'minin Ali and *'A'immah* (Leaders with Divine Authority), *'Alayhim al-Salam*, after him is part of the religion of Allah and this is the authority and the covenant before Allah.'

"I then asked about the words of Allah: 'To the righteously striving believers Allah will grant love.' (19:96)

"The Imam said, 'It is the love for Amir al-Mu'minin Ali, *'Alayhi al-Salam*, and to acknowledge his *Wilayah*. It is this love of which Allah speaks in His words, "(Muhammad), We have given it to you (the Book, the Holy Quran) in your own language so that you can easily give the glad news to the pious ones and warn the quarrelsome ones.'" (19:97) The Imam said, 'It was made easy for him when Allah appointed Amir al-Mu'minin Ali, *'Alayhi al-Salam*, as the standard of truth. With him He gave glad news to the true believers and warning to the unbelievers. It is these unbelievers whom He in His book has called, "The quarrelsome ones."

"I (the narrator) then asked him about the words of Allah: '. . . so that you may warn a people who are unaware because their fathers were not warned.' (36:6)

"The Imam said, 'It was to warn the people with whom the Holy Prophet, *'Alayhi al-Salam*, lived just as their forefathers were warned and they were unaware of Allah, His messenger and His warning. ". . . (I swear) that most of them are doomed to be punished [for not acknowledging the *Wilayah* of Ali and *'A'immah*, *'Alayhim al-Salam*, after him]. '. . . They have no faith. . . .'" (36:7) [in the *Wilayah* of Ali and the executors of the will after him, *'Alayhi al-Salam*. Since they did not believe and their punishment was as such as Allah has mentioned, ". . . We have enchained their necks up to their chins. Thus, they cannot bend their heads [in hell] (to find their way)." (36:8) [Then Allah has said], ". . . We have setup a barrier in front and behind them and have made them blind. Thus, they cannot see." (36:10) [It will be the punishment for not acknowledging the *Wilayah* of Ali and *'A'immah* after him. This is in this world and in the next life it will be hell wherein they will not be able to raise their heads. Then Allah has said], ". . . Whether you, Muhammad, warn them or not, they will not believe," (36:10) [in Allah and the *Wilayah* of Ali and the *'A'immah*, *'Alayhi al-Salam*, after him. Then Allah has said], ". . . You should warn only those who follow the Holy Quran [meaning thereby Amir al-Mu'minin Ali, *'Alayhi al-Salam*], '. . . and have fear of the Beneficent without seeing Him. Give them [O Muhammad], the glad news of their receiving forgiveness and an honorable reward (from Allah).'" (36:11)."

Note: in the following *Hadith* as the previous one, inside brackets are the words of the Imam, and the words of the Holy Quran are placed inside single or double quotation marks.

H 1168, Ch. 108, h 91
Ali ibn Muhammad has narrated from certain persons of our people from ibn Mahbub from Muhammad ibn al-Fudayl who has said the following:

"The narrator has said that once I asked abu al-Hassan, *'Alayhi al-Salam*, about the words of Allah, the Most Majestic, the Most Gracious: 'They want to put out the light of Allah with their mouths. . . .' (61:8) The Imam said, 'They want to banish *Wilayah* of Amir al-Mu'minin, Ali, *'Alayhi al-Salam*, with their mouths.' I then read from the Holy Quran, '. . . but Allah will certainly make His light shine forever. . . .' (61:8) The Imam said, 'Allah will complete Imamat (Leadership with Divine Authority) as He, the Majestic, the Glorious, has said in His words, ". . . Those who have faith in Allah, His Messenger and the light which We have revealed . . ." (64:8) 'Light' stands for the Imam.' I then asked about, 'It is He who has sent His Messenger with guidance and the true religion. . . .' (61:9) The Imam then said, 'It is He Who sent His Messenger with *Wilayah* for the executor of his will and *Wilayah* is the true religion.'

"I then read from the Holy Quran: '. . . make the true religion to stand supreme over all religions. . . .' (61:9) The Imam said, 'He will make it stand supreme at the time of (the rise of al-Mahdi with Divine Authority and power) as Allah has said, ". . . He will make the true religion [*Wilayah of al-Qa'im*] stand supreme over all religions, . . . even though the pagans may dislike it.'" (61:9) The Imam said, 'They are the unbelievers in the *Wilayah* of Ali, *'Alayhi al-Salam*.'"I then asked, 'Is it revelation from Allah?' He, *'Alayhi al-Salam*, replied, 'These words are revelation (things that Jibril brought as part of the Holy Quran) but the others are interpretation.'

"I then read from the Holy Quran: 'This is because they accepted the faith and then rejected it. . . .' (63:3) The Imam said, 'Allah, the Most Holy, the Most High, has called those who do not follow His Messenger in the matter of *Wilayah,* as hypocrites. He has considered those who reject *Imamat* just as those who rejected Muhammad, *'Alayhi al-Salam*, and to this effect He has revealed certain verses in the Holy Quran: "When the hypocrites . . . [in the matter of *Wilayah* of the executor or your will, Ali, *'Alayhi al-Salam*] . . . come to you, they say, 'We testify that you are the Messenger of Allah.' Allah knows that you are His Messenger. Allah testifies that the hypocrites. . . . [in the matters of *Wilayah* of Ali, *'Alayhi al-Salam*] . . . are liars. (63:1) They have chosen their oaths as a shield to obstruct others from the way of Allah. [*The way* is the executor of the will]. How terrible is what they do! (63:2) This is because they accepted the faith [your message] and then rejected it [*Wilayah* of the executor of your will]. Allah has sealed their hearts, thus, they do not have any understanding.'" (63:3)

"I (the narrator) then asked, 'What is the meaning of: ". . . they do not have any understanding?'" (63:3) The Imam said, 'Allah has said that they do not think about your prophecy.' I then asked about the meaning of Allah's words: 'When they are told, "Come forward so the Messenger of Allah (can) seek forgiveness for you. . . ."'" (63:6) The Imam said, 'It means that when they are asked to come back to the *Wilayah* of Ali, *'Alayhi al-Salam*, so the Messenger of Allah, *'Alayhi al-Salam*, will ask Allah to forgive your sins, ". . . they shake their heads [Allah says] and you can see them turning away arrogantly," (63:6) [from the *Wilayah* of Ali, *'Alayhi al-Salam*. Allah then has reiterated His words about the fact that they know the *Wilayah* very well saying], '. . . It is all the same whether you seek forgiveness for them or not, Allah will never forgive them. Allah does not guide the evildoing people.' (63:6) The Imam said, 'It refers to the unjust ones against the executor of will.'

"I then asked the Imam about the meaning of the words of Allah: 'Can one who walks with his head hanging down be better guided than one who walks with his head upright?' (67:22) The Imam said, 'Allah has considered the ones who deviate from *Wilayah* of Ali, *'Alayhi al-Salam*, as those who walk with their heads bent down without knowing what is around them. He, on the other hand, has considered those who acknowledge *Wilayah* of Ali, *'Alayhi al-Salam*, as those who walk by the straight path. Amir al-Mu'minin Ali, *'Alayhi al-Salam*, is the straight path.'

"I (the narrator) then asked the Imam about the words of Allah: '. . . the Holy Quran is certainly the word of a reverent messenger.' (69:40) The Imam said, 'It is the words of Jibril from Allah about *Wilayah* of Ali, *'Alayhi al-Salam*.'

"I then asked about the words of Allah: 'It is not the word of a poet but only a few of you have faith.' (69:41) The Imam said, 'They had said that Muhammad, *'Alayhi al-Salam*, is not truthful about his Lord and Allah has not commanded him anything about Ali, *'Alayhi al-Salam*. Allah then revealed in the Quran (a reading) about it that said, ". . . It [*Wilayah* of Ali, *'Alayhi al-Salam*] is a revelation from the Lord of the worlds. (69:43) Had Muhammad invented certain words against Us, (69:44) We would have caught hold of him by his right hand (69:45) and cut off his main artery." (69:46). [Then Allah has turned to *Wilayah* of Ali, *'Alayhi al-Salam*, saying], 'Certainly [*Wilayah* of Ali, *'Alayhi al-Salam*] is a reminder for the [worlds of] pious ones. (69:48) We certainly know that certain ones of you have rejected it (69:49) and (on the Day of Judgment) this [*Wilayah* of Ali, *'Alayhi al-Salam*] will be a great source of regret for the unbelievers (69:50). This [*Wilayah* of Ali, *'Alayhi al-Salam*] is the Truth beyond any doubt. (69:51) (Muhammad), speak of the Glory of the name of your Lord, the Great

One.' (69:52) The Imam also said that Allah has said, 'Thank (O Muhammad) your Lord, the Great, Who has granted you this distinction.'

"I (the narrator) then asked the Imam, *'Alayhi al-Salam*, about the words of Allah: 'Now that we have listened to the guidance, we believe in it. . . . (72:13) [The Imam said, 'Guidance is *Wilayah* of Ali, *'Alayhi al-Salam*. We have established belief in *Wilayah* of our guardian and those who do so], . . . Whoever believes in his Lord [whoever establishes belief in the Divine Authority of his guardian] does not fear loss or oppression.' (72:13)

"I then asked the Imam, 'Is it (the words of the Imam) or the revealed words of Allah?' He (the Imam) said, 'No, it is interpretation.'

"I then asked him about the words of Allah: 'Say, I do not possess any power to harm or benefit you.' (72:21) The Imam said, 'The Messenger of Allah called people to acknowledge *Wilayah* of Ali, *'Alayhi al-Salam*. Quraysh came to him and said, "O Muhammad, absolve us from such acknowledgment." The Messenger of Allah said, "It is not from me but it is up to Allah." They accused him and left him. Allah then revealed this reading: "Say, 'I do not possess any power to harm or benefit you.'" (72:21) "Say, 'No one can protect me from Allah, [if I disobey Him] nor can I find any place of refuge but with Him (72:22). My only (means of protection) is to convey the message of Allah. . . .'" (72:23) [about Ali, *'Alayhi al-Salam*].'

"I then asked, 'Is it the revealed words of Allah?' He (the Imam) said, 'Yes, it is the revealed word of Allah.' Allah has, to place more emphasis, said, '. . . whoever disobeys Allah and His Messenger [in the matters of *Wilayah* of Ali, *'Alayhi al-Salam*] is doomed to hell, wherein he will live forever.' (72:23)

"I then read the words of Allah: '. . . until the unbelievers witness that with which they have been warned. They will then know whose helpers are weaker and fewer in number.' (72:24) The Imam said, 'It is a reference to the rise of al-Mahdi with Divine Authority and power and his supporters.'

"I then read the words of Allah: 'Bear patiently whatever they say. . . .' (73:10) The Imam said, 'Be patient in what they say about you, ". . . and leave them and distance from them in an honorable manner. (73:10) Leave [O Muhammad,] the prosperous unbelievers [in *Wilayah* of Ali, *'Alayhi al-Salam*, the executor of your will] to Me and give them respite for a little while." (73:11)

"I then asked him, 'Is it the revealed words of Allah?' He (the Imam) said, 'Yes, it is.'

"I then read the words of Allah: 'It gives more certainty to the people of the Book. . . .' (74:31) The Imam said, 'They had certainty that Allah, His Messenger and the executor of his will are true.'

"I then read the words of Allah: '. . . and strengthens the faith of the believers . . .' (74:31) The Imam said, '*Wilayah* of Ali, *'Alayhi al-Salam*, strengthens their faith.'

"I then read the words of Allah, '. . . The people of the Book and the believers have no doubt about it. . . .' (74:31) The Imam said, 'They have no doubts in the *Wilayah* of Ali, *'Alayhi al-Salam*.'

"I then asked, 'What is this doubt?' He (the Imam) said, 'It refers to people of the Book and the believers that Allah has mentioned. He (the Imam) said that they do not doubt the *Wilayah* of Ali, *'Alayhi al-Salam*.'

"I then read the words of Allah: '. . . This parable is a reminder for mankind.' (74:31) The Imam said, 'Yes, it is the *Wilayah* of Ali, *'Alayhi al-Salam*.' I then recited: '. . . it is certainly one of the two great things.' (74:35) The Imam said, 'It is the *Wilayah* of Ali, *'Alayhi al-Salam*.'

"I then read the words of Allah: '. . . whether one steps forward to embrace the faith or one turns away from it.' (74:37) The Imam said, 'One who steps forward to our *Wilayah* has stepped away from hell and one who steps away from our *Wilayah* has stepped closer to hell.'

"I then read the words of Allah: '. . . except the people of the right hand.' (74:39) The Imam said, 'They, by Allah, are our Shi'a (followers).'

"I then read the words of Allah: '. . . We did not pray,' (74:43) The Imam said, 'It refers to their saying, "We did not believe in *Wilayah* of Ali, *'Alayhi al-Salam*, and *'A'immah* (Leaders with Divine Authority) after him and they do not offer the special greeting for them."'"

"I then read the words of Allah: '. . . why do they run away from guidance?' (74:49) The Imam said, 'It means running away from our *Wilayah*.'

"I then read the words of Allah: 'There is no doubt that it is a guide.' (74:54) The Imam said, 'It refers to *Wilayah* of Ali, *'Alayhi al-Salam*.'

"I then read the words of Allah: 'The servants of Allah fulfill their vows. . . .' (76:7) The Imam said, 'They fulfill the vow and covenant that they had made to acknowledge our *Wilayah*.'

"I then read the words of Allah: '(Muhammad), We have revealed the Holy Quran to you in gradual steps.' (76:23) The Imam said, 'It means, revealed with *Wilayah* of Ali, *'Alayhi al-Salam*.'

"I then asked, 'Is it of the revealed words of Allah?' He (the Imam) said, 'Yes, with interpretation.'

436

"I then read the words of Allah: 'This (chapter) is a reminder. . . .' (76:29) The Imam said, 'It is a reminder of *Wilayah*.'

"I then read the words of Allah: 'He admits to His mercy whomever He wants. . . .' (76:31) The Imam said, 'He admits in our *Wilayah*.' The Imam also recited the words of Allah: '. . . for the unjust He has prepared a painful punishment.' (76:31) [Consider that Allah has said], '. . . they (children of Israel) did not wrong Us but wronged themselves.' (2:57) The Imam further said, 'Allah is by far more Glorious than to do injustice or ascribe injustice to Himself. However, Allah has mixed our affairs with Hisown, thus, He has called injustice to us as injustice to Himself and our *Wilayah* as His own *Wilayah* and guardianship. About this matter He revealed Quran (a reading) to His Prophet that reads: "We did not do any wrong to them but they wronged themselves."' (16:118)

"I then asked, 'Is it the revealed word of Allah?' He (the Imam) said, 'Yes, it is.'

"I then read the words of Allah: 'On that Day, woe will be to those who have rejected Allah's revelations.' (77:15) The Imam said, 'Allah will say, "O Muhammad, woe is to those who reject what I have revealed. . . ." [about the *Wilayah* of Ali (ibn abu Talib), *'Alayhi al-Salam*]. Did We not destroy the ancient people (77:16) and make others settle after them in their land?" (77:17) [The Imam said that the ancient people were those who refused to obey the prophets about the executors of their will]. 'Thus do We deal with the sinful ones.' (77:18) [The Imam said, 'It refers to those who sinned in the matters of the *Ahl al-Bayt* (family) of Muhammad, *'Alayhim al-Salam*, and did to them what they did].'

"I then read the words of Allah: 'The pious ones . . .' (77:41) The Imam said, 'By Allah, only we and our Shi'a (followers) follow truly the religion of Abraham (Ibrahim). Other people have no relationship with it.'

"I then read the words of Allah: 'On that day, the Spirit and the angels who stand in lines will not speak. . . .' (78:38) The Imam said, 'We, by Allah, on the Day of Judgment will have the permission to speak the truth.' I asked him, 'What will you say when you speak?' The Imam said, 'We will praise our Lord, greet our Holy Prophet, *'Alayhi al-Salam*, and intercede for our Shi'a. Our Lord will not reject our request.'

"I then read the words of Allah: '. . . the records of the sinner's deeds are in Sijjin.' (83:7) The Imam said, 'They are the ones who did injustice to *'A'immah, 'Alayhim al-Salam*, and treated them with hostility.'

"I then read the words of Allah: '. . . This is what you had called a lie.' (83:17) The Imam said, 'It refers to Amir al-Mu'minin Ali, *'Alayhi al-Salam*.'

"I then asked, 'Is it the revealed word of Allah?' The Imam, *'Alayhi al-Salam*, said, 'Yes, it is.'"

H 1169, Ch. 108, h 92

Muhammad ibn Yahya has narrated from Salama ibn al-Khattab from al-Husayn ibn 'Abd al-Rahman from Ali ibn abu Hamza from abu Basir from abu 'Abd Allah, *'Alayhi al-Salam*, who has said the following:

"About the words of Allah, the Most Majestic, the Most Gracious, 'Whoever ignores My guidance will live a woeful life. . . .' (20:124), the Imam, *'Alayhi al-Salam*, said, 'It means ignoring *Wilayah* of Ali, *'Alayhi al-Salam*.'

"I then read the words of Allah: '. . . and will be brought blind in Our presence on the Day of Judgment.' (20:124) The Imam said, 'It means blind of eyes in the next life and blind of heart toward *Wilayah* of Amir al-Mu'minin Ali, *'Alayhi al-Salam*, in this life.' The Imam also said, 'He will be confused on the Day of Judgment and will ask, ". . . he will say, My Lord, why have you brought me back to life blind when before I could see? (20:125) The Lord will say, this is true. But just as you forgot Our revelations that had come to you, so, also, you are forgotten on this day." (20:126) The Imam said, 'Revelations stand for *'A'immah* (Leaders with Divine Authority), *'Alayhim al-Salam*, that you rejected so also you are rejected and left to the fire today. You did not obey their commands and did not listen to their words.'

"I then read the words of Allah: 'Thus We recompense those who are unjust and have no faith in Our revelations. The torment in the life to come will be more severe and of extended duration.' (20:127) The Imam said, 'It refers to those who accept others as partners of Amir al-Mu'minin Ali, *'Alayhi al-Salam*, in the matters of *Wilayah*. It refers to those who do not believe in the revelations of his Lord and have left *'A'immah*, *'Alayhim al-Salam*, on account of hostility, who have not followed their teachings and have not acknowledged their *Wilayah* (Leadership with Divine Authority).'

"I then read the words of Allah: 'Allah is kind to His servants. He gives sustenance to whomever He wants. . . .' (42:19) The Imam said, 'Sustenance is the *Wilayah* of Ali, *'Alayhi al-Salam*.'

"I then read the words of Allah: 'We shall increase the harvest of those who seek a good harvest in the life hereafter. . . .' (42:20) The Imam said, 'It is recognition of Amir al-Mu'minin Ali and *'A'immah*, *'Alayhim al-Salam*, from whom they receive additional gains. He also said, such people will receiver their share in the government (of *'A'immah*).' '. . . however, those who want to have their harvest in this life, We will give to them thereof but they will have no share in the hereafter.' (42:20) The Imam said, 'They will have no share in the government of truth at the time of *al-Qa'im*, the one who will rise with Divine Authority and power).'"

Chapter 109 - Notable Points and Comprehensive Ahadith about Wilayah (Divine Authority)

H 1170, Ch. 109, h 1

Muhammad ibn Ya'qub al-Kulayni has narrated from Muhammad ibn al-Hassan and Ali ibn Muhammad from Sahl ibn Ziyad from ibn Mahbub from ibn al-Ri'ab from Bukayr ibn 'A'yan who has said the following:

"Abu Ja'far, *'Alayhi al-Salam*, would often say, 'Allah made our Shi'a (followers) to acknowledge our *Wilayah* (Leadership with Divine Authority) when they were only in the realm of small particles. It was the day when Allah made the small particles to acknowledge Him as the Lord and Muhammad, *'Alayhi al-Salam*, as His prophet.'"

H 1171, Ch. 109, h 2

Muhammad ibn Yahya has narrated from Muhammad ibn al-Husayn from Muhammad ibn 'Isma'il ibn Bazi' from Salih ibn 'Uqba from 'Abd Allah ibn Muhammad al-Ja'fari from abu Ja'far, *'Alayhi al-Salam*, and from 'Uqba from abu Ja'far, *'Alayhi al-Salam*, who has said the following:

"Abu Ja'far, *'Alayhi al-Salam*, has said, 'Allah created the creatures. He created whatever He loved from whatever He loved. He created those most beloved to Him from the clay of paradise. He created those He disliked from that which He disliked. Thus, He created from the clay of fire that which He disliked most. Then He sent them to the shadow.'

'I asked him, "What is the shadow?" The Imam asked, 'Have you not seen your own shadow in the sun that when you look at, it is nothing. Allah then sent to them the prophets who called them to acknowledge Allah as the Creator. This is the meaning of His words. "(Muhammad), if you ask them, 'Who has created them (idols)?' They will certainly say, 'Allah has created them. . . .' (43:87)

'Then He called them to acknowledge the prophets. Certain ones of them acknowledged and others did not acknowledge. Then He called them to acknowledge our *Wilayah* (Leadership with Divine Authority). Those whom He loved, by Allah, acknowledged and those whom He disliked did not acknowledge as He has said, "However, how could the people believe what they had previously called lies? . . ." (10:74) Abu Ja'far, *'Alayhi al-Salam*, then said, 'Refusal to acknowledge was then and there.' ' "

H 1172, Ch. 109, h 3

Muhammad ibn Yahya has narrated from Salama ibn al-Khattab from Ali ibn Sayf from al-'Abbass ibn 'Amir from Ahmad ibn Rizq al-Ghumushani from Muhammad ibn 'Abd al-Rahman from abu 'Abd Allah, *'Alayhi al-Salam*, who has said the following:

"Abu 'Abd Allah, *'Alayhi al-Salam*, has said, 'Our *Wilayah,* Leadership with Divine Authority is the *Wilayah,* Guardianship and Authority of Allah without which no prophet was ever sent.'"

H 1173, Ch. 109, h 4

Muhammad ibn Yahya has narrated from 'Abd Allah ibn Muhammad ibn 'Isa from Muhammad ibn 'Abd al-Hamid from Yunus ibn Ya'qub from 'Abd al-'Ala who has said the following:

"I heard abu 'Abd Allah, *'Alayhi al-Salam*, say, 'No prophet has ever been sent without his acknowledgement of our rights and our having distinction over others.'"

H 1174, Ch. 109, h 5

Muhammad ibn Yahya has narrated from Ahmad ibn Muhammad ibn 'Isa from Muhammad ibn 'Isma'il ibn Bazi' from Muhammad ibn al-Fudayl from abu al-Sabbah al-Kinani who has said the following:

"I heard abu Ja'far, *'Alayhi al-Salam*, say, 'By Allah, in the heavens there are seventy lines of angels. Even if all the inhabitants of earth try to count one line of them they will not be able to count them. All of these angels acknowledge our *Wilayah* (Leadership with Divine Authority).'"

H 1175, Ch. 109, h 6

Muhammad ibn Yahya has narrated from Ahmad ibn Muhammad from ibn Mahbub from Muhammad ibn al-Fudayl from abu al-Hassan, *'Alayhi al-Salam*, who has said the following:

"Abu al-Hassan, *'Alayhi al-Salam*, has said, *'Wilayah* of Ali, *'Alayhi al-Salam*, (Leadership with Divine Authority) is written in all the books of the prophets. Allah never sent a messenger who did not acknowledge the prophet-hood of Muhammad, *'Alayhi al-Salam*, and Ali, *'Alayhi al-Salam*, as the executor of his will."

H 1176, Ch. 109, h 7

Al-Husayn ibn Muhammad has narrated from Mu'alla ibn Muhammad from Muhammad ibn Jumhur who has said that Yunus narrated to him from Hammad ibn 'Uthman from al-Fudayl ibn Yasar from abu Ja'far, *'Alayhi al-Salam*, who has said the following:

"Abu al-Hassan, *'Alayhi al-Salam*, has said, 'Allah, the Most Majestic, the Most Gracious, has appointed Ali, *'Alayhi al-Salam*, as a lighthouse between His creatures and Himself. Whoever recognizes him (Ali) is a believer and whoever does not recognize him is an unbeliever. Those ignorant of him (Ali) are lost. Those who consider others like him (Ali) are Mushrik (considering those who do not have any Divine Authority as having Divine Authority). Those who come with his (Ali's) *Wilayah* are admitted in paradise." ' "

H 1177, Ch. 109, h 8

Al-Husayn ibn Muhammad has narrated from Mu'alla ibn Muhammad from al-Washsha' from 'Abd Allah ibn Sinan from abu Hamza who has said the following:

"I heard abu Ja'far, *'Alayhi al-Salam*, say, 'Ali, *'Alayhi al-Salam*, is a door that Allah, the Most Holy, the Most High, has opened. Those who enter this door are true believers and those who go out of it are unbelievers. Those who neither go out nor enter are under the category (of people) about whom Allah has said, "I have a decision to make.'"

H 1178, Ch. 109, h 9

Muhammad ibn Yahya has narrated from Ahmad ibn Muhammad from ibn Mahbub from ibn al-Ri'ab from Bukayr ibn 'A'yan who has said the following:

"Abu Ja'far, *'Alayhi al-Salam*, would say, 'Allah made our Shi'a to make a covenant to acknowledge our *Wilayah* (Leadership with Divine Authority) when they were small particles. It was the day when He made all particles to make a covenant to acknowledge Him as the Lord and Muhammad, *'Alayhi al-Salam*, as the Prophet. Allah, the Most Majestic, the Most Gracious, presented to Muhammad his 'Umma (followers) in clay and they were shadows. He created them from the clay out of which Adam was created. Allah created the spirits of our Shi'a two thousand years before their bodies were created. He presented them to the Holy Prophet, *'Alayhi al-Salam*, and introduced them to the Messenger of Allah as well as to Ali, *'Alayhi al-Salam*, and we recognize them by their accent.' "

Chapter 110 - 'A'immah (Leaders with Divine Authority), *'Alayhim al-Salam*, Know Their Friends and That They Are the People in Charge of Their Affairs

H 1179, Ch. 110, h 1
Muhammad ibn Yahya has narrated from Ahmad ibn Muhammad from ibn Mahbub from Salih ibn Sahl from abu 'Abd Allah, *'Alayhi al-Salam*, the following:

"Once, when Amir al-Mu'minin Ali, *'Alayhi al-Salam*, was in the company of his companions, a man came to him. The man offered greetings of peace and said, 'By Allah, I love you and acknowledge your *Wilayah* (Leadership with Divine Authority).' Amir al-Mu'minin Ali, *'Alayhi al-Salam*, said to him, 'What you say is not true.' He said, 'Yes, by Allah, I love you and acknowledge your *Wilayah*,' repeating it three times. Amir al-Mu'minin Ali, *'Alayhi al-Salam*, said, 'What you say is not true. You are not what you say you are. Allah created the spirits two thousand years before creating the bodies. He then presented to us those who love us. By Allah, I did not see your spirit among those presented to us. Where were you?' The man remained silent and did not talk back.'"

In another *Hadith* it is said that abu 'Abd Allah, *'Alayhi al-Salam*, said, "He was in the fire."

H 1180, Ch. 110, h 2
Muhammad ibn Yahya has narrated from Ahmad ibn Muhammad from al-Husayn ibn Sa'id from 'Amr ibn Maymun from 'Ammar ibn Marwan from Jabir from abu Ja'far, *'Alayhi al-Salam*, who has said the following:

"Abu al-Hassan, *'Alayhi al-Salam*, has said, 'We know men when we see them through the reality of belief and the reality of hypocrisy.'"

H 1181, Ch. 110, h 3
Ahmad ibn Idris and Muhammad ibn Yahya have narrated from al-Hassan ibn Ali al-Kufi from 'Ubays ibn Hisham from 'Abd Allah ibn Sulayman who has said the following:

"Once I asked abu 'Abd Allah, *'Alayhi al-Salam*, about the Imam. 'Has Allah made him the person in charge of and in full control (over the affairs of the people) as Sulayman ibn Dawud was?'

'The Imam said, "Yes, (as the person in charge of affairs) he is given control. It is because a man asked him (the Imam) a question and he gave the answer. Another person asked the same question and he gave him a different answer (although the question was the same). A third person asked him the same question and he gave an answer that was different from both the previous answers. Then he (the Imam) recited: 'This is Our gift to you, so give them away free or keep them as you like.' (38:39) The Imam also said, 'This is charity from us, enjoy it with thanks or (give to others) without being questioned,' according to Imam Ali's recitation.'

"I (the narrator) said to him, 'May Allah grant you well being, when he (the Imam) gives such answers does he know them?' The Imam said, 'Glory belongs to Allah, have you not heard Allah's words? "In this there is evidence (of the Truth) for the judicious ones," (15:75) such people are *'A'immah* (Leaders with Divine Authority), *'Alayhim al-Salam*, ". . . it [Leaders with Divine Authority] is on a straight path," (15:76) [it will remain there forever].' Then he said to me, 'Yes, when the Imam looks at a person he recognizes him and his color. On hearing his words even from behind the wall he recognizes him and what he is. Allah has said, "Other evidence of His existence is the creation of the heavens and the earth and the differences of languages and colors. In this there is evidence (of the truth) for the scholars." (30:22) *'A'immah*, *'Alayhim al-Salam*, are the scholars. Whatever they hear that is spoken they recognize, the one who has received salvation or otherwise. For this reason they answer them as they answer them.' "

Chapters on History

Chapter 111 - The Birth of the Holy Prophet, *'Alayhi al-Salam,* and His Demise

Al-Kulayni has said, "The Holy Prophet, *'Alayhi al-Salam,* was born on the twelfth of the month of Rabi' al-Awwal, in the year of the Elephant on a Friday at noon. Also it is narrated that it was at dawn forty years before his receiving Divine messages. His mother conceived him on the days of Tashriq (1, 12, 13) of Dhu al-Hajj near the middle Jamara (a pillar of stones) and she was in the house of 'Abd Allah ibn 'Abd al-Muttalib. At Sha'b of abu Talib, peace be upon him, (Sha'b, a place in Makkah) she gave birth when she was in the house of Muhammad ibn Yusuf at the left far corner of the house, as you enter. Al-Khayzuran made that house into a mosque and people ever since use it for prayers. After receiving Divine commands as the Messenger of Allah he remained in Makkah for thirteen years. Thereafter he migrated to Madina wherein he lived for ten years. He passed away on Monday the twelfth of the month of Rabi' al-Awwal at the age of sixty-three. His father 'Abd Allah ibn 'Abd al-Muttalib died in Madina among his maternal uncles when he (Muhammad) was only two months old. His mother, 'Amina daughter of Wahab ibn 'Abd Manaf, ibn Zuhra ibn Kilab ibn Murra ibn Ka'b ibn Luway ibn Ghalib, died when he was a boy of four years old. 'Abd al-Muttalib died when the Holy Prophet, *'Alayhi al-Salam,* was about eight years old. He married Khadija when he was twenty and some years old. From Khadija, before receiving the Divine commands, of his children born were al-Qasim, Ruqiyya, Zaynab and 'Umm Kulthum. Of his children born after he received Divine commands were al-Tayyib, al-Tahir and *Fatimah, 'Alayha al-Salam.* It is also narrated that after he received Divine commands no other children besides *Fatimah, 'Alayha al-Salam,* were born and that al-Tayyib and al-Tahir were born before he received divine commands.

"Khadija (peace be upon her) died at the time the Messenger of Allah, *'Alayhi al-Salam,* came out of Sha'b of abu Talib. This was one year before his migration to Madina. Abu Talib died one year after the death of Khaija. When the Messenger of Allah lost these two people it became very difficult for him to live in Makkah. He became extremely sad and complained about it to Jibril. Allah, the Most High, then sent him the message to 'leave the town, the town of the unjust people'; after abu Talib there was no one in Makkah to support him. He was commanded to migrate."

H 1182, Ch. 111, h 1

Muhammad ibn Yahya has narrated from Ahmad ibn Muhammad from ibn Faddal from 'Abd Allah ibn Muhammad son of the brother of Hammad al-Katib from al-Husayn ibn 'Abd Allah who has said the following:

"Once I asked abu 'Abd Allah, *'Alayhi al-Salam,* 'Was the Messenger of Allah the master of the children of Adam?' The Imam said, 'By Allah, he was the master of all whom Allah has created. Allah has not created any creature better than Muhammad, *'Alayhi al-Salam.'''*

H 1183, Ch. 111, h 2

Muhammad ibn Yahya has narrated from Ahmad ibn Muhammad from al-Hajjal from Hammad from abu 'Abd Allah, *'Alayhi al-Salam,* who has said the following:

"Once the Imam, *'Alayhi al-Salam,* mentioned the Messenger of Allah and said, 'Amir al-Mu'minin Ali, *'Alayhi al-Salam,* has said, "Allah has not created any creature better than Muhammad, *'Alayhi al-Salam.'''*

H 1184, Ch. 111, h 3

Ahmad ibn Idris has narrated from al-Husayn ibn 'Abd Allah from Muhammad ibn 'Isa and Muhammad ibn 'Abd Allah from Ali ibn Hadid from Murazim from abu 'Abd Allah, *'Alayhi al-Salam,* who has said the following:

"Abu 'Abd Allah, *'Alayhi al-Salam,* has said, 'Allah, the Most Holy, the Most High, has said, "O Muhammad I have created you and Ali a light, a spirit, without body before I created My heavens, My earth, My Throne, and My ocean. You continued to acknowledge Me as your Lord and speak of My Glory. I then collected the spirits of both of you and made it one spirit. This spirit continued to speak of My Glory, My Holiness and acknowledge Me as the Lord. I then divided it into two and two which became four: one Muhammad, one Ali, al-Hassan and al-Husayn, the other two. Then Allah created *Fatimah, 'Alayha al-Salam,* from a light beginning with a spirit that was created first without a body. He then wiped us with His right hand to allow His light reach us all.'''

H 1185, Ch. 111, h 4

Ahmad has narrated from al-Husayn from Muhammad ibn 'Abd Allah from Muhammad ibn al-Fudayl from abu Hamza who has said the following:

"I heard abu Ja'far, *'Alayhi al-Salam,* say, 'Allah, the Most High, sent revelation to Muhammad, *'Alayhi al-Salam,* "O Muhammad I created you. You did not exist. I blew into you from My spirit. It was an honor with which I honored you when I made it an obligation on all of My creatures to obey you. Whoever will obey you obeys Me and whoever will disobey you disobeys Me. I have made such obedience to Ali, *'Alayhi al-Salam,* also obligatory as well as to those of his descendents whom I have chosen for Myself.'''

H 1186, Ch. 111, h 5

Al-Husayn ibn Muhammad al-Asha'ari has narrated from Mu'alla ibn Muhammad from abu al-Fadl 'Abd Allah ibn Idris from Muhammad ibn Sinan who has said the following:

"Once I was in the presence of abu Ja'far, *'Alayhi al-Salam,* the 2nd, and I mentioned the differences among the Shi'a.

"The Imam said, 'O Muhammad, Allah, the Most Holy, the Most High, is One and eternal. He created Muhammad, Ali and Fatimah, *'Alayhim al-Salam.* They were there for a thousand Dahr (one Dahr equals the amount of time from beginning to present of earth's existence). Then He created all other things. He made them witness the creation of all other things. He made obedience to them obligatory and gave them control of the affairs of the creation. They can, thus, make lawful whatever they wish and unlawful whatever they wish and they never wish anything unless Allah, the Most Holy, the Most High, wishes.' He then said, 'O Muhammad, this is a religion that, if exaggerated, will lead to disproportionate belief and ignoring it will cause degradation. Those holding to it properly will have proper contact. Keep it with you, O Muhammad.'"

H 1187, Ch. 111, h 6

A number of our people have narrated from Ahmad ibn Muhammad from ibn Muhbub from Salih ibn Sahl from abu 'Abd Allah, *'Alayhi al-Salam*, who has said the following:

"Certain persons from Quraysh asked the Messenger of Allah, 'By what means did you excel the prophets and you came into this world as the last prophet?' The Messenger of Allah said, 'I was the first to believe in my Lord, and the first to answer Allah when He called the prophets to make a covenant and bear testimony against their own souls to acknowledge and answer positively when asked, "Am I not your Lord?" They all had answered, 'Yes, You Are our Lord.' I was the first prophet that said, "Yes, You Are our Lord." I, thus, excelled them in acknowledgment of the Oneness of Allah.'"

H 1188, Ch. 111, h 7

Ali ibn Muhammad has narrated from Sahl ibn Ziyad from Muhammad ibn Ali ibn Ibrahim from Ali ibn Hammad from al-Mufaddal who has said the following:

"Once I asked abu 'Abd Allah, *'Alayhi al-Salam*, 'How did you exist when you existed in the shadows?' The Imam said, 'O Mufaddal, we were in the presence of our Lord and there was no one else in the green shadow. We spoke of His Glory, Holiness, acknowledged Him as the Lord and spoke of His Majesty. There was no angel even of the ones close to Allah or a living being except us in His presence until He decided to create all things. He then created whatever He wanted, in the way He wanted of the angels and others. He then made the knowledge of that to reach and come to us.'"

H 1189, Ch. 111, h 8

Sahl ibn Ziyad has narrated from Muhammad ibn al-Walid, who has said that he heard Yunus ibn Ya'qub narrated from Sinan ibn Turayf who has said the following:

"I heard abu 'Abd Allah, *'Alayhi al-Salam*, say, 'We are the first family whose names Allah has exalted. When He created the heavens and earth He commanded an announcer to proclaim three times: "I testify that no one other than Allah deserves to be worshipped, I testify that Muhammad is the Messenger of Allah, three times: and that Ali, *'Alayhi al-Salam*, is Amir al-Mu'minin (Leader with Divine Authority) in all truth, three times." ' "

H 1190, Ch. 111, h 9

Ahmad ibn Idris has narrated from al-Husayn ibn 'Abd Allah al-Saghir from Muhammad ibn Ibrahim al-Ja'fari from Ahmad ibn Ali ibn Muhammad ibn 'Abd Allah ibn 'Umar ibn Ali ibn abu Talib, *'Alayhi al-Salam*, from abu 'Abd Allah, *'Alayhi al-Salam*, who has said the following:

"Abu 'Abd Allah, *'Alayhi al-Salam*, has said, 'Allah existed when there was no other 'being'. He created the 'being' and place and the light of lights from which all lights lit up. And He made to flow to it (light of lights) from His own light, which lighted up all lights. It was the light from which Muhammad and Ali were created. They both continued to be the first two lights; nothing had come into being before them. They continued to flow pure and clean through the clean generations until they separated in two clean persons; namely 'Abd Allah and abu Talib, peace be upon them."

H 1191, Ch. 111, h 10

Al-Husayn has narrated from (Muhammad) ibn 'Abd Allah from Muhammad ibn Sinan from al-Mufaddal from Jabir ibn Yazid who has said the following:

"Once abu Ja'far, *'Alayhi al-Salam*, said to me, 'O Jabir, the first thing that Allah created was Muhammad, *'Alayhi al-Salam*, and his offspring who are the rightly guided guides. They existed in *'Ashbah* (form) of light in the presence of Allah.'

"I then asked, 'What is *'Ashbah*? The Imam said, 'It is the shadow of light, the lighting bodies without the spirit. It was supported by one spirit, the Holy Spirit. In that state he and his offspring worshipped Allah and for this reason He created them forbearing scholars, conscientious pure ones who worship Allah through prayer, fasting, prostration, speaking of His Glory and the acknowledgment that He is the only Lord. They perform prayers, perform Hajj and fast.'"

H 1192, Ch. 111, h 11

Ali ibn Muhammad and others have narrated from Sahl ibn Ziyad from Muhammad ibn al-Walid Shabab al-Sayrafi from Malik ibn 'Isma'il al-Nahdi from 'Abd al-Salam ibn Harith from Salim ibn abu Hafsa al-'Ijli from abu Ja'far, *'Alayhi al-Salam*, who has said the following:

"Abu Ja'far, *'Alayhi al-Salam*, has said, 'The Messenger of Allah had three qualities that no one else had. He did not have any shadow. Whatever path he walked even after two or three days one could still notice his passing thereby due to his fragrance that remained along the path. On his passing by, out of respect, every stone and tree prostrated before him.'"

H 1193, Ch. 111, h 12

Ali ibn Ibrahim has narrated from his father from Ahmad ibn Muhammad ibn abu Nasr from Hammad ibn 'Uthman from abu Basir from abu 'Abd Allah, *'Alayhi al-Salam*, who has said the following:

"Abu 'Abd Allah, *'Alayhi al-Salam*, has said, 'When the Messenger of Allah was taken for the ascension Jibril took him to a place and left him there alone. He said, 'Jibril, why do you leave me in such a condition?' Jibril said, 'Go on. By Allah, you have stepped at a place whereat no human has ever stepped and no human has ever walked before you.'"

H 1194, Ch. 111, h 13

A number of our people have narrated from Ahmad ibn Muhammad from al-Husayn ibn Sa'id from al-Qasim ibn Muhammad al-Jawhari from Ali ibn abu Hamza who has said that abu Basir asked abu 'Abd Allah, *'Alayhi al-Salam*, when I was also present:

"May Allah keep my soul in service for your cause, how many times was the Messenger of Allah taken for ascension? The Imam, *'Alayhi al-Salam*, said, 'It happened twice. Jibril asked him to stop at a place saying wait right there, O Muhammad, you have stood at a place whereat no angel or prophet has ever stood before you. Your Lord is praying.' He (the Holy Prophet) asked, 'O Jibril, how does He pray?' Jibril said, 'He says, "The Glorious, the Holy, I Am the Lord of the angels and the Spirit. My mercy exceeds My anger."' The Holy Prophet, *'Alayhi al-Salam*, then said, 'O Lord, I beg forgiveness from You, I beg forgiveness from You.'

"The Imam said, 'It was as Allah has said, ". . . until he was as close to him as the distance of two bows, or even less." (53:9) Abu Basir then asked, 'May Allah keep my soul in service for your cause, what is ". . . the distance of two bows, or even less?"' (53:9) The Imam said, 'It is the distance of the radius of the bow.' The Imam then said, 'Between the two there was a barrier (curtain) that shined with oscillation.' I (narrator) do not know except that he said it was *Zabarjad* (Beryl; chrysolite). He (the Holy Prophet) looked into the light of Greatness of the size of a needle's eye or so that Allah willed. Allah, the Most Holy, the Most High, said, 'O Muhammad.' He replied, 'Yes, my Lord.' He (the Lord) asked, 'Who will be after you to guide your followers?' He (Muhammad) replied, 'Allah knows best.' He (the Lord) said, 'Ali ibn abu Talib, *'Alayhi al-Salam*, will be Amir al-Mu'minin (Leader with Divine Authority), the master of the Muslims, the leader of the ones marked with brightness on their foreheads.'

"The narrator has said that then abu 'Abd Allah, *'Alayhi al-Salam*, said to abu Basir, 'O abu Muhammad, by Allah, *Wilayah* of Amir al-Mu'minin Ali, *'Alayhi al-Salam*, did not come from earth. It (*Wilayah*) came from the heavens in words that Allah personally spoke.'"

H 1195, Ch. 111, h 14
A number of our people have narrated from Ahmad ibn Muhammad from Ali ibn Sayf from 'Amr ibn Shimr from Jabir who has said the following:
"Once I asked abu Ja'far, *'Alayhi al-Salam*, 'Describe to me the Prophet, *'Alayhi al-Salam*, of Allah.' The Imam said, 'The Holy Prophet, *'Alayhi al-Salam*, had a white reddish complexion, large sharp black and white eyes, the eyebrows almost joined, chubby hands and feet as if gold molded to the form of his fingers and toes and with manifest shoulder bones. When he would turn to a person he did so with the whole of his body, due to kind and tenderheartiness. A line of hair extended from the front cavity of his neck down to his bellybutton as if it was a clear and pure silver line. His neck was long and clear, his nose almost touched the water when he wanted to drink and when walking he somehow leaned forward as if walking on a downward slope. No one similar to him was seen as such before or after the Holy Prophet, *'Alayhi al-Salam*, of Allah.'"

H 1196, Ch. 111, h 15
A number of our people have narrated from Ahmad ibn Muhammad from Faddal from abu Jamila from Muhammad al-Halabi from abu 'Abd Allah, *'Alayhi al-Salam*, who has said the following:
"Abu 'Abd Allah, *'Alayhi al-Salam*, has said, 'The Messenger of Allah has said, "Allah presented my *'Umma* (followers) to me in the realm of clay and taught me their names just as He had taught all the names to Adam. The (groups of) people bearing flags passed by and I prayed and asked forgiveness for Ali, *'Alayhi al-Salam*, and his followers. My Lord has promised me a quality for the Shi'a of Ali, *'Alayhi al-Salam*.'"

"It was asked, 'What is that quality O Messenger of Allah, *'Alayhi al-Salam*?' He replied, 'It is forgiveness for those of them who are believers and that none of their minor or major sins will be left without being changed to good deeds.'"

H 1197, Ch. 111, h 16

Ali ibn Ibrahim has narrated from his father from al-Hassan ibn Sayf from his father from those he mentioned from abu 'Abd Allah, *'Alayhi al-Salam*, who has said the following:

"Abu 'Abd Allah, *'Alayhi al-Salam*, has said, 'Once the Messenger of Allah, *'Alayhi al-Salam*, addressed the people and he raised his right hand while holding his fingers closed and said, 'Do you know, O people, what is in my hand?' They said, 'Allah and His Messenger know best.' He then said, 'In my hand there are the names of the people of paradise, the names of their fathers and the names of their tribes up to the Day of Judgment.' He then raised his left hand and asked, 'O people, do you know what is my hand?' They said, 'Allah and His Messenger know best.' He then said, 'In my hand there are the names of the people of hell, the names of their fathers and the names of their tribes up to the day of Judgment.' Then he said, 'Allah has decreed and He has done justice. Allah has decreed and He has done justice. One group will go to paradise and the other group to hell.'"

H 1198, Ch. 111, h 17

Muhammad ibn Yahya has narrated from Ahmad ibn Muhammad ibn 'Isa from al-Hassan ibn Mahbub from Ishaq ibn Ghalib from abu 'Abd Allah, *'Alayhi al-Salam*, who has the following:

"Abu 'Abd Allah, *'Alayhi al-Salam*, in a special sermon has described the Holy Prophet and *'A'immah* (Leaders with Divine Authority), *'Alayhi al-Salam*, and their qualities as follows:

"The great sins and people's bad deeds did not prevent Our Lord, due to His forbearance, caring and kindness, from choosing for the people the best of His prophets. (The Lord chose) Muhammad ibn 'Abd Allah, the most respectable one to Him, and he was born in an honorable environment and to a noble family. His association was unsuspicious and his lineage was not unknown to the people of knowledge to describe. The glad news of his coming was mentioned in the books of the prophets and spoken of in the words of the scholars and his qualities were discussed in the thinking of the people of wisdom. No person of Hashimite descent has ever reached the level of his discipline or paralleled to him and no person of the inhabitants of *Abtah* has ever climbed to his high position. Restraint (from meaningless matters) was of his attributes and generosity was part of his nature. He was made with the dignity of prophet-hood and its discipline. His nature was formed out of the qualities of Divine messenger and its wisdom. The means and measures of Allah brought him to the appointed time and the decree by the commands of Allah proceeded to their goals. The determined decision of Allah delivered him to their objects. Every nation gave the glad news about him to the one thereafter and every father delivered to the next one from one generation to the next. No indecency ever mixed his element and no conjugal relation ever made him unclean from Adam to his father, 'Abd Allah. He was in the best group and of most honorable descent, the tribe of glory, in the well-preserved womb and in the best protective hands. Allah had chosen him as it pleased Him, selected him, and gave him the keys to knowledge and the sources of wisdom. He (the Lord) raised him as the mercy and blessings for His servants and as the season of spring for His lands. Allah sent to him the Book in which there is communication and explanations. It is a reading in Arabic free of complexities, so that they (people) may perhaps observe piety (before Allah). He has explained it to people.

He has arranged it into a system with the knowledge that explains in detail and a religion that He has clarified its obligations, determined its limits for the people and has clarified them.

"There are matters that He has stated to His servants openly. In it (the Book) there is guidance to salvation and evidence to show the right guidance. The Messenger of Allah has preached the message that he had brought and demanded obedience to what he was ordered to preach and delivered the responsibilities of a prophet toward his followers. He exercised patience for the sake of his Lord and strove hard in the way of the Lord. He gave good advice to his followers and called them to salvation. He exhorted them in the matters of al-Dhikr (reminder) and showed them the right guidance. He did so with systems and potentials that he established on certain foundations for the servants (of Allah) and with the sources of light for which he raised proper beacons. He did so, so that they will not be misled after him and he was very compassionate and kind to them.'"

H 1199, Ch. 111, h 18

Muhammad ibn Yahya has narrated from Sa'd ibn 'Abd Allah from a group of our people from Ahmad ibn Hilal from 'Umayya ibn Ali al-Qaysi who has said that narrated to me Durust ibn abu Mansur who has said the following:

"I once asked abu al-Hassan, the 1ª, *'Alayhi al-Salam*, 'Did the Messenger of Allah live under the authority of abu Talib, peace be upon him?' The Imam said, 'No, but abu Talib was the trustee of certain (items) of will that he delivered to the Holy Prophet, *'Alayhi al-Salam*.'

"I then said, 'So abu Talib delivered the wills to the Holy Prophet because of his authority over him.' The Imam said, 'If so he did not have to deliver the wills to him (the Holy Prophet).'

"I then asked, 'What was the condition of abu Talib?' The Imam said, 'He (abu Talib) acknowledged the Holy Prophet, *'Alayhi al-Salam*, and his Divine message and delivered to him (Prophet) the (items of) wills and died on that day.'"

H 1200, Ch. 111, h 19

Al-Husayn ibn Muhammad al-Asha'ari has narrated from Mu'alla ibn Muhammad from Mansur ibn al-'Abbass from Ali ibn Asbat from Ya'qub ibn Salim from a man from abu Ja'far, *'Alayhi al-Salam*, who has said the following:

"Abu Ja'far, *'Alayhi al-Salam*, has said, 'When the Messenger of Allah passed away the family of Muhammad, *'Alayhi al-Salam*, experienced the longest night. They had a feeling as if the sky did not provide them shadow and the earth did not hold them up anymore. The Messenger of Allah had united all people just for the sake of Allah. In such a condition someone came to them whom they did not see but they could hear his words. He offered them greetings saying, 'Peace be with you, O members of the family of the Holy Prophet, *'Alayhi al-Salam*, and may Allah's mercy and blessings be with you. With Allah is the best of condolences for all kinds of suffering and the salvation from all forms of destruction and a remedy for the losses.

"He then read the words of Allah: 'Every soul is destined to experience the agony of death. You (Muslims) will receive the recompense for your deeds on the Day of Judgment. To be saved from the fire and admitted to paradise is certainly a great triumph. The worldly life is no more than a deceitful possession.' (3:185)

"He then continued, 'Allah has selected you, granted you distinction, purified and made you members of the family of His prophet. He has entrusted you with His knowledge and has made you inherit His book. He has made you the chest (Ark) of His knowledge and the staff of His Majesty. He has given for you an example of His light and has protected you from all sins and mistakes. He has protected you against all forms of mischief. Accept the condolences of Allah. Allah has not withdrawn His blessings away from you and He will never remove any of His bounties from you. You are the people of Allah, the Most Majestic, the Most Gracious, through whom the bounties increase, different groups become united and words receive harmony. You are His friends. Those who love you achieve success and those who do injustice to you will vanish. To love you is obligatory, because of the commands of Allah in His book, on His believing servants. Besides, Allah has full power to help and support you whenever He would wish. Exercise patience against the consequences of the matters because they all proceed to Allah. Allah has accepted you as the Holy Prophet, *'Alayhi al-Salam*, has entrusted you with Him and He has entrusted you with His believing faithful friends on earth. Whoever is truthful to the trust with him, Allah will give him the reward for his truthfulness. You are the entrusted trust and to love you is obligatory on people and obedience to you is a duty. Allah has taken His Messenger away from this world and He has completed the religion for you. He has explained to you how to come out of (difficulties). He has not left any excuse for anyone.

"Whoever does not know or pretends to be ignorant, deny, forget or pretend to forget will be held accountable before Allah. Allah will always look forward to fulfill your needs. I entrust you with Allah. May peace and blessings be with you.'

"The narrator has said, 'I asked the Imam, "From whom did the condolences come?"' The Imam said, 'They came from Allah, the Most Holy, the Most High.'"

H 1201, Ch. 111, h 20

A number of our people have narrated from Ahmad ibn Muhammad from al-Husayn ibn Sa'id from Muhammad ibn Sinan from ibn Muskan from Isma'il ibn 'Ammar from abu 'Abd Allah, *'Alayhi al-Salam*, who has said the following:

"Abu 'Abd Allah, *'Alayhi al-Salam*, has said, 'If one looked at the Messenger of Allah in the dark night he could see a light like that from the moon radiating from him."

H 1202, Ch. 111, h 21

Ahmad ibn Idris has narrated from al-Husayn ibn 'Ubayd Allah from abu 'Abd Allah al-Husayn al-Saghir from Muhammad ibn Ibrahim al-Ja'fari from Ahmad ibn Ali ibn Muhammad ibn 'Abd Allah ibn 'Umar ibn Ali ibn abu Talib, *'Alayhi al-Salam*, from abu 'Abd Allah, *'Alayhi al-Salam*, and Muhammad ibn Yahya from Sa'd ibn 'Abd Allah from Ya'qub ibn Yazid from ibn Faddal from certain persons of his people from abu 'Abd Allah who has said the following:

"Abu 'Abd Allah, *'Alayhi al-Salam*, has said, 'Once Jibril came to the Holy Prophet, *'Alayhi al-Salam*, and said, "O Muhammad, Allah offers you greetings of peace and says, 'I have prohibited the fire to harm the man and woman who carried your seed and the man whose lap provided you protection and guardianship. The man who carried your seed is 'Abd Allah ibn 'Abd al-Muttalib and the woman whose womb carried you is 'Amina, daughter of Wahab, and the man whose lap provided you protection and guardianship is abu Talib.'"

In the *Hadith* of ibn Faddal it says, ". . . and Fatimah daughter of Asad."

H 1203, Ch. 111, h 22

Muhammad ibn Yahya has narrated from Ahmad ibn Muhammad ibn 'Isa from ibn abu 'Umayr from Jamil ibn Darraj from Zurara ibn 'A'yan from abu 'Abd Allah, *'Alayhi al-Salam*, who has said the following:

"On the Day of Judgment 'Abd al-Muttalib will be resurrected as a whole nation and he will have a complexion like those of the prophets and a majestic presence like those of the kings."

H 1204, Ch. 111, h 23

Ali ibn Ibrahim has narrated from his father from 'Abd Allah ibn 'Abd al-Rahman al-'Asamm from al-Haytham ibn Waqid from Muqarrin from abu ''Abd Allah, *'Alayhi al-Salam*, who has said the following:

"'Abd al-Muttalib is the first one who believed in Bada' (Allah's revised plan). He will be resurrected as a whole nation. He will have an august presence like kings and a countenance like that of the prophets."

H 1205, Ch. 111, h 24

Certain persons of our people have narrated from ibn Jumhur from his father from ibn Mahbub from ibn al-Ri'ab from 'Abd al-Rahman ibn al-Hajjaj (and) from Muhammad ibn Sinan from al-Mufaddal ibn 'Umar all from abu 'Abd Allah, *'Alayhi al-Salam*, who has said the following:

"'Abd al-Muttalib will be resurrected as a whole nation (one *'Umma*) with the grandeur of the kings and the complexion of the prophets. It is because he was the first one who believed in Bada' (Allah's revised plan). Once, 'Abd al-Muttalib sent the Messenger of Allah to the shepherds of his camels to help them with a runaway camel. He collected them all but had delayed in returning home. 'Abd al-Muttalib out of anxiety was holding the ring of the door of Ka'ba. He kept pleading, 'O Lord, will you destroy your own people? (Please do not do so). If You do so then it means that You have changed Your decision.' The Messenger of Allah came with camels and 'Abd al-Muttalib had sent people to search him in all directions and valleys of (Makkah). He kept crying, 'O Lord, will you destroy Your own people? (Please do not do so). If You do so then You may have revised Your decision and plan.' When he saw the Messenger of Allah he held him to kiss and said, 'Son, I will not send you thereafter for anything. I am afraid for you to be kidnapped and killed.'"

H 1206, Ch. 111, h 25

A number of our people have narrated from Ahmad ibn Muhammad ibn 'Isa from ibn abu 'Umayr from Muhammad ibn Humran from Aban ibn Taghlib who has said the following:

"Abu 'Abd Allah, *'Alayhi al-Salam*, has said, 'When the fellow from Ethiopia marched with horses and elephants to destroy the Ka'ba they passed by the camels of 'Abd al-Muttalib and they herded them together. When 'Abd al-Muttalib learned about it, he went to the man from Ethiopia and asked permission for a meeting. His men told him that 'Abd al-Muttalib ibn Hashim had asked permission for a meeting. He asked, 'What does he want?' The translator said, 'He has come asking that his camels be released.' The king of Ethiopia said to his people, 'This is the leader and the chief of the people here. I have come to destroy his house of worship but he asks me to order the release of his camels. Had he asked me not to destroy the house I might have agreed. Release his camels.'

"'Abd al-Muttalib asked the translator, 'What did the king say?' When the words of the king were explained to him, he said, 'I am the owner of the camels. The house has an owner who is to protect it.' His camels were released and 'Abd al-Muttalib returned home. He passed by the elephant on his way home. He said to the elephant, 'O Mahmud. The elephant shook his head. Then he asked, 'Do you know why they have brought you here?' The elephant said by shaking his head, 'No, I do not know.' 'Abd al-Muttalib said, 'They have brought you to destroy the house of your Lord. Will you do so?' The elephant by shaking his head said, 'I will not do so.' 'Abd al-Muttalib returned home. The next morning they tried to make the elephant enter the Holy precinct to destroy it but the elephant refused.

"'Abd al-Muttalib at that time said to certain ones of his servants, 'Climb up the hill and see if you can observe anything.' He said, 'I can see black spots in the direction of the sea (in the air). He asked, 'Do you see all of it?' He said, 'Not all of it but almost.' When the black spots came closer he said, 'They are a great many birds. I can see that every bird has a pebble in his beak of the size thrown with a finger.' 'Abd al-Muttalib said, 'I swear by my Lord that the birds aim only at those people.' When the birds arrived over their heads they threw the pebbles on their heads and every pebble fell on top of their skulls and pierced its way down to their bottom end and left them dead. Only one man was left alive who went with the news to the others. When he gave them the news a pebble fell on his head and killed him.'"

H 1207, Ch. 111, h 26

Ali ibn Ibrahim has narrated from his father from Ahmad ibn Muhammad ibn abu Nasr from Rifa'a from abu 'Abd Allah, *'Alayhi al-Salam*, who has said the following:

"At a certain place around the Ka'ba 'Abd al-Muttalib's people would spread house furnishings for him only and for no one else. His sons stood around him for protection. Once the Messenger of Allah, then a small child who had just begun to walk, came to 'Abd al-Muttalib and sat in his lap. One of the people standing as a guard came to remove the child away but 'Abd al-Muttalib said, 'Leave my child alone. The angel has just come to him.'"

H 1208, Ch. 111, h 27

Muhammad ibn Yahya has narrated from Sa'd ibn 'Abd Allah from Ibrahim ibn Muhammad al-Thaqafi from Ali ibn Mu'alla from his brother, Muhammad from Durust ibn abu Mansur from Ali ibn abu Hamza from abu Basir from abu 'Abd Allah, *'Alayhi al-Salam*, who has said the following:

"When the Holy Prophet, *'Alayhi al-Salam*, was born he remained for days without milk. Abu Talib himself breast-fed him and Allah sent milk through his nipples. It continued for several days until abu Talib found Halima al-Sa'diya and the child was given to her." Note: The mother of the Holy Prophet, *'Alayhi al-Salam*, died when he was four years old and 'Abd al-Muttalib died when the Holy Prophet, *'Alayhi al-Salam*, was about eight years old. With these two people still alive abu Talib did not have to play such a role. The above *Hadith* does not seem very consistent.

H 1209, Ch. 111, h 28
Ali ibn Ibrahim has narrated from his father from ibn abu 'Umayr from Hisham ibn Salim from abu 'Abd Allah, *'Alayhi al-Salam*, who has said the following:
"Abu 'Abd Allah, *'Alayhi al-Salam*, has said, 'The case of abu Talib is like the case of the people of the cave who hid their belief and expressed polytheism. Allah gave them twice as much reward.'"

H 1210, Ch. 111, h 29
Al-Husayn ibn Muhammad and Muhammad ibn Yahya have narrated from Ahmad ibn Ishaq from Bakr ibn Muhammad al-Azdi from Ishaq ibn Ja'far from his father, *'Alayhi al-Salam*, who has said the following:
"They think that abu Talib was an unbeliever. They speak lies. How could he be an unbeliever when he said such words as follows: 'Do they not know that we found Muhammad as a prophet like Musa (Moses) whose name is written in the ancient books?'"

According to another *Hadith* he has asked, "How can abu Talib be called an unbeliever when he has said in the following lines?

'They certainly know that our child is not accused of speaking,

'To us lies and the false words do not receive any attention.

'The (beautiful) white face (of the Holy Prophet),

'That prays thus, the clouds send rain,

'Is the helper of the orphans and the protector of the widows.'"

H 1211, Ch. 111, h 30
Ali ibn Ibrahim has narrated from his father from ibn abu 'Umayr from Hisham ibn al-Hakam from abu 'Abd Allah, *'Alayhi al-Salam*, who has said the following:
"Once when the Holy Prophet, *'Alayhi al-Salam*, was in the sacred Mosque wearing new clothes, the pagans threw the contents of the stomach of camel on him and his new clothes were ruined. Allah knows how hard it was for him. He (the Holy Prophet) went to abu Talib and asked, 'What is my honor worth to you?' He asked, 'What is the matter, O son of my brother?' The Holy Prophet, *'Alayhi al-Salam*, informed him of the incident. Abu Talib, while picking up a sword, called and asked Hamza to take up arms. He then asked Hamza to pick up the stomach of the camel and they came to the people along with the Holy Prophet, *'Alayhi al-Salam*. They found people of Quraysh around the Ka'ba. When they saw him (abu Talib) they read trouble from his face. Abu Talib asked Hamza to

spread the contents of the stomach of the camel against everyone's mustache and Hamza did so to the last person. Abu Talib then turned to the Holy Prophet, *'Alayhi al-Salam*, and said, 'Son of my brother, this is how much we value your honor (ready to face such great risk for it).'"

H 1212, Ch. 111, h 31

Ali has narrated from his father from ibn abu Nasr from Ibrahim ibn Muhammad al-Ash'ari from 'Ubayd ibn Zurara from abu 'Abd Allah, *'Alayhi al-Salam*, who has said the following:

"When abu Talib, peace be upon him, passed away, Jibril came to the Messenger of Allah and said, 'O Muhammad, migrate from Makkah. There is no one to help protect you.' Quraysh revolted against the Holy Prophet, *'Alayhi al-Salam*, and he came out of Makkah running away until he reached one of the mountains of Makkah, called al-Hajun. He went there.'"

H 1213, Ch. 111, h 32

Ali ibn Muhammad ibn 'Abd Allah and Muhammad ibn Yahya have narrated from Muhammad ibn 'Abd Allah who in a *marfu'* manner has narrated it from abu 'Abd Allah, *'Alayhi al-Salam*, who has said the following:

"Abu Talib acknowledged Islam through the expression of al-Jummal, a universal language. (Al-Jummal is a system wherein each letter of the alphabet is given a certain numerical value and instead of a letter its numeric value is used for secrecy or other reasons). The Imam said, 'He used a universal language.'"

H 1214, Ch. 111, h 33

Muhammad ibn Yahya has narrated from Ahmad and 'Abd Allah sons of Muhammad ibn 'Isa from their father from 'Abd Allah ibn al-Mughira from 'Isma'il ibn abu Ziyad from abu 'Abd Allah, *'Alayhi al-Salam*, who has said the following:

"Abu 'Abd Allah, *'Alayhi al-Salam*, has said, 'Abu Talib acknowledged Islam through the expression of al-Jummal. He formed number sixty-three with his hands.'"

H 1215 Ch. 111, h 34

Muhammad ibn Yahya has narrated from Ahmad ibn Muhammad from ibn al-Faddal from al-Husayn ibn 'Ulwan al-Kalbi from Ali ibn al-Hazawwar al-Ghanawi from Asbagh ibn Nubata al-Hanzali who has said the following:

"Once I saw Amir al-Mu'minin Ali, *'Alayhi al-Salam*, on the day of victory in Basra while he was riding on the mule of the Messenger of Allah, (then) he said, 'O people, do you want me to tell who the best of the creatures of Allah will be on the Day when Allah will bring all of them at one place?' Abu Ayyub al-Ansari stood up and said, 'Yes, O Amir al-Mu'minin, *'Alayhi al-Salam*, please explain it to us. You were present and we were absent.' The Imam then said, 'The best of the people, on the Day of resurrection when Allah will bring all people together, are seven people descended from 'Abd al-Muttalib whose distinction no one except an unbeliever can deny and no one can reject except a deviant.'

'Ammar ibn Yasir (may Allah grand him blessings) then stood up and said, 'O Amir al-Mu'minin, *'Alayhi al-Salam*, tell us their names so we can recognize them properly.' The Imam said, 'The best in the creatures of Allah on the Day when He will bring all creatures together are the messengers and the best of the messengers is Muhammad, *'Alayhi al-Salam*. The best in every *'Umma* (nation) after the prophet is the executor of his will until a prophet comes. There is no doubt that the best among the executors of the wills of the prophets is the executor of the will of Prophet Muhammad, *'Alayhi al-Salam*. There is also no doubt that the best among the people after the executors of the will of the prophets are the martyrs and the best of the martyrs are Hamza ibn 'Abd al-Muttalib and Ja'far ibn abu Talib who was given two fresh wings with which he flies in paradise. No one else besides him from this 'Umma received two wings. With him Allah honored and granted dignity to Muhammad, *'Alayhi al-Salam*. Also of the seven people are the two grandsons of the Holy Prophet, *'Alayhi al-Salam*, and *al-Mahdi*, *'Alayhi al-Salam*. Whoever Allah wants will be *al-Mahdi* from our *Ahl al-Bayt*.'

"Then he read this verse of the Holy Quran: 'One who obeys Allah and the Messenger is the friend of the Prophets, saints, martyrs, and the righteous ones to whom Allah has granted His favors. They are the best friends that one can have (4:69). The favors of Allah are such, and He knows very well (how to reward you).'" (4:70)

H 1216, Ch. 111, h 35
Muhammad ibn al-Husayn has narrated from Sahl ibn Ziyad from ibn al-Faddal from Ali ibn al-Nu'man from abu Maryam al-Ansari who has said the following:
"Once I asked abu Ja'far, *'Alayhi al-Salam*, 'How was the prayer for the dead body of the Holy Prophet, *'Alayhi al-Salam*?'

"The Imam said, 'When Amir al-Mu'minin Ali, *'Alayhi al-Salam*, washed his body and placed him in the shroud and covered his body, ten persons came in and walked around him. Amir al-Mu'minin Ali, *'Alayhi al-Salam*, then stood in the middle of them and said, "Allah showers His blessings upon the Prophet and the angels seek forgiveness for him. Believers, pray for the Prophet and greet him with the greeting of peace." (33:56) The group also continued reciting what the Imam said until the people of Madina and people of 'Awali also said the prayer (for burial) in the same way.'"

H 1217, Ch. 111, h 36
Muhammad ibn Yahya has narrated from Salama ibn al-Khattab from Ali ibn Sayf from abu al-Maghra' from 'Uqba ibn Bashir from abu Ja'far, *'Alayhi al-Salam*, who has said the following:
"Abu Ja'far, *'Alayhi al-Salam*, has said, 'Once the Holy Prophet, *'Alayhi al-Salam*, said to Ali, *'Alayhi al-Salam*, "O Ali, bury me in this place, raise the surface of my grave from the ground by the width of four fingers and sprinkle water on it."'"

H 1218, Ch. 111, h 37
Ali ibn Ibrahim has narrated from his father from ibn abu 'Umayr from Hammad from al-Halabi from abu 'Abd Allah, *'Alayhi al-Salam*, who has said the following:
"Abu 'Abd Allah, *'Alayhi al-Salam*, who has said, 'Al-'Abbass came to Amir al-Mu'minin Ali, *'Alayhi al-Salam*, and said, 'O Ali, people have come in a group to bury the Messenger of Allah in Baqi', the prayer place, and one of them as an Imam led the prayer.' Amir al-Mu'minin Ali, *'Alayhi al-Salam*, then came out to

the people and said, 'O people, the Messenger of Allah is the Imam whether dead or living. He had said that he must be buried in the place where he died. He then stood at the door and prayed for him. Then he commanded every ten people to come in and pray for him and leave.'"

H 1219, Ch. 111, h 38

Muhammad ibn Yahya has narrated from Salama ibn al-Khattab from Ali ibn Sayf from 'Amr ibn Shimr from Jabir from abu Ja'far, *'Alayhi al-Salam*, who has said the following:

"Abu Ja'far, *'Alayhi al-Salam*, has said, 'When the Holy Prophet, *'Alayhi al-Salam*, passed away, the angels, *al-Muhajirun* (the immigrant Muslims) and *al-Ansar* (the helping Muslims, people of Madina) prayed over his body group after group.'

"The narrator has said that Amir al-Mu'minin Ali, *'Alayhi al-Salam*, has said, 'I heard the Messenger of Allah saying while in good health, "This verse is revealed to me about praying for me after Allah will take me away from this world. 'Allah showers His blessings upon the Prophet and the angels seek forgiveness for him. Believers, pray for the Prophet and greet him with the greeting of peace.' " ' " (33:56)

H 1220, Ch. 111, h 39

Certain persons of our people have narrated in a *marfu'* manner from Muhammad ibn Sinan from Dawud ibn Kathir al-Raqqi who has said that he asked abu 'Abd Allah, *'Alayhi al-Salam*, the following:

"I asked abu 'Abd Allah, *'Alayhi al-Salam*, 'What is the meaning of 'Peace be with the Messenger of Allah (or offering him the greeting of peace)?' The Imam said, 'When Allah, the Most Holy, the Most High, created His Prophet, the executor of the will of His Prophet, the daughter of His Prophet, their two sons, all *'A'immah* (Leaders with Divine Authority), *'Alayhim al-Salam*, and their Shi'a (followers), He made a covenant with them to exercise patience, help to exercise patience, establish good relations and live piously before Allah. He promised to give them the blessed land, the sacred sanctuary, to bring down to them the constructed house (*al-Bayt al-Ma'mur*), to manifest to them the raised ceiling (*al-Saqf al-Marfu'*) and grant them relief against their enemies. Also Allah grants them the earth that He will change with peace and protect all that is therein for them without any quarrels therein against the enemies and there will exist all that they love. The Messenger of Allah made a similar covenant with all *'A'immah* and their Shi'a.

"Offering of peace to him is a mention of that covenant and renewing it before Allah, so that perhaps He, the Most Majestic, the Most Gracious, will allow that peace to take place soon for all of you with all that is therein.'"

H 1221, Ch. 111, h 40

Ibn Mahbub has narrated from 'Abd Allah ibn Sinan who has said the following:

"I heard abu 'Abd Allah, *'Alayhi al-Salam*, say, 'O Lord, grant blessings upon Muhammad, Your chosen one, Your friend and Your selected one who manages Your affairs.'"

Chapter 112 - Climbing Over the Grave of the Holy Prophet, *'Alayhi al-Salam*, Prohibited

H 1222, Ch. 112, h 1

A number of our people have narrated from Ahmad ibn Muhammad al-Barqi from Ja'far ibn al-Muthanna al-Khatib who has said the following:

"I was in Madina when the section of the roof of the Mosque that covers the grave of the Holy Prophet, *'Alayhi al-Salam*, had crumbled down and the workers were climbing up and down (for repairs). We were a group and asked our people, 'Who has an appointment with abu 'Abd Allah, *'Alayhi al-Salam*?' Mihran ibn abu Nasr said, 'I have an appointment with the Imam.' 'Isma'il ibn 'Ammar al-Sayrafi said, 'I have an appointment with the Imam.' I said to them, 'Ask the Imam if it is permissible to climb up and look on to the grave of the Holy Prophet, *'Alayhi al-Salam.*' Next day we met them and we all came together. 'Isma'il said, 'We asked your question and he said this: "I do not want anyone to climb above him. I do not feel safe for anyone whose eyesight may go away because of catching sight of something that causes him such loss or sees him (the Holy Prophet) standing in prayer or sees him with anyone of his wives.'""

Chapter 113 - The Birth of Amir Al-Mu'minin Ali, *'Alayhi al-Salam*

Al-Kulayni has said, "Amir al-Mu'minin Ali, *'Alayhi al-Salam*, was born thirty years after the year of elephant. He was martyred on the twenty-first of the month of Ramadan on Sunday night in the fortieth year after Hijra (migration). He was sixty-three years old at that time. He lived for thirty years after the death of the Holy Prophet, *'Alayhi al-Salam*. His mother was Fatimah, daughter of Asad ibn Hashim ibn 'Abd Manaf. He was the first person whose parents both belonged to Hashim."

H 1223, Ch. 113, h 1

Al-Husayn ibn Muhammad has narrated from Muhammad ibn Yahya al-Farisiy from abu Hanifa Muhammad ibn Yahya from al-Walid ibn Aban from Muhammad ibn 'Abd Allah ibn Muskan from his father who has said the following:

"Abu 'Abd Allah, *'Alayhi al-Salam*, has said, 'Once Fatimah, daughter of Asad, came to abu Talib with the glad news of the birth of the Holy Prophet, *'Alayhi al-Salam*. Abu Talib said, 'Wait for a *sabt,* then I will give you similar glad news, except prophet-hood (the new born will not be a prophet).'

"The Imam has said, 'A *sabt* is thirty years. Amir al-Mu'minin Ali, *'Alayhi al-Salam*, was born thirty years after the birth of the Messenger of Allah, *'Alayhi al-Salam.*'"

H 1224, Ch. 113, h 2

Ali ibn Muhammad ibn 'Abd Allah has narrated from al-Sayyariy from Muhammad ibn Jumhur from certain persons of our people from abu 'Abd Allah, *'Alayhi al-Salam*, who has said the following:

"Fatimah, mother of Amir al-Mu'minin Ali, *'Alayhi al-Salam*, was the first woman who migrated to the Messenger of Allah from Makkah to Madina on foot.

She was the kindest person to the Messenger of Allah. She heard the Messenger of Allah say, 'On the Day of Judgment people will be raised naked as they were born.' She said, 'My goodness, what a lamentable lack of privacy!'

"The Messenger of Allah then said, 'I will pray to Allah to resurrect you all dressed up.' When she heard him speak of the constraint in the grave, she then said, 'Alas! How pitiful is my weakness!' The Messenger of Allah said, 'I will pray to Allah to make it easy for you.' One day she said to the Messenger of Allah, 'I want to set my female slave free.'

"He said, 'If you do so, Allah will set free for every part of her a part of you from fire. When she died she made her will to the Messenger of Allah and ordered that her female slave be set free. At the time of death her tongue could not move. She made (a great deal of) gestures to the Messenger of Allah. The Messenger of Allah accepted her will. One day when he was sitting, Amir al-Mu'minin Ali, *'Alayhi al-Salam*, came weeping. The Messenger of Allah asked him about the reason for his weeping and he answered, 'My mother, Fatimah, has died.' The Messenger of Allah, *'Alayhi al-Salam*, said, 'By Allah, and (she is) my mother also.' He went to her quickly and looked at her and wept. He directed the ladies to wash her and said, 'When you complete your task do not do anything else without informing me first. When the ladies informed him of the completion of their task he gave them one of his shirts that he would wear under all of his other clothes to be used as her shroud. He said to the Muslims, 'If you see me doing something that I have not done before you may ask me why I have done so.'

"When the ladies completed the washing and shrouding he went to pick up her remains. He lifted upon his shoulder (one side of) the coffin and continued all the way to the gravesite. When her body was placed on the ground near the grave he entered the grave and lay down in it. He then got up and (helped) with his hands to place the body in the grave. Then he bent over the body for a long time whispering certain words and said to her, 'Your son, your son, [your son]. He then came out and leveled the gravesite. Then he bent over the grave and said, 'I testify that no one deserves to be worshipped and obeyed except Allah. O Lord, I entrust her to you.' He then left the graveyard. The Muslims said to him, 'We found you doing certain things that you had not done before this day.' He said, 'Today I lost the kindness of abu Talib. If she ever had anything good in her possession she would make it available to me before herself and her own children. Once I mentioned the Day of Judgment when everyone will be resurrected naked; she said, 'My goodness, what a lamentable lack of privacy!' I said to her, 'I will pray to Allah to resurrect you all dressed up.' She heard me speak of the constraint in the grave. She then said, 'Alas! How pitiful is my weakness!' I guaranteed her that Allah will make it easy for her. Thus, I gave my shirt to use for her shroud and lay down in her grave for this reason. I then bent myself over her body to dictate to her the answer to the questions that she was asked. She was asked who her creator was. She gave the right answer. She was thereafter asked to tell who the messenger to her from Allah was. She gave the right answer. She then was asked who her *Wali*, the Imam (Leader and Guardian with Divine Authority) was. She stuttered. I said to her, 'It is your son, it is your son, [it is your own son].'"

H 1225, Ch. 113, h 3

Certain persons of our people have narrated from those he mentioned from ibn Mahbub from 'Umar ibn Aban al-Kalbi from al-Mufaddal ibn 'Umar who has said the following:

"Once I heard abu 'Abd Allah, *'Alayhi al-Salam*, say, 'When the Messenger of Allah was born the white houses of the Persian kingdom and the palaces of Sham (Syria) were shown to Amina, his mother, openly (conquered). Fatimah daughter of Asad, mother of Amir al-Mu'minin Ali, *'Alayhi al-Salam*, came to abu Talib laughing with glad news and explained to him what Amina had said. Abu Talib asked her, 'Has it surprised you so much? You will conceive a child who will be the executor of the will and the Vizier of this newborn.'"

H 1226, Ch. 113, h 4

A number of our people have narrated from Ahmad ibn Muhammad ibn 'Isa from al-Barqi from Ahmad ibn Zayd al-Naysaburi who has said that narrated to me 'Umar ibn Ibrahim al-Hashimi from 'Abd al-Malik ibn 'Umar from 'Asid ibn Safwan the companion of the Messenger of Allah who has said the following:

"On the day that Amir al-Mu'minin Ali, *'Alayhi al-Salam*, passed away the place shook as people wept and cried, and they were frightened as on the day the Holy Prophet, *'Alayhi al-Salam*, passed away. A man came weeping. He seemed in a hurry and was saying the words of the Holy Quran, 'We are the servants of Allah and to Him we shall all return.' (2:156) He continued, 'Today the government as succession of that of the Holy Prophet, *'Alayhi al-Salam*, is discontinued.' He stood at the door of the house in which Amir al-Mu'minin Ali, *'Alayhi al-Salam*, was and said, 'May Allah grant you blessing, O abu al-Hassan.

'You were the first in the nation who accepted Islam and were of the purest faith among them (people of the nation). You were of the most solid certainty and feared Allah the most among them. The degree of your hard work (for the cause of Allah) was the greatest and you were the most cautious in protecting the Messenger of Allah among them. You were the most trusted in the affairs of his companions and of the most distinguished in excellence, of the most honorable past credentials, of the highest degree of virtue and the closest as relatives to the Messenger of Allah among them. You were the most similar among them to him (the Messenger of Allah) in the matters of providing guidance, moral discipline, mannerism and deeds. You were the most valuable person to him (the Messenger of Allah) among them, in importance and the most honorable to him among them. May Allah grant you good rewards on behalf of Islam, His Messenger and the Muslims. You exercised strength when his (the Messenger of Allah's) companions became weak. You would come out (to face the enemy) when they showed humiliation; you rose up whenever they showed laziness. You maintained steadfastness in adherence to the system of the Messenger of Allah whenever his companions inclined otherwise. You, indeed, were his undisputed successor and you did not cause strife (in the community) despite the mischief of the hypocrites, the anger of the unbelievers, the dislike of the jealous ones and the lowliness of the transgressors.

'You stood firm for the truth when they failed, spoke clearly when they became speechless, marched forward in the light of Allah when they halted; and if they followed you they found the right guidance.

'You were the softest in tone and of the highest degree of prayer among them, of the smallest amount of speech and of the most correct and valid statements. You were of the greatest ideas, of the bravest heart, of the most solid certainty, of the best of deeds and the most knowledgeable of the issues among them. You, by Allah, were the lead figure in religion at first and at last. You were the first when people digressed in chaos and the last (to remain steadfast to the end) when they failed. You were as a kind father to the believers as they became dependent upon you and you bore such burdens that others felt much too weak to carry. You protected what they had lost and guarded what they had ignored. You tightened your belt (due to hunger) when they accumulated (wealth with greed); you rose high when they despaired (in humiliation). You exercised patience when they rushed and you achieved what they had never dreamed of achieving and through you they gained what they had never expected to gain.

'You were an overwhelming calamity and disaster upon the unbelievers and the fortress and support for the believers. You by Allah, were invented for the task of Leadership with Divine Authority with its blessing and you succeeded in achieving its awards, establishing its prerequisite and left with its distinctions. Your evidence in support of your Divine Authority never lost its cutting edge and your heart never wavered, your intelligence never weakened, your soul did not falter or become frightened. You were like a mountain that strong winds could not move. It is just as the Holy Prophet, *'Alayhi al-Salam*, has said, "People lived secure in your company and their property well-preserved in your hands." You were just as the Holy Prophet, *'Alayhi al-Salam*, has said, 'Physically weak but very strong to support the cause of Allah,' of a very humble soul, but very great in the sight of Allah, the Chief on earth and majestic in the sight of the believers. No one could ever find fault with you or advance criticism against you. No one could ever involve you in corruption. You never showed anyone (corrupt) compliance. The weak and feeble to you were strong and popular until you restored their rights and the powerful and popular were weak and feeble to you until you made them yield to others' rights.

'People of close relation or otherwise were equal before you in such cases. Your method was reality, the truth and kindness. Your words were law and final, and your commands were based on forbearance and determination, your view was knowledge and the final decision in what you did. The system is established, the pitfalls are routed, the fires (of mischief) are extinguished, religious issues are balanced and through you Islam has become strong. The guidance of Allah has become manifest even though the unbelievers dislike it. Through you Islam and the believers are strengthened. You have raced (for Divine excellence) a long race and caused a great deal of weariness to those behind you.

'Losing you can never be compensated for with weeping, and your death is a great issue in heaven and it has threatened the people (with the emergence of chaos). 'We are the servants of Allah and to Him we shall all return.' (2:156) We accept the decision of Allah and submit to His commands. By Allah, the Muslims will never find anyone like you. You were a fortress and a stronghold like a heavy mountain and the intense anger against the unbelievers. May Allah join you with His Holy Prophet, *'Alayhi al-Salam*. May Allah not deprive us of your rewards, and keep us safe against misguidance after you.'

'People remained silent until he finished his words. He wept and the companions of the Messenger of Allah wept. Thereafter, they searched for him but he was nowhere to be found.' "

H 1227, Ch. 113, h 5
A number of our people have narrated from Ahmad ibn Muhammad from Ali ibn al-Hakam from Safwan al-Jammal who has said the following:
"Once, 'Amir, 'Abd Allah ibn Jiza'a, al-'Azdi and I were in the presence of abu 'Abd Allah, *'Alayhi al-Salam*. The narrator has said that 'Amir said to the Imam the following:

'May Allah keep my soul in service for your cause, people think Amir al-Mu'minin Ali, *'Alayhi al-Salam*, was buried in al-Rahba (an open space near the mosque of Kufa).' The Imam said, 'No, he was not buried there.'

"He then asked, 'Where is he buried?' The Imam said, 'After his death, al-Hassan, *'Alayhi al-Salam*, carried him to a place, behind Kufa which is near al-Najaf, toward the right of al-Ghari and the left of al-Hira. He buried him among the small dunes of white sands.' Later on, I went to the place and I thought of one place as being his gravesite. I then returned and informed the Imam about it. The Imam said, 'You, may Allah grant you blessing, found it (the gravesite) three times.'"

H 1228, Ch. 113, h 6
Ahmad ibn Muhammad has narrated from ibn abu 'Umayr from al-Qasim ibn Muhammad from 'Abd Allah ibn Sinan who has said the following:
"Once, 'Umar ibn Yazid came to me and said, 'Ride with us, and I rode with them and went until we came to the house of Hafs al-Kunasi. We took him also with us and continued the journey until we arrived at al-Ghari and the gravesite. He (Hafs) said, 'Dismount, this is the grave of Amir al-Mu'minin Ali, *'Alayhi al-Salam*.' We asked him, 'How did you find out?' He said, 'I have come here several times with abu 'Abd Allah, *'Alayhi al-Salam*, when he was in al-Hira and he told me that this is his (Amir al-Mu'minin Ali, *'Alayhi al-Salam*) gravesite.'"

H 1229, Ch. 113, h 7
Muhammad ibn Yahya has narrated from Salama ibn al-Khattab from 'Abd Allah ibn Muhammad from 'Abd Allah ibn al-Qasim from 'Isa Shalqan who has said the following:
"I heard abu 'Abd Allah, *'Alayhi al-Salam*, say, "'Amir al-Mu'minin Ali, *'Alayhi al-Salam*, had maternal uncles in the tribe of the descendent of Makhdhum and a young man from them came to him (Amir al-Mu'minin Ali, *'Alayhi al-Salam*)

and said, "Uncle, my brother has died and I am very sad because of his death." The narrator has said that he (Amir al-Mu'minin Ali, *'Alayhi al-Salam*) asked him, 'Do you want to see him?' He said, 'Yes, I want to see him.' He said, 'Show me his grave.' The narrator has said that he (Amir al-Mu'minin Ali, *'Alayhi al-Salam*) came out with him with the gown of the Messenger of Allah on him. When he reached at the gravesite he moved his lips and knocked the grave with his foot and he came out of his grave speaking in Persian. Amir al-Mu'minin Ali, *'Alayhi al-Salam*, asked, 'Did you not die as an Arab man?' He said, 'Yes, but we died in the tradition of so and so, son of so and so; thus our language changed.'"

H 1230, Ch. 113, h 8

Muhammad ibn Yahya has narrated from Ahmad ibn Muhammad and Ali ibn Muhammad from Sahl ibn Ziyad all from ibn Mahbub from abu Hamza from abu Ja'far, *'Alayhi al-Salam*, who has said the following:

"When Amir al-Mu'minin Ali, *'Alayhi al-Salam*, passed away, al-Hassan ibn Ali stood up in the Mosque of Kufa. He praised Allah and spoke of His Glory. He prayed to Allah to grant blessings up on the Holy Prophet, *'Alayhi al-Salam*, and then he said this: 'People, tonight a man has passed away the like of whom cannot be found in previous and the coming generations. He was the standard bearer of the Messenger of Allah, with Jibril on his right and Micha'il on his left. He would not turn back until Allah granted him victory. All that he has left of the worldly belongings is seven hundred Dirhams extra from his gifts with which he wanted to buy (hire) a servant for his household. By Allah, he died during a night in which the executor of the will of Musa (Moses) Yusha' ibn Nun had passed away, the night in which Jesus, son of Mary, was taken to heaven and the night in which the Holy Quran was revealed.'"

H 1231, Ch. 113, h 9

Ali ibn Muhammad has narrated in a *marfu'* manner from abu 'Abd Allah, *'Alayhi al-Salam*, who has said the following:

"Abu 'Abd Allah, *'Alayhi al-Salam*, has said, 'When Amir al-Mu'minin Ali, *'Alayhi al-Salam*, was washed for burial they were called from the side of the house, 'If you lift up the front of the coffin you do not need to lift up the back of the coffin and if you lift up the back side then you do not need to lift up the front side.'"

H 1232, Ch. 113, h 10

'Abd Allah ibn Ja'far and Sa'd ibn 'Abd Allah both have narrated from Ibrahim ibn Mahziyar from his brother, Ali ibn Mahziyar from al-Hassan ibn Mahbub from Hisham ibn Salim from Habib al-Sajistani who has said the following:

"I heard abu Ja'far, *'Alayhi al-Salam*, say, 'Fatimah, daughter of the Holy Prophet, *'Alayhi al-Salam*, was born five years after he proclaimed his being the Messenger of Allah and she passed away when she was eighteen years and seventy-five days old.'"

H 1233, Ch. 113, h 11

Sa'd ibn 'Abd Allah has narrated from Ahmad ibn Muhammad ibn 'Isa from al-Hassan ibn Ali ibn Faddal from 'Abd Allah ibn Bukayr from certain persons of our people who have said the following:

"I heard abu 'Abd Allah, *'Alayhi al-Salam*, say, 'When Amir al-Mu'minin Ali, *'Alayhi al-Salam*, died, al-Hassan and al-Husayn, *'Alayhim al-Salam*, and two other men carried his body out until they went out of Kufa. They continued with Kufa on their right and then they moved forward on the path of Jabana until they passed al-Ghari. They then buried him and leveled his grave and then returned (home).'"

Chapter 114 - The Birth of Al-Zahra', Fatimah, *'Alayha al-Salam*

Al-Kulayni has said, "Fatimah, *'Alayha al-Salam*, was born five years after the Messenger of Allah declared his message. She died when she was eighteen years and seventy-five days old. She lived for seventy-five days after the death of her father, *'Alayhi al-Salam*."

H 1234, Ch. 114, h 1

Muhammad ibn Yahya has narrated from Ahmad ibn Muhammad from ibn Mahbub from ibn al-Ri'ab from abu 'Ubayda from abu 'Abd Allah, *'Alayhi al-Salam*, who has said the following:

"Abu 'Abd Allah, *'Alayhi al-Salam*, has said, 'Fatimah, *'Alayha al-Salam*, lived for seventy-five days after the death of the Messenger of Allah. She had become extremely sad for her father. Jibril would come to her with condolences because of the death of her father and to provide solace. He would inform her about where her father was and about what might happen after her death to her descendents and Ali, *'Alayhi al-Salam*, would write down such information.'"

H 1235, Ch. 114, h 2

Muhammad in Yahya has narrated from al-'Amrakiy ibn Ali from Ali ibn Ja'far from his brother from abu al-Hassan, *'Alayhi al-Salam*, who has said the following:

"Abu al-Hassan, *'Alayhi al-Salam*, has said, 'Fatimah is truthful and a martyr. The daughters of the prophets do not experience menses.'"

H 1236, Ch. 114, h 3

Ahmad ibn Mihran, may Allah grant him blessing, has narrated in a *marfu'* manner and Ahmad ibn Idris has narrated from Muhammad ibn 'Abd al-Jabbar al-Shaybani who has said that narrated to me al-Qasim ibn Muhammad al-Razi who has said that narrated to him Ali ibn Muhammad al-Hurmuzani from abu 'Abd Allah al-Husayn ibn Ali, *'Alayhi al-Salam*, who has said the following:

"Abu 'Abd Allah al-Husayn ibn Ali, *'Alayhim al-Salam*, has said, 'When Fatimah, *'Alayha al-Salam*, passed away Amir al-Mu'minin Ali, *'Alayhi al-Salam*, buried her secretly, camouflaged her gravesite and then stood up facing the grave of the Messenger of Allah and said, "O Messenger of Allah, may Allah grant you blessings on my behalf and on behalf of your daughter who is visiting you and will pass this night in the soil of your location. Allah chose to make her join you the fastest. O Messenger of Allah, my patience has reached its limits and I miss so much your chosen one (daughter) and my self-control has vanished due to the departure of the leader of the ladies of the world. The only solace for me is to follow your tradition and be mournful for your own departure from us. A little while ago I placed you in your grave and your spirit left your body between my own throat and chest. Yes, in the book of Allah (for me) there is the best example for expressing acceptance of Allah's decision, 'We are the servants of Allah and to Him we shall all return.'" (2:156)

'The trust is returned, the commitment is recalled and al-Zahra' is taken away from us. How sad, O Messenger of Allah, the green skies and the dusty earth seem to us. My sadness has become perpetual and my nights have become sleepless. There is an anxiety that will not relieve my heart until Allah will choose for me a dwelling like that where you are. I have a heart bleeding, sorrowful, and a restlessess and anxiety. How quickly the separation took place. Before Allah I lament, and your own daughter will explain to you how your 'Umma (followers) succeeded in committing injustice against her. You may ask her questions and find information about the case from her. How great was her sorrow for which she could not find a place for expressing, but now she has found a place and an ear to express it to. She would say, 'Allah will judge because He is the best judge'. I offer my prayer to Allah to grant you blessings as a note of farewell, but not because of disappointment and desperation. If I return it is not because I have become tired and if I stand up it will not be because of pessimism toward the promise of Allah to those who exercise patience. Indeed to exercise patience is more safe and fruitful. Had I not feared the mischief of the enemies I would have liked to turn the place into a place of worship, to keep my worship continuous and to cry like the mothers for the death of their son, for the great loss. In the sight of Allah your daughter is buried secretly, her rights are taken away unjustly, her inheritance is withheld for no valid reason. It all happened just after you left and your memories are still fresh. To Allah, O Messenger of Allah, we lament and from you, O Messenger of Allah, we seek condolences. May Allah grant blessings to you and to her. May the peace and happiness from Allah be with you.'"

H 1237, Ch. 114, h 4

A number of our people have narrated from Ahmad ibn Muhammad ibn 'Isa from Ahmad ibn Muhammad ibn abu Nasr from 'Abd al-Rahman ibn Salim from al-Mufaddal who has said the following:

"Once I asked abu 'Abd Allah, *'Alayhi al-Salam*, 'Who washed Fatimah (for burial)?' He said, 'Amir al-Mu'minin Ali, *'Alayhi al-Salam*, did.' My reaction to his words seemed to be an extraordinary one. He said, 'You seem to be constrained by what I said.'

"I (the narrator) replied, 'Yes, may Allah keep my soul in service for your cause, it is so.' The narrator has said that the Imam then said, 'Do not be constrained. She was the most truthful person and no one has the authority to wash an all-truthful person but another all-truthful person. Did you not know that no one could wash Mary but Jesus.'"

H 1238, Ch. 114, h 5

Muhammad ibn Yahya has narrated from Muhammad ibn al-Husayn from Muhammad ibn 'Isma'il from Salih ibn 'Aqaba from 'Abd Allah ibn Muhammad al-Ju'fi from abu Ja'far and abu 'Abd Allah, *'Alayhim al-Salam*, who have said the following:

"Abu Ja'far and abu 'Abd Allah, *'Alayhim al-Salam*, have said, 'During the time of their doing (setting the door on fire) what they did, Fatimah, *'Alayha al-Salam*, held 'Umar by his collar and pulled (down) saying, 'By Allah, O son of al-Khattab, had I not disliked inflicting calamity upon innocent people, you would have learned how my swearing upon Allah could bring swift response (with the wrath of Allah upon you).'"

H 1239, Ch. 114, h 6
Through the same chain of narrators it is narrated from Salih ibn 'Aqaba from Yazid ibn 'Abd al-Malik from abu Ja'far, *'Alayhi al-Salam*, who has said the following:

"Abu Ja'far, *'Alayhi al-Salam*, has said, 'When Fatimah, *'Alayha al-Salam*, was born Allah sent an angel to make the tongue of Muhammad, *'Alayhi al-Salam*, call (name) her 'Fatimah'. Then he said, 'I set you free (from ignorance) with knowledge and set you free from menses.' Abu Ja'far, *'Alayhi al-Salam*, then said, 'By Allah, He had granted her full freedom in knowledge (against ignorance) and from menses at the time of formation of universal covenant (al-Mithaq).'"

H 1240, Ch. 114, h 7
Through the same chain of narrators it is narrated from Salih ibn 'Aqaba from 'Amr ibn Shimr from Jabir from abu Ja'far, *'Alayhi al-Salam*, who has said the following:

"Abu Ja'far, *'Alayhi al-Salam*, has said, 'Once, the Holy Prophet, *'Alayhi al-Salam*, said to Fatimah, 'Rise and bring that tray.' She went and took out the tray with fresh bread and steaming meat on it. The Holy Prophet, Ali, Fatimah, al-Hassan and al-Husayn, *'Alayhim al-Salam*, continued to have their meals from it for thirteen days. Then 'Umm Ayman saw al-Husayn, *'Alayhi al-Salam*, with certain things with him. She asked, 'Where did you get it from?' He replied, 'We have been having this for our meal for the past thirteen days.' 'Umm Ayman came to *Fatimah, 'Alayha al-Salam*, and said, 'O Fatimah, if 'Umm Ayman finds anything it is all for *Fatimah, 'Alayha al-Salam*, and her sons but if *Fatimah, 'Alayha al-Salam*, finds something then there is nothing in it for 'Umm Ayman.' She (Fatimah) then took out food for her from the tray and 'Umm Ayman ate but the food from the tray vanished. The Holy Prophet, *'Alayhi al-Salam*, said to *Fatimah, 'Alayha al-Salam*, 'Were you not to feed her (a non-infallible) from it, you and your descendents could have found food in it up to the Day of Judgment.'

"Abu Ja'far, *'Alayhi al-Salam*, then said, 'The tray is with us and our *al-Qa'im* (the one who will rise with Divine Authority and power) will take it out at his time.'"

H 1241, Ch. 114, h 8
Al-Husayn ibn Muhammad has narrated from Mu'alla ibn Muhammad from Ahmad ibn Muhammad ibn Ali from Ali ibn Ja'far who has said the following:

"I heard abu al-Hassan, *'Alayhi al-Salam*, say, 'Once, when the Messenger of Allah was sitting an angel who had twenty four faces came to him. The Messenger of Allah said to him, 'My friend Jibril, I had not seen you in this form before.' The angel said, 'I am not Jibril, O Muhammad. Allah, the Most Majestic, the Most Gracious, has sent me to join in marriage the light with the light.' He then asked, 'Who with whom?' The angel said, 'Fatimah and Ali, *'Alayhim al-Salam*.' The Imam said, 'When the angel turned around on his shoulder it said, 'Muhammad the Messenger of Allah, and Ali, *'Alayhi al-Salam*, the executor of his will.' The

Messenger of Allah asked, 'Since when has this been written on your shoulder?' The angel replied, 'It was there twenty two thousand years before Allah created Adam.'"

H 1242, Ch. 114, h 9
Ali ibn Muhammad and others have narrated from Sahl ibn Ziyad from Ahmad ibn Muhammad ibn abu Nasr who has said the following:

"I asked al-Rida, *'Alayhi al-Salam*, about the grave of *Fatimah, 'Alayha al-Salam.* He said, 'She was buried in her own house. When the Amawids enlarged the Mosque it became part of the Mosque.'"

H 1243, Ch. 114, h 10
A number of our people have narrated from Ahmad ibn Muhammad from al-Washsha' from al-Khaybari from Yunus ibn Zabyan who has said the following:

"I heard abu 'Abd Allah, *'Alayhi al-Salam*, say, 'If Allah had not created Amir al-Mu'minin Ali, *'Alayhi al-Salam*, no match could be found for Fatimah, *'Alayha al-Salam*, on earth from Adam to the end.'"

Chapter 115 - The Birth of al-Hassan ibn Ali, *'Alayhi al-Salam*

Al-Kulayni has said, "Al-Hassan ibn Ali, *'Alayhi al-Salam*, was born in the month of Ramadan in the year that the battle of Badr took place, the second year after Hijra (A.H.) (migration of the Holy Prophet, *'Alayhi al-Salam*, from Makkah to Madina). It is also narrated that he was born in the third year. He passed away in the end of the month of Safar in the year forty-nine A.H. He lived for forty-seven years and a few months. His mother was *Fatimah, 'Alayha al-Salam*, daughter of the Messenger of Allah."

H 1244, Ch. 115, h 1
Muhammad ibn Yahya has narrated from al-Husayn ibn Ishaq from Ali ibn Mahziyar from al-Husayn ibn Sa'id from al-Nadr ibn Suwayd from 'Abd Allah ibn Sinan from the one who heard from abu Ja'far, *'Alayhi al-Salam*, who has said the following:

"Abu Ja'far, *'Alayhi al-Salam*, has said, 'When al-Hassan, *'Alayhi al-Salam*, was about to die he wept. He was asked, 'O grandson of the Messenger of Allah, why do you weep, when you have such a position with the Messenger of Allah and all the (good things) said about you? You have performed Hajj twenty times on foot and distributed all of your belongings among the needy three times exactly.' He replied, 'I weep for two reasons: It is the fear of resurrection and separation from loved ones.'"

H 1245, Ch. 115, h 2
Sa'd ibn 'Abd Allah and 'Abd Allah ibn Ja'far have narrated from Ibrahim ibn Mahziyar from his brother, Ali (ibn Mahziyar) from al-Hassan ibn Sa'id from Muhammad ibn Sinan from ibn Muskan from abu Basir from abu 'Abd Allah, *'Alayhi al-Salam*, who has said the following:

"Abu 'Abd Allah, *'Alayhi al-Salam*, has said, 'Al-Hassan ibn Ali, *'Alayhi al-Salam*, passed away at the age of forty-seven in A.H. year fifty. He lived forty years after the death of the Messenger of Allah, *'Alayhi al-Salam*.'"

H 1246, Ch. 115, h 3

A number of our people have narrated from Ahmad ibn Muhammad from Ali ibn al-Nu'man from Sayf ibn 'Amira from abu Bakr al-Hadrami who has said the following:

"Ju'ada daughter of 'Ash'th ibn Qays al-Kindi poisoned al-Hassan ibn Ali, *'Alayhi al-Salam*, and a female servant of the Imam. The female servant, however, vomited the poison but in the case of al-Hassan, *'Alayhi al-Salam*, the poison remained in his digestive system and caused swelling that killed him."

H 1247, Ch. 115, h 4

Muhammad ibn Yahya and Ahmad ibn Muhammad have narrated from Muhammad ibn al-Hassan from al-Qasim al-Nahdi from 'Isma'il ibn Mihran from al-Kunasi from abu 'Abd Allah, *'Alayhi al-Salam*, who has said the following:

"Abu 'Abd Allah, *'Alayhi al-Salam*, has said, 'Once, al-Hassan ibn Ali, *'Alayhi al-Salam*, went outside the town with a man from the children of al-Zubayr who believed al-Hassan to be the Imam. They stopped for rest on one of the oases under a palm tree that had dried up due to lack of water. A furnishing was spread for Imam al-Hassan, *'Alayhi al-Salam*, under that tree and for al-Zubayri the furnishings were arranged under a tree just next to it. The narrator has said that al-Zubayri looked up the tree and said, 'I wish this tree had fruits so we could eat from them.' Al-Hassan, *'Alayhi al-Salam*, asked, 'Do you wish to have dates?' He said, 'Yes, I do wish to have dates.' He (al-Hassan, *'Alayhi al-Salam*) raised his hands to the sky and spoke certain words that I did not understand. The tree turned green. It returned to its normal condition, its leaves grew and it became loaded with dates. The man from whom they had hired camels begun to say, 'It by Allah, is magic.' Al-Hassan, *'Alayhi al-Salam*, said, 'Woe is upon you, it is not magic. It is a prayer of the grandson of a prophet that is answered.' They climbed the tree to pick the dates that were there and it provided enough for their needs.'"

H 1248, Ch. 115, h 5

Ahmad ibn Muhammad and Muhammad ibn Yahya have narrated from Muhammad ibn al-Hassan from Ya'qub ibn Yazid from ibn abu 'Umayr from his people from abu 'Abd Allah, *'Alayhi al-Salam*, who has said the following:

"Abu 'Abd Allah, *'Alayhi al-Salam*, has said, 'Al-Hassan, *'Alayhi al-Salam*, has said, "Allah has two cities. One is in the east and the other is in the west. They have a boundary around them that is made of iron and each one has a million doors. Seven thousand different languages exist therein and I know all those languages and all that is in and between the two cities. No one possesses Leadership with Divine Authority over them except me and my brother al-Husayn, *'Alayhi al-Salam*.'"

H 1249, Ch. 115, h 6

Al-Husayn ibn Muhammad has narrated from Mu'alla ibn Muhammad from Ahmad ibn Muhammad from Muhammad ibn Ali ibn al-Nu'man from Sandal from abu 'Usama from abu 'Abd Allah, *'Alayhi al-Salam*, who has said the following:

"Abu 'Abd Allah, *'Alayhi al-Salam*, has said, 'One year al-Hassan ibn Ali left for Makkah on foot. On the journey his feet swelled and his servants said, 'If you travel riding, the swelling will go away.' He said, 'I will not ride up to the coming place for rest where you will see a black person who has oil with him. Buy from him oil without trying to reduce the price.' The servant said, 'May Allah keep my soul and the souls of my parents in service for your cause, we had never been up to a place of rest where anyone sold such medicine.'

"The Imam said to him, 'Yes, there are such people right ahead of you before reaching the place for rest.' They walked for a mile and they met the black person. Al-Hassan, *'Alayhi al-Salam*, said to his servant, 'There is the man. Take the oil from him and pay him.' The black man asked the servant, 'For whom do you want this oil?' He replied, 'I want it for al-Hassan ibn Ali, *'Alayhi al-Salam*. He said, 'Take me to him.' They came to al-Hassan, *'Alayhi al-Salam*, and the man said, 'May Allah keep my soul and the souls of my parents in service for your cause; I did not know that you need this. If you want to have it you can have it free of charges. I am only one of your servants. Just pray for me to Allah to grant me a healthy son who would love you, *Ahl al-Bayt*. When I left, my wife was about to give birth.' The Imam said, 'Go to your place. Allah has gifted you with a healthy son who is of our Shi'a (followers).'"

Chapter 116 - The Birth of Al-Husayn Ibn Ali, *'Alayhi al-Salam*

Al-Kulayni has said, "Al-Husayn ibn Ali, *'Alayhi al-Salam*, was born in the third year A.H. (after Hijrah, migration of the Holy Prophet). He left this word in the month of Muharram in the year sixty-one A.H. He lived for fifty-seven years and few months. 'Ubayd Allah ibn Ziyad (may he fall in condemnation of Allah) murdered him during the Caliphate of Yazid ibn Mu'awiya (may he fall in condemnation of Allah). He was the governor of Kufa. The horsemen who murdered him were led by 'Umar ibn Sa'd (may he fall in condemnation of Allah) in the plane of Karbala. It took place on Monday the tenth of the month of Muharram. His mother was *Fatimah, 'Alayha al-Salam*, daughter of the Messenger of Allah."

H 1250, Ch. 116, h 1

Sa'd and Ahmad ibn Muhammad both have narrated from Ibrahim ibn Mahziyar from his brother, Ali ibn Mahziyar from al-Husayn ibn Sa'id from Muhammad ibn Sinan from ibn Muskan from abu Basir from abu 'Abd Allah, *'Alayhi al-Salam*, who has said the following:

"Abu 'Abd Allah, *'Alayhi al-Salam*, has said, 'Al-Husayn, *'Alayhi al-Salam*, passed away a martyr on the day of 'Ashura' (tenth of the month of Muharram) and he was fifty-seven years old."

H 1251, Ch. 116, h 2

A number of our people have narrated from Ahmad ibn Muhammad from Ali ibn al-Hakam from 'Abd al-Rahman al-'Arzami from abu 'Abd Allah, *'Alayhi al-Salam*, who has said the following:

"Abu 'Abd Allah, *'Alayhi al-Salam*, has said, 'The time between the birth of al-Hassan, and the conception for al-Husayn, *'Alayhim al-Salam*, was like one cycle of menses and the time between the birth of the two was six months and ten days.'"

H 1252, Ch. 116, h 3

Muhammad ibn Yahya has narrated from Ahmad ibn Muhammad from al-Washsha' and al-Husayn ibn Muhammad from Mu'alla ibn Muhammad from al-Washsha' from Ahmad ibn 'A'idh from abu Khadija from abu 'Abd Allah, *'Alayhi al-Salam*, who has said the following:

"Abu 'Abd Allah, *'Alayhi al-Salam*, has said, 'When *Fatimah, 'Alayha al-Salam*, conceived al-Husayn, *'Alayhi al-Salam*, Jibril came to the Messenger of Allah and said, '*Fatimah, 'Alayha al-Salam*, will soon give birth to a son. Your 'Umma (followers) will murder him after you die.' When Fatimah had conceived al-Husayn she was unhappy and when she gave birth she was unhappy. The Imam then said, 'No mother has ever been seen in the world to bear a child that she would not like. However, she was unhappy; she knew that he will be murdered.' The Imam has said, 'It is this case for which the following verse of the Holy Quran came: "We have advised the human being to be kind to his parents; his mother bore him with (unhappiness) hardship and delivered him while suffering a great deal of pain (unhappiness). The period in which his mother bore and weaned him lasted for thirty months. . . .'" (46:15)

H 1253, Ch. 116, h 4

Muhammad ibn Yahya has narrated from Ali ibn 'Isma'il from Muhammad ibn 'Amr al-Zayyat from a man from our people from abu 'Abd Allah, *'Alayhi al-Salam*, who has said the following:

"Abu 'Abd Allah, *'Alayhi al-Salam*, has said, 'Once Jibril came to Muhammad, *'Alayhi al-Salam*, and said to him, 'O Muhammad, Allah gives you the glad news of the birth of a son from *Fatimah, 'Alayha al-Salam*. Your 'Umma (followers) will murder this child after you die.' He (the Holy Prophet) said, 'O Jibril peace is from my Lord. I do not need a child from *Fatimah, 'Alayha al-Salam*, who will be murdered by my 'Umma after I die.' Jibril ascended and then descended back and said to him the same thing. He said, 'O Jibril peace is from my Lord. I do not need a child who will be murdered by my 'Umma after I die.' Jibril ascended to the heavens and then descended back and said, 'O Muhammad, *'Alayhi al-Salam*, your Lord sends you greetings and gives you the glad news of His placing Imamat (Leadership with Divine Authority), the guardianship and the executor-ship of the will in the descendents of this child.' Then he (the Holy Prophet) said, 'I agree and accept the arrangement.' He then sent to *Fatimah, 'Alayha al-Salam*, the message of the glad news of the birth of a child from her who will be murdered by his 'Umma. She returned the answer, 'I do not need a child who will be murdered by your 'Umma after you die.' He then sent the message to her that Allah will place Imamat (Leadership with Divine Authority), guardianship and the executorship of the will in the descendents of this child. She then sent back with the answer that she has agreed to the arrangement. '. . . His mother bore him with hardship and delivered him while suffering a great deal of pain. The period in which his mother bore and weaned him lasted for thirty months. When he grew up to manhood and became forty years old, he then said, "Lord, inspire me to give You thanks for the bounties you have granted to me and my parents, and to act righteously to please You. Lord, make (people of) my offspring virtuous . . ."' (46:15)

"The Imam said, 'Had he not said, ". . . Lord, make (people in) my offspring virtuous. . . ." (46:15) all of his offspring would have been *'A'immah* (Leaders with Divine Authority).' (The word 'in' indicates part, not the whole or all of something). Al-Husayn, *'Alayhi al-Salam*, did not have any milk from *Fatimah, 'Alayha al-Salam*, nor from other females. They would bring him to the Holy Prophet, *'Alayhi al-Salam*, to place his thumb in the child's mouth. The child would receive food therefrom and it sufficed him for three days. The flesh of al-Husayn, *'Alayhi al-Salam*, grew from that of the Messenger of Allah, *'Alayhi al-Salam*, and his blood from his blood. No one has ever been born after six months except Jesus son of Mary and al-Husayn ibn Ali, *'Alayhi al-Salam*.'"

In another *Hadith* from abu al-Hassan al-Rida, *'Alayhi al-Salam*, it is said that they (people of the family) would bring al-Husayn to the Holy Prophet, *'Alayhi al-Salam*, and he would place his tongue in his mouth. This sufficed him (for food) and he did not have any milk from any female.

H 1254, Ch. 116, h 5
Ali ibn Muhammad has narrated in a *marfu'* manner from abu 'Abd Allah, *'Alayhi al-Salam*, who has said the following:

"About the words of Allah, the Most Majestic, the Most Gracious, '. . . then he (Abraham) contemplated when looking at the stars (37:88) and said, "I am sick."' (37:89) Abu 'Abd Allah, *'Alayhi al-Salam*, has said, 'He calculated and found what had happened to al-Husayn, *'Alayhi al-Salam*, then he said, "I am sick because of what will happen to al-Husayn, *'Alayhi al-Salam.*"'"

H 1255, Ch. 116, h 6
Ahmad ibn Muhammad has narrated from Muhammad ibn al-Hassan from Muhammad ibn 'Isa ibn 'Ubayd from Ali ibn Asbat from Sayf ibn 'Amira from Muhammad ibn Humran who has said the following:

"Abu 'Abd Allah, *'Alayhi al-Salam*, has said, 'When all that happened to al-Husayn, *'Alayhi al-Salam*, had happened, the angels wept and cried before Allah and said, "How could such a thing happen to al-Husayn, *'Alayhi al-Salam*? Your chosen one and the grandson of Your Prophet?" The Imam has said that Allah, then showed them the shadow of *al-Qa'im* (the one who will rise with Divine Authority and power) and said, 'Through him I will bring the perpetrators to My justice.'"

H 1256, Ch. 116, h 7
A number of our people have narrated from Ahmad ibn Muhammad ibn 'Isa from Ali ibn al-Hakam from Sayf ibn 'Amira from 'Abd al-Malik ibn 'A'yan from abu Ja'far, *'Alayhi al-Salam*, who has said the following:

"Abu Ja'far, *'Alayhi al-Salam*, has said, 'When (Divine) support came to al-Husayn ibn Ali, *'Alayhi al-Salam*, it filled from earth to the heavens and then he was given the choice to have victory or meet Allah, but he chose the latter.'"

H 1257, Ch. 116, h 8
Al-Husayn ibn Muhammad has said that abu Kurayb and abu Sa'id al-Ashja' narrated to him that 'Abd Allah ibn Idris narrated to them from his father, Idris ibn 'Abd Allah al-'Awdi who has said the following:

"When al-Husayn, *'Alayhi al-Salam*, was murdered people wanted to run horses over his (al-Husayn's) body. Fizza then said to Zaynab, (sister of al-Husayn) 'My lady, there was a shipwreck and Safina came out on an Island face to face with a lion. He (Safina) said to the lion, "O abu al-Harith, I am a slave of the Messenger of Allah." The lion murmured in front of him and showed him the way. There lives a lion in this area. Allow me to go and inform him of what the people intend to do to al-Husayn, *'Alayhi al-Salam*, tomorrow. The narrator has said that she (Fizza) went to the lion and said, 'O abu al-Harith, and the lion raised his head. She asked, "Do you know what these people intend to do to abu 'Abd Allah, *'Alayhi al-Salam*? They intend to run horses over his body.'"

"The narrator has said that the lion walked (all the way) and placed both of his hands over the body of al-Husayn, *'Alayhi al-Salam*. When the horsemen came they found the lion in that position and 'Umar ibn Sa'd (may he fall in condemnation of Allah) told them, 'It is mischief. Do not bother and turn back. They turned back."

H 1258, Ch. 116, h 9
Ali ibn Muhammad has narrated from Sahl ibn Ziyad from Muhammad ibn Ahmad from al-Hassan ibn Ali from Yunus from Masqala al-Tahhan who has said the following:
"I heard abu 'Abd Allah, *'Alayhi al-Salam*, say, 'After al-Husayn was murdered his wife, who was from the tribe of al-Kalb, began to organize a mourning gathering. She wept and the ladies and servants wept until their tears dried up. There was one female servant (slave) who wept and her tears would not stop. She called her and asked, 'How is it that our tears have dried up and your tears have not?' She said, 'When I suffer I drink Sawiq (a kind of soup made of wheat and or barley).' She then ordered to prepare Sawiq and food. She would drink and eat and give others to drink and eat and say, 'We need to find energy to weep for al-Husayn, *'Alayhi al-Salam*.'"

"The Imam has said, 'Certain birds were given to al-Kalbia lady to help her in her mourning for al-Husayn, *'Alayhi al-Salam*. When she saw them she asked, 'What are these?' They told her that they were a gift from so and so to help you in mourning for al-Husayn, *'Alayhi al-Salam*. She said, 'We are not in a wedding. What do we do with them?' She told her servants to take them out of the house. When they were taken out of the house they just disappeared as if they did not exist or flew between the heavens and earth and afterwards no trace of them was found anywhere.'"

Chapter 117 - The Birth of Ali ibn Al-Husayn, *'Alayhi al-Salam*

Al-Kulayni has said, "Ali ibn al-Husayn was born in the year thirty-eight A.H. He passed away in the year ninety-five at the age of fifty-seven. His mother was Slama, daughter of Yazdjurd ibn Shahryar ibn Shiruwayh ibn kisra 'A Perwiz. Yazdjurd was the last Persian ancient king."

H 1259, Ch. 117, h 1
Al-Husayn ibn al-Hassan al-Hassani, may Allah grant him blessings, and Ali ibn Muhammad ibn 'Abd Allah all of them from Ibrahim ibn Ishaq al-Ahmar from 'Abd al-Rahman ibn 'Abd Allah al-Khuza'i

from Nasr ibn Muzaham from 'Amr ibn Shimr from Jabir from abu Ja'far, *'Alayhi al-Salam*, who has said the following:

"The girls of Madina loved to see the daughter of Yazdjurd when she was brought before 'Umar. When she entered the Mosque it became all delightful and bright. When 'Umar looked at her she covered her face and said in her own language, "'Uff, bay ruj ba' da Hurmuz (May the life of Hurmuz turn black).' 'Umar asked, 'Is she abusing me?' He turned to her (with a certain attitude). Amir al-Mu'minin Ali, *'Alayhi al-Salam*, said, 'You do not have such a right (over her). Give her the chance to choose whoever of the Muslims she likes and then count as his share of the booty (of the properties seized from the Persian army).' He ('Umar) allowed her to choose and she came all the way to place her hand on the head of al-Husayn, *'Alayhi al-Salam*. Amir al-Mu'minin Ali, *'Alayhi al-Salam*, asked her, 'What is your name?' She said, 'It is Jahan Shah.' Amir al-Mu'minin Ali, *'Alayhi al-Salam*, said, 'In fact, it is Shahra Ba'nuwayh.' He then said to al-Husayn, *'Alayhi al-Salam*, 'O abu 'Abd Allah, she will give birth to a son for you who will be the best of the inhabitants of earth.' She gave birth to Ali ibn al-Husayn, *'Alayhi al-Salam*. Ali ibn al-Husayn was called the son of the two best. The chosen from Arabs was the tribe of Hashim and from non-Arab were Persians. It is narrated that abu al-Aswad al-Du'ili said about it:

'A boy from Kisra and Hashim;

'The most noble one on whom sacred symbols are stitched for safety.'"

H 1260, Ch. 117, h 2
A number of our people have narrated from Ahmad ibn Muhammad from ibn al-Faddal from ibn Bukayr from Zurara who has said the following:
"I heard abu Ja'far, *'Alayhi al-Salam*, say, 'Ali ibn al-Husayn, *'Alayhi al-Salam*, had a she-camel. He had taken this camel twenty two times to Hajj (pilgrimage to Makkah) and had not used a whip against it, not even once. The Imam has said that the camel came after he passed away and we were not aware but we noticed only when one of the servants or slaves came and said, 'The she-camel has gone out all the way to the grave of Ali ibn al-Husayn, *'Alayhi al-Salam*. She rubs her neck against the grave and moans.' I then asked them to quickly get to her before they (the enemies) might know about her or see her. The Imam has said, the she-camel had never seen the grave before.'"

H 1261, Ch. 117, h 3
Ali ibn Ibrahim ibn Hashim has narrated from his father from Muhammad ibn 'Isa from Hafs ibn al-Bakhtari from the person he mentioned from abu Ja'far, *'Alayhi al-Salam*, who has said the following:
"Abu Ja'far, *'Alayhi al-Salam*, has said, 'When my father, Ali ibn al-Husayn, *'Alayhi al-Salam*, passed away the she-camel that belonged to him came from the pasture and placed her neck against his grave and rolled her body on the ground. I commanded to return her back to her pasture. My father would take her for the journey to Hajj and 'Umra (pilgrimage to Makkah) and had never used a whip against her.'"

Note: The following Hadith is from the book of ibn Babuwayh.

H 1262, Ch. 117, h 4

Al-Husayn ibn Muhammad ibn 'Amir has narrated from Ahmad ibn Ishaq ibn Sa'd from Su'dan ibn Muslim from abu 'Imara from a man from abu 'Abd Allah, *'Alayhi al-Salam*, who has said the following:

"Abu 'Abd Allah, *'Alayhi al-Salam*, has said, 'When it was the night that Ali ibn al-Husayn, *'Alayhi al-Salam*, passed away he asked Muhammad, *'Alayhi al-Salam*, his son, 'Son bring me water for Wudu (cleaning for prayer).' Muhammad has said, 'I then brought water for him.' He said, 'I do not like this water. There is something dead in it.' I then brought the water in the light and found a dead mouse in it. I then brought him other water. He said, 'Son this is the night in which I am promised to be taken out of this world.' He explained his recommendations about his shecamel and that a stable be prepared for her and that she should be fed properly. I personally did as he had asked. Very shortly thereafter the she-camel came out of the stable and reached the grave, placed her neck on it, rolled her body on the ground and her eyes were flooded with tears. Muhammad ibn Ali, *'Alayhi al-Salam*, was informed that the she-camel had gone. He came to her and said, 'Control your emotion and get up. May Allah grant you good fortune.' She did not stop. The Imam has said, 'When he would take the camel to Makkah, he used to hang the whip from the luggage where it remained unutilized until he returned to Madina.' The Imam has said, 'Ali ibn al-Husayn, *'Alayhi al-Salam*, used to come out in the dark at night with a sack containing Darahim and Dananir (units of money) and would go door-to-door, knock them and gave a certain amount to the person who came out. When Ali ibn al-Husayn passed away, these people did not see the person with money anymore. Then they realized that Ali ibn al-Husayn, *'Alayhi al-Salam*, must have been the distributor of money among them.'"

H 1263, Ch. 117, h 5

Muhammad ibn Ahmad has narrated from his uncle, 'Abd Allah ibn al-Salt from al-Hassan ibn Ali ibn bint 'Ilya's who has said the following:

"I heard abu al-Hassan, *'Alayhi al-Salam*, say, 'When Ali ibn al-Husayn, *'Alayhi al-Salam*, was about to leave this world he passed out then he opened his eyes and recited Chapters 48 and 56 from the Holy Quran and said, "All praise belongs to Allah Who has fulfilled His promise to us and made us to have the earth as our legacy and choose from paradise whatever we might like. Thus, is the reward for those who work." At that time he passed away and did not say anything further.'"

H 1264, Ch. 117, h 6

Sa'd ibn 'Abd Allah and 'Abd Allah ibn Ja'far al-Himyari have narrated from Ibrahim ibn Mahziyar from his brother, Ali ibn Mahziyar from al-Husayn ibn Sa'id from Muhammad ibn Sinan from ibn Muskan from abu Basir from abu 'Abd Allah, *'Alayhi al-Salam*, who has said the following:

"Abu 'Abd Allah, *'Alayhi al-Salam*, has said, 'Ali ibn al-Husayn, *'Alayhi al-Salam*, passed away at the age of fifty-seven in A.H. year ninety-five. He lived for thirty five years after al-Husayn, *'Alayhi al-Salam*.'"

Chapter 118 - The Birth of abu Ja'far, Muhammad ibn Ali, *'Alayhi al-Salam*

Al-Kulayni has said, "Abu Ja'far, *'Alayhi al-Salam*, was born in the year fifty-seven A.H. He passed away in the year one hundred fourteen at the age of fifty-seven. He was buried in al-Baqi' cemetery, Madina, near the grave of his father, Ali ibn al-Husayn, *'Alayhi al-Salam*. His mother was 'Umm 'Abd Allah, daughter of al-Hassan ibn Ali ibn abu Talib, *'Alayhi al-Salam*, may Allah grant him and his rightly guided offspring blessings."

H 1265, Ch. 118, h 1

Muhammad ibn Yahya has narrated from Muhammad ibn Ahmad from 'Abd Allah ibn Ahmad from Salih ibn Mazid from 'Abd Allah ibn al-Mughira from abu al-Sabbah from abu Ja'far, *'Alayhi al-Salam*, who has said the following:

"Abu Ja'far, *'Alayhi al-Salam*, has said, 'Once, my mother was sitting next to a wall. The wall began to break apart and we heard an intense crumbling noise. She pointed out with her hands saying, 'No, for the sake of al-Mustafa (one of the titles of the Messenger of Allah), Allah has not granted you permission to fall.' The wall remained hanging in the air until she moved away from that place. My father gave one hundred Dinars as charity in appreciation and as an expression of gratitude for Allah's favor.

"Abu al-Sabbah has said, 'Once abu 'Abd Allah, *'Alayhi al-Salam*, mentioned his grandmother and said, "She was a truthful person. No woman was ever found in the descendents of al-Hassan, *'Alayhi al-Salam*, like her (in excellence).'"

Muhammad ibn al-Hassan has narrated from 'Abd Allah ibn Ahmad a similar *Hadith*.

H 1266, Ch. 118, h 2

A number of our people have narrated from Ahmad ibn Muhammad from Muhammad ibn Sinan from Aban ibn Taghlib from abu 'Abd Allah, *'Alayhi al-Salam*, who has said the following:

"Abu 'Abd Allah, *'Alayhi al-Salam*, has said, 'Jabir ibn 'Abd Allah al-Ansari was the last surviving of the companions of the Messenger of Allah. He was a devoted follower of our *Ahl al-Bayt*. He would sit in the Mosque of the Messenger of Allah wearing a black turban. He would call, '*O Baqir al-'Ilm, O Baqir al-'Ilm* (a person of deep knowledge).' The people of Madina would say, 'Jabir is hallucinating.' He would say, 'No, by Allah, I do not hallucinate, but I heard the Messenger of Allah say, "You will soon meet a man from me whose name will be as my name and his manners as my manners. He will dig very deep in knowledge." This is what makes me say what I say.' The Imam has said, 'Jabir would still come and go, and one day in one of the roads of Madina, when passing, he found a few of the school children among whom Muhammad ibn Ali, *'Alayhi al-Salam*, was also present (for a reason other than schooling. Attending schools was not necessary for *'A'immah* (Leaders with Divine Authority)). He looked at him and called him (Muhammad ibn Ali) to himself. The boy came to him and then he said, 'go back.' The boy went back. Then he said, 'I swear by the One in Whose hand is my life, (that I see) manners as the manners of the Messenger of Allah. O (little) boy, what is your name?' He replied, 'My name is Muhammad ibn Ali ibn al-Husayn,' *'Alayhi al-Salam*. Jabir came forward and began to kiss his head and say 'May Allah keep my soul and the souls of my parents in service for your cause, the Messenger of Allah, your great-great grandfather, told me to convey his greetings of peace to you and would speak of all that (I see in you).'

"The Imam has said, 'Once Muhammad ibn Ali ibn al-Husayn came to his father and he was anxious. He explained to him about Jabir. His father asked, 'Did Jabir really do this?' He replied, 'Yes, he did so.' The Imam said, 'My son, stay home (and do not expose yourself to the enemy).' Jabir thereafter would come to him mornings and evenings and the people of Madina would say, 'It is so strange that Jabir, the only surviving companion of the Messenger of Allah, comes to a boy on both ends of the day every day.' Very shortly Ali ibn al-Husayn, *'Alayhi al-Salam*, passed away. Muhammad ibn Ali, *'Alayhi al-Salam*, then normally went to visit Jabir out of respect for his being a companion of the Messenger of Allah and spoke to people from Allah, the Most Holy, the Most High. The people of Madina would say, 'We have not seen anyone as bold as he is.' On hearing this from them he began to speak to them from the Messenger of Allah. The people of Madina began to say, 'We have not seen a greater liar as he is because he speaks from one whom he has never seen.' On hearing this from them he began to narrate to them from Jabir ibn 'Abd Allah.

"The Imam has said, 'They would accept what he narrates from Jabir ibn 'Abd Allah. However, Jabir would come to him and learn from him (Muhammad ibn Ali ibn al-Husayn, *'Alayhi al-Salam*).'"

H 1267, Ch. 118, h 3

A number of our people have narrated from Ahmad ibn Muhammad from Ali ibn al-Hakam from al-Muthanna al-Hannat from abu Basir who has said the following:

"Once I went to see abu Ja'far, *'Alayhi al-Salam*, and asked him, 'Are you the heir of the Messenger of Allah?' He said, 'Yes, we are his heir.' I then asked, 'Was the Messenger of Allah the heir of the prophets and did he know all that they knew?' He said to me, 'Yes, it is true.' I then asked, 'Do you have the power to bring the dead back to life and cure the lepers, and the blind?' He said, 'Yes, we do have such powers by the permission of Allah.' Then he said to me, 'Come closer to me, O abu Muhammad.' I went closer to him and he rubbed my face and my eyes and I saw the sun, the skies, the earth, the houses and all things in the town. Then he asked me, 'Do you like to live this way, you will have what others have and be responsible for whatever they will be held responsible for on the Day of Judgment or wopuld you like to live as before and have paradise purely?' I said, 'I would like to live as I lived before.' He rubbed my eyes and I found myself as before.'

"I (the narrator) told it to ibn abu 'Umayr who said, 'I testify that this is true just as the day is true.'"

H 1268, Ch. 118, h 4

Muhammad ibn Yahya has narrated from Muhammad ibn Ahmad from Muhammad ibn al-Husayn from Muhammad ibn Ali from 'Asim ibn Humayd from Muhammad ibn Muslim who has said the following:

"One day I was in the presence of abu Ja'far, *'Alayhi al-Salam*, when a pair of turtledoves came and sat on the wall and exchanged cooing as they usually do. Abu Ja'far, *'Alayhi al-Salam*, then also responsed to their queries for a while. They then flew away and on the other wall the male sounded to the female for a while and then both of them flew away. I then asked the Imam, 'May Allah keep my soul in service for your cause, what were these birds?' The Imam said, 'O ibn Muslim, all that Allah has created, such as birds, animals or other things that have life, they obey us better than people. The male dove was suspicious about the female and she denied it on oath, which the male did not accept. Then she asked if he would abide by the decision of Muhammad ibn Ali, *'Alayhi al-Salam*. He agreed and I told him that he had wronged his mate, then he believed her.'"

H 1269, Ch. 118, h 5

Al-Husayn ibn Muhammad has narrated from Mu'alla ibn Muhammad from Ali ibn Asbat from Salih ibn Hamza from his father from abu Bakr al-Hadrami who has said the following:

"Once abu Ja'far, *'Alayhi al-Salam*, was taken to al-Sham (Damascus) to the court of Hisham ibn 'Abd al-Malik. When he arrived at his door he (Hisham) instructed his people from the Amawids, 'When I finish scolding Muhammad ibn Ali, *'Alayhi al-Salam*, and stop, then each of you one after the other should reprimand and level blame on him.' He then ordered to allow Muhammad ibn Ali, *'Alayhi al-Salam*, to come in his presence. When abu Ja'far, *'Alayhi al-Salam*, arrived he made a gesture with his hand to all of them and offered a general greeting. He then sat down. This increased the disappointment of Hisham because he did not address him as the Caliph and sat down without his permission. Hisham then began to reprimand and scold him. He said to him among other things, 'O Muhammad ibn Ali, why is it that one or the other from you cause disunity among the Muslims and call people to follow him thinking that he is the Imam? It is nothing but because of his ignorance and foolishness.' He scolded him as much as he wanted. When he became quiet others one after the other began to annoy and nag him.

"When they all became quiet, he rose and stood up and asked, 'O people, what is it that you want and where are you headed? Through us, Allah granted you guidance to the first one among you and through us the last among you can receive guidance. You do have a temporary power but to us belongs the future power and there will be no power after our power; to us belongs the final good end as Allah, the Most Majestic, the Most Gracious, has said, "The final victory is for the pious ones." (7:128)

"He (Hisham) ordered him imprisoned. In the prison whoever he spoke to he would sympathize with him. The guard came to Hisham and said, 'O Amir al-Mu'minin, I am afraid for you from the people of al-Sham (Damascus). They may remove you from this position.' He gave him the full report. Hisham then ordered the Imam and his people escorted to Madina. He ordered his people not to allow the Imam and his people to go to marketplaces. They were denied food and water. They traveled three days without food and water until they arrived at Madyan. They were left behind the locked doors therein. People of the Imam complained to him of hunger and thirst. The Imam has said that he then climbed a hill above them and said loudly, 'O people of Madyan, the town of unjust people. I am Baqiyat Allah (the power that Allah has kept in reserve) as He has said, "If you are true believers then you must know that the profit (the reserved power) which Allah has left for you is better for you (than what you may gain through deceitful ways). I am not responsible for your deeds."' (11:86)

"The Imam has said that among them there was an old man who went to them (people of the town) and said, 'By Allah, this is the call of Shu'ayb, the Prophet of Allah. If you do not go to this man in the marketplace, you will be seized from the above and below. Believe me and obey me this time, but you may reject me next time. I am giving you good advice.' He has said, 'They came out quickly to Muhammad ibn Ali, 'Alayhi al-Salam, and his people in the marketplace. The news reached Hisham ibn 'Abd al-Malik who summoned the old man and he was taken to the court but it is not known what he did to him.'"

H 1270, Ch. 118, h 6

Sa'd. ibn 'Abd Allah and al-Himyari both have narrated from Ibrahim ibn Mahziyar from his brother, Ali ibn Mhaziyar from al-Husayn ibn Sa'id from Muhammad ibn Sinan from ibn Muskan from abu Basir from abu 'Abd Allah, 'Alayhi al-Salam, who has said the following:

"Abu 'Abd Allah, 'Alayhi al-Salam, has said, 'Muhammad ibn Ali, al-Baqir, 'Alayhi al-Salam, passed away at the age of fifty-seven, in A.H. one hundred fourteen. He lived for nineteen years and two months after Ali ibn al-Husayn, 'Alayhi al-Salam."

Chapter 119 - The Birth of abu 'Abd Allah Ja'far ibn Muhammad, 'Alayhi al-Salam

Al-Kulayni has said, "Abu 'Abd Allah, 'Alayhi al-Salam, was born in A.H. eighty-three. He passed away in the month of Shawwal in the year one hundred forty-eight at the age of sixty-five. He was buried in al-Baqi' cemetery, Madina in the graveyard, where his father and grandfather and al-Hassan ibn Ali, 'Alayhi al-Salam, were buried. His mother was 'Umm Farwah, daughter of al-Qasim ibn Muhammad ibn abu Bakr, and her mother was 'Asma' daughter of 'Abd al-Rahman ibn abu Bakr."

H 1271, Ch. 119, h 1

Muhammad ibn Yahya has narrated from Ahmad ibn Muhammad from 'Abd Allah ibn Ahmad from Ibrahim ibn al-Hassan who has said that Wahab ibn Hafs narrated to me from Ishaq ibn Jarir who has said the following:

"Abu 'Abd Allah, 'Alayhi al-Salam, has said, 'Sa'id ibn al-Musayyib, al-Qasim ibn Muhammad ibn abu Bakr and abu al-Khalid al-Kabuli were of the trusted and reliable companions of Ali ibn al-Husayn, 'Alayhi al-Salam. The Imam has said, 'My mother was a true believer, pious and a person of good deeds. Allah loves the people of good deeds.' He has said, 'My mother has said that my father said,

"O 'Umm Farwah, I pray to Allah to forgive the sins of the sinners of our Shi'a (followers) a thousand times a day because we exercise patience in the face of hardships knowing well the facts of reward (in the next life) but they exercise patience in that of which they have no knowledge.'"

H 1272, Ch. 119, h 2

Certain persons of our people have narrated from ibn Jumhur from his father from Sulayman ibn Sama'a from 'Abd Allah ibn al-Qasim from al-Mufaddal ibn 'Umar who has said the following:

"Once abu Ja'far al-Mansur ordered his governor of Makkah and Madina, al-Hassan ibn al-Zayd, to set fire to the house of Ja'far ibn Muhammad, *'Alayhi al-Salam*, to burn him to death. The house of abu 'Abd Allah, *'Alayhi al-Salam*, was set on fire and it burned the door and the corridor. Abu 'Abd Allah, *'Alayhi al-Salam*, came out walking in the fire and stepping on it and said, 'I am the son of 'A'raq al-Thara ('Isma'il), I am the son of Ibrahim (Abraham), the beloved friend of Allah.'"

H 1273, Ch. 119, h 3

Al-Husayn ibn Muhammad has narrated from Mu'alla ibn Muhammad from al-Barqi from his father from those he mentioned from Rufayd, slave of Yazid ibn 'Amr ibn Hubayra who has said the following:

"Once Hubayra became angry with me and swore to kill me. I ran away from him in fear and sought refuge with abu 'Abd Allah, *'Alayhi al-Salam*. I informed him of my story and he said, 'go back and convey my greetings to him and say to him, on my behalf, "I have given refuge and protection against you to your slave, Rufayd. Do not harm him with your anger.'" I said to him, 'May Allah keep my soul in service for your cause, he is a Shami (from Damascus) and has filthy opinions.' He said, 'go to him and say what I have told you to say.' I then returned back and on the way in the wilderness I met an Arab man who asked me, 'Where are you going? I see the face of a man to be killed.' He then said, 'Show me your hand.' I showed him my hand. He said, 'It is the hand of a person to be murdered.' He then said, 'Show me your foot.' I showed him my foot. He said, 'It is the foot of a person to be murdered.' He then said, 'Show me your body.' When I did so, he said, 'It is the body of a person to be murdered.' He then said, 'Show me your tongue.' I showed him my tongue. He said, 'go on. Nothing will happen to you. On your tongue there is a message that if you take it even to the tall mountains they will obey you.'

"I (the narrator) then went on until I was at the door of ibn Hubayra and I asked permission to see him and then I went in his presence. He said, 'The traitor has come on his own legs. O slave, get the leather rope and the sword,' he shouted. He ordered to tie up my hands and head. The sword man stood over my head to cut my head off. I said, 'O commander, you have not captured me just like that. I came to you from a living person. There is a certain matter that I want to say to you. Thereafter it will be up to you to do whatever you may choose.' He said, 'Say it.' I said, 'First, you must allow me to speak to you in private.' He ordered everyone to go out of the room and they went out. I said, 'Ja'far ibn Muhammad, *'Alayhi al-Salam*, asked me to convey his greetings of peace to you. He also said, "I have given protection against you to your slave, Rufayd. Do not harm him with your words." He then said, 'I swear you to Allah, did Ja'far (ibn Muhammad) really say these words and convey greetings of peace to me?' I then swore before him and he asked Allah to grant peace to Ja'far ibn Muhammad. He did so three times. Then he opened my hands and then said, 'This does not convince me until you do to me what I just did to you.' I said, 'My hands will not move for such things and my conscience will not accept it.' He said, 'By Allah, my conscience will not agree unless you do what I asked.' I then did what he had done to me and then released him. He then gave me his own seal and said, 'I hereby place all of my affairs in your hands to manage as you would like.'"

H 1274, Ch. 119, h 4

Muhammad ibn Yahya has narrated from Ahmad ibn Muhammad from 'Umar ibn 'Abd al-'Aziz from al-Khaybari from Yunus ibn Zabyan and al-Mufaddal ibn 'Umar and abu Salama al-Sarraj and al-Husayn ibn Thuwayr ibn abu Fakhita who have said the following:

"Once we were in the presence of abu 'Abd Allah, *'Alayhi al-Salam*, and he said, 'We (*Ahl al-Bayt*) have the key to the treasures of the earth. If I tell one of my feet to say to the earth, "Let out whatever gold that is there in you," it will do so.'

"The narrator) has said that he then said to one of his feet and made a line with it on earth, the earth ripped open, then he told his hand that took out a brick of gold of the size of a hand (about a foot). He then said, 'Watch carefully.' We then looked again and saw many such pieces of gold one over the other shining. A certain person among us said, 'May Allah keep my soul in service for your cause, you have been granted whatever there is but your Shi'a are needy.'

"The narrator has said that the Imam then said, 'Allah will soon grant to our Shi'a and to us the bounties of both this and the next life. He will admit them in paradise and its blessings. There will be hell for our enemies.'"

H 1275, Ch. 119, h 5

Al-Husayn ibn Muhammad has narrated from Mu'alla ibn Muhammad from certain persons of his people from abu Basir who has said the following:

"I had a neighbor who followed the Sultan (the ruler) and he had gained certain properties. He often arranged parties and invited female singers. They would drink wine and disturb me. I complained to the man several times but he did not pay any attention. When I insisted he said, 'O man, I am an addicted person and you are sober. I wish you would take me to your master and I hope Allah will save me through him.' His words impressed me a great deal. Upon my visiting abu 'Abd Allah, *'Alayhi al-Salam*, I mentioned the condition of the man to him. The Imam said, 'When you will go back to Kufa he may come to you, say to him, "Ja'far ibn Muhammad, *'Alayhi al-Salam*, said to you, 'Stay away from what you are involved in. I guarantee that Allah will admit you in paradise.'"' When I returned to Kufa he came to me. I kept him with me until just two of us were there alone. I then said to him, 'O man, I mentioned you to abu 'Abd Allah, Ja'far ibn Muhammad, al-Sadiq, *'Alayhi al-Salam*, and he said to me, "When you will return to al-Kufa, the man will soon come to you. Say to him, 'Ja'far ibn Muhammad said to you, "Stay away from what you are involved in and I will guarantee that Allah will admit you in paradise."'"'"

479

"The narrator has said that the man then wept and asked me, 'I swear you to Allah, did abu 'Abd Allah, *'Alayhi al-Salam*, really say this to you?' I then swore before him that abu 'Abd Allah, *'Alayhi al-Salam*, did really say so.' He said, 'This is enough for you' and he left. After few days he called me while he was behind his house and had no clothes on him and he said to me, 'O abu Basir, by Allah, there is nothing left in my house. I gave all of them away and I am left as you see.'

"The narrator has said, 'I then went to our people and made a collection to clothe him. Shortly thereafter he sent someone to inform me that he was ill and that I must see him. Thereafter I often went to him to provide treatment until he was about to die. I was sitting near him and he was experiencing the agony of death. He fainted and then regained conscience and said to me, 'O abu Basir, your master has fulfilled his promise to me.' He then passed away. May Allah grant him blessings. When I went for Hajj I went to see abu 'Abd Allah, *'Alayhi al-Salam*, and asked permission for a meeting. As I was about to enter in his presence, one foot in the corridor and one inside, the Imam, before my saying anything, said from the inside, 'O abu Basir, we have fulfilled our promise to your friend.'"

H 1276, Ch. 119, h 6
Abu Ali al-Ash'ari has narrated from Muhammad ibn 'Abd al-Jabbar from Safwan ibn Yahya from Ja'far ibn Muhammad ibn al-'Ash'ath who said to me the following:
"Do you know the reason why we came in this matter (became Shi'a) and recognized it even though there was no mention of it among us and we had no knowledge of what other people (Shi'a) had?" I (the narrator) asked him, "What then is the reason for it?"

"He said, 'Abu Ja'far, abu Dawaniq once said to abu Muhammad ibn al-'Ash'ath, 'O Muhammad, I want a person of reason who can represent me.' My father said, 'I have found one for you. He is so and so ibn Muhajir, my maternal uncle.' He (abu Dawaniq) said, 'Bring him to me.' He has said that he brought him to abu Dawaniq. Abu Ja'far, abu Dawaniq said, 'O son of Muhajir, take this property to Madina and give it to 'Abd Allah ibn al-Hassan ibn al-Hassan and a number of the people of his family among whom is Ja'far ibn Muhammad and say to them, "I am from Khrusan and a stranger in this area. One of your Shi'a (followers) from Khurasan gave me this property to deliver to you." Then give to each of them from the property with such and such conditions. When they take the property then, as a messenger, ask them for a receipt for the amount and the kind of the property they received from you."

"He then took the property, went to Madina and came back to abu Dawaniq when Muhammad ibn al-'Ash'th was also present. Abu Daqwaniq asked, 'What did you leave behind?' He said, 'I met the people and this is the receipt in their own handwritings for what they received, except Ja'far ibn Muhammad, *'Alayhi al-Salam*. I went to see him when he was praying in the Mosque of the Messenger of Allah. I sat behind him to wait until he finished so then I could give him the message as I had done with the others. He hurried up, finished, then turned to me and said, 'O you, have fear of Allah and do not deceive *Ahl al-Bayt* (the family) of Muhammad, *'Alayhi al-Salam*. They have just experienced the government of the sons of Marwan and they all are needy.' I then asked, 'What are you talking about, may Allah grant you well being?' He said, 'Then he brought his head closer to me and told me about all that had passed between me and you as if he had been the third person with us.' He has said that abu Ja'far, al-Dawaniq said, 'O ibn Muhajir take notice and pay attention that the family of a prophet has never been without a *Muhaddath* (a person to whom angels speak) among them. Today the *Muhaddath* among us is Ja'far ibn Muhammad.'

"This was the reason for our receiving guidance and acceptance of this matter and belief (belief of Shi'a Muslims)," al-'Ash'ath explained.

H 1277, Ch. 119, h 7

Sa'd ibn 'Abd Allah and 'Abd Allah ibn Ja'far both have narrated from Ibrahim ibn Mahziyar from his brother Ali Mahziyar from al-Husayn ibn Sa'id from Muhammad ibn Sinan from ibn Muskan from abu Basir who has said the following:

"Abu 'Abd Allah, Ja'far ibn Muhammad, *'Alayhi al-Salam*, passed away at the age of fifty-six in A.H. one hundred forty-eight He lived after abu Ja'far, *'Alayhi al-Salam*, his father, for thirty-four years."

H 1278, Ch. 119, h 8

Sa'd ibn 'Abd Allah has narrated from abu Ja'far ibn 'Umar ibn Sa'id from Yunus ibn Ya'qub from abu al-Hassan, the 1ᵗ *'Alayhi al-Salam*, who has said the following:

"Abu al-Hassan, the 1ᵗ *'Alayhi al-Salam*, has said, 'I shrouded my father with two pieces of winter cloth that he had used as clothes for Ihram (special clothes used during performing Hajj). One of his shirts, the *'Amama* (turban) that belonged to Ali ibn al-Husayn, *'Alayhi al-Salam*, and a gown he had bought for forty Dinars were also used."

Chapter 120 - The Birth of abu al-Hassan Musa ibn Ja'far, *'Alayhi al-Salam*

Al-Kulayni has said, "Abu al-Hassan Musa, *'Alayhi al-Salam*, was born in Abwa' in A.H. one hundred twenty-eight. Certain historians have said that it was the year one hundred twentysix. He passed away on the sixth of the month of Rajab in the year one hundred eighty-three at the age of fifty-five or fifty-six in Baghdad in the prison of al-Sindi ibn Shahik. Harun had summoned him from Madina on twentieth of the month of Shawwal in the year one hundred seventy-nine. Harun went to Madina on his way back from 'Umra (pilgrimage to Makkah) in the month of Ramadan. Thereafter Harum went for Hajj and took abu al-Hassan Musa ibn Ja'far, *'Alayhi al-Salam*, with him to Basra. He then imprisoned him in the control of 'Isa ibn Ja'far. Then he summoned him to Baghdad and imprisoned him in the control of al-Sindi ibn Shahik and in his prison he, *'Alayhi al-Salam*, died. He was buried in Baghdad in the graveyard of Quraysh. His mother was 'Umm Walad, called Hamida."

H 1279, Ch. 120, h 1

Al-Husayn ibn Muhammad al-Ash'ari has narrated from Mu'alla ibn Muhammad from Ali ibn al-Sindi al-Qummi who has said that narrated to us 'Isa ibn 'Abd al-Rahman from his father the following:

"Once ibn al-'Ukkasha ibn Muhsin al-Asadi went to see abu Ja'far, *'Alayhi al-Salam*, and abu 'Abd Allah, *'Alayhi al-Salam*, was also standing in his presence. Grapes were offered to him. The Imam then said, 'The old man and the small boy eat grapes one piece at a time. One who is anxious for filling himself up eats three or four pieces at a time but you should take two pieces at a time because it is mustahab (preferable) to do so.'

"He (ibn al-'Ukkasha) then asked abu Ja'far, *'Alayhi al-Salam*, 'Why do you not arrange a marriage for abu 'Abd Allah, *'Alayhi al-Salam*, who has grown up already?' He has said that before abu Ja'far, *'Alayhi al-Salam*, there was a sealed bag filled with money and he said, 'Very soon traders will come from Barbar and find accommodation in the house of Maymun and with the money in this bag we will buy for him a slave girl.'

"The narrator has said that time went by and one day we went to see abu Ja'far, *'Alayhi al-Salam*, and he asked, 'Do you want me to tell you about the trader of whom I had spoken to you? He has just arrived. Go and with the money in this bag buy for him a slave girl'.

"The narrator has said, 'We went to the trader but he had sold all of his slave girls accept two of them who were ill and one of them was more beautiful than the other. We said that we wanted to know about them. He then showed them to us and we asked for how much he might sell the more beautiful one.' He said, 'Seventy Dinars is the price.' We asked him to reduce the price but he said that he does not accept anything less than seventy Dinars. We then said, 'We will give all the money that is in the bag but we do not know how much is in it.' There was a man with gray hair and beard, who said, 'Open the bag and weigh it.' The trader said, 'Do not open it because if it is less then seventy Dinars I do not accept.' The old man said, 'Come close.' We went closer and opened the bag and weighed the Dinars in it and there were exactly seventy Dinars, no more and no less. We brought the slave girl to abu Ja'far, *'Alayhi al-Salam*, and Ja'far, *'Alayhi al-Salam*, was also there. We informed abu Ja'far, *'Alayhi al-Salam*, of the whole story. He offered thanks to Allah and praised Him. He then asked the girl, 'What is your name?' She said, 'My name is Humayda.' He said, 'You are Humayda in this world and a praised one in the next life. Tell me more, 'Are you virgin or not virgin?' She said, 'I am virgin.' He asked, 'How can that be true? The traders corrupt whatever may come in their hands.' She said, 'He would come to me and sit next to me just as men and women do but Allah would make a man with gray hair and gray beard appear and force him to go away from me. This happened several times between him and the man with gray hairs and beard.'

"The Imam said, 'O Ja'far take her for yourself.' She then gave birth to the best person on earth who was Musa ibn Ja'far, *'Alayhi al-Salam*.'"

H 1280, Ch. 120, h 2

Muhammad ibn Yahya has narrated from Muhammad ibn Ahmad from 'Abd Allah ibn Ahmad from Ali ibn al-Husayn from ibn Sinan from Sabiq ibn al-Walid from al-Mu'alla ibn Khunays who has said the following:

"Abu 'Abd Allah, *'Alayhi al-Salam*, said, 'Humayda is clean of uncleanness like purified gold. The angels continuously guarded her until she reached me due to Allah's regard for me and the possessor of Leadership with Divine Authority after me."

H 1281, Ch. 120, h 3

A number of our people have narrated from Ahmad ibn Muhammad and Ali ibn Ibrahim from his father all of them from abu Qatada al-Qummi from Ali ibn Khalid al-Zabali who has said the following:

"When abu al-Hassan Musa, *'Alayhi al-Salam*, was brought before al-Mahdi ('Abbassid ruler) the first time he was accommodated in Zabala and I talked to him. He found me depressed and asked, 'O abu Khalid, why is it that I see you depressed?' I asked, 'How can I be not depressed when you are being taken to this transgressor and I do not know what will happen to you?' He said, 'I will be all right. In such and such month and day come to meet me on a mile's distance.' I then had no worries but to count the months and days pass by until that particular day. I then went up to a mile's distance and spent the day there until it was almost sunset. Suddenly, Satan caused temptations to my heart and I feared doubting in what he had said. At this point I saw figures coming from the direction of Iraq. I went to meet them and abu al-Hassan, *'Alayhi al-Salam*, was in front of them on a mule. He asked, 'Is it you O abu Khalid?' I said, 'Yes, O great, great, great grandson of the Messenger of Allah.' He said, 'Do not doubt; Satan loved that you had doubts.' I then said, 'Thanks to Allah Who saved you from them.' He said, 'I will have a return to them in which I will not find any safety.'"

H 1282, Ch. 120, h 4

Ahmad ibn Mihran and Ali ibn Ibrahim both have narrated from Muhammad ibn Ali from al-Hassan ibn Rashid from Ya'qub ibn Ja'far ibn Ibrahim who has said the following:

"Once I was in the presence of abu al-Hassan Musa, *'Alayhi al-Salam*, when a Christian man came to see him. At this time we were with him in al-'Urayd. The Christian man said, 'I have come to you from a far away place after a difficult journey. I have been praying to my Lord for thirty years to guide me to the best of the religions and to the best of the servants (of Allah) and the most knowledgeable among them. I saw a person in my dream that described a man who lived in 'Ulya' (upper) Damascus. I went to see that man and I talked to him. He said, 'I am the most knowledgeable one among the people who follow my religion but there are people more knowledgeable than me.' I (Christian man) then asked him to guide me to the one who is more knowledgeable than him; I like traveling and can endure difficulties; having read the whole Gospel, the Psalms of David and the four parts of Torah, I have also read the apparent text of the whole Quran. The scholar (of upper Damascus) then said to me (Christian man), 'If you like Christianity I am the most knowledgeable person in it amongst the Arab and non-Arab people. If you want the knowledge of Judaism then Bati ibn Shurahbil al-Samari is the most knowledgeable person in that religion today.

However, if you want to learn the knowledge of Islam, the knowledge of Torah, the knowledge of the Gospel, the knowledge of Psalms, the book of Hud and all that is revealed to any of the prophets in your time or in the times of the others, if you like to learn all that has come from the heavens in the form of information, people may have learned or not learned such information, in which there is the explanation for everything, the cures for the worlds, the spirit for those who wish to have comfort, understanding in what Allah has willed to be for their good and seek comfort with the truth, I can guide you to a person (who can teach you all such things). Go to him even if you have to walk to him on foot. If you cannot walk then you must crawl to him on your knees. If you cannot do that also then you must drag yourself on your hips. If you cannot reach him that way you must move to him on your face.'

"I (Christian man) then said, 'No, none of this is necessary. I can walk to him. Physically I am prepared and financially I am capable.' He (the scholar from upper Demascus) then said, 'Go on to him without any delay until you reach Yathrib.' I (Christian man) said, 'I do not know where Yathrib is?' He said, 'Go until you reach Madina of the Holy Prophet, *'Alayhi al-Salam*, who was raised among the Arabs. He was a prophet from the Arabs, from the tribe of al-Hashim. When you will arrive there ask for banu Ghanam ibn Malik ibn al-Najjar who is near the door of the Mosque in that city. Show yourself to him in the Christian dress; their governor is strict on them and the Caliph is even harsher to them. Thereafter ask for the tribe of banu 'Amr ibn Mabdhul that is in the area of al-Zubayr. Then ask for Musa ibn Ja'far, *'Alayhi al-Salam*, and his house and where he himself is, that is, is he on a journey or at home? If he will be on a journey then you must reach him; his destination is shorter than the distance you have to travel. When you will meet him say that the chief monk of al-Ghuta, Ghuta of Damascus, guided you to him. That he asked you to convey a great deal of greetings of peace to him and has said to him the following: "I pray to my Lord very often to make my Islam to take form in your hands."'"

"The Christian man told this story of his dream while he was standing and supporting himself with his staff. Then he said, 'My master, if you grant me permission I want to fold my hands before you and sit down.' He (the Imam) said, 'Yes, you have my permission to sit down but I will not give permission to fold your hands before me.' He sat down and removed his hat and said, 'May Allah keep my soul in service for your cause, will you grant me permission to speak'? The Imam said, "Yes, you have come just for it." The Christian man said, 'Return the greetings to my friend. Do you not return the greetings of peace?' Abu al-Hassan, *'Alayhi al-Salam*, said, 'The answer to your friend is that he must accept Islam. The greeting of peace will be returned when he will accept our religion.' The Christian man then said, 'I want to ask you questions, may Allah grant you well being.' The Imam said, 'Ask your questions.' He said, 'Tell me about the book that Allah has revealed to Muhammad who read, followed it and said, "Ha Mim. (44:1) I swear by the illustrious Book (44:2) that We have revealed the Holy Quran on a blessed night to warn mankind (44:3). On this night, every absolute command coming from Us becomes distinguishable." (44:4) What is its intrinsic interpretation and meaning?'

"The Imam said, 'Ha Mim stands for Muhammad, *'Alayhi al-Salam*, who is mentioned in the book of Hud which was revealed to him and its letters are abbreviated. The "Illustrious Book" stands for Amir al-Mu'minin Ali, *'Alayhi al-Salam*. The blessed night stands for *Fatimah, 'Alayha al-Salam*. ". . . absolute command coming from Us becomes distinguishable," (44:4) means that in that night there comes a great deal of good. There is the man of wisdom, the man of wisdom and the man of wisdom. (It is a reference to the first three *'A'immah* (Leaders with Divine Authority) from the descendents of *Fatimah, 'Alayha al-Salam*.'

"The man said, 'Describe to me the first and last of these men.' The Imam then said, 'qualities are similar. However I will describe the third of these people and his descendents and he is mentioned to you in the books revealed to you. If you have not altered and changed and rejected them as you have been doing for a long time.'

"The Christian man said, 'I will not hide from you what I know and will not lie to you and you already know what I will say is true and what is false. By Allah, He has granted you through His grace so much distinction and has given the opportunity through His bounties so much that people cannot even think how much they are. No one can hide them and falsify them, even those who reject (the truth). My words in the matter are true as I mentioned and it is as such that I said.'

"Abu Ibrahim (the Imam), *'Alayhi al-Salam*, then said to him, 'I can tell you news that only very few people who read books know. Tell me, what was the name of the mother of Mary and when the spirit was blown in Mary and in which hour of the day? What was the date when Jesus was born and during which hour of the day?'

"The Christian man said, 'I do not know.' Abu Ibrahim then said, 'The name of the mother of Mary was Martha, and *Wahiyba* in Arabic. The day Mary conceived Jesus was a Friday at noontime. It was the day in which the trusted spirit descended and among the Muslims there is no holiday of greater preference than this. Allah, the Most Holy, the Most High, has advanced it with greatness and Muhammad, *'Alayhi al-Salam*, has venerated it with greatness. He commanded it to be observed as a holiday, thus, it is the day of congregation. The day in which Mary was born was a Tuesday four and a half-hours before noon. Do you know the river on the side of which Mary gave birth to Jesus?' The Christian man said, 'No, I do not know it.' The Imam then said, 'It was Euphrates that has palm trees and vineyards on its banks. No other place is like Euphrates for vineyards and palm trees. Have you noticed the day in which her tongue was curtained in speaking and Qaydus (the king of Israel) called his sons and subjects for support to take the family of 'Imran out and look at Mary?' They asked her, 'What has Allah told you in His book and against us in His book?'

485

"The Imam then asked, 'Have you understood it (the book)?' The Christian man said, 'Yes, I read it this day the last time.' The Imam then said, 'Therefore, you will not rise from this meeting before Allah will grant you the right guidance.' The Christian man asked, 'What was the name of my mother in Asyrian and in Arabic.' The Imam said, 'In Asyrian it was 'Anqalia. 'Unqura was the name of your grandmother from your father's side. The name of your mother in Arabic was Mayyata. The name of your father was 'Abd al-Masih and it is 'Abd Allah in Arabic. Al-Masih (Messiah) did not have any servant.' The Christian man said, 'You have spoken the truth and you have done a good deed. Can you tell me what the name of my grandfather was?' The Imam said, 'The name of your grandfather was Gabriel and I call him 'Abd al-Rahman in this our meeting.' The Christian man asked, 'Was he a Muslim?' Abu Ibrahim, *'Alayhi al-Salam*, said, 'Yes, he was a Muslim and he was martyred. Soldiers attacked him and murdered him in his home senselessly and the soldiers were from the people of Damascus.'

"The Christian man asked, 'What was my name before my Kunya (such as 'abu' of so and so or 'ibn' of so and so)?' The Imam then said, 'It was 'Abd al-Salib.' The Christian man asked, 'What name would you like to give me? The Imam then said, 'I will call you 'Abd Allah.' The Christian man said, 'I then declare my belief in Allah the Great and testify that no one deserves to be worshipped and obeyed besides Allah Who is One and no one is His partner. He is One, self-sufficient. He is not like how the Christians describe Him. He is not like how the Jews describe Him. He is not a genus of the categories of polytheism. I testify that Muhammad, *'Alayhi al-Salam*, is His servant and His Messenger. He has sent him with all truth. He has manifested the truth to the people of truth and has turned the people of falsehood blind. That Muhammad, *'Alayhi al-Salam*, is the Messenger of Allah to all mankind, red and black alike. Thus, those who have understanding have understood and those who sought guidance have received guidance. The people of falsehood have turned blind and have lost what they were calling (as their Lord).'

"I testify that His representative and His *Wali* (Leader with Divine Authority) have spoken with His wisdom. That all the prophets before him had spoken with pure wisdom, supported each other in obedience to Allah, stayed away from falsehood and the people of falsehood, from filth and the people of filth. That they kept aloof from error, that Allah supported them through obedience to Him, kept them infallible and sinless. Thus, they were the *Awliya'* of Allah (people possessing Divine Authority) and the protectors of religion. They encouraged others to do good and commanded them to do so. I declare my belief in the small ones among them and greater ones among them, those of them whom I have mentioned as well as those that I have not mentioned. I declare my belief in Allah, the Most Holy, the Most High, the Lord of the worlds.

"He then cut off his relic and the cross that was made of gold and hung from his neck. He then said, 'Command me as you wish to whom I must pay charities due on me.' The Imam said, 'There is one of your brethren in religion and he is of your own people, from Qays ibn al-Tha'laba, and is doing well financially like yourself. You must cooperate with each other and be lenient to each other. I will not allow that your rights in Islam be ignored'.

"He then said, 'By Allah, may Allah grant you well being, I am doing very well financially. In my town I have three hundred horses male and female and a thousand camels. Your right in them is more than mine.' The Imam said, 'You are the slave of Allah and His Messenger and your lineage is natural.' He improved himself in Islam and married a lady from the tribe of Fihr. Abu Ibrahim, *'Alayhi al-Salam*, paid her dowry (marriage gift), which was fifty Dinars from the charities of Ali ibn abu Talib, *'Alayhi al-Salam*. He hired for him a servant and provided him accommodation until abu Ibrahim, *'Alayhi al-Salam*, was taken (to Baghdad). Thereafter he died after only twenty-eight days.'"

H 1283, Ch. 120, h 5

Ali ibn Ibrahim and Ahmad ibn Mihran all have narrated from Muhammad ibn Ali from al-Hassan ibn Rashid from Ya'qub ibn Ja'far who has said the following:

"Once I was in the presence of abu Ibrahim, *'Alayhi al-Salam*, when a monk and a nun from the people of Najran, Yemen, came to see him. Al-Fadl ibn Sawwar sought permission for them and the Imam said, 'Tomorrow bring them to the well of 'Umm Khayr.'

"The narrator has said that on the next day we went to see him and we found the people (the monk and the nun) there also. The Imam ordered to spread a mat that was made of palm tree fibers. He then sat down on it and the people also sat down with the Imam. The nun began asking questions. She asked many questions. The Imam answered them all. Abu Ibrahim, *'Alayhi al-Salam*, asked her certain questions but she could not answer. She then accepted Islam.

"The monk then began to ask questions and the Imam answered whatever he asked. The monk then said, 'I was very strong in my religion and no one of the Christians was as knowledgeable as I. I heard of a man from India who could go for pilgrimage to the Holy House in one day and one night and then go back to India to his home. I asked, 'Where did he live'? I was told that he lived in Sibdhan. The one who informed me about him said that he knew the knowledge with which Asaf the companion of Solomon brought the throne of Sheba before Solomon. He is the one whom Allah has mentioned in your book and in the books of the followers of the Bible.'

"Abu Ibrahim, *'Alayhi al-Salam*, then asked, 'How many are the names of Allah that if invoked do not leave one without the desired result?' The monk said, 'They are many but the ones with perfect effects that do not leave the person invoking them without the desired results are seven.' Abu al-Hassan, *'Alayhi al-Salam*, asked him, 'Tell of whichever that you know.' The monk said, 'I swear by Allah, who has sent the Torah to Moses and has made Jesus to be a lesson for the worlds and a trial for the thankfulness of the people of reason. (I swear by Allah), Who has made Muhammad, *'Alayhi al-Salam*, to be a blessing and mercy and has made Ali, *'Alayhi al-Salam*, a lesson and the source of understanding, Who has made the executors of his will from his descendents and the descendents of Muhammad,

'Alayhi al-Salam, that I do not know. Had I known them you would not have to ask me, I would not have to come to you and would not have asked you questions.'

"Abu Ibrahim, *'Alayhi al-Salam*, then said, 'Tell me more about the man from India.' The monk said, 'I had heard certain names but I did not know their sense and details. I did not know what and how they were and how they were read? I journeyed to Sibdhan in India, asked about the man. I was told that he has built a monastery in the mountain and can only be seen twice a year. The people of India believe that Allah has made a stream flow through his monastery. They think that a different kind of farming is done for him therein, all is done without normal labor. I then went to his door and waited for three days without knocking and trying to open the door. On the fourth day Allah opened the door. A cow loaded with firewood came. Her breast was so heavily filled with milk that it almost touched the ground and the milk almost came out. The cow pushed the door open and I followed her. I found the man in a standing position looking toward the sky and wept. Then he looked to the earth and wept. He looked at the mountains and wept.' I said, 'glory belongs to Allah. How few are the people like you in our times.' He said, 'By Allah, I am only one good deed of the deeds of the one whom you have left behind you.' I then said, 'I am told that you know certain names of the names of Allah through which you can reach, every day and night, the Holy house that is in al-Sham (Syria). Is it true?' He asked me, 'Do you recognize the Holy House?' I replied, 'I do not know any other Holy House besides that in al-Sham.' He said, 'It is not Bayt al-Maqdis (the mosque in Jerusalem). It is the Holy House, that is, the House of the family of Muhammad, *'Alayhi al-Salam*.'

"I then said, 'What I have heard up to this day is the Holy House that I just mentioned.' He said, 'That is the place where the prophets worshipped Allah. It had been called the center of the places of worship until the period between the time of Jesus and the coming of Muhammad, *'Alayhi al-Salam*, in which the calamities approached the pagans and misfortune entered the houses of Satan. They moved, changed and transferred those names as Allah, the Most Holy, the Most High, has said in His words whose intrinsic meanings stand for the family of Muhammad, *'Alayhi al-Salam*, and its apparent meanings stand as a proverb, "These are only names given by yourselves and your fathers. Allah has not given them any authority. . . ."' (53:23)

"I (Christian man) then said, to him, 'I have come to you from a faraway land. On the way I crossed oceans, sadness, anxieties and fear. I have passed days and nights in despair for failing to reach my goal.'

"He said to me, 'I do not see that your mother conceived you at any time without a noble angel with her. I never found your father without formal purification whenever he would go to bed with your mother. He went to bed with her in a purified condition. I do not think there was any other reason except his reading the fourth part of the Torah during his nightly vigil, thus, it lead him to the good end. Go back just as you came. Go until you reach Madina of Muhammad, *'Alayhi al-Salam*, which is also called *Taybah*. In the age of darkness of ignorance they called it Yathrib. Then go to a place therein called al-Baqi'. Then ask for a house called the house of Marwan. Lodge there for three days. Then ask for a black old man who works with the fibers of the palm tree (to make mats and other such things) that they call al-Khasf. Be kind to him and tell him, 'I am sent to you by your guest who would stay with you in the corner of the house wherein there are the four pieces of woods. Then ask him about so and so son of so and so. Ask him where he forms his gathering and what time he passes thereby. He will show him to you or will give a full description and you recognize him through the description as I will describe him for you.'

I said, 'After meeting him what should I do?' He said, 'Ask him of whatever happened and whatever will happen. Ask him about religious guidance of those of the past and those yet to come.' The narrator has said that abu Ibrahim, *'Alayhi al-Salam*, said to him, 'Your friend whom you met has given you very good advice.' The monk then asked the Imam, 'What is his name, may Allah keep my soul in service for your cause?'

"The Imam said, 'His name is Mutammim ibn Firuz, from the people of Persia. He established belief in Allah Who is only One and has no partners and worshipped Him sincerely with certainty and devotion. He ran away from his people when he was afraid of them. His Lord granted him authority and guided him to the way of right guidance and progress. He made him to be of the pious ones and granted him the knowledge of who His sincere servants are. Every year he visits Makkah for Hajj. He performs 'Umra once at the beginning of every month. He comes from his place in India to Makkah because of the distinction that Allah has granted him and His support and, thus, Allah rewards those who give thanks.'

"The monk then asked him many questions. The Imam answered them all. He asked the monk certain questions, which he could not answer but the Imam himself answered them. The monk then said, 'Tell me of the eight letters (code words) that were revealed out of which four were manifested on earth and the other four remained in space. To whom were the four that remained in space sent? Who will interpret them?'

"The Imam then said, 'He will be our *al-Qa'im* (the one who will rise with Divine authority and power). Allah will send them to him and he will interpret them. He will send to him what has not even been sent to the truthful ones, the messengers and the rightly guided ones.'

"Then the monk said, 'Tell me about the two of the four that were sent to earth. What are they?" The Imam said, 'I will tell you about all four. The first one was, No one deserves to be worshipped and obeyed except Allah Who is One and has no partners and that He is eternal. The second was, Muhammad is the Messenger of Allah purely. The third one was we the *Ahl al-Bayt* (infallible members of the family of Muhammad, *'Alayhim al-Salam*).The fourth one was our Shi'a (followers) who are from us and we are from the Messenger of Allah and the Messenger of Allah is from Allah through a means.'

"The monk then said, 'I testify that no one deserves to be worshipped and obeyed except Allah, that Muhammad is the Messenger of Allah, that whatever he brought from Allah is true, that you, *Ahl al-Bayt* (the infallible members of the family of Muhammad, *'Alayhi al-Salam*) are the chosen ones of Allah from His creatures and that your Shi'a are pure who are the replacement (of those who oppose you). They will have the good end. All thanks are due to Allah, Lord of the worlds.'

"Abu Ibrahim, *'Alayhi al-Salam*, called to bring for him a gown, a shirt made in Gha'in Khurasan, a scarf, a shoe and a hat. He gave them to him, prayed the noontime prayer and asked him to circumcise. He said, 'It had been done when he was seven years old.'"

H 1284, Ch. 120, h 6
A number of our people have narrated from Ahmad ibn Muhammad from Ali ibn al-Hakam from 'Abd Allah ibn al-Mughira who has said the following:
"The pious servant of Allah once passed by a woman in Mina who was weeping and her children around her also were weeping because her cow was dead. He went close to her and asked, 'What has caused you to weep O slave of Allah?' She said, 'O servant of Allah, we have orphan children. Our cow that was the means for our living has died and we are left without any means of living.'

"He asked, 'Will you be happy if I will bring your cow back to life?' She was just inspired to say, 'Yes, O servant of Allah I will be very happy.'

"He stepped aside and said two Rak'at prayers. He then raised his hands and gently moved his lips. He then stood up and called the cow to get up. He pushed the cow with his foot or a staff and she was up straight standing. When the woman looked at the cow she cried and said, 'Jesus, son of Mary, I swear by the Lord of the Ka'ba (he is Jesus).' Many people gathered around and he disappeared among them and went.'"

H 1285, Ch. 120, h 7
Ahmad ibn Mahziyar, may Allah grant him blessings, has narrated from Muhammad ibn Ali from Sayf ibn 'Umayra from Ishaq ibn 'Ammar who has said the following:
"Once I heard the pious servant of Allah giving the news of his own death to a man. I thought that he may or may not know when a person from his Shi'a (followers) dies. He turned to me as if angry and said, 'O Ishaq, Rushayd al-Hajriy possessed the knowledge of deaths and suffering, the necessity for such knowledge for the Imam is much greater.' Then he said, 'O Ishaq, do whatever you may like. Your life is destroyed and you will die within two years. Your brothers and family will very soon after you scatter in disunity and turn as traitors against each other so much so that even their enemies will scold them. Was this in your mind?'

"I said, 'I seek refuge with Allah for what went in my center (heart or chest).' After that meeting Ishaq did not live very long and he died. Very soon after banu (children of) 'Ammar began to live on loans and they became very poor and destitute."

H 1286, Ch. 120, h 8
Ali ibn Ibrahim has narrated from Muhammad ibn 'Isa from Musa ibn al-Qasim al-Bajali from Ali ibn Ja'far who has said the following:

"Muhammad ibn 'Isma'il came to me when we were still in Makkah after completing our 'Umra in the month of Rajab. He said, 'Uncle, I intend to go to Baghdad but I want to say farewell to my uncle, abu al-Hassan Musa ibn Ja'far, *'Alayhi al-Salam*, and I want you also to come with me.'

"I went with him to my brother (the Imam), *'Alayhi al-Salam*, and he was in his house in al-Hawba. It was just after sunset. I knocked at the door and my brother answered the door asking, 'Who is it?' I replied, 'It is Ali.' He said, 'I am just coming.' He would do his Wudu very slowly. I said, 'Be quick please.' He said, 'I will be quick.' He came out wearing dyed cloths that he had secured around his neck and sat down just below the doorsteps. I (Ali ibn Ja'far) bowed toward him and kissed his head and said, 'I have come for a matter to find out if you agree then Allah may grant him success, if you do not agree then it is one of those mistakes that we make.' He asked, 'What is it?' I said, 'This is the son of your brother. He wants to say farewell to you; he wants to go to Baghdad.' He said to me, 'Call him.' I called him and he had kept some distance. He came close to him and kissed his head and said, 'May Allah keep my soul in service for your cause, please advise me.'

"The Imam said, 'I advise you to be pious before Allah and spare my life.' He in answer said, 'Whoever has bad intentions toward you, may Allah have the same for him.' He continued to pray against those who have bad intentions against the Imam. He then kissed the head of the Imam again and said, 'Please advise me.' The Imam said, 'I advise you to be pious before Allah and spare my life.'

"He in answer said, 'Whoever has bad intentions against you, may Allah have the same for him, and He has already done so.' He kissed the head of the Imam and said, 'Please advise me.' The Imam said, 'I advise you to be pious before Allah and spare my life.' He prayed against those having bad intentions against the Imam, and moved away and I left along with him.

"My brother called me and said, 'O Ali, wait where you are.' I waited. He went inside and then called me inside. I went inside and he gave me a bag with a hundred Dinars in it and said, 'Tell your nephew to use it during his journey.'

"I (the narrator) secured the money in my dress and he gave me another hundred Dinars to give to him also and then he gave me one more bag to give to him. I said, 'May Allah keep my soul in service for your cause, 'When you are afraid of him so much then why do you give him all this money and why do you support him against your own self?'

491

"He said, 'If I maintain good relations with him and he cuts off such relationships Allah will cut his life short.' Then he gave to me a pillow with three hundred pure Dirhams (units of money) in it and asked to also give it to him. The narrator has said, 'I then left and gave him the first one hundred. He became extremely happy and prayed for his uncle. I then gave him the other money and he became so happy that I thought he might not want anymore to go to Baghdad. I then gave him all the Dirhams and he left for Baghdad. He greeted Harun as the Caliph and said, 'I did not think that there could be two Caliphs on earth at the same time. I also saw my uncle Musa ibn Ja'far being greeted as the Caliph.'

"Harun sent him one hundred thousand Dirhams. He fell sick with Diphtheria or scrofulous and died before seeing or touching any of the money."

Sa'd ibn 'Abd Allah and 'Abd Allah ibn Ja'far all have narrated from Ibrahim ibn Mahziyar from his brother Ali ibn Mahziyar from al-Husayn ibn Sa'id from Muhammad ibn Sinan from ibn Muskan from abu Basir who has said the following:

"Musa ibn Ja'far, *'Alayhi al-Salam*, died at the age of fifty-five in the year one hundred eighty-three. He lived for thirty-five years after Ja'far ibn Muhammad, *'Alayhi al-Salam*."

Chapter 121 - The Birth of abu al-Hassan al-Rida, *'Alayhi al-Salam*

Al-Kulayni has said, "Abu al-Hassan al-Rida, *'Alayhi al-Salam*, was born in A.H. one hundred forty-eight He passed away in the month of Safar in the year two hundred and three at the age of fifty-five. All the views about this date are not the same but it is more accurate, if Allah so wills. He died in Tus in the town called Sanabad that is within the reach of human voice from Nawqan. He was buried there. Al-Ma'mun (an 'Abbassid ruler) had summoned him from Madina to Marw via Basra to Persia. When al-Ma'mun left for Baghdad he took the Imam, *'Alayhi al-Salam*, along with him and he (the Imam) passed away in this town. His mother was 'Umm Walad called 'Umm al-Banin."

H 1287, Ch. 121, h 1
Muhammad ibn Yahya has narrated from Ahmad ibn Muhammad from ibn Mahbub from Hisham ibn Ahmar who has said the following:

"Once abu al-Hassan, *'Alayhi al-Salam*, the 2nd. asked me, 'Do you know if anyone from Morocco (or the west) has arrived?' I replied, 'No, no one has come.' He said, 'Yes, a man has come. Come with us.' He rode and I also rode and went until we reached the man. He was a man from Madina who had a few slaves with him for sale. I asked him to show the slaves for sale and he showed me seven slave-girls. Abu al-Hassan, *'Alayhi al-Salam*, said, 'I do not need any of these.' Then he asked, 'Show us more.' The man said, 'There is no more except one who is ill.' The Imam asked, 'Why do you not show her to us?' The man refused and the Imam returned. The next day he sent me and said to ask him for how much is the girl who is ill and if he said for so and so amount say, 'I pay.'

"I went to him and he said, 'I will not accept less than such and such amount for her.' I said, 'I agree to take her.' He said, 'She is yours but tell me who was the man with you yesterday?' I said, 'A man from the clan of banu Hashim.' He asked, 'From which family is he?' I said, 'That is all I know.' He said, 'I want to tell you about this girl. I bought her in the far corner of the west (or Morocco). A woman from the followers of the Bible came and asked, "What is she doing with you?" I said, 'I have purchased her for myself.' She said, 'This girl should not be with one like you. This girl should be with the best of the people on earth. With such a person she will not live very long before giving birth to a boy whose like will not be born in the west or east of the earth.' I brought her to the Imam and shortly afterwards she became the mother of Imam al-Rida, *'Alayhi al-Salam.'*"

H 1288, Ch. 121, h 2
Muhammad ibn Yahya has narrated from Ahmad ibn Muhammad from those he mentioned from Safwan ibn Yahya who has said the following:

"When abu Ibrahim, *'Alayhi al-Salam,* passed away abu al-Hassan (al-Rida), *'Alayhi al-Salam,* spoke of his Imamat (Leadership with Divine Authority) and it was troubling to us. It was said to him, 'You have declared a very great issue and we are afraid for your life from this rebel.' The Imam said, 'Allow him to strive hard but he will not find any way against me.'"

H 1289, Ch. 121, h 3
Ahmad ibn Mihran, Allah grant him blessings, has narrated from Muhammad ibn Ali from al-Hassan ibn al-Mansur from his brother who has said the following:

"Once I went to see al-Rida, *'Alayhi al-Salam,* in a room inside his house in the middle of the night. He raised his hand and it was as if there were ten lamps inside the house. A man asked permission for a meeting. He lowered his hand and then gave him permission."

H 1290, Ch. 121, h 4
Ali ibn Muhammad has narrated from ibn Jumhur from Ibrahim ibn 'Abd Allah from Ahmad ibn 'Abd Allah from al-Ghifari who has said the following:

"I owed money to a man from the family of abu Rafi', slave of the Holy Prophet, *'Alayhi al-Salam,* called Tays. He demanded payment and pressed me hard and people also assisted him. When I found myself in such condition I prayed the morning prayer in the Mosque of the Messenger of Allah and then headed to al-Rida, *'Alayhi al-Salam,* who was in al-'Arid those days. When I had almost reached his door he appeared on his donkey wearing a shirt and a gown. When I looked at him I felt shy. When he approached me he looked at me and I offered him the greeting of peace. It was the month of Ramadan. I said, 'May Allah keep my soul in service for your cause, I owe money to your slave, Tays, and he has defamed me. I thought he would order him to stop pressuring me and by Allah, I did not tell him how much I owed nor did I mention any amount. He ordered me to sit until he returned. I remained there until I said my sunset prayer and I was fasting. I felt depressed and I thought of returning home. At that time he appeared before me with people around him. Beggars had surrounded him and he gave them charity. He passed by and entered his house. Then he came out and called me inside. We both sat down and I began to speak to him about ibn al-Musayyib, the governor of Madina, as I used to speak to him about the governor often. When I finished he said, 'I do not think you have ended your fast yet.' I said, 'No, I have not ended it yet.' He asked for food and ordered the boy (servant) to join me at the table. The boy and I had our meal and when we finished he said to me, 'Lift up the furnishing and pick up whatever is underneath.' I lifted it up and found Dinars therein. I picked them up and placed them in my pocket. He ordered four of his slaves to escort me to my house. I said, 'May Allah keep my soul in service for your cause, the spies of ibn al-Musayyib check around all the time and I would not like them to see me with your slaves. He said, 'You are right, may Allah keep you rightly guided.' He ordered them to return whenever I wanted them to do so.

"When I almost reached my house and felt safe I asked them to go back. I went home and asked for a lamp. I looked at the Dinars and there were forty-eight of them. I owed twenty-eight to the man. Among them one Dinar caught my sight. I picked it up and brought it near the lamp. I found a clear mark on it that said, 'Pay to the man twenty-eight Dinars and keep the rest for yourself.' By Allah, I did not tell him (the Imam) how much I owed him. All praise belongs to Allah Who has granted honor to those whom He has given authority.'"

H 1291, Ch. 121, h 5
Ali ibn Ibrahim has narrated from his father from certain persons of our people who have said the following:

"Abu al-Hassan al-Rida, *'Alayhi al-Salam*, came out of Madina in the year that Harun wanted to perform Hajj. When he arrived near the mountain called Fari' on the left going to Makkah, abu al-Hassan, *'Alayhi al-Salam*, looked at it and then said, 'The builder at Fari' and the demolisher will be cut in pieces.' We had no idea what it meant. When he returned Harun arrived and camped at that place. Ja'far ibn Yahya climbed the mountain and ordered to build a resting place for him. When he (Ja'far) returned from Makkah he climbed there and ordered demolished what he had ordered to build. When he (Ja'far) returned to Iraq he was cut into pieces.'"

H 1292, Ch. 121, h 6
Ahmad ibn Muhammad has narrated from Muhammad ibn al-Hassan from Muhammad ibn 'Isa from Muhammad ibn Hamza ibn al-Qasim from Ibrahim ibn Musa who has said the following:

"I urged abu al-Hassan al-Rida, *'Alayhi al-Salam*, in a matter that I demanded from him and he asked to give him time. One day he went out to receive the governor of Madina and I was with him. He came near the castle of so and so and stopped for rest among a few trees. Just the two of us and not a third was there. I said, 'May Allah keep my soul in service for your cause, this holiday is upon us, by Allah, all I have is one Dirham only and nothing else.' He broke the surface of the earth with his whip and with his hand picked up a mold of gold and said, 'Use it and keep secret what you just saw.'"

H 1293, Ch. 121, h 7
Ali ibn Ibrahim has narrated from Yasir al-Khadim and al-Rayyan ibn al-Salt and both have said the following:

"When the matter of the deposed Caliph (Amin) ended and it (rule) was established for al-Ma'mun he wrote to al-Rida, *'Alayhi al-Salam*, asking to come to Khurasan. Abu al-Hassan, *'Alayhi al-Salam*, in reply presented certain reasons to justify his disagreement with the proposal but al-Ma'mun continued writing until the Imam found it unavoidable and that he (al-Ma'mun) would not leave him alone. He, *'Alayhi al-Salam*, then decided to leave for Khurasan and at that time abu Ja'far, *'Alayhi al-Salam*, was only seven years old. Al-Ma'mun wrote to him, 'Do not travel through the mountains and Qum. Take the road through Basra, al-Ahwaz and Persia.' The Imam arrived at Marw. Al-Ma'mun offered him to command and lead the task of Khilafat (leadership) but abu al-Hassan, *'Alayhi al-Salam*, declined. He then offered the Imam to accept the position of a crown prince. The Imam said that he might accept it under certain conditions. Al-Ma'mun said, 'Say whatever conditions you like.'

"The Imam wrote, 'I will assume this position with the conditions that I will not issue any order or prohibitions nor issue any *fatwa* or judgment nor any appointment or dismissal of officers or change anything in the current system. You must excuse me in all such matters.' Al-Ma'mun agreed to all such conditions.

"The narrator has said that Yasir narrated to me saying, 'When it was 'Id (the holiday) al-Ma'mun asked al-Rida, *'Alayhi al-Salam*, to attend the program, lead the prayer and deliver the sermon. Al-Rida, *'Alayhi al-Salam*, replied to him saying, 'You know the conditions between us. They did not consist of any such matters. Al-Ma'mun sent the message, 'I only want thereby to build confidence in the people by knowing your distinction.' He continued insisting until the Imam said, 'O Amir al-Mu'minin, I will appreciate it greatly if you excuse me from such task and if you still insist then I will do this task in the manner that the Messenger of Allah and Amir al-Mu'minin Ali, *'Alayhi al-Salam*, would do.'

"Al-Ma'mun then said, 'You may do as you choose.' Al-Ma'mun ordered the servants and guides to lead a procession to the door of abu al-Hassan, *'Alayhi al-Salam*, saying '*Allahu Akbar*,' Allah is great.

"The narrator has said that Yasir al-Khadim narrated to me, 'People lined up waiting for the Imam on the roads and roof tops, men, women and children. The guides and people from the army gathered at the door of abu al-Hassan, *'Alayhi al-Salam*. At sunrise the Imam took a shower and wore a white turban made of cotton. He let one end of the turban hang over his chest and the other end between his shoulders on his back. He tied his belt and said to his followers, 'Do as I have done.' He picked up an arrow-shaped staff and came out and we were along with him. He was barefoot and his gown was raised halfway between his feet and knees and so were his other (long) clothes. When he walked and we walked along with him he raised his head toward the sky and said, '*Allahu Akbar*' (Allah is great) four times. It seemed to us as if the sky and the walls responded to him. The guides and the people at the door were ready and armed and decorated with the best dresses. When we came out in such fashion along with al-Rida, *'Alayhi al-Salam*, he stood at the door briefly. He then said, '*Allahu Akbar* (Allah is great). *Allahu Akbar* (Allah is great). *Allahu Akbar* (Allah is great). *Allahu Akbar* (Allah is great). He has granted us guidance. *Allahu Akbar* (Allah is great). He has granted us the cattle. All praise belongs to Allah. He has granted us blessings.' We all raised our voices. Yasir al-Khadim has said that the whole Marw shook with the weeping cries and shouts when they looked at abu al-Hassan, *'Alayhi al-Salam*. Many of the guides fell from their horses. The horses kicked. The guides threw away their boots when they saw abu al-Hassan, *'Alayhi al-Salam*, barefoot. He would walk about ten steps and pause and say, '*Allahu Akbar*' three times. Yasir al-Khadim has said that to us it seemed as if the sky, earth and mountains responded along with him. The whole Marw had become one voice loud and tearful. It was reported to al-Ma'mun. Sahl ibn al-Fadl, who had two official posts, said to him, 'O Amir al-Mu'minin, if al-Rida, *'Alayhi al-Salam*, will reach the place of prayer in this manner people will devotedly be attracted to him. In my opinion, ask him to return home.'

"Al-Ma'mun sent his people to ask abu al-Hassan, *'Alayhi al-Salam*, to return home. He asked to bring his shoes and wore them and rode back home.'"

H 1294, Ch. 121, h 8

Ali ibn Ibrahim has narrated from Yasir al-Khadim who has said the following:

"When al-Ma'mun left Khurasan for Baghdad along with him came Fadl, Dhu al-Ri'asatayn and we came out with abu al-Hassan, *'Alayhi al-Salam*. Fadl ibn Sahl had received a letter from his brother Hassan while we were on our journey. Hassan had said in the letter, 'I studied the Zodiac changes this year according to the astrological calculations. I have found out that in the month of so and so on a Wednesday you will feel the test of iron and fire. I urged you to go to a Turkish bath with al-Ma'mun and Imam al-Rida, *'Alayhi al-Salam*, and perform phlebotomies and stain your hands with blood, which will help remove this misfortune from you.'

"Fadl ibn Sahl wrote about it to al-Ma'mun requesting him to request His Holiness Imam Ali ibn Musa al-Rida, *'Alayhi al-Salam*, to also join them on the appointed day. Al-Ma'mun informed the Holy Imam of the contents of that letter and demanded the consent of His Holiness. In reply to the caliph's letter Imam al-Rida, *'Alayhi al-Salam*, wrote, 'I will not go to the Turkish bath tomorrow. You and Fadl also must not go there tomorrow.' He sent that letter to the Imam twice. Abu al-Hassan, *'Alayhi al-Salam*, wrote to him, 'O Amir al-Mu'minin, I will not go to the Turkish bath. I have seen in a dream the Messenger of Allah forbidding me to go to that Turkish bath. You and Fadl also must not go to the Turkish bath.'

"Al-Ma'mun replied to the letter saying, 'You have spoken the truth and so has the Messenger of Allah. I will not go to the Turkish bath tomorrow and Fadl knows best (to decide for himself).' The narrator has said that Yasir said, 'When the night fell al-Rida, *'Alayhi al-Salam*, told us to say, 'We seek refuge in Allah against the misfortune in this night.' We continued saying the expression. When al-Rida, *'Alayhi al-Salam*, prayed the Morning Prayer he asked me to climb to the roof and to listen if there is anything. When I climbed I heard a great deal of commotion and crying and it was increasing. We saw al-Ma'mun enter from the door that opened to his quarter from the quarter of abu al-Hassan, *'Alayhi al-Salam*, and he said, 'My master, abu al-Hassan, may Allah grant you good reward for suffering the death of Fadl. He refused to cancel his decision for the bath and he went to the Turkish bath. A group of people attacked him with swords and killed him. Three of the attackers were arrested and one of them was the son of his maternal uncle, the son of Dhu al-Qalamayn.'

"He (Yasar) then said, 'The police and the guides and the people of Fadl present at the door of al-Ma'mun said, 'He (al-Ma'mun) has murdered him. We avenge him.' They want to set the door on fire. Al-Ma'mun said to abu al-Hassan, *'Alayhi al-Salam*, 'My master, please come out to them to calm them down and ask them to disperse.'

"The narrator has said that Yasir said, 'Abu al-Hassan, *'Alayhi al-Salam*, rode and asked me to ride also.' When we were out of the door of the house he looked at the people who were crowded there. He made hand gestures to ask them to disperse. Yasir has said, 'The people created a stampede while rushing to disperse and to whomever he made a hand gesture, he would run and pass quickly by the Imam.'"

H 1295, Ch. 121, h 9
Al-Husayn ibn Muhammad has narrated from Mu'alla ibn Muhammad from Musafir and from al-Washsha' from Musafir who has said the following:

"When Harun ibn al-Musayyib decided to fight Muhammad ibn Ja'far, abu al-Hassan, al-Rida, *'Alayhi al-Salam*, told me to go to him and say, 'Do not go out tomorrow. If you do so you will be defeated and your people will be killed. If he asks, 'How do you know that'? say, 'I saw it in my dream.' I (the narrator) went to him and said, 'May Allah make me of service to you; do not go out tomorrow to fight. If you do so you will be defeated and your people will be killed.' He asked, 'How do you know this?' I said, 'I saw it in my dream.' He said, 'A slave goes to sleep (to dream) and his behind is not even washed.' He went out to fight. He was defeated and his people were killed.'

"The narrator has said that Musafir narrated, 'I was in the presence of abu al-Hassan al-Rida, *'Alayhi al-Salam*, in Mina, Makkah when Yahya ibn Khalid passed by and he covered his head from the dust. The Imam said, 'Poor people do not know what will happen to them this year and stranger than this is the case of Harun and me.' The Imam made a gesture with his two fingers side by side. I, by Allah, could not understand the meaning of his statement until we buried him (Yahya ibn Khalid).'"

H 1296, Ch. 121, h 10
Ali ibn Muhammad has narrated from Sahl ibn Ziyad from Ali ibn Muhammad al-Qasani who has said the following:

"A certain person of our people has said that he wanted to deliver an amount of property to abu al-Hassan al-Rida, *'Alayhi al-Salam*. It was a large amount. When he (al-Rida), *'Alayhi al-Salam*, saw it he did not manifest any sign of happiness. I became depressed and said to myself, 'I delivered this property to him but he did not become happy.' The Imam called, 'O boy, bring water and the receptacle.'

"The narrator has said that the Imam then sat on the chair and made a hand gesture to the boy to dispense water on his hand. The narrator has said that from his hand gold began to fall in the receptacle. He then turned to me and said, 'One who is capable of doing this, he does not become happy for whatever you have delivered to him.'"

H 1297, Ch. 121, h 11
Sa'd ibn 'Abd Allah and 'Abd Allah ibn Ja'far both have narrated from Ibrahim ibn Mahziyar from his brother Ali ibn Mahziyar from al-Husayn ibn Sa'id from Muhammad ibn Sinan who has said the following:
"Ali ibn Musa, *'Alayhi al-Salam*, died at the age of forty-nine and a few months in A.H. two hundred and two. He lived for nineteen years and two or three months after the death of Musa ibn Ja'far, *'Alayhi al-Salam*."

Chapter 122 - The Birth of Muhammad ibn Ali, abu Ja'far the 2nd, *'Alayhi al-Salam*

Al-Kulayni has said, "Abu Ja'far, Muhammad ibn Ali, *'Alayhi al-Salam*, was born in the month of Ramadan in the year one hundred ninety-five and passed away in the year two hundred twenty at the end of the month of Dhu al-Qa'da at the age of twenty-five and two months and eighteen days. He was buried in Baghdad in the graveyard of Quraysh near the grave of his grandfather, Musa ibn Ja'far, *'Alayhi al-Salam*. Al-Mu'tasam (an 'Abbassid ruler) had summoned him to Baghdad at the beginning of the year in which he left this world. His mother was 'Umm Walad, called, Sabika Nuwbiyya. It is also said that her name was Khizuran. It also is narrated that she was from the family of Maria', mother of Ibrahim, son of the Messenger of Allah."

H 1298, Ch. 122, h 1
Ahmad ibn Idris has narrated from Muhammad ibn Hassa'n from Ali ibn Khalid who has said the following:
"Muhammad, who belonged to Zaydi sect, said this to me: 'I was in the army camp and I was told that a prisoner was brought from the area of al-Sham (Syria) tied up and that he has proclaimed himself a prophet.'

"Ali ibn Khalid has said that I went to him and found my way through the guards until I reached him. I found him to be a man of understanding. I asked him, 'O you, what is your story and your case?' He said, 'I am a man from al-Sham. I was praying to Allah at a place called the "Place of the head of al-Husayn." During my prayer a man came to me and said, "Come with me." I went with him and I found myself in the Mosque of al-Kufa. He asked me, 'Do you recognize this Mosque?' I replied, "Yes, I recognize it." He (now a prisoner) said, 'He prayed and I prayed with him. Then I found us in the Mosque of the Messenger of Allah in Madina. He offered greetings of peace to the Messenger of Allah and I did the same. He prayed and I prayed with him. He offered the special prayer for the Messenger of Allah. I was with him and found us in Makkah. I continued to find myself with him until we finished all the acts to be performed there. Then I found myself with him at the place in which I was praying to Allah in al-Sham. The man left for his own destination. The next year I was with him again and we did as in the year before. When we finished all of the activities of prayers and he returned me to my place of prayer in al-Sham and was about to leave I asked him this: 'I swear you to the One Who has given all these capabilities to you, tell me who are you?' He said, 'I am Muhammad ibn Ali ibn Musa, *'Alayhi al-Salam.*' The news spread and it reached Muhammad ibn 'Abd al-Malik al-Zayyat. He sent his people who arrested me and tied me up in chains and transferred me to Iraq.'

"I (the narrator) then asked him to send a petition to Muhammad ibn 'Abd al-Malik. He did so explaining the whole story but the answer to his petition bearing the signature of Muhammad ibn 'Abd al-Malik said, 'He should ask the one who took him from al-Sham to al-Kufa, then to al-Madina then to al-Makkah then back to al-Sham to release him from prison also.' I felt very sad for him with a great deal of sympathy. I tried to cheer him up and asked him to exercise patience. Next early morning when I went to see him I found people from the army, the chief of the security men, the prison guard and the crowd of creatures of Allah around and in the area. I asked, 'What is the matter?' They said, 'The prisoner from al-Sham who had proclaimed himself a prophet has disappeared and no one knows if the earth has swallowed him up or birds have snatched him away.'"

H 1299, Ch. 122, h 2

Al-Husayn ibn Muhammad al-Ash'ari has said that a shaykh from our people called 'Abd Allah ibn Razyn narrated to me the following:

"I lived in al-Madina of the Messenger of Allah. Abu Ja'far, *'Alayhi al-Salam,* would come every day to the mosque at noontime. He would enter the compound, turn to the shrine of the Messenger of Allah and offer his greeting of peace. He would then turn to the house of *Fatimah, 'Alayha al-Salam,* take off his shoes, stand up and pray. Satan induced temptation in my heart and said, 'When he (the Imam) comes, go and pick up the dust on which he has just stepped.' I waited that day for that purpose. When it was noontime he came riding on his donkey but he did not dismount at the place where he had done so before. He came and dismounted on the rock in front of the door of the Mosque. He then entered the Mosque, turned to the Shrine of the Messenger of Allah and offered his greetings of peace to the Messenger of Allah. He then turned to the place where he would pray. He did the exact thing for several days. I then said to myself, 'When he will come this time and remove his shoes I will go and pick up the gravel on which he has just stepped.' When he came the next day at noontime he dismounted on the rock then entered the Mosque, turned to the Shrine of the Messenger of Allah and offered his greetings of peace. He then came to the place where he would pray but prayed without removing his shoes and did the same thing for several days. I then said to myself, 'I could not succeed this way but now I must find which public bathhouse he uses to take a shower. I must wait at the door of the place and when he comes to enter the public bathhouse I can pick up the dust from the place on which he steps. I asked about such public bathhouse and found out that it is such a place in al-Baqi' that belongs to a man from the family of al-Talha. I found out about the day that he comes to this bathhouse. I then, on that day, went to the place, met the man from the family of al-Talha and began to talk to him while waiting for him (the Imam, *'Alayhi al-Salam*) to come. The owner of the place said to me, 'If you want to use the bathhouse you must do so now; later on it will not be available.' I asked, 'Why is that?' He said, 'Ibn al-Rida, *'Alayhi al-Salam*, will come to use it.' I then asked, 'Who is ibn al-Rida?' He said, 'A man from the family of Muhammad, *'Alayhi al-Salam*. He is very pious and well disciplined.' I then asked, 'Is it unlawful to use the public bathhouse at the time that he is there?' He said, 'We just vacate the place and leave it that way just for him.'

"The narrator has said that at that time he came with a few of his slaves. In front of him there was a slave who carried a piece of mat and brought it in all the way to the dressing room where he spread it down. He (the Imam) also came in, offered his greetings of peace and entered the dressing room while still riding on the donkey. He then dismounted on the mat. I then said to the man from the family of al-Talha, 'Is this the one whom you mentioned with all the superlative words in his praise?' He said, 'O you, by Allah, he has never done this before. It only has happened today.' I said to myself, 'This is because of what I have committed against my own soul.' I then said to myself, 'I will wait until he comes out, perhaps I will succeed in my plan.' When he came out he asked his people to bring the donkey. The donkey was brought into the dressing room and he rode on the donkey while over the mat and left. I said to myself, 'By Allah, this is enough. I have troubled him so much, I will not do any such thing again and will not even think about doing such things.' My decision was complete and solid. When it became noontime of that day he came to the Mosque while riding on his donkey and dismounted on the exact spot in the compound of the Mosque where he had normally been doing. Then he turned to the shrine of the Messenger of Allah and offered his greetings of peace and went to the place where he prayed in the house of *Fatimah, 'Alayha al-Salam*. He took off his shoes and stood up for prayer.'"

H 1300, Ch. 122, h 3
Al-Husayn ibn Muhammad has narrated from Mu'alla ibn Muhammad from Ali ibn Asbat who has said the following:

"Once he (abu Ja'far Muhammad ibn Ali al-Rida, *'Alayhi al-Salam*) came out to me and I looked at his head and legs so I could describe him physically to our people in Egypt. I kept looking until he sat down and said, 'O Ali, Allah's presentation of proofs in support of *'A'immah's* Imamat (Leadership with Divine Authority) is the same as those in support of the prophet-hood of a prophet. Allah has said, "... we gave knowledge and wisdom to John during his childhood." (19:12) "... When he attained maturity, Allah gave him strength, wisdom and knowledge. Thus, do We reward those who do good." (12:22) "... When he grew up to manhood and became forty years old...." (46:15) Allah may give authority to a child and He may do so when he is a forty years old man.'"

500

H 1301, Ch. 122, h 4

Ali ibn Muhammad has narrated from certain persons of our people from Muhammad ibn al-Rayyan who has said the following:

"Al-Ma'mun did all he could to prove that abu Ja'far, Muhammad ibn Ali al-Rida, *'Alayhi al-Salam,* was only a young man with worldly desires. However, al-Ma'mun could not succeed. When he became frustrated he gave his daughter in marriage to abu Ja'far, Muhammad ibn Ali al-Rida, *'Alayhi al-Salam.* For the ceremony he sent two hundred most beautiful entertaining girls each with a bowl in her hand with a precious pearl in it to welcome abu Ja'far, Muhammad ibn Ali al-Rida, *'Alayhi al-Salam,* when he would sit on the special seat prepared for him. They, however, were not of any attraction to the Imam to disturb him. There was a man called Mukhariq who had a voice, musical skills, a guitar and a long beard. Al-Ma'mun called him and he said, 'O Amir al-Mu'minin, if he is a worldly man I will prove myself as dealing him deadly blows on your behalf.' He sat in front of abu Ja'far, Muhammad ibn Ali al-Rida, *'Alayhi al-Salam,* and began to bray, which made all the people of the house gather around him. He began to play his guitar and sing. He did it for an hour but abu Ja'far, *'Alayhi al-Salam,* did not pay any attention to the right or left. Then he, *'Alayhi al-Salam,* raised his head and said, 'O you, long-bearded one, be pious before Allah.'

"The narrator has said that the musical instrument and guitar fell off his hand and he could not use his hands thereafter until he died. When al-Ma'mun asked him about his condition he said, 'When abu Ja'far, *'Alayhi al-Salam,* expressed his disappointment at me it struck me with a huge degree of fear from which I have not been able to relieve myself ever since.'"

H 1302, Ch. 122, h 5

Ali ibn Muhammad has narrated from Sahl ibn Ziyad from Dawud ibn al-Qasim al-Ja'fari who has said the following:

"Once I went to see abu Ja'far, *'Alayhi al-Salam,* and I had a few questions on three pieces of material with improper markings and they were mixed as such that I could not distinguish. I felt sad. He picked one and said, 'This is the letter of Ziyad ibn Shabib.' Then he picked up the other one and said, 'This is the letter of so and so.' I became awestruck. He looked at me and smiled.

"The narrator (Dawud) has said that the Imam then gave me three hundred Dinars and asked me to deliver them to certain persons of the sons of his uncle. He said, 'He will ask you to show him a professional person who could help him to buy goods, help show him one.' I (Dawud) then went to him and gave him the Dinars and he asked me, 'O abu Hashim, can you show me a professional person who may help me to buy goods?' I said, 'Yes, I can do so.'

"The narrator has said that once a camel man asked me to speak on his behalf to abu Ja'far, *'Alayhi al-Salam,* to take part in certain matters of his affairs. I went to see him (abu Ja'far), *'Alayhi al-Salam,* to speak to him but he was having a meal with a group of people and I did not get a chance to speak to him. He (abu Ja'far), *'Alayhi al-Salam,* said, 'O abu Hashim, eat.' He placed food before me.

Then he said, initiating and without any question from me, 'O boy, take good care of the camel man that abu Hashim has brought for us. Keep him with you.'

"The narrator has said that one day I entered a garden along with him and said, 'May Allah keep my soul in service for your cause, I am addicted to eating fig. Pray to Allah for me.' He was calm and then after three days on his own initiation he said, 'O abu Hashim, Allah has removed your addiction.' It (fig) ever since, is the thing that I hate most."

H 1303, Ch. 122, h 6

Al-Husayn ibn Muhammad has narrated from Mu'alla ibn Muhammad from Muhammad ibn Ali from Muhammad ibn Hamza al-Hashimi from Ali ibn Muhammad or Muhammad ibn Ali al-Hashimi who has said the following:

"Once I went to see abu Ja'far, *'Alayhi al-Salam*, in the morning of his marriage to the daughter of al-Ma'mun. The night before I had taken medicine and I was the first to meet him that morning. I was thirsty but did not like to ask for water. Abu Ja'far, *'Alayhi al-Salam*, looked at me and said, 'I think you are thirsty.' I said, 'Yes, I am thirsty.' He called, 'O Ghulam (male slave or servant) or Jariya (female slave or servant) bring us water.' I said to myself, 'They may poison the water.' For this reason I felt depressed. The servant then came with water. He (abu Ja'far, *'Alayhi al-Salam*) looked at me with a smile and said, 'O Ghulam, give the water to me.' He drank from it and gave the rest to me and I drank. I was thirsty again and did not like to ask for water. He then did as he had done before. When the Ghulam (servant) came with the bowl of water I thought as I did before. He then took the bowl, drank from it and gave the rest to me with a smile.'

"Muhammad ibn Hamza has said that this Hashimi told me, 'I think what they (Shi'a) say (that the Imam possesses Divine Authority) about him is true.'"

H 1304, Ch. 122, h 7

Ali ibn Ibrahim has narrated from his father who has said the following:

"Once a group of Shi'a from the suburbs asked permission to meet abu Ja'far, *'Alayhi al-Salam*. He granted them permission and they came in his presence. They asked him thirty thousand questions in one meeting (place). He answered them all and at that time he was ten years old."

Note: Thirty thousand questions may have been answered in one place in several sessions.

H 1305, Ch. 122, h 8

Ali ibn Muhammad has narrated from Sahl ibn Ziyad from Ali ibn al-Hakam from Di'bil ibn Ali who has said the following:

"Once I went to see abu al-Hassan al-Rida, *'Alayhi al-Salam*, and he ordered his people to give me a certain gift, but I did not thank Allah. The Imam, *'Alayhi al-Salam*, then asked, 'Why did you not thank Allah?' I went again to see abu Ja'far, *'Alayhi al-Salam*, and he ordered his people to give me a gift and I said, 'All praise belongs to Allah.' The Imam said, 'Now you have learned discipline.'"

H 1306, Ch. 122, h 9
Al-Husayn ibn Muhammad has narrated from Mu'alla ibn Muhammad from Ahmad ibn Muhammad ibn 'Abd Allah from Muhammad ibn Sinan who has said the following:

"Once I went to see abu al-Hassan, *'Alayhi al-Salam*. He said, 'O Muhammad, has something happened to the family of al-Faraj (the governor of al-Madina)?' I said, 'Yes, 'Umar (a member of al-Faraj family) has died.' The Imam then said, 'All thanks and praise belong to Allah.' He said it twenty-four times. I then said, 'My master, had I known it could make you this happy I should have come to you running and barefoot with the news (to congratulate you).' The Imam said, 'Do you not know what he, may Allah condemn him, once had said to Muhammad ibn Ali, my father?' I (the narrator) then said, 'No, I do not know it.' The Imam said, 'He spoke to my father about an issue and then said to him, "I think you are drunk." My father then said, "O Lord, if you know that I have been fasting this day, then make him feel the wrath of war, and the humiliation of captivity." By Allah, in just a few days his belongings were looted and he was captured. Now he is dead, may Allah deprive him of His mercy. Allah, the Most Majestic, the Most Gracious, has exacted revenge from him and He continues to exact revenge for His friends from His enemies.'"

H 1307, Ch. 122, h 10
Ahmad ibn Idris has narrated from Muhammad ibn Hassa'n from abu Hashim Al-Ja'fari who has said the following:

"Once I prayed with abu Ja'far, *'Alayhi al-Salam*, in the Mosque of al-Musayyib. He led the prayer with us and for the direction of Makkah he stood up facing straight. He also has said that a berry tree that was in the Mosque had dried up and had no leaves. The Imam asked for water and prepared himself under that tree for prayer. The berry tree came alive with leaves and fruits in that year."

H 1308, Ch. 122, h 11
A number of our people have narrated from Ahmad ibn Muhammad from al-Hajjal and 'Amr ibn 'Uthman from a man of the people of al-Madina from al-Mutrifiy who has said the following:

"Abu al-Hassan al-Rida, *'Alayhi al-Salam*, passed away and owed me four thousand Dirhams. I said to myself, 'My money is lost.' Abu Ja'far, *'Alayhi al-Salam*, sent me a message to meet him the next day and bring with me a balance and weighing stones. I went to see him and he said, 'Abu al-Hassan, *'Alayhi al-Salam*, has passed away. Did he owe you four thousand Dirhams?' I said, 'Yes, he did.' He then lifted up his prayer rug on which he was sitting and there were the Dinars that he gave to me.'" (The balance and weighing stones were to weigh the money.)

H 1309, Ch. 122, h 12
Sa'd ibn 'Abd Allah and al-Himyari both have narrated from Ibrahim ibn Mahziyar from his brother Ali from al-Husayn ibn Sa'id from Muhammad ibn Sinan who has said the following:

"Muhammad ibn Ali, *'Alayhi al-Salam*, passed away at the age of twenty-five years, three months and twelve days. He died on a Tuesday on the sixth of Dhi al-Hajj in A.H. two hundred twenty He lived nineteen years less twenty five days after his father."

Chapter 123 - The Birth of abu al-Hassan Ali ibn Muhammad, *'Alayhi al-Salam*

Al-Kulayni has said, "He was born on Dhi al-Hajj fifteen in the year two hundred twelve. It is said that he was born in the month of Rajab in the year two hundred and fourteen A.H. He passed away on twenty-sixth of Jamadi al-Akhir in the year two hundred fifty-four A.H. It is narrated that he passed away in the month of Rajab in the year two hundred fifty-four A.H. He lived for forty-one years and six months. According to the previously mentioned date he lived for forty years. Al-Mutawakkil had summoned him from al-Madina with Yahya ibn Harthama ibn 'Ayan to Surra man Ra'a. He left this world there and he was buried in his house. His mother was 'Umm Walad, called Samana."

H 1310, Ch. 123, h 1

Al-Husayn ibn Muhammad has narrated from Mu'alla ibn Muhammad from al-Washsha' from Khayrana al-Asbati who has said the following:

"Once I went to al-Madina to see abu al-Hassan, *'Alayhi al-Salam*. He asked me, 'What is the news from al-Wathiq (Abbassid ruler)?' I said, may Allah keep my soul in service for your cause, I left him in good health and I am of all people the last who met him. I met him just ten days ago.' The Imam then said, 'People of al-Madina say that he has died.' When he said, 'People say' I understood that it is he himself. He then said, 'What has Ja'far (an Abbassid man) done?' I said, 'I left him in the worst condition of all people. He was in prison.' He (the Imam) then said, 'He has become the ruler. What has ibn al-Zayyat (the Vizier of Wathiq) done?' I said, 'May Allah keep my soul in service for your cause, people are with him and whatever he says it takes place.' The Imam then said, 'His progress has proved to be a misfortune for him.'

"The Imam then paused for a while and said to me, 'The measures of Allah, the Most High, and His decrees must go on. O Khayaran, al-Wathiq has died, Al-Mutawakkil, Ja'far has replaced him and ibn al-Zayyat is killed.' I then asked, 'May Allah keep my soul in service for your cause, when has this happened?' He said, 'Six days after the time you left.'"

H 1311, Ch. 123, h 2

Al-Husayn ibn Muhammad has narrated from Mu'alla ibn Muhammad from Ahmad ibn Muhammad ibn 'Abd Allah from Muhammad ibn Yahya from Salih ibn Sa'id who has said the following:

"Once I went to see abu al-Hassan, *'Alayhi al-Salam*, and I said, 'May Allah keep my soul in service for your cause, they wanted to extinguish your light by all means and be unjust to you. It is so much so that they have lodged you in this disgraceful place for the homeless.' He said, 'O ibn Sa'id, look here. He pointed out with his hand and said, 'Look there.' When I looked I saw gardens. I saw very delightful gardens. There lived lovely boys and girls as if they were well-protected and secure pearls. There lived birds and beautiful deer. It had fountains and rivers that poured out and gushed forth. My sight was bewildered and my eyes turned dull. He then said, 'Wherever we may live, these are for us. We are not in the lodging for the homeless.'"

H 1312, Ch. 123, h 3

Al-Husayn ibn Muhammad has narrated from Mu'alla ibn Muhammad from Ahmad ibn Muhammad ibn 'Abd Allah from Ali ibn Muhammad from Ishaq al-Jallab who has said the following:

"Once I bought a large number of sheep for abu al-Hassan, *'Alayhi al-Salam*. He called and admitted me into the barn area of his house into a vast location that I could not recognize. He ordered me to distribute the sheep among certain people and of such people were abu Ja'far (his son) and his mother and others. Thereafter I requested permission to leave for Baghdad to see my father. It was the day of Tarwiya (eighth of the month of Dhi al-Hajj). He wrote to me, 'Stay with us tomorrow and thereafter leave.' I stayed that day and then it was the day of 'Arafah (ninth of Dhi al-Hajj) but I stayed with them that day as well as the tenth night in the balcony of his house. At dawn he came to me and said, 'O Ishaq, wake up.' I then got up. I then opened my eyes and found myself at my own door in Baghdad. I went inside and met my father among my people and told them that I spent the day of 'Arafah (ninth of Dhi al-Hajj) in the army camp (Samarra) and for 'Id (tenth of Dhi al-Hajj) I am in Baghdad.'"

H 1313, Ch. 123, h 4

Ali ibn Muhammad has narrated from Ibrahim ibn Muhammad al-Tahiri who has said the following:

"Al-Mutawakkil became so seriously ill because of a boil that he was about to die and no one had the courage to touch to operate him. His mother vowed to send a large sum of money to abu al-Hassan, *'Alayhi al-Salam*, from her own property if her son recovered. Fath ibn Khaqan had advised him (Al-Mutawakkil) to ask him (the Imam) about it saying, 'He might know something that could help relieve you.' He (Al-Mutawakkil) sent the message to him (the Imam) and explained his illness. The messenger returned with a message that said, 'Warm up oil residue from sheep mixed with extracts from roses and place it on the boil.' When the messenger explained it to them they laughed at his words. However, al-Fath said, 'He, by Allah, knows best about what he has said.' They brought the oil and prepared it as explained and placed it on the boil. The patient soon after was fast asleep and his active pain had calmed down. Afterwards it opened up, the substance in it was discharged and his mother was given the glad news of his recovery. She sent ten thousand Dinars to him (abu al-Hassan), *'Alayhi al-Salam*, marked with her own insignia. He had fully recovered from his illness, al-Bat ha'i al-'Alawi acting as a spy reported to him, 'Large sums of money and weapons are delivered to him (abu al-Hassan), *'Alayhi al-Salam*.' He (al-Mutawakkil) ordered Sa'id, the police chief, to search his (Imam's) house during the night, confiscate whatever money and weapons were found therein and bring them to him (al-Mutawakkil).' Ibrahim ibn Muhammad has said, 'Sa'id, the chief of police, told me that when I went to his house during the night I had a ladder to climb over the wall. When I climbed on the roof and then climbed down few steps in the dark I did not know how to reach the house. He (abu al-Hassan, *'Alayhi al-Salam*, called me, 'O Sa'id, hold on until they bring you candles. In a little while they brought me a candle, I climbed down and found him with a woolen gown on him and woolen cap. In front of him there was a prayer rug with a mat on it. I then had no doubt that he was praying. He said to me, 'There are the rooms.' I then searched them and did not find anything there but I found the bag of money in his house that was sealed with the insignia of the mother of al-Mutawakkil on it and another sealed bag of money. He said to me, 'There is the prayer rug.' I lifted it up and there was a sword underneath in a sheath. I took them to al-Mutawakkil. When he saw the insignia of his mother on it he called her for inquiry and she came to him. Private servants informed me that she said to him, 'When you were very ill, I had vowed out of frustration that if you recovered I would pay him (the Imam) ten thousand Dinars from my own properties. I paid him and this is my own seal.' He opened the other bag and there were four hundred Dinars in it. He added another bag of money to it and asked me to deliver them to him (abu al-Hassan), *'Alayhi al-Salam*. I returned the sword and the bags of money to him saying, 'My master, (I wish you knew) how much this assignment has depressed me.' He said, 'The unjust ones will find out very soon at what kind of destination they will end up.'"

H 1314, Ch. 123, h 5
Al-Husayn ibn Muhammad has narrated from Mu'alla ibn Muhammad from Ahmad ibn Muhammad ibn 'Abd Allah from Ali ibn Muhammad al-Nawfali who has said the following:
"Muhammad ibn al-Faraj told me that abu al-Hassan, *'Alayhi al-Salam*, had written to him this. 'O Muhammad, organize your affairs and be careful.' He (Muhammad ibn al-Faraj) said, 'I began to organize my affairs and did not know what the Imam meant thereby until police came to me and took me out of Egypt as a captive. All of my belongings were confiscated and I remained in prison for eight years. In the prison I received a letter from him that said, 'O Muhammad, do not reside in the western location.' I read the letter and said to myself, 'He writes me this and I am in prison. This is strange.' Shortly afterwards, I was released, thanks to Allah.

"The narrator has said that Muhammad ibn al-Faraj wrote to him about his properties. The Imam wrote to him (Muhammad ibn al-Faraj) in response, 'Your properties will soon be returned to you and even if they are not returned to you it will not harm you.' When Muhammad al-Faraj left for the army camp (Samarra) an order was issued to release his properties but he (Muhammad ibn al-Faraj) died before receiving them.

"The narrator has said that Ahmad ibn al-Khadib wrote to Muhammad ibn al-Faraj asking him to come to the army camp. He wrote to the Imam, abu al-Hassan, *'Alayhi al-Salam*, for his advice in the matter and the response was this, 'Go out. In it there will be happiness and relief for you, by the will of Allah, the Most High.' He left for the journey but very shortly afterwards he died.'"

H 1315, Ch. 123, h 6
Al-Husayn ibn Muhammad has narrated from a man from Ahmad ibn Muhammad who has said the following:
"Abu Ya'qub informed me saying, 'I saw him (Muhammad ibn al-Faraj) before his death in the army camp in an evening. Abu al-Hassan, *'Alayhi al-Salam*, received him and looked at him and he became ill the next day. After several days I went to visit him during his illness and his illness was worsening. He informed me that he (abu al-Hassan), *'Alayhi al-Salam*, had sent him cloths which he had folded to use as a pillow. The narrator has said that he was shrouded in that cloth.

Ahmad has said that abu Ya'qub said, 'I saw abu al-Hassan, *'Alayhi al-Salam*, with ibn al-Khadib who said to him, 'May Allah keep my soul in service for your cause, go ahead.' The Imam said, 'You go first.' Only after four days he was put in shackles and the news of his death was given out.

"The narrator has said that it is narrated that when ibn al-Khadib insisted in his demanding the house from him (the Imam), he sent him this messages: 'I will ask Allah, the Most Majestic, the Most Gracious, to place you as such that not even your traces could be found.' Allah, the Most Majestic, the Most Gracious, took him away in those days.'"

H 1316, Ch. 123, h 7
Muhammad ibn Yahya has narrated from a number of our people the following:
"I took a copy of the letter of al-Mutawakkil to abu al-Hassan, *'Alayhi al-Salam*, the 3ʳᵈ· from Yahya ibn Harthama in the year two hundred forty-three that read as follows: '(I begin) in the name of Allah, the Beneficent, the Merciful. Thereafter, Amir al-Mu'minin acknowledges your position, takes good care of you as a relative, and deems it obligatory to observe your rights. He pays attention toward your welfare and the well being of your family through the means with which Allah will grant wellbeing to you and to them and establish your honor and honor to them, grant blessings and security to you and to them. He seeks thereby the pleasure of his Lord and to fulfill his obligations toward you and to them. Amir al-Mu'minin, believes that it is best to remove 'Abd Allah ibn Muhammad as commander of the army and prayer leader in al-Madina of the Messenger of Allah since you have mentioned his ignorance and his disregard of your rights. That he has not respected you properly. Also it is because of his accusing you of matters that Amir al-Mu'minin has learned are unfounded and he acquits you of such charges. It is because of your sincere intentions in not leading an attempt to achieve what you consider yourself unfit for. Amir al-Mu'minin has replaced him ('Abd Allah ibn Muhammad) with Muhammad ibn al-Fadl and has ordered him to honor and revere you and abide by your orders and opinions. He must seek nearness to Allah and to Amir al-Mu'minin in this way. Amir al-Mu'minin looks forward to seeing you and loves to see you soon to look at you in person. If you want to visit him and stay with him as long as you like along with whoever of the members of your family and friends and servants you may do so whenever convenient for you and desirable. You may start your journey whenever you like, stopping on the way whenever and wherever you like. If you like, Yahya ibn Harthama, the slave of Amir al-Mu'minin, and the elements of the army will escort you. They will travel, as you like them to do so. All the matters will be up to you to decide until you arrive at Amir al-Mu'minin's place. No one of his (al-Mutawakkil's) brothers, sons, family members and persons special to him could be deserving more kindness, respected position, more praiseworthiness and preference to him than you do. He (al-Mutawakkil, the ruler) will not be more caring, compassionate and helpful to them and happier with any of them as much as he will be with you. If Allah may so will. May (Allah grant you) peace, kindness and blessings.'"

Written by Ibrahim ibn al-'Abbass. May Allah grant blessing upon Muhammad and his family.

H 1317, Ch. 123, h 8
Al-Husayn ibn al-Hassan al-Hassani has said that narrated to me abu al-Tayb al-Muthanna, Ya'qub ibn Yasir the following:

"Al-Mutawakkil would say, 'Woe is you (people). Ibn (the son of) al-Rida, (Ali al-Hadi), *'Alayhi al-Salam*, has frustrated me. He refuses to share a drink (liquor) with me and associate with me and I never get a chance in it.' They (al-Mutawakkil's associates) told him, 'If he does not give you a chance, his brother Musa plays music, sings, eats, drinks and seeks carnal love.' He asked them to call him so that we may confuse people with ibn al-Rida (by considering Musa, as Ali al-Hadi, *'Alayhi al-Salam*) an associate of al-Mutawakkil. He wrote to Musa and invited him honorably. All the people from the clan of Hashim present, the officials and people received him with the condition that on his arrival a piece of land would be given to him on which proper accommodations would be built for him. People who love to drink liquor and the singers will come to meet him there. He (al-Mutawakkil) maintained good relations with him cared for him and prepared a gorgeous lodging for him where he would visit him therein. When Musa arrived, abu al-Hassan, *'Alayhi al-Salam*, met him at al-Qantra Wasif, the place where the visitors were being received. He met him, offered him the greeting of peace and observed his rights. Then he (the Imam) said to him, 'This man has invited you to insult and humiliate you. Do not confess to him that you have ever drunk any liquor.' Musa said, 'If he has invited me for this purpose then what should I do?' The Imam said, 'Do not humiliate yourself and do not drink any liquor because he wants to insult you.' He (Musa) refused and he (abu al-Hassan, *'Alayhi al-Salam*) repeated his advice. When he found out that he (Musa) did not agree, he said, 'Remember, this is a place where you will never be able to meet him (al-Mutawakkil).' He (Musa) lived there for three years. Every day he would wake up and his people tell him that al-Mutawakkil is busy today; you can meet him next time. He would go and they tell him that he (al-Mutawakkil) is drunk. He would go again and they say he (al-Mutawakkil) has just had medicine. It continued this way for three years until al-Mutawakkil was killed and Musa never had a chance to meet him.'"

H 1318, Ch. 123, h 9
Certain persons of our people have narrated from Muhammad ibn Ali that Zayd ibn Ali ibn al-Husayn ibn Zayd narrated to me the following:

"Zayd ibn Ali has said, 'I became ill and a doctor came to see me at night. He prescribed a medicine for me to be taken at night for so and so many days. I could not find the medicine that night. The physician was still there that Nasr (the servant of Imam) came in with a bottle containmg the medicine that the physician had prescribed for me and said, 'Abu al-Hassan, *'Alayhi al-Salam*, has sent you the greeting of peace and has asked you to take this medicine for so and so many days.' I took the medicine and recovered from my illness.

"Muhammad ibn Ali has said that Zayd ibn Ali told me, 'The critics refused to accept this *Hadith* saying, 'Wherefrom the extremist have brought this *Hadith*?'"

Chapter 124 - The Birth of abu Muhammad, al-Hassan ibn Ali, *'Alayhi al-Salam*

Al-Kulayni has said, "Abu Muhammad al-Hassan ibn Ali, *'Alayhi al-Salam*, was born in the month of Ramadan (in another copy it is in the month of Rabi' al-Awwal) in the year two hundred thirty two. He died on a Friday on the eighth of the month of Rabi' al-Awwal in the year two hundred sixty at the age of twenty-eight. He was buried in the house where his father was buried in the city of Surra man Ra'a (Samarra), Iraq. His mother was 'Umm Walad called Hudayth (or Suwsan)."

H 1319, Ch. 124,h 1
Al-Husayn ibn Muhammad al-Ash'ari and Muhammad ibn Yahya and others have narrated the following:
"Ahmad ibn 'Ubayd Allah ibn Khaqan was in charge of collecting property and other taxes in the city of Qum. One day in his presence the 'Alawids and their beliefs were mentioned. He was a hardheaded Nasibi (abusive of 'Alawids). He said, 'In the city of Surra man Ra'a, I never saw a man from the 'Alawids like al-Hassan ibn Ali ibn Muhammad ibn al-Rida, *'Alayhim al-Salam*, in guidance, calmness, piety, nobility and generosity to his family and among banu Hashim. They as well as the official, the ministers and common people gave preference to him over their elders and the noble ones.

"One day I was standing next to my father (as an assistant or guard) and it was the day of his meeting people. His guards came and said; 'Abu Muhammad ibn al-Rida is at the door.' He said loudly, 'Allow him to come in.' I was surprised at their mentioning so boldly someone with his Kunya (i.e. father of so and so) before my father while only a Caliph, a crown Caliph or one who by the command of the Sultan were to be addressed that way could have been treated as such. A man with a fair complexion came in. His height was good and his face looked handsome, physically very good and young. He looked majestic and awesome. When my father looked at him he stood up and walked toward him several steps. I had not seen him doing this to a person from the clan of banu Hashim and the officers. When he (my father) approached him (ibn al-Rida) he embraced him, kissed his face and chest and holding his hand led him to sit on his own place for prayer and himself sat next to him turning his face toward him. He talked to him and said often, 'May Allah keep my soul in service for your cause.' I was surprised at what I saw. At this time the servant came and said, 'Al-Muwaffaq (brother and commander in chief of the Caliph) has come.' Whenever he (al-Muwaffaq) came to my father he received preference over the officers and other personalities. They stood up in the presence of my father between the door and the seat of my father until he came in and left. My father was still paying attention to abu Muhammad, *'Alayhi al-Salam*, and was talking to him until he looked at his special servants and said, 'May Allah keep my soul in service for your cause, now you may leave if you so wish.' He then said to his guards to lead him through the back so that he (al-Muwaffaq) would not see him. He stood up and my father also stood up and embraced him and he left. I asked the guards of my father and his servants, 'Woe is you, who was the man whom you addressed by his Kunya before my father and my father treated him as he did?' They said, 'This 'Alawid man is called al-Hassan ibn Ali, *'Alayhi al-Salam*, known as ibn al-Rida, *'Alayhi al-Salam.*' This surprised me even more. The whole day I thought anxiously about his affairs and the behaviors of my father and I did not see him until it was night. He usually said his 'Isha (late evening) prayer and studied the things that he needed of the issue to present before the Sultan. When he prayed and began to study I went and sat before him while he was alone. He asked, 'O Ahmad, do you need something?' I said, 'Yes, my father. If you allow me I want to ask.' He said, 'You have permission, my son, say whatever you like.' I said, 'Father, who was the man you met in the morning and behaved with him the way you did toward him with so much glorification, greatness and reverence with such expressions as, "May Allah keep my soul and the soul of my parents in service for your cause?" He said, 'My son, he was the Imam (Leadership with Divine Authority) of the al-Rafida (those who refuse to accept the leadership of people other than Ali ibn abu Talib and his infallible descendents). He is al-Hassan ibn Ali, *'Alayhi al-Salam*, known as ibn al-Rida.' He remained quiet for a while and then said, 'My son if the Imamat (leadership) would be removed from the Abbassid Caliphs no one from the clan of banu Hashim could deserve to become the Imam except this man. He deserves it because of his distinctions, piety, guidance, safety (from mistakes), his chastity, his worship, his beautiful moral characteristics and perfection. Had you had a chance to see his father you would have seen a man of great intelligence, nobility and excellence.' This increased my anxiety, thinking with anger toward my father and I thought his dealing and behavior toward him and his words for him were excessive.

"Thereafter, there was nothing more important to me than to ask more about him and investigate his affairs. Whoever of the members of Hashimit clan or the guards, the clerks, the judges, the scholars of the law (Fuqha') and other people I asked I found him being glorified, mentioned with greatness and high position. I would hear very beautiful words about him and see him given preference over all members of Hashimit clan and their elders. The feeling of greatness for him increased in my heart because I did not find anyone of his friends or foe that did not speak well of him and praise him.

"A certain person from the al-Ash'ari beliefs present asked him, 'What is the news about his brother, Ja'far, O abu Bakr?' He said, 'Who is Ja'far that you ask about or compare him with al-Hassan, *'Alayhi al-Salam*? Ja'far was an evildoer in public, polluted with sins, an addict drunkard, the lowest of all man and the most humiliating of his own self among men. He was worthless and mean to his own self. What happened during the time of the death of al-Hassan ibn Ali, *'Alayhi al-Salam*, to the Sultan and his people astonished me and I did not think such a thing could happen. When he became ill my father was informed that ibn al-Rida, *'Alayhi al-Salam*, had become ill. He immediately rode to reach the capital of the Caliphate. He came back in a hurry with five people of the servants of the Amir al-Mu'minin. They all were of his confidants and trustworthy ones among whom one was Nihriyr. He (my father) commanded them to stay close to the house of al-Hassan, *'Alayhi al-Salam*, to learn about him and his conditions. He called a few physicians and commanded them to maintain contact with him and be around him mornings and evenings. After two or three days he was informed that he (the patient) was weakening. He commanded the physicians to remain around his house and sent for the chief judge who came in his presence. He then commanded him (the judge) to select ten people from his most trustworthy ones in the matters of their religion, trust and restraint in the worldly matters. They were called in his presence and he sent them to the house of al-Hassan, *'Alayhi al-Salam*. He commanded them to be there day and night and they were there until he, *'Alayhi al-Salam*, passed away. The city of Surra-man-Ra'a turned into one huge voice of weeping and lamentation. The Sultan sent people to search his house and search all the rooms therein and seal the contents thereof. They searched for his son and called certain women with knowledge to deal with pregnancy. They examined his ladies. A certain woman had said that one of the ladies is pregnant. She was accommodated in a certain quarter and Nihriyr, al-Khadim, and his people and the women with him were ordered to stay guard around her. Thereafter they began to prepare for the burial. Markets were to remain closed. Members of the clan of al-Hashim, the guards, my father and other people formed the burial procession. The city of Surra-man-Ra'a on that day had turned into a day similar to the Day of resurrection. When the body was readied for burial the Sultan sent a message to abu 'Isa ibn al-Mutawakkil and commanded him to lead the prayer. When the body was placed at the prayer area abu 'Isa went close and uncovered his face. He then asked all members of al-Hashim clan of the 'Alawid and 'Abbassid branch, the guards, the clerks, the judges and juries to bear witness that al-Hassan ibn Ali ibn Muhammad ibn al-Rida, *'Alayhim al-Salam*, had died a natural death in his own bed. That this had taken place in the presence of the servants of Amir al-Mu'minin, his confidants, so and so persons of the judges and so and so persons of the physicians. He (abu 'Isa) then covered his face and ordered to pick up the body. The body was then picked up from the central area of the house and was buried in the room where his father was buried."

"After his burial, the Sultan and people began to search for his son. The search was carried out extensively. All the houses and rooms were searched. The distribution of his legacy was suspended. The people appointed to guard one of the ladies who was thought of as pregnant continued their task until it was found out that such thought was invalid. When pregnancy was proved invalid they distributed his legacy between his mother and brother, Ja'far. His mother claimed to be the executor of his will and her claim was confirmed before the judge. The Sultan, even after searching so much for his son continued his search to find traces of his son.

"Thereafter, Ja'far came to my father and asked, 'Assign the position of my brother to me. I will pay you twenty thousand Dinars every year.' My father treated him harshly and rebuked him saying, 'You are a fool. The Sultan puts to the sword whoever he just thinks is a Shi'a, follower and supporter of your father and brother to stop them from holding such belief but he fails to achieve such goal. Had you been considered an Imam among the Shi'a of your father and brother you would not need any help from the Sultan or others to give you such position as that of your father and brother. If you are not considered an Imam among the Shi'a of your father and brother you will not have such position from us.' My father belittled him, considered him weak and ordered his people to keep him away from his office. My father did not give him permission for a meeting as long as he lived. We left and he remained in the same condition. The Sultan continued his search for the traces of the son of al-Hassan ibn Ali, *'Alayhi al-Salam.*'"

H 1320, Ch. 124, h 2

Ali ibn Muhammad has narrated from Muhammad ibn 'Isma'il ibn Ibrahim ibn Musa ibn Ja'far, *'Alayhi al-Salam*, who has said the following:

"Once, abu Muhammad, *'Alayhi al-Salam*, wrote to abu al-Qasim Ishaq ibn Ja'far al-Zubayri before the death of al-Mu'tazz by about twenty days as follows: 'Stay home until what is to happen will happen.' When Burayha was killed he wrote to him (the Imam), *'Alayhi al-Salam*, 'A happening has happened. What do you command me to carry out?' He wrote back, 'This is not the happening. It is another happening.' Then there was the case of al-Mu'tazz the way it was."

"It is narrated from the same narrator that the Imam wrote to another person, 'Ibn Muhammad ibn Dawud ibn 'Abd Allah will be killed.' It (the writing) was ten days before his assassination. On the tenth day he was killed."

H 1321, Ch. 124, h 3

Ali ibn Muhammad has narrated from Muhammad ibn Ibrahim, known as ibn al-Kurdiy, from Muhammad ibn Ali ibn Ibrahim ibn Musa ibn Ja'far, *'Alayhi al-Salam*, who has said the following:

"We were under pressure and constraint. My father said, 'We should go to abu Muhammad, *'Alayhi al-Salam*, for help. People describe him as very generous and considerate.' I asked, 'Do you know him?' He said, 'No, I do not know him and I have not even seen him as yet.' We decided to go and meet him. My father said on the way, 'I hope he will grant us five hundred Dirhams. Two hundred for clothes, two hundred to pay the debts and one hundred for expenses. We need this much very badly.' I then said to myself, 'I hope he will grant me three hundred Dirhams, one hundred to buy a donkey, one hundred for expenses and one hundred for clothes and I will go to the mountains.'

"The narrator has said that when we arrived at the door a slave came out and said, 'Ali ibn Ibrahim and his son Muhammad, please come inside.' When we were in his (the Imam's) presence we said the greetings of peace. He (the Imam) said to my father. 'O Ali, what held you back from coming to us until now?' He said, 'My master, I felt shy to come to you in this condition.' When we left him his slave came to us and gave a bag of money to my father saying, 'This is five hundred Dirhams. Two hundred for clothes, two hundred to pay debts and one hundred for expenses.' He gave me a bag and said, 'This is three hundred Dirhams, one hundred for the donkey, one hundred for clothes and one hundred for expenses. Do not go to the mountains. Go to Sawra.' He then went to Sawra' and married a woman and now his income from properties is a thousand Dinar. Despite this he belongs to the waqifi sect in matters of beliefs. Muhammad ibn

Ibrahim has said that I said to him, 'Woe is you! What more clear proof do you want to believe in him as your Imam?' He said, 'This (belief in Waqifi sect) is a habit that has been with us (and it does not go away).'"

H 1322, Ch. 124, h 4
Ali ibn Muhammad has narrated from abu Ali Muhammad ibn Ali ibn Ibrahim who has said that narrated to me Ahmad ibn al-Harith al-Qazwini who has said the following:

"I was with my father in the city of Surra man Ra'a. My father was a veterinarian at the animal farm of abu Muhammad, *'Alayhi al-Salam*. Al-Musta'in (the 'Abbassid ruler) had a mule the like of which in beauty and size has not been seen. No one could touch that mule to ride, saddle or harness. He had called all the trainers and they had failed to ready the mule for riding. Certain people close to him had said, 'O Amir al-Mu'minin, why do you not ask al-Hassan, ibn al-Rida, *'Alayhi al-Salam*, who may either ready it for riding or get killed in which case it will be a great relief for you?' The narrator has said that he sent for abu Muhammad, al-Hassan, *'Alayhi al-Salam*, and my father went with him (the Imam). My father has said, 'When abu Muhammad, *'Alayhi al-Salam*, entered the compound of the Sultan, he, *'Alayhi al-Salam*, looked at the mule that was standing in the facility. He went forward and placed his hand over the rear of the mule. I (the narrator) then saw the mule perspire and perspiration began to flow down. Then he, *'Alayhi al-Salam*, went to al-Musta'in. He offered him greeting of peace and received welcome. The Sultan asked him to sit just next to him and asked abu Muhammad, *'Alayhi al-Salam*, to harness the mule (that has become obstinate).' Abu Muhammad, *'Alayhi al-Salam*, said to my father, 'Young man harness the mule.' Al-Musta'in said, '(please) you harness the mule.' The Imam took off his gown, harnessed the mule and returned back to his place. Al-Musta'in asked him to saddle the mule but he said to my father, 'Young man, saddle the mule.' Al-Musta'in asked him (the Imam) to saddle the mule. He stood again, saddled the mule and returned back to his place and said, 'Do you want that I ride it also?' He said, 'Yes, please do so.' He (the Imam) rode the mule without any resistance. The mule ran in the facility and then he took the mule for an amble, which the mule performed in the best way that can be. He came back and dismounted. Al-Musta'in said to him, 'O abu Muhammad, *'Alayhi al-Salam*, how was the mule?' He said, 'O Amir al-Mu'minin, I had not seen like it before in beauty and skill. Only Amir al-Mu'minin deserves to have such a mule.'

"The narrator has said that al-Musta'in then said, 'O abu Muhammad, *'Alayhi al-Salam*, Amir al-Mu'minin wants you to ride it.' Abu Muhammad, *'Alayhi al-Salam*, then said to my father, 'O young man take the mule with you and he led the mule away.'"

H 1323, Ch. 124, h 5
Ali has narrated from abu Ahmad ibn Rashid from abu Hashim al-Ja'fari who has said the following:

"I requested abu Muhammad, *'Alayhi al-Salam*, for something that I needed. He scratched the earth with his whip. I (the narrator) think he then covered it with a handkerchief and then took out five hundred Dinars. He then said, 'O abu Hashim this is for you and (please) accept our apologies.'"

H 1324, Ch. 124, h 6

Ali ibn Muhammad has narrated from abu 'Abd Allah ibn Salih from his father from abu Ali al-Mutahhar the following:

"Once He (abu Ali al-Mutahhar) wrote to him (abu Muhammad, *'Alayhi al-Salam*, in the year of Qadisiyya, the year of draught that forced people to return home without performing Hajj for fear of thirst. He wrote back in reply, 'Continue your journey and you will have no fear by the will of Allah.' They continued their journey to Hajj safely and all thanks belong to Allah, Lord of the worlds.'"

H 1325, Ch. 124, h 7

Ali ibn Muhammad has narrated from Ali ibn al-Hassan ibn al-Fadl al-Yamani who has said the following:

"Al-Ja'fari from the family of Ja'far (al-Tayyar) was attacked by such a large number of people that it seemed impossible for them to defend themselves. He wrote to abu Muhammad, *'Alayhi al-Salam*, about his endangered condition. He (abu Muhammad), *'Alayhi al-Salam*, wrote back to him in reply, 'You will be adequately defended by the will of Allah, the Most High. He came out with just a few people to defend themselves against the attackers who were in excess of twenty thousand while on his side there were fewer than a thousand but the attackers all vanished.'"

H 1326, Ch. 124, h 8

Ali ibn Muhammad has narrated from Muhammad ibn 'Isma'il al-'Alawi who has said the following:

"Abu Muhammad, *'Alayhi al-Salam*, was imprisoned under the supervision of Ali ibn Narmasha who was extremely hostile toward the descendents of abu Talib, peace be upon him. He was told to treat him (abu Muhammad), *'Alayhi al-Salam*, as he (the guard) wished. He stayed with him only for a day and the guard who was hostile toward him, turned into such a submissive person before him that he could not even dare to look up into his face out of glorification and reverence. He (abu Muhammad), *'Alayhi al-Salam*, came out from his prison and he (the guard) had found the highest degree of understanding of him and spoke the best words about him."

H 1327, Ch. 124, h 9

Ali ibn Muhammad and Muhammad ibn abu 'Abd Allah have narrated from Ishaq ibn Muhammad al-Nakha'i who has said that narrated to me Sufyan ibn Muhammad al-Duba'i who has said the following:

"Once I wrote to abu Muhammad, *'Alayhi al-Salam*, and asked him about the meaning of the word *al-Walija* (relying) in the words of Allah, the Most High: 'Do you think that Allah will not make any distinction between those of you who have fought for His cause and have relied on no one other than Allah, His Messenger, and the believers, and other people?' (9:16) I said to myself, not in the letter, 'To whom does the "believers" refer in this verse?' The answer came as this: '*Walija* refers to a person who is appointed in place of the Leader with Divine Authority. You have said to yourself, 'To whom does the "believers" refer in this verse?' They are the *'A'immah* (Leaders with Divine Authority) who ask Allah to grant security to the people and He grants their request.'"

H 1328, Ch. 124, h 10

Ishaq has said that abu Hashim al-Ja'fari has said the following:

"Once I complained to abu Muhammad, *'Alayhi al-Salam*, about the constraining cell of the prison and the weight of the shackles on me. He wrote back in reply to me, 'Today you will pray your noontime prayer in your own home.' I then was released that day and prayed the noontime prayer in my own home as he had said. I was under financial constraints and I decided to ask him for a certain amount of Dinars in writing but I felt shy. When I was going to my home he sent me a hundred Dinars and had written to me this: 'If you need anything do not feel shy or embarrassed. Ask and you will find it as you wanted, by the will of Allah.'"

H 1329, Ch. 124, h 11
Ishaq has narrated from Ahmad ibn Muhammad al-Aqra' who has said that narrated to me abu Hamza, Nasir al-Khadim the following:

"I had heard many times that abu Muhammad, *'Alayhi al-Salam*, spoke to each of his Roman, Turkish and Saqaliba slaves in their own languages. It was astonishing to me and I would think that he was born in al-Madina and had not been exposed to anyone until abu al-Hassan, *'Alayhi al-Salam*, passed away and no one had seen him. How is it that he speaks such languages? I was talking to myself when he came to me and said, 'Allah, the Most High, the Most Holy, grants distinction to Leaders with Divine Authority over the other creatures in all matters. He gives them distinction in the matters of languages, knowledge of the genealogical issues, of the duration of lives and events. Without such distinctions there will be no difference between Leaders with Divine Authority and others.'"

H 1330, Ch. 124, h 12
Ishaq has narrated from al-Aqra' who has said the following:

"Once I wrote to abu Muhammad, *'Alayhi al-Salam*, asking him if *'A'immah* (Leaders with Divine Authority) experience wet dreams? I said to myself after the letter had gone, 'Wet dream is something Satanic, and Allah, the Most Holy, the Most High, has protected those whom He has given authority against such things.' The answer came. 'The conditions of *'A'immah* (Leaders with Divine Authority) when asleep are the same as when they are awake. Sleep does not change anything in them. Allah has given protection to those whom He has given authority from Satanic encounters as you spoke to yourself.'"

H 1331, Ch. 124, h 13
Ishaq has said that al-Hassan ibn al-Zarif narrated to me the following:

"Two issues would nudged in my chest which made me write to abu Muhammad, *'Alayhi al-Salam*. I wrote about *al-Qa'im* (the one who will rise with Divine Authority and power). 'When he will rise, by what means will he judge among the people and where will be his court house?' I also wanted to ask him about alternating fever but I had forgotten to mention it in writing. The answer came. 'You had asked about *al-Qa'im*. When he will rise he will judge among people through his own knowledge just the way David would judge. He will not call any witness to testify. You also wanted to ask about alternating fever but you forgot to do so. Write this on a sheet (of material), 'We said to the fire, be cool and peaceful (with Abraham).' (21:69) The narrator has said that we did just as he had said and the suffering person was relieved.'"

H 1332, Ch. 124, h 14

Ishaq has said that narrated to him 'Isma'il ibn Muhammad ibn Ali ibn 'Isma'il ibn Ali ibn 'Abd Allah ibn 'Abbass ibn 'Abd al-Muttalib who has said the following:

"Once I sat on the side of the road waiting for abu Muhammad, *'Alayhi al-Salam*, to pass by so that I could present before him my complaint against a need. When he was passing by I presented my complaint before him and swore that I did not have even a Dirham, and nothing for lunch or dinner. The narrator has said that the Imam said, 'You falsely swore by Allah. You have buried two hundred Dinars. My words are not to deny you any grants. Young man, give him whatever is with you. His servant gave me one hundred Dinars. He then turned to me and said, 'You will be deprived of it in your worst days.' He meant those Dinars that I had buried for a difficult day. What he said was true. I had buried two hundred Dinars thinking that they would only be used in a very difficult day. When I faced such a difficult day and all the ways to find a living were closed I went to take out the two hundred Dinars but soon I found that there was not even a single Dinar left. In fact, my son had learned about where the Dinars were buried and he had taken them and had run away. I could not benefit from any of those Dinars.'"

H 1333, Ch. 124, h 15

Ishaq has said that narrated to me Ali ibn Zayd ibn Ali ibn al-Husayn ibn Ali, *'Alayhi al-Salam*, the following:

"I had a horse that I liked very much and I admired it often in social gatherings. One day I went to see abu Muhammad *'Alayhi al-Salam*, and he said, 'How is your horse doing?' I said, 'I still have it and it is in front of your door. I just dismounted it.' He said, 'Change it before this evening if you can and if you find a buyer do not delay.' Someone came in and our conversation discontinued. I then left anxiously for home and informed my brother about it and he said, 'I do not know what to say about it.' I felt covetous about it and procrastinated in offering for sale until it was evening. We had just prayed the late evening prayer when the horse trainer came in saying, 'My master your horse has died.' I felt sad and realized that this was what abu Muhammad, *'Alayhi al-Salam*, meant. After several days I went to see abu Muhammad, *'Alayhi al-Salam*, and I was saying to myself, 'I wish he would replace my horse with another one. It was his words that made me so sad.' When I sat down he said, 'Yes, we will replace your horse. Young man, give to him my dark brown bay (type of horse) which is better than his horse to ride and will live longer.'"

H 1334, Ch. 124, h 16

Ishaq has said that Muhammad ibn al-Hassan Shammun has said that Ahmad ibn Muhammad narrated to me the following:

"Once I wrote to abu Muhammad, *'Alayhi al-Salam*, when al-Muhtadi (an 'Abbassid ruler) had begun to kill the Turkish *Mawali* (slave or supporters), 'My master, we thank Allah for diverting his (al-Muhtadi's) attention from us. I have heard that he had threatened you and has said, "By Allah, I will wipe them out from the face of the earth."

"Abu Muhammad, *'Alayhi al-Salam*, sent in response with his own signature. 'This will be shortening his life very much. Count five days from today. On the sixth day he will be killed, humiliated, with insults and suffering that he will go through.' It then happened exactly as he had said.'"

H 1335, Ch. 124, h 17
Ishaq has said that Muhammad ibn al-Hassan Shammun narrated to me the following:
"Once I wrote to abu Muhammad, *'Alayhi al-Salam*, requesting him to pray for me because of the pain that I suffered in my eyes. One of my eyes had gone and the other was about to go. He wrote back to me in reply, 'Allah has kept your eye for you.' My painful eye then recovered. He had signed at the end with these words, 'May Allah grant you good rewards and best recompense.' I felt sad and I did not know anyone just passed away from my family. After a few days I received information of the death of my son, Tayyib. I then realized what his condolences to me were for."

H 1336, Ch. 124, h 18
Ishaq has said that narrated to me 'Umar ibn Muslim the following:
"We were in the city of Surra man Ra'a when a man, called Sayf ibn al-Layth, from Egypt came with a complaint to al-Muhtadi against Shafi' al-Khadim who had usurped his property and expelled him from the city. We hinted to him to write to abu Muhammad, *'Alayhi al-Salam*, and request him to facilitate his affairs. Abu Muhammad, *'Alayhi al-Salam*, wrote back to him, 'You will be fine. Your property will be given back to you. Do not forward your complaints to Sultan. Go and meet the agent (of Shafi' al-Khadim) who has your property and frighten him with the power of the Greatest Sultan, Allah, Lord of the worlds.' He met the agent. The agent who had the property with him said, 'It was written to me at the time of your leaving Egypt to find you and return your property to you. He returned the property by the order of the judge, ibn abu al-Shawarib, in the presence of witnesses and he did not have to present his complaints to al-Muhtadi. He procured his property and nothing was heard about him thereafter."

"The narrator has said that it was Layth who said the following also.

"When I left Egypt one of my sons was ill and my elder son was the executor of my will and the supervisor over my family in case I died. I wrote to abu Muhammad, *'Alayhi al-Salam*, requesting him to pray for my son who was ill. He wrote back to me in reply, 'Your son has recovered but your elder son, the executor of your will and the supervisor over your family has died. Pay thanks to Allah, do not be impatient lest your rewards will be withheld.' The news came to me that my son who was ill has recovered and my elder son died on the day I received the reply letter from abu Muhammad, *'Alayhi al-Salam.*"

H 1337, Ch. 124, h 19
Ishaq has said that narrated to me Yahya ibn al-Qushayri from the town called Qira, the following:
"Abu Muhammad, *'Alayhi al-Salam*, had an agent who lived in a room in the house with the white servant of the Imam. The agent invited the servant to have evil activities with him and the servant refused to do so unless he brought him wine. The agent managed to find wine and took it to him. There were three closed doors between them and the quarters of the Imam. The narrator has said that the

agent narrated to me that I was awake and I saw the doors open until I saw the Imam in person standing at the door. He then said, 'O you, have fear of Allah and be pious before Him. In the morning he ordered the servant sold and discharged me from the job.'"

H 1338, Ch. 124, h 20
Ishaq has said that narrated to me Muhammad ibn al-Rabi' al-Sa'i the following:
"I debated a man who believed in dualism in Ahwaz, then I went to Surra man Ra'a. However, his words were stuck in my heart. I was sitting in front of the door of Ahmad al-Khadib when I saw abu Muhammad, *'Alayhi al-Salam*, coming from the house for public gathering. It was the house wherein on a certain day the Sultan allowed the common people to visit him. The Imam looked at me and made a gesture with his forefinger, saying, 'One, single and only One.' I fainted and fell on my face.'"

H 1339, Ch. 124, h 21
Ishaq has narrated from abu Hashim al-Ja'fari who has said the following:
"One day I went to see abu Muhammad, *'Alayhi al-Salam*, and I wanted him to give me a certain amount of silver so I could make a ring out of it and keep it for blessing. I sat down but forgot to ask what I had come for. When I was leaving and said farewell to him he threw a ring to me and said, 'You wanted silver and we could give you a ring. You profited the gems and the cost of the goldsmith works. May Allah grant you blessings, O abu Hashim.' I then said, 'I testify that you are the *Wali* (Leader with Divine Authority) from Allah, and my Imam through my obedience to whom I follow the religion of Allah.' He then said, 'May Allah grant you forgiveness, O abu Hashim.'"

H 1340, Ch. 124, h 22
Ishaq has said that narrated to me Muhammad ibn al-Qasim abu al-'Ayna' al-Hashimi, the slave of 'Abd al-Samad ibn Ali 'Ataqa, the following:
"Oftentimes I went to see abu Muhammad, *'Alayhi al-Salam*. When in his presence I felt thirsty but I, due to shyness and respect for him, could not ask for water but he would call the people of his household to bring water for me. Oftentimes I thought to myself of leaving and he would say, 'Young man, bring his horse.'"

H 1341, Ch. 124, h 23
Ali ibn Muhammad has narrated from Muhammad ibn 'Isma'il ibn Ibrahim ibn Musa ibn Ja'far ibn Muhammad, *'Alayhi al-Salam*, from Ali ibn 'Abd al-Ghaffar who has said the following:
"When abu Muhammad, *'Alayhi al-Salam*, was imprisoned in the control of Salih ibn Wasif, the 'Abbassids, Salih ibn Ali and others who were not Shi'a all came to Salih ibn Wasif asking him to exert more pressure on abu Muhammad, *'Alayhi al-Salam*. Salih told them, 'What should I do? I managed to find two people who were of the harshest manners and appointed them to guard him. They both turned into most assiduous worshippers in prayers and fasting. When I asked them about their behaviors they replied, 'What can you say about a man who fasts every day, worships the whole night and does not speak or busy himself with anything?

When we look at him a feeling of trembling and shivering overtakes us and we lose control over our own selves.' When they heard this they returned in despair.'"

H 1342, Ch. 124, h 24

Ali ibn Muhammad has narrated from al-Hassan ibn al-Husayn who both have said that narrated to us Muhammad ibn al-Hassan al-Makfuf that certain persons of our people have narrated from a Christian cupping expert who served in the army the following:

"One day at noontime abu Muhammad, *'Alayhi al-Salam*, sent for me at the time of noon prayer and told me to perform cupping on this vein. He showed me a vein that was not known to me as one of the veins used for cupping. I thought to myself, 'I have not seen anything stranger than this: To perform cupping at noontime which is not the time for it and on a vein that I do not know.' He then told me, 'Wait in the house.' When it was evening he called me and said, 'Open the vein.' I opened the vein. He said, 'Hold it' I held the vein and stopped the blood. He then told me to remain in the house. At midnight he called me and said to open the vein. It increased my astonishment, but I did not want to ask him. I opened the vein and white blood like salt came out. He has said that he (the Imam) told me to stop it and I stopped it. He has said that he (the Imam) told me to remain in the house. In the morning he (the Imam) ordered his clerk to pay me three Dinars. I took the Dinars and left. I then went to see Bakhtishu' who was a Christian and told him the whole story. The narrator has said that he (Bakhtishu') said, 'By Allah, I do not understand what you say and I do not know anything about medicine. I have not read any such thing in the books. I do not know anyone more knowledgeable in Christianity than so and so, a Persian man. Go to him.' He has said that I then hired a boat and went to Basra then to Ahwaz and to Persia to the man I was looking for. I explained to him the story. He has said, 'He asked me to give him time.' I waited for few days and then went to him for an answer. He said, 'What you say this man did is something that Jesus had done only once in his life.'"

H 1343, Ch. 124, h 25

Ali ibn Muhammad has narrated from certain persons of our people who have narrated the following:

"Muhammad ibn al-Hujr once wrote to abu Muhammad, *'Alayhi al-Salam*, complaining against 'Abd al-'Aziz ibn Dulafa and Yazid ibn 'Abd Allah. He wrote back in reply, 'As far as 'Abd al-'Aziz is concerned I have relieved you from his troubles. As far as Yazid is concerned for each of you there is a position before Allah.' 'Abd al-'Aziz died and Yazid killed Muhammad ibn Hujr.'"

H 1344, Ch. 124, h 26

Ali Muhammad has narrated from certain persons of our people who have said the following:

"Abu Muhammad, *'Alayhi al-Salam*, was placed under the supervision of a zookeeper who caused constraints and suffering to him. He (the zookeeper) has said that his wife told him, 'Woe is you, be pious before Allah. Do you not know who is in your house?' She then explained to him the good manners of the Imam and said, 'I am afraid for you from him.' He then said, 'I can throw him to the beasts.' He in fact did so and the Imam was seen standing among them for prayer and the beasts circled around him.'"

H 1345, Ch. 124, h 27

Muhammad ibn Yahya has narrated from Ahmad ibn Ishaq who has said the following:

"Once I went to see abu Muhammad, *'Alayhi al-Salam*, and asked him to write for me few lines so that whenever I see his handwriting I can recognize it. The Imam said, 'Yes,' and then said, 'O Ahmad the writing with a fine pen and with thick pen will look different to you. Do not have doubts He then asked for a pen and inkpot and began writing. He made the pen to have ink from the bottom of the inkpot. I thought to myself when he was writing, 'I will request him to gift me the pen with which he is writing.' When he finished writing he turned to me and began speaking while he was wiping the pen with the handkerchief of the inkpot for a while and then said, 'Here, O Ahmad it is for you.' He gave it to me. I then said, 'May Allah keep my soul in service for your cause, I feel sad about something that is in my soul. I wanted to ask your father about it but I did not have the chance.' He asked, 'What is it, O Ahmad?' I said, 'My master, it is narrated to us from your holy ancestors that the prophets sleep on their backs, the true believers sleep on their right side, the hypocrites sleep on their left side and Satans sleep on their belly.' He, *'Alayhi al-Salam*, said, 'That is how it is.' I then said, 'My master I struggle to sleep on my right side but I cannot do so and I cannot go to sleep on my right side.' He remained calm for a while and then said, 'O Ahmad, come close to me.' I went close to him and he said, 'Place your hand under your clothes.' I did so. He then took his hand from under his clothes and placed under my clothes. He wiped with his right hand my left side and with his left hand my right side three times. Ahmad has said that ever since I have not been able to sleep on my left side and cannot go to sleep on my left side.'"

Chapter 125 - The Birth of the Possessor (of Divine Authority), *'Alayhi al-Salam*

Al-Kulayni has said, "He was born on fifteenth of the month of Sha'ban in the year two hundred fifty five A.H."

H 1346, Ch. 125, h 1

Al-Husayn ibn Muhammad al-Ash'ari has narrated from Mu'alla ibn Muhammad from Ahmad ibn Muhammad who has said the following:

"When al-Zabayri was killed this letter came from abu Muhammad, *'Alayhi al-Salam*, 'Such as this is the retribution for those who lie against Allah in the matters of those who possess Authority from Him. He thought that he would kill me and I would leave no children behind. How has he then experienced the power of Allah?' A child was born to him, whom he named M.H.M.D, in the year two hundred fifty-six A.H.'"

H 1347, Ch. 125, h 2

Ali ibn Muhammad has said that narrated to me Muhammad and al-Hassan sons of Ali ibn Ibrahim in the year two hundred seventy nine saying that narrated to them Muhammad ibn Ali ibn 'Abd al-Rahman al-'Abdi of 'Abd Qays from Daw' ibn Ali al-'Ijli from a man from Persia, whose name he mentioned, who has said the following:

"Once I went to the city of Surra man Ra'a and kept myself at the door of abu Muhammad, *'Alayhi al-Salam*. He called me inside without any request from me.

When I went inside and offered greeting of peace, he said to me, 'How are you, O father of so and so?' Then he told me, 'Sit down O so and so.' He then asked me about a group of men and ladies from my family. He then said to me, 'What brings you here?' I said, 'It is the wish to serve you.'

"The narrator has said that he said, 'Alright, stay here.' I then remained in the house with the servants. Then I would do the purchases for them from the market. I could go in his presence without first requesting permission when he was present in the men's quarters. One day I went to him when he was in the men's quarters. I heard the sound of movement in the house and he said, 'Do not move from your place.' I could not dare to go out or inside. Then a female servant came out to me who had something with her, which was covered. He then called me inside and I went inside. He called the female servant and she came back. He told her to uncover what she had with her. She uncovered the very handsome face of a white baby boy. And she uncovered his chest. A line of hairs had grown from his neck down to his bellybutton, which seemed to be greenish in color and not totally black. He said, 'This is your master (Leader with Divine Authority).' He then ordered her to take the baby inside and after that I could not see him until abu Muhammad, *'Alayhi al-Salam*, passed away."

"Daw' ibn Ali has said, 'I asked the man from Persia, 'How old do you think he was?' He said, 'Two years old.' Al-'Abdi has said, 'I asked Daw', 'How old do you think he was?' He said, 'Fourteen years old.' Abu Ali and abu 'Abd Allah has said that we think he is twenty one years old.'"

H 1348, Ch. 125, h 3

Ali ibn Muhammad has narrated from more then one person of our people of Qumm from Muhammad ibn Muhammad al-'Amiri from abu Sa'id Ghanim al-Hindi who has said the following:

"I lived in interior Kashmir, India. My friends would sit on chairs on the right and left of the King. They were forty people and all of them read the four books, Torah, Gospel, Psalms and the books of Abraham. We judged among the people, provided them understanding of their religion and issued legal opinions for them in the lawful and unlawful matters. All people sought assistance from us including their King. Once we discussed about the Messenger of Allah and said that this prophet who is mentioned in the books has remained unidentified to us. We must investigate about him and lead a fact-finding task in his affairs. We agreed that I should go out and lead the fact-finding task. I then set out with a large amount of money and journeyed for twelve months until I reached near Kabul. Turkish bandits robbed and wounded me seriously. They sent me to Kabul where their King saved my life. When he learned about my case, he sent me to Balkh which was under the control of Dawud ibn al-'Abbass ibn abu al-Aswad. Information had reached him that I have come out of India in search of religion and that I have learned Persian and have debated the scholars of law and theology. Dawud ibn al-'Abbass summoned me to his presence. He gathered the scholars of law against me. They debated me. I then informed them that I have come in search of the prophet about whom we have learned in the books.

"He asked, 'Who is he and what is his name?' I said, 'His name is Muhammad.' They said, 'You are searching for our prophet.' I asked them about his laws and they provided me information. I said, 'I know that Muhammad is the prophet but I do not know the one you describe to me. Is he the one I search for or not? You should show where he is so I can go and find out whether the signs that I have are found in him or not. If he is the one I am looking for I will accept his religion.'

"They said, 'He has passed away.' I asked them, 'Who is the executor of his will and his successor?' They said, 'Abu Bakr was his successor.' I asked them, 'Tell me about his name. This is (Abu Bakr) his Kunya?' They said, 'It is 'Abd Allah ibn 'Uthman.' They ascribed him to Quraysh. I then asked them to tell me about the genealogy of your prophet, Muhammad, *'Alayhi al-Salam*. They informed me of his genealogy. I said, 'This is not the person I am looking for. The one I am searching for is the one whose successor is his brother in religion and his cousin genealogically, the husband of his daughter and the father of his sons. This prophet will have no children on earth except the sons of this man who is his successor.'

"He has said that they attacked me and said, 'O commander, this man has come out a polytheist and has entered disbelief. It is lawful to tip out his blood.' I said to them, 'O people, I already have a religion and I strongly believe in it. I do not want to give it up until I find a religion stronger than this. I have found the description of this man in the books that Allah has revealed to His prophets. I came out of my country, India, leaving behind all the honor and respect that I had only to find him. When I examined your prophet the way you described him to me I found out that it did not match the description of the Prophet mentioned in the books. So leave me alone.'

"The agent (of the government) sent for a man called al-Husayn ibn Eshkib and said to him, 'Debate this Indian man.' He said, 'May Allah grant you well-being. There are the scholars of the law and the other scholars. They know better how to debate him.' He said to him, 'Debate him as I say, and you can meet privately and be kind to him.' Al-Husayn ibn Eshkib said to me after our consultations, 'The prophet that you are looking for is the one these people have described for you but their description of his successor is not the true describtion. This prophet is Muhammad ibn 'Abd Allah ibn 'Abd al-Muttalib. His successor is Ali ibn abu Talib, *'Alayhi al-Salam*, ibn 'Abd al-Muttalib. He is the husband of *Fatimah, 'Alayha al-Salam*, daughter of Muhammad, *'Alayhi al-Salam*, and the father of al-Hassan and al-Husayn, the grandsons of Muhammad, *'Alayhi al-Salam*.'

"Ghanim abu Sa'id has said that I then said, 'Allahu Akbar, (Allah is great). This is the one I have been looking for.' I then returned to Dawud ibn al-'Abbass and said to him, 'O commander, I have found what I was searching for. I testify that no one deserves to be worshipped and obeyed besides Allah and I testify that Muhammad is the Messenger of Allah.'

"The narrator has said that he treated and helped me with kindness and asked al-Husayn to look after me. Thereafter I went to him until we were acquainted properly and he taught me understanding of the law of the matters that I needed such as prayer, fasting and the obligations.

"I (the narrator) then said to him, 'We read in our books that Muhammad, *'Alayhi al-Salam*, is the last of the prophets and there will be no other prophets after him. The task (Leadership with Divine Authority) after him will be with the executor of his will, his successor and heir. Thereafter it will be with the executor of the will of the preceding one and so on in their descendents until the end of the world. Who is the executor of the will of the executor of the will of Muhammad, *'Alayhi al-Salam*?' He said, 'They are al-Hassan then al-Husayn, *'Alayhim al-Salam*, the grandsons of Muhammad, *'Alayhi al-Salam*.' He then continued speaking of the executors of the will of the Holy Prophet, *'Alayhi al-Salam*, until the Sahib al-Zaman (the one who possesses Divine Authority today). Then he explained to me what had happened (with *'A'immah*, the Leaders with Divine Authority). Thereafter I had no other goals but to search for the Holy Location. He ('Amiri) has said that he came to us in Qum. He sat with our people in the year two hundred sixty-four A.H. He then left with them and arrived in Baghdad with his friend from al-Sind who had accompanied him in religion. 'Amiri has said that Ghanim said to me, 'I disliked certain things about my companion and I departed him and went out to al-'Abbassia and prepared myself for prayer. I began the prayer but I was anxious and thinking about my goal. At this time someone came to me and called me with my Indian name. I replied, 'Yes, it is I.' He said, 'Your master is calling you.' I went with him and he walked from this to that street until he came to a house and a garden and I saw him, *'Alayhi al-Salam*, sitting. He said, 'Welcome, O so and so,' in Indian language. 'How are you? How was so and so,' until he mentioned all the forty people (mentioned in the beginning of the *Hadith*). He then asked me about every one of them. Then he told all that had happened among us, all in Indian language. Then he asked, 'did you want to perform Hajj with people of Qum?' I said, 'Yes, my master.' He then said, 'Do not go to Hajj with them this year. Go back and perform Hajj in future.' He then gave me a bag of money that was in front of him. He said to me, 'Spend it for your needs and do not go to Baghdad to so and so.' He mentioned his (so and so's) name and said, 'Do not tell him anything.'

"'Amiri has said that he came to us at Qum. He then informed us of the triumph and that our people had returned from al-'Aqaba. Ghanim went to Khurasan. Next year he went for Hajj and sent us souvenirs from Khurasan. He lived there for some time and then he died. May Allah grant him blessings."

H 1349, Ch. 125, h 4
Ali ibn Muhammad has narrated from Sa'id ibn 'Abd Allah who has said the following:
"Al-Hassan ibn al-Nadr and abu Sidam and a group of people, after abu Muhammad, *'Alayhi al-Salam*, had passed away spoke about the property (of religious dues) in their possession and how to find out (who should they give it to). Once al-Hassan ibn al-Nadr came to abu Sidam and said, 'I want to go for

Hajj this year.' Abu Sidam said, 'Postpone it this year.' Al-Hassan ibn al-Nadr said, 'I experience nightmares in my sleep. I must go this year for Hajj.' He prepared his will and appointed Ahmad ibn Ya'li ibn Hammad as the executor of his will. He said in his will to pay a certain amount of money to the Holy Location with his own hand into his (Imam's) own hand when he might appear in public. The narrator has said that al-Hassan has said, 'When I arrived in Baghdad I rented a house and a certain person of the representatives came to me with clothes and Dinars and left them with me. I asked him, 'What is all this?' He said, 'It is, as you know, what it is.' Others also came to me with such properties until the house was filled up. Then Ahmad ibn Ishaq came with all that was with him. I was astonished and remained thinking. A letter came to me from the man, *'Alayhi al-Salam*, that said, 'When it will become such and such hours of the day then take all (money and property) with you.' I then left with what was with me and on the way there was a robber that looted the travelers with his sixty men thieves. I passed him safely by the help of Allah. I arrived at the army camp and stopped there. A letter came that told me to take everything along with me. I loaded everything in the carriages of the porters and when I reach the corridor a black man was standing there. He asked, 'Are you al-Hassan ibn al-Nadr?' I said, 'Yes, I am he.' He then said, 'Enter.' I then entered the house and then a room and unloaded the goods from the carriages of the porters therein. In a corner of the room there was a large quantity of bread. He gave two loaves to each of the porters and told them to leave. Then I found out that there was a room behind the curtain and someone called me therefrom: 'O al-Hassan ibn al-Nadr, thank Allah for the favor that He has done to you and do not complain. Satan loves that you doubt. He gave me two pieces of cloth and said, 'Take these; you will soon need them.' I took them and left.'

"Sa'd has said, 'Al-Hassan ibn Nadr came back, died in the month of Ramadan and was shrouded in the pieces of cloth the Imam, *'Alayhi al-Salam*, had given to him.'"

H 1350, Ch. 125, h 5

Ali ibn Muhammad has narrated from Muhammad ibn Hamawayh al-Suwaydawiy from Muhammad ibn Ibrahim ibn Mahziyar who has said the following:

"At the time abu Muhammad, *'Alayhi al-Salam*, passed away I had doubts. Large quantities of commodities (of religious dues) were accumulated with my father. He loaded them in a boat and he also embarked. I was with him to say farewell to him. He began to feel severe fever and asked me to take him back home; he said, 'It is death.' He then said to me, 'Be pious before Allah about these commodities.' In his will he appointed me to watch over the commodities. He then died. I then said to myself, 'My father was not such a person to make a will for an incorrect cause. I must take these commodities to Iraq and rent an accommodation on the bank of the river and I will not tell anyone of anything with me. If the matter becomes clear to me as it was at the time of abu Muhammad, *'Alayhi al-Salam*, I will deal accordingly, otherwise, throw them into the river.'

"I then went to Iraq, rented a place on the bank of the river and stayed there for several days. Then I received a letter with a messenger. The letter said, 'O Muhammad, there is so and so things inside so and so thing with you. It explained to me everything in detail even about the things of which I had no knowledge. I then submitted everything to the messenger and remained there for several more days. No one asked who I was. I felt depressed and sad. Then a letter came that said, 'We have appointed you in the place of your father. Therefore be thankful to Allah.'"

H 1351, Ch. 125, h 6
Muhammad ibn abu 'Abd Allah has narrated from abu 'Abd Allah al-Nisa'iy who has said the following:

"I delivered certain items from al-Marzabani al-Harithi to the Holy Location (the house where Imam al-Hassan ibn Ali al-Hadi, *'Alayhi al-Salam*, lived). One item was a gold bracelet. Other items were accepted but the bracelet was returned. I was ordered to break it. When I did so inside there were certain amounts of iron, brass and zinc. I took them out and sent the gold back. It was accepted."

H 1352, Ch. 125, h 7
Ali ibn Muhammad has narrated from al-Fadl al-Khazzaz al-Mada'ini, the slave of Khadija daughter of Muhammad, abu Ja'far, *'Alayhi al-Salam*, who has said the following:

"Certain people of the city of al-Madina belonged to al-Talibiyin group who believed in the truth (about Ahl al-Bayt). They would receive their financial grants regularly on time. When abu Muhammad, *'Alayhi al-Salam*, passed away a few of them disregarded the belief that abu Muhammad, *'Alayhi al-Salam*, has left behind a son. The financial grants thereafter came only to those who still believed in the son of abu Muhammad, *'Alayhi al-Salam*, and stopped coming to the others. They are mentioned no more along with those who are mentioned. All praise belongs to Allah, Lord of the worlds."

H 1353, Ch. 125, h 8
Ali ibn Muhammad has said the following:

"A man from Bedouins sent a certain quantity of commodity (as religious dues) but it was returned to him and he was told, 'Pay first the rights of the children of your uncle. It is four hundred Dirhams.' The property of the children of his uncle was in his possession in a sharing manner and he had withheld their property. When he did the accounting, their right in that shared property was four hundred dirhams. He paid that amount and sent the rest to the Imam, *'Alayhi al-Salam*, and it was accepted."

H 1354, Ch. 125, h 9
Al-Qasim ibn al-'Ala' has said the following:

"Several boys were born to me and each time I would write (to the Imam, *'Alayhi al-Salam*, and request for prayer. Nothing in response had ever been written to me about them. They all died. When my son al-Hassan was born I wrote and requested for prayer. The answer came, 'He lives and all praise belongs to Allah.'"

H 1355, Ch. 125, h 10
Ali ibn Muhammad has narrated from 'Abd Allah ibn Salih who has said the following:

"I lived in Baghdad and during one year I requested permission (from the twelfth Imam, *'Alayhi al-Salam*) to travel out but permission was not granted. I waited for twenty-two days and the caravan had already left for al-Nahrawan, then I was granted permission. It was a Wednesday and I was told to leave. I then left but I did not have any hope of reaching the caravan. I arrived at al-Nahrawan and the caravan was still there. I then had enough time to feed my camels only and then the caravan left. I journeyed with the caravan and he, *'Alayhi al-Salam*, had prayed for my safety. I did not face any difficulties. All praise belongs to Allah."

H 1356, Ch. 125, h 11
Ali has narrated from al-Nadr al-Bajali from Muhammad ibn Yusuf al-Shashi who has said the following:
"A boil had grown on my hips. I sought treatment from several physicians and spent money but they said that they knew of no medicine for it. I then wrote a letter to him (the twelfth Imam), *'Alayhi al-Salam*, requesting him to pray. He wrote back to me with his signature, 'May Allah grant you good health and place you with us in this life and in the life hereafter.' The narrator has said that before the coming of the Friday the boil was gone and it became like the palm of my hand (clean and flawless). I then called one of the physicians and showed him the place of the boil and he said, 'We had no knowledge of any medicine to cure it.'"

H 1357, Ch. 125, h 12
Ali has narrated from Ali ibn al-Husayn al-Yamani who has said the following:
"I lived in Baghdad. Once the caravan for the people of Yemen was about to leave, I also decided to leave with them. I then wrote to him (the twelfth Imam), *'Alayhi al-Salam*, requesting his permission. The response came, 'Do not leave with them. There is nothing good for you in leaving with them. Stay in al-Kufa.'

"The narrator has said, 'I stayed in al-Kufa and the caravan left but the tribe of Hanzala attacked and looted them. I then wrote for permission to leave by ships on water. Permission was denied. I then found out that of the ships that had traveled that year, none reached the destination safely. Indian groups called al-Bawarij had looted the ships. I then visited the army camp. Near sunset I went to the door (of the shrine of the two Imam) quietly. I did not speak to anyone nor did I introduce myself to anyone. I was praying in the mosque after offering my greeting of peace (to the tenth and eleventh Imam). A servant came and said, 'Rise up and come with me.' I asked him, 'Where should we go?' He said, 'We will go home.' I then asked, 'Do you know who I am? Perhaps you are sent for someone else.' He said, 'I have been sent for you only. You are Ali ibn al-Husayn, the messenger of Ja'far ibn Ibrahim.' He took me to the house of al-Husayn ibn Ahmad. He then spoke to him secretly and I did not hear what they spoke about. Everything that I needed was brought for me. I stayed with him for three days. I asked his permission to offer my greetings of peace from inside the house. He granted me permission and I offered my greetings of peace during the night.'"

H 1358, Ch. 125, h 13
Al-Hassan ibn al-Fadl ibn Yazid al-Yamani has said the following:

"My father wrote (to the sacred location) in his own handwriting and he received a response. I then wrote in my own handwriting. I also received a response. One of our Fuqaha' (scholar of law) wrote in his own handwriting but he did not receive any response. We then began to think about it and we found out that the man had changed his belief into that of the Qirmati sect.

"Al-Hassan ibn al-Fadl has said, 'I visited (the holy places in Iraq) and arrived at Tus. I decided not to leave until I experienced evidence in support of my belief and success in achieving my needs even if it took my staying until I received confirmation.' He has said, 'In the meantime I felt depressed because of fear that I might lose the opportunity to perform Hajj.' He has said, 'One day I went to see Muhammad ibn Ahmad for help.' He said to me, 'Go to so and so mosque. A man will meet you there.' I then went to the mosque and a man came to me. He looked at me and laughed and said, 'Do not be sad and depressed. You will perform Hajj this year and will return back to your wife and children safely.'

"The narrator has said, 'I gained confidence and my heart felt at peace. I say that is how my wish came true. All praise belongs to Allah. I then went to the army camp (city of Surra man Ra'a) and a bag of money with few Dinars and a piece of cloth were sent to me (from the Imam's office). I felt depressed and said to myself, 'Is this how these people treat me and this is how much my reward is with them?' I used ignorance and returned the gift and wrote a letter. The person who brought them to me did not explain or say anything. I then felt very strongly regretful and said to myself, 'I have become ungrateful to my master in rejecting his gift.' I wrote a letter and begged for forgiveness of my misbehavior. I confessed my sins and begged for pardon. I sent the letter and remained rubbing my hands against each other (in despair). In such condition I was thinking and saying to myself, 'If the money is sent to me I will not open the bag and will not say anything about it. I will take it to my father. He knows more than me and will do whatever he will like. At that time a letter had come to the messenger who had brought the bag of money. He was told, 'What you did was wrong. You did not inform the man that we sent gifts to our friends and followers and sometimes they ask us for such gifts for blessings.' A letter came to me also and it said, 'You made a mistake in rejecting the gift but when you asked Allah to forgive you, Allah will forgive you. It was your intention not to open the gift or spend it; we have spent it on your behalf. However, you must take the cloth so you can use it for Ehram (during performing certain acts of Hajj).'

"The narrator has said, 'I wrote him about two issues and I wanted to write about a third issue but I did not do so for fear that he, *'Alayhi al-Salam*, might not like it.' The answer for the two issues came back and the meaning of the third one was also explained. All praise belongs to Allah.

"Once I made a contract with Ja'far ibn Ibrahim al-Naysaburi in Naysabur to share a ride on our journey to Makkah. When we arrived in Baghdad I decided to change our agreement. I then went around to find another person for sharing a ride. Ibn al-Wajna' came to see me after I had already proposed to him to share a ride and

527

hiring a ride and he had expressed his dislike to my proposal. He said, 'I am looking for you and I am told (by the people of the sacred location), "He will accompany you. Treat him kindly, find for him ride sharing and hire for him a ride."'

H 1359, Ch. 125, h 14
Ali ibn Muhammad has narrated from al-Hassan ibn 'Abd al-Hamid who has said the following:
"I had doubts in the case of Hajiz (as whether he had been authorized or not). I then collected a few items and left for the army camp (the city of Surra man Ra'a). The notification that came to me said, 'There is no doubtfulness in us nor in those who represent us in our affairs. Whatever is with you take them to Hajiz ibn Yazid.'"

H 1360, Ch. 125, h 15
Ali ibn Muhammad has narrated from Muhammad ibn Salih who has said the following:
"When my father died and the task (of working as representative of the *'A'immah* (Leaders with Divine Authority), *'Alayhim al-Salam*, was left to me, with my father there were promissory notes from those who owed (religious dues). I wrote to him (the Imam) about the case. He wrote back to me, 'Demand from them and make them pay.' People paid what they owed except one man who had signed a promissory note for four hundred Dinars. I went to demand from him what he owed but he procrastinated and took it lightly and his son behaved foolishly. I complained to his father and he said, 'So what!' I then held him by his beard and leg and pulled him toward the center of the house and kicked him many times. His son went out and cried for help from the people of Baghdad saying, 'He is a Qumi, Rafidi (derogatory name for Shi'a) he has killed my father.' A large number of Baghdad people gathered around me. I rode my horse and said, 'Very nice of you people of Baghdad. You support the unjust against a lonely stranger. I am a man from the Sunni sect and he calls me a man from Qum and a Rafidi so that he can destroy my rights.'

"The narrator has said that people then turned against him and they wanted to enter his store. I then calmed them down. The signatory in the promissory note called me and set upon himself a stipulation with an oath that said, 'His wife will be divorced if he does not pay his dues.' My part of the stipulation was to ask the people to leave his place.'"

H 1361, Ch. 125, h 16
Ali has narrated from a number of our people from Ahmad ibn al-Hassan and al-'Ala' ibn Rizq Allah from Badr Ghulam Ahmad ibn al-Hassan who has said the following:
"I began to live in al-Jabal (a town between Baghdad and Azarbayjan) and I did not believe in Imamat (the Divine Authority of al-Mahdi, *'Alayhi al-Salam*, but I loved them (descendents of Amir al-Mu'minin Ali, *'Alayhi al-Salam*). When Yazid ibn 'Abd Allah (a representative of al-Mahdi, *'Alayhi al-Salam*) died he said in his will that I must deliver his Shahri Samand (famous Persian horse), sword and belt to his master (al-Mahdi), *'Alayhi al-Salam*. I was afraid that if I did not give the horse to Edhkutakin (a Turkish official of 'Abbassid rulers) he might harm me. I by myself then evaluated the items at seven hundred Dinars and

no one knew about it. A letter then came from Iraq that said, 'Send us our seven hundred Dinars that are with you for the Shahri (famous Persian horse), the sword and the belt.'"

H 1362, Ch. 125, h 17

Ali has narrated from the one who narrated to him the following:

"A boy was born to me. I wrote to him (al-Mahdi), *'Alayhi al-Salam*, for his permission to give the baby a special bath for the ceremony on the seventh day of his birth. The answer came back and it said, 'Do not do so.' The boy died on the seventh or the eighth day. I then wrote to him about the death of the boy. He wrote back to me, 'He will be succeeded by another and another. Let his name be Ahmad and the name for the one after Ahmad will be Ja'far.' It came to be as he, *'Alayhi al-Salam*, had said.

"The narrator has said, 'Once I made preparation for the journey to Hajj, said farewell to (my) people and I was about to leave. The message came to me that said, 'We do not like it but it is up to you.' I felt depressed and sad and I wrote, 'I am steadfast to obey your commands and listen to your words except that I feel sad for missing Hajj.' He then had signed (a note to me) that said, 'Do not be depressed. You will soon perform Hajj by the will of Allah.' The next year I wrote to ask his permission and the permission came. I then wrote that I had chosen Muhammad ibn al-'Abbass as a ride sharing partner and that I trusted him for his religion and safety. The message that then came said, 'Al-Asadi is a good ride sharing partner. If he will come do not choose anyone else besides him.' Al-Asadi came and I chose him as the ride sharing partner.'"

H 1363, Ch. 125, h 18

Al-Hassan ibn Ali al-'Alawi has said the following:

"Al-Majruh left a certain amount of commodities that were of the dues to the Holy Location with Mirdas ibn Ali. With Mirdas there were already such commodities that Tamim ibn Hanzala had left. A message came to Mirdas and it said, 'Send (to us) the commodities of Tamim and whatever al-Shirazi (Majruh) has left with you.'"

H 1364, Ch. 125, h 19

Ali ibn Muhammad has narrated from al-Hassan ibn 'Isa al-'Uraydi abu Muhammad who has said the following:

"When abu Muhammad, *'Alayhi al-Salam*, passed away a man from Egypt came to Makkah with a certain amount of commodities that were due to the Holy Location (office of the Imam). People expressed different opinions on the issue. Certain persons said, 'Abu Muhammad, *'Alayhi al-Salam*, has passed away and has left no one behind as his successor and Ja'far is his successor.' Others said, 'Abu Muhammad, *'Alayhi al-Salam*, passed away and he has left his successor behind.' A man called abu Talib was sent to the army camp (the city of Surra man Ra'a) with a letter. He went to see Ja'far and ask him for the evidence to prove that he is the successor of abu Muhammad, *'Alayhi al-Salam*, and Ja'far said, 'It is not available at this time.' He then went to the door (of the house where al-Hassan ibn Ali al-Hadi, *'Alayhi al-Salam*, lived) and gave the letter to our people.

The response that came said, 'We present our condolences to you for the death of your friend (the man from Egypt). He has died and he has a will in which he has said that the commodities must be given to the trustworthy person to deal with in a proper manner. His letter was answered.' (When he came back to Makkah it was just the way he was informed by the Holy Location (the office of the Imam, *'Alayhi al-Salam*)."

H 1365, Ch. 125, h 20
Ali ibn Muhammad has said the following:

"From A'ba (name of a town) certain items of property that belonged to the Holy Location (office of the Imam) were delivered to him (the Imam) but a sword that was part of such property was forgotten and remained in A'ba. When the delivery was made a letter came to him that said, 'What about the sword that you forgot and left in A'ba?'"

H 1366, Ch. 125, h 21
Al-Hassan ibn Khafif has narrated from his father who has said the following:

"Imam al-Mahdi, *'Alayhi al-Salam*, had sent certain servants to al-Madina of the Messenger of Allah and among them were two servants. He had written to Khafif to leave with them for Al-Madina. He then left with them and they reached al-Kufa where one of the two servants had consumed alcohol. Before they left al-Kufa a letter came to them from the army camp (city of Surra man Ra'a) that said, 'Send back the servant who has consumed alcohol and remove him from the service.'"

H 1367, Ch. 125, h 22
Ali ibn Muhammad has narrated from Ahmad ibn abu Ali ibn Ghiyath from Ahmad ibn al-Hassan who has said the following:

"Yazid ibn 'Abd Allah has said in his will to send a horse, a sword and certain other properties to the Holy Location (office of the Imam, *'Alayhi al-Salam*). The money from the sale of the horse along with other properties were delivered to the Holy Location but the sword was forgotten. A message then came that said, 'With the items that you sent there was a sword that has not reached us,' or in similar such words, the message was expressed."

H 1368, Ch. 125, h 23
Ali ibn Muhammad has narrated from Muhammad ibn Ali ibn Shadhan al-Naysaburi who has said the following:

"Five hundred Dirhams less twenty were collected with me. I decided to send them but I did not like sending five hundred less twenty. I then added twenty Dirhams to it from my own money and sent them to al-Asadi without any mention of what was therein. The message that came to me said, 'We have recived five hundred Dirhams of which twenty were your money (that you had added to it).'"

H 1369, Ch. 125, h 24
It is narrated from al-Husayn ibn Muhammad al-Ash'ari who has said the following:

"The letters of abu Muhammad, *'Alayhi al-Salam*, would come about the matters related to al-Junayd, who eliminated Faris, abu al-Hassan and others. When he passed away letters about the issues related to abu al-Hassan and his friend continued coming from (Imam al-Mahdi, *'Alayhi al-Salam*) but there was no mention of al-Junayd. I felt depressed about it. (Soon) thereafter, the news of the death of al-Junayd reached us.'"

H 1370, Ch. 125, h 25
Ali ibn Muhammad has narrated from Muhammad ibn Salih who has said the following:
"I had a female slave that had attracted my attention. I wrote to him (Imam al-Mahdi), *'Alayhi al-Salam*, requesting permission to have a child from her. The answer came, 'You may do so but Allah does whatever He wants.' I went to bed with her and she became pregnant. The fetus fell off prematurely and she died.'"

H 1371, Ch. 125, h 26
Ali ibn Muhammad has said the following:
"Ibn al-'Ajami in his will had set aside one third of his properties for the Holy Location (office of the Imam, *'Alayhi al-Salam*) and had written about it to the office of the Imam. Before he took the one third out of his properties he gave a certain amount to his son, abu al-Miqdam, of which no one had any knowledge. He (Imam al-Mahdi), *'Alayhi al-Salam*, wrote to him, 'Where is the property that you took out for abu al-Miqdam?'"

H 1372, Ch. 125, h 27
Ali ibn Muhammad has narrated from abu 'Aqil 'Isa ibn Nasr who has said the following:
"Ali ibn Ziyad al-Saymari wrote a letter to request a shroud. He (al-Mahdi), *'Alayhi al-Salam*, wrote back to him, 'You will need it in the year eighty.' He died in the year eighty and the shroud was sent to him a few days before his death."

H 1373, Ch. 125, h 28
Ali ibn Muhammad has narrated from Muhammad ibn Harun ibn 'Imran al-Hamadani who has said the following:
"I owed five hundred Dinars to the Holy Location (office of Imam al-Mahdi, *'Alayhi al-Salam*). I felt extremely depressed about it. I said to myself, 'The stores that I have bought were for five hundred thirty Dinars. I will set them aside for the Holy Location (office of Imam al-Mahdi, *'Alayhi al-Salam*).' However I had not said anything in words. He wrote to Muhammad ibn Ja'far, 'Take possession of the stores from Muhammad ibn Harun as payment for the five hundred Dinars that he owed us.'"

H 1374, Ch. 125, h 29
Ali ibn Muhammad has said the following:
"Ja'far (the impostor) sold certain items. Of the items that he sold was a Ja'fari (descendents of Ja'far ibn abu Talib) female child that they (family of abu Muhammad, *'Alayhi al-Salam*) had brought up. A certain 'Alawi person informed the buyer all about the female child and the buyer said, 'I will be glad to return her if someone will pay me what I have paid.' He then informed the people of the Holy Location (office of Imam al-Mahdi, *'Alayhi al-Salam*). They sent forty one Dinars to the slave trader and asked him to return her to her people.'"

H 1375, Ch. 125, h 30
Al-Husayn ibn al-Hassan al-'Alawi has said the following:

"A man who was an informer for Ruz Hassani with another man with him once said to Ruz, 'This man (al-Mahdi), *'Alayhi al-Salam*, is out there. Money is collected for him. He has representatives in many places. They mentioned his representatives by their names in different areas. This news reached 'Ubayd Allah ibn Sulayman, the Vizier. The Vizier decided to arrest these representatives. The Sultan said, 'Find out. Where is this man? This is a serious matter.' 'Ubayd Allah ibn Sulayman then said, 'We will arrest the representatives, the agents.' The Sultan said, 'No, you must send your undercover agents who should pose to them as devotees ready to pay their dues to their Imam. If they accept the funds then arrest them.' The narrator has said that a message came out from the Holy Location (office of Imam al-Mahdi, *'Alayhi al-Salam*) to inform all the representatives not to accept any dues from anyone, deny knowing anything about the Imam and say that they have no information. A man who was an undercover agent came to Muhammad ibn Ahmad whom he did not know. The undercover agent spoke to him privately and said, 'I have certain funds with me and I want them to be delivered to the Holy Location (office of Imam al-Mahdi, *'Alayhi al-Salam*).' Muhammad said to him, 'You have made a mistake. I do not know anything about it.' He insisted and tried to show kindness and Muhammad denied having any knowledge of it. The spies spread to all places but the representatives would refuse to accept any funds because of the message that was delivered to them beforehand."

H 1376, Ch. 125, h 31
Ali ibn Muhammad has said the following:

"A prohibition to visit the Quryash cemetery and al-Hira (Karbala) came out of the Holy Location (office of Imam al-Mahdi, *'Alayhi al-Salam*). After a few months the Vizier (abu al-Fath Ja'far ibn Furat) summoned al-Baqtia, and said to him, 'Meet the clan of banu Furat and al-Bursiyin and tell them not to visit Quraysh cemetery; the Sultan has decided to have all those who visit these places be arrested.'"

Chapter 126 - The Statements and the Explicit Texts that Confirm Leadership with Divine Authority of the Twelve Imam (Leaders with Divine Authority), *'Alayhim al-Salam*

H 1377, Ch. 126, h 1
A number of our people have narrated from Ahmad ibn Muhammad al-Barqi from abu Hashim Dawud ibn al-Qasim al-Ja'fari from abu Ja'far al-Thani who has said the following:

"Once Amir al-Mu'minin Ali came, with al-Hassan ibn Ali, *'Alayhim al-Salam*, and he was holding the hand of Salman for support. He entered the sacred Mosque (in Makkah) and sat down. Then a handsome and well-dressed man came. He offered the greeting of peace to Amir al-Mu'minin Ali, *'Alayhi al-Salam*, who answered his greetings likewise and he sat down. He then said, 'I will ask you, O Amir al-Mu'minin, three questions. If you answer them I then acknowledge that the people who have acted against you in the matters of leadership after the Holy Prophet, *'Alayhi al-Salam*, have acted against their own selves. Their actions have taken away peace from them in this world as well in the next life. Otherwise (if you cannot answer) you and those people will be the same.'

"Amir al-Mu'minin Ali, *'Alayhi al-Salam*, said, 'Ask whatever you like.' He said, 'Tell me about the man who sleeps. Where does his spirit go? Tell me about the man, how he remembers and forgets? Tell me about the man, how do his children become similar to the aunts and uncles?'

"Amir al-Mu'minin Ali turned to al-Hassan, *'Alayhi al-Salam*, and said, 'O abu Muhammad, answer him.' Al-Hassan, *'Alayhi al-Salam*, answered his questions. The man then said, 'I testify that no one deserves to be worshipped and obeyed besides Allah and I continue to testify to this fact. I testify that Muhammad is the Messenger of Allah and I continue to testify to this fact. I testify that you are the executor of the will of the Messenger of Allah and that you are the person in charge of this task (Leadership with Divine Authority) with His authorization.' He pointed out to Amir al-Mu'minin, *'Alayhi al-Salam*, with his hand. He then said, 'I continue to testify to this fact. I testify that you are the executor of his (Amir al-Mu'minin's will and the person in charge of this task (Leadership with Divine Authority) by His authorization after him (Amir al-Mu'minin, *'Alayhi al-Salam*).'

"He pointed out with his hand to al-Hassan, *'Alayhi al-Salam*. Then he said, 'I continue to testify to this fact. I testify that al-Husayn ibn Ali, *'Alayhi al-Salam*, will be the executor of the will of his brother and the person in charge of this task (Leadership with Divine Authority) with His authorization after him. I testify in support of Ali ibn al-Husayn, *'Alayhi al-Salam*, that he will be the person in charge of the task of al-Husayn, *'Alayhi al-Salam*, after him.

"I testify that Muhammad ibn Ali will be the person in charge of the task of Ali ibn al-Husayn, *'Alayhi al-Salam*, after him.

"I testify that Ja'far ibn Muhammad, *'Alayhi al-Salam*, will be the person in charge of the task of Muhammad ibn Ali, *'Alayhim al-Salam*.

"I testify that Musa ibn Ja'far, *'Alayhi al-Salam*, will be the person in charge of the task of Ja'far ibn Muhammad after him.

"I testify that Ali ibn Musa, *'Alayhi al-Salam*, will be the person in charge of the task of Musa ibn Ja'far, *'Alayhi al-Salam*.

"I testify that Muhammad ibn Ali, *'Alayhi al-Salam*, will be the person in charge of the task of Ali ibn Musa, *'Alayhi al-Salam*, after him.

"I testify that Ali ibn Muhammad, *'Alayhi al-Salam*, will be the person in charge of the task of Muhammad ibn Ali, *'Alayhi al-Salam*, after him.

"I testify that al-Hassan ibn Ali, *'Alayhim al-Salam*, will be the person in charge of the task of Ali ibn Muhammad, *'Alayhim al-Salam*, after him.

"I testify in support of a man from the children of al-Hassan, *'Alayhi al-Salam,* who will not be mentioned by his Kunya (father or son of so and so) or his name until he will rise with Divine Authority and power to fill the earth with justice after its being filled with injustice.

"I offer you my greeting of peace O Amir al-Mu'minin, *'Alayhi al-Salam,* and pray to Allah to grant you blessings and holiness.' He then stood up and left.

"Amir al-Mu'minin, *'Alayhi al-Salam,* said, 'O abu Muhammad, *'Alayhi al-Salam,* follow him to look where he went.' Al-Hassan ibn Ali, *'Alayhi al-Salam,* went outside to find out (and came back) and said, 'As soon as he stepped out of the Mosque I could not figure out in which direction of the earth of Allah did he disappear. Thus I have returned to Amir al-Mu'minin, *'Alayhi al-Salam,* and informed him (what I saw).' He said, 'O abu Muhammad, do you know him?' I (al-Hassan ibn Ali, *'Alayhi al-Salam*) said, 'Allah, the Messenger of Allah and Amir al-Mu'minin, *'Alayhi al-Salam,* know best.' He said, 'He was al-Khidr, peace be up on him.'"

H 1378, Ch. 126, h 2
Also Muhammad ibn Yahya has narrated from Muhammad ibn al-Hassan al-Saffar from Ahmad ibn abu 'Abd Allah from abu Hashim a similar *Hadith:*
"Muhammad ibn Yahya has said, 'I said to Muhammad ibn al-Hassan, 'O abu Ja'far I wish this was narrated through a chain of narrators other then Ahmad ibn 'Abd Allah.' He said, 'He, Ahmad ibn 'Abd Allah, had narrated this to me ten years before the confusion.'"

Note: Ahmad ibn abu 'Abd Allah is Ahmad ibn Khalid Barqi who is one of the trusted narrators of *Hadith.* He has written many books of which only "Mahasin" is available. He narrated from weak narrators also for which reason Ahmad ibn Muhammad ibn 'Isa sent him away from Qum. However, later they made peace and apologized. "Confusion" is a hint of his very old age or to his sending him out of Qum.

H 1379, Ch. 126, h 3
Muhammad ibn Yahya and Muhammad ibn 'Abd Allah have narrated from 'Abd Allah ibn Ja'far from al-Hassan ibn Zarif and Ali ibn Muhammad from Salih ibn abu Hammad from Bakr ibn Salih from 'Abd al-Rahman ibn Salim from abu Basir from abu 'Abd Allah, *'Alayhi al-Salam,* who has said the following:
"Abu 'Abd Allah, *'Alayhi al-Salam,* has said, 'Once, my father said to Jabir ibn 'Abd Allah al-Ansari, 'I need your help in a certain issue. When do you think it will be convenient for you that we meet privately and I will ask you about it?' He (Jabir) said, 'Whenever you like it will be alright for me.' One day when they met each other he, *'Alayhi al-Salam,* said, 'O Jabir, tell me about the tablet that you saw in the hand of my great-great-great grandmother, Fatimah, *'Alayha al-Salam,* daughter of the Messenger of Allah. Tell me of what she said to you about the tablet and the writing on it?'

"Jabir then said, 'I ask Allah to testify (to the truth of what I experienced that day). Once I went to see your great-great-great grandmother, Fatimah, *'Alayha al-Salam*, in the lifetime of the Messenger of Allah. I congratulated her for the birth of al-Husayn, *'Alayhi al-Salam*, and I saw in her hand a green tablet that I think was made of Emerald (precious gem). I saw on it a white writing that was shining like the color of sun.

"I then said to her, 'May Allah keep my soul and the souls of my parents in service for your cause, O daughter of the Messenger of Allah, what is this tablet?' She said, 'This is a tablet that Allah has given as a gift to His Messenger. In it there is the name of my father, the name of my husband, the names of my two sons and the names of the executors of the wills of my (special) descendents. My father gave it to me as a gift and glad news.'

"Jabir then said, 'Your great-great-great grandmother, *'Alayhi al-Salam*, then gave the tablet to me. I read it and made a copy of it.' My father then said, 'O Jabir can you show that copy (that you made from the tablet) to me?' He said, 'Yes, I can show it to you.' My father went with him to his house and he brought to light a tablet of parchment. He then said, 'O Jabir, look carefully at your writing to see how I read it for you.' Jabir then kept looking at his handwriting while my father read and his reading was exactly letter by letter the same as what Jabir had in his copy. Jabir then said, 'I ask Allah to testify to the truth of my words that this is what I saw was written on the tablet:

(I begin) in the Name of Allah, the Beneficent, the Merciful.

This is a document from Allah, the Most Majestic, the Most Wise, for Muhammad, His Prophet, *'Alayhi al-Salam*, His light, His ambassador, His barrier (Hijab) and His guide (for people). The trusted Spirit has brought it from the Lord of the worlds. O Muhammad, acknowledge the greatness of My names and pay thanks for My bounties. Do not hide My favors. I Am Allah and no one deserves to be worshipped and obeyed besides Me. I break down the transgressors and grant wealth to the oppressed. I Am the One Who has established the religion. I Am Allah. No one deserves to be worshipped and obeyed besides Me. Whoever expects to receive any distinction from someone other than Me or have fear of the justice of someone other Me I will cause him to suffer a torment the like of which I will cause no one else of the creatures of the worlds to suffer. Worship only Me and place your trust only in Me.

"I have not sent any prophet without, upon the completion of his days, appointing the executor of his will. I have given preference to you over the prophets and I have given preference to the executor of your will over the executors of the wills (of the other prophets). I have granted you honor through your two brave grandsons, al-Hassan and al-Husayn, *'Alayhim al-Salam*. I have made al-Hassan, *'Alayhi al-Salam*, to be the treasurer of My knowledge after the completion of the time of his father. I have made al-Husayn,

'*Alayhi al-Salam*, to be the keeper of My revelation *Wahy* (inspiration). I have granted him nobility through martyrdom and made his end triumphant. He will be the best of the martyrs and of the highest degree in the rank of the martyrs. I have kept My perfect word with him and My extremely clear authority and proof available for him. Through his descendent I will give good rewards to people or cause them to suffer torments. The first of them will be Ali (ibn al-Husayn), master of the worshippers, and the beauty of My friends of the past. Then will be his son who will be very similar to his grandfather, the praised one, Muhammad al-Baqir, the one very deeply founded in My knowledge and the source and mine of My wisdom. Those who have doubts about Ja'far will soon be destroyed. Whoever rejects him will be like one who rejects Me. The true words have already come from Me that I will dignify the position of Ja'far and will grant him joy and happiness for his followers, supporters and friends.

"After him Musa will live at the time of a blind, confusing and dark mischief. (He will live among the people) because the system of obedience to Me does not break down and my authority (proof of My existence) does not remain obscure. The thirst (for knowledge and guidance) of My friends will be quenched with sufficient measures. Whoever rejects any one of them has rejected my favors. Whoever changes my signs and verses of my book has accused Me with lies.

"Woe is to those who fabricate lies and reject (the truth) after the completion of the time of Musa, My servant, My beloved, My chosen one about Ali (al-Rida). (Ali al-Rida) who is My *wali* (the one who possesses Divine Authority), My supporter, the one on whom I will place the task of prophet-hood and examine how he will deal with it. An arrogant devil will murder him. He will be buried in the city built by the virtuous servant (of Allah) next to the worst of My creatures. The words of truth have already been established that I will grant him joy and happiness with the birth of his son, Muhammad, his successor and the heir of his knowledge. He is the source and fountainhead of My knowledge, the right place for My secrets and My authority over My creatures. Whoever believes in him I will make paradise his dwelling and will grant him the ability to intercede for seventy people from his family of whom everyone may have become subject to hell-fire.

"I will make the end for his son, Ali, to arrive at salvation. Ali is My *wali* (the one who possesses Divine Authority), My supporter, the testimony in My creatures and My trustee in My revelation. From him I will make to come out a preacher to My way and a treasure of My Knowledge, al-Hassan. I will complete it with his son (M.H.M.D.), a blessing for the worlds. One will be able to find in him the perfection of Musa (Moses), the beauty of Jesus and the patience of Ayyub. My friends in his time will become weak. Their heads will be sent as gifts like the heads of the Turks and Daylam. They will be murdered and burned. They will live in fear, frightened and fearful. The earth will be stained with their blood and wailing and lamentations will become widepread in their women. These will possess My authority and through them I will remove the blind and dark mischief. Through them I will remove uncertainties, sufferings and shackles. These are the ones upon whom the blessings and forgiveness of their Lord descend and they are the ones who provide guidance.'"

"'Abd al-Rahman ibn Salim has said that abu Basir said, 'Even if you hear no other *Hadith* expect this, it will be enough for you. Protect it against everyone except the deserving people.'"

H 1380, Ch. 126, h 4

Ali ibn Ibrahim has narrated from his father from Hammad ibn 'Isa from Ibrahim ibn 'Umar al-Yamani from Aban ibn abu 'Ayyash from Sulaym ibn Qays and Muhammad ibn Yahya from Ahmad ibn Muhammad from ibn abu 'Umayr from 'Umar ibn 'Udhayna and Ali ibn Muhammad from Ahmad ibn Hilal from ibn abu 'Umayr from 'Umar ibn 'Udhayna from Aban ibn abu 'Ayyash from Sulaym ibn Qays who has said the following:

"I heard 'Abd Allah ibn Ja'far al-Tayyar say, 'Once al-Hassan, al-Husayn, *'Alayhim al-Salam*, 'Abd Allah ibn 'Abbass, 'Umar ibn 'Umm Salama and 'Usama ibn Zayd and I were in the court of Mu'awiya. A conversation started between Mu'awiya and I. I said to Mu'awiya, 'I heard the Messenger of Allah say, "I have more authority over the believers' souls than they themselves do. Then my brother Ali ibn abu Talib, *'Alayhi al-Salam*, will have more authority over the believers' souls than they themselves will have. When Ali, *'Alayhi al-Salam*, will become a martyr al-Hassan ibn Ali will have more authority over the believers' souls than they themselves will have. Thereafter my son al-Husayn after him (al-Hassan) will have more authority over the believers' souls than they themselves will have. When he will become a martyr, his son Ali ibn al-Husayn after him (al-Husayn) will have more authority over the believers' souls than they themselves will have. O Ali, you will see him (Ali ibn al-Husayn). Thereafter his son Muhammad ibn Ali will have more authority over the believers' souls than they themselves will have. O al-Husayn, you will see him. Then the twelve will complete the number of *'A'immah* (Leaders with Divine Authority). Nine will be of the descendents of al-Husayn.'

"'Abd Allah ibn Ja'far said, 'I asked al-Hassan, al-Husayn, *'Alayhim al-Salam*, 'Abd Allah, ibn 'Abbass, 'Umar ibn 'Umm Salama and 'Usama ibn Zayd to bear witness. They all bore witness for me before Mu'awiya.'

"Sulaym ibn Qays has said, 'I heard such *Hadith* from Salman, abu Dhar and al-Miqdad who said that they heard such *Hadith* from the Messenger of Allah.'"

H 1381, Ch. 126, h 5

A number of our people have narrated from Ahmad ibn Muhammad ibn Khalid his father from 'Abd Allah ibn al-Qasim from Hanan ibn al-Sarraj from Dawud ibn Sulayman al-Kisa'i from abu al-Tufayl who has said the following:

"I was present in the funeral procession of abu Bakr the day it took place. I was also present when 'Umar took oath of allegiance and Ali, *'Alayhi al-Salam*, was sitting on the side. A young, handsome, well-dressed Jewish boy came. He was a descendent of Harun and he stood (on a place that was) above 'Umar and asked, 'O Amir al-Mu'minin, are you the most knowledgeable person in this nation in their book and the commands of their prophet?'

"The narrator has said that 'Umar kept his head down. He then said, 'I meant you.' He repeated his words. 'Umar said, 'Why is that?' He said, 'I have doubts about my religion and I have come to you for guidance.' He ('Umar) said, 'go to this young man.' He said, 'Who is this young man?' He said, 'He is Ali ibn abu Talib, *'Alayhi al-Salam*, the cousin of the Messenger of Allah and he is the father of al-Hassan and al-Husayn, *'Alayhim al-Salam*, the grandsons of the Messenger of Allah and he is the husband of *Fatimah, 'Alayha al-Salam*, daughter of the Messenger of Allah.'

"The young Jewish man then went to Ali, *'Alayhi al-Salam*, and said, 'Are you such a person?' He said, 'Yes, I am such a person.' He said, 'I want to ask you about three and three and one.' The narrator has said that Amir al-Mu'minin Ali, *'Alayhi al-Salam*, then smiled a different smile and said, 'O Haruni, what prevents you from saying seven?' He said, 'I ask about three. If you answer me then I will ask you about the rest. If you cannot answer then I will assume that there are no scholars among you.'

"Ali, *'Alayhi al-Salam*, said, 'I swear you to the Lord in whom you believe, if I answer whatever you will ask, will you then leave your religion and accept our religion?' He said, 'I have come for no other reason but that.' Ali, *'Alayhi al-Salam*, said, 'Ask your questions.' He said, 'Tell me about the first drop of blood that was spilled on earth, what drop was that? Tell me about the first fountain that gushed out of earth, which one was it? Tell me about the first thing that moved on earth, what was that?' Amir al-Mu'minin Ali, *'Alayhi al-Salam*, answered him. He then said, 'Tell me about the other three. Tell me about Muhammad, *'Alayhi al-Salam*. How many Imam (Leaders with Divine Authority) who possess the quality of justice will be there as his successors? In which paradise will he be? Who will be with him in paradise?' He said, 'O Haruni, there will be twelve just Imam (Leader with Divine Authority) as successors of Muhammad, *'Alayhi al-Salam*. No one's betrayal will harm them and they will not feel frightened because of people's opposition to them. In the matters of religion they will be stronger than the firm mountains on earth. In paradise Muhammad will dwell with the twelve Imam who possess the noble quality of justice.' He then said, 'You have spoken the truth by Allah, besides whom no one deserves to be worshipped and obeyed. I find them in the book of my father Harun. He has written it in his own handwriting. My uncle Moses had dictated to him.' He then said, 'Tell me about the "one." Tell me about the executor of the will of Muhammad, *'Alayhi al-Salam*. For how long will he live after him? Will he die or will he be killed?' He (Ali), *'Alayhi al-Salam*, said, 'O Haruni, he will live after him thirty years, not one day less and not one day more. Then he will be hit with an strike here, meaning over his head, and then this (beard) will be stained with this (blood from his head).'

"The Jewish man screamed loudly and broke his Kustija (a Jewish religious object) and he said, 'I testify that no one deserves to be worshipped and obeyed besides Allah Who is One and has no partner and I testify that Muhammad, *'Alayhi al-Salam*, is His servant and His Messenger and that you are the executor of his will. You must be above all and no one must be above you. Your greatness must be acknowledged and you must not be weakened.' The narrator has said that Ali, *'Alayhi al-Salam*, then took him to his house and taught him the Divine guidance."

H 1382, Ch. 126, h 6
Muhammad ibn Yahya has narrated from Muhammad ibn Ahmad from Muhammad ibn al-Husayn from abu Sa'id al-'Usfuriy from 'Amr ibn Thabit from abu Hamza who has said the following:

"I heard Ali ibn al-Husayn, *'Alayhi al-Salam*, say, 'Allah created Muhammad, Ali and the remaining eleven *'A'immah* (Leaders with Divine Authority) from his descendents out of the light of His greatness. He then placed them as figures in the brightness of His light where they worshipped Him before the creation of the creatures. They would speak of the Glory of Allah and of His Holiness. They are the *'A'immah* (Leaders with Divine Authority) from descendents of the Messenger of Allah.'"

H 1383, Ch. 126, h 7
Muhammad ibn Yahya has narrated from 'Abd Allah ibn Muhammad al-Khashshab from ibn Sama'a from Ali ibn al-Hassan ibn Ribat from ibn 'Udhayna from Zurara who has said the following:

"I heard abu Ja'far, *'Alayhi al-Salam*, say, 'The twelve Imam (Leaders with Divine Authority) all from the family of Muhammad, *'Alayhi al-Salam*, are *Muhaddath* (the ones to whom angels speak). They all are from the descendents of the Messenger of Allah and the descendents of Ali, *'Alayhi al-Salam*. The Messenger of Allah and Ali, *'Alayhi al-Salam*, are their ancestors.'

"Ali ibn Rashid has said that Ali ibn al-Husayn, *'Alayhi al-Salam*, had a brother from his (foster mother, not his real mother, the Persian princess) who did not believe in the *Hadith*. He expressed denial. The Imam, abu Ja'far, *'Alayhi al-Salam*, said to him loudly, "The son of your mother is one of them."

H 1384, Ch. 126, h 8
Muhammad ibn Yahya has narrated from Muhammad ibn al-Husayn from Mas'ada ibn Ziyad from abu 'Abd Allah and Muhammad ibn al-Husayn from Ibrahim from ibn abu Yahya al-Madyani from abu Harun al-'Abdi from abu Sa'id al-Khudriy who has said the following:

"I was (in the city of al-Madina) when abu Bakr was no more and he had appointed 'Umar as his successor. Once, one of the great Jewish men of Yathrib came to 'Umar. The Jewish people in the city of al-Madina thought that he, 'Umar, was the most knowledgeable person of his time. He came to 'Umar and said, 'O 'Umar, I have come to accept Islam if you can answer what I will ask. Are you the most knowledgeable person among the companions of Muhammad, *'Alayhi al-Salam*, in the matters of the book, the *Sunnah* (his traditions) and all that I want to ask from you?'

"The narrator has said that 'Umar than said to him, 'I am not the one you are looking for. However, I can guide you to the one who is the most knowledgeable person in our nation in the matters of the book, the *Sunnah* (traditions of the Holy Prophet, *'Alayhi al-Salam*) and all that you would like to ask.' He pointed out Ali, *'Alayhi al-Salam*. The Jewish man then said, 'If what you say is true then why have you taken the oath of allegiance from people? The most knowledgeable among you is that man.' 'Umar then treated him harshly. The Jewish man went to

Ali, *'Alayhi al-Salam*, and said, 'Are you as such as 'Umar has said?' He (Ali, *'Alayhi al-Salam*) then asked, 'What has 'Umar said?' He then informed him of what 'Umar had said. The Jewish man said, 'If you are as he has said you are, I would like to ask you certain questions to know if anyone of you knows the answer so I will know that your claim is true that you are the best and the most truthful among the nations. In such case I will accept your religion, Islam.

"Amir al-Mu'minin, *'Alayhi al-Salam*, said, 'Yes, I am as 'Umar has said I am. Ask whatever you want to ask. I will give the answer by the will of Allah.' He said, 'Tell me about three and three and one.' Ali, *'Alayhi al-Salam*, said, 'O Jewish man, why do you not say, 'Tell me about seven?' The Jewish man then said, 'If you can tell me the answer to the three then I will ask you other questions, otherwise, I will abstain. If you provide me the answer to these seven you then are the most knowledgeable person on earth, the best of them and have more authority over the people than they themselves do.' He then said, 'Ask your questions O Jewish man.' He said, 'Tell me about the first stone that was placed on the face of earth, the first tree that was planted on earth and the first water fountain that gushed out of earth.'

"Amir al-Mu'minin, *'Alayhi al-Salam*, answered his questions. The Jewish man then said to him, 'Tell me how many Imam (Leaders with Divine Authority) will this nation have? Tell me about your Prophet: where will be his place in paradise and who will be with him therein?'

"Amir al-Mu'minin, *'Alayhi al-Salam*, said, 'This nation will have twelve *'A'immah*. All of them will be from the descendents of the Holy Prophet, *'Alayhi al-Salam*, of this nation. They will be from my descendents. The place of our Holy Prophet, *'Alayhi al-Salam*, in paradise will be the best and holiest of them in Eden. Those who will be with him therein in his dwelling will be these twelve people from his descendents. Their mother and grandmother and the mother of their mother and their descendents will live with them therein. No one else will live therein as their partner.'"

H 1385, Ch. 126, h 9
Muhammad ibn Yahya has narrated from Muhammad ibn al-Husayn from ibn Muhbub from abu al-Jarud from abu Ja'far from Jabir ibn 'Abd Allah al-Ansari who has said the following:
"Once I went to see Fatimah, *'Alayha al-Salam*, daughter of the Holy Prophet, *'Alayhi al-Salam*, and I saw with her a tablet in which the names of the executors of the wills (of Leaders with Divine Authority) from her descendents were written. I then counted them to twelve. The last one's name was *al-Qa'im* (the one who will rise with Divine Authority and power). The name of three of them was Muhammad and the name of another three was Ali."

H 1386, Ch. 126, h 10
Ali ibn Ibrahim has narrated from Muhammad ibn 'Isa ibn 'Ubayd from Muhammad ibn al-Fudayl from abu Hamza from abu Ja'far, *'Alayhi al-Salam*, who has said the following:
"Allah sent Muhammad, *'Alayhi al-Salam*, to all Jinn and man and appointed twelve executors of the will after him. Of these people are those who have left this

world and there are those who will have to complete their task. All the executors of the wills (of the prophets) experienced certain traditions, *Sunnah*. The executors of the will after Muhammad, *'Alayhi al-Salam*, experienced the traditions, *Sunnah*, of the executor of the will of Jesus were twelve in number. Amir al-Mu'minin, *'Alayhi al-Salam*, experienced the tradition of Jesus."

H 1387, Ch. 125, h 11

Muhammad ibn Yahya has narrated from Ahmad ibn Muhammad ibn 'Isa and Muhammad ibn abu 'Abd Allah and Muhammad ibn al-Husayn from Sahl ibn Ziyad all from al-Hassan ibn al-'Abbass ibn al-Jarish from abu Ja'far al-Thani, *'Alayhi al-Salam*, who has said the following:

"Amir al-Mu'minin Ali, *'Alayhi al-Salam*, said to ibn 'Abbass, 'Layla al-Qadr (the night of destiny) comes every year and in that night the command for the whole year descends down. To receive that command are the Leaders with Divine Authority after the Messenger of Allah.'

"Ibn 'Abbass then asked, 'Who are they?' He said, 'I and the eleven persons from my descendents who all are *'A'immah* (Leaders with Divine Authority), and *Muhaddathun*, such persons to whom angels speak.'"

H 1388, Ch. 126, h 12

Through the same chain of narrators the following is narrated:

"The Messenger of Allah once said to his companions, 'You must believe in the Layla al-Qadr (night of destiny). It is Ali ibn abu Talib, *'Alayhi al-Salam*, and his eleven descendents after me.'"

H 1389, Ch. 126, h 13

Through the same chain of narrators the following is narrated:

"Amir al-Mu'minin Ali, *'Alayhi al-Salam*, one day said to abu Bakr, 'Do not think of those slain for the cause of Allah as dead. "They are alive with their Lord and receive sustenance from Him." (3:169) I testify that Muhammad, the Messenger of Allah, died as a martyr. He, by Allah, comes to you and do not have any doubts when he will come to you. Satan cannot appear in his disguise." Ali, *'Alayhi al-Salam*, took the hand of abu Bakr and showed the Holy Prophet, *'Alayhi al-Salam*, to him, who said, 'O abu Bakr, believe in Ali, *'Alayhi al-Salam*, and in the eleven *'A'immah* (Leaders with Divine Authority) from his descendents. They are all like me except prophet-hood. Repent before Allah because of what you are involved in. You have no right in it.'

"The narrator has said that then he, *'Alayhi al-Salam*, went and was not seen around."

H 1390, Ch. 126, h 14

Abu Ali al-Ash'ari has narrated from 'Ubayd Allah from al-Hassan ibn Musa al-Khashshab from Ali ibn Sama'a from Ali ibn al-Husayn ibn Ribat from 'Udhayna from Zurara who has said the following:

"I heard abu Ja'far say, 'There will be twelve *'A'immah* (Leaders with Divine Authority) from the family of Muhammad and they all will be *Muhaddathun*, persons to whom angels speak. They will be of the descendents of the Messenger of Allah and Ali ibn abu Talib, *'Alayhi al-Salam*. The Messenger of Allah and Ali are their ancestors.'"

H 1391, Ch. 126, h 15

Ali ibn Ibrahim has narrated from ibn abu 'Umayr from Sa'id ibn Ghazwan from abu Basir who has said the following:

"Abu Ja'far, *'Alayhi al-Salam*, has said, 'After al-Husayn ibn Ali, *'Alayhi al-Salam*, there will be nine *'A'immah* (Leaders with Divine Authority). The ninth of them will be *al-Qa'im* (the one who will rise with Divine Authority and power).'"

H 1392, Ch. 126, h 16

Al-Husayn ibn Muhammad has narrated from Mu'alla ibn Muhammad from al-Washsha' from Aban from Zurara who has said the following:

"I heard abu Ja'far, *'Alayhi al-Salam*, say, 'We are twelve *'A'immah* (Leaders with Divine Authority). Al-Hassan and al-Husayn, *'Alayhim al-Salam*, are of them. Thereafter *'A'immah* (Leaders with Divine Authority) are from the descendents of al-Husayn.'"

H 1393, Ch. 126, h 17

Muhammad ibn Yahya has narrated from Muhammad ibn Ahmad from Muhammad ibn al-Husayn from Sa'id al-'Usfuriy from 'Amran ibn Thabit from abu al-Jarud from abu Ja'far, *'Alayhi al-Salam*, who has said the following:

"The Messenger of Allah has said, 'I and twelve persons from my descendents and you, O Ali, are the safety anchor of the earth, that is, the pillars thereof and its ropes. Through us Allah has secured the earth from devouring the inhabitants. If all the twelve persons from my family will no longer be there, the earth will devour her inhabitants without delay.'"

H 1394, Ch. 126, h 18

Through the same chain of narrators it is narrated from abu Sa'id in a *marfu'* manner from abu Ja'far, *'Alayhi al-Salam*, who has said the following:

"The Messenger of Allah has said, 'From my descendents there will be twelve noble supervisors, who are *Muhaddathun*, persons to whom angels speak, and very intelligent. The last of them will be *al-Qa'im* (the one who will rise with Divine Authority and power and with truth) who will fill the earth with justice after being filled with injustice.'"

H 1395, Ch. 126, h 19

Ali ibn Muhammad and Muhammad ibn al-Hassan have narrated from Sahl ibn Ziyad from Muhammad ibn al-Hassan ibn Shammun from 'Abd Allah ibn 'Abd al-Rahman al-Asamm from Karram who has said the following:

"Once I took an oath with myself that I would not eat any food during the day until the rise of *al-Qa'im* (the rise of al-Mahdi with Divine Authority and power). I then went to see abu 'Abd Allah, *'Alayhi al-Salam*.

"The narrator has said, 'A man from your Shi'a (followers) has imposed on himself an oath not to eat any food during the day until the rise of *al-Qa'im* from the family of Muhammad, *'Alayhi al-Salam*.'

"The Imam said, 'Fast, then, O Karram. Do not fast on the two 'Id days and the three days of Tashriq (11,12,13) of the month of Dhi al-Hajj. Also do not fast when you are on a journey or when you will have an illness. It is because when al-Husayn, *'Alayhi al-Salam*, was murdered, the heavens and the earth and all the angels in them mourned and lamented before the Lord. They said, "Lord, grant us permission to destroy the creatures and purge the earth from them because of their disregard of Your reverence and their murdering Your chosen people." Allah then inspired them, "My angels, My heavens and My earth be patient and relieved." He then removed a barrier of the barriers and there appeared Muhammad and the twelve executors of his will. He held the hand of so and so (*al-Qa'im*, the one who will rise with Divine Authority and power) from among them. He (the Lord) said, "O My angels, My heavens and My earth through this I will grant support for this (cause of al-Husayn)." He said it three times.'"

H 1396, Ch. 126, h 20

Muhammad ibn Yahya and Ahmad ibn Muhammad have narrated from Muhammad ibn al-Husayn from abu Talib from 'Uthman ibn 'Isa from Sama'a ibn Mihran who has said the following:

"Once abu Basir, Muhammad ibn 'Imran, the slave of abu Ja'far, *'Alayhi al-Salam*, and I were in his (Imam's) house in Makkah. Muhammad ibn 'Imran said, 'I have heard abu 'Abd Allah, *'Alayhi al-Salam*, say, "We, all twelve of us, are *Muhaddath* (the ones to whom angels speak)." Abu Basir then said, 'Did you hear abu 'Abd Allah, *'Alayhi al-Salam*, say so?' He made him to swear once or twice that he has heard so. Abu Basir then said, 'However, I have heard it from abu Ja'far, *'Alayhi al-Salam*.'"

Chapter 127 - What Applies to a Man May Apply to His Descendents Also. (If a man is promised to find something with his son but it is found in his sons or grandsons then it still is the same promise.)

H 1397, Ch. 127, h 1

Muhammad ibn Yahya has narrated from Ahmad ibn Muhammad and Ali ibn Ibrahim from his father both from ibn Mahbub from ibn Ri'ab from abu Basir from abu 'Abd Allah, *'Alayhi al-Salam*, who has said the following:

"Allah sent revelation to 'Imran saying, 'I will grant you a perfect and holy son who can cure the blind and the lepers and bring the dead back to life by My permission and I make him a messenger to the Israelites.' 'Imran then told it all to his wife, Hanna, mother of Mary. When she conceived with the baby Mary, she believed it would be the birth of baby boy. When she gave birth to Mary she said, 'Lord, I have given birth to a girl and boys are not like girls. A girl can not be a messenger.' Allah, the Most Majestic, the Most Gracious, said, 'Allah knows to whom you have given birth.' Allah, the Most High, granted Jesus to Mary. He was the boy promised to 'Imran. He promised Jesus to 'Imran. When we say something about a man from us and that thing is found in his sons or grandsons then you must not deny it.'"

H 1398, Ch. 127, h 2

Muhammad ibn 'Isma'il has narrated from al-Fadl ibn Shadhan from Hammad ibn 'Isa from Ibrahim ibn 'Umar al-Yamani from abu 'Abd Allah, *'Alayhi al-Salam*, who has said the following:

"Abu 'Abd Allah, *'Alayhi al-Salam*, has said, 'If we say something about a man and it is not found in him but it is found in his son or his grandson, you must not reject it. It is because Allah does what he wants.'"

H 1399, Ch. 127, h 3

Al-Husayn ibn Muhammad has narrated from Mu'alla ibn Muhammad from al-Washsha' from Ahmad ibn 'A'idh from abu Khadija who has said the following:

"I heard abu 'Abd Allah, *'Alayhi al-Salam*, say, 'Sometimes a man is considered as practicing justice or acting unjustly and such acts are ascribed to him even if he may not have committed them but such acts are found in his son or his grandson after him. Therefore, he, the son or grandson is the one, in reality (who has, in fact, practiced such acts).'"

Chapter 128 - 'A'immah (Leaders with Divine Authority), *'Alayhim al-Salam* Rise for and With Authority of Allah, the Most High, and Guide to Allah

H 1400, Ch. 128, h 1

A number of our people have narrated from Ahmad ibn Muhammad ibn 'Isa from Ali ibn al-Hakam from Zayd ibn abu al-Hassan from al-Hakam ibn abu Nu'aym' who has said the following:

"Once I went to see abu Ja'far, *'Alayhi al-Salam*, when he was in the city of al-Madina and I said to him, 'I decided to make a vow and a covenant, while I was between the corner of the Ka'ba and the place where Abraham had prayed, that when I might meet you I would not leave al-Madina until I knew with certainty that you were *al-Qa'im* (the one who will rise with Divine Authority and power) from the family of Muhammad, *'Alayhi al-Salam.'* The Imam did not say anything. I then stayed in the city of al-Madina for thirty days. One day he came face to face with me on a road. He said, 'O al-Hakam, are you still here?' I said, 'Yes, I am still here. I had explained to you about my vow and commitment and you did not command me anything or prohibit from anything nor did you answer me with anything.' The Imam then said, 'Early tomorrow, come to my house.' Next morning I went to see him and he said to me, 'Ask what you need.' I said, 'I have a commitment of vow, of fasting and paying charity. I made a decision while I was between the corner of the Ka'ba and the station of Abraham. Its object was that after my meeting with you I would not leave until I knew with certainty that you were *al-Qa'im* (the one who rises with Divine Authority and power) from the family of Muhammad, *'Alayhi al-Salam*, or not. If you were he I would then maintain relations with you, otherwise, I should go in the land to find how to make a living.'

"The Imam then said, 'O Hakam, we all are *al-Qa'im* (the one who rises with Divine Authority and power) because of the commands of Allah.' I then asked, 'Are you al-Mahdi (the guide)?' He said, 'We all guide to Allah.' I asked, 'Are you the owner of the sword?' He said, 'We all are owners of the sword, the heirs of the sword.' I asked, 'Are you the one who does away with enemies of Allah, through whom honor will come to the friends of Allah and with whom the religion of Allah will stand supreme?' The Imam said, 'O Hakam how could I be he. I have already become forty-five years old while the master of this task will be much younger than I and much lighter for the saddle of the horse.'"

544

H 1401, Ch. 128, h 2

Al-Husayn ibn Muhammad al-Ash'ari has narrated from Mu'alla ibn Muhammad from al-Washsha' from Ahmad ibn 'A'idh from abu Khadija from abu 'Abd Allah, *'Alayhi al-Salam*, who has said the following:

"The Imam, *'Alayhi al-Salam*, when he was asked about *al-Qa'im*, said, 'We all are *al-Qa'im* (the one to rise with Divine Authority) with the command of Allah one after the other until the time when the owner of the sword will rise. When the owner of the sword will rise he will rise with a command different from what others (his predecessors) had (which was *taqiyah*).'"

H 1402, Ch. 128, h 3

Ali ibn Muhammad has narrated from Sahl ibn Ziyad from Muhammad ibn al-Hassan ibn Shammun from 'Abd Allah ibn 'Abd al-Rahman from 'Abd Allah ibn al-Qasim al-Batal from 'Abd Allah ibn Sinan who has said the following:

"Once I asked abu 'Abd Allah, *'Alayhi al-Salam*, about the meaning of, 'On the Day when We will call every nation with her Imam (leader) . . .' (17:71)

"The Imam then said, 'It refers to the Imam who is with them and he is *al-Qa'im* of the people of that time.'"

Chapter 129 - Compensation to the Imam, *'Alayhi al-Salam*

H 1403, Ch. 129, h 1

Al-Husayn ibn Muhammad ibn 'Amir through his chain of narrators has narrated in a *marfu'* manner the following:

"Abu 'Abd Allah, *'Alayhi al-Salam*, has said, 'Whoever thinks that the Imam is needful of what people own he becomes an unbeliever. It is the people who need acceptance from the Imam. Allah, the Most Majestic, the Most Gracious, has said, 'Collect religious tax (*Zakat*) from them to purify and cleanse them and pray for them. . . .'" (9:103)

H 1404, Ch. 129, h 2

A number of our people have narrated from Ahmad ibn Muhammad from al-Washsha' from 'Isa ibn Sulayman al-Nahhas from al-Mufaddl ibn 'Umar from al-Khaybari and Yunus ibn Zabyan who both have said we heard abu 'Abd Allah, *'Alayhi al-Salam*, say the following:

"Abu 'Abd Allah, *'Alayhi al-Salam*, has said, 'There is nothing more beloved to Allah than the Dirhams taken out (of one's property) to pay to the Imam. On the Day of Judgment Allah will make his Dirham in paradise as big as the mountain of 'Uhud."

"He then said, 'Allah, the Most High, has said in His book, "One who generously lends to Allah will be paid back in many multiples of the loan . . ." (2:245) The Imam said, "This is a special reference to the payment made to the Imam.""

H 1405, Ch. 129, h 3

Through the same chain of narrators it is narrated from Ahmad ibn Muhammad from Muhammad ibn Sinan from Hammad ibn abu Talha from Ma'adh Sahib al-Akyisa who has said the following:

"I heard abu 'Abd Allah, *'Alayhi al-Salam*, say, 'Allah does not ask His creatures to lend Him from their properties to meet His needs. In fact, whatever of such rights Allah has (on people) they are for His appointed guardian (over His creatures).'"

H 1406, Ch. 129, h 4

Ahmad ibn Muhammad has narrated from Ali ibn al-Hakam from abu al-Maghra' from Ishaq ibn 'Ammar from abu Ibrahim, *'Alayhi al-Salam*, who has said the following:

"I asked abu Ibrahim, *'Alayhi al-Salam*, about the words of Allah, the Most Majestic, the Most Gracious: 'Whoever gives a virtuous loan to Allah will receive in multiples from Him in addition to an honorable reward.' (57:11)

"The Imam said, 'It was revealed about the payments to the Imam, *'Alayhi al-Salam*.'"

H 1407, Ch. 129, h 5

Ali ibn Ibrahim has narrated from Muhammad ibn 'Isa from al-Hassan ibn Mayyah from his father who has said the following:

"Once abu 'Abd Allah, *'Alayhi al-Salam*, said to me, 'O Mayyah, one Dirham paid to the Imam is greater in weight than the mountain of 'Uhud.'"

H 1408, Ch. 129, h 6

Ali ibn Ibrahim has narrated from Muhammad ibn 'Isa from Yunus from certain persons of his people who have narrated from abu 'Abd Allah, *'Alayhi al-Salam*, the following:

"Abu 'Abd Allah, *'Alayhi al-Salam*, has said, 'One Dirham paid to the Imam earns more reward than two million Dirhams paid for other charities.'"

H 1409, Ch. 129, h 7

Muhammad ibn Yahya has narrated from Ahmad ibn Muhammad from ibn Faddal from ibn Bukayr who has said the following:

"I heard abu 'Abd Allah, *'Alayhi al-Salam*, say, 'I procure payment of one Dirham from a person among you when I am the wealthiest of the people of the city of al-Madina. I accept such payments for no other reason but to purify you.'"

Chapter 130 - The Fay', al-Anfal, al-Khums (Kinds of Taxes), Its Rules and the Properties Subject to al-Khums

Al-Kulayni, May Allah grant him blessing, has said the following:

"Allah, the Most Holy, the Most High, has invented the whole world for His deputy as He said to His angels. 'When your Lord said to the angels, "I am appointing someone as my deputy on earth. . . ."'" (2:30) The whole world was for Adam and after him it belonged to the good ones among his descendents and his successors. Whatever their enemies had taken away from them and came back to them through war or conquest is called "Fay'." It is the property that comes to them as a result of conquest or war. The rules for such properties in it (the Book) are as Allah, the Most High, has said: 'You must know that whatever property you may gain, one-fifth belongs to Allah, the Messenger, the kindred, orphans, the needy and those who need money while on a journey . . .' (8:41)

"Such properties belong to Allah, the Messenger and the relatives of the Messenger. Such properties are called *"al-Fay'"* (taken back). It is the property taken back from others by force. However, whatever may come to them without the use of force and resources such as horses and man, it is called *'al-Anfal'*. Such properties belong to Allah and the Messenger only and no one else will have any share in it. Others can have shares only in what is acquired through fighting. All those who take part in the struggle will have certain shares. Properties taken in such way are divided into four portions out of which one belongs to the Messenger of Allah. The portion that belongs to the Messenger of Allah is divided into six portions. Three will be for him and the other three for the orphans, the destitute and those left without means on a journey.

"However, the case of *'al-Anfal'* is different. It belongs to the Messenger of Allah only. Of such properties was Fadak that belonged to the Messenger of Allah only. It is because he and Amir al-Mu'minin Ali, *'Alayhi al-Salam*, conquered it and no one else took part. The name *"al-Fay'"* therefore does not apply to it. The term *'al-Anfal'* applies to it. Similar to *'al-Anfal'* are such properties as the marshes, mines, oceans and the wilderness. They all belong to Imam exclusively. If people work in them by the permission of the Imam four fifths will belong to them for labor and one-fifth will belong to the Imam. Such one-fifth is like al-Khums. If people work in such properties without the permission of the Imam, the Imam will have all of it and no one will have anything in them.

"The same is the case if someone works, revives, improves, develops and builds on a land without the permission of the Imam. It is up to the Imam to leave it with him or take it away from him or settle it differently."

H 1410, Ch. 130, h 1

Ali ibn Ibrahim has narrated from his father from Hammad ibn 'Isa from Ibrahim ibn 'Umar al-Yamani from Aban ibn abu 'Ayyash from Sulaym ibn Qays who has said the following:

"I heard Amir al-Mu'minin Ali, *'Alayhi al-Salam*, say, 'We, by Allah, are the ones to whom Allah has referred by the words *Dhi al-Qurba'* (relatives) and He has brought us near to Himself and His Holy Prophet saying, "Whatever Allah grants to His Messenger (out of the property) of the people of the towns, belongs to Allah, the Messenger, the *Dhi al-Qurba'* (relatives), the orphans, the destitute . . ." (59:7) It (*Dhi al-Qurba'*) applies to such persons from us exclusively. In the charity no portion is appropriated to us. It is the way Allah has honored His Holy Prophet and has honored us instead of feeding us the filthy things in the hands of people.'"

H 1411, Ch. 130, h 2

Al-Husayn ibn Muhammad has narrated from Mu'alla ibn Muhammad from al-Washsha' from Aban from Muhammad ibn Muslim from abu Ja'far, *'Alayhi al-Salam*, who has said the following about the words of Allah, the Most High:

"Abu Ja'far, *'Alayhi al-Salam*, has said, 'You must know that whatever property you may gain, one-fifth belongs to Allah, the Messenger (of Allah), the *Dhi al-Qurba'* (relatives)." (8:41)

547

"The Imam said, 'It refers to the relatives of the Messenger of Allah. Al-Khums (one-fifth) belongs to Allah, the Messenger (of Allah) and to us.'"

H 1412, Ch. 130, h 3

Ali ibn Ibrahim has narrated from his father from ibn abu 'Umayr from Hafs ibn al-Bakhtari from abu 'Abd Allah, *'Alayhi al-Salam*, who has said the following:

"Abu 'Abd Allah, *'Alayhi al-Salam*, has said, *'Al-Anfal* is such property for the acquisition of which no camels or horses are used and no armed expeditions are undertaken. It is the property that may come as a result of negotiated settlement or certain people may give (to us) with their own hands or it may come from a barren land or from inside the valleys. Such properties belong to the Messenger of Allah and they will belong to the *'A'immah* (Leaders with Divine Authority), *'Alayhim al-Salam*, after the Messenger of Allah. The Imam will spend them as he may consider proper."

H 1413, Ch. 130, h 4

Ali ibn Ibrahim ibn Hashim has narrated from his father from Hammad ibn 'Isa from certain persons of our people from the virtuous servant of Allah who has said the following:

"*Al-Khums* (one-fifth tax) is due on five categories of properties. It is due on (1) spoils of war or general net income, (2) properties acquired from diving deep waters, (3) the treasures found, (4) the mines and (5) salt mines. On each of such categories *al-Khums* is due. *Al-Khums*, such one-fifth, is distributed just as Allah, the Most High, has done. The remaining four portions are distributed among those who have taken part in the actual fighting or those lending support behind the front. The one-fifth is distributed in six portions as follows: One portion for Allah, one for the Messenger of Allah, one for the relatives (of the Messenger of Allah), one for the orphans, one for the destitute and one portion for those who become needy on a journey.

"Thus, the portion for Allah and the Messenger of Allah belongs to Leadership with Divine Authority after the Messenger of Allah as the portion of inheritance. He (Leader with Divine Authority) will have three portions. Two portions are inheritance and one is that which Allah has granted to him.

"Fifty percent of *al-Khums* (one-fifth) belongs to him, the Imam (Leader with Divine Authority). The other fifty percent of *al-Khums* belongs to his (the Holy Prophet's) family members. One portion is for the orphans thereof, one portion for the destitute thereof, one portion for those of them who become needy while on a journey. It is distributed among them according to the rules in the Book and the *Sunnah*. The limit is an amount that can suffice for their expenses for a whole year. If anything is left extra it will go to the *Wali,* (Leader with Divine Authority). In the case of deficit the *Wali* is responsible for providing and paying the deficit to meet their needs.

"*Wali* is responsible for paying the deficit; the extra is given to him. Allah has given this one-fifth exclusively to them, not to the destitute from the masses. It is also given to those of them (relatives) who become needy on a journey as a replacement for the charities due on people. It is a sign of distinction from Allah

548

for them because of their being the relatives of the Messenger of Allah and an honor from Allah to keep them secure from the filth in the hands of people. Thus, it is for them only as sustenance to save them from humiliation and destitution. They may receive other forms of charities from each other.

"These are those for whom Allah has assigned *al-Khums*. They are the relatives of the Holy Prophet, *'Alayhi al-Salam*, as Allah has mentioned in His words, 'Warn your close relatives.' (26:214) They are the children of 'Abd al-Muttalib themselves, male and female. No one of the families of Quraysh or the Arabs is of them. Among them or from them also is none of their slaves to have a portion in *al-Khums*. The charities of the masses of people are lawful for their slaves to consume. Their slaves and the masses of people are the same. One whose mother is from the family of Hashim and his father from the masses of Quraysh, the charities are lawful for such person to consume. Such person is not entitled to receive from *al-Khums*; Allah, the Most High has said, 'Call them sons of their own fathers.' (33:5)

"The properties of the best quality in the taxable properties are as the portion of the Imam. The female slave, the best horse, the best clothes and other items that are liked and desired for; such items are for him before the distribution and before the subtraction of *al-Khums*.

"He will pay and maintain with such properties, the causes where he may need to pay such as grants to people who are inclined to the system of belief and so forth. If anything is left extra then *al-Khums* is taken out therefrom and is distributed to the causes for which it is. If anything is left extra then it is given to the *Wali*. If nothing is left after the expenses then there is nothing for the *Wali*. Nothing from the land is for the fighters. So also are the properties that are acquired by overwhelming (the enemy) except for what the army has physically captured."The Bedouins have no share in the distribution even if they take part in fighting in support of the *Wali*. It is because the Messenger of Allah reached a settlement with them. It said, 'They will not be exiled, and that if the Messenger of Allah will be attacked by his enemies they will come to help to fight the enemy but will have no share in the properties of the enemies confiscated.' This practice has been continuous ever since about them and others.

"The lands that were captured by the forces of the army will remain in the public domain. The developers may keep them and reach a settlement with the *Wali* who uses his discretion in the matter. They may find a fair and proportionate agreement on the basis of proper protection of all parties rights and interests. The apportionment may take shape in the form of a half, a one-third or two-thirds and so forth.

"The tax on whatever is harvested, after necessary deductions, will be ten percent if the plantation is irrigated by rain. It is five percent if irrigation is by mechanical means such as *al-Dawaliy* and *al-Nawadih*. *Wali* collects this tax and spends on the causes that Allah has described which are eight categories: (1) The needy, (2) the destitute, (3) the employees of the taxation office, (4) the people who sympathize with the faith, (5) to set free the slaves, (6) to help the bankrupt, (7) for the cause of Allah and (8) to help those who become needy on a journey.

"Each cause can receive an amount enough for its expenses and maintenance for up to one year in a reasonable manner. If anything is left extra it is for the *Wali*. If it is not sufficient the *Wali* must provide the needed funds from his resources. The ten-percent tax is divided between the *Wali* and his partners such as workers and supervisors of the land. They will receive their shares according to the standing agreements. The remaining will be spent on those who help him in the matters of religion of Allah and in the interest of Islam and the strengthening of the religion such as defense and so forth, in which there is general but not personal interest. It is not for his personal interests small or large.

"Besides *al-Khums* for Imam there is '*al-Anfal*'. Al-Anfal is every kind of abandoned land whose owners are no more and all the lands that are acquired without the use of force and fighting but are achieved through settlement or the owners may have given them to the Imam without fight.

"To the Imam belongs the mountain, inside of the valleys, marshes and undeveloped lands that have no owners. To the Imam belong the properties of the kings (defeated) if such properties are not usurped. The usurped properties are all returned to the owner. The Imam is the heir of those who have no heirs. He supports those who have no supporters (financially).

"The Imam has said, 'There is no category of the properties that Allah may not have distributed and has given every rightful person his or her rights of the general or particular nature of the needy and the destitute and all categories of people.'

"Also the Imam has said, 'If justice is practiced among the people they will become free from want.' The Imam then said, 'Justice is more sweet than honey. No one practices it properly except those who are good in justice.'

"The Imam then said, 'The Messenger of Allah would distribute the charities of the rural areas in the rural areas and the charities of the towns to the people of the towns. He would not divide every amount of charity received into eight portions. He would divide it proportionate to the categories of the causes present before him and to the degree for each cause that would suffice it for one year. There was no limit of time or a certain date or the combination of both. He based it on what was available and who was present and how much of the need of each category could have been fulfilled. He offered the remaining to other people.

"*Al-Anfal* belongs to the *Wali* and so are all the lands that were captured during the time of the Holy Prophet, '*Alayhi al-Salam*, to eternity. It does not matter whether the conquest was made through the people of justice or otherwise. The responsibility of the Messenger of Allah is one and the same in the past, present or future generations. It is because the Messenger of Allah said, 'Muslims as brothers are equal in the matters of lives. Even the small ones among them strive for the fulfillment of their responsibilities.'

"There is no *zakat* on *al-Khums* property. It is because the shares of the needy from the masses are placed in the properties of the people in eight categories. No one of the needy in the masses is left out. The needy from the relatives of the Messenger (of Allah) have their share in the fifty percent of *al-Khums*. This suffices them and they do not need the charities of the masses, the charities of the Holy Prophet, *'Alayhi al-Salam*, and the charities of *Wali* (Leadership with Divine Authority). In this way the system leaves no one as a needy person of the masses or of the relatives of the Messenger of Allah without proper coverage and welfare benefits, so all the needy benefit. For this reason there is no *zakat* (tax) on the properties of the Holy Prophet, *'Alayhi al-Salam*, or *Wali*. It is due to the fact that for all kinds of needs there are resources in the system to facilitate them. There are responsibilities as well as rights on the parts of the Holy Prophet and the *Wali*.'"

H 1414, Ch. 130, h 5

Ali ibn Muhammad ibn 'Abd Allah has narrated from certain person of our people (that I think is al-Sayyari) from Ali ibn Asbat who has said the following:

"In one of the meetings of abu al-Hassan Musa, *'Alayhi al-Salam*, with al-Mahdi (one of 'Abbassid ruler) the Imam found him paying reparations (for the damages caused to people). The Imam said, 'O Amir al-Mu'minin, what has happened to the reparations due to us?' He then asked, 'What damage is caused to you, O abu al-Hassan, *'Alayhi al-Salam*?' He (the Imam) said, 'Allah, the Holy, the Most High, granted victory to His Holy Prophet, *'Alayhi al-Salam*, and the land of Fadak and its surrounding areas came under his control without any armed struggle. Allah sent a message to His Holy Prophet, *'Alayhi al-Salam*. It said, "Give the relatives their rights." The Messenger of Allah did not know who they were. He turned to Jibril to find out and Jibril turned to his Lord for the answer. Allah then sent revelation to him to give possession of Fadak to *Fatimah, 'Alayha al-Salam*. Thereupon, the Messenger of Allah called *Fatimah, 'Alayha al-Salam*, and said to her. "O Fatimah, Allah has commanded me to give possession of Fadak to you." She then said, "O Messenger of Allah, I have accepted the offer from Allah and from you." Thereafter her representatives lived there during the lifetime of the Messenger of Allah. When abu Bakr took control he expelled her representatives therefrom. She went to abu Bakr and asked him to reverse his decision and return Fadak to her but he said to *Fatimah, 'Alayha al-Salam*, "Bring to me a black or white person to testify that Fadak belonged to you." *Fatimah, 'Alayha al-Salam*, brought Amir al-Mu'minin Ali, *'Alayhi al-Salam*, and 'Umm Ayman who both testified in favor of *Fatimah, 'Alayha al-Salam*. He then wrote, "Fatimah must not be disturbed in the matters of Fadak." *Fatimah, 'Alayha al-Salam*, then left with the document. On the way 'Umar came from the opposite direction and asked, "What is it in your hand, O daughter of Muhammad?" *Fatimah, 'Alayha al-Salam*, said, "It is a document that ibn abu Quhafa has written for me." He said, "Show it to me." *Fatimah, 'Alayha al-Salam*, refused to hand it over to him but he snatched it away from her hand and read it. He then spit on it wiped out its writing and tore it into pieces. He said, "This was not captured by forces of the camels and horses of your father so that you can tie the rope around our necks.'"

"Al-Mahdi said, 'O abu al-Hassan define for me the boundaries of Fadak.' The Imam said, 'On one side it borders the mountain of 'Uhud. On the other side is 'Arish Misr. Also it borders Sayf al-Bahr and on one of it's sides is Dawmat al-Jandal.' Then he asked the Imam, 'All of it?' He said, 'Yes, O Amir al-Mu'minin, this is all that came to the Messenger of Allah without the use of the forces of the camels and horses.'

"He said, 'This is a large area but I will look into it.'"

H 1415, Ch. 130, h 6
A number of our people have narrated from Ahmad ibn Muhammad from Ali ibn al-Hakam from Ali ibn abu Hamza from Muhammad ibn Muslim who has said the following:
"I heard abu Ja'far, *'Alayhi al-Salam*, say, '*Al-Anfal* (also name of a chapter in the Holy Quran) means *al-Nafl* (optional). In this chapter, *al-Anfal* stands for the amputation of the nose (of enemies and proof of their humiliation)."

H 1416, Ch. 130, h 7
Ahmad has narrated from Ahmad ibn Muhammad ibn abu Nasr who has said the following:
"Once a person asked al-Rida, *'Alayhi al-Salam*, about the words of Allah, the Most Majestic, the Most Gracious, 'You must know that whatever property you may gain, one-fifth belongs to Allah, the Messenger of Allah, and the relatives, . . .' (8:41) It then was asked, 'The portion that belongs to Allah to whom is it given?'

"The Imam said, 'It belongs to the Messenger of Allah and whatever belongs to the Messenger of Allah belongs to the Imam.' Another question said, 'If one of the categories of welfare recipient is more and the other category less, how then it is dealt with?' The Imam said, 'It is left to the discretion of the Imam. Consider how the Messenger of Allah dealt with such cases. Is it not the case that he used his own discretion to distribute, as he considered proper? The Imam deals with such case in the same way.'"

H 1417, Ch. 130, h 8
Ali ibn Ibrahim ibn Hashim has narrated from his father from ibn abu 'Umayr from Jamil ibn Darraj from Muhammad ibn Muslim who has said the following:
"Abu Ja'far, *'Alayhi al-Salam*, was asked about the minerals such as gold, silver, iron, lead and zinc. He said, 'They all are subject to *al-Khums*.'"

H 1418, Ch. 130, h 9
Ali has narrated from his father from ibn abu 'Umayr from Jamil from Zurara who has said the following:
"The Imam, *'Alayhi al-Salam*, has the right, before the distribution, to spend from (booties of war), to give as gifts, grants and other causes. The Messenger of Allah had a confrontation with a people and he did not leave anything for them from *al-Fay'*. He may have given them a share if he wanted."

H 1419, Ch. 130, h 10
Muhammad ibn Yahya has narrated from Ahmad ibn Muhammad from Muhammad ibn Sinan from 'Abd al-Samad ibn Bashir from Hakim Mu'adhin ibn 'Isa who has said the following:
"Once I asked abu 'Abd Allah, *'Alayhi al-Salam*, about the words of Allah, the Most High: 'You must know that whatever property you may gain, one-fifth belongs to Allah, the Messenger of Allah, the relatives, . . .' (8:41)

"Abu 'Abd Allah, *'Alayhi al-Salam*, placing his elbows on his knees and making hand gestures, said, 'By Allah, such gains are the daily gains except that my father had given more freedom and ease to his Shi'a (to pay the one-fifth any time during or at the end of the year).'"

H 1420, Ch. 130, h 11
Ali ibn Ibrahim has narrated from his father from ibn abu 'Umayr from al-Husayn ibn 'Uthman from Sama'a who has said the following:
"I asked abu al-Hassan, *'Alayhi al-Salam*, about al-Khums. He said, 'It is due on all small and large gains that people make.'"

H 1421, Ch. 130, h 12
A number of our people have narrated from Ahmad ibn Muhammad ibn 'Isa ibn Yazid who has said the following:
"Once I wrote to the Imam, *'Alayhi al-Salam*, 'May Allah, keep my soul in service for your cause, explain to me what is gain and profit? What is its limit? What is your opinion? May Allah, the Most High, grant you long life. I will be grateful for your explanation so I will not continue in unlawful activities with invalid prayer and fasting.'

"He wrote to me, 'gain and profit is the income from trade from its net profit or from farming after the deduction of expenses and prizes.'"

H 1422, Ch. 130, h 13
A number of our people have narrated from Ahmad ibn Muhammad from ibn abu Nasr who has said the following:
"Once I wrote to abu Ja'far, *'Alayhi al-Salam*, 'Is al-Khums paid before or after deducting the expenses?' He wrote back in answer, 'It is paid after the deduction of the expenses.'"

H 1423, Ch. 130, h 14
Ahmad ibn Muhammad has narrated from Ali ibn al-Hakam from Ali ibn abu Hamza from abu Basir from abu Ja'far, *'Alayhi al-Salam*, who has said the following:
"Abu Ja'far, *'Alayhi al-Salam*, has said, *'Al-Khums* (one-fifth) of whatever is gained from a war that is fought to establish the testimony: 'No one deserves to be worshipped and obeyed besides Allah and that Muhammad is the Messenger of Allah,' belongs to us. It is not lawful for anyone to buy anything with money for which al-Khums, our right, is not paid, until payment is made to us.'"

H 1424, Ch. 130, h 15
Ahmad ibn Muhammad has narrated from Muhammad ibn Sinan from Yunus ibn Ya'qub from 'Abd al-'Aziz ibn Na'fi' who has said the following:

"Once we asked permission from abu 'Abd Allah, *'Alayhi al-Salam*, and sent him a message. He then sent us a message that said two of us should meet him at one time. A man and I went to meet him. I said to the man, 'I want you to ask permission to ask questions.' He said, 'Yes, I will do so.' He then said to the Imam, 'May Allah keep my soul in service for your cause, my father was taken as a captive by the 'Umayyids. I know that 'Umayyids did not consider lawful and unlawful matters and that they did not have any right in all that was in their possession in large or small quantities but that they rightfully belonged to you. When I think how much must I return to you I get a feeling that almost destroys my power of reason.' The Imam said, 'You are free from such obligation as well as all those who are in the same conditions as you are. They are also free from such obligations after me.' The narrator has said that we then left and Mu'attib (the servant) reached the next group who were to meet the Imam and said, "'Abd al-'Aziz ibn Na'fi' has succeeded in what no one before him had ever done.' They asked, 'What is it?' He then explained it to them.

"Then two of them (people) went to see the Imam. One of them said, 'May Allah keep my soul in service for your cause, my father was a captive in the hands of the 'Umayyids. I knew that the 'Umayyids had no legal control over all that they had in small or large amounts. I would like that you set me free from the liabilities.'

"The Imam said, 'Is that up to us? It is not up us. We have no right to make things lawful or unlawful.' The two men then left. Abu 'Abd Allah, *'Alayhi al-Salam*, became angry. Abu 'Abd Allah, *'Alayhi al-Salam*, then, to every one who went to see him, began to say, 'Are you not surprised at so and so? He comes to me to legalize what the 'Umayyids had done? He thinks it is up to us. That night no one benefited little or in large amounts except the first two people. They gained what they needed.'"

H 1425, Ch. 130, h 16
Ali ibn Ibrahim has narrated from his father from ibn Mahbub from Durays al-Kunasi who has said the following:
"Once abu 'Abd Allah, *'Alayhi al-Salam*, said, 'Why do people get in the course of adultery?' I said, 'I do not know, may Allah keep my soul in service for your cause.' He said, 'It is because of not paying our *al-Khums* (one-fifth religious dues) except our pure Shi'a. It helps clean their birth.'"

H 1426, Ch. 130, h 17
Ali ibn Ibrahim has narrated from his father from ibn abu 'Umayar from Shu'ayb from abu al-Sabbah who has said the following:
"Abu 'Abd Allah, *'Alayhi al-Salam*, said to me, 'We are the people, obedience to whom is obligatory by the commands of Allah. *Al-Anfal* (properties acquired without the use of armed forces) and the best of the properties of the gains from war belong to us.'"

H 1427, Ch. 130, h 18
A number of our people have narrated from Ahmad ibn Muhammad from al-Husayn ibn Sa'id from al-Qasim ibn Muhammad from Rifa'a from Aban ibn Taghlib from abu 'Abd Allah, *'Alayhi al-Salam*, who has said the following:

"About a man who dies without an heir the Imam, *'Alayhi al-Salam*, said, 'To him this verse applies: "They (the believers) ask you (Muhammad) about the booty captured (from the enemies) during a war. Tell them, "It belongs to Allah and the Messenger. If you have faith, have fear of Allah. Settle the disputes among yourselves and obey Allah and His Messenger." (8:1)

H 1428, Ch. 130, h 19
Ali ibn Ibrahim has narrated from his father from ibn abu 'Umayar from Hammad from from al-Halabi from abu 'Abd Allah, *'Alayhi al-Salam*, who has said the following:

"A certain person asked, 'How much tax is on treasures?' Abu 'Abd Allah, *'Alayhi al-Salam*, said, '*Al-Khums*, one-fifth of treasure found is paid as tax.' The question said, 'How much is on minerals?' The Imam said, 'One fifth. So are lead, zinc and iron. All minerals are like gold and silver on which the religious due is *al-Khums*, one-fifth.'"

H 1429, Ch. 130, h 20
Muhammad ibn Yahya has narrated from Ahmad ibn Muhammad from Muhammad ibn Sinan from Sabbah al-Azraq from Muhammad ibn Muslim from one of them (abu Ja'far or abu 'Abd Allah, *'Alayhi al-Salam*, who has said the following:

"Abu 'Abd Allah, *'Alayhi al-Salam*, has said, 'The most serious trouble that one may face on the Day of Judgment is when a person with the right to receive *al-Khums* will stand up and say, 'Lord, my *al-Khums* (was not paid).' However, we have gifted it to our Shi'a to cleanse and purify their birth."

H 1430, Ch. 130, h 21
Muhammad ibn Yahya has narrated from Muhammad ibn al-Husayn from Ahmad ibn Muhammad ibn abu Nasr from Muhammad ibn Ali from abu al-Hassan, *'Alayhi al-Salam*, who has said the following:

"The narrator has said, 'Once I asked him about what is taken out of the sea, such as pearls, rubies and gems and minerals such as gold and silver and others, how much is the tax on them?' The Imam, *'Alayhi al-Salam*, said, 'If it is worth up to a Dinar then *al-Khums* (one-fifth) is due on it.'"

H 1431, Ch. 130, h 22
Muhammad ibn al-Husayn and Ali ibn Muhammad have narrated from Sahl ibn Ziyad from Ali ibn Mahziyar who has said the following:

"Once I wrote to him (the Imam, *'Alayhi al-Salam*), 'My master, a man is given money to perform Hajj. Is there *al-Khums* on such money when he receives it or is there *al-Khums* only on what remains extra from the expenses after Hajj?' He wrote, 'There is no *al-Khums* on him.'"

H 1432, Ch. 130, h 23
Sahl ibn Ziyad has narrated from Muhammad ibn 'Isa from Ali ibn al-Husayn ibn 'Abd Rabbihi who has said the following:

"Once al-Rida, *'Alayhi al-Salam*, sent a gift to my father and my father wrote to him, 'Is there *al-Khums* on the gift you just sent to me?' He wrote back to him in answer, 'There is no *al-Khums* on the gift that the recipient of *al-Khums* has sent to you.'"

H 1433, Ch. 130, h 24
Sahl has narrated from Ibrahim ibn Muhammad al-Hamadani who has said the following:
"Once I wrote to abu al-Hassan, *'Alayhi al-Salam*, 'Ali ibn Mahziyar read to me the letter of your father, *'Alayhi al-Salam*, that said, "The owners of gardens pay three percent after deducting the expenses. Those whose gardens do not produce even the expenses, there is nothing due on them." A difference of opinion has risen among our people. They say that on the produce of the gardens there is *al-Khums* (one-fifth) after the deduction of the expenses, the expenses of the garden, not the expenses of the owner and his family. The Imam wrote back in answer, *'Al-Khums* is due after the deduction of the taxes to government and the expenses of one's family.'"

H 1434, Ch. 130, h 25
Sahl has narrated from Ahmad ibn al-Muthanna who has said the following:
"Muhammad ibn al-Tabari has said that a businessman from Persia who was of the friends of abu al-Hassan al-Rida, *'Alayhi al-Salam*, wanted permission about *al-khums*. The Imam wrote:

"(I begin) in the name of Allah, the Beneficent, the Merciful.

"Allah increases people's sustenance and He is generous. He has guaranteed rewards for work and sadness for constraints. The use of a property is not lawful unless it is used in the way Allah has made lawful. *Al-Khums* helps us in our religion, in the expenses of our dependents and our friends. It helps us to gift and buy protection for our dignity against those whom we fear. Do not withhold it from us and do not deprive yourselves from our prayers as far as it is possible for you. Paying *al-Khums* increases your earnings, cleanses your sins and whatever you preserve for yourselves for the day when you will need help the most. A Muslim is one who fulfills his promise to Allah. One is not a Muslim if he says, 'yes' with his tongue but opposes it in his heart. With peace.'"

H 1435, Ch. 130, h 26
Through the same chain of narrators it is narrated from Muhammad ibn Zayd who has said the following:
"Once a group of people came from Khurasan to abu al-Hassan al-Rida, *'Alayhi al-Salam*. They asked him to set them free from the obligation of payment of *al-Khums*. The Imam said, 'What kind of plan is this? Do you try to love us purely only with your tongue and withhold from us the right that Allah has set for us? That right is *al-Khums*. We do not, do not, and do not relinquish it to any one of you.'"

H 1436, Ch. 130, h 27
Ali ibn Ibrahim has narrated from his father who has said the following:
"Once I was in the presence of abu Ja'far al-Thani, *'Alayhi al-Salam*, that Salih ibn Muhammad ibn Sahl came and he was his supervisor of endowments in Qum.

He said, 'My master, write off for me ten thousand because I have already spent it.' The Imam said, 'It is relinquished in your favor.' When Salih left then abu Ja'far, *'Alayhi al-Salam*, said as follows: 'Once one of them gets his hand on the property that belongs to *Ahl al-Bayt* of Muhammad, *'Alayhi al-Salam*, to their orphans, to their destitute, to their needy and to those of them who become needy on a journey and then he comes to us and says, "Relinquish it in my favor," do you think I can say, "No, I will not relinquish it in your favor?"

"By Allah, Allah will soon question them on the Day of Judgment without any concession.'"

H 1437, Ch. 130, h 28
Ali has narrated from his father from ibn abu 'Umayar from Hammad from al-Halabi who has said the following:
"Once I asked abu 'Abd Allah, *'Alayhi al-Salam*, about the corral (under sea treasure) and diving for pearls. The Imam said, 'There is *al-Khums* due on them.'"

This is the End of First Volume of the Book about the People who Possess Divine Authority (of the Book al-Kafi) that is followed by the Book, 'Belief and Disbelief'.

All praise belongs to Allah, Lord of the worlds. May peace and blessings be showered upon Muhammad and his family, the clean and pure ones.

Made in United States
Troutdale, OR
02/27/2024

18031951R00335